G000055841

Understanding the Chinese Economies

Understanding the Chinese Economies

Rongxing Guo

ELSEVIER

AMSTERDAM • BOSTON • HEIDELBERG • LONDON • NEW YORK • OXFORD • PARIS
SAN DIEGO • SAN FRANCISCO • SINGAPORE • SYDNEY • TOKYO
Academic Press is an imprint of Elsevier

Academic Press is an imprint of Elsevier
The Boulevard, Langford Lane, Kidlington, Oxford OX5 1GB, UK
225 Wyman Street, Waltham, MA 02451, USA

First edition 2013

Copyright © 2013 Elsevier Inc. All rights reserved

No part of this publication may be reproduced, stored in a retrieval system or transmitted in any
form or by any means electronic, mechanical, photocopying, recording or otherwise without the
prior written permission of the publisher

Permissions may be sought directly from Elsevier's Science & Technology Rights
Department in Oxford, UK: phone (+44) (0) 1865 843830; fax (+44) (0) 1865 853333;
email: permissions@elsevier.com. Alternatively you can submit your request online by visiting the
Elsevier web site at http://elsevier.com/locate/permissions, and selecting *Obtaining permission to
use Elsevier material*

Notice

No responsibility is assumed by the publisher for any injury and/or damage to persons or property
as a matter of products liability, negligence or otherwise, or from any use or operation of any
methods, products, instructions or ideas contained in the material herein. Because of rapid advances
in the medical sciences, in particular, independent verification of diagnoses and drug dosages should
be made

British Library Cataloguing-in-Publication Data
A catalogue record for this book is available from the British Library

Library of Congress Cataloging-in-Publication Data
A catalog record for this book is available from the Library of Congress

ISBN–13: 978-0-12-397826-4

For information on all Academic Press publications
visit our web site at books.elsevier.com

Typeset by MPS Limited, Chennai, India
www.adi-mps.com

Printed and bound in China

12 13 14 15 16   10 9 8 7 6 5 4 3 2 1

**Working together to grow
libraries in developing countries**

www.elsevier.com | www.bookaid.org | www.sabre.org

ELSEVIER   BOOK AID International   Sabre Foundation

This book is dedicated to the memory of
my mother, Hè Yǘhuā (1927–2005)
who taught me to do something helpful
for the American people.

Contents

List of Boxes

List of Case Studies

List of Figures

Contents of the Companion Site

1. PowerPoint slides (Introduction and 15 chapters).
2. Case studies (including five in-depth research papers).
3. Suggested reading.

To download a free copy of these materials, please visit the companion site at:
http://www.elsevierdirect.com/companions/9780123978264.

ABC	Agriculture Bank of China	M&A	merger and acquisition
AIC	Administration of Industry and Commerce	MES	market economy status
ARATS	Association for Relations across the Taiwan Strait	MOFCOM	Ministry of Commerce
		MPS	material product system
BAIC	Beijing Automotive Industry Holding Co	NBS	National Bureau of Statistics of China
BECZ	trans-province border economic cooperative zone	NDRC	National Development and Reform Commission
BOC	Bank of China	NIE	newly industrialized economy
CASS:	Chinese Academy of Social Sciences	NMP	net material product
CCB	China Construction Bank	NOC	national oil company
CCP	Chinese Communist Party	NPC	National People's Congress
CCPCC	Chinese Communist Party Central Committee	NPL	non-performing loan
CEPA	closer economic partnership arrangement	ODI	outward foreign direct investment
CIC	China Investment Corporation	PBC	People's Bank of China
CNOOC	China National Offshore Oil Corporation	PCS	people's commune system
CNPC	China National Petroleum Corporation	PPP	purchasing power parity
COE	collectively-owned enterprise	PRC	People's Republic of China
CPE	centrally planned economy	PSE	private, shareholding, or other enterprise
CPPCC	Chinese People's Political Consultative Congress	R&D	research and development
		RMB	renminbi, Chinese currency
ECFA	Economic Cooperation Framework Agreement	SAFE	State Administration for Foreign Exchange
		SAR	special administrative region
EIBC	Export-Import Bank of China	SARS	severe acute respiratory syndrome
FDI	foreign direct investment	SASAC	State-Owned Assets Supervision and Administration Commission
FIE	foreign (including Taiwan, Hong Kong, and Macau) invested enterprise	SEF	Straits Exchange Foundation
FYP	five-year plan	SEZ	special economic zone
GDP	gross domestic product	Sinopec	China Petroleum & Chemical Corporation
GHG	greenhouse gas	SNA	system of national accounts
GNP	gross national product	SOE	state-owned enterprise
GVAO	gross value of agricultural output	SPC	State Planning Commission
GVIAO	gross value of industrial and agricultural output	SSB	State Statistical Bureau
		TFP	total-factor productivity
GVIO	gross value of industrial output	TVE	township and village enterprise
GVSP	gross value of social product	UNCTAD	United Nations Conference on Trade and Development
HRS	household responsibility system		
ICBC	Industrial & Commercial Bank of China	WHO	World Health Organization
IPR	intellectual property right	WTO	World Trade Organization

Acknowledgments

The completion of this book has been facilitated by various factors. The Award for Outstanding Research on Development received from the Global Development Network (GDN) and Government of Japan in 2007 and the fund from the Organization for Economic Cooperation and Development (OECD) in 2011 made it possible for me to collect some specific micro-level data on China's regional economies. The early grants from National Social Science Foundation of China (1992), the National Science Foundation of China (1994; 1998), the Ministry of Coal Industry of China (1998), the Chinese Academy of Social Sciences (CASS) (2003), the East Asian Development Network (EADN) (2002; 2006), and the GDN (2004) have enabled me to conduct a series of field inspections in China. All of these research projects have contributed to the writing of this book.

This book includes some previously published material. Specifically, the case study in Chapter 2 is based on an article published by the *Journal of Contemporary China* (2012, vol. 21, No. 57); the case study in Chapter 8 is based on an article published in Chinese by *Management World* (guanli shijie) with Li Shi and Xing Youqiang (2003, No. 4); and the Annex in Chapter 12 is based on an article published by the *Asian Economic Journal* (2007, vol. 21, No. 1). Thanks go to the co-authors and the copyright owners of the above publications for their kind permission to use these materials in this edition. Some materials included in this book are published in my monographs such as *How the Chinese Economy Works* (three editions, published by Palgrave-Macmillan in 1999, 2007, and 2009, respectively) and *An Introduction to the Chinese Economy* (Wiley, 2010). All the materials and data included in the present book have been fully revised and updated.

Many individuals have contributed to the publication of this book. The annual Northeast Asian Policy meetings sponsored by the Brookings Institution in Seoul (in 2010) and Hong Kong (in 2011) enabled me to exchange ideas with international audiences, which have contributed to the structural design of the present book. I have benefited from the valuable comments received from Professor Zhao Renwei (CASS). During my visits to South Korea and Germany, I benefited from many discussions with Professors Eui-Gak Hwang (Korea University) and Thomas Heberer (University of Trier). I have also benefited from various joint research projects with Professor Hu Xuwei, Professor Zhao Renwei, Professor Li Shi, Mr Zhang Yong, Mr Guo Liqing, Mr Zhao Gongzheng, Mr Xing Youqiang, Ms Xie Yanhong, and Ms Wang Xiaoping. I have also benefited from research assistance by Ms Wang Huayan.

Some micro-level findings used in this book are based on field inspections and surveys. The following organizations and agencies provided generous help in carrying out my field-trips and research activities:

Chuangda Company, Zichuan District, Shandong Province
Development and Research Center of the State Council, Beijing
Government of Peixian County, Jiangsu Province
Government of Weishan County, Shandong Province
Guangzheng Company, Zichuan District, Shandong Province
Jinggezhang Coalmine, Tangshan City, Hebei Province
Kailuan Group Corporation, Tangshan City, Hebei Province
Linnanchang Coalmine, Yutian County, Hebei Province
Linyi Municipal Planning Commission, Linyi, Shandong Province
National Development and Reform Commission, Beijing
Suqian Municipal Planning Commission, Suqian, Jiangsu Province
Xuzhou Municipal Planning Commission, Xuzhou, Jiangsu Province
Zaozhuang Municipal Planning Commission, Zaozhuang, Shandong Province
Zhengzhou Huijin Company, Zhengzhou, Henan Province
Zibo Mining Group, Zibo City, Shandong Province

Many valuable comments and suggestions on part of or the whole manuscript have been received from the following individuals:

Professor Pieter Bottelier (Johns Hopkins University SAIS, Washington, DC),

Dr Lyn Squire (Founder and First President of the Global Development Network, New Delhi; and Nonresident Senior Fellow of the Brookings Institution, Washington, DC),

Professor José María Fanelli (University of Buenos Aires, Argentina),

Dr Gary McMahon (Senior Specialist, The World Bank, Washington, DC),

Dr Richard C Bush (Senior Fellow, and Director of the Center of Northeast Asian Policy Studies, The Brookings Institution, Washington, DC),

Professor David SG Goodman (Director of Social Sciences, University of Sydney, Sydney),

Professor Giles Chance (Guanghua Business School, Peking University),

Ms Isher Ahluwalia (Chairperson, Indian Council for Research on International Economic Relations, New Delhi),

Professor Richard Cooper (Harvard University, Boston, MA),

Professor Amara Pongsapich (Chulalongkorn University, Thailand),

Professor Leong Liew (Griffin University, Australia),

Professor Shigeyuki Abe (Doshisha University, Japan),

Dr Chalongphob Sussangkarn (former President, Thailand Development and Research Institute, Bangkok),

Dr Chia Siow Yue (Senior Fellow, Singapore Institute for International Affairs),

Dr Josef T Yap (Director, Philippines Institute for Development Studies, Manila),

Professor Zhang Yunling (CASS, Beijing),

Professor Hiro Lee (*Asian Economic Journal*, Japan),

Dr Jun Li (Senior Lecturer, University of Essex, UK), and over ten anonymous reviewers (of whom, eight were kindly arranged by Elsevier Inc., San Diego, CA).

Among the Elsevier staff contributing to the publication of this book, Dr J Scott Bentley (Senior Acquisition Editor) merits particular mention. I would also like to thank Ms Kathleen Paoni (Editorial Project Manager) for keeping the production on track.

I have also learnt a lot from Ms Susan Li (also known as Li Xia, Senior Project Manager, Elsevier, Oxford, UK) who has refined various bits of this book.

Finally, I would like to thank Luc Guo for his assistance during the process of writing this book and Liu Yuhui for constant moral support.

Guo Rong Xing
Qiaozi, Huairou, Beijing
January 2012

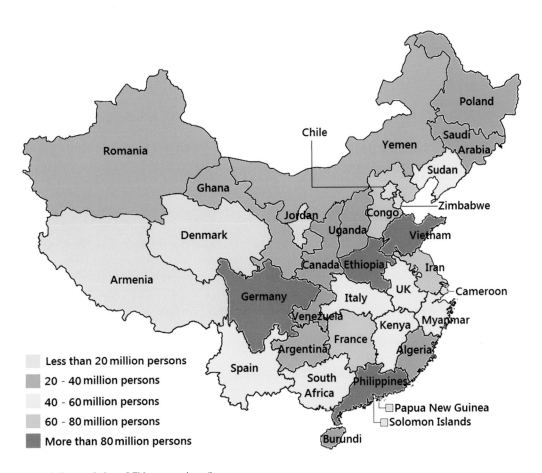

Which countries match the population of Chinese provinces?

Notes: (1) The equivalents are as follows: Algeria=Fujian, Argentina=Guizhou, Armenia=Tibet, Burundi=Hainan, Cameroon=Shanghai, Canada=Shaanxi, Chile=Beijing, Congo (Dem. Rep. of)=Hebei, Denmark=Qinghai, Ethiopia=Henan, France=Hunan, Germany=Sichuan, Ghana=Gansu, Iran=Jiangsu, Italy=Hubei, Jordan=Ningxia, Kenya=Jiangxi, Myanmar=Zhejiang, Papua New Guinea=Hong Kong, Philippines=Guangdong, Poland=Heilongjiang, Romania=Xinjiang, Saudi Arabia=Jilin, Solomon Islands=Macau, South Africa=Guangxi, Spain=Yunnan, Sudan=Liaoning, Uganda=Shanxi, UK=Anhui, Venezuela=Chongqing, Vietnam=Shandong, Yemen=Inner Mongolia, and Zimbabwe=Tianjin. (2) Data are as of 2010. *Source: Author based on http://www.economist.com/content/all_parities_china*

Copyright © 2012 by Rongxing Guo.
Tiantan (temple of heaven), Beijing – a place where Chinese emperors came every winter solstice to worship heaven and to solemnly pray for a good harvest.

The world is watching the miraculous development of the Chinese economy with a mixture of emotions: envy, hope, concern. This has been pointed out by Mr. Lyn Squire (Founder and First President of the Global Development Network, New Delhi, India) in his foreword to my book *How the Chinese Economy Works*: 'Even a country such as India, which is experiencing its own miracle, can still cast a jealous eye at the success of the Chinese economy. Other less fortunate countries are looking to China for lessons to guide and accelerate their own development. And still others worry that China's emergence will squeeze them out of markets for their exports or their sources of energy.'[1]

The present book is intended to provide information and explanations of the operational mechanisms of the Chinese economy during the pre- and post-reform periods and through national, regional, and local dimensions. It examines the driving forces – both exogenous and endogenous – for and how they have influenced China's economic development for the period since the People's Republic of China (PRC) was founded in 1949, especially since 1978, when China took the decision to transform its economy

[1]See 'Foreword' to *How the Chinese Economy Works*, 3rd edn. (Palgrave-Macmillan, 2009).

from a centrally planned system to a market-oriented one. In this book, a multiregional comparison of the Chinese economy is conducted in terms of natural and human resources, institutional evolution, and social and economic performances; and there is some clarification of the positive and negative consequences of the Chinese economic transformation.

Indeed, writing a book incorporating all of the details about the diversified Chinese economies is never an easy job, since China *per se* is on a larger scale and perhaps more complex than any other country in the world. This job is especially difficult for me – a native Chinese who was born in China's poorest rural area and grew during the most difficult period in recent Chinese history. I did not receive a world-class education; and my English was taught in China and, of course, only with Chinese characteristics. Nevertheless, it is still gratifying to note that, through reading a book written in my *Chinglish*, one could have an easy understanding of how the Chinese economy has worked through the so-called socialist market system with Chinese characteristics.

Over the course of recent decades, the Chinese economy has worked, and is expected to continue working in the years to come, through a path or approach that is to some extent similar to the one that I have applied to the writing of this book – grammatically or stylistically. In the meantime, I am quite satisfied, as I have felt that my working experience in China, including the entire writing process of the present book and myself as well, has become to some extent another part of the Chinese economy.

EXECUTIVE SUMMARY

Starting with a brief history of China (called 'zhongguo' in Chinese, meaning 'center under heaven'), Chapter 1 is focused on various factors that could have shaped China's existing political, economic, and cultural characteristics. It investigates the causes and consequences of China's periodic changes of feudal dynasties as well as their political, economic, and cultural implications to China in the years to come.

The Chinese economy is one of the most complicated and diversified spatial systems to be found anywhere in the world. The only feasible approach one can adopt is, therefore, to divide it into smaller geographic elements through which one can gain a better insight into the spatial mechanisms and regional characteristics. In Chapter 2, we will divide the Chinese economy into: (1) provincial administrations; (2) great regions; (3) geographical belts; (4) southern and northern parts; and (5) ethno-cultural areas. It is common for the method of spatial division of the Chinese economy to differ, depending on the analytical purposes.

A huge population does not represent an advantage in human resources for economic development. This is particularly true for China, which is being transformed from an agricultural society that has used mainly traditional methods of production to an industrial society that requires not only advanced sciences and technologies but also qualified workers. A well-educated and law-abiding population that possesses a strong work ethic is the *sine qua non* of China's economic growth. In addition, Chinese culture, which aims to achieve a harmonious balance between Confucianism, Buddhism, and Taoism, worked particularly well over a very long period of time. However, the early cultural achievements sometimes may become an inability to innovate…

The vast size and diversified natural conditions of China have generated many regional differences in terms of climate, geography, soil fertility, and other natural resource endowments. This in turn means that social and economic developments vary from region to region. In particular, South and East regions have natural advantages for agriculture over the Northwest region. Except for a few deposits of non-ferrous metals, minerals and energy resources are much richer in the North and West areas than in the Southern coastal area. One of the most important implications of Chapter 4 is that the unevenly distributed and coal-dominated energy structure is the major obstacle to Chinese industrialization and sustainable development. All of these factors have inevitably resulted in great spatial economic disequilibria and disparities in China. This chapter also discusses China's worsening environmental problems.

China's political and administrative systems are mysteries to many Westerners. At one level, China is a one-party state that has been ruled by the Chinese Communist Party since 1949. In the late 1950s, the same authoritarian regime was waging a massive campaign under the name of the 'Great Leap Forward', which resulted in the loss of a large number of lives. From 1966 to 1976, the same regime was launching a so-called 'Great Cultural Revolution', causing serious cultural and economic damages to this nation. Furthermore, influential theories of the political economy of the former socialist systems emphasizes that unless the one-party monopoly is abolished, reforms are doomed to fail. Obviously, the achievements of China's modernization defy conventional explanations. Consequently, this will lead to the asking of questions like: How has the Chinese political system worked during the past decades? Can it be sustained in the long run?

The economic system of any nation is the mechanism that brings together natural resources, labor, technology, and the necessary managerial talents. Anticipating and then meeting human needs through the production and distribution of goods and services is the end purpose of every economic system. The Chinese economy is no exception to this rule. The advocates of new institutional economics recognize that a good market economy requires 'getting institutions right'. The institutional economists thus regard the conventional wisdom of transition focusing on stabilization, liberalization, and privatization as inadequate, because it overlooks the important institutional dimension. Standing in marked contrast with the failures of some former socialist economies, which were to some extent based on a 'blueprint' or 'recipe' from Western advisors, has been the enormous success of China. This is the so-called Chinese characteristics of economic transitions…

In Chapter 7, we will examine various cases of economic reforms (which can be further divided into 'radical' and 'gradual/partial' reforms). The analytical narrative of the successful and unsuccessful cases of the Chinese-style reform shows that the efficiency of a reform depended upon: (i) the initial institutional conditions; (ii) the external environment; and (iii) the reform strategy. The empirical evidence suggests that a radical reform tends to be more efficient than a gradual/partial one during the early stages (the late 1970s and the early 1980s), while a gradual/partial reform tends to be more efficient than a radical (big-bang) one in the later stages. We also find that the Chinese-style reform has evolved from the collusion of the CCP radicals and conservatives to that of the political, economic, and cultural elites, at the cost of retarding political reforms and of sacrificing the benefits of the rest of the people.

Chapter 8 sets out to examine various factors (sources) contributing to China's rapid economic growth. While China's reform since the late 1970s has been a strong driver of its economic growth and of the increased levels of income, it has also caused a series of socioeconomic problems. In the initial stage of the reform, the policy of 'letting some people get rich first', adopted to overcome egalitarianism in income distribution, to promote efficiency with strong incentives and ultimately to realize common prosperity based on an enlarged pie, has quickly increased income gaps between different groups of people. This chapter tests, qualitatively and quantitatively, the causes and consequences of China's increasing income inequalities. Finally, China's poverty reduction and social security are briefly discussed.

Since economic reform and open-door policies were implemented in the late 1970s, the Chinese economy has demonstrated an increasing asymmetry between different regions and resulted in a series of regional economic problems which need to be addressed properly by policymakers. Due to the application of different statistical systems in the pre- and post-reform periods as well as the unavailability of statistical data in some provinces, a complete multiregional comparison of the Chinese economy is extremely difficult and, to some extent, meaningless. Using the best data and the regression approach, we try to estimate a set of time-series data on GDP for all provinces, on which the multiregional comparison of the Chinese economy is based. Finally, regional economic disparity indexes are computed for the past decades. Not surprisingly, China's interregional economic differences have been posing considerable challenges to its societal harmony.

Despite the mutually complementary conditions between many of its different regions, the Chinese economy has been internally affected by various geographical, administrative, and cultural barriers that exist between provincial administrations. Following an empirical analysis of the spatial efficiency of the Chinese economy, Chapter 10 studies the possibilities and conditions under which the Chinese economy can (or cannot) be optimized spatially. We will analyze the negative economic impacts of China's interprovincial barriers. The result shows that the multiregional complementarities have not been utilized fully and that due to this existing cross-border separation the Chinese economy cannot be spatially optimized. During recent decades, China's economic reform and open-door policies have developed its provincial and local economies disproportionally. The particular focus of the final part of this chapter will examine China's various efforts on the search for spatial economic integration.

In the newly industrialized economies (NIEs), industrialization has served as the key engine in the early period of economic takeoff. Therefore, most developing nations (especially poor and agrarian nations) have placed great emphasis upon it. Despite its long history of civilization, China lagged behind the advanced nations in industrial modernization during the past centuries. During the prereform period China's industrialization had been affected to a large extent by political movements. Generally, the poor industrial performances had been ascribed to China's 'self-reliance and independence' policies and the irrational industrial structure in which heavy industry was given priority. If the leapfrogging theory can be used to describe the dynamic pattern of the world economy, it appears likely that, in the decades to come, China's technological gap with advanced nations will be narrowed.

The Chinese economy has been transforming from the autarkic to an outward-oriented pattern. The open-door policy was first implemented in the coastal area in the early 1980s, resulting in a rapid economic growth for China and the Eastern belt in particular. In the early 1990s, China embarked on another outward-looking policy to promote the cross-border trade and economic development of the inland frontier area. China has been industrializing and is becoming a major exporter of manufactured goods. China's

efforts on economic internationalization have greatly benefited every sphere of Chinese life. The Chinese government has attempted to adjust further its economic policies so as to meet gradually the needs of the multilateral trading system. Since China joined in the WTO, the Chinese economy has become freer and more internationalized. But many pressing issues still exist.

Foreign investment has played an increasing role in the Chinese economy. What is more important, the foreign enterprises have promoted the importation of advanced technology, equipment, and management and, above all, competition mechanisms from the advanced economies. Although China's outward direct investment (ODI) is still smaller than its massive inward FDI, China's overseas companies have been gaining momentum in moving international capital, investing across a broad spectrum of sectors ranging from natural resources to manufacturing to telecommunications and many others. As China's economy continues to grow, China faces shortages in many raw materials (particularly oil, iron ore, aluminum, and uranium), and it must therefore build trade linkages with resource-rich countries (such as Australia, Russia, Brazil, and the Middle East countries) to secure supplies.

Although the laws and regulations are fundamentally the same throughout the country, provincial and local officials have a large degree of discretion in terms of the enforcement of national legislation. This resulted in the fact that investment climate varies widely across provinces. In Chapter 14, in addition to demonstrating the fundamentals of doing business in China, we will compare, internationally and interprovincially, four key indicators (starting a business, registering property, getting credit, and enforcing contracts). While these indicators are not a full reflection of the local investment climate, they do suggest that coastal areas scored highest overall on the ease of doing business. At last, this chapter gives some details about China's business culture.

Despite their common history and cultural homogeneity, the greater China area has followed during the past decades divergent political and economic systems, from which different social and economic performances have resulted. In Chapter 15, the social and economic influences of Hong Kong, Macau, Taiwan, and overseas Chinese, as well as their influences on the economic development of mainland China, are examined. Our focus is due to the great potential of comparative advantages as well as the close cultural linkages between Hong Kong, Macau, Taiwan, and mainland China. The remaining part of this chapter analyzes the cross-Strait economic relations and the overseas Chinese economics.

HOW TO USE THIS BOOK

In this book, numerous photographs and maps are adopted to enhance the text. In each chapter one or two boxed examples are inserted where appropriate. It is hoped that this will be illuminating for readers from different academic backgrounds who are seeking to gain more knowledge about the ways in which the Chinese economies have been working. In addition, a few ancient Chinese fables, some of which have become popular idioms in contemporary Chinese society, are selected as epigraphs.

I provide some end-of-chapter case studies, some of which are based upon my previous field inspections and micro-level surveys in China. They are, therefore, very useful for researchers and students attempting to study Chinese economics and for ordinary readers who wish to keep a close watch on China and the Chinese economy in particular. In addition, a few mathematical and technical materials that have close connections to the text are annexed to the end of the relevant chapters.

The following notes may help readers to have a clear and concrete understanding of the entire text:

- Unless stated otherwise, the geographical scope of China covers only mainland China, although Hong Kong, Macau, and Taiwan are mentioned in a number of the chapters.
- The term 'Chinese economies' refers either to China's provincial/local economies or to the larger extent of all the Chinese-speaking economies.
- Chinese names are customarily written in the order of family name (which is in the single syllable in most cases) followed by given name.
- Chinese names and geographic terms in mainland China are written in China's official (pinyin) form, while those outside mainland China are in the conventional form.
- Unless stated otherwise, the statistical data used in this book are from *China Statistical Yearbooks* (NBS, all issues).
- For the sake of convenience, specific autonomous regions and municipalities directly under the central government will be referred to alongside provinces by a single name.

SUGGESTED READING

For further reading related to specific economic of each chapter, please visit the publisher's companion web site (URL shown in next section). A wide variety of academic journals now carry articles on the Chinese economy. Of the China-related journals, a short list includes *The China Quarterly* (Cambridge University Press); *Journal of Contemporary China* (Taylor & Francis); and *The China Journal* (Australian National University).

Of the economics journals, the most consistently interesting China-related articles come in the *China Economic Review* (Elsevier) and *Journal of Comparative Economics* (Elsevier).

In addition, the statistical data on China's national and provincial economic development can be found in the following table:

Title	Version(s)	Year(s)	Author(s)	Publisher
China Statistical Yearbook[a]	Chinese/English	1981–99 2000–	SSB NBS	CSP
Regional China: A Business Economic Handbook	English	2000; 2010	Guo	PM
A Compilation of Historical Statistical Materials of China's Provinces, Autonomous Regions and Municipalities	English	1949–89	SSB (1990) Hsueh et al. (1993)	CSP WVP
Historical Data on China's Gross Domestic Product	Chinese	1952–95	SSB	NCUFE
Almanac of China's Economy	Chinese	1981–		EMP
China Industrial Economic Statistical Yearbook	Chinese	1988–	SSB	CSP
Price Yearbook of China[b]	Chinese	1990–	ECPYC	CPP

Notes:
(a)Also available at the website (http://www.stats.gov.cn/eng/) for the data from 1996 onwards.
(b)Some price information is available at http://www.chinaprice.gov.cn. CPP=China Price Press; CSP=China Statistics Press; ECPYC=editing committee of Price Yearbook of China; EMP=Economics and Management Press; NBS=National Bureau of Statistics of China; NCUFE=Press of Northeast China University of Finance and Economics; PM=Palgrave-Macmillan; and WVP=Westview Press; SSB=State Statistical Bureau.

USEFUL WEBSITES

The supplement materials (including the PowerPoint slides and some in-depth case studies, and a list of readings suggested for each chapter) are available at the publisher's companion site:

http://www.elsevierdirect.com/companions/9780123978264

For news and information about China's current political, administrative and economic conditions, please visit the following websites:

http://www.cpcchina.org/ (the website of the Communist Party of China) http://english.gov.cn/ (the website of Central People's Government of the PRC)

http://www.npc.gov.cn/englishnpc/news/index.htm (the website of the National People's Congress of the PRC)

http://www.cppcc.gov.cn/ (the website of the Chinese People's Political Consultative Congress)

Useful websites that have the most popular topics relating to the Chinese economy or from which the reader can get access to the recent statistical data on the Chinese economy include the following:

http://www.chinaprice.gov.cn

http://www.stats.gov.cn/

http://www.cei.gov.cn/

http://www.economist.com/topics/chinese-economy

http://www.economist.com/content/all_parities_china

http://www.chinaeconomicreview.com/

http://www.economywatch.com/world_economy/china/?page=full

http://en.wikipedia.org/wiki/Economy_of_China

http://en.wikipedia.org/wiki/Economy_of_the_Peoples_Republic_of_China

For more information see the companion site at:

http://www.elsevierdirect.com/companions/9780123978264

Chapter 1

A Brief History of China

The Yellow River. *Source: The Yellow River Conservancy Commission of the Ministry of Water Resources of the People's Republic of China.*

The Yellow River (Huanghe) originates at the foot of the Kunlun mountains in the west and flows over 5,000 kilometers eastward to the Pacific Ocean. The river has been generally regarded as the cradle of the Chinese nation. It was along the banks of the river that the Chinese civilization first developed. The geographical and hydrological characteristics of the Yellow River have shaped the Chinese nation, its 5,000-year civilization, as well as its distinctive philosophy and history.

Here [Luoyi, a place in central China] is the center under heaven, from which all other states bear same distance when they come to pay tributes. (ci tianxia zhi zhong, sifang rugong daoli jun.)

– King Wu (*c.* 1066 BC)

1.1 THE ORIGINS OF THE NATION

China, shaped like a rooster, and situated in East Asia, has a 14,500 km coastline extending along the Bohai Sea, the Korean Bay, the Yellow Sea, the East China Sea, the South China Sea, and the Tokin Gulf. It has a total length of approximately 22,140 km, with land boundaries with North Korea, Russia and Mongolia in the northeast and north, Kazakhstan, Kyrgyzstan, Tajikistan, Afghanistan, and Pakistan in the west, India and Nepal in the southwest, and Myanmar, Laos, and Vietnam in the south. Over the course of thousands of years of history, there have been many legendary stories about this huge nation, as well as its people, culture, and history.

Understanding the Chinese Economies. DOI: http://dx.doi.org/10.1016/B978-0-12-397826-4.00001-9
© 2013 Elsevier Inc. All rights reserved.

1.1.1 Cradle of the Nation

In the prehistoric period, the progenitors of the Chinese people were scattered across small tribes over the middle reaches of the Yellow River. The present-day Chinese see themselves as descendants of the Hua-Xia people. The Hua people, who first settled around Mount Hua, near the middle reaches of the Yellow River valley, together with the Xia people, who established themselves near the Xia River (the upper course of the Han River, a tributary of the Yangtze River), were referred to as the Hua-Xia people. Both of these areas were located in the central southern region of Shaanxi province. Towards the end of the Neolithic period, these tribes were already using a primitive form of writing, and had developed a system to measure time and count numbers. They had also developed a variety of articles for daily use, including clothing, houses, weapons, pottery, and money.

According to mythology, the Chinese nation began with Pangu, the creator of the universe. However, Chinese culture began to develop with the emergence of Emperor Yan (Yandi) and Emperor Huang (Huangdi) around 2300 BC. For this reason the Chinese today refer to themselves as the *yanhuang zisun* (the descendants of Emperors Yan and Huang). During the period of the reign of Emperors Yan and Huang and their successors, people were taught to observe five basic relationships, including good relations between: sovereign and minister; father and son; husband and wife; brother and brother; and friend and friend. This code of conduct, which was later systematically developed by Confucius (551–475 BC) and his disciples, established an ethical philosophy which has influenced Chinese society for the past two thousand years.

1.1.2 Xia, Shang, and Zhou Dynasties

From the twenty-first to the second century BC, three ancient dynasties – Xia, Shang and Zhou – were established in the Yellow River valley. The Xia dynasty, founded by the great Yu and his son, Qi, lasted until the sixteenth century BC. At the very least, the Xia dynasty marked an evolutionary stage between the late Neolithic cultures and the characteristic Chinese urban civilization of the Shang dynasty. During this period, the territorial boundaries of the Chinese nation began to take shape. The country was divided into nine administrative prefectures and a system of land taxes was established.

The Shang dynasty lasted from the sixteenth century BC to around 1046 BC. The Shang dynasty (which was also called the Yin dynasty in its later stages) was founded by a rebel leader, Tang, who overthrew the last of the Xia rulers. Its civilization was based on agriculture, augmented by hunting and animal husbandry. Two of the most important events of the period were the development of a writing

system, as revealed in archaic Chinese inscriptions found on tortoise shells and flat cattle bones (commonly called oracle bones), and the use of bronze metallurgy. A number of ceremonial bronze vessels with inscriptions date from the Shang period; the workmanship on the bronzes attests to a high level of civilization. For example, in the ruins of the city of Anyang (located at northern Henan province), the last capital of the Shang dynasty, archeologists have unearthed over 150,000 pieces of oracle bones and other relics of the dynasty, suggesting that China experienced relative stability and prosperity in that period.

In a war with the 28th ruler of the Shang dynasty, the allied forces, under the command of King Wu, defeated the Shang army, leading to the foundation of a new dynasty named Zhou. The power of the rulers in the Zhou dynasty was based on 'Zongfa' – a system of inheritance and ancestral worship at a time when polygamy was a customary practice among the royalty and nobility.[1] In this way, a huge structure was built up, radiating from a central hub through endless feudal and in-feudal systems. Particularly noteworthy is that, in the dynasty, education was widespread with a national university in the capital and various grades of schools named. Scholars and intellectuals were held in high esteem, and art and learning flourished as never before.

The Chinese name *zhongguo* (or 'China') derives from the term 'center under heaven', a term that was first coined by King Wu of the Zhou dynasty (see Box 1.1). The king's intention was to move the Zhou capital from Haojing in western China to Luoyi (now known as Luoyang) in central China, in order to maintain more effective control over the entire nation.

During the second half of the Zhou dynasty (also known as the Warring States period), a new group of regional rulers sought to obtain the services of talented individuals who could help to increase their political influence. The result was an unprecedented development in independent thinking and original philosophies. The most celebrated philosophers of this period were Laozi, Confucius, Zhuangzi, Mencius, Mozi, Hanfei, and Xunzi. These individuals became the leading sprits of the Taoist, Confucian, Mohist, and Legalist schools of thought.

1.2 THE RISE AND FALL OF THE EMPIRE

1.2.1 Qin, Han, and Jin Dynasties

In 221 BC, China was unified by Ying Zheng (also called Qin Shihuang), the first emperor of the Qin dynasty. The most important contribution of the Qin dynasty was the

---

1. According to the Zongfa system, the eldest son born of the highest-ranking wife of a member of the royal household or nobility was called the 'major branch' and inherited the right of succession to his father's throne or noble title. Other sons were known as 'minor branches'.

Box 1.1 Hezun and 'Zhongguo'

Hezun is a wine vessel made in the first years of the Zhou dynasty (1046–221 BC). With a height of 38.8 cm, a top-opening diameter of 28.8 cm and a weight of 14.6 kg, Hezun is named after 'He', the owner of the vessel.

Unearthed in the fall of 1963 on the level of the Jiacun village, Baoji city, Shaanxi province, Hezun is now part of a collection of the Baoji Bronze Ware Museum. There is an inscription of 122 Chinese characters at the bottom inside. The main idea is: In 1039 BC King Cheng of the Zhou dynasty (reign 1043–1007 BC) was offering a sacrifice to his father (King Wu of the Zhou), saying: 'Once capturing Luoyi [today's Luoyang at central China's Henan province, the major city of the Shang dynasty], King Wu notified his liegemen that "it will, as the center under heaven, become a place in which I can govern the whole nation". The remaining characters of the inscription tell that King Cheng taught a young man, named He, of the King's family, a lesson on how the former Kings of the Zhou dynasty reigned the people.

The inscription in Hezun has been regarded as the earliest literal record for the name 'China' ('zhongguo').

foundation of a completely new social and political order, under a strict system of rewards and punishment, favored by a group of scholars known as Legalists. In place of feudalism, the country was reorganized into 36 prefectures and a number of counties. Under this prefecture-county administration, all authority was vested in the central government. For the first time in history, China's written language, currency, and weights and measures were all unified and standardized. In order to consolidate and strengthen his imperial rule, the Emperor Qin Shihuang undertook large-scale construction projects, including national roadways, waterways, and the Great Wall, which was 5,000 kilometers long. At its greatest extent, the Great Wall reaches from eastern Liaoning to northwestern Gansu. These activities required enormous levels of manpower and resources, not to mention repressive measures.

After the conquest of the 'barbarians' in the south, the Chinese territory was extended to the shores of the South China Sea. In spite of many political and military achievements, its multicultural development was monopolized by the Qin dynasty. Excessive trust was placed in the efficacy of the Legalist methods, while the books on Confucianism and other schools of thought were burned in order to keep the people in a state of ignorance. Even worse, those intellectuals and scholars who criticized the government were either executed or were forced to work as slave labor. Due to its cruel and despotic rule, the Qin dynasty was overthrown less than twenty years after its rise to power. The imperial system initiated during the Qin dynasty, however, set a pattern that was to be repeated over the next two millennia.

Five years later, Liu Bang reunited China and established a lasting dynasty, the Han (206 BC–AD 220). Strong military forces made it possible for the Han dynasty to expand China's territories to the Western Dominion in today's Xinjiang and Central Asia and also to Taiwan Island in the East China Sea. The Han dynasty represented a glorious era in Chinese history. The political institutions of the Qin and the Han dynasties were typical of all the dynasties that were to follow. The nine-chapter legal code drawn up in the early days of the Han served as a model for all later versions of Chinese codes. The political and military might of the Han dynasty was so impressive that, since this time, the Chinese have referred to themselves as the 'Han' people.

Under the Han rulers, Confucianism was given special emphasis and those doing research on Confucian studies were given priority for public positions. Emperor Wudi (140–87 BC) listed the Confucian classics as subjects of study for his ministers, and appointed well-read scholars to positions of authority, labeled *Boshi* (doctor). Confucianism thus gained official sanction over competing philosophical schools and became the core of Chinese culture. The Han period also produced China's most famous historian, Sima Qian (145–87 BC), whose *Shiji* (historical records) provides a detailed chronicle from the time of a legendary Huang emperor to the period of Emperor Wudi of the Han. This period was also marked by a series of technological advances, including two of the great Chinese inventions, paper and porcelain.

At the end of the Eastern Han period (AD 25–220)[2] political corruption and social chaos, together with widespread civil disturbances and royal throne usurpation, led

---

2. Historically, the Han dynasty is divided into two periods: the Western Han had its capital in Chang'an in the west; while the Eastern Han had its capital in Luoyang in the east.

eventually to the creation of three independent kingdoms – the Wei (AD 220–265) in the north, the Shu (AD 221–263) in the southwest and the Wu (AD 222–280) in the southeast. China remained divided until AD 265 when the Jin dynasty was founded in Luoyang in central China.

The Jin was not militarily as strong as the non-Han counterparts in the north, which encouraged the southwards move of its capital to where is now called Nanjing (southern capital). Large-scale migration from the north to the south led to the Yangtze River valley becoming more prosperous than before, and the economic and cultural center therefore shifted gradually to the southeast of the country. This transfer of the capital coincided with China's political fragmentation into a succession of dynasties that lasted from AD 420 to 589. In the Yellow River valley, the non-Han peoples lived alongside the indigenous Han people, forming a more diverse and dynamic Chinese nation than ever before. Despite the political disunity of the times, there were notable technological advances, including the invention of gunpowder and the wheelbarrow. During this period, Buddhism became increasingly popular in both northern and southern China.

1.2.2 Sui, Tang, and Song Dynasties

China was reunified during the Sui dynasty (AD 581–618). The Sui is famous for its construction of the Grand Canal which linked the Yellow River and the Huai and Yangtze Rivers, in order to secure improved communication between the south and the north of the country. In terms of human costs, only the Great Wall – which was constructed during the Qin dynasty – is comparable with the Canal. Like the Qin, the Sui was also a short-lived dynasty, which was succeeded by the more powerful Tang dynasty (AD 618–907).

The Tang period was the golden age of literature and art. A government system supported by a large class of Confucian literati, selected through a system of civil service examinations, was perfected under Tang rule. This competitive procedure was designed to draw the best talents into government. But perhaps an even greater consideration for the Tang rulers, aware that imperial dependence on powerful aristocratic families and warlords would have destabilizing consequences, was to create a body of career officials that had no autonomous territorial or functional power base. As it turned out, these scholar-officials acquired considerable status within their local communities, family ties, and shared values that connected them to the imperial court. From the Tang times until the closing days of the Qing Empire in AD 1911, scholar-officials often functioned as intermediaries between the grassroots level and the government.

By the middle of the eighth century, Tang power had ebbed. Domestic economic instability and military defeat

in AD 751 by Arabs at Talas, in Central Asia, marked the beginning of five centuries of steady military decline for the Chinese empire. Misrule, court intrigues, economic exploitation, and popular rebellions weakened the empire, making it possible for northern invaders to terminate the dynasty in AD 907. The next half-century saw the gradual fragmentation of China into five Dynasties and ten Kingdoms (AD 907–960).

In AD 960, China was reunited once again. The founders of the Song dynasty built an effective centralized bureaucracy staffed with civilian scholar-officials. Regional military governors and their supporters were replaced by centrally appointed officials. This system of civilian rule led to a greater concentration of power in the hands of the emperor and his palace bureaucracy than had been achieved in the previous dynasties. Unlike the Tang dynasty, the Song dynasty (AD 960–1279) was confronted by powerful military enemies from the north. The conflict between the Song and the Liao (a non-Han dynasty in northern China from AD 907 to 1125) lasted for more than a century before another non-Han dynasty, the Jin (AD 1115–1234), first defeated the Liao and then, in 1127, took control of the Song's capital, Kaifeng, and captured two Song emperors as hostages. With northern China falling into the hands of the Jin, the Song capital moved from the Yellow River valley to Lin'an (today's Hangzhou). As a result, the economic and cultural centers shifted from the central to the southeastern areas of China.

Despite its military weakness, the Song dynasty contributed a great deal to the civilization of the world. Many Chinese inventions, including the compass, gunpowder and movable-type printing, were introduced to the West during this period. Culturally, the Song also refined many of the developments of previous centuries. The Neo-Confucian philosophers found certain purity in the originality of the ancient classical texts of Confucianism. The most influential of these philosophers was Zhu Xi (AD 1130–1200), whose synthesis of Confucian thought and Buddhist, Taoist, and other ideas became the official imperial ideology from late Song times to the late nineteenth century. Neo-Confucian doctrines also came to play a dominant role in the intellectual life of Korea, Vietnam, and Japan.

1.2.3 Yuan, Ming, and Qing Dynasties

In AD 1279 the Mongol cavalry, under the leadership of Genghis Khan, controlled the entire Chinese territory. The 88-year-long Yuan dynasty was an extraordinary one. Under Mongol rule, China once again expanded its borders. During the strongest period of the Yuan dynasty, China's territory even extended as far as eastern Europe.

The Mongols' extensive West Asian and European contacts led to a substantial degree of cultural exchange. This led to the development of rich cultural diversities.

Western musical instruments were introduced and helped to enrich the Chinese performing arts. This period marks the conversion to Islam of growing numbers of Chinese in the northwest and southwest by Muslims from Central Asia. Nestorianism and Roman Catholicism also enjoyed a period of toleration during this period. Tibetan Buddhism (Lamaism) flourished, although native Taoism endured Mongol persecutions. Confucian governmental practices and examinations based on the Classics, which had fallen into disuse in north China during the period of disunity, were reinstated by the Mongols in the hope of maintaining order over Han society. Certain key Chinese innovations, such as printing techniques, porcelain production, playing cards and medical literature, were introduced in Europe, while the production of thin glass and cloisonné became increasingly popular in China. European people were also enthralled by the account given by Venetian Marco Polo of his trip to 'Cambaluc', the Great Khan's capital (now Beijing), and of the ways of life he encountered there.

In internal affairs, however, the Mongolian caste system – in which the majority of the Han people were seen as inferior to non-Han peoples – was not ideal. Widespread famines, resulting from natural disasters, political corruption, and misgovernment, eventually resulted in a successful anti-Mongol revolution led by Zhu Yuanzhang, who founded the Han-based dynasty, the Ming (AD 1368–1644) in Nanjing. In 1421, the Ming dynasty moved its seat to Beijing, after defeating the nomadic tribes of the northern part of the Great Wall. In Southeast Asia the Chinese armies reconquered Annam, as northern Vietnam was then known, and they also repelled the Mongols, while the Chinese fleet sailed the China seas and the Indian Ocean, venturing even as far as the east coast of Africa. The maritime Asian nations sent envoys with tributes for the Chinese emperor.

The maritime expeditions stopped suddenly after 1433, probably as a result of the great expense of large-scale expeditions at a time of preoccupation with securing northern borders against the threat from the Mongols. Pressure from the powerful Neo-Confucian bureaucracy led to a revival of a society that was centered on agriculture. Internally, the Grand Canal was expanded to its farthest limits and proved to be a stimulus to domestic trade. The stability of the Ming dynasty, which suffered no major disruptions of the population (then around 100 million), economy, arts, society and politics, promoted a belief among the Chinese that they had achieved the most satisfactory civilization on earth and that nothing foreign was either needed or welcome.

As the Ming dynasty declined, China's last, also the last minority-based dynasty, the Qing (AD 1644–1911), was set up by the Manchus, who rose to power in Manchuria (today's northeastern part of China). Compared with the Mongols, the period of Manchu rule over China can be viewed as more successful. At the height of the Qing dynasty, the Manchus utilized the best minds and richest human resources of the nation, regardless of race. Although the Manchus were not Han Chinese and were subjected to strong resistance, especially in the south, they had assimilated a great deal of the Han-Chinese culture before conquering China Proper.

Realizing that in order to dominate the empire they would have to do things in the Chinese manner, the Manchus retained many institutions of Ming and earlier Chinese derivation. Furthermore, the Han-based political ideologies and cultural traditions of the Chinese were adopted by the Manchus, resulting in virtually total cultural assimilation of the Manchus by the Han Chinese. After the subduing of China Proper, the Manchus conquered Outer Mongolia (now the Mongolian People's Republic) in the late seventeenth century. In the eighteenth century they gained control of Central Asia as far as the Pamir Mountains and established a protectorate over Tibet. The Qing thus became the first dynasty to successfully eliminate all danger to China Proper from across its land borders. Under the rule of the Manchu dynasty the empire grew once again; during this period Taiwan, the last outpost of anti-Manchu resistance, was incorporated into China for the first time. In addition, the Qing emperors received tributes from many neighboring states.

1.2.4 The Fall of the Empire

The 1840s marked a turning point in Chinese history. In the early nineteenth century, Britain was smuggling large quantities of opium into China, causing a substantial outflow of Chinese silver and grave economic disruption. In an effort to protect its opium trade, in 1840 Britain initiated the First Opium War. The war ended in 1842, after the Qing court signed the Treaty of Nanjing with Britain, bartering away China's national sovereignty. Subsequently, China declined into a semi-colonial and semi-feudal country. After the Opium War, Britain and other Western powers, including Belgium, the Netherlands, Prussia, Spain, Portugal, the USA, and France, seized 'concessions' and divided China into 'spheres of influence'.

The second half of the nineteenth century saw many peasant leaders and national heroes. The Revolution of 1911, led by Dr Sun Yatsen, is of great significance in modern Chinese history, since with the founding of the Republic of China (ROC) in 1912, it discarded the feudal monarchical system that had ruled China for more than 2,000 years. In the following decades, however, the Chinese nation was on the edge of bankruptcy. The major events that occurred in Chinese society during the twentieth century are listed below in chronological order:

- 1912, China's final dynasty, the Qing, was replaced by the Republic of China (ROC)
- 1921, the Chinese Communist Party (CCP) was founded

- 1931, Japan invaded the Northeast of China (Manchuria)
- 1937, Japan invaded China and the War of Resistance against Japan began
- 1945, Japan surrendered unconditionally and, thereafter, the Civil War between the Nationalists and the Communists broke out
- 1949, the People's Republic of China (PRC) was founded, followed by large-scale land reform and socialist transformation

1.3　CHINA IN THE NEW MILLENNIUM

1.3.1　Socialism in Transition

During the past century, China's economic development had been interrupted on a number of separate occasions. The Chinese economy was nearly bankrupt at the end of the Civil War in the late 1940s, and was seriously damaged by both the Great Leap Forward (1958–60) and the Cultural Revolution (1966–76) movements. However, since the late 1970s, when the Chinese government began the gradual transformation of its centrally planned Stalinesque system, the Chinese economy has grown extremely rapidly. In the reform era since 1978, China has become one of the world's fastest-growing economies. Since 1978, China's real GDP has grown at an average annual rate of almost 10 percent.

With China achieving vigorous economic growth since the implementation of market-oriented reform in the late 1970s, the Chinese model has been generally regarded as having achieved the most successful transformation of all of the former Soviet-type economies in terms of improvements in economic performance. However, it should also be noted that China still lags behind many market-based, industrialized economies. The per capita income of China has remained significantly lower than that of the USA, Japan and other newly industrialized economies. While China's over-centralized planning system was largely responsible for its poor socioeconomic performance, there were also historical, social, and cultural factors that hindered its socioeconomic development. Indeed, it is not easy to develop a market-system framework within a short period of time – China utilized the centrally planned system for nearly 30 years and this was, in particular, deeply influenced by long periods of feudalism, but rarely by economic democracy.

Modern Western civilization has undoubtedly attained a far higher level of development than those found in the rest of the world. As mentioned in Weber (1904, pp. 1–2), only in the West has science attained such an advanced stage of development. However, a consideration of the evolution of the world's civilizations over the past many

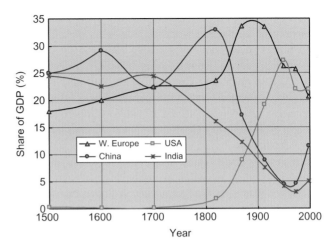

FIGURE 1.1　A dynamic view of the Chinese economy, AD 1500–2000. *Source: Based on Maddison (2001).*

thousands of years clearly reveals that no civilizations (or countries) have been economic and technological leaders throughout the ages. If the current world growth pattern (see Figure 1.1) persists for two or more decades, we may be seeing the USA overtaken by China or India in the twenty-first century.

1.3.2　Capitalism, Chinese Style?

Over recent decades, the Chinese economy has experienced dramatic changes and a more rapid pace of development than many other transitional centrally planned economies (CPEs). This has been the result of a combination of both internal and external circumstances. In these first few years of the twenty-first century, we can see that China is scheduled to develop its economy along its own distinctive lines. At the same time, China's current situation poses many significant challenges to its economy. Many inherent problems in relation to economic development still persist. If the Chinese government does not address these properly, its efforts, based on the successful introduction of Chinese-style reforms, will inevitably be jeopardized.

More than two thousand years ago, Confucius instructed his pupils through the telling of this autobiographical story:

Since the age of 15, I have devoted myself to learning; since 30, I have been well established; since 40, I have understood many things and have no longer been confused; since 50, I have known my heaven-sent duty; since 60, I have been able to distinguish right and wrong in other people's words; and since 70, I have been able to do what I intended freely without breaking the rules.

Hopefully, after the celebration of the 60th anniversary of the PRC, the Chinese leaders will finally be emerging from their past confused age and will now better know where to go and what to do next.

Case Study 1

Understanding Chinese Culture

When considering the world's great ancient civilizations, we find that most of them are centered in river valleys. The Sumerians were located along the Euphrates and the Tigris Rivers and their tributaries, and the Egyptians around the Nile. Roots of the ancient Indus civilization originated along the Indus River, and the earliest Chinese dynasties centered their culture on the Yellow River. Not only were rivers used for irrigating crops and daily water needs, but societies also relied on the rivers for communication and transportation.

The hydrological characteristics of rivers heavily influenced ancient riparian civilizations. Large workforces were needed to divert water for irrigation and build protective works to minimize flood damage. This led to increasing sedentism, high population density, and the need for a centralized administration along the river valley. The development of 'hydraulic societies' in China, that were dependent on complex irrigation systems, is a good example of this. The cost of hydraulic constructions and its subsequent maintenance required a political and social structure capable of forceful extraction of labor. Furthermore, upstream communities usually had a strategic advantage over downstream residents regarding the control of water. As a result, social stratification and armed military forces emerged alongside large-scale water control. These are very important processes in the development of ancient civilizations.

If ancient civilizations commonly originated along ancient river systems, then why did some river systems such as the Amazon, Yangtze, Mississippi, Volga, and Rhine not experience the rise of *in situ* sociopolitical complexity? This may be related to more local environmental and hydrological factors that influence the frequency and magnitude of natural disasters and create variable adaptive stress. Natural disasters have economic and emotional effects on people. The ability, therefore, to predict and to combat, or prevent, natural disasters that threaten us is crucial in the development of human civilizations. However, not all natural disasters are the same, and they vary in how they can stimulate the development of social and political complexity. For the sake of brevity, I here focus on the cyclical nature of riverine floods.

One of the hallmark creations of early civilizations is the calendar. A device to mark cyclical time is not easily related to droughts, earthquakes, volcanic eruptions, famine, windstorms, or other natural disasters. However, calendars were closely related to the regularity of river flooding. For example, in ancient Egypt, the 15th day of June, or the start of the flooding season of the Nile, was selected as the first day of a new year. Moreover, because natural disasters tied to flooding are more frequently found in large river valleys (especially in their lower reaches), people living in such areas have a need to develop technological tools in order to survive.

The development of the ancient Chinese civilization along the valley of the Yellow River provides even stronger evidence to support the hypothesis that civilization originates as a human response to river floods. China has had a particularly long and terrible history of devastating flooding. More than five thousand kilometers long, the Yellow River begins much higher above sea level in the western mountain area and ends at the Yellow Sea. During the long history of China, the Yellow River has been dubbed as 'China's Sorrow', because it has killed more people than any other river in the world. Much of the problem stems from the high silt content of the river. Millions of tons of yellow mud choke the channel, causing the river to overflow and change its course. Water is held in by dikes of ever-increasing height. In its lower reaches, the riverbed has actually become 20 meters higher than the level of the surrounding countryside. At the same time, the river has also been known as the 'cradle of Chinese civilization' and considered a blessing, with the nickname 'China's Pride'.

During the course of Chinese history, attempts to control the Yellow River have been categorized by different strategic approaches. One strategy is the active control of the river: to confine it within a narrow channel through the use of a system of high levees. More often than not, Chinese scholars have seen the close confinement of the river as a 'Confucian' solution of discipline and order imposed upon nature – this contrasts with the 'Taoist' solution of allowing the river a more 'natural' course within lighter constraints. In either case, however, river engineering represented a tremendous interference with any 'natural' regime; and the contrasting solutions were more accurately characterized as being opposites of engineering than philosophical approaches. Certainly, these contradicting phenomena are the defining results of the differing living conditions on which Confucian and Taoist founders were based (see Table 1.1).

Specifically, the Confucians, including Confucius and Mencius and early followers, all of whom lived within the lower reaches of the Yellow River, had either suffered more seriously from river floods, or had been more deeply impressed by such flood-related stories as told by their elders than Laozi, the founder of Taoism. For example, the following story is included in the analects of Mencius (372–289 BC):

In the time of Emperor Yao [around the 22nd century BC], the waters flowing out of their channels inundated the Central

TABLE 1.1 Confucianism Versus Taoism: Some Basic Facts

	Confucianism	Taoism
Founder's name	Kongzi (Confucius)	Laozi (Lao Tzu)
Founder's year of birth	551 BC	c. 600 BC
Founder's place of birth/living	Qufu – lower reaches of Yellow River	Luyi/Luoyi[a] – middle and upper reaches of Yellow River
How the founder suffered from river flood	Very seriously	Not seriously
Overall goal	Find peaceful and harmonious place of life	No overall goal
Rule of behavior	Follow a certain relationship between people	Follow life according to the Tao
Attitude towards flood control	Narrow channel by high levees	Wider flood plain between lower levees

[a]Laozi spent most of his career first at Luoyi (the capital of the eastern Zhou dynasty) and later at the mountain areas in western China.

Kingdom. Snakes and dragons occupied it, and the people had no place in which they could settle themselves. In the low grounds they made nests for themselves on the trees or raised platforms, and in the high grounds they made caves. It is said in the Book of History, 'The waters in their wild course warned me.' Those 'waters in their wild course' were the waters of the great inundation. Emperor Shun dispatched Yu to reduce the waters to order. Yu dug open their obstructed channels, and conducted them to the sea. He drove away the snakes and dragons, and forced them into the grassy marshes. On this, the waters pursued their course through the country, even the waters of the Jiang, the Huai, the He, and the Han, and the dangers and obstructions which they had occasioned were removed. The birds and beasts which had injured the people also disappeared, and after this men found the plains available for them.[3]

Subject to differing living conditions within the valley of the Yellow River, the Confucian and Taoist schools each had its own unique view on basic beliefs, overall goals, goals of individual behavior, views of life, rules of behavior, and views about society. The overall goal of Confucianism was to find a peaceful and harmonious place in life, whereas that of Taoism had no overall aim. The Taoists simply had to follow life according to the Tao, but the Confucians followed a certain behavior and sought to be in harmony with nature. The Confucians believed that you should be improved by education and the development of your character and that you needed to understand the complicated relationships with your family members, with the government and with society as a whole, while the Tao believed that the life you lived with the Tao was good and following society's ways was bad.

Indeed, the historical evolution of the Yellow River provides a useful analogy for explaining the differences between Chinese culture and other cultures in the rest of the world. The changes of the river's course have been spectacular, and the river mouth has sometimes changed drastically by hundreds of kilometers. It has had dozens of major and numerous minor changes in course over thousands of years, each leading to a great amount of not only human casualties but also property losses. All of these features have influenced the lifestyles of the Chinese people, especially of those with close proximity to the Yellow River. For example, after having compared the architectures of the Yellow River valley and of the southeastern provinces (such as Guangdong and Fujian), we find that the houses and other buildings at the Yellow River valley, especially at the lower reaches of the river, are much simpler and, of course, less firm in structure, with fewer valuable materials. Since the majority of the Han population living in the southeast provinces are descended from those who emigrated from the Yellow River valley, only geographical features can explain this difference. People living at the Yellow River valley must have frequently abandoned their homes in order to escape from the unruly disastrous floodwaters.

The Yellow River can provide us with more details about Chinese society. For example, the difficulties in securing sufficient food within the valley of the Yellow River, probably a result of the frequent natural disasters, have built the economical foundations for Chinese cuisine. In contrast to the Westerners, the Chinese have a much smaller percentage of fat and meat as the main ingredient

---

3. Cited from Mencius (c. 300 BC, Teng Wen Gong II). Note that the term 'dragon', which has also been known as the 'God of water or rain' in traditional Chinese culture, probably referred to the 'crocodile' or other amphibious lizards.

in their daily diet. This instantly reminds me of the hypothesis that it is the shortage of food in quantity and category that drove the Chinese to develop many cooking methods (including braising, boiling, braising with soy sauce, roasting, baking, grilling, scalding, deep-frying, steaming, drying, and salt-preserving) in order to make their food more delicious. In addition, the scarcity of food has resulted in a distinctive eating habit (that is, dishes are placed in the center of a table so that everybody can share the meal) in ancient China. In the meantime, the above conditions have also contributed to the development of a collectivist-style culture in China.

REFERENCES

Maddison, A. (2001). *The world economy: a millennial perspective.* Paris: OECD Development Center.

Mencius (c. 300 BC) (1999). *Analects of mencius* (an English-Chinese edition). Beijing: Foreign Languages Press.

Chapter 2

Spatial and Administrative Divisions

The Great Wall at Badaling, Changping, Beijing. *Source: https://www.cia.gov/library/publications/the-world-factbook/photo_gallery/ch/*

As one of the greatest construction projects in the world, the Great Wall, which once served as China's political and administrative boundaries in ancient times, was first built during the Spring and Autumn Period (770–476 BC) and the Warring States Period (475–221 BC). The Wall extends from Linyao (located around the Min-xian county of Gansu province) in the west, to Yin-shan in the north and to Liao-dong in the east. Almost all the emperors of the Han (206 BC–220 AD), the Northern Wei (386–534 AD), the Northern Qi (550–577 AD), the Northern Zhou (557–581 AD) and the Sui (581–618 AD) dynasties invested heavily in the rebuilding of the Wall, in order to prevent their territories from being attacked from the north.

During the early period of the Ming dynasty (1368–1644 AD), the border wall was restored to its current state.

Baigui [a minister of the state of Wei in today's Henan province during the Warring States period] said, 'My management of the waters is superior to that of Yu.' Mencius replied, 'You are wrong, Sir. Yu's regulation of the waters was according to the natural laws of water. He therefore made the four seas their receptacle, while you make the neighboring states their receptacle. Water flowing out of its channels is called an inundation. The inundating waters are disastrous to the neighboring states, and what a benevolent man detests. You are wrong, my dear Sir!'

– Analects of Mencius (6B: 6)

Understanding the Chinese Economies. DOI: http://dx.doi.org/10.1016/B978-0-12-397826-4.00002-0
© 2013 Elsevier Inc. All rights reserved.

2.1 ADMINISTRATIVE DIVISIONS

2.1.1 Historical Evolution

During ancient times, the Chinese nation was generally regarded as being divided into nine states (or prefectures). More often than not, China, which is now called *zhongguo* (center under heaven or central state) in pinyin form, had an alternative name, *jiuzhou* (nine states). However, there have been a number of different viewpoints as to the precise classification of these nine states.

For example, according to *Yugong* (the geographical records of the tribute to the Yu), a book which was probably written in the Xia dynasty (c. 1988–1766 BC),[1] the nine states are Jizhou (on the northern side of the Yellow River), Yanzhou (on the eastern side of the Yellow River), Qingzhou (on the Shandong peninsula), Yangzhou (in the southeast), Jingzhou (in the south), Yuzhou (on the southern side of the Yellow River), Yongzhou (in the near west), Liangzhou (in the far west) and Xuzhou (in the east, comprising the northern Jiangsu and southeast Shandong provinces).[2]

Since the founding of the feudal system, China's provincial administrations have been named, *inter alia*, as:

- *jun* in the Qin dynasty (221–206 BC)
- *junguo* in the Western Han dynasty (206 BC–AD 25)
- *zhou* in the Eastern Han (AD 25–220) and the Wei (AD 220–265), the Jin (AD 266–420) and the North and South (AD 420–589) dynasties
- *dao*[3] in the Tang dynasty (AD 618–907)
- *lu* in the North and South Song (AD 960–1279) and the Jin (AD 1115–1235) dynasties
- *zhongshu-xingsheng* in the Yuan dynasty (AD 1279–1368)
- *xingsheng* in the Ming (AD 1368–1644) and the Qing (AD 1644–1911) dynasties.

Notice that the Chinese character *sheng* originally refers to the term 'ministry' (it is still being used in Japan and Korea). *Zhongshu-xingsheng* and *xingsheng* (the latter has evolved to the term *sheng* in contemporary Chinese language) refer to the 'ministerial representative agencies of central government to provinces'.

2.1.2 China's Administrative Hierarchy

At present, China's territorial-administrative hierarchy has three different types of provincial-level units: *sheng* (province), *zizhiqu* (autonomous regions) and *zhixiashi* (municipalities directly under the central government). In the Chinese state administration 'autonomous' refers to self-government by a large and single (but not necessarily majority) ethnic minority in any given unit within the territorial hierarchy. Autonomous regions are provincial-level units of state administration where the presence of an ethnic minority is officially recognized. They have the name of the specific ethnic minority incorporated in their title, as, for example, in the Guangxi Zhuang autonomous region, where Guangxi is the geographic name of the region and the Zhuang is the name of a nationality. Municipalities are large cities, directly subordinate to the Chinese Communist Party Central Committee (CCPCC) and the State Council.

It should be noted that the three kinds of provincial administrations (*sheng*, *zizhiqu* and *zhixiashi*) have different functions. More often than not, top *zhixiashi* leaders have been appointed as members of the Politburo of the CCPCC, something which has only happened to a small number of *sheng* and *zizhiqu* leaders. The autonomous regions (*zizhiqu*) are only established in areas where the ethnic minorities consist of the major portion of the population. Compared to other forms of provincial administrations, the *zizhiqu* is, at least in form, the most politically and culturally autonomous of the three kinds of provincial administrations. In addition, Hong Kong and Macau – which returned to China in 1997 and 1999, respectively – are now China's two special administrative regions (SARs). It was agreed on handover that the existing political and economic systems that prevailed prior to these dates would be maintained for 50 years.

While the formation of most provinces had taken place well before the foundation of the PRC, in recent decades a few of the others were either incorporated with their neighboring provinces or divided into new provinces. For example, in 1954, Pingyuan province, which was composed of the marginal administrative areas of present-day Hebei, Shanxi, Shandong and Henan provinces, was abolished. In 1988, Hainan island, Guangdong province, was established as a new province; and, in 1997, Chongqing city and its surrounding areas, all of which had belonged to Sichuan province, became a province-level municipality under the direct control of the central government. In addition, during the history of the PRC, some provincially marginal areas have been administratively transposed between the neighboring provinces. For example, in 1953, Xuzhou administrative region, Shandong province, was placed under the administration of Jiangsu province; and, in 1955, Yutai county was transferred from Anhui to Jiangsu provinces.

There are five hierarchies of administrative divisions in China: provincial level; prefectural level; county

---

1. The book *Yugong* was probably written or revised in the middle of the Warring States period (475–221 BC) since one tribute mentioned in this book, iron, had not been found until that period.

2. In another book entitled *Lvshi Chunqiu* (historical records compiled by Lv Buwei), these states include Jizhou, Yanzhou, Qingzhou, Yangzhou, Jingzhou, Yuzhou, Yongzhou, Youzhou (in the northeast), and Bingzhou (in the north).

3. Notice that the Chinese character *dao* is still being used to refer to 'province' in both North and South Korea.

TABLE 2.1 Names of Various Hierarchies of Administrative Divisions in China

Provincial Level	Prefectural Level	County Level	Township Level	Village Level
Autonomous Region (zìzhì qū)	Sub-provincial-level autonomous prefecture (fu shengji zizhi zhou); Prefectural-level city (diji shi); Autonomous prefecture (zihi zhou); Prefecture (diqu); Leagues (meng)	District (shixia qu); County-level city (xianji shi); County (xian); Autonomous county (zizhi xian); Banner (qi); Autonomous banner (zizhi qi)	Sub-district (jiedao); Town (zhen); Township (xiang); Ethnic township (minzu xiang); Sub-county district (xianxia qu); Sumu; Ethnic Sumu (minzu sumu)	Neighborhood committee (jumin weiyuan hui); Community (shequ); Village (cun); Gacha
Province (shěng)	Sub-provincial-level city (fu shengji shi); Prefectural-level city (diji shi); Autonomous prefecture (zizhi zhou); Prefecture (diqu)	District (shixia qu); Ethnic district (minzu qu); Special district (tequ); County-level city (xianji shi); County (xian); Autonomous county (zizhi xian)		
	Sub-prefectural-level city (fu diji shi); Administrative office (fu diji banshichu); Forestry district (linqu)			
Municipality directly under central government (zhíxiá shì)	Sub-provincial-level new area (fu shengji shixia qu); Prefectural-level district (diji shixia qu); County (xian)			

Notes: (1) 'Sub-provincial-level' (fu shengji) administrative divisions are included in the 'Prefectural level' administrative divisions. (2) Hong Kong and Macau are not included.

level; township level; and village level (see Table 2.1). The first-class administrative divisions include provinces, autonomous regions, and municipalities directly under the central government. The second-class administrative divisions refer to prefectures, autonomous prefectures, municipalities, and other prefecture-level administrative divisions. The third-class administrative divisions relate to counties, autonomous counties, and other county-level administrative divisions. An organizational pattern involving more classes of administrative divisions has been generally observed to have a lower level of administrative efficiency.

Recently, some provinces have been granted permission by the central government to reform the administrative divisions (that is, to eliminate the second-class administrative divisions) in order to increase spatial economic efficiency. However, this administrative reform has encountered difficulties in dealing with large provinces. For example, in Henan or Shandong province, there are more than 100 counties and county-level administrative divisions. Without the participation of the prefecture-level administrations, it would be very difficult, if not impossible, for a provincial governor to exert any direct effective influence on all of these county magistrates concurrently.

2.1.3 Large Versus Small Administrations

Most of China's provinces, autonomous regions and municipalities that are under the direct control of the

central government,[4] which are the average size and scale of a European country in population and land area, are considerable political and economic systems in their own right (see Table 2.2). These large provincial administrations, although they have some comparative advantages over the small ones in some circumstances, have been known to lack spatial administrative efficiency. Generally, the sources of benefits for large administrations may be grouped into two categories:

(i) The large administrations can make relatively efficient use of their fixed costs and hence gain considerable advantages over small administrations.

(ii) Marketing in a larger economy has many benefits, but the main economies of scale from marketing include the bulk purchase opportunities and distribution potential.

A number of advantages can lead to larger administrations experiencing risk-bearing economies. The underlying factor is that large administrations frequently engage in a range of diverse activities, so that a fall in the return from any one unit of economy does not threaten the stability of the whole economy. While increases in size frequently confer advantages on an administration, there is a limit to the gains from growth in many cases. In other

---

4. In what follows, unless stated otherwise, we will use the term 'province' to denote all of the three kinds of administrative divisions.

TABLE 2.2 Status of China's Current Provincial Administrations

Provincial Administration	Political Form	Population (Millions)	Land Area (1,000 km²)	Capital City	Official Website[a]
Anhui	S	59.5	130.0	Hefei	www.ah.gov.cn
Beijing	ZXS	19.6	16.8	Beijing	www.beijing.gov.cn
Chongqing	ZXS	28.8	82.4	Chongqing	www.cq.gov.cn
Fujian	S	36.9	120.0	Fuzhou	www.fj.gov.cn
Gansu	S	25.6	390.0	Lanzhou	www.gs.gov.cn
Guangdong	S	104.3	180.0	Guangzhou	www.gd.gov.cn
Guangxi	ZZQ	46.0	230.0	Nanning	www.gx.gov.cn
Guizhou	S	34.7	170.0	Guiyang	www.gz.gov.cn
Hainan	S	8.7	34.0	Haikou	www.hainan.gov.cn
Hebei	S	71.9	190.0	Shijiazhuang	www.hebei.gov.cn
Heilongjiang	S	38.3	460.0	Harbin	www.hlj.gov.cn
Henan	S	94.0	160.0	Zhengzhou	www.henan.gov.cn
Hubei	S	57.2	180.0	Wuhan	www.hubei.gov.cn
Hunan	S	65.7	210.0	Changsha	www.hunan.gov.cn
Inner Mongolia	ZZQ	24.7	1,100.0	Huhehaot	www.nmg.gov.cn
Jiangsu	S	78.7	100.0	Nanjing	www.jiangsu.gov.cn
Jiangxi	S	44.6	160.0	Nanchang	www.jiangxi.gov.cn
Jilin	S	27.5	180.0	Changchun	www.jl.gov.cn
Liaoning	S	43.7	150.0	Shenyang	www.ln.gov.cn
Ningxia	ZZQ	6.3	66.0	Yinchuan	www.nx.gov.cn
Qinghai	S	5.6	720.0	Xi'ning	www.qh.gov.cn
Shaanxi	S	37.3	190.0	Xi'an	www.shaanxi.gov.cn
Shandong	S	95.8	150.0	Ji'nan	www.sd.gov.cn
Shanghai	ZXS	23.0	5.8	Shanghai	www.shanghai.gov.cn
Shanxi	S	35.7	150.0	Taiyuan	www.shanxi.gov.cn
Sichuan	S	80.4	477.6	Chengdu	www.sc.gov.cn
Tianjin	ZXS	12.9	11.0	Tianjin	www.tj.gov.cn
Tibet (xizhang)	ZZQ	3.0	1,200.0	Lasha	www.xizhang.gov.cn
Xinjiang	ZZQ	21.8	1,600.0	Wurumuqi	www.xinjiang.gov.cn
Yunnan	S	46.0	380.0	Kunming	www.yn.gov.cn
Zhejiang	S	54.4	100.0	Hanzhou	www.zj.gov.cn

Notes: (1) All data are as of 2010. (2) S (sheng) = province; ZZQ (zizhiqu) = autonomous region; ZXS (zhixiashi) = municipality directly under the central government. (3) Hong Kong, Macau and Taiwan are not included.
[a]In the homepage (in either Chinese or Chinese/English) of each website, there is also a link to its English homepage.

words, there is an optimal level of capacity, and increases in size beyond this level will lead to a loss of economies of scale and manifest themselves in rising average cost (see Figure 2.1). Without doubt, the increasing complexity of managing a large administration is the major source of administrative inefficiencies when its size grows beyond a certain level, and management of diverse socioeconomic affairs and risks becomes increasingly difficult.

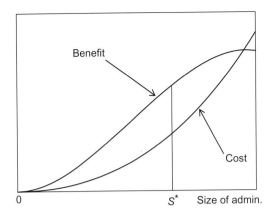

FIGURE 2.1 The optimum size (S*) of administrative divisions.

2.1.4 How Many Provinces Should There Be in China?

Given China's huge size and enormous population, establishing new provincial administrations (including provinces or other provincial-level units) in the border areas of some adjacent, large provinces seems to serve two positive functions. The first concerns increases in efficiency of spatial administration over the marginal, adjacent areas by transferring the multitude of administrative systems into a unitary administrative structure; and the second relates to the realization of increased economies of scale for provincial administration by separating the marginal areas out of the over-sized provinces.

Over recent decades, the total number of China's provincial administrations has increased from 29 in the mid-1950s, to 30 in 1988, and 31 in 1997. But economic geographers and regional scientists still believe that the introduction of more provinces, which are smaller in size, may help to improve the spatial efficiency of the Chinese economy.[5]

However, it seems unlikely that, under current political and economic systems, the central government will be willing to create, and, of course, be able to deal with any more provincial administrations.

2.2 GREAT REGIONS

2.2.1 Historical Evolution

When the People's Republic of China (PRC) was founded on 1 October 1949, China's provincial economies were managed through six great administrative regions (North, Northeast, East, Central South, Southwest, and Northwest).

With the exception of the North region, which was under the administration of the central government, the other five great regions also had their own governmental bodies in charge of agriculture and forestry, industry, public finance, trade, and so on.

In 1954, the six great administrative regions were abolished and, three years before their final reorganization in 1961, seven cooperative commissions were established in the North, Northeast, East, Central, South, Southwest, and Northwest regions. The six great regional administrations were destroyed during the Cultural Revolution period (1966–76).

In 1970 the Chinese economy was spatially organized via ten economic cooperative zones (namely Southwest, Northwest, Center, South, East, Northeast, North, Shandong, Fujian and Jiangxi, and Xinjiang). It is generally believed that this arrangement was based on the centrally planned system and reflected the state's efforts to meet the desperate need for regional self-sufficiency at the high point of the Cold War era.

From 1981 to 1985, and guided by the State Council (1980), six economic zones were organized in the Northeast, North, East, Central South, Southwest and Northwest regions. Notice that Shandong was excluded from this list of six economic zones; Guangxi was included in both Central South and Southwest economic zones; and eastern Inner Mongolia was included in both the North and Northeast economic zones.

In 1992, when the Chinese government decided to develop a market-oriented economy, the State Planning Commission (SPC) was authorized to map out the development plans for the following economic regions (*People's Daily*, 1992, p. 1):

- Yangtze delta (Jiangsu, Zhejiang and Shanghai)
- Bohai Sea rim (Beijing, Tianjin, Hebei, Shandong, Shanxi, central Inner Mongolia and Liaoning)
- Southeast Coastal area (Guangdong, Fujian and Hainan)
- Northeast area (Liaoning, Jilin, Helongjiang and eastern Inner Mogolia)
- Southwest area (Sichuan, Guizhou, Yunnan, Tibet and Guangxi)
- Central area (Henan, Anhui, Hubei, Hunan and Jiangxi)
- Northwest area (Shaanxi, Gansu, Ningxia, Qinghai, Xinjiang and western Inner Mongolia).

2.2.2 Statistical and Economic Regions

Since the early 1980s, the great regions have not had any political or administrative relevance in China. However, they are still widely used by various departments and divisions. For example, China's official statistical authorities (such as the State Statistical Bureau (SSB) or, as it is now

5. For example, as reported in Liu (1996, pp. 153–6), the optimum number of China's provinces have been suggested as 58 by Hong (1945a and b), 40–43 by Hu (1991) and 43 by Guo (1993).

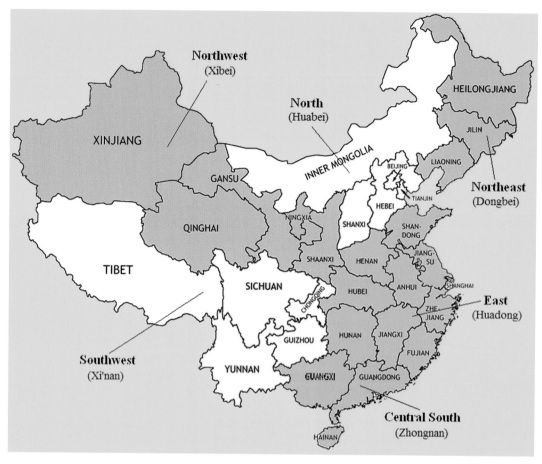

FIGURE 2.2 The six great regions.

called, the National Bureau for Statistics (NBS)), and other statistical departments and divisions under ministries or administrations, have used the six great regions (as shown in Figure 2.2):

- Huabei (North) region (including Beijing, Tianjin, Hebei, Shanxi, and Inner Mongolia, with 16.3 percent of the land area)
- Dongbei (Northeast) region (including Liaoning, Jilin, and Heilongjiang, with 8.2 percent of the land area)
- Huadong (East) region (including Shanghai, Jiangsu, Zhejiang, Anhui, Fujian, Jiangxi, and Shandong, with 8.3 percent of the land area)
- Zhongnan (Central South) region (including Henan, Hubei, Hunan, Guangdong, Guangxi, and Hainan, with 10.6 percent of the land area)
- Xi'nan (Southwest) region (including Sichuan, Chongqing, Guizhou, Yunnan, and Tibet, with 24.6 percent of the land area)
- Xibei (Northwest) region (including Shaanxi, Gansu, Qinghai, Ningxia, and Xinjiang, with 32.0 percent of the land area).

This method of dividing the country into six great regions has been applied in many scholarly research works.[6] Besides, regional scientists and economic geographers have also defined Chinese great regions, with differing numbers and geographical scope, for their own purposes.[7] Since the late 1990s, due to their distinguishable comparative advantages and remarkable economic achievements, three economic areas have attracted attention. They are:

- The Bohai Sea rim (BSR) area (including Beijing, Tianjin, the coastal Hebei, and the peninsulas of Shandong and Liaodong)
- The Pearl River delta (PRD) area (including Guangdong, and northern Hainan, Hong Kong and Macau)

---

6. Examples of literature on the application of the six great regions includes Hu et al. (1988, pp. 171–381), Yang (1989, p. 92), and Wei (1992, pp. 62–3).
7. These include, for example, Wright (1984, p. 78), Yang (1993, p. 270), Hu (1993, pp. 193–203) and Liu (1994, pp. 36–7) for six great regions; Li et al. (1994, pp. 139–65), and Keidel (1995) for seven great regions; and Yang (1989, pp. 238–40), Yang (1990, pp. 38–40) and Liu (1994, p. 36) for ten great regions.

TABLE 2.3 China's Three Economic Engines (Areas)

	Bohai Sea Rim	Pearl River Delta	Yangtze River Delta
Provinces included	Beijing, Tianjin, coastal Hebei, peninsulas of Shandong and Liaodong	Guangdong, and N. Hainan, Hong Kong, Macau	Shanghai, Zhejiang, S. Jiangsu
Climate zone	Semi-arid	Tropical	Semi-tropical
Ethnic minorities	Hui, Manchu	Yao, Zhuang	Hui, She
Oral language	Mandarin	Cantonese (Yue)	Wu
Food-style	Shandong (Lu)	Cantonese (Yue)	Jiangsu (Su)

- The Yangtze River delta (YRD) area (including Shanghai, Zhejiang, and southern Jiangsu).

In terms of physical environment, the three Chinese economic areas are different from each other (see Table 2.3). For example, most of the BSR area belongs to the semi-arid zone, while the PRD area is classified as tropical. Nevertheless, the YRD area has a semi-tropical temperature. Culturally, all the three areas are dominated by the ethnic Han community. But there also exist some differences. For example, although written Chinese is used widely throughout the country, people in the BSR area speak Mandarin, while those in the PRD and YRD areas use Cantonese and Wu as their native spoken languages, respectively. However, the most important feature is their comparative advantages (we will analyze this in Section 10.1 of Chapter 10).

2.3 GEOGRAPHICAL BELTS

2.3.1 Coastal and Inland Areas

The 12 provinces surrounded by the Yellow, East China and South China Seas are classified as the 'coastal area', while the remaining provinces are regarded as the 'inland area' (see Figure 2.3). Generally, the coastal area is more developed than the inland area, as a result of its proximity to the market economies along the western shore of the Pacific Ocean as well as the fact that it was the region that experience the earlier introduction of economic reform and opening up to the outside world. There have been different definitions of the coastal and inland areas. For example, Mao (1956, p. 286) treats Anhui and eastern Henan provinces as a part of the coastal area according to the principle of geographical proximity to the coastal area, while the State Council (1993) classifies the two coastal provinces of Guangxi and Hainan into the inland area according to the principle of economic similarity.

Even though China's economic divergence has not been as large within the inland area as it has between the

inland and coastal areas, there are still some plausible reasons to explain why the inland area needs to be further divided into smaller geographical units. As the western part of the inland area has less-developed social and economic infrastructures than the eastern part, China's inland area can be further divided into two sections – the Central belt which is next to the coastal area (here it is referred to as the Eastern belt) and the Western belt.

2.3.2 Eastern, Central and Western Belts

The concepts of the Eastern, Central and Western belts first appeared in the proposal for national economic and social development in the seventh Five-Year Plan (1986–90), which was adopted in April 1986 by the National People's Congress (NPC). In this document, the government advocated that, 'The development of the Eastern coastal belt shall be further accelerated and, at the same time, the construction of energy and raw material industries shall be focused on the Central belt, while the preparatory works for the further development of the Western belt shall be actively conducted.'[8] Since this time, the three-belt definition has been widely used in government policy documents as well as in the literature.[9]

The Eastern, Central and Western belts (shown in Figure 2.3) have their component provinces, as follows:

- Eastern belt (including Liaoning, Hebei, Beijing, Tianjin, Shandong, Jiangsu, Shanghai, Zhejiang, Fujian, Guangdong, Hainan, and Guangxi, with 13.5 percent of the land area)
- Central belt (including Shanxi, Jilin, Heilongjiang, Anhui, Henan, Hubei, Hunan, Jiangxi, and Inner Mongolia, with 29.8 percent of the land area)

---

8. See *Guangming Daily*, 6 April 1986, p. 1.
9. See, for example, Yao and Zhang (2001a, b), Brun et al. (2002), and Wu (2004).

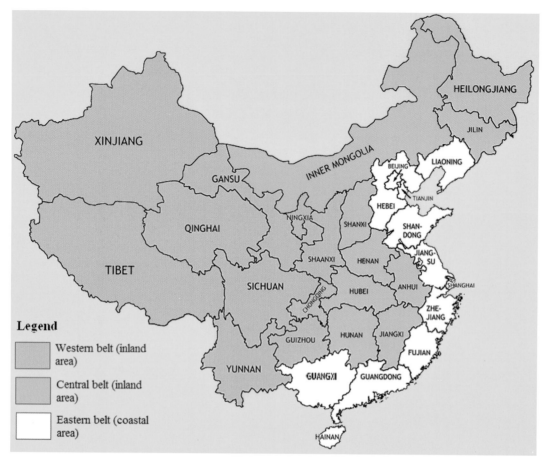

FIGURE 2.3   The coastal/inland areas and the Eastern/Central/Western belts.

- Western belt (including Sichuan, Chongqing, Guizhou, Yunnan, Shaanxi, Gansu, Qinghai, Tibet, Ningxia, and Xinjiang, with 56.7 percent of the land area).

The above definition has been applied in many government documents and much of the scholarly literature.[10] It should be noted that the government's definition changed slightly after 1999, when the southern province of Guangxi, which was originally part of the Eastern belt, was reallocated to the Western belt and similarly Inner Mongolia, originally part of the Central belt, was reallocated to the Western belt. In addition, there have been other different definitions on the tripartite division of the Chinese economy.[11]

2.4   SOUTHERN AND NORTHERN PARTS

2.4.1   Natural and Social Contexts

In this book, the introduction of the concept of the 'Northern part' (beifang) and the 'Southern part' (nanfang) of China seems to be necessary for the bi-regional comparison of the Chinese economy. From the south to the north, the landmass of China is characterized by dramatic geographical, geological and hydro-geological diversities. Its land surface ascends from north to south in four distinct climate zones: the arid zone, the semi-arid zone, the semi-humid zone, and the humid zone.

In addition to the natural and climatic diversities, social and cultural conditions also differ between northern and southern China. Without good reason, the Chinese are usually identified as Northerners and Southerners in terms of their birthplaces and, occasionally, the homes of their parents or relatives, when they are introduced to one another. While it is not quite clear when the saying 'South China raises intelligent scholars while marshals mainly come from the North' was aired, and whether or not it can be used to spatially characterize China's ethnic nature, many

---

10. For example, Wu and Hou (1990, p. 116), Hu et al. (1988, pp. 182–4), Yang (1990, pp. 38–43), Liu (1994, pp. 1–13) and Hsueh (1994a, pp. 22–56) give the same definition.

11. For instance, Guangxi, a coastal province along the Gulf of Tonkin, is included in the Western belt by Yang (1989, pp. 90–6), Gu (1995, pp. 45–51) and Chen (1994, p. 57). In Gu's analysis, moreover, Jilin and Heilongjiang, two inland provinces in Northeast China, are included in the Eastern belt.

Box 2.1 Where are Shaanxi and Gansu?

During a visit to the Beijing No. 35 Middle School on September 4, 2009, Wen Jiabao – China's Premier (2003–2012) – shared a lesson with students.

After sitting at the back of a class, Premier Wen took notes carefully. He suddenly pointed out an error in the geographic textbook, which gave an incorrect description of China's geographic regions. In the textbook, Shaanxi and Gansu provinces and Ningxia Hui autonomous region are included in 'North China' (*Huabei*). Premier Wen pointed out that they should be regarded as part of 'Northwest China' (*Xibei*).

Premier Wen's speech unwittingly stirred a debate over the criteria by which to group China's provinces and autonomous regions. The publisher of this textbook reportedly retorted that, geographically speaking, their definition of 'North China' is correct. This is perhaps the first time for an academic unit (the publisher) to seemingly disregard the voice from the highest authority in China.

The main point of the differences lies in that the publisher used a bi-national divide approach in which *Huabei* (northern China) includes all of the northern part of China (as shown in Figure 2.4), while Wen applied the great-regions approach (as shown in Figure 2.2).

However, the definition of *Huabei* that Premier Wen used has been more popular in general Chinese usage.

conflicts and wars in Chinese history did take place in the Northern part[12] (see Box 2.1).

The first major Han-Chinese migration from the northern to the southern part of the Yangtze River took place during the Wei (AD 220–265), the Jin (AD 265–420) and the South and North dynasties (AD 420–589), and was accelerated during the Five Dynasties and Ten Kingdoms period (AD 907–960) when China's northern part became the nation's battlefield. Large-scale Han-Chinese migration was later promoted by frequent wars between the Chinese and the Liao, Jin, Mongol, and other non-Han minorities in the North Song (AD 960–1126) and the South Song (AD 1127–1279) dynasties. In the wars with their far northern enemies, the Han-Chinese first lost their northern part after the late North Song dynasty. Naturally, the frequent wars greatly accelerated the emigration of northern intellectuals to the Southern part of the country.

2.4.2 Criteria for the Bifurcation

The geographic definition of the Southern and Northern parts may differ slightly. For example, the Qinling range and the Huaihe River are traditionally used to divide the South and North, while the Yangtze River is sometimes known as the boundary of northern and southern China. The only difference between the two definitions lies in the fact that the Qinling range and the Huaihe River are located in Shaanxi, Henan, Anhui, and Jiangsu provinces, while the Yangtze River runs through Sichuan, Chongqing, Hubei, Anhui, Jiangsu, and Shanghai provinces. In most cases, nevertheless, there are approximately an equal number of provinces in each of the Northern and Southern parts (as shown in Figure 2.4):

- Northern part (including Beijing, Tianjin, Hebei, Shanxi, Inner Mongolia, Liaoning, Jilin, Heilongjiang, Shaanxi, Gansu, Qinghai, Ningxia, Xinjiang, Shandong, and Henan, with 59.8 percent of the land area)
- Southern belt (including Shanghai, Jiangsu, Zhejiang, Anhui, Fujian, Jiangxi, Sichuan, Chongqing, Guizhou, Yunnan, Tibet, Hubei, Hunan, Guangdong, Guangxi, and Hainan, with 40.2 percent of the land area).

2.5 ETHNO-CULTURAL AREAS

2.5.1 Historical Evolution

China is not a culturally or ethnically homogeneous country. In addition to the Han majority, which is linguistically and religiously heterogeneous (we will discuss this further in Section 3.4 of Chapter 3), 55 other ethnic minorities also exist in China.[13] In 1947 China's first, and ethnically based, autonomous region, Inner Mongolia, was established at the provincial level by the CCP. Then, after the foundation of the PRC in 1949, the Chinese government began to introduce a system of regional autonomy for other non-Han ethnic areas. In 1952, the Chinese government issued the Program for the Implementation of Regional Ethnic Autonomy of the People's Republic of China, which included provisions for the establishment of ethnic autonomous areas and the composition of organs of self-government, as well as the right of self-government for such organs.

The first National People's Congress (NPC), convened in 1954, included a system of regional autonomy for ethnic

12. Note that care should be taken when the terms 'North China' (huabei) and 'Northern part' (beifang) are used.

13. As at 2010, the main minority ethnic groups are Zhuang (16.1 million), Manchu (10.6 million), Hui (9.8 million), Miao (8.9 million), Uyghur (8.3 million), Tujia (8 million), Yi (7.7 million), Mongol (5.8 million), Tibetan (5.4 million), Buyei (2.9 million), Dong (2.9 million), Yao (2.6 million), Korean (1.9 million), Bai (1.8 million), Hani (1.4 million), Kazakh (1.2 million), Li (1.2 million), and Dai (1.1 million) – NBS (2011).

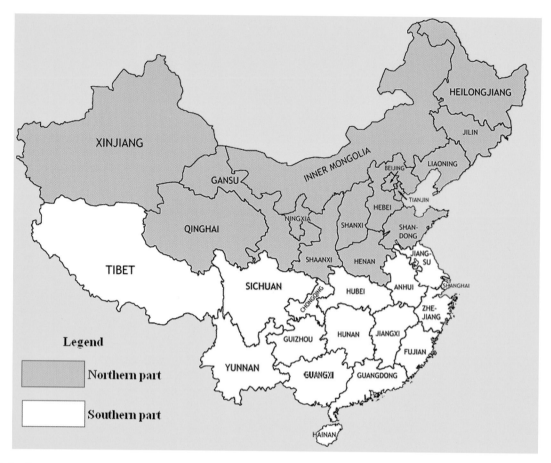

FIGURE 2.4   The Northern and Southern parts.

minorities in the Constitution of the People's Republic of China. Thereafter, four autonomous regions appeared in China: they were Xinjiang Uygur autonomous region (October 1955), Guangxi Zhuang autonomous region (March 1958), Ningxia Hui autonomous region (October 1958), and Tibet autonomous region (September 1965).

On May 31, 1984, on the basis of summarizing the experience of practicing regional autonomy for non-Han ethnic minorities, the second session of the Sixth NPC adopted the 'Law on Regional Ethnic Autonomy'. The law, which was further amended in 2001, has been the basic legal document for implementing the system of regional autonomy for ethnic minorities. It defines the relationship between the central government and the ethnic autonomous regions, as well as the relationship between different ethnic groups in ethnic autonomous regions.

2.5.2   Organization

In most cases, the name of an ethnic autonomous area consists of the name of the place, the name of the ethnic group, and the character indicating the administrative status, in that order. Take the Ningxia Hui autonomous region as an example: 'Ningxia' is the name of the place, 'Hui'

is the name of the ethnic group, and 'region' indicates the level of administration. By the end of 2005, China's non-Han ethnic administrative areas included:

- five autonomous regions including
  - Guangxi Zhuang autonomous region
  - Inner Mongolia autonomous region
  - Ningxia Hui autonomous region
  - Tibet autonomous region
  - Xinjiang Uygur autonomous region

- 30 autonomous prefectures (APs) in nine provincial administrations including
  - Gansu province: Gannan Tibetan AP; Linxia Hui AP.
  - Guizou province: Qiandongnan Miao-Dong AP; Qiannan Buyi-Miao AP; Qianxi'nan Buyi-Miao AP.
  - Hubei province: Enshi Tujia-Miao AP.
  - Hunan province: Xiangxi Tujia-Miao AP.
  - Jilin province: Yanbian Korean AP.
  - Qinghai province: Yushu Tibetan AP; Hainan Tibetan AP; Huangnan Tibetan AP; Haibei Tibetan AP; Guoluo Tibetan AP; Haixi Mongolian-Tibetan AP.
  - Sichuan province: Ganzi Tibetan AP; Liangshan Yi AP; A'ba Tibetan-Qiang AP.

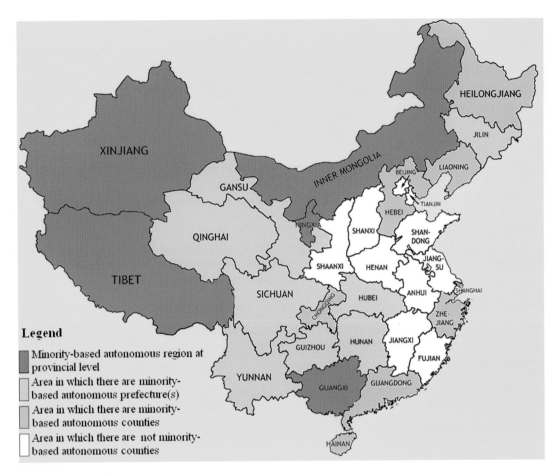

FIGURE 2.5 The ethno-cultural areas.

- Xinjiang Uygur autonomous region: Bayin'guole Mongolian AP; Bo'ertala Mongolian AP; Kezilesu Kirgiz AP; Changji Hui AP; Yili Kazak AP.
- Yunnan province: Xishuangbanna Dai AP; Dehong Dai-Jingpo AP; Nujiang Lisu; Dali Bai AP; Diqing Tibetan AP; Honghe Hani-Yi AP; Wenshan Zhuang-Miao AP; Chuxiong Yi AP.

- 119 county-level autonomous administrations in 18 provincial administrations (see Figure 2.5).[14]

Communities of one ethnic group may establish different autonomous administrations, according to their respective sizes. If we take the Hui ethnic group as an example, this includes:

- A provincial administration, called Ningxia Hui autonomous region
- A sub-provincial administration, called the Linxia Hui autonomous prefecture of Gansu province

- A sub-prefecture administration, called the Mengcun Hui autonomous county of Hebei province.

In places where different ethnic groups live, each autonomous administration can be established based on either one ethnic group (such as Tibet autonomous region; Liangshan Yi autonomous prefecture of Sichuan province; and Jingning She autonomous county of Zhejiang province); or two or more ethnic groups (such as Haixi Mongolian-Tibetan autonomous prefecture of Qinghai province; and Jishishan Bao'nan-Dongxiang-Salar autonomous county of Gansu province). If a minority ethnic group lives in an autonomous area of a bigger ethnic group, the former may establish their own subordinate autonomous areas. For example, Yili Kazak autonomous prefecture and Yanqi Hui autonomous county are both to be found in the Xinjiang Uygur autonomous region.

Organizationally, China's non-Han ethnic administrative areas are oriented in a multi-ethnic manner. For example, in addition to deputies from the ethnic group or groups exercising regional autonomy in the area concerned, the people's congresses of the autonomous areas also include an appropriate number of members from other

---

14. More detailed information about all these county-level autonomous administrations can be found on the official website of the Chinese National Museum of Ethnology (www.cnmuseum.com).

ethnic groups who live in that autonomous area. Among the chairman or vice-chairmen of the standing committee of the people's congress of an autonomous area there will be one or more citizens of the ethnic group or groups exercising regional autonomy in the area concerned. The head of an autonomous region, autonomous prefecture or autonomous county alike will be a citizen of the ethnic group exercising regional autonomy in the area concerned. Other members of the people's governments of the autonomous areas should include an appropriate number of members of the ethnic group exercising regional autonomy alongside members of other ethnic minorities. The functionaries of the working departments subsidiary to the organs of self-government should be composed in a similar fashion.

2.6 SUMMARY

In any discussion of the Chinese economy, at least two important points must be noted: first, China's vast territorial size and the diversity of physical environments and natural resources have inevitably resulted in considerable regional economic differences; secondly, China has a population of more than 1.3 billion, comprised of 56 ethnic groups. It is geographically divided by 31 provincial administrations, each of which would have been roughly equivalent in size to a medium-sized country. Furthermore, all of the provinces are independent from one another in designing local fiscal, tax, labor and trade policies, and economic development plans which have, *ceteris paribus*, resulted in differing levels of regional economic performance in China.

In short, the Chinese economy is one of the most complicated and diverse spatial systems to be found anywhere in the world. The only feasible approach one can adopt is, therefore, to divide it into smaller geographic elements, through which one can gain a better insight into the spatial mechanisms and regional characteristics. In this chapter, we have divided the Chinese economy into: (1) provincial administrations; (2) great regions; (3) geographical belts; (4) southern and northern parts; and (5) ethno-cultural areas. It is common for the method of spatial division of the Chinese economy to differ, depending on the purposes of the analysis.

Case Study 2

Who Owns Lake Weishan?[15]

Lake Weishan is located on the border of Shandong and Jiangsu provinces in East China mid-way between Shanghai and Beijing. It is composed of four connected

sub-lakes: Dushan, Nanyang, Zhaoyang, and Weishan. As the largest freshwater reservoir in northern China (with an area of 1,260 square kilometers), Lake Weishan receives water from 53 rivers in a broad catchment area spread across 32 counties and cities of four provinces (Jiangsu, Shandong, Henan, and Anhui). The maximum capacity of the lake is 4.73 billion cubic meters.[16] For centuries, Lake Weishan has been an important storage area for fresh water, but it also assists in the prevention of flooding, the development of water-related industries, as the route for local shipping, and the source of water for agricultural and industrial production. It remains vital to the daily life of the residents of 14 cities and counties (districts) in Jiangsu and Shandong provinces. High-quality coal resources have also been discovered beneath the lake. These are seen as extremely important by the economic policy makers at both central and provincial level government in China.

Prior to 1953, most of Lake Weishan was part of the Xuzhou Administrative Region, and under the jurisdiction of Shandong province. Ninety percent of the southern part of Lake Weishan was shared by two counties (Peixian and Tongshan); and the eastern part of the lake was part of the Seventh District of Peixian county, with Xiazhen township being the administrative center of the district, which comprised eight towns and more than 100 villages. In 1953, Xuzhou Administrative Region was transferred from Shandong to Jiangsu province. During the process of territorial readjustment, Shandong province submitted a proposal that, for the sake of the unified administration and the public security of the entire lake area, the sub-lakes of Zhaoyang and Weishan, together with some villages in Tongshan county (all of which had been under the jurisdiction of Jiangsu province), should comprise a new county (Weishan) and be placed under the administration of Shandong province.[17]

The interprovincial border established at that time followed the principles set by the Central Government: Shandong's Weishan county was to be separated from Jiangsu's Peixian and Tongshan counties by the border between the lake's waterline and lakeside land, with the exception of a few villages located outside the lakeside land. These villages were set as border markers between the two provinces. The State Administrative Council, the former State Council, approved this proposal on August 22, 1953 (zhengzhengbuzi [53] official letter, No. 136).

15. A full version of this research can be found on the companion site (http://www.elsevierdirect.com/companions/9780123978264).

16. *Weishan Statistical Yearbook 2001*, Statistical Bureau of Weishan County, May 2002, p. 1.

17. This proposal was submitted to the Ministry of Civil Affairs (MCA) by the Administrative Commission of East China Region on July 17, 1953 (dongbanzi [53] official letter, No. 0643) and supported by the People's Government of Shandong province on May 4, 1953 (luminzi [53] official letter, No. 1533).

The newly established county of Weishan was entitled to administer 267 villages and four towns.[18] In March 1956, the counties of Fushan and Xuecheng were also placed under the administration of Weishan county. However, between May and September of the same year, some villages were transferred from Weishan county to Xuzhou municipality of Jiangsu province and others were transferred from Yixian, Jiaxiang and Jining counties of Shandong province to Weishan county. In early 1984, another 14 villages from Peixian county in Jiangsu province were transferred to Weishan county in Shandong province.

As a result of the administrative readjustments outlined above, the county of Weishan now contains 565 administrative villages and five neighborhood committees, covering a total geographical area of 1,780 square kilometers (this includes 514 square kilometers of lake). As of 2001, Weishan county had a total population of 682,000. The majority are Han Chinese, but 25 other ethnic minorities, including Hui (Muslims), Miao, Mongol, Zhuang, Manchu, Korean, Yi and Hani, are also resident in Weishan.[19]

During the twentieth century, the Lake Weishan area has experienced a number of drastic changes in provincial administration. This has placed the Shandong–Jiangsu interprovincial relation on an unstable foundation. The 1953 border readjustment scheme created many problems. The fact that changes in natural conditions could result in either a rise (during the rainy season) or a fall (during the dry season) of the water level in Lake Weishan, which would in turn either reduce or increase the size of lake and lakeshore land, was not taken into consideration. Naturally, this would cause frequent changes in the location of the interprovincial borderline which followed the decision that: 'Wherever water reaches is under Shandong's jurisdiction; but the land is regarded as Jiangsu's territory.'

In addition, it was clearly assumed in the 1953 border delimitation scheme that the whole area of the lake should be under the exclusive administration of Weishan county in Shandong province. Jiangsu residents living along the lakeside were permitted to continue conducting their lake-related businesses, such as fishing in the lake and farming in the lakeside land.

During the first years, when Shandong province exercised its governance over the entire area, Jiangsu province did not fully realize the lake's crucial importance to the agricultural and industrial economy of the region, nor was there sufficient recognition of the area's importance to

the people's livelihood. It was only when Jiangsu province attempted to build an iron-ore mine in Liguo at the southern side of Lake Weishan, in an area near the provincial borders, that the debate strengthened. The mining proposal was impeded in 1956 and this stimulated the Jiangsu administrators to demand the return of 35 villages which had been transferred to Shandong province in 1953.

The central government in Beijing agreed to Jiangsu's request in principle, but still kept the whole lake under the sole administration of Weishan county.[20] Since that time Jiangsu has increasingly sought to gain strategic recognition of the lake as part of its provincial economy.

In 1958, Shandong province decided to construct a dam, which effectively divided the whole lake into two parts – an upper lake and a lower lake. While the construction of the dam in the middle of the lake was good for the provincial economy of Shandong province, it was not beneficial to the economy of Jiangsu province. Jiangsu had no administrative jurisdiction over Lake Weishan, and could neither change Shandong's construction scheme nor exercise any control over water rights. Not only did the dam result in 90 percent of the lake's water reserves being contained on the Shandong side of the border, but it also submerged 210,000 mu (one mu is approximately equal to 667 square meters) of arable land on the Jiangsu side. Even worse, it made the farmers of Peixian district completely unable to irrigate their crops during a drought or to drain their waterlogged fields after heavy rain.[21]

The central government made great efforts to resolve the Lake Weishan disputes and these attempts can be traced through three documents issued by the Chinese Communist Party Central Committee and the State Council in 1984. The three documents, which transferred disputed areas and villages from Jiangsu to Shandong, provide a large part of the present administrative picture of the Shandong–Jiangsu border area issues (see Figure 2.6a).

However, the Shandong and Jiangsu provincial governments have each chosen to interpret the three central documents in a different manner. The result has been uncertainty over the interprovincial border and a lack of resolution of what is a fundamental border demarcation issue. Over the course of the following years, the Shandong administrators emphasized an exact implementation of the three central documents, insisting that Lake Weishan should be under the sole administration of Weishan county. However, the Jiangsu administrators argued that the

18. Source: The State Administrative Council of the PRC (under the form of Letter zhengzhengbuzi, No. 136), 22 August 1953. According to the *Weishan Statistical Yearbook 2001* (p. 1), the total number of villages was 302.

19. Source: *Weishan Statistical Yearbook 2001*, p. 2.

20. See: Statistics on Status of the Lakeside Land and Lake-related Resources in Lake Weishan, Peixian County (peixian guanyu zai weishanhu nei hutian, huchan qingkuang tongji), Office of Lakeside land, Peixian county, 8 June 1996.

21. Ibid.

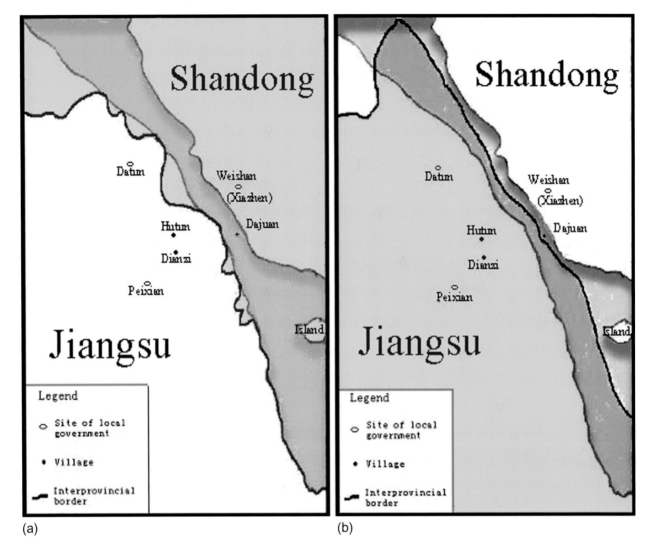

(a)   (b)

FIGURE 2.6   The differently defined borders between Shandong and Jiangsu provinces.

decisions made by the central government were unfair.[22] Jiangsu suggested that the use of the widely recognized principle on water-area delimitation that 'shared lakes are divided along the deepest line' (see Figure 2.6b). Both provinces found that there were far too many differences between them to enable them to reach an agreement.[23]

The argument about the ownership of Lake Weishan continued, as did the border conflict between the provinces. In the period from the founding of the People's Republic of China in 1949 and the year 2000 there have been nearly 400 cases of cross-border conflicts in the region, with nearly 400 people being either killed or seriously wounded. The figures include the following:

16 people died and 24 people were disabled in Peixian county; four people died in Weishan county; and there were numerous casualties in Tongshan and Fengxian counties of Jiangsu province.[24] The main causes for these casualties came from fights between the cultivators of the lakeside land and fishermen operating other lake-related business, as well as workers involved in the construction of various water conservancy, public security, construction of communication equipment programs, and the collectors of fees and taxes for the use of lake-related resources.

The border disputes between Shandong and Jiangsu provinces have had a serious effect on the social solidarity and public security of the Lake Weishan area. In addition, owing to the lack of appropriate coordination between

22. See: Report on the Work of the Delimitation between Peixian and Weishan Counties (guanyu peiwei bianjie kanjie gongzuo de huibao), the Working Office of Lake Area, Peixian County, 17 February 1998.
23. Based on the author's two talks with officials in Weishan and Peixian counties on 1 and 2 June 2000, respectively.

24. Source: Report on the Work of the Delimitation between Peixian and Weishan Counties (guanyu peiwei bianjie kanjie gongzuo de huibao), the Working Office of Lake Area, Peixian County, 17 February 1998.

all stakeholders concerned, natural and environmental resources have been either over-exploited or destroyed. The border disputes have damaged the ecological sustainability of the lake and caused a substantial amount of environmental degradation. During our field inspections, we found that five major rivers, the Chengguo, Xiaoni, Peiyan, Zhengji and the Sulu, have been the major sources of pollution. Freshwater fish and important limnobiological plants were no longer present around the mouths of these rivers. Water pollution has not only endangered the local fishery and the collection of limnological plants; it has also affected the daily lives and health of the nearby residents. According to a survey conducted by a correspondent of the Qilu Evening News, the frequency of cancer-causing illnesses and tumors has been much higher in the lake region than in the nearby inland areas. Reported health events related to liver diseases, diarrhea and birth defects have also been much more frequent in the polluted area than in the non-polluted area. For example, the following case was reported in a newspaper:

Located at the mouth of Chengguo River, Shadi village, Liuzhuang township in Weishan county, has a population of 1000 people and an area of over 20,000 mu of shoaly land. Due to the lack of arable land (with a per capita area of only 0.013 mu), most of the residents were used to taking reeds, lotus-roots and other lake-related resources. Fishing and fishery cultivation have been their major sources of living. During recent years, as industrial and living waste water discharged from Tengzhou city into Lake Weishan via Chengguo River has increased, water sources on which the residents have depended for their living have been seriously polluted. Consequently, fish stocks have been extinguished, and limnological plants have died. Even worse, the health conditions of the residents living in the region have been seriously affected. Since 1988, 26 young residents have died from diseases caused by, as diagnosed by hospitals at county or higher levels, the drinking of polluted well water.[25]

Usually, armed disputes in the Lake Weishan area were resolved by the relevant local authorities. However, there have been a few extremely serious examples. These have been resolved by higher-level authorities from both sides concerned. It was said that the self-resolved cases have not been documented[26] but that from the 1960s to the mid-1980s, there were six jointly resolved cases for armed fights in 1961, 1967, 1973, 1980, 1981, and 1984. The resolution of the conflicts required participation by officials from both provinces and the related counties. However, since most of the resolutions were not mediated by the central government, they did not resolve the fundamental problems underlying the disputes. Each side, Shandong and Jiangsu, only emphasized their own interests. As a result, only some minor border-related problems were resolved.

During the field research carried out in the Lake Weishan area, we noted that local officials doubted the fairness of the central government's final decisions in relation to the resolution of the Lake Weishan disputes. Their most serious concern was that those key central government officials who had provincial ties to either Shandong or Jiangsu were inclined to make resolutions in favor of one side or the other. According to our talks with the local officials of Peixian county, the final decision made by the central government concerning the resolution of the Weishan lake disputes was seen as unfair by Jiangsu provincial authorities since the top decision makers, Wan Li and Tian Jiyun – both of whom held the position of vice premier of the State Council during the 1980s – had been born in Shandong province. Jiangsu officials complained that the speech given by Mr Wan Li had set the scene for the final resolution of the disputes in 1983. For example, Wan Li pointed out: 'In order to find a thorough resolution to this problem, the State Council has made a fairly definite decision. After having taken into account all gains and losses, it seems better to put all disputed villages under the administration of Shandong province.'[27]

In our meetings with the local officials in Peixian county, the Jiangsu side stated that since some key central officials were natives of Shandong province, Jiangsu province had been placed in a disadvantageous position. By contrast, there was also a growing fear from the Shandong side that the resolution of the local disputes had favored Jiangsu province since, during the 1990s, more key central government officials came from southern China. For example, with regard to their victory in the resolution of the interprovincial taxation disputes, the Jiangsu officers admitted in an internal, confidential, report that they had done 'hard and meticulous work'.[28] The key issues that were not included in the final resolution were: (1) the legality of the ownership transfer of Shandong's underground resources to Jiangsu province; and (2) the entitlement by Shandong province to levy taxes and fees on the exploitation of resources underlying its territory.[29]

25. See: The Village Surrounded by Polluted Water (bei wushui baowei de cunzhuang), *Qilu Evening News*, 14 December 1997.
26. Based on the author's talks with county officials in Peixian township, Jiangsu province on 2 June 2000.

27. Cited from Comrade Wan Li's Speech at the Meeting of Report Delivered by Comrade Cui Naifu of Minister of Civil Affairs on the Issues Concerning the Resolution of the Disputes over Lake Weishan.
28. See: Report on the Work of the Delimitation between Peixian and Weishan Counties.
29. For instance, Article 12 of Temporary Regulations Concerning the Resource Taxation of the People's Republic of China (Beijing, State Council, No. 139 document, December 25, 1993) states that: 'Tax payers shall pay taxes to the taxation bureau in charge of places from which the taxed products originate.'

The Shandong–Jiangsu border disputes have resulted in a long history of human suffering and environmental damage. Any situation as complex as this can rarely be found in any other disputed interprovincial border areas in mainland China. The border disputes have been fought over lakeside land, submerged resources, drainage and irrigation projects, water conservancy projects, the communication infrastructure, and public security. The disputes have received urgent attention from many ministries and even the State Council and the CCP's Central Committee. For decades, the border conflicts have peaked during periods of seasonal calamity. It has been recognized that 'A great drought occurred in the lake for every eight or nine years; this "drought" has usually lasted for three years and during this period conflicts have reached their highest levels.'[30]

The interprovincial conflicts have wasted energy and resources at all levels of provincial and local government. This has impeded the economic and social development of the lake area as a whole. In Weishan county, the position of magistrate deputy has been established principally for the purpose of dealing with border conflicts and related matters; while in Peixian county, an office has been established to take charge of the lakeside land cultivation and border-related affairs. Given the difficulties in the current administrative arrangements, is there an alternative to the present situation of continual interprovincial border disputes?

REFERENCES

Brun, J. F., Combes, J. L., & Renard, M. F. (2002). Are there spillover effects between the coastal and no-coastal regions in China? *China Economic Review, 13*, 161–169.

Chen, G. (1994). *China's regional economic development: a comparative study of the east, central, and west belts* [zhongguo quyu jingji fazhan: dongbu zhongbu he xibu de bijiao yanjiu]. Beijing: Beijing University of Technology Press.

Gu, J. (1995). Analyses on the causes of income variable among regions in China. Proceedings of the fifth annual meeting of the Congress of Political Economists (COPE), International. Seoul, South Korea, January 5–10, pp. 45–51.

Guangming Daily, 6 April 1986, p. 1.

Guo, R. (1993). *Economic analysis of border-regions: theory and practice of China* [zhongguo shengji bianjie diqu jingji fazhan yanjiu]. Beijing: China Ocean Press.

Hong, F. (1945a). On the new provincial regions [xin shengqu lun]. *Dagong pao* October 2.

Hong, F. (1945b). Reconstructing provincial regions: a preliminary discussion [chonghua shengqu fang'an chuyi]. *Oriental Journal, 43*(6).

Hu, H. (1991). The past, present, and future administrative divisions in China [zhongguo xingzheng qu de guoqu, xianzai he weilai] In Chinese Society for Administrative Divisions (Ed.), *Studies of China's administrative divisions* [zhonguo xingzheng quhua yanjiu] (pp. 144–167). Beijing: China Social Press.

Hu, X. (1993). On the typology and organization of economic regions in China [lun zhonguo jingjiqu de leixing yu zhuzhi]. *ACTA Geographica Sinica, 48*(3), 193–202.

Hu, X., Shao, X., & Li, F. (1988). *Chinese economic geography* [zhonguo jingji dili]. Lixin Financial Economics Series, Shanghai: Lixin Accounting Books Press.

Keidel, A. (1995). *China's regional disparities*. Washington, DC: World Bank.

Li, S., Wu, Z., & Wu, C. (1994). A quantitative analysis of the interregional linkages in China [zhongguo quji lianxi de shuliang fenxi] Development Research Center of the State Council (Ed.), *The regional coordinate development strategy in China* [zhonguo quyu xietiao fazhan zhanlue] (pp. 139–175). Beijing: China Economy Press.

Liu, G. (1994). China's regional economic development strategy – an evaluation and prospect [zhongguo diqu jingji fazhan zhanlue de pinggu yu zhaiwang]. In S. Liu, Q. Li, & T. Hsueh (Eds.), *Studies on China's regional economic development* [zhongguo diqu jingji yanjiu] (pp. 1–13). Beijing: China Statistics Publishing House.

Liu, J. (1996). *China's administrative divisions: theory and practice* [zhongguo xingzheng quhua de lilun yu shijian]. Shanghai: East China Normal University Press.

Mao, Z. (1956). On the ten major relations. In *Selected works of Mao Tse-tung* (Vol. 5). Beijing: Foreign Languages Press, 1975.

NBS. (various years). *China statistical yearbook*, various issues, Beijing: China Statistics Publishing House.

People's Daily (1992). On regional economy [lun quyu jingji]. (editorial), November 5, Beijing.

State Council (1980). *Provisional regulations concerning the promotion of economic unification*. Beijing: State Council.

State Council (1993). *Resolution concerning the promotion of the development of the TVEs in the central and western area*. Beijing: State Council. December

Wei, H. (1992). On the changing pattern of the interregional income gaps in China [lun woguo quji shouru chaju de biandong geju]. *The Economic Research* [jingji yanjiu], *4*, 61–65.

Wright, T. (1984). *Coal mining in China's economy and society 1895–1937*. Cambridge: Cambridge University Press.

Wu, C., & Hou, F. (1990). *Territorial development and planning* [guotu kaifa ahengzi yu guihua]. Nanjing: Jiangsu Educational Press.

Wu, Y. (2004). *China's economic growth: a miracle with Chinese characteristics*. London: Routledge Curzon.

Yang, D. (1990). Patterns of China's regional development strategy. *The China Quarterly, 122*, 230–257.

Yang, K. (1989). *A study of regional development in China* [zhongguo quyu fazhan yanjiu]. Beijing: China Ocean Press.

Yang, K. (1993). *For a spatial integration: China's market economy and regional development strategy* [maixiang kongjian yiti hua: zhongguo shichang jingji yu quyu fazhan zhanlue]. Across the Century Series. Chengdu: Sichuan People's Press.

Yao, S., & Zhang, Z. (2001a). Regional growth in China under economic reforms. *Journal of Development Economics, 38*, 16–46.

Yao, S., & Zhang, Z. (2001b). On regional inequality and divergence clubs: a case study of contemporary China. *Journal of Comparative Economics, 29*, 466–484.

---

30. Source: Report on the Work of the Delimitation between Peixian and Weishan Counties.

Chapter 3

Human and Cultural Contexts

The Terracotta Army, Xi'an. *Copyright © 2007 Maros Mraz (for the main photo)*

The Terracotta Army (or the Terra Cotta Warriors and Horses) is a collection of terracotta sculptures depicting the armies of Qin Shi Huang, the first emperor of the Qin dynasty (221–209 BC). The figures were discovered in 1974, near the Mausoleum of Qin Shi Huang in Lintong district, Xi'an, Shaanxi province. Current estimates are that in the Terracotta Army there were over 8,000 soldiers, 130 chariots with 520 horses, and 150 cavalry horses, many of which are still buried in the pits.

Mt. Tai did not refuse every block of soil, so it has become a great mountain; the Yellow River and the East Sea did not refuse small streams, so they achieved their depth; and the Kings did not refuse a large number of people, so they enjoyed respect of merit. Therefore, land should not be divided into the East and the West; and no people should be treated as foreigners... Now Your Majesty intends to abandon the people to subsidize the enemy and expel the guest scholars who might contribute to the other states' achievements. Consequently, the Magi around the world would stop their footsteps at the entrance into the state of Qin. Ah! This is what people said, 'lending weapons to enemies, and giving dry rations to thieves'.

– Li Si (c. 280–208 BC)

Understanding the Chinese Economies. DOI: http://dx.doi.org/10.1016/B978-0-12-397826-4.00003-2
© 2013 Elsevier Inc. All rights reserved.

3.1 POPULATION

3.1.1 General Situation

At the beginning of the twenty-first century, China's population has risen above 1.3 billion, which accounts for more than 20 percent of the global total; it is nine times that of Japan, five times that of the USA, and three times that of the entire European Union. The dynamic mechanism of population growth has been substantially influenced by China's population policies.

When the People's Republic of China (PRC) was founded in 1949, the population of mainland China was about 450 million. Since then China has experienced two major peaks of population growth. From 1949 to 1958, when the Great Leap Forward movement was launched, the birth rate was as high as 3 to 4 percent while, in contrast, the death rate decreased significantly. This dramatic growth in population was largely encouraged by the government in line with Mao Zedong's thought 'the more population, the easier are the things to be done'. China's population began to grow rapidly once again after the Famine period (1959–61), during which many people died from starvation.[1] The birth rate peaked at 4.3 percent in 1963 and then decreased gradually but still ran at over 2 percent until the early 1970s when the government realized the importance of population control (see Figure 3.1).

Unfortunately, it was too late for China to control its population, which has continued to grow at a rate of more than 10 million per annum. According to UN population predictions, in the coming decades, China will continue to be the world's most populous nation before being overtaken by India in the 2030s (see Table 3.1).

TABLE 3.1 Population Forecasts for Selective Countries (Million Persons)

Country	1950	2000	2010	2025	2050
China	555	1,270	1,330	1,476	1,437
India	358	1,046	1,173	1,391	1,747
USA	158	289	310	349	420
Indonesia	80	211	243	271	297
Brazil	54	174	201	229	260
Pakistan	40	144	177	229	295
Bangladesh	42	139	158	190	231
Nigeria	30	125	152	205	282
Russia	NA	147	139	129	109
Japan	84	127	127	119	95

Source: United Nations Statistical Division for the years of 1950, 2000 and 2010; and UNPD (2007) for the years of 2025 and 2050.

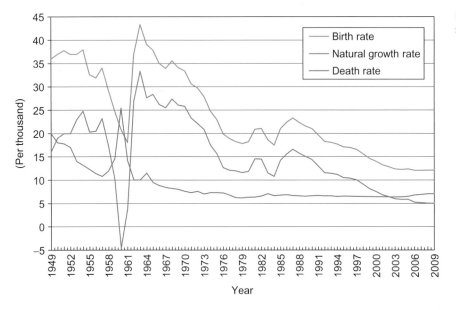

FIGURE 3.1 Birth, death, and natural growth rates, 1949–2009. *Source: NBS, various years.*

---

1. Wakabayashi (1989, p. 14) estimates that 14 million people died from starvation between 1959 and 1961. In addition, Minami (1994, p. 197, fn. 8) puts a higher figure on the number of deaths.

The Chinese government's promotion of its 'sea of manpower' approach led simultaneously to the development of a number of population problems. During recent decades, when the population densities of some developed countries have either stayed constant or decreased gradually, China's population density has increased sharply from 40 persons per square kilometer of land area in 1949 up to 130 persons per square kilometer of land area at the end of the 1990s – a figure which is more than three times greater than that of the world as a whole.

In fact, China's population density is not very high when compared with South Korea (443 persons per km^2), Japan (329 persons per km^2), India (290 persons per km^2), the UK (237 persons per km^2) or Germany (226 persons per km^2). However, because much of China's territory consists of mountains, desert and other uninhabitable lands, the number of persons per square kilometer of the *inhabitable* land area is much larger than the nominal population density in China. For instance, the population densities of many provinces in East China are more than 400 persons per square kilometer of land area (see Figure 3.2), much higher than that of the majority of the most populous nations in the world.

3.1.2 Population Control

Today, when considering the poor living conditions which exist in the countryside and the unemployment problem in the urban areas, one cannot help but remember the ridiculous debate about whether or not population growth should be subjected to effective controls. Stimulated by the idea that population equals production, some people believed blindly in the link 'more people→more labor force→more production→faster economic development', which led eventually to China's problem of over-population.[2] In fact, faced by the grim reality of population growth, in his later years even Mao Zedong acknowledged the increasing pressure of over-population on the Chinese economy, when he began to puzzle about his earlier prediction that:

Of all things in the world, people are the most precious… Even if China's population multiplies many times, she is fully capable of finding a solution.

(Mao, 1949, pp. 453–4.)

In the early 1970s, the Chinese government had to implement a birth control policy that aimed to encourage late marriages, prolong the time period between births and reduce the number of children in each family. In 1978, the encouragement of birth control made its first official appearance in Article 53 of the PRC Constitution.

Following the implementation of a population control policy, the first National Conference on Birth Control (NCBC) was held in Beijing in 1979. The conference requested that 'one couple has only one child, and at most two children, but with a three year interval. Those couples who do not plan to have a second child will be rewarded and those who have a third child will receive economic punishment.'

Since the 1970s, and especially since the early 1980s, China has effectively controlled its population trends by the introduction of a series of strict measures. The rate of population growth declined dramatically – from 3 percent in the 1960s to less than 1 percent by the end of the 1990s. Obviously, without this reduction, China's population would have increased by more than 20 million (that is, $(0.03–0.01) \times 1$ billion) per annum. In other words, as a result of China's population control efforts, every two or three years the increase in population has been reduced by an amount equal to the size a medium-sized European nation (such as the UK or France).

3.1.3 Problems

Despite the above successes, the 'one-child' policy has also resulted in some problems. First, China's population control policy has generated a gender imbalance. In the poorest and most remote rural areas, the traditional discrimination against women has remained very strong. Because there is very little social security in those rural areas, sons offer the best hope for parents who are still earning their living by physical labor. This provides a strong incentive for people to have more than one child until they have sons. Partly as a result of the birth control policy and partly because of the increasing burden of having an additional female child, the inhumane practices of feticide and infanticide can be occasionally found, especially in rural areas, where men generally have a higher social position than women. China's national birth gender ratio (i.e., male to female) is much higher than that found in the developed nations.[3] If only the rural area is taken into account, the birth gender ratio would, of course, be much larger.

Secondly, a lower birth rate will eventually result in a higher proportion of aged people. This is already a social problem in the advanced nations and, sooner or later, it will also affect Chinese society. Thanks to the government's efforts in raising the social position of women and the strict domicile system for urban citizens, China's 'one-child' policy has been successfully implemented in the urban areas since the early 1980s. At present, it is

---

2. The literature on this argument includes Wang and Dai (1958, pp. 10–14), He et al. (1960, pp. 20–5), and Zhang (1982, pp. 12–14).

3. According to a sampling survey conducted on 1 October 1995, the birth gender ratios for population at the ages of 0, 1, 2, 3, and 4 years were 116.57:100, 121.08:100, 121.26:100, 119.17:100, and 115.01:100, respectively (SSB, 1996, p. 72).

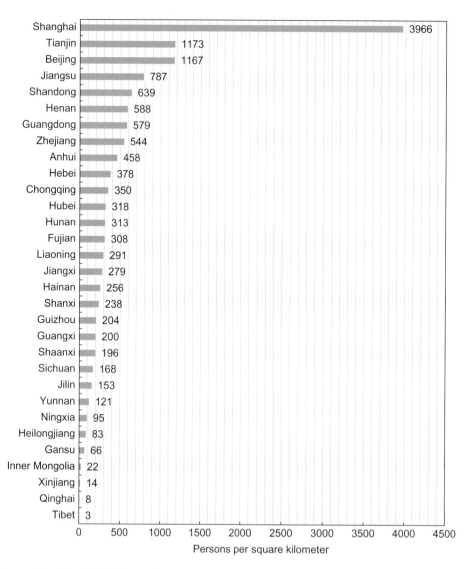

FIGURE 3.2 China's population density (2010), by province.

very common in urban China for a couple to have only one child. However, the policy is to rigidly transform China's urban family pattern into a reverse pyramid in the coming decades.[4]

The population age composition also differs from region to region. In 1982, Shanghai became the first province where the percentage of the population aged 65 years or over exceeded 7 percent of the total – a criterion that is generally thought to characterize an aged society. At the end of the 1990s, a number of other provinces could also share this classification including Beijing, Tianjin, Jiangsu, Zhejiang, Shandong, Guangdong, Liaoning, Sichuan, and

so on. According to Du (1994, p. 88), the proportion of the aged population in China will increase steadily to 8.1 percent in 2010, 10.9 percent in 2020, 14.7 percent in 2030, 19.8 percent in 2040, and 20.9 percent in 2050.

Thirdly, patterns of population growth show considerable differences between the rural and urban areas of China. In some poor rural areas, where labor productivity is to a large extent physically determined, parents have strong incentives to have large numbers of children. By contrast, in urban and other relatively well-off areas, parents who receive higher education and have lifetime social welfare can usually make a trade-off between having more children and improving their living standards and quality of life.

Faced with cramped living conditions and the high cost of education, as well as severe competition for university entrance, urban parents have little incentive to have a second child, not to mention the fact that those who illegally

---

4. In 1953, the proportion of the population aged 65 or over was only 4.4 percent. This proportion was further reduced to 3.6 percent in 1964, but rose again to 4.9 percent in 1982, 5.6 percent in 1990, and 7.0 percent in 2000 (NBS, 2002).

raise more than one child would not receive subsidies from the government and could be fired from their current posts. As an only child is, in general, better protected by its family than one with siblings, those children born in urban areas usually receive better care and education than those born in rural areas. In brief, the fact that the rural poor have more children than the urban and well-educated people will reduce the overall educational level of the Chinese population.

As a result of the diverse regional natural and geographical conditions, the population of China is unevenly distributed. Generally, population density is higher in the Eastern belt than in the Central belt, while the Central belt has a higher density than the Western belt. The most populous provinces are Shanghai (3,966 persons per km²), followed by Tianjin, Beijing, Jiangsu, Shandong and Henan. On the other hand, however, Tibet, Qinghai, Xinjiang, and Inner Mongolia have only 3, 8, 14, and 22 persons for each square kilometer of land area, respectively (see Figure 3.2).

3.2 LABOR FORCE

3.2.1 General Situation

The size of the labor force in a country can be defined as the population in the productive age group multiplied by the labor force participation rate. In turn, the labor force participation rate can be calculated as the ratio of the labor force to the population at or above a certain age. The international standard for the productive age is defined as 15 years or over. In a market economy, labor force demand is positively related to gross production output. When labor supply exceeds labor demand, unemployment occurs.

According to China's official definition, the registered unemployment rate in urban areas refers to the ratio of the number of the registered unemployed persons to the sum of the number of employed persons and the registered unemployed persons. Registered unemployed persons in urban areas are defined as 'persons who are registered as permanent residents in the urban areas engaged in non-agricultural activities, aged within the range of laboring age (for males, 16 years or older but younger than 50 years; for females, 16 years or older but younger than 45 years), capable of work, unemployed but wishing to be employed and registered with the local employment service agencies.'

Table 3.2 gives a cross-national comparison of the economically active population, a term defined by economists as 'all men or women who simply work for the production of economic goods and services during a specific period'. It is noticeable that China had an incredibly high level of per capita annual labor input (947 hours), compared with the African nations (608 hours), and the Western nations

TABLE 3.2 Characteristics of Human Capital, China and the Rest of the World

Item	Africa	China	Western Nations	World
Proportion of female labor (%)[a]	38.1	37.3	42.5	36.2
Ratio of employment to population (%)[a]	39.3	44.0	44.5	40.5
Per capita labor input (in hours)[a]	608	947	709	736
Gross enrollment ratios[b]	53	99	104	86
(1) Male	58	100	104	89
(2) Female	50	98	105	82

[a]Calculated by the author based on Maddison (1996, Table J-1).
[b]Gross enrolment in primary education (UNESCO, 1999).

(709 hours). The high labor input of China may help us to understand, at least in part, its levels of rapid economic growth over the course of recent decades.

A human development index (HDI) has been computed by the United Nations Development Program (UNDP) for a number of countries. This is simply the average of indices for life expectancy, literacy, and school enrollment, and price-adjusted PPP GDP per capita. Figure 3.3 and Table 3.3 show that: (i) internationally, China's HDI has improved significantly since 1980; and (ii) domestically, there is significant variation among China's provinces. For example, we can see that, in 2008, Shanghai's HDI is comparable to Hong Kong's or Taiwan's; and several coastal provinces have, like Mexico, inched into the high HDI category. However, several western provinces, such as Guizhou, Gansu and Yunnan, are similar to Indonesia and Vietnam; and Tibet HDI in 2008 is the same as China's in 1990.

3.2.2 Rural-To-Urban Migration

Since the 1970s the Chinese economy has been characterized by a labor surplus problem – a result of the uncontrolled population growth during the 1950s and 1960s. While China's urban unemployment rate is not as high as is found in the developed nations,[5] there have been more unemployment problems in rural China. Thus, it is inevitable that the situation of a rapidly increasing rural population combined with a limited amount of cultivable land will generate a large rural labor surplus, particularly with

---

5. The definition of 'unemployment' differs from country to country, so it is difficult to conduct meaningful international comparisons.

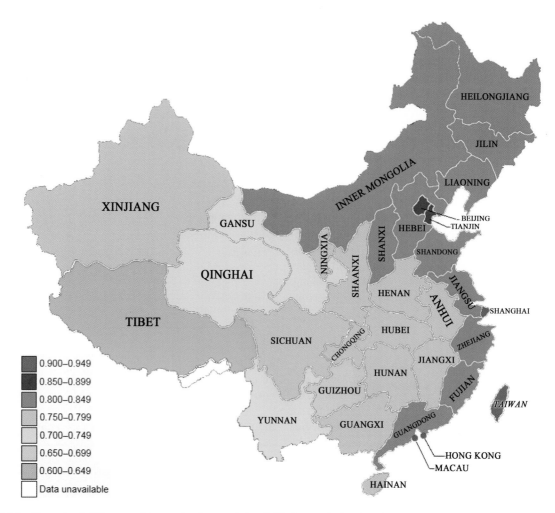

FIGURE 3.3 The regional differences of human development index, 2008. *Source: Author based on http://www.undp.org.cn/pubs/nhdr/nhdr2010cn. pdf. Accessed on 11/25/2011.*

the increased productivity resulting from the introduction of advanced technologies.

Since the 1980s, the seasonal movement of tens of millions of rural laborers (*mingong*) between the rural and urban areas has created a special scenario for the Chinese economy. Following the Spring Festival – the Chinese New Year which begins in late January or early February and lasts for about a month – the rural laborers leave for the urban areas and are employed as industrial workers or self-employed as retailers and servants. During the planting and harvesting seasons in the summer and autumn, some of them may return home to take part in agricultural work. As migration from the countryside to the cities is strictly controlled by the government through a system of registration of urban residents, most of the *mingong* are still treated as 'agricultural residents'. The *mingong* phenomenon has been having a dramatic effect on Chinese society. First of all, it has met the needs of the workers in urban construction and other labor-intensive sectors. Secondly, it has become an important source of increases

in rural income level and has been mainly responsible for the socioeconomic changes in rural China.

In any consideration of the factors that have contributed to China's dramatic urban growth, particular emphasis should be given to the role of the large numbers of rural workers. In Beijing, for example, each year there are more than one million temporary migrants from the countryside. As a permanent resident in Beijing, I have found that these rural workers have carried out most of Beijing's physical work. Without these workers, Beijing's urban constructions (such as those of the Bird's Nest and other new facilities used by the 2008 Olympic Games) would have been impossible. By contrast, very few, if any, of Beijing's 'officially registered' and economically active population are now to be found carrying out physical and menial jobs in the low-level service sectors of the economy.[6] This phenomenon stems mainly from the fact that China's

---

6. There is a saying that, 'without rural workers, Beijing would stop running'.

TABLE 3.3 Human Development Differences, Selected Nations and Chinese Provinces

Nations	HDI	Chinese Provinces	HDI
Norway	0.96		
Hong Kong, Taiwan	0.92	Shanghai	0.91
South Korea	0.90	Beijing	0.89
Argentina	0.86	Tianjin	0.88
Mexico	0.81	Guangdong, Liaoning, Zhejiang, Jiangsu	0.83–0.84
China 2008	0.79	Shandong, Jilin, Hebei, Heilongjiang	0.81–0.82
Brazil, Malaysia, Colombia	0.79	Fujian, Inner Mongolia, Shanxi	0.80
Thailand	0.78	Henan, Inner Mongolia, Hubei, Hainan, Chongqing, Hunan	0.78–0.79
Philippines	0.76	Guangxi, Xinjiang, Shaanxi, Jiangxi, Sichuan, Anhui	0.76–0.77
China	*0.75*		
Turkey	0.75		
China in 1999	*0.72*	Qinghai	0.72
Indonesia, Vietnam	0.70	Yunnan, Gansu	0.71
		Guizhou	0.69
China in 1990	*0.63*	Tibet	0.63
India	0.60		
Myanmar	0.58		
China in 1980	0.56		
Pakistan	0.53		

Notes: *(1) HDI = human development index. (2) Unless stated otherwise, national data are as of 2003 and provincial data are as of 2008.*
Sources: UNDP (2005, pp. 219–23) and http://www.undp.org.cn/pubs/nhdr/nhdr2010cn.pdf. Accessed on 11/25/2011.

'one-child' policy has been implemented more strictly in urban than in rural areas. It is expected that, over the course of the next few years, this part of the rural population will continue to contribute to China's urban development, especially in those areas experiencing physical expansions and therefore physical workers play a crucial role.

In China, the majority of rural-to-urban migrants are classified as 'temporary residents'. The prefix 'temporary' is misleading because there is no time limit to the status. Under the present system the migrants must remain 'temporary residents' all their lives. Most migrants in urban China are not covered by the city's medical insurance scheme, even though they have been employed in urban areas for more than 10 years. The other factor was the regulation governing the registration of births. The children of the 'temporary residents' have to be registered in the localities that were officially their fathers' or mothers' permanent places of residence. Thus, even

if they were born in, for example, Beijing, their parents would have to go to rural areas to obtain the birth certificates and have their names included in the *hukouben* (family registration books, which record various family events including births, deaths, marriages, and divorces, and complementary data such as permanent place of residence). Like their parents, they must be classified as 'agricultural' in their *hukouben*. However, these children all grow up in urban areas and have nothing to do with agricultural activity!

3.3 EDUCATION

3.3.1 Historical Evolution

Education was highly regarded by Guangzhong (?–645 BC) – a famous primary minister in the state of Qi during the Spring and Autumn period (771–475 BC):

If you plan for a year, sow a seed; if for ten years, plant a tree; if for a hundred years, teach the people. You will reap a single harvest by sowing a seed once and ten harvests by planting a tree; while you will reap a hundred harvests by teaching the people.

For more than one thousand years, and as a result of the Confucian influences, people in China have placed a substantial value on education. At present, most Chinese parents still believe it to be a glorious thing for their children to attain the highest school degrees. However, for the majority of the past one hundred years, the development of education in China has not been particularly successful.

In 1964, when the second national population census was conducted, 56.76 percent of the total population aged 16 years of age and above, were classified as either illiterate or semi-literate. Thereafter, the illiterate and semi-literate rate decreased considerably, but it was still estimated at 31.88 percent and 20.61 percent in the third and fourth national population census in 1982 and 1990, respectively (SSB, 1996, p. 71). According to UNESCO (1995, tab. 1.3), in 1990 the literacy rates for China were 87 percent for males and 68 percent for females, which were higher than the corresponding figures for India (62 percent and 34 percent), Pakistan (47 percent and 21 percent), and many other low-income countries, while being lower than those of Indonesia (88 percent and 75 percent), the Philippines (90 percent and 89 percent), Thailand (95 percent and 91 percent), Malaysia (86 percent and 70 percent), and many other low- and upper-middle income countries, and much lower than those found in Japan, the USA, Germany, and other high-income countries.

China's moderately high illiteracy has been determined by both historic and institutional factors. Before 1949, China's education was very limited and had been seriously damaged by the long-lasting wars. For instance, more than 60 percent of people born in the 1930s and more than 70 percent of people born in the 1920s were either illiterate or semi-literate. During the two peaks of population growth in the 1950s and 1960s, neither the government nor their families were capable of providing an adequate educational opportunity for each child.

The period of the Cultural Revolution (1966–76) saw a substantial revision of China's education system which had, to a large extent, been grounded in the principles of Confucianism. The length of primary school education was reduced from six years to five years; and that of junior- and senior-middle schools was cut by one year in each instance. In addition, the textbooks were heavily revised and simplified. Even worse, the status of schoolteachers, who had been highly regarded in traditional Chinese society, became subject to political discrimination. At the same time, the destruction of the higher education system was even more severe because universities were closed between 1966 and 1970 and operated in line with political,

rather than academic, considerations between 1971 and 1976. The Cultural Revolution resulted in a 'break-point' of ages for scientists and engineers, which has already had a negative effect on China's socioeconomic development.

China's educational system began to return to a more normal path as soon as the Cultural Revolution came to an end. In 1977 there was a resumption of the national entrance examinations for higher learning institutes. One year later, the Chinese government made the first recognition, during the First National Conference on Science and Technology (NCST), that 'science and technology is a productive force' and began to treat intellectuals as 'a branch of the working class'. Since this declaration education has been the subject of much state attention. In 1995, the Chinese government decided to implement a nine-year compulsory education system (that is, six years of primary school followed by three years of junior-middle school), with the aim of achieving universal access to junior-middle school within six years in urban and coastal areas and within ten years in other parts of the country.

3.3.2   Progress and Problems

China's primary and junior-middle education has achieved substantial progress in recent years, with the enrollment rates increased to nearly 100 percent in the early years of the twenty-first century. During this time, China's higher learning institutions (including three- and four-year colleges), which were only able to absorb a small proportion of graduates from senior-middle schools before the 1990s and an even smaller proportion of them before the 1980s (data are shown in Figure 3.4), have provided opportunities to more than two-thirds of senior-middle school graduates. However, problems still remain in senior-middle school education. For instance, almost one-third of graduates from junior-middle schools have not been able to enter senior-middle schools in the 2000s (see Figure 3.4).

In China, expenditure on public education as a percentage of GNP is still lower than that of many developed nations such as Canada (7.6 percent, 1992), Hungary (7.0 percent, 1992), Bulgaria (5.9 percent, 1992), Portugal (6.1 percent, 1990), USA (5.3 percent, 1990), and Japan (4.7 percent, 1991) (UNESCO, 1995). As early as 1993, the Chinese government had already set a long-term target for educational development in China: i.e., to invest 4 percent of its GDP in public education by 2000. However, this goal has not been achieved, even though the government budget on education has risen significantly in recent years (see Figure 3.5). In 1978, China's expenditure on public education accounted for 2.07 percent of its GDP. In later years, this ratio rose gradually, reaching 2.69 percent in 1986. In the following ten years, however, it did not change significantly, and finally dropped back to 2.08

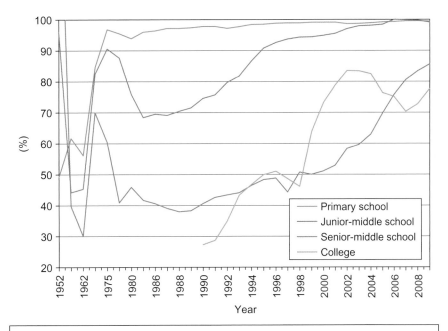

Notes: (1) The proportion of graduates of junior-middle schools entering senior-middle schools was higher than 100% in the early 1950s as the students graduating from junior-middle schools were less than the students enrolled in senior-middle schools.
(2) Graduates of junior-middle school include vocational schools.
(3) 'College' includes three- and four-year colleges.

FIGURE 3.4 Enrollment ratios of various educational institutions, 1952–2009. *Source: NBS (various years).*

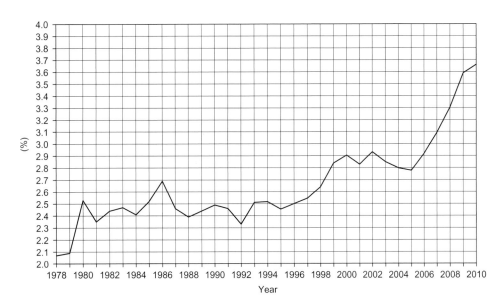

FIGURE 3.5 Government expenditure on education as a percentage of GDP. *Source: NBS, various years.*

percent in 1995. From 1995 to 2000, the ratio increased considerably. But since then, till 2005, there were not any significant changes.

A regression based on the data on China's educational expenditure and national income from the 1980s and early 1990s reveals that at a time when the per capita national income grew from 250 yuan to 1,000 yuan, the ratio of educational expenditure to national income decreased from 6.3 percent to 2.8 percent (Hsueh, 1994, pp. 80–1). Obviously, the empirical estimate is inconsistent with the hypothesis that there is a positive correlation between the income level and the ratio of educational expenditure to

GNP, as estimated by Chenery and Syrquin (1975, p. 20).[7] Even though the two estimates are based on different statistical definitions, it can still be seen that China's expenditure on education lagged behind its economic growth.

China's education is provided unevenly across the provinces. Usually, the mean value of education is much higher in the eastern coastal areas (such as Beijing and Shanghai) than in the western inland provinces (such as Qinghai and Tibet). However, the mean values of education in years are more even in the urban areas, the reasons for which may be twofold. First, the central government attempts to equalize educational opportunities across provinces: the richer provinces tend to receive less and the poorer provinces tend to receive more central government funding for education. Secondly, the assignment of college graduates to employment is carried out on a national basis. The government gives preferential treatment to the poor provinces by assigning graduates from colleges in rich provinces to work in poor provinces (Knight and Li, 1993, p. 300).

3.3.3 Institutional Constraints

In recent years, especially since Beijing successfully sponsored the 29th Olympic Games in 2008, during which China received the largest number of gold medals, the Chinese have been predicting when China will produce a Nobel Laureate. This is a serious problem, which is worthwhile considering. Whenever the Nobel Prizes are awarded each year, the Chinese will ask the same question since China's academic and intellectual achievements are not as great as its sporting successes. 'Why do our schools fail to nurture outstanding talents?' This is the question asked several times by Qian Xuesen – a famous scientist who received his university degrees in the United States in the 1930s – before his death in 2009. Then, there was an open letter issued jointly by several professors to the Chinese Minister of Education and to the national educational circles. In contrast to China's recent economic achievements, there have also been serious concerns about China's political and economic sustainability. How then does one explain the Qian Xuesen question?

Published in November 2009 by the Shanghai Jiao Tong University, the seventh annual Academic Ranking of World Universities (ARWU) offers a comparison of over 1,000 colleges worldwide. What is interesting is that the Chinese groups apparently carried out the study without bias. Unfortunately, no Chinese schools featured in the list of the ARWU's top 200 schools, in which Harvard University took the top ranking. The following phenomenon is more ridiculous. Since 2009, China has produced more PhDs than the United States, making China the No. 1 country holding doctorate degrees in the world. That is the good news. Less than cheering is that half of Chinese doctorates become government officials.[8] This phenomenon reflects a serious problem in China's policy on higher education. It is argued that this trend can only be harmful to social development. Producing so many doctorates to be officials – or, more specifically, awarding so many officials with doctorates – is in itself a misused function. Does one need a doctorate degree to be an official? From the perspective of educational development, this is an absurd and ridiculous phenomenon.

Since the late 1970s, a large number of university graduates and PhD students have traveled to Western nations to pursue their advanced studies. A majority of them, living primarily in the USA, have remained abroad and these people constitute an important 'brain-pool' for China's technological development.[9] Since the late 1990s, the Chinese government has sought to create a more favorable climate in order to encourage these overseas Chinese scholars to return home, in order to take over the running of laboratories, high-tech firms, or scientific parks. Yes, this kind of knowledge borrowing can recharge the batteries of economic growth for a short period of time. But, in order to achieve sustainable, long-term economic development, China must be able to provide an academic environment in which the world-class talents will be produced consistently.

Although the Chinese government has so far managed the rising tensions between economic modernization on the one hand, and the many institutional flaws of authoritarian rule (e.g., lack of political accountability, weak rule of law, bureaucratic ossification, and endemic corruption) on the other, China will not likely continue this course of rapid growth without undertaking the necessary political reforms to make the Chinese political system more responsive and respectful of individual rights. Indeed, it is no surprise that Chinese schools fail to nurture outstanding talents. Now, China's colleges and universities have 'no lack of money'. They are able to build a campus which can give California Institute of Technology (where Professor Qian received his degree) 'a sense of inferiority'. But they are unable to produce an outstanding talent like Qian

---

7. According to Chenery and Syrquin (1975, p. 20), when the per capita GNP grows from US$100 to US$400 in developing countries, the ratio of educational expenditure to GNP increases from 3.3 percent to 3.5 percent accordingly.

8. During the past decade, an increasing number of key Chinese officials – at both central, ministerial and provincial levels – have been awarded with PhD degrees, regardless of whether or not they had academic qualifications.

9. It is estimated that the total number of Chinese graduates now living in the USA may be in the region of 200,000 to 300,000. Of these, around 10,000 to 15,000 are world-class scientists and engineers (Sigurdson et al., 2005, p. 65).

Xuesen. With so many universities competing to build luxury school buildings, there is still a lack of an open and free academic atmosphere. So, when executive power is always higher than academic power in schools, and if the executive order is much higher than academic freedom, Chinese schools will continue to find it impossible to nurture outstanding talents.

3.4 CULTURAL DIVERSITY

While others usually suggest more complicated compositions for a culture, in this section we will only discuss three elements – ethnicity, language, and religion. Of course, our discussion of these cultural elements is not definitive and perhaps would not satisfy anthropologists. Nevertheless, our consideration is due to the concerns that:

(i) 'ethnicity' provides a genetic basis on which socioeconomic behaviors between same and different groups of people can be easily differentiated

(ii) 'language' is an effective tool for communication

(iii) 'religion' can provide insights into the characteristics of culture.

3.4.1 Ethnicity

For the majority of the Christian era members of the ethnic majority in China have traditionally been referred to as the Han race. This may well be because of the relatively long period of social, political, economic, and military consolidation and stability enjoyed by the Chinese nation during the period of the Han dynasty (206 BC–AD 220). The term 'Han', however, does not offer a full account of the cultural and ethnic origins of the Chinese people. It was, instead, an inclusive name for the various tribes that lived together on the Central China Plains well before the time of Christ. The trend over the ages was for many ethnic groups living adjacent to the Hua-Xia people to be assimilated at different times and to different degrees into what the Chinese have ultimately termed the Han culture. The original ethnic stock for this amalgam seems to have primarily included the Hua-Xia, Eastern Yi, Chu-Wu, and Baiyue groups. Other non-Han peoples were assimilated into the Han culture at different points in China's history.[10]

While the Han majority can be found throughout the country, China's ethnic minorities are scattered over vast areas of China (see Table 3.4). Historically, the total number of ethnic groups has never been fixed precisely. For example, in 1953, only 42 ethnic peoples were identified, while the number increased to 54 in 1964 and 56 in 1982. Geographically, most ethnic minorities are concentrated on the western inland areas, such as Hui in Ningxia, Ugyur in Xinjiang, Mongols in Inner Mongolia and Qinghai, and Tibetans in Tibet and the surrounding areas. However, the ethnic Zhuang form the majority in the Guangxi Zhuang autonomous region in the southern coastal area.

During their histories, many ethnic groups have also established differing economic and cultural backgrounds. For example, the names of some ethnic groups can reveal certain information about their particular economic and cultural conditions, with a number of these highlighting a group's characteristic occupation. For example, in the language of the Lahu people, 'Lahu' means 'roasting tiger-meat on fire', from which it can be understood that the Lahu people used to live by hunting. This can also be witnessed by their neighbors in Southwest China, the Dai and Hani, who called themselves Mushe ('the hunters'). There is a small ethnic group entitled the 'Oroqen' (a word which has two meanings: 'people who herd tamed deer' and 'people who live on the mountains') living in the Greater and Lesser Xing'an Mountains in Northeast China. Another ethnic group, also living in Northeast China, call themselves the Daur (meaning 'cultivator'), indicating that the Daur people engaged in agriculture during ancient times.

Since the dawning of China's Neolithic period, agriculture has been the economic mainstay of the Han people. In the embryonic stages of its ethnic development, the Han group lived primarily along the banks of China's major rivers. The area along the Yellow River, characterized by a semi-arid climate, with loose, fertile soil, was suitable for the growing of millet; while the tropical and semi-tropical climate of the areas along the Pearl and Yangtze Rivers was good for rice production. Thus millet and rice could be said to be the staple crops that delineated early Han culture. While the Han culture continued to develop, commerce, industry, education and government service were also viable livelihoods, as, for example, in the case of the transportation of food, clothing and jewelry between the large walled cities and smaller, more remote towns. The non-Han minorities, such as the Tibetans, in western China, on the other hand, have traditionally had a mixed nomadic economy. The minority peoples in northeast China rely on either fishing and hunting or nomadism, while the Mongols have been mainly nomadic. The other minorities, such as the Uygurs in Xinjiang, have historically engaged in either agriculture or nomadism, but have supplemented their incomes through commerce.

Transnational migrants – with both legal and illegal status – are joining Chinese society on an unprecedented scale, and in unexpected ways. In late 2010, China conducted its sixth national population census, for the first time counting foreigners (including residents of Hong Kong,

---

10. They are, for example, the Huns (Xiongnu) and Xianbei between the third and fifth century AD, the Eastern Hu and the Jurchens (ancestors of the Manchus) from the tenth through the early thirteenth century, and the Manchus through their conquest of China in the seventeenth century.

TABLE 3.4 Basic Conditions of the 55 Ethnic Minorities in China (2010)

Name	Population (000 persons)	Geographic Distribution	Language(s)	Religion(s)
Achang	33.94	Yunnan	Achang	Buddhism
Bai	1,858.06	Yunnan, Guizhou	Bai, most also speak Chinese	animism
Baonan	91.88	Gansu	Baonan, Chinese (spoken and written)	Islam
Blang	16.51	Yunnan	Blang, Dai	Buddhism
Bouyei	2,971.46	Guizhou, Yunnan, Guangxi	Dai	Buddhism
Dai	1,158.99	Yunnan	Dai, most also speak Chinese	Buddhism
Daur	132.39	Inner Mongolia, Heilongjiang, Xinjiang	Daur (spoken), Chinese (written)	Lamaism
Deang	17.94	Yunnan	Deang	Buddhism
Derung	7.43	Yunnan	Derung	
Dong	2,960.29	Guizhou, Hunan, Guangxi	Dong, Chinese	animism
Dongxiang	513.81	Gansu, Xinjiang	Dongxiang, most also speak Chinese	Islam
Ewenki	30.51	Inner Mongolia, Heilongjiang	Ewenki (spoken), Mongolian (written), Chinese (written)	shamanism
Gaoshan	458.00	Taiwan, Fujian	Gaoshan (spoken), Chinese	
Gelao	579.36	Guizhou, Guangxi	Gelao, Chinese	Islam
Hani	22.52	Yunnan	Hani	animism
Hezhe	1,439.67	Heilongjiang	Hezhe (spoken), Chinese	
Hui	4.64	Ningxia, Gansu, Henan, Hebei, Qinghai, Shandong	Chinese	Islam
Jing	9,816.80	Guangxi	Jing, Chinese (spoken and written)	
Jingpo	132.14	Yunnan	Jingpo	animism
Jino	20.90	Yunnan	Jino	
Kazak	1,420.46	Xinjiang, Gansu, Qinghai	Kazaki	Islam
Kirgiz	160.82	Xinjiang, Heilongjiang	Kirgiz, Uygur (written), Kazaki (written)	Islam, Lamaism
Korean	1,923.84	Jilin, Liaoning, Heilongjiang	Korean, Chinese	individual choice
Lahu	453.71	Yunnan	Lahu	animism
Lhoba	2.97	Tibet	Lhoba (spoken)	Lamaism
Li	1,247.81	Hainan	Li, some also speak Chinese	animism
Lisu	634.91	Yunnan, Sichuan	Lisu	
Manchu	10,682.26	Liaoning, Jilin, Heilongjiang, Beijing, Inner Mongolia	most speak Chinese; only a small portion speak Manchu	individual choice
Maonan	107.17	Guangxi	Maonan, Zhuang, Chinese (written)	Islam
Miao	8,940.12	Guizhou, Sichuan, Hunan, Hubei, Guangdong	Miao; the majority also assimilated into Chinese language	animism
Monba	8.92	Tibet	Monba, Tibetan	Lamaism

(Continued)

TABLE 3.4 (Continued)

Name	Population (000 persons)	Geographic Distribution	Language(s)	Religion(s)
Mongol	5,813.95	Inner Mongolia, Xinjiang, Liaoning, Jilin, Heilongjiang, Gansu, Hebei, Henan, Qinghai	Mongolian, Mandarin	Lamaism
Mulam	207.35	Guangxi	Mulam and Zhuang (spoken), Chinese (written)	Lamaism
Naxi	308.84	Yunnan, Sichuan	Naxi, most also speak Chinese	Dongba
Nu	28.76	Yunnan	Nu	
Oroqen	8.20	Inner Mongolia, Heilongjiang	Oroqen (spoken), Chinese (written)	shamanism
Pumi	33.60	Yunnan	Pumi	
Qiang	306.07	Sichuan	Qiang (spoken)	Lamaism
Russian	15.61	Xinjiang, Heilongjiang	Russian	Eastern Orthodox
Salar	104.50	Qinghai, Gansu	Salar (spoken), Chinese (spoken and written)	Islam
She	709.59	Fujian, Zhejiang, Jiangxi, Guangdong	Chinese	animism
Shui	406.90	Guizhou, Guangxi	Shui, most also speak Chinese	animism
Tajik	41.03	Xinjiang	Tajik (spoken), Uygur	Islam
Tatar	4.89	Xinjiang	Tatar, Uygur, Kazaki	Islam
Tibetan	5,416.02	Tibet, Qinghai, Sichuan, Gansu, Yunnan, Xinjiang	Tibetan	Lamaism
Tu	241.20	Qinghai, Gansu	Tu, Chinese	Lamaism
Tujia	8,028.13	Hunan, Hubei	Tujia, most also speak Chinese	animism
Uygur	8,399.39	Xinjiang	Uygur	Islam
Uzbek	12.37	Xinjiang	Uzbek, Uygur, Kazaki	Islam
Va	396.61	Yunnan	Va	animism
Xibe	188.82	Xinjiang, Liaoning, Jilin	Xibe	Islam
Yao	2,637.42	Guangxi, Hunan, Yunnan, Guangdong	Yao, most also speak Chinese	animism
Yi	7,762.29	Sichuan, Hunan, Guizhou, Guangxi	Yi (spoken), males also speak and write Chinese	animism
Yugur	13.72	Gansu	Yugur, Chinese (spoken and written)	Lamaism
Zhuang	16,178.81	Guangxi, Guangdong, Yunnan and Guizhou	Zhuang (spoken), most also speak and write Chinese	animism

Sources: NBS (2011) for the population data and author for others.

Macau, and Taiwan) who were residing in mainland China. The census counted 1,020,145 people from outside mainland China, mainly coming from the Republic of Korea, the United States, Japan, Myanmar, Vietnam, Canada, France, India, Germany, and Australia (see Figure 3.6).

International communities are beginning to emerge within Chinese society. Shanghai and Beijing municipalities, Guangdong, Jiangsu, Fujian, Yunnan, Zhejiang, Shandong, and Liaoning provinces, and Guangxi Zhuang autonomous region are home to the largest concentrations of foreign residents. It is estimated that Beijing's 'Korea Town', Wangjing, is home to more than 200,000 Koreans. Approximately 50,430 Japanese lived in Shanghai for more than three months in 2010, the largest enclave of which is in the city's Gubei district. *Xinhua News* reported that in 2007 the number of long-term Japanese residents

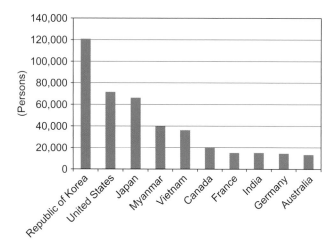

FIGURE 3.6 The top ten countries of origin of foreigners residing in China (2010). *Source: NBS (2011).*

was greater in Shanghai than in New York. Some communities may be a bit more unexpected. 'Middle-East Street', a bazaar in Yiwu, Zhejiang province that is frequented by Muslims, is the largest international small commodities wholesale market in the world. Guangzhou is home to a so-called 'African Zone' (also named 'China's Brooklyn'), where an estimated 200,000 African peddlers have lived with their families during the last decade.[11]

3.4.2 Language

China's linguistic system is understood in terms of its lexicon, grammar, syntax, phonetics, and so on. Chinese, the language spoke by the Han people – China's official language, which belongs to the Sino-Tibetan language family – is the most commonly used language in China and one of the most common languages in the world. Written Chinese emerged in its embryonic form of carved symbols approximately 6,000 years ago. The Chinese characters used today evolved from those used in bone and tortoise shell inscriptions more than 3,000 years ago and the bronze inscriptions produced soon after. Drawn figures were gradually reduced to patterned strokes, pictographs were reduced to symbols; the complicated became simplified. Earlier pictographs and ideographs were joined by pictophonetic characters. Chinese is monosyllabic. The vast majority of Chinese characters used today are composed of an ideogrammatic portion on the left and the phonetic on the right.[12]

In addition to Chinese, a number of other languages are also used regionally and locally in China (see Figure 3.7). Specifically, 23 of these languages have taken written forms. Five linguistic systems are represented: 29 languages, including Zhuang, Dai, Tibetan, Yi, Miao, and Yao, are within the Han-Tibetan language family; 17 languages, including Uygur, Kazak, Mongolian, and Korean, are within the Altaian language family; three languages, the Va, Deang, and Blang, are within the South Asian language family; and Gaoshan is an Austronesian language. The Jing language has yet to be classified typologically. The main non-Han Chinese languages used in China are: Zhuang (spoken) in most parts of Guangxi and some parts of Guangdong, Yunnan, and Guizhou; Ugyur (spoken and written) in Xinjiang and some parts of Qinghai; Tibetan (spoken and written) in Tibet and the surrounding areas; Mongolian (spoken and written) in Inner Mongolia, Qinghai, and the surrounding areas; Yi (spoken) in some parts of Sichuan, Yunnan, Guizhou and Guangxi provinces; and English (spoken and written) in Hong Kong, and so on.

Although Mandarin is standardized nationwide as *putonghua*, each region speaks its own local version, usually reflecting influence from the native dialect of the area (see Box 3.1). The main unifying force of China's many diverse dialects is the shared written system. It is generally believed that the unified Chinese characters used by people speaking different dialects make it possible for the central government to maintain control effectively over a vast size of territory. However, achieving mastery of the many thousands of Chinese characters is a very long and time-consuming process. This, as argued by Maddison (1996, p. 54), strengthened Chinese ethnocentrism, encouraged self-satisfaction, and inhibited the intellectuals' deviance or curiosities.

On the other hand, Fairbank (1980, p. 41) notes that 'written Chinese is not a wide open door through which the mass peasants gain access to truth and knowledge; rather, all too often it is the stumbling block for their progresses'. However, since the end of the twentieth century, Fairbank's hypothesis has no longer been an issue. Thanks to the fast development of computer technology, the Chinese have been liberalizing from past heavy and time-consuming office work in relation to the hand writing of Chinese characters. As a result, this has enabled China to significantly increase its macroeconomic efficiency. Even if office computerization has also been realized in the Western nations, its marginal effects on the increase of labor productivity are much larger in China than in the rest of the world.

3.4.3 Religion

Religion has been defined as 'belief in the existence of a supernatural ruling power, the creator and controller of the

---

11. Source: Shen (2011), which also provides further references.

12. For example, the Chinese character for the tree that produces tung oil is composed of an ideogram on the left representing a tree, and a phonogram on the right indicating that the word should be pronounced *tong* (as would this phonetic element if it were an independent character).

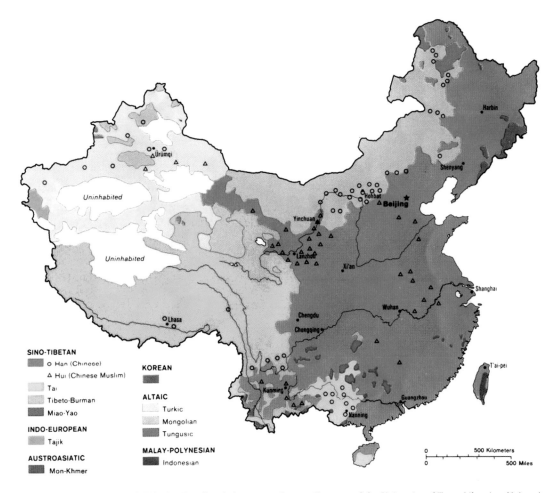

FIGURE 3.7 The spatial distribution of China's ethno-linguistic groups. *Source: Courtesy of the University of Texas Libraries, University of Texas at Austin.*

Box 3.1 The Main Chinese Dialects

Chinese dialects are spoken in three-quarters of the country by two-thirds of the population throughout China. Generally, these dialects can be classified into the following groups:

- The Xiang dialect (in the Hunan area) and the Gan dialect (in the Jiangxi area) each has six tones, including the entering tone. In some areas such as Changsha and Nanchang, these dialects do not distinguish between the constants *l-* and *n-*.
- The Kejia dialect, whose speakers are mostly found in Guangdong, Taiwan, and other scattered areas in Southeast Asia, also has six tones.
- The Wu dialect (mostly spoken in Shanghai, Jiangsu and Zhejiang provinces) has a great deal of variation. The Suzhou dialect of Jiangsu province, representing the

northern Wu, has seven tones; the Wenzhou dialect of Zhejiang province, treated as the southern Wu, has eight tones; and the Shanghai dialect has five tones.

- The Min dialect (spoken widely in Fujian, Taiwan, Hainan, and many areas of Southeast Asia) includes Northern and Southern Min. While the Northern Min is represented by Fuzhou, the Southern Min dialect, which has seven tones, is mostly spoken in eastern Fujian and most parts of the Taiwan area.
- Cantonese (Yue), with a total of nine tones which is more than any other dialect, is the main dialect of Guangdong, Hong Kong, Macau, and many overseas Chinese communities.

---

universe, who has given to man a spiritual nature which continues to exist after the death of the body' (*Oxford Advanced Learner's Dictionary*, 1974, 3rd edn, p. 712). The main religions in China are Confucianism, Buddhism,

Taoism, Islam, Catholicism, Protestantism, along with shamanism, Orthodox Christianity, and the Naxi people's Dongba religion. The native religions are Confucianism, Buddhism, Taoism, shamanism, and animism, while

Buddhism was imported from India and evolved later into a Chinese-style religion. The section below discusses the features of some of these religions.

Founded by Kongzi or Confucius (551–479 BC), Confucianism was reputed to have served as the basis of traditional Chinese culture. *Lunyu* (Analects of Confucius) records the sayings and deeds of Confucius and his disciples. It covers a wide range of subjects, ranging from politics, philosophy, literature, and art to education and moral cultivation. With only 12,000 characters, it is terse but comprehensive, rich yet profound; as the major classic of Confucianism as well as the most authoritative, it has influenced Chinese society for over two thousand years. Its ideas have taken such firm root in China that all Chinese – both Han and non-Han ethnicities – have been more or less influenced by it. Since the Han dynasty, every ruler has had to pay at least some heed to this, and people also expected their ruler to act accordingly in China. Confucian philosophy concerning the relationship between politics and morality serves as the basis of the Confucian school's emphasis on moral education. This can be found in the Analects of Confucius: 'Regulated by the edicts and punishments, the people will know only how to stay out of trouble, but will not have a sense of shame. Guided by virtues and the rites, they will not only have a sense of shame, but also know how to correct their mistakes of their own accord.' This idea also represented the distinguishing feature of the Oriental culture realm under the influence of Confucianism.

Taoism originated from sorcery, the pursuit of immortality and other supernatural beliefs that were present in ancient China. Taoists look to the philosopher Laozi (or Lao Tzu, born in about 600 BC) as their great leader, and take his work *The Classic of the Way and its Power* ('Daode Jing' or 'Tao Te Ching') as their canon. Mystifying the philosophical concept of 'Dao' or 'Tao' (the way, or path), they posit that man could become one with the 'Dao' through self-cultivation and can thereby achieve immortality. As an escape from Confucianism, Taoism has been promoted by a group of scholars working against the ritualism and detailed prescriptions of Classical texts. It has also denoted the common people's belief in certain traditional super-institutions. Applying the idea of balance in all things, Taoism argues that human moral ideas are the reflection of human depravity, that the idea of filial piety springs from the fact of impiety, that the Confucian statement of the rules of propriety is really a reflection of the world's moral disorder. Later, Taoism developed via two directions. The first one, represented by Zhuangzi (c. 369–295 BC), resulted in so-called nihilism. The second one, with the Tao as the basis of proprieties and laws, led to the founding of the Legalist school.

Through the entire course of Chinese history, Chinese culture has been reconstructed as the result of external influences. Among the first, and the most important, is the importation of Buddhism from India in the first century BC. At the heart of Buddhism there are Four Noble Truths:

1. Existence is suffering
2. Suffering has a cause, namely craving and attachment
3. There is a cessation of suffering, which is Nirvana
4. There is a path to the cessation of suffering, which includes the noble eightfold path – that is, right view, right intention, right speech, right action, right livelihood, right effort, right mindfulness, and right concentration.

Nirvana is the ultimate goal of Buddhism. It represents the extinction of all cravings and the final release from suffering. To the extent that such an ideal reflects the thinking of masses of people, a Buddhist society's values would be considered antithetical to goals such as acquisition, achievement, or affluence. Buddhism became increasingly popular after the fourth century AD and has now become a Chinese religion and an important part of Chinese culture. Tibetan Buddhism, or Lamaism as it is sometimes called, is founded primarily in Tibet and Mongolia. One of the tenets of Buddhism is that life is painful and that it is not limited to the mortal span with which we are familiar.

In the mid-seventh century, Muslim Arab and Persian merchants came overland through Central Asia to northwest China and by sea to Guangdong and other southeastern ports, bringing with them the Islamic faith. Christian belief was first introduced to China approximately one thousand years ago. During the Ming (AD 1368–1644) and the Qing (AD 1644–1911) dynasties, a large number of Christian missionaries began to arrive in China. They brought not only their religion but also new concepts of science and technology.

Today, China is a country which displays considerable spatial diversities in religion. Apart from the Protestants and Roman Catholics, who are scattered across the nation, most of the other religious followers have either a geographical or an ethnic orientation in China. Most Han people traditionally engage in folk religious practices, usually mixed with elements from Confucianism, Taoism, and Buddhism. The Hui, Uygur, Kazak, Kirgiz, Tatar, Ozbek, Tajik, Dongxiang, Salar, and Bonan people, mostly in the area of Northwest China, adhere to Islamic culture. The Tibetans, Mongols, Lhoba, Moinba, Tu, and Yugur follow a creed of Tibetan Buddhism (also known as Lamaism); whereas the Blang and Deang in Southwest China favor Theravada Buddhism. The minorities of Southwest China such as the Dai tend to be adherents of the Hinayana school of Buddhism. Some minorities in Jilin and Heilongjinag provinces subscribe to shamanism, while other ethnic groups living in the valleys of the southwestern mountain ranges embrace animist beliefs.

3.5 SUMMARY

A huge population does not represent an advantage in human resources for economic development, particularly for a country that has been transformed from an agricultural society using mainly traditional methods of production to an industrial society that requires not only advanced sciences and technologies but also qualified workers. A well-educated and law-abiding population that possesses a strong work ethic is the *sine qua non* of modern economic growth. At present, the development of its educational system is a particularly pressing matter for China – a country with a high proportion of illiteracy and whose educational system had been seriously damaged in the Cultural Revolution period (1966–76). At the same time, ways must be found to raise the technical and professional level of the workers already in employment.

Historical evidence suggests that the Western countries gradually pulled ahead of the rest of the world from the sixteenth century.[13] Northern Italy and Flanders played the leading role from the sixteenth to the seventeenth century, the Netherlands from then until the end of the eighteenth century, the UK and Germany in the nineteenth, and the USA since that time. The main institutional characteristics of Western society that have favored its development can be broadly summarized as follows: (1) the recognition of human capacity to transform the forces of nature through rational investigation and experiment; and (2) the ending of feudal constraints on the free purchase and sale of property, followed by a whole series of developments which gave scope for successful entrepreneurship (Maddison, 1996, p. 50).

Creativity and innovation have been the most fundamental elements in promoting, either directly or indirectly, economic development and social change. In China, there were great thinkers such as Confucius, Mencius, Laozi, and Zhuangzi. But these achievements go back to the periods of the Spring and Autumn (770–476 BC) and the Warring States (475–221 BC), and there has not been a similar breakthrough within the past 1,000 years. Throughout its history, Chinese culture has two obvious historical traits. One is that it had a very long period of feudalism. The second trait is that the Imperial Examination (keju) system was too rigid and deeply entrenched. The feudal period in Europe was, by contrast, shorter and was followed by over 200 years (from the fourteenth to the sixteenth century AD) of the Renaissance, a revolutionary movement in intellectual thought and inventiveness spurred on by the call to revive the arts of classical Greece. The Enlightenment and the Industrial Revolution that followed caused a tumultuous transformation in Europe. Shaking off its feudal shackles in ideology and social systems, Europe created a brave new world for itself. Under such circumstances, Europe produced many new creations and inventions in the realms of art, science, music, architecture and so on. Over the course of the past 200 years, the United States has attracted many high caliber immigrants and provided very favorable conditions for creativity and inventiveness, making it the world's only present-day superpower.

Chinese culture is perhaps the most sophisticated in East Asia. Its religious package, which aims to achieve a harmonious balance between Confucianism, Buddhism, and Taoism, worked particularly well over a very long period of time. It is probably for this very reason that the Chinese remained intoxicated by past prosperity and still proudly regarded China as the *zhongguo* (center under heaven) of the world, even when it was beginning to lag far behind the Western nations. This kind of ethnocentrism and self-satisfaction eventually made China a typical autarkic society. The following were blamed for China's problems: the attachment to the family becomes nepotism; the importance of interpersonal relationships rather than formal legality becomes cronyism; consensus becomes the greasing of wheels and political corruption; conservatism and respect for authority become rigidity and an inability to innovate; much-vaunted educational achievements become rote-learning and a refusal to question those in authority.

Case Study 3

Age, Gender, Ethnicity, Education, and Earnings[14]

J and L are two state-owned mining firms that belong to the Kailuan Group Corporation.[15] Firm J is located near Jinggezhuang village, northeast Tangshan city, Hebei province. It was established in 1958 and went into operation in 1979, with a production capacity of 1.2 million tons per year. Following some technological readjustments in 1981, production has risen to more than 1.7 million tons per year since this time. About 100 km from Tianjin city and 72 km from Tangshan city, Firm L is located at Linnanchang town, southwest Yutian county, Hebei province. The firm was originally established by Tianjin municipal government in April 1970 and was transferred to Kailuan Group in April

---

13. See North and Thomas (1973), North (1981, 1990) and Abramovitz (1986) for the varieties of European experience on the importance of institutions or differential social capability.

14. A full version of this research can be found on the companion site (http://www.elsevierdirect.com/companions/9780123978264).

15. I conducted two surveys on these two firms in January 2001. Mr Chen Tianchi and Mr Tian Guogang (Director and Deputy Director of the General Managers' Office of Kailuan Group, respectively) accompanied me during my field work. As requested, the two firms are named only as two abbreviated letters, J and L, respectively. Research assistance by Zhao Gongzheng and Guo Liqing are acknowledged.

1978. In November 1985 the firm went into operation, with a production capacity of 0.6 million tons per year, down from 1.2 million tons per year in the first year.

At the end of 2000, there were 5,605 and 2,926 staff in Firms J and L, respectively. In our surveys, we only collected the data on 617 staff for Firm J, and 554 staff for Firm L (see Table 3.5). In general, Firm J's average educational level (in length of years) is 11.83, which is higher than Firm L's at 8.10. Restricted by bad working environments in underground mines, China's retirement ages are officially defined as 45 years for underground miners and 60 years (for males) and 55 years (for females) in other industrial sectors. In Firms J and L, the average ages of employees are 35.98 and 35.26 years, respectively. These figures are less than the average age (39.64) of employees in China's state-owned enterprises as a whole in the mid-1990s (Zhao, 1999, p. 455).

Since Firms J and L were established during the 1970s and the 1980s, their organizational behaviors in production and business activities have reflected, to a certain extent, the outcome of a centrally planned system. Moreover, economic performance differed between these two firms. For example, in 1999 Firm J produced 1.794 million tons of raw coal with a gross profit of 14.28 million yuan; however, Firm L only produced 0.600 million tons of raw coal, with a loss of 4.20 million yuan.

Table 3.6 compares the two firms' average wage levels between various groups of staff. Generally speaking, in Firms J and L the basic wages are not so different as the bonuses and subsidies. But in both firms the total wage levels are significantly different between male and female staff. This is quite easily understood, since female workers only engaged in the jobs with low work intensities and with, accordingly, relatively low compensation.[16] Besides,

TABLE 3.5 About the Samples (October 2000): Firms J and L

		Firm J	Firm L
Total samples (persons)		617	554
As % of total staff		11.01	18.93
Proportion of female staff (%)		5.51	4.51
Proportion of CCP members (%)		16.86	2.53
Proportion of ethnic minorities (%)[a]		0.72	1.06
Proportion of underground miners (%)		68.07	65.88
Composition by education[b]	Average length of education (years)[c]	11.88	8.10
	Primary school (%)	0.00	5.60
	Junior high school (%)	2.43	53.43
	Senior high school (%)	17.50	8.30
	Technical school (%)	11.67	0.18
	College (3 or 4 years)	15.56	0.00
Composition by age group	Average age (years)	35.98	35.26[d]
	20 years or younger (%)	3.57	0.00
	21–30 years (%)	27.23	28.80
	31–40 years (%)	35.98	47.73
	41–50 years (%)	29.66	21.60
	51 years or older (%)	3.57	1.87

TABLE 3.6 Average Wages by Groups of Workers (Yuan/Person): Firms J and L

By Group of Workers		Total Wage (October 2000)[a]	
		Firm J	Firm L
All samples		1,232.18	972.00
Gender	Male	1,244.04	990.68
	Female	1,028.67	576.68
Political status	CCP membership	1,607.05	1,128.64
	Non-CCP	1,156.18	967.94
Ethnicity	Han ethnic	1,260.33	1,112.49
	Non-Han ethnic	1,045.02	1,150.25
Occupation	Underground miner	1,187.12	1,120.94
	Office worker	1,328.23	684.36
Education	College	1,523.08	NA
	Technical school	1,219.32	2,172.00
	Senior high school	1,013.65	1,139.52
	Junior high school	1,097.17	1,095.42
	Primary	1,227.96	1,213.19
	Others[b]	1,227.96	678.03
Age group	20 years or younger	804.67	
	21–30 years	984.94	1,026.59
	31–40 years	1,281.52	1,121.75
	41–50 years	1,422.48	1,209.36
	50 years or older	1,466.72	1,057.57

Notes:
[a]'Total wage' includes such items as 'basic wage', 'bonus', and 'subsidy', whose data are not shown here.
[b]These include illiterate and unidentified staff.

16. Females are not allowed to work as underground miners in China.

since most, if not all, high-ranking staff were also Chinese Communist Party (CCP) members, whereas very few low-ranking staff were, the wage levels differed significantly between CCP and non-CCP members.

Although Han ethnic staff accounted for the majority of employees, some non-Han ethnic minorities (such as the Hui, Mongol, and Manchu) were also employed in both Firms J and L. According to the Chinese constitution, every employee should be treated fairly and paid equally if they carry out the same jobs, no matter which ethnic groups they belong to. Nevertheless, we found two ethnically related items in the list of wages in both firms:

- 'Penalty on the birth of a second child': since the non-Han ethnic minorities are permitted a more flexible birth-control policy than Han ethnic couples, this item applies more frequently to the Han ethnic staff.
- 'Subsidy to the Hui ethnic staff': since Muslims do not eat pork, which is a common food in Chinese cafeterias, they may use this subsidy to prepare their own food by themselves.

Generally, wage levels vary with respect to age. According to Machin (1996, p. 52, Table 4), the ratio of wage levels of those aged 40–49 to those aged 21–24 was 1.36 in the UK and 2.14 in the USA in 1990. In our surveys, comparable ratios of wage levels were 1.58 for Firm J (which is higher than the UK's) and 1.29 for Firm L (which is lower than the UK's), and wage level ratios for those aged 45–49 to those aged 20–24 were 1.59 for Firm J and 1.28 for Firm L (which is much lower than the figure for the USA). From Table 3.6, we can also see that the monthly wage level was the highest for the group aged >50 in Firm J (i.e., 1,466.72 yuan), while it was the highest for the group aged 41–50 in Firm L (i.e., 1,209.36 yuan).

Table 3.6 also shows that, in the case of both firms, staff with higher levels of education usually received higher wages. However, some exceptions do exist in Firm J in which the average level of wages of the 'Senior high school' staff (1,013.65 yuan) was lower than that of the 'Junior high school' staff (1,097.17 yuan) and even lower than that of the 'Primary school' staff (1,227.96 yuan).[17]

Theoretically, in firms the levels of wages are decided by many factors through very complicated patterns which are either linear, non-linear, random, or even fuzzy. According to Kotlikoff and Gokhale (1992), the compensation of office workers and marketing staff follow the following patterns with respect to age:

(i) For office workers, the level of compensation is lower than that of labor productivity before the age of 50 years and is higher than that of labor productivity thereafter.

(ii) For marketing staff, the level of compensation is higher than that of labor productivity near the age of retirement and lower than that of labor productivity thereafter.

It should be noted that firms with different types of production techniques have different requirements in respect of the educational and professional backgrounds for their staff. All of these will decide the distributions of earnings in different firms. In addition, the mechanism of earnings distribution for unskilled workers with unlimited supply is also different from that of skilled workers with limited supply. In fact, as Prendergast (1999) points out, since most workers have been employed under the condition that 'performances are achieved not individually but collectively', the determinants of wage levels are very complicated.

In order to understand and compare the determinants of earnings distributions in Firms J and L, we may use the data collected in our surveys to estimate the wage functions with respect to various explanatory variables, including age, age-squared, gender, CCP membership, ethnicity, position, and education. The estimated coefficients, which can be found on the companion site (http://www.elsevierdirect.com/companions/9780123978264), show that the wage level (in natural log form) rises with increasing age before the ages of 27.5 years (for Firm J) and 25.0 years (for Firm L) and decreases with age thereafter. In addition, the estimated results of the two firms have the following differences:

(i) the coefficients on 'Male', 'Han ethnic', 'Technical school', 'Senior high school' and 'Junior high school' are not significantly estimated in Firm J.

(ii) the coefficients on 'CCP member', 'Han ethnic' and 'Education in years' are not significantly estimated in Firm L.

The estimated coefficients on 'Underground miner', which are statistically significant in both firms, show that the underground miners' wages are 21.29 percent and 40.92 percent higher than those of the other staff in Firms J and L, respectively.

During the 1980s and early 1990s, there was an unusual phenomenon in terms of the distribution of earnings in China, which is called 'nao ti daogua': this indicates that physical labor is paid more than technical labor (Zhao, 1990). Since the mid-1990s, however, that situation has been changed significantly (Liu, 1998; and Lai, 1999, p. 452). Table 3.6 shows that in Firms J and L the coefficients on higher education dummies are always larger than

---

17. It should be noted that this does not mean that wages decrease with increasing levels of education. As a matter of fact, the staff in each educational group are also characterized by other variables such as age, gender, and occupation, each of which also decides the level of wages. We will discuss this issue in more detail later on.

those on lower education ones. The estimated coefficient on education in years, also called 'ratio of return to education' by labor economists, is 0.0436 for Firm J. Obviously, this coefficient is larger than that for urban and rural China (0.038 and 0.020, respectively) in 1988 (Li and Li, 1994, p. 445) and of state-owned enterprises and collectively owned enterprises (0.042 and 0.032, respectively) in 1996, but smaller than that of foreign invested enterprises (0.0791) in 1996 (Zhao, 2001).

By contrast, Firm L's ratio of return to education is not only smaller than that of Firm J, it is also insignificantly estimated in the statistics. Does this phenomenon result from the fact that Firm L's production technologies are less efficient and its economic performance is much poorer than Firm J's? We leave this question for future research.

REFERENCES

Abramovitz, M. (1986). Catching up, forging ahead, and falling behind. *Journal of Economic History*, 56(June), 23–34.

Chenery, H., & Syrquin, M. (1975). *Patterns of Development, 1950–1970*, published for the World Bank, New York: Oxford University Press.

Du, P. (1994). *A study of the process of population aging in China* [zhongguo renkou laohua yanjiu]. Beijing: The People's University of China Press.

Fairbank, J. K. (1980). *The United States and China: policies in Chinese–American relations*. Cambridge, MA: Harvard University Press.

He, J., Zhu, Z., & Liao, J. (1960). Criticizing Ma Yinchu's reactionary 'New Population Theory' [pipan Ma Yinchu fandong de 'xin renkou lun']. *The Economic Research [jingji janjiu]*, 4, 20–25.

Hsueh, T. (1994). The regional economic development pattern in China and its international comparison [zhongguo diqu jingji fazhan de xingtai, jianyu guoji jian de biaojiao]. In S. Liu, Q. Li, & T. Hsueh (Eds.), *Studies on China's regional economic development [zhongguo diqu jingji yanjiu]* (1994, pp. 74–99). Beijing: China Statistics Publishing House.

Knight, J., & Song, L. (1993). Why urban wages differ in China. In K. Griffin & Zhao Renwei (Eds.), *The distribution of income in China*. London: Macmillan.

Kotlikoff, L., & Gokhale, J. (1992). Estimating a firm's age-productivity profile using the present value of a worker's earnings. *Quarterly Journal of Economics*, 107, 1215–1242.

Lai, D. (1999). *Education, labor and income distribution* [jiaoyu, laodongli yu shouru fenpei]. In Zhao et al. (eds, 1999), pp. 451–474.

Li, S., & Li, W. (1994). *Estimating the ratios of return to investment in education in China* [zhongguo jiaoyu touzi de geren shouyilv de guji]. In Zhao et al. (eds, 1999), pp. 442–456.

Liu, Z. (1998). Earnings, education, and economic reform in urban China. *Economic Development and Cultural Change*, 46(4), 697–725.

Maddison, A. (1996). *A retrospect for the 200 years of the world economy, 1820–1992*. Paris: OECD Development Center.

Mao, Z. (1949). The bankrupt of the idealist conception of history. In *Selected works of Mao Tse-tung* (Vol. 4). Beijing: Foreign Languages Press. 1975, (pp. 451–459).

NBS (2011). *Major figures on residents from Hong Kong, Macao and Taiwan and foreigners covered by 2010 population census*. Beijing: National Bureau of Statistics (NBS). April 29, available at <http://www.stats.gov.cn/english/newsandcomingevents/t20110429_402722638.htm>. Accessed on June 24, 2011.

NBS. (various years). *China statistical yearbook*. Beijing: China Statistics Publishing House.

North, D. C. (1981). *Structure and change in economic history*. New York: Norton.

North, D. C., & Thomas, R. P. (1973). *The rise of the western world*. Cambridge: Cambridge University Press.

Shen, H. (2011). *Inflow of international immigrants challenges China's migration policy*. The Brookings Institution. September 8. Available at: <http://www.brookings.edu/opinions/2011/0908_china_immigrants_shen.aspx>. Accessed on October 28, 2011.

Sigurdson, J., et al. (2005). *Technological superpower China*. Cheltenham, UK: Edward Elgar.

SSB. (various years). *China statistical yearbook*. various issues, Beijing: China Statistics Publishing House.

UNDP (2005). *Human development report 2005: international cooperation at a crossroad*. New York: Oxford University Press.

UNESCO. (various years). *Statistical yearbook*. Paris: UNESCO.

UNPD (2007). *World population prospects: the 2006 revised population data sheet*. New York: United Nations Population Division (UNPD).

Wakabayashi, K. (1989). *China's population problem*. Tokyo: University of Tokyo Press. (in Japanese).

Wang, Z., & Dai, Y. (1958). A critique on the 'New Population theory' ['xin renkou lun' pipan]. *The Economic Research (jingji yanjiu)*, 2, 10–14.

Zhang, L. (1982). A review of the discussions on two production theories [liangzhong shengchan lilun de taolun zhongshu]. *Population Studies [renkou yanjiu]*, 5, 12–14.

Zhao, R. (1990). Two contrasting phenomena in China's income distribution. *Cambridge Journal of Economics*, 14, 345–349.

Zhao, R. (1999). Review of economic reform in China: features, experiences and challenges. In R. Garnaut & L. Song (Eds.), *China: twenty years of reform* (pp. 185–200). Canberra: Asia Pacific Press.

Zhao, R. (2001). Increasing income inequality and its causes in China. In C. Riskin, R. Zhao, & Li Shi (Eds.), *China's retreat from equality: income distribution and economic transition* (pp. 25–43). New York: M.E. Sharpe.

Chapter 4

Natural and Environmental Resources

The Dujiangyan Irrigation System. *Source: http://en.wikipedia.org*

Located in the Min River in Sichuan province, Dujiangyan is an irrigation infrastructure built by the State of Qin in 256 BC during the Warring States Period. Unlike contemporary dams where water is blocked with a huge wall, Dujiangyan is composed of a small artificial levee to redirect a portion of the river's flow and then to cut a channel through Mt. Yulei to discharge the excess water upon the dry Chengdu Plain beyond. The irrigation infrastructure is still in use today to irrigate over 5,300 square kilometers of land in the region. In 2000, Dujiangyan became a UNESCO World Heritage Site.

Xishi, known for her peerless beauty, was beset by some sort of heart trouble, and so she was often seen knitting her brows and walking with a hand on her chest. Now there was an ugly woman, named Dongshi, in the neighborhood who one day saw Xishi in the village street. In admiration she returned home determined to imitate Xishi's way of walking and mannerisms. But this only increased her ugliness. So much so that every time she walked abroad the rich would shut their doors tight and disdain to come out, while the poor with their wives and children would avoid her and quickly turn their steps away. Alas, that woman mistook frowning for something invariably beautiful, and was unaware that it only adds beauty to a real beauty.

– Zhuangzi (c. 368–286 BC)

Understanding the Chinese Economies. DOI: http://dx.doi.org/10.1016/B978-0-12-397826-4.00004-4
© 2013 Elsevier Inc. All rights reserved.

4.1 NATURAL RESOURCES

4.1.1 Land and Agriculture

China's vast size, which is comparable to that of the USA or Canada, means that it possesses an abundance of natural resources. For example, China's cropland accounts for near seven percent of the world total, making it the fourth largest (after Russia, the USA, and India); China has nine percent of the world's total permanent pasture (exceeded only by Australia and Russia), and more than three percent of the world's forestland and woodland (after Russia, Brazil, Canada, and the USA). However, if population size is taken into account, China's natural resources are not richer than in the world as a whole. For instance, China's per capita cultivated land area is less than one-third the world's; its per capita forestland and woodland is approximately one-seventh the world's.[1]

Does this entire situation suggest that China's development pattern should be different from the one that has been adopted by many Western nations during the past century?

China has provided sustenance and other basic necessities for one-fifth of the world's population, although it has a smaller share of the world's cultivated land. China is now an important consumer of agricultural commodities, leading the world in the consumption of wheat, rice, cotton, palm oil and rubber. The United States or India is ranked first or second in terms of the consumption of maize, soybeans, soy oil, sugar and tea; but China is usually in second or third place. It is noteworthy that this kind of development pattern has created many serious environmental problems that are the result of inappropriate policies and approaches in agricultural production. During the 1960s and 1970s, the Chinese government saw 'taking grain production as the key link' (*yi liang wei gang*) in order to maximize self-sufficiency in the supply of foodstuffs. This policy has been generally known to ignore the comparative advantages between the regions differing in natural conditions, and accelerated the conversion of forestland, wetland, and marginal land into cropland.

The landmass of China is characterized by dramatic geographical, geological and hydrogeological diversities. Its land surface ascends from north to south in four distinct zones: arid zone, semi-arid zone, semi-humid zone, and humid zone. The climate ranges from the tropical zone in the south to the frigid zone in the north and from the arid and semi-arid zones in the northwest to the humid and semi-humid zones in the southeast. As a result, the regional distribution of natural resources is extremely unequal in China. The precipitation is more than 1,000 mm/yr in the Southern part and more than 1,600 mm/yr in the southern coastal area, while it only ranges between 100 and 800 mm/yr in the Northern part (see Figure 4.1).[2] In addition, monthly precipitation has been rather uneven in both southern (such as Guangzhou and Shanghai) and northern (such as Beijing, Lanzhou, Shenyang, and Yinchuan) cities. Throughout China, rainfall usually occurs heavily in summer but not in winter. This is particularly so for cities in the northwest (such as Lanzhou and Yinchuan), where there is almost no rainfall during the seasons from October to May.

In general, the agricultural and biological resources diminish from the south to the north and from the east to the west. As a result of the suitable climate and adequate rainfall, the Southern part is the dominant rice producer; and wheat is the main foodstuff in the lower Yellow River valley (such as Henan, Shandong, Hebei, northern Jiangsu, and Anhui provinces) and the area south of the Great Wall. A selection of the top five agriculturally-based provinces is shown below:

- Hunan, Sichuan, Jiangsu, Hubei, and Guangdong for rice
- Henan, Shandong, Jiangsu, Hebei, and Sichuan for wheat
- Shandong, Jilin, Hebei, Sichuan, and Henan for maize
- Heilongjiang, Henan, Jilin, Shandong, and Anhui for soybean
- Shandong, Hebei, Henan, Hubei, and Jiangsu for cotton
- Shandong, Sichuan, Anhui, Jiangsu, and Henan for rapeseeds
- Henan, Yunnan, Shandong, Guizhou, and Hunan for tobacco
- Zhejiang, Hunan, Sichuan, Anhui, and Fujian for tea
- Shandong, Hebei, Guangdong, Sichuan, and Liaoning for fruits

4.1.2 Mineral Resources

China is a country rich with mineral resources. It has proven reserves, more or less, of all kinds of metallic mineral resources that have so far been discovered worldwide. Of these, the proven reserves of tungsten, tin, antimony, rare earth, tantalum and titanium rank first in the world; those of vanadium, molybdenum, niobium, beryllium and lithium rank second; those of zinc rank fourth; and those of iron, lead, gold and silver rank fifth. Metallic mineral resources feature wide distribution with relatively concentrated deposits in several regions. For instance, iron deposits are mainly found in three areas – Anshan-Benxi

---

1. Calculated by author based on WRI (1992, pp. 322–3 and 262–3).

2. In particular, the Talimu, Tulufan, and Chaidamu basins in the Northwest region have less than 25 mm of precipitation per annum (NBS, 2011, p. 4).

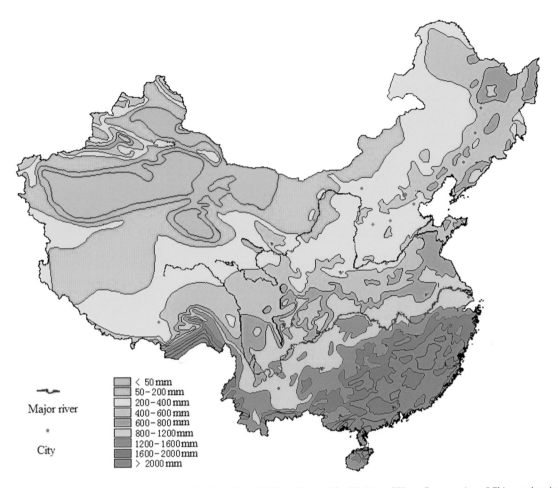

FIGURE 4.1 Regional differences in annual precipitation in mainland China. *Source: The Ministry of Water Conservation of China and author.*

Major river

City

□ < 50 mm
□ 50–200 mm
□ 200–400 mm
□ 400–600 mm
□ 600–800 mm
□ 800–1200 mm
□ 1200–1600 mm
□ 1600–2000 mm
□ > 2000 mm

(in Liaoning province), north Hebei province and Shanxi province. Bauxite reserves are mainly distributed in Shanxi, Henan and Guizhou provinces and Guangxi Zhuang autonomous region. Tungsten deposits are chiefly distributed in provinces of Jiangxi, Hunan and Guangdong, and tin deposits in Yunnan, Guangdong and Hunan provinces and Guangxi autonomous region.

China is one of the few countries in the world that have a relatively complete range of nonmetallic mineral resources. Most of the nonmetallic mineral resources in China have large proven reserves.[3] Of these, the proven reserves of magnesite, graphite, fluorite, talc, asbestos, gypsum, barite, wollastonite, alunite, bentonite and rock salt (halite) are among the largest in the world, while those of phosphorus, kaolin, pyrite, mirabilite, tripolite, zeolite,

pearlite and cement limestone hold major positions. Some natural stone materials such as marble and granite in China are of high quality, with rich reserves. However, if population size is taken into account, China's natural resources are not richer than in the world as a whole. For instance, with the exceptions of tin and tungsten, China's per capita metal reserves are fewer than the world's, as shown in Table 4.1.

Some of China's metallic minerals such as tungsten, tin, molybdenum, antimony and rare earth have large reserves, and are of high quality and competitive in world markets. However, many important metallic minerals such as iron, manganese, aluminum and copper are of poor quality, with ores lean and difficult to smelt. Most of the metallic mineral deposits are small or medium-sized, whereas large and super-large deposits account for a small proportion of the total. For example, most of the iron ore reserves are found to be ferriferously poor, and the iron-rich ore that can be directly processed by refineries accounts for a little proportion of the proven reserves; China's copper ore reserves can only be refined at a much

---

3. According to a report published by the World Resources Institute, China has 8.39 percent of the world's reserves of 15 major metals (copper, lead, tin, zinc, iron ore, manganese, nickel, chromium, cobalt, molybdenum, tungsten, vanadium, bauxite, titanium and lithium), after Russia, South Africa and the USA (WRI, 1992, pp. 262–3).

TABLE 4.1 Major Metal Reserves of China and the World

Item	Million Tons of Contents			Per Capita Kg		
	China (1)	World (2)	(1)/(2) (%)	China (3)	World (4)	(3)/(4) (%)
Bauxite	150	21,559	0.70	128.2	3,934.1	3.26
Copper	3.00	321.00	0.93	2.56	58.58	4.37
Iron ore	3,500	64,648	5.41	2,992	11,797	25.36
Lead	6.00	70.44	8.52	5.13	12.85	39.92
Manganese	13.6	812.8	1.67	11.62	148.32	7.83
Molybdenum	0.55	6.10	9.02	0.47	1.11	42.34
Nickel	0.73	48.66	1.50	0.62	8.88	6.98
Tin	1.50	5.93	25.30	1.28	1.08	118.52
Titanium	30.0	288.6	10.40	25.64	52.66	48.68
Tungsten	1.05	2.35	44.68	0.90	0.43	209.30
Vanadium	0.61	4.27	14.29	0.52	0.78	66.67
Zinc	5.00	143.90	3.47	4.27	36.26	16.26

Source: WRI (1992, pp. 322–3).

lower rate of copper products than in many other countries. The phosphoric ore also has very little composition of phosphorus pentoxide (P_2O_5).

With the exception of hydropower resources, which are concentrated in the Southwest and Central South regions, energy resources are richer in the north than in the south; while metals are distributed principally in the geologically-transitional area (such as Sichuan, Gansu, Hunan, and so on) between the plateau in the west and the mountain and hilly areas in the east (see Figure 4.2).

The major resource-rich provinces (in order of reserves) are provided as follows:[4]

- Argentum (Ag): Jiangxi, Guangdong, Guangxi, Yunnan, Hunnan
- Bauxite: Shanxi, Henan, Shandong, Guangxi, Guizhou
- Bismuth (Bi): Hunan, Guangdong, Jiangxi, Yunnan, Inner Mongolia
- Chromium (Cr): Tibet, Inner Mongolia, Gansu
- Coal: Shanxi, Inner Mongolia, Shaanxi, Guizhou, Ningxia
- Cobalt. (Co): Gansu, Yunnan, Shandong, Hebei, Shanxi
- Copper (Cu): Jiangxi, Tibet, Yunnan, Gansu, Anhui
- Gold (Au): Shandong, Jiangxi, Heilongjiang, Jilin, Hubei

- Hydragyrum (Hg): Guizhou, Shaanxi, Hunan, Sichuan, Yunnan
- Iron (Fe) ore: Liaoning, Sichuan, Hebei, Shanxi, Anhui
- Kaolin (Ka): Hunan, Jiangsu, Fujian, Guangdong, Liaoning
- Lead (Pb): Yunnan, Guangdong, Hunan, Inner Mongolia, Jiangxi
- Manganese (Mn): Guangxi, Hunan, Guizhou, Liaoning, Sichuan
- Molybdenum (Mo): Henan, Jilin, Shaanxi, Shandong, Jiangxi
- Natural gas: Sichuan, Liaoning, Henan, Xinjiang, Hebei, Tianjin
- Nickel (Ni): Gansu, Yunnan, Jilin, Sichuan, Hubei
- Petroleum: Heilongjiang, Shandong, Liaoning, Hebei, Xinjiang
- Platinum (Pt): Gansu, Yunnan, Sichuan
- Silica stone (SiO_2): Qinghai, Beijing, Liaoning, Gansu, Sichuan
- Stibium (Sb): Hunan, Guangxi, Guizhou, Yunnan
- Tantalum (Ta): Jiangxi, Inner Mongolia, Guangdong, Hunan, Sichuan
- Tin (Sn): Guangxi, Yunnan, Hunan, Guangdong, Jiangxi
- Titanium (Ti): Sichuan, Hebei, Shaanxi, Shanxi
- Tungsten (WO_3): Hunan, Jiangxi, Henan, Fujian, Guangxi
- Vanadium (V): Sichuan, Hunan, Gansu, Hubei, Anhui
- Zinc (Zn): Yunnan, Inner Mongolia, Guangdong, Hunan, Gansu

---

4. Judged by the author based on CISNR (1990, p. 644). Note that Hainan province is included in Guangdong province and Chongqing municipality is included in Sichuan province.

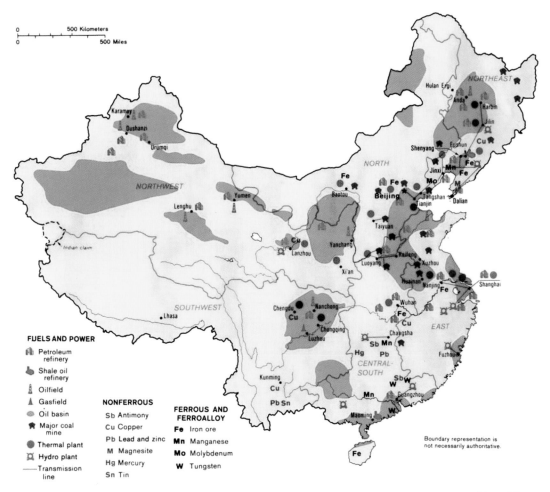

FIGURE 4.2 The distribution of minerals and energy resources in mainland China. *Source: Courtesy of the University of Texas Libraries, University of Texas at Austin.*

China's three resource-rich provinces are Sichuan, Shanxi, and Inner Mongolia. Between them, they have almost a half of the nation's minerals. However, the 12 provinces (Guangdong, Hainan, Jilin, Guangxi, Jiangsu, Hubei, Beijing, Tianjin, Fujian, Zhejiang, Tibet, and Shanghai) as a whole only account for 5 percent of the total reserves (see Figure 4.3).

4.1.3 Water Availability

China now faces almost all of the problems related to water resources that are faced by countries across the globe. China's rapid economic growth, industrialization and urbanization have outpaced infrastructural investment and management capacity, and have created widespread problems of water scarcity. In the areas of the North China Plain, where about half of China's wheat and corn is grown and there are extensive peach orchards, drought is an ever-looming threat. With one-fifth of the world's population, China has only eight percent of the world's fresh water. China's annual renewable water reserves were about 2.8

trillion cubic meters, which ranked it fifth in the world, behind Brazil, Russia, Canada and Indonesia, but ahead of the USA. However, in terms of per capita availability of water reserves, China is one of the lowest in the world – barely one-quarter of the world average (WRI, 2003). In the coming decades, China will be under severe water stress as defined by the international standard.

Large-scale underground water extraction began in the 1950s and has increased significantly over the course of the past 20 years. Accordingly, underground water use as a percentage of the total water supply has also increased. The over-exploitation of groundwater has led to a marked and continuous drawdown of underground water levels in China. From time to time deeper wells have to be installed. Recent surveys indicate that the cones of depression in the deep aquifers have joined together to form a huge interprovincial cone of depression in the North China Plain. There is growing competition for water between communities, sectors of the economy, and individual provinces. There are already a dozen seawater desalination plants in China. China has also invested in a seawater desalination project to carry

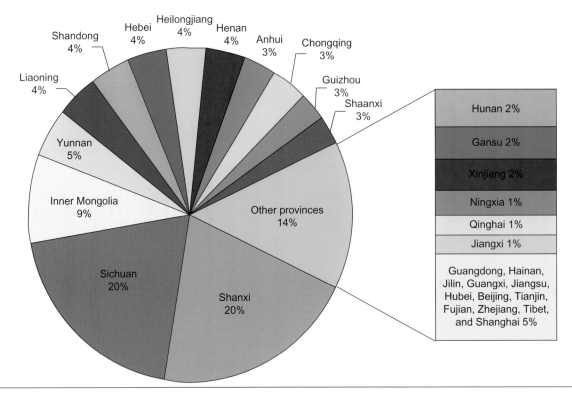

Notes: (1) Each of Guangdong, Hainan, Jilin, Guangxi, Jiangsu, Hubei, Beijing, Tianjin, Fujian, Zhejiang, Tibet, and Shanghai is less than 1%.
(2) Sichuan and Chongqing are estimated by the author based proportionally on their total reserves and land areas.

FIGURE 4.3   Spatial distribution of major mineral resources in China. *Source: Sun (1987, pp. 4–8) and author.*

desalinated seawater to the Beijing municipality. However, the problem with respect to the wide utilization of the desalinated seawater in the vast rural area is the cost. Many farmers in China are still neither able nor willing to offer such a high price, since, in traditional culture, the waters in rivers and lakes have been free of any such charge.

In addition to water scarcity for China as a whole, there is considerable unevenness in terms of the amount of water resources available in different regions of the country. In general, the Southern part is water-rich; whereas the Northern part is poor in surface water, but modestly rich in groundwater in a few provinces, including Qinghai, Xinjiang, Inner Mongolia and Heilongjiang.[5] As a result of the uneven distribution, the per capita water rate in northern China (especially the areas in the Liaohe River valley in the northeast of China and in the Haihe River valley around Tianjin municipality) is much lower than that of the national average. Water shortage has become a major economic bottleneck to these areas.

Given the existence of surface water surplus in southern China and freshwater shortage in northern China, is it feasible to transfer water from the water-rich south to the north? A water transfer project had been discussed for more than two decades before it was started on December 27, 2002. The South-North Water Transfer Project involves the construction of three canals across the eastern, middle and western parts of China, linking the country's four major rivers – the Yangtze, Yellow, Huai, and Hai Rivers. The gigantic project is expected to take 50 years to complete. If all goes well, the project will carry annually more than 40 billion tons of water from the Yangtze River basin to northern China. However, this project alone cannot completely solve the water shortage problems in China.[6]

4.2   ENERGY PRODUCTION

Energy resources are also unevenly distributed in China. Specifically, most of the hydropower reserves are concentrated in the Southwest and Central South regions; most coal reserves are distributed in the North region, with only a small proportion, sparsely distributed, in the Northeast,

---

5. The areas south of the Yangtze River, which account for only 37 percent of the country's total territory, have 81 percent of its total water resources. By contrast, the areas north of the Yangtze, which make up 63 percent of China's territory, possess only 19 percent of the country's total water resources (Chen and Cai, 2000).

6. See Case study 4 for a detailed analysis of this project.

TABLE 4.2 Composition of Energy Resources, by Region and by Type of Energy (%)

Region	Coal	Hydropower[a]	Petroleum[b]	All Energy[c]
North	64.0 (98.2)	1.8 (1.3)	14.4 (0.5)	43.9 (100.0)
Northeast	3.1 (54.6)	1.8 (14.2)	48.3 (31.2)	3.8 (100.0)
East	6.5 (72.9)	4.4 (22.5)	18.2 (4.6)	6.0 (100.0)
Central South	3.7 (44.5)	9.5 (51.8)	2.5 (3.7)	5.6 (100.0)
Southwest	10.7 (25.2)	70.0 (74.7)	2.5 (0.1)	28.6 (100.0)
Northwest	12.0 (66.7)	12.5 (31.3)	14.0 (2.0)	12.1 (100.0)
China	100.0 (85.9)	100.0 (13.1)	100.0 (1.0)	100.0 (100.0)

Notes: *(1) The geographical scopes of the great regions are defined in Figure 2.1. (2) Figures in parentheses are energy structures.*
[a]*The theoretical reserves multiplied by 100 years.*
[b]*Includes natural gas and shale oil.*
[c]*Standard coal equivalent conversion rates are 0.714 t/t for coal, 1.43 t/t for petroleum, 1.33 t/1,000 m^3 for natural gas, 0.143 t/t for oil shale, and 350 g/kWh for hydropower.*
Source: MOE (1991, p.101).

Northwest, East, and Central South regions; the Northeast and Northwest regions account for more than half of the nation's petroleum and natural gas reserves. In addition, the Northwest is the only region which is modestly rich in coal, hydropower, petroleum and natural gas.

Energy resources are also unevenly distributed in China. For example, as shown in Table 4.2, about 70 percent of the hydropower reserves are concentrated in the Southwest region, while the North, Northeast and East regions as a whole share only less than 10 percent; more than 60 percent of coal reserves are distributed in the North region, with only a small proportion, sparsely distributed, in the Northeast, East and Central South regions; the Northeast region accounts for nearly one half of the nation's petroleum and natural gas reserves, while the Central South and Southwest regions as a whole only share a mere 5 percent. Nevertheless, the Northwest is the only region which is modestly rich in coal, hydropower, petroleum and natural gas. In addition, the energy structure is disproportional among regions. For example, coal nearly monopolizes the North region, while the Southwest and Central South regions are mostly dominated by hydropower. Nevertheless, the East, Northwest and Northeast regions are principally served by coal rather than by petroleum and hydropower.

4.2.1 Coal

Coal resources are concentrated in northern China, around 600–1,000 km away from the most industrialized provinces and municipalities in the Southeast. Coal is transported mainly by train and it accounts for more than 40 percent of the country's rail freight. On the other hand, the building of thermal power stations near the coal mines (*kengkou dianzhan*) seems to be an efficient practice, but faces substantial obstacles because of the shortage of water needed for turbine cooling. With an annual production of nearly 2.5 billion tons in 2008, coal accounts for more than 70 percent of China's primary energy production (shown in Figure 4.4). This figure already makes China the world's leading coal producer. Furthermore, the Chinese coal industry is planning to increase its levels of annual coal production and it is unclear whether or not the Chinese government will be willing to introduce significant decreases in the current proportion of coal in total energy consumption in the foreseeable future. Environmental problems associated with the entire process of coal extraction, transportation, processing, and consumption will, therefore, continue to have a serious effect on the sustainable development in China if no sustainability measures are adopted.

China's dependence on coal continues amid the frequent occurrence of coal mine accidents, which cause thousands of casualties each year. Furthermore, China is much more inefficient in its coal exploitation than developed nations. At present, China uses about 3.3 tons of coal reserves in order to produce one ton of raw coal. In the USA, for example, the production of one ton of raw coal uses only 1.25 tons of reserves.[7] The Chinese government

---

7. According to a report released by the Chinese Academy of Social Sciences, the mining recovery ratio has been less than 44 percent in China's large state-owned coal mines and only 10 percent in the small and private coal mines; by contrast, those in developed nations including Australia, Canada, Germany and the United States reportedly achieve figures as high as 80 percent (Cui, 2007).

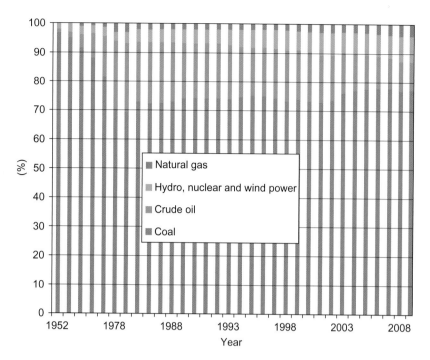

FIGURE 4.4 China's energy production structure, 1952–2009. *Source: NBS, various years.*

had planned to raise the average recovery ratio of coal exploitation from the current figure of 30 percent to at least 50 percent by 2010 (Si, 2008). However, this has met various obstacles from local governments which have close ties with those low efficient small coalmines. As part of its efforts to achieve these goals, China has decided to consolidate the coal industry by building several large mining conglomerates (each with a production capacity of 100 million tons of raw coal per year), as well as to shut down those small and inefficient coal pits. However, this seems to be a difficult job to be realized within a short period of time, since many stakeholders, especially local governments, would be unwilling to support this kind of reform.

4.2.2 Petroleum and Natural Gas

Currently, petroleum and natural gas are supplied mainly by the Northeast and the Northwest regions. Oil and gas reserves are rich in China's continental shelves. However, China has maritime disputes with Japan in the East China Sea, with North Korea and, possibly, South Korea in the Yellow Sea, and with other Southeast nations in the South China Sea. In addition, the locational disadvantages of offshore oil and gas fields at these sea areas will pose difficulties for China's seabed oil and gas exploitation and transportation. Theoretically, the structure of energy consumption may be largely readjusted through foreign trade. As a result of its rapidly growing consumption – and relatively stagnant production – of petroleum, in 1993 China became a net importer of oil (see Figure 4.5).

China's consumption of petroleum has increased by more than five times from 3.81 quadrillion BTU in 1980, while its production of crude oil has increased only at a relatively slow speed from 4.55 quadrillion BTU in 1980, creating an ever-growing oil shortage. In addition, China's oil deficit, which already stands at several million barrels per day, is expected to quadruple to 13.1 million barrels per day over the period to 2030, when the country's oil consumption is projected to reach 15.7 million barrels per day (EIA, 2006). That is to say, more than 80 percent of China's oil demand should be met by either imports or technological substitution. (See subsection 13.3.3 of Chapter 13 for a detailed analysis of China's overseas investment in the oil sector.)

4.2.3 Clean/Green Energy

The government hopes to reduce the share of thermal-power in its power generation mix through the construction of large hydroelectric dams. The main hydroelectric dams are Gezhouba Dam in Hubei province, followed by Liujiaxia Dam in Gansu province, Longyang Dam in Qinghai province, Manwan Dam in Yunnan province, and Baishan Dam in Jilin province. China has now also completed the world's largest dam in the Three Gorges on the Yangtze River. This dam increases the supply of affordable electricity throughout the Yangtze valley, as well as controlling floods, boosting the growing economy and reducing the levels of air pollution. The economic advantages coming from such a big dam, however, could also be reduced by the losses arising from the ecological and environmental costs and risks.

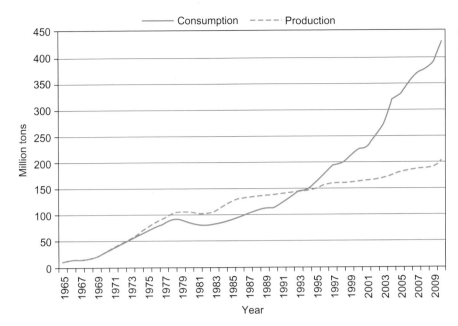

FIGURE 4.5 China's oil production and consumption (million tons), 1965–2010. *Source: BP Statistical Review of World Energy, 2011.*

The Chinese leadership realizes that the development of nuclear power is an appropriate solution to improve local energy shortages in those eastern and southern coastal areas that lack coal and petroleum resources. However, after the 2011 Japan earthquake, it is unlikely that China will see any sharp increase in investing in nuclear power. Currently, the nuclear power stations are at Qinshan in Zhejiang province, Daya Bay in Guangdong province, and Hongyanhe in Liaoning province.

With its large land mass and long coastline, China has relatively abundant wind resources. The windiest areas of the country are located mainly along the southeast coast and the nearby islands and in Inner Mongolia, Xinjiang, western Gansu, and in some parts of Northeast China, Northwest China, North China, and the Qinghai-Tibetan Plateau. Apart from this, there are also certain areas in China's interior that are rich in wind resources. China has large marine areas, and ocean-based wind resources are plentiful.

China has emerged as the dominant player in solar power. The Chinese solar power sector has been growing at an unprecedented rate during recent years. In 2006, there were two companies from China in the list of top ten cell producers. In 2010, there were six. China's Big Three solar power companies are Suntech Power, Yingli Green Energy, and Trina Solar – and all grew very rapidly during recent years. China has had a very clear strategy toward solar energy development. In the year 2000, China accounted for at least a half the world's solar power production, and its market share is rising rapidly. Within four years, the world's solar manufacturing sector shifted from being led by a geographically dispersed number of companies to being dominated by Chinese companies. In 2010 alone, its state-owned banks handed out US$30 billion in low-cost loans to the top five manufacturers (Lacey, 2011). This has helped China's solar producers to become world leading exporters of solar.

4.3 ENVIRONMENTAL QUALITY

China's environmental concerns stem from two kinds of human activities:

(i) Resource depletion, which covers the activities of the losses reflecting the deterioration of land and depleting reserves of coal, petroleum, timber, and groundwater

(ii) Resource degradation, which covers the consequences associated with air and water pollution, land erosion, and solid wastes.

Resource depletion is a concern because it would mean the quantitative exhaustion of natural resources that are an important source of revenues, obtained through exploitation and the discovery of new reserves. In the case of resource degradation, the issue is not the quantitative exhaustion of natural resources, but rather the qualitative degradation of the ecosystem, for example, through amongst other things the contamination of air and water, as a result of the generation and deposit of residuals, and as a result of the environmental impact of producing garbage and solid wastes.

In order to make an assessment of China's environmental situation, let's consider air, water, land, and deforestation and desertification.

TABLE 4.3 Greenhouse Gas (GHG) Emissions, China and USA

Item	China		USA	
	1990	2006	1990	2006
GDP (billion US$)[a]	372.4	2,626.3	5,672.6	13,194.7
GHGs (million ton)	2,524	6,200	5,163	5,800
GHGs/POP (ton/person)	2.18	4.72	21.0	19.4
GHGs/LA (ton/km²)	262.9	645.8	551.6	619.7
GHGs/GDP (kg/US$)	6.78	2.36	0.91	0.44

Notes: *GDP = gross national product, POP = population, LA = land area.*
[a]*Measured in exchange rates (for China) and in current prices (for China and USA).*
Sources: WRI (1992), NEAA (2007) and author.

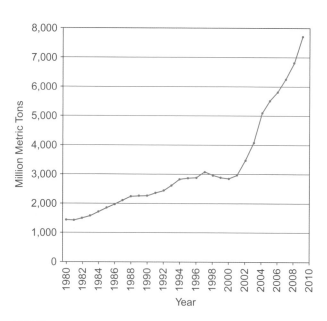

FIGURE 4.6 China's carbon dioxide emissions from consumption. *Source: EIA (2011).*

4.3.1 Air

Recent decades have seen a worsening of China's air quality, particularly in urban areas. According to European satellite data, pollutants in the sky over China have increased by about 50 percent between 1995 and 2005. The satellite data also revealed that the city of Beijing – China's capital – is one of the worst environmental victims of China's spectacular economic growth, which has led to air pollution levels that have been blamed for more than 400,000 premature deaths a year. According to the European Space Agency, Beijing and its neighboring northeast provinces have the planet's worst levels of nitrogen dioxide, which can cause fatal damage to the lungs (Watts, 2005). An explosive increase in car ownership is blamed for a sharp rise in unhealthy emissions.

In 2006 China became the largest national producer of greenhouse gas (GHG) emissions, with an estimated annual production of about 6,200 million tons, followed by the USA, with about 5,800 million tons (see Table 4.3). When discussing the situation of China's GHG emissions, one comes across two different opinions: first, it is posited that the country's per capita emissions are very low in comparison with the industrially developed countries and that the onus of global warming must rest elsewhere; secondly, compared with other countries, China's GHG emissions have grown rapidly (see Figure 4.6) and the emissions per unit of GDP are already very high – approximately 5.36 times that of the USA in 2006, although this figure is lower than that for 1990. According to its long-term commitment, which was announced at the United Nations Climate Change Conference, held in Copenhagen from 7–18 December 2009, China has also agreed to cut the intensity of carbon dioxide emissions per unit of GDP by 40–45 percent from 2005 levels by 2020.

In China, atmospheric pollution comes mainly from the burning of coal and its associated products which, under the most optimistic scenario, will be unlikely to contribute less than the current three-quarters of total primary energy consumption by the year 2025 or even by the year 2050. China's chlorofluorocarbon (CFC) and halon compound use is relatively low given the size of the country. However, the potential for much greater use of CFCs is enormous. Moreover, it is projected that CFC emissions are likely to increase as a result of both China's economic growth and its increase in population size. The specific sources of these emissions are, in order of quantity produced, livestock, wet rice, natural gas pipeline leakage, solid waste disposal, and coal mining. In addition, China's large and still expanding population also suggests a concomitant increase of methane (CH_4).

Most of China's proven coal reserves are bituminous, with only a small proportion being lignite and anthracite. Therefore, coal is mainly responsible not only for the high carbon dioxide (CO_2) emissions, but also for the high emissions of sulfur (SO_2), nitrogen oxide (NO_x), and total suspended particulate (TSP). In addition, as the northern (especially urban) areas usually use coal for heating in the winter, it is unsurprising that the level of air pollution in these areas is much more serious than that in the Southern part. All of these pollutants have posed serious threats to public health. There has been a rise in the share of chronic obstructive pulmonary disease and cancers. In addition, acid rain is becoming an increasingly critical issue. The high sulfur content of burning coal contributes widely to the high acidity levels of rainfall. Nationwide acid rain measurement shows that the situation is particularly serious in southern China, where the pH values are often lower than 5.6 – a value indicative of acid rain.

Another noticeable factor is that the wind coming from the Northwest region increases the neutralizing capability of atmosphere and transfers air pollutants to Southeast China and the neighboring countries.

4.3.2   Water

The constant and excessive extraction of groundwater has led to the continuous dropping of the watertable and the subsidence of land. The area of subsidence around large municipalities such as Beijing, Tianjin and Shanghai has been reported to be the most serious. In the coastal areas of Hebei and Shandong provinces, the excessive drop in the groundwater level has led to the leeching of saline water into the freshwater aquifers. In the Loess Plateau area of Northwest China, the drawing of underground water for irrigation is becoming extremely difficult, with increasing energy costs. Another key issue is the pollution of drinking water in both urban and rural areas. Many groundwater sources have been affected as a result of infiltration of polluted surface water in urban areas. Rural water resources are even more contaminated due to fertilizers and pesticide runoff, human and animal waste, and pollutants from the township and village-owned enterprises. As a result, many people residing in the rural areas do not have access to safe drinking water.

River water pollution in those sections of rivers that run through or near cities is the most serious in terms of ammonia nitrogen, fecal bacteria, volatile phenols, and biological oxygen demands (BOD).[8] The Huaihe River, which many people now refer to as the *black river*, has been the most polluted river in China. The Yangtze River, which closely connects China's large industrial bases such as Chongqing, Wuhan, Nanjing and Shanghai, will become, as believed by many observers, more seriously polluted, if no countermeasure is carried out. In addition,

pollution from heavy metals, such as mercury (Hg), lead (Pb), and other toxic chemicals are also having a serious impact on river water.

Nitrogen and phosphorus pollution is common in China's lakes. Water pollution has not only endangered the local fishery and the collection of limnological plants, but has also affected the daily lives and health of the nearby residents. In addition, petropollutants, inorganic nitrogen and inorganic phosphorus are common in the coastal water sources. Marine environments near large coastal cities are degraded as a result of the discharge of raw sewage and coastal construction. As a result, incidences of red tides have become frequent in many coastal areas, contaminated fish and mollusks have been commonplace and consequently many fragile marine environments have been destroyed. Marine pollution in northeastern and southern China is of particular concern since the industrial development is outpacing the environmental protection efforts in these areas.

The excessive use of water without adequate drainage leads to waterlogging, salinization and soil erosion. Salinization and alkalization are increasingly affecting irrigated farmland. In the Northeast region, cropping activities have increased the soil alkalinity to such a high level that it is very difficult to put them back into pasture. In the sandy soils of the Northwest region, where the irrigation water seeps away quickly, strong winds and high evaporation contribute to easy alkalization of the soil. The rapid development of individually- and collectively-owned industrial enterprises are generally known to be responsible for the increasing levels of water pollution in rural areas. More than two-thirds of China's industrial wastewater has flown directly into rivers, lakes, seas and reservoirs. The chemical industry is the largest wastewater producer. Other main sectors discharging wastewater include ferrous metals, papermaking and paper products, the production and supply of power, steam, and hot water.

4.3.3   Land

Since the introduction of economic reforms in the late 1970s, the transference of farmland to residential and industrial uses has been promoted. Consequently, the area of land under cultivation has decreased substantially. This has meant that in order to increase the level of agricultural production, the only way was to increase the levels of land productivity, which resulted in the intensive use of chemical fertilizers, continuous cropping, greatly expanded irrigation and the use of improved plant varieties. In practice, it is almost impossible for farmers to make an accurate count of the proportion of nutrients that is required by the soil. In most cases, the marginal cost and benefit do not determine the use of fertilizers. The government's subsidies on fertilizer consumption could distort the pricing mechanism and induce farmers to the even more excessive and inefficient use of chemical fertilizers, which has,

---

8. As oxygen is required to aerobically decompose biologically degradable compounds, the higher the level of BOD, the poorer the water quality.

through the leaching of nitrates, caused the contamination of groundwater and the deterioration of soil structure.

Organic manure and the leavened crop residues, stalks, and straws have many advantages when used as fertilizers, even if their value of nutrient per unit volume is lower than that of chemical fertilizers. Many farmers, however, have ignored the advantages of these *clean* fertilizers. In addition, in rural China the shortage of fuelwood for both cooking and heating results in the burning of straws, stalks and crop residues. Continuous cropping, instead of crop rotation, may cause the soil to be deficient in some nutrients. For example, the cropping of soybeans causes a deficiency of phosphorus and potassium in the soil. The use of high-yielding and improved plant varieties has made crops more vulnerable to pest damage, which in turn results in the use of pesticides. Since the 1970s the use of pesticides has increased in both tonnage and concentration of active ingredients and, as a result, has had a serious effect on water, soil and food.

The more widespread use of plastic sheeting is a further threat. Farmers have been increasingly interested in the application of plastic sheets to conserve soil moisture and speed up the maturation of crops, particularly in northern China. But many farmers have ignored the fact that plastic sheets, if not treated properly after cropping, may be mixed with the soil and hence hinder the flow of water and root growth. Farmland is also suffering from the damages of industrial wastes and urban rubbish, occupied by piles of solid waste and seriously damaged as a result of the improper use of garbage and sludge. The sum of these circumstances has led to soil loss, especially in the area where ground cover was removed. The ecosystems of forests, wetlands, sloping and marginal lands are particularly fragile. Another form of soil contamination is the use of wastewater for irrigation, which ignores the fact that acids and toxic heavy metals in much of this water impair the soil chemistry and render it useless for agriculture.

Apart from the soil loss deriving from the erosion process, another consequence of soil over-exploitation and removal of ground cover is the increase of silt materials flowing into rivers. This leads to the rising of riverbeds undermining flood control, navigation and power generating capacity. The Loess Plateau area between Gansu, Shaanxi and Shanxi provinces has been cultivated since the Neolithic period and is now perhaps one of the most erodible areas in the world. Through this area, the Yellow River carries billions of tons of sediment annually into the Bohai sea by seriously degrading the land. The average riverbed has been rising by approximately one meter per decade with a consequent growing risk of catastrophic flooding. The Yangtze River's load raises lake levels, particularly in Hubei and Hunan provinces. As a result, over the course of recent decades most lakes in East Hubei have disappeared, owing to the combination of silting and conversion to farmland.

With the formation of cones of depression, many cities, especially those coastal cities which have thick unconsolidated soft soil layers, are suffering from land subsidence caused by the withdrawal of underground water in deep aquifers. The cities of Shanghai and Tianjin, with a maximum subsidence of about three meters, are the most severe cases. Ground subsidence has caused a series of problems, such as the sinking and splitting of railway bases, buildings, and underground pipelines, and an emerging flooding crisis in areas near major rivers or the sea. For example, embankments have had to be constructed to prevent flooding of seawater into some areas of Tianjin after significant ground subsidence.

4.3.4 Deforestation and Desertification

The causes of deforestation come mainly from the rapidly growing population in rural areas and the economic interests of the state. As the size of the population expands, the needs of food, housing, and energy will increase accordingly. The conversion of forestland, grassland and wetland to cropland therefore also increases, as does the illegal felling of trees for lumber and fuel. In the rural areas, the lack of fuels led to use of wood for both heating and cooking. But the traditional rural stoves have low combustion efficiency. In addition, much of the fuelwood consumed is low quality brush and weeds collected from already deforested hills.

From the 1950s to the 1970s, a period during which a series of political and social movements (such as the Great Leap Forward and the Cultural Revolution) were under way, many of China's natural and tropical forests were suffering serious damage. In Tibet and many other provinces and autonomous regions, the process of forest degradation began with the large-scale cutting of forests by the state or its contractors for commercial logging. This large-scale cutting combined with fuel necessities has denuded hillsides, resulting in soil erosion and water loss. Covering about one-third of its total land area, China's grassland is concentrated in the Inner Mongolia, Xinjiang and Tibet autonomous regions and a few other provinces and autonomous regions, located mostly in the North and Northwest regions. As grassland is regarded as 'wasteland' in some rural areas, the conversion of it into productive uses has been promoted as a result of the growth in population. The conversion of grassland into crop cultivation has led to a continuing decrease in the amount of grassland.

Heavy and frequent sand storms in northern China have resulted in damage to the sustainability of the Chinese economy. Dust storms are caused by turbulent wind systems which contain particles of dust that reduce visibility to less than 1,000 m. A dust storm may cause soil erosion, loess formation, climate change, air pollution, and a reduction in the level of solar irradiance. Although the number of annual dust days has decreased over past decades, the frequency of severe dust storms (where visibility <200 m) has increased during the same period in northern China, with four in the 1950s, seven in the 1960s, 13 in the 1970s, 14 in the 1980s, and 23 in the 1990s (Qian and Zhu, 2001; and Chen et al., 2003). An extremely dry environment can induce more severe dust storms such as the 'Black Storm' (in which visibility <10 m).

The variability of dust storms over time is associated with climate fluctuations in terms of both temperature and precipitation. The arid and semi-arid areas of northern China make up 30 percent of the country's total land area; and the dry mid-latitude climate is dominated by continental polar air masses much of the year. Most dust events occur during the spring season from March to May when cyclonic cold fronts meet warm air mass influxes, leading to strong seasonal atmospheric instability, a favorable synoptic condition for dust storms. However, human activities have also had a substantial impact on dust storms at both regional and local levels. In northern China, there was a rapid escalation of the level of decertified land, as a direct result of human activity. In recent decades the Chinese government has invested substantial social and economic resources to suppress dust storms. Despite some successful cases, the present-day desertification situation is not optimistic.

4.4 CHINESE ENVIRONMENTAL POLICY

Using a way to fish by drying up lakes – how cannot you catch the fisheries? Then there would be no fisheries next year. Using a way to hunt by firing woods – how cannot you catch the animals? Then there would be no animals next year.

— Lvshi Chunqiu (Yishang, 2)

4.4.1 About Sustainable Development

It was not until the late 1960s and the early 1970s that the 'environment' became a significant part of the political agenda in developed nations. This was largely a response not only to the spectacular growth of the Western economies, but also to the continued extensive industrialization of the rest of the world. The phrase 'sustainable development' was firstly popularized by the World Commission for Environment and Development (WCED, 1987). Since that time, much attention for defining 'sustainable development' has been given by the worldwide environmentalists and economists. For example, Pearce et al. (1988, p. 6) state 'We can summarize the necessary conditions for sustainable development as constancy of the natural capital stock; more strictly, the requirement for non-negative changes in the stock of natural resources, such as soil and soil quality, ground and surface water and their quality, land biomass, water biomass, and the waste assimilation capacity of the receiving environments.'

Another example cited by Solow (1991) from an UNESCO document is as '... every generation should leave

water, air and soil resources as pure and unpolluted as when it came on earth'.

The above two passages, however, involve a categorical mistake, that being to identify the determinants of well-being with the constituents of well-being (for example, welfare, freedom, and so on), as sustainable development is defined as an impossible goal by these authors.

To be sure, a number of authors writing on sustainable development have recognized that the starting point ought to be the realization of well-being over time. On the basis of this point, Dasgupta and Mäler (1995, p. 2394) give a more general interpretation of the idea of sustainable development that well-being (and, therefore, consumption) must never be allowed to decline over time. However, this definition also suggests that sustainable development is very difficult or, sometimes, impossible to achieve. In what follows in this chapter, we will define sustainable development less strictly (but more practically) as 'the maximization of total well-being over a long period of time'.

There are at least two key striking characteristics of China: its population is huge and its economy has been growing very fast for at least a quarter of a century. China has become the world's major player in both output and input markets. The data on the total consumption of various primary products presented in Table 4.4 reinforce the importance of China in world consumption markets. In the areas of both metals and coal, China is always ranked first, with shares of between 15 percent and one-third of world consumption, and the United States is ranked either second or third; in other energies, the United States is first and China is either second or third. China is also an important consumer of agricultural commodities, leading the world in the consumption of wheat, rice, cotton, palm oil, and rubber. India is ranked first in terms of the consumption of sugar and tea. Increasing commodity demand from the giants obviously supports prices, other things being equal, but prices also depend upon supply. Most analysts hold that, in recent years, Chinese demand has increased the prices of most metals because the growth in supply has not kept pace with growth in demand (Winters and Yusuf, 2007, pp. 16–17).[9]

During recent decades, China's rapid economic development has resulted in a substantial improvement in the standard of living of ordinary people. However, it has also generated environmental problems at an impressively high rate. Carbon dioxide (CO_2), sulfur (SO_2), nitrogen oxide (NO_x), methane (CH_4), chlorofluorocarbons (CFCs) and other hazardous waste and toxic materials have been

---

9. The exception that proves the rule is aluminum, for which China is a net exporter and produces about 25 percent of the world total. Compared with price increases of 379 percent for copper from January 2002 to June 2006, aluminum prices have increased modestly – up only 80 percent (Streifel, 2006).

TABLE 4.4 Shares in Consumption of Primary Commodities for China, India, and USA (%)

Commodity		China	India	USA
Metals 2005	Aluminum	22.5 (1)	3.0 (8)	19.4 (2)
	Copper	21.6 (1)	2.3 (11)	13.8 (2)
	Lead	25.7 (1)	1.3 (15)	19.4 (2)
	Nickel	15.2 (1)	0.9 (17)	9.5 (3)
	Tin	33.3 (1)	2.2 (7)	12.1 (2)
	Zinc	28.6 (1)	3.1 (8)	9.0 (2)
	Iron ore	29.0 (1)	4.8 (5)	4.7 (6)
	Steel production	31.5 (1)	3.5 (7)	8.5 (3)
Energy 2003	Coal	32.9 (1)	7.1 (3)	20.6 (2)
	Oil	7.4 (2)	3.4 (7)	25.3 (1)
	Total primary energy	12.6 (2)	3.6 (5)	23.4 (1)
	Electricity generation	11.4 (2)	3.8 (5)	24.3 (1)
Agriculture 2003	Wheat	15.2 (1)	13.5 (2)	5.4 (4)
	Rice	29.7 (1)	21.4 (2)	1.0 (12)
	Maize	17.0 (2)	2.2 (6)	32.5 (1)
	Soybeans	19.2 (2)	3.7 (5)	24.0 (1)
	Soy oil	24.4 (2)	6.4 (4)	25.7 (1)
	Palm oil	15.8 (1)	15.3 (2)	0.6 (37)
	Sugar	6.6 (3)	15.2 (1)	12.5 (2)
	Tea	14.4 (2)	17.5 (1)	3.8 (7)
	Coffee	0.4 (45)	0.8 (27)	16.8 (1)
	Cotton	31.2 (1)	12.8 (2)	6.9 (5)
	Rubber	23.5 (1)	8.4 (4)	12.9 (2)

Note: *Figures within parentheses are world rankings.*
Source: Streifel (2006).

increasingly produced in parallel with industrial growth in China. Air pollution stemming from the burning of coal – China's major source of energy – has reached the approximate level of the developed countries in the 1950s and 1960s. Today, air, water, noise pollution, and land erosion, together with unprocessed garbage, have had a considerable impact upon Chinese society.[10]

Three elements have made substantial contributions to the environmental damage that has been brought in China in recent decades: population growth, economic growth driven by highly polluting manufacturing industries and an energy industry that is dominated by coal. In 1949, the new government adopted the Soviet-style development model in which heavy industry was given priority while seeking the maximum level of self-sufficiency in the national economy. The Chinese leadership believed strongly that economic independence and national defense could only be guaranteed by the development of heavy industry. But the latter is also the main source of pollution within the country. Without good reason, the rapidly growing population, with its increasing demand for energy and food, will accelerate the deforestation and transference of forestland and wetland into cropland. But the fragile ecosystem can only accelerate the vicious circle of poverty (see Figure 4.7).

10. One striking example is that air pollution is estimated to have caused more than 400,000 excess deaths in 2003, and this figure will increase if no action is taken (Winters and Yusuf, 2007, p. 26).

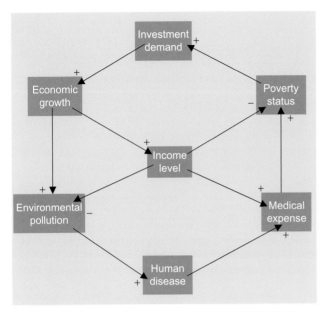

Notes: '+' denotes positive relations; '–' denotes negative relation;
'→' denotes causal direction.

FIGURE 4.7 Economic, environmental, and health relations.

If these problems are not addressed properly, all efforts to achieve the sustainable development of the Chinese economy would inevitably be jeopardized.

4.4.2 China's Commitment to the Environment

Since the late 1970s, several changes have taken place in the legislation of environmental protection in China, along with the economic reforms and opening up to the outside world. 1978 saw the first insertion of a clause for environmental protection in the Constitution of the People's Republic of China. China's first Law on Environmental Protection (*huanjing baohu fa*) was formally promulgated in 1989 and was further revised in 1995. Since the early 1980s, a series of laws, regulations, and national standards (*guobiao*, or GB) concerning environmental protection (including four environmental laws, eight natural resource protection laws, more than 20 administrative decrees, more than 30 ministerial regulations for pollution prevention and 300-plus environmental standards) have been promulgated in China.[11]

A relatively comprehensive legal system concerning environmental protection has initially taken shape, ending the past situation of there being no laws in this regard. Since

1980, China has joined or approved many international protocols on environmental protection, including the United Nations Convention on the Law of the Sea (UNCLOS), the Antarctic Treaty, the Convention on International Trade in Endangered Species, the Vienna Conference for the Protection of the Ozone Layer, the Basel Convention on Transboundary Hazardous Waste Disposal, the Montreal Protocol for Limiting use of CFCs, and the Kyoto Protocol.

However, a number of problems still remain. For example, in the field of the environment and resources, for a long period up to the late 1990s there was no appropriate legislation in relation to solid wastes and toxic chemicals, radioactive pollution prevention, and the sustainable management of natural resources. Chinese legislation also faces problems of attempting to achieve coordination and consistency with international treaties and conventions. Moreover, as the Chinese legislation relating to sustainable development was to a large extent promulgated on the basis of a centralized planning system, many problems arose from China's economic transition. For example, there have been no environmentally related laws and regulations that are directly applicable to diversified economic sectors, that is, for the environmental administration of township and village-based enterprises, foreign-funded enterprises and the tertiary sector.

In China, environmental concerns have stemmed from two kinds of human activities: resource depletion, which covers the activities of the losses reflecting the deterioration of land and depleting reserves of coal, petroleum, timber, and groundwater; resource degradation, which covers the activities associated with air and water pollution, land erosion, and solid wastes. Resource depletion is a concern because it would lead to the quantitative exhaustion of natural resources that are an important source of revenues, obtained through exploitation and the discovery of new reserves. In the case of resource degradation, the issue is not the quantitative exhaustion of natural resources, but rather the qualitative degradation of the ecosystem – for example, through the contamination of air and water, as a result of the generation and deposit of residuals, and as a result of the environmental impact of producing garbage and solid waste (see Box 4.1).

To preserve the richness of forestry and stabilize the soil structure, the Chinese government has begun a massive reforestation program. The first afforestation project was initiated in 1978 to plant trees covering 551 counties, cities, and townships of 13 provinces and autonomous regions in the northern, western, central and eastern China areas. The other afforestation projects include:

- 'Forest System of the Upper and Middle Reaches of the Changjiang River', with a planned afforestation space of around 66,000 square kilometers
- 'Coastal Shelter-Forest System' with 25,000 square kilometers

---

11. These laws, regulations, and other relevant official documents have covered a broader range from air, inland water pollution control, and protection of endangered wildlife, to the control of domestic marine pollution from offshore oil drilling, and waste release into territorial seas (ACCA21, 1994, p. 1-1A-1).

Box 4.1   What is the Environmental Kuznets Curve?

There is a long line of thought suggesting that environmental quality changes with respect to income level. Theoretical papers by Gruver (1976), John and Pecchenino (1992), and Seldon and Song (1995) have derived transition paths for pollution, abatement effort and development under alternative assumptions about social welfare functions, pollution damage,

the cost of abatement, and the productivity of capital. Empirical studies (Hettige et al., 1992; Shafik, 1994; Selden and Song, 1994; and Grossman and Krueger, 1995) have searched for systematic relationships by regressing cross-country measures of ambient air and water quality on various polynomial specifications of income per capita.

In a more synthesized term, the relationship between environmental pressures and income levels has been summarized to follow an inverted-U curve (see, for example, Lucas et al., 1992, World Bank, 1992 and 1995, Panayton, 1993, Selden and Song, 1994, Shafik, 1994, Grossman and Krueger, 1995, Holtz-Eakin and Selden, 1995, and Rock, 1996). This phenomenon is known as the environmental Kuznets curve (EKC), due to the similarity with the relationship between the level of inequality and income per capita considered by Kuznets (1955). According to the EKC hypothesis, environmental pressures increase as income level increases at the initial stage of economic development, but later these pressures diminish along with the income levels.

- 'Afforestation Project of the Taihang Mountains between Shanxi, Hebei, and Henan provinces and Beijing and Tianjin Municipalities', with 33,000 square kilometers (NEPA, 1992).

4.4.3   Unresolved Issues

There are further constraints on Chinese sustainable development. For example, China has expressed a willingness to participate in an international global warming treaty. However, it is unlikely that the Chinese are going to push GHG reductions up to the 'no-regrets' level, because they have more pressing problems. In addition, China has also promised to protect endangered species in order to maintain a diversified ecosystem.

The gains of today might eventually become the costs of tomorrow. The environmental costs resulting from industrialization often build up slowly and do not become critical in the first few years. By contrast, the benefits of industrialization are usually immediate. However, if the government, industrialists, and consumers are prepared to continue with various practices and leave future generations to worry about their environmental consequences, the problem is therefore a re-election of the importance that people attach to the present relative to the future.

It should also be noted that some articles of the laws relating to the environment have so far only been defined in principle, but are not actionable. For example, Article 44 of the 'Law of Mineral Resources of the People's Republic of

China' (kuangcan ziyuan fa), which was adopted on March 19, 1986, and revised on August 29, 1996, states:

...those who use destructive methods to extract mineral resources should refund the loss of damages and, if the resources have been seriously damaged, be additionally charged till the withdrawal of their certificates for mining permission at the most serious situation...[12]

However, this article should be further clarified at least in the following respects:

- the specific types of extraction methods which are considered 'destructive' to mineral resources should be defined
- how to define 'serious damages' to resources
- how to calculate the 'loss of damages'
- how to determine the amount of 'additional charges'
- what should be defined as the 'most serious situation'.

Before the early 1980s, China had no formal administrative organs in charge of environmental protection. In 1984, the National Environmental Protection Agency (NEPA) was established. Thereafter, environmental protection bureaus, divisions, or offices have been established at all governmental levels, such as 'environmental protection offices' of the commissions, ministries, and other government branches and the state-owned

---

12. Cited from http://www.chinasafety.gov.cn/zhengcefagui/1986-03/19/content_48.htm. Accessed on December 15, 2011.

corporations at ministry or semi-ministry level, 'environmental protection bureaus' of the provinces and autonomous regions, and so on. In 2008, the NEPA was upgraded, becoming the Ministry of Environmental Protection (MEP).

China's environmental protection network has been virtually a complete one. Directly under the State Council, the MEP has eight specific departments including planning, policy regulation, development supervision, pollution control, science and technology, nature conservation, personnel, and foreign affairs. The MEP supervises China's environmentally related activities through two parallel channels:

1. Provinces and autonomous regions → prefecture or municipalities → counties and urban districts → non-state and private enterprises
2. State commissions → ministries and other government branches and state corporations at ministry and semi-ministry levels → state-owned enterprises.

However, China's current administrative organs in charge of environmental protection and its environmentally related law enforcement are still weak, particularly at the grassroots level, compared to its increasing economic growth and social demands for environmental quality. The MEP can only exert its policy and professional directions to the provincial environmental protection bureaus, while the latter are appointed by and, naturally, mainly responsible to *their* respective provincial governments.

Furthermore, the importance of coordinating the economic development and environmental protection has not been brought home to some local governments and enterprises, because of their lack of awareness of their responsibility for the implementation of the environmental protection laws. Motivated partially by economic interest, the government officials and enterprise managers often ignore environmental costs and benefits, as the yardstick of their achievements has been largely confined to the economic growth index. They are reluctant to make a careful study of whether such growth could be sustained, and have even seen the developing economy as an excuse to evade the restraints of laws and regulations. The irrational aspects of the administrative system and unclear defined responsibility in various departments have impaired the efficiency of environmental management.

4.5 POLICY IMPLICATIONS

The uneven distribution of natural resources in China has had a considerable influence on the disequilibrated regional structures of exploitation and the supply of those resources used as inputs of production to produce desired final goods and services for society. China's mineral and energy resources are principally distributed in the northern and western inland areas, while the largest industrial consumers are located in the eastern and southern coastal areas. Therefore, the long distance transfers of raw materials and semi-finished products from the northern and western inland areas to the eastern and southern coastal areas should be the only feasible approach by which to efficiently create an equilibrium between supply and demand in the Chinese economy. The Chinese government should recognize this fact and try to deal carefully with national economic cooperation.

In contrast to the development pattern of most industrialized economies, the Chinese economy has been fueled principally by coal rather than by petroleum and natural gas. Given its abundance in reserves compared with other energy resources such as hydropower, petroleum and natural gas, coal, which accounts for more than 80 percent of China's total energy resources, has until recently supplied almost 70 percent of the nation's total energy supply. Without stressing the low heating conversion rate of coal consumption, the serious environmental damage resulting from the exploitation, transportation and consumption of coal resources has already posed challenges to the sustainable development of the Chinese economy.

Since the late 1970s, several changes have taken place in the legislation of environmental protection in China, along with the economic reform and opening up to the outside world. A relatively comprehensive legal system concerning environmental protection has initially taken shape. China has also joined or approved many international protocols on environmental protection. However, Chinese legislation faces problems in attempting to achieve coordination and consistency with international treaties and conventions.

China has essentially followed a traditional development model that is characterized by high resource and energy (mainly coal) consumption and extensive management. This has led not only to damage to the environment of today, but has also affected its economic sustainability. Therefore, shifting the development strategy and embarking on the path to sustainable development is the only correct choice for the Chinese economy.

It should be noted that China, like many other developing countries, is facing many pressing problems related to economic development which might, at least in the short run, be contradicted by a system of environmental protection. However, environmental policies and measures should never be treated independently from economic policies. Moreover, they can serve as a dynamic mechanism for the maximization of the real well-being of the whole people.

Case Study 4

The South-North Water Transfer Project

China is plagued with unevenly distributed water and land resources: more water vis-à-vis less land in southern China and less water vis-à-vis more land in northern China. North

China accounts for over one-third of the country's total population, nearly one-half of cultivated land, but only one-eighth of the total water resources. Over 80 per cent of the direct water runoff in China takes place in the south. Since the 1980s the Haihe and Yellow River valleys have been stricken by chronic drought. Yet, further south, large amounts of water from the Yangtze empty into the sea each year.

The northern part of China has long been a center of population, industry and agriculture. However, the per capita share of the region's limited water resources has inevitably kept falling. Inevitably, this has led to the over-exploitation of groundwater – often supplying urban and industrial development at the expense of agriculture – leading to severe water shortages in rural areas. In addition, land subsidence and the region's frequent sandstorms have also been linked to the excessive use of groundwater. Given the existence of surface water surplus in southern China and freshwater shortage in northern China, is it feasible to transfer water from the water-rich south to the north?

On August 23, 2002, the South-North Water Diversion Project – the largest of its kind ever undertaken in the world – was approved by the State Council. Later in this year, work began on the eastern route of the project. A special limited liability company (the South- to- North Water Transfer Project Company) has been created to cover the construction, operation and maintenance of the main project, with each province being required to set up a water supply company to manage the local administration and infrastructure elements.

The project involves drawing water from southern rivers and supplying it to the dry northern provinces. This massive scheme has already taken several decades from conception to commencement. The project will link China's four main rivers – the Yangtze, the Yellow, the Huai, and the Hai. This requires the construction of three diversion routes, namely, stretching south to north across the eastern, central and western parts of the country, respectively (see Figure 4.8).

I   The Eastern Route

The eastern route has supplied Shandong and the northern part of Jiangsu since 2007 – a year ahead of the original schedule – linking Shandong with the Yangtze River and bringing water north to the Huang-Huai-Hai Plain via the Beijing-Hangzhou Grand Canal. However, completion of this route has also suffered delays in other areas. Diverted from a major branch of the Yangtze River, near Yangzhou city, the water will travel along existing river channels to Lake Weishan of Shandong, before crossing the Yellow River via a tunnel and flowing to Tianjin.

The finished diversion will be slightly over 1,155 km long and involves the construction of 23 pumping stations with the installed capacity of 453.7 MW in the first stage alone to complement the seven existing ones, which will themselves

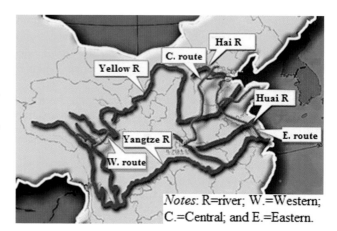

FIGURE 4.8 The three routes of the South-North Water Transfer Project. *Source: Author.*

be rehabilitated and upgraded. This part of the project will also include nearly 9 km of tunnels, from the outlet of Dongping Lake to the inlet of the Weilin Canal, including a 634 m long siphon section, together with two 9.3 m diameter horizontal tunnels 70 m under the Huanghe riverbed.[13]

The Beijing-Hangzhou Grand Canal is currently being upgraded. Water from the Yangtze River will be drawn into the canal in Jiangdu, where a giant $400\,m^3/s$ pumping station was already built in the 1980s, and is then fed uphill by pumping stations along the Grand Canal and through a tunnel under the Yellow River, from where it can flow downhill to reservoirs near Tianjin. Construction on the eastern route officially began on December 27, 2002.

II   The Central Route

Construction of the central route began in December 2003. The central route diverts water from the Danjiangkou reservoir on the Han River via new canals to flow through Henan and Hebei provinces to Beijing – a diversion route totaling some 1,267 km in length. The nearby city of Tianjin will also draw water from the trunk line near Xushui in Hebei province. Initially designed to transfer 9.5 billion cubic meters of water, by 2030 some 13–14 billion cubic meters will be flowing along this system. The work also includes the construction of two tunnels of 8.5 m internal diameter some 7 km long, with a flow design of $500\,m^3/s$.

The central route is from the Danjiangkou Reservoir on the Han River – a tributary of the Yangtse River – to Beijing. This route is built on the North China Plain and, once the Yellow River has been crossed, water can flow all the way to Beijing by gravity. The main engineering challenge is to build a tunnel under the Yellow River. Construction on the central route began in 2004. In 2008

13. Data source: http://www.water-technology.net/projects/south_north/. Accessed on November 6, 2011.

TABLE 4.5 The Basic Indicators of the South-North Water Transfer Project

	Annual Diverted Volume of Water (billion cu.m.)	Estimated Costs (Billion Yuan)		
		Stage I (2000–10)	Stage II (2010–20)	Long-range (2020–50)
Eastern route	14.8	17.9	11.3	–
Central route	13.0	23.4	31.5	–
Western route	17.0	–	0–20	230–250
Total	44.8	41.3	42.8–62.8	230–250

Sources: Qian and Zhang (2001, p. 244) and author.

the 307 km long northern stretch of the central route was completed at a cost of US$2 billion. Water in that stretch of the canal does not yet come from the Han River, but from various reservoirs in Hebei Province south of Beijing.[14]

The whole project was expected to be completed around 2010. This has recently been set back to 2014 to allow for increased environmental protections. A problem is the influence on the Han River, where one-third of the water is diverted. One long-term consideration is to build another canal to divert water from the Three Gorges Dam to Danjiangkou reservoir. Another major difficulty is the resettlement of residents around the Danjiangkou reservoir and along the route. In 2009, the Chinese government began to relocate residents from the areas of the Hubei and Henan provinces that will be affected by the reservoir.

III The Western Route

The western route, also called the Big Western Line, is to divert water from the headwater of the Yangtze River into the upper stream of the Yellow River. The original plan that began in the 1950s and 1960s called for diverting the Nu (Salween), Lancang (Mekong), Tongtian, Yalong, Dadu Rivers into upstream Yellow River. The project was considered too costly to be undertaken at that time. At present, however, new technology has made it possible to connect the three latter rivers (Tongtian, Yalong, and Dadu, Rivers that flow entirely within the borders of China) and to divert them into the Yellow River.

In order to move the water through the drainage divide between these rivers, huge dams and long tunnels are needed to be built to cross the Qinghai-Tibetan Plateau. In addition, water will be diverted from the upstream sections of six rivers (including the Mekong, the Yarlung Zangbo and the Salween) through a system of reservoirs, tunnels and natural rivers. The feasibility of this route is still under study.

Construction of the western route – which involves working on the Qinghai-Tibet Plateau 3,000–5,000 m above

sea level – will involve overcoming some major engineering and climatic challenges. Once completed, the project will bring a huge amount of water from three tributaries of the Yangtze – the Tongtian, Yalong, and Dadu Rivers – across the Bayankala Mountains and then on to northwest China.

The complete project is expected to cost much more than that of the country's 'Three Gorges Dam' project. Planned for completion in 2050, it will eventually divert 44.8 billion cubic meters of water annually. Projected costs in yuan terms (and dollar terms, given the almost fixed yuan-dollar peg of recent years) have tended to increase, reflecting inflation and perhaps the addition of unforeseen costs, such as for pollution control along the eastern route and for the preservation of cultural and historical relics. Shortly before the diversions were approved, the total estimated cost for all three routes, to the end of construction in 2050, was 314–354 billion yuan at the 1995 price (see Table 4.5).

Since the introduction of the project, it has created widespread controversy. According to the State Administration of Cultural Heritage, at least 788 cultural heritage sites will be affected by the diversions. The central government has so far approved 50 million yuan to protect 45 sites along the eastern and central routes.[15] Like China's other megaproject – the Three Gorges Dam – the diversion scheme has provoked many environmental concerns, principally regarding the loss of antiquities, the displacement of people, and the destruction of pasture land. In addition, plans for industrialization along the routes of the project pose a serious risk of pollution to the diverted water. To counter this risk of pollution, the Chinese government has built treatment facilities to help ensure that water in the areas of the diversion project will meet minimum drinking standards.

Opponents of the project object to it on the grounds that it is a waste of resources, it could create a large number of migrant people, it could waste massive amounts of water through evaporation and pollution, the project's huge cost

---

14. See *The Economist*, October 11, 2008, p. 61.

15. Source: http://www.yellowriver.gov.cn/lib/top2/2005-11-16/jj_08303-7124307.html. Accessed on November 6, 2011.

would make the water prohibitively expensive for consumers, the dry season could cause the Yangtze River to suffer from water shortages, it would be detrimental to the Yangtze River's transportation, and it could cause an environmental disaster. According to official estimates, between 300,000 and 400,000 people will be displaced by the projects, mostly along the Middle Route. For some who formerly lived in the Danjiangkou Reservoir area, this will be their second displacement. In April 2005, the central government issued a provisional regulation on land requisition, compensation, and resettlement for the project (Nickum, 2006).

Regardless of these negative impacts, government officials and defenders of the project claim the Yangtze River has a plentiful supply of water, with most of the water currently flowing into the Pacific Ocean. They argue that transferring one portion to the poorly irrigated areas of the North could solve the North's water scarcity issue.

REFERENCES

ACCA21 (1994). *Priority programs for China's agenda 21*, First Tranche, Beijing: Administrative Committee of China Agenda 21 (ACCA21) of State Planning Commission and State Science and Technology Commission.

BP Statistical Review of World Energy. 2011, London, UK.

Chen, M., & Cai, Z. (2000). *Groundwater resources and the related environ-hydrogeologic problems in China (in Chinese).* Beijing: Seismological Press.

Chen, Y., Cai, Q., & Tang, H. (2003). Dust storm as an environmental problem in north China. *Environmental Management, 33*, 413–417.

CISNR (Ed.). (1990). *Handbook of natural resources in China* (zhongguo zhiran zhiyuan scouche). Commission of Integrated Survey on Natural Resources (CISNR) of Chinese Academy of Sciences. Beijing: Science Press.

Cui, M. (Ed.). (2007). *China energy development report – 2007.* Beijing: Social Sciences Literature Press. in Chinese.

Dasgupta, P., & Mäler, K.-G. (1995). Poverty, institutions, and the environmental resource-base. In J. Behrman & T. N. Srinivasan (Eds.), *Handbook of development economics* (Vol. 3, pp. 2331–2463). Amsterdam: Elsevier Science BV.

Economist, The (2008). China's water-diversion scheme: a shortage of capital flows. *The Economist.* October 11, p. 61.

EIA (Economist Intelligence Agency) (2006). *International energy outlook 2006.* London: Economist Intelligence Agency.

EIA (Energy Information Agency) (2011). *China's carbon dioxide emissions from consumption.* Washington DC: U.S. Energy Information Agency (EIA).

Lacey, S. (2011). How China dominates solar power: huge loans from the Chinese Development Bank are helping Chinese solar companies push American solar firms out of the market. <guardian.co.uk>, 12 September (Monday).

Ministry of Energy (1991). *Energy in China.* Beijing: Ministry of Energy.

NBS. (various years). *China statistical yearbook.* various issues, Beijing: China Statistics Publishing House.

NEAA (2007). *China now No. 1 in CO2 emissions; USA in second position.* Netherlands Environmental Assessment Agency (NEAA). available at <www.mnp.nl>.

NEPA. (various years). *Report on the State of the environment.* Beijing: National Environment Protection Agency.

Nickum, J.E. (2006). *The status of the south-north water transfer plans in China.* draft, Tokyo Jogakkan College. Available at <http://hdr.undp.org/en/reports/global/hdr2006/papers/james_nickum_china_water_transfer.pdf>. Accessed on November 6, 2011.

Pearce, D., Barbier, E., & Markandya, A. (1988). Sustainable development and cost–benefit analysis. *Paper presented at the Canadian assessment workshop on integrating economic and environment Chinese economic sustainability assessment.*

Qian, W., & Zhu, Y. (2001). Climate change in China from 1880 to 1998 and its impact on the environmental condition. *Climate Change, 50,* 419–444.

Qian, Z., & Zhang, G. (Eds.). (2001). *A strategic research on China's sustainable development of water resources: the synthetic and specialized reports* [zhongguo kechixu fazhan shui ziyuan zhanlue yanjiu zonghe baogao ji ge zhuanti baogao]. Beijing: Zhongguo Shuili Dianli Chubanshe.

Si, T. (2008). Coal efficiency set to get boost. *China Daily, November 3*(Monday), 2.

Solow, R. M. (1991). *Sustainability – an economist's perspective.* Cambridge, MA: Department of Economics, Massachusetts Institute of Technology.

Streifel, S. (2006). *Impact of China and India on global commodity markets: focus on metals and minerals and petroleum.* draft, Development Prospects Group, World Bank, Washington DC.

Sun, J. (1987). *Territory, resources, and regional development* [guotu, zhiyuan kaifa he quyu fazhan]. Beijing: People's Education Press.

Watts, J. (2005). Satellite data reveals Beijing as air pollution capital of world. *The Guardian* October 31, available at <www.guardian.co.uk/news/2005/oct/31/china.pollution>

Winters, L. A., & Yusuf, S. (2007). Introduction: dancing with giants Winters Yusuf (Eds.), *Dancing with Giants: China, India, and the Global Economy* (pp. 1–34). Washington, DC: World Bank Publications.

World Commission for Environment and Development (1987). *Our common future.* New York: Oxford University Press.

World Resources Institute (1992). *World resources 1992–93.* Oxford: Oxford University Press.

World Resources Institute (2003). *Water resources and freshwater ecosystems.* Washington, DC: World Resources Institute.

Political and Administrative Systems

A ding from the Shang dynasty. *Source: http://en.wikipedia.org*

A ding is an ancient Chinese cauldron with legs. Dings were originally made of ceramic materials, then later, at the time of the Shang dynasty (1766–1046 BC), cast in bronze. They were used for cooking, storage, and the preparation of ritual offerings to ancestors. Perhaps the most famous ancient dings were the set of nine bronze vessels (jiu-ding), which is said to have been cast by King Yu of the Xia dynasty when he divided his nation into the Jiuzhou or nine territories. During the Zhou dynasty (1046–221 BC), only the kings could have a set of nine vessels, while people with lower positions were only allowed to have a smaller number of vessels. Since then the idiom 'yiyan jiuding' has been used in Chinese language to represent a sign of rightful authority over all.

Bianque stood looking at Duke Huang of Cai for a while and spoke, 'Your Majesty is suffering from an ailment, which now remains in between the skin and the muscles. But it may get

Understanding the Chinese Economies. DOI: http://dx.doi.org/10.1016/B978-0-12-397826-4.00005-6
© 2013 Elsevier Inc. All rights reserved.

worse without treatment.' 'I am not at all indisposed,' replied the Duke complacently. When Bianque left, the Duke remarked, 'It is the medical man's usual practice to pass a healthy person as a sick man in order to show his brilliance.' Ten days later, when Bianque saw the Duke, he pointed out: 'The ailment has developed into the muscles. It will go from bad to worse if no treatment is conducted.' To this the ruler showed a greater displeasure than before. Another ten days went by. On seeing the Duke again, Bianque warned him that the illness had gone into the stomach and the intestines and that unless an immediate treatment be given, it would go on worsening. Again the Duke looked angrier. After a third ten days, when Bianque saw the Duke, he simply turned round and went away… (to be continued)[1]

– Hanfeizi (c. 280–233 BC)

5.1 PARTY VERSUS STATE

5.1.1 What Does the Constitution Say?

According to the Constitution of the People's Republic of China (PRC), all the power in the country belongs to the people who exercise their power through the NPC and local people's congresses at all levels; and the people manage the state, economy, culture, and other social affairs through a multitude of means and forms. However, the Constitution also stipulates that the PRC was founded by the Chinese Communist Party (CCP) which is the leader of the Chinese people. The socialist system led by the working class and based on the alliance of the workers and farmers is the fundamental system of the PRC.

The State Council is the official government of China. It initiates legislation and controls the civil service. The State Council is indirectly elected by the NPC, which assembles in plenary every year to scrutinize and ratify its decisions on domestic and foreign affairs. The Chinese People's Political Consultative Congress (CPPCC) – an institution similar to the Senate in the United States – consists of representatives from the CCP, several democratic parties, democrats with no party affiliations, various people's organizations and ethnic groups, and other specially invited individuals. The primary functions of the CPPCC are to conduct political consultations and democratic supervisions, and to discuss and manage state affairs.

The approximately 3,000 deputies that attend the NPC are elected indirectly every five years by the People's Congresses of provinces, autonomous regions, municipalities under central government, and by the People's Liberation Army (PLA). The supreme legislative organ of China, the NPC, holds regular (annual) meetings in the Great Hall of the People in Beijing to discuss state affairs, to approve those whom are recommended by the Chinese Communist Party Central Committee (CCPCC) as central

government officials, and to issue laws and regulations. In addition to indirectly electing the State Council, the NPC can also dismiss the holders of the top offices of state. The Standing Committee of the NPC, which is further composed of a series of special committees and working and administrative bodies (see Figure 5.1) is empowered to modify legislation between plenary sessions of, and carry out the daily work of, the NPC on a more permanent basis. In practice, although its scrutiny role has been enhanced in recent years and unanimous votes have become less frequent, the independent power of the NPC remains limited.[2]

5.1.2 How the Communist Party Works

Although there are other political organizations in China, the only organization that matters is the Chinese Communist Party (CCP). Some 2,000 CCP delegates are elected to the National Congress of the CCP, which is held every five years. The National Congress elects the members and alternates of the Chinese Communist Party Central Committee (CCPCC), which normally sits once a year. The 17th CCPCC, which was elected in 2007, is composed of 371 members and hundreds more alternates. The Central Committee for Discipline Inspection (CCDI) is also elected at this congress. Immediately after the closing ceremony of the National Congress, the CCPCC members indirectly elect, in addition to the Central Military Commission, the General Secretary, members of the Politburo and its Standing Committee, and the Secretariat (see Figure 5.2). The Politburo and particularly the smaller Standing Committee of the Politburo are where the overall policy of the Chinese government is really decided.

The CCP has been virtually the most important body of power in China and holds real political power in China's *de facto* one party state. Party organizations run in parallel to those of the government at all levels. The CCP's structure is characterized by 'democratic centralism' (*minzhu jizhong*), a system whereby the individual party member is subordinate to the organization, and where minority groups or opinions are subordinate to the wishes of the majority, embodied by the CCPCC. At the bottom of this pyramid are 'primary party organizations' in workplaces and villages. The overwhelming majority of delegates to the NPC are party members. CCP membership remains essential for a successful career, particularly in the public sector. Party membership now stands at nearly 80 million, and this figure continues to increase.

Indeed, the CCP's 'three represents' theory states clearly that the CCP is no longer the single representative

---

1. To be continued at the end of this chapter.

2. For example, the tenth National People's Congress (NPC) of March 2008 elected Hu Jintao as President with a total of 2,937 votes. Just four delegates voted against him, four abstained, and 38 did not vote (Guo, 2010, p. 107).

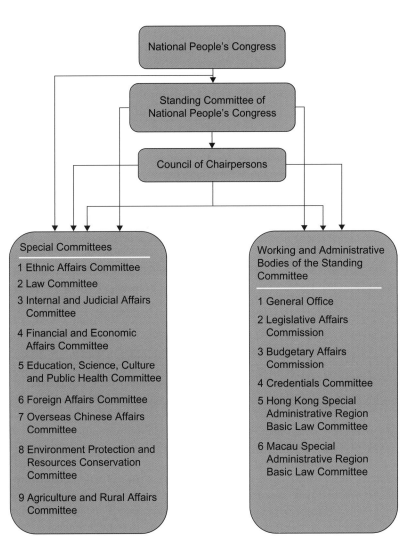

FIGURE 5.1 The structure of the National People's Congress (NPC) of China.

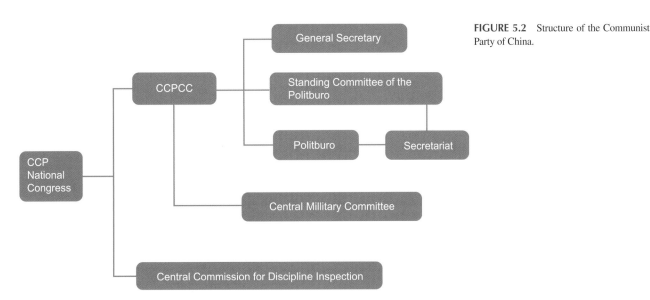

FIGURE 5.2 Structure of the Communist Party of China.

Notes: CCP = Chinese Communist Party; CCPCC = Chinese Communist Party Central Committee

of poor, working-class people; rather, it has also become the representative of the economic and cultural elites in China. By openly proclaiming itself a party of the 'economic elite' that has benefited from its free market agenda, the CCP has been hoping to consolidate a reliable base of support for its continued rule. The party's alliance with the rich is just as tight. With its pro-growth policies, its ban on independent trade unions, and its low environmental standards, the CCP has created an advantageous atmosphere for the economic elite to make money. Many successful entrepreneurs have also been party members. Policies so favor the rich and business that China's economic program, in the words of one Western ambassador, resembles 'the dream of the American Republican Party' (Pomfret, 2002).

5.1.3   CCP and 'Baiping'

Since the late 1990s, a new Chinese terminology – Baiping – has been popularized in mainland China. The term 'Baiping' is composed of two Chinese characters – 'bai' (to place, to put, to arrange, etc.) and 'ping' (flat, uniform, fair, etc.). The original meaning of Baiping is 'to put flat; or to arrange uniform'. The term had been so informal before the twenty-first century that even the 1999 edition of Cihai – the largest and most influential Chinese dictionary published by Shanghai Cishu Publishing House – didn't mention it. Notice that the frequently used Baiping has extended from its original meaning to 'to treat fairly', 'to compromise', 'to tradeoff', 'to punish' and so on.

After the death of Deng Xiaoping in 1997, Jiang Zemin must deftly play its various wings against each other. In this scenario, Li Peng, Chairman of the eighth National People's Congress (NPC), was selected to hold the No. 2 post of the CCPCC, higher than that of Zhu Rongji, Premier of the State Council, during the 1998–2003 tenure. This was the first time in the PRC's history that the NPC Chairman held a political rank higher than that of Premiership.

Moreover, a large number of non-Communist party and non-party individuals were selected as state leaders with the titles of vice Chairpersons of the NPC and of the Chinese People's Political Consultative Congress (CPPCC) in exchange for their support of the CCP as the permanent ruler of the state. For example, during the 2003–08 and the 2008–13 tenures, China's state-level leaders included nine standing members of the CCPCC Politburo (some of whom also held the posts of President, Premier, the NPC and CPPCC Chairmen) and dozens of vice Chairpersons of the NPC and of the CPPCC. The total number has been the highest since the 1980s.

5.2   GOVERNMENT AND ADMINISTRATIVE SYSTEMS

5.2.1   Central Government

In China, the central administrative system includes the central administrative organs under the system of the National People's Congress (NPC), and the leadership of the central administrative organs over local administrative organs at various levels. The central administrative organ is the State Council of the PRC. The State Council is the highest administrative organ of the state. The State Council is the executive body of the highest organ of state power and the highest organ of state administration in the People's Republic of China. The State Council exercises leadership over local administrative organs at various levels throughout the country, regulates the specific division of power and function of the state administrative organs at the central level and the provincial, autonomous, regional, and municipal level.

The premiership assumes overall responsibility for the work of the State Council and is responsible to the NPC and its Standing Committee on behalf of the State Council. The vice premiers and state councilors, together with the secretary-general of the state council, and ministers, are responsible to the premier. However, in all circumstances, the premier has the final decision making power on all major issues in the work of the State Council. For example, the premier has the power to suggest to the NPC and its Standing Committee the appointment or removal of the vice premiers, state councilors, ministers, and secretary-general of the State Council. Decisions, decrees, and administrative rules and regulations promulgated by the State Council, bills, and suggestions of appointments and removals submitted by the State Council to the NPC and its Standing Committee are legally valid only after the premier has signed them.

The State Council is composed of the premier, vice premiers, state councilors, ministers, auditor-general, and the secretary-general. The premier is nominated by the president of the PRC, decided by the NPC, appointed and removed by the president. The vice premiers, state councilors, ministers, auditor-general, and secretary-general of the State Council are nominated by the premier, decided by the NPC, appointed and removed by the president of the PRC. When the NPC is not in session, the choice of state councilors, ministers, auditor-general, and secretary-general are decided by the Standing Committee of the NPC according to nomination by the premier and appointed or removed by the President of the PRC.

The State Council serves for a term of five years. The premier, vice premiers, and state councilors may serve no more than two consecutive terms. Entrusted by the premier or the executive meeting of the State Council, state councilors may take charge of work in certain aspects or special tasks. They may also represent the State Council in conducting foreign affairs. Under the leadership of the premier, the secretary-general of the State Council is in charge of the day-to-day work of the State Council. The auditor-general is in charge of the supervision of state revenue and expenditure, and other financial and monetary activities.

All in all, the State Council convenes three categories of meetings:

- General meetings
- Executive meetings
- Working meetings.

The general meeting of the State Council, which is convened once every two months, or once every quarter of a year under normal conditions, is attended by all members of which the State Council is composed, convened and presided over by the premier. The meeting is convened to discuss issues of major importance or matters involving more than one department.

The executive meeting of the State Council, which is convened once a month under normal conditions, is convened and presided over by the premier and participated by vice premiers, state councilors and the secretary-general. The meeting sets out to discuss major issues in the work of the State Council, bills to be submitted to the Standing Committee of the NPC, administrative rules and regulations and important issues submitted by various departments and localities for decision by the State Council.

The working meeting of the premier, which is convened, whenever necessary, by the premier (or by a vice premier entrusted by the premier) is to discuss and deal with major issues in the daily work of the State Council. According to the Constitution of 1982, the State Council exercises the following functions and powers:[3]

1. To adopt administrative measures, enact administrative rules and regulations, and issue decisions and orders in accordance with the Constitution and the law; and to submit proposals to the National People's Congress or its Standing Committee.

2. To formulate the tasks and responsibilities of the ministries and commissions of the State Council, to exercise unified leadership over the work of the ministries and commissions and to direct all other administrative work of a national character that does not fall within the jurisdiction of the ministries and commissions; to exercise unified leadership over the work of local organs of state administration at various levels throughout the country, and to formulate the detailed division of functions and powers between the central government and the organs of state administration of provinces, autonomous regions, and municipalities directly under the central government; to alter or annul inappropriate orders, directives and regulations issued by the ministries or commissions; and to alter or annul inappropriate decisions and orders issued by local organs of state administration at various levels.

3. To draw up and implement the plan for national economic and social development and the state budget; to direct and administer economic affairs and urban and rural development; to conduct foreign affairs and conclude treaties and agreements with foreign states; to direct and administer the building of national defense; to direct and administer the affairs of education, science, culture, public health, physical culture and family planning; to direct and administer civil affairs, public security, judicial administration, supervision and other related matters; to direct and administer affairs concerning the ethnic groups and to safeguard the equal rights of ethnic minorities and the right to autonomy of the ethnic autonomous areas; to protect the legitimate rights and interests of Chinese nationals residing abroad and protect the lawful rights and interests of returned overseas Chinese and of the family members of Chinese nationals residing abroad; to approve the geographic division of provinces, autonomous regions and municipalities directly under the central government, and to approve the establishment and geographic divisions of autonomous prefectures, counties, autonomous counties and cities; to decided on the imposition of martial law in parts of provinces, autonomous regions, and municipalities directly under the central government; and to examine and decide on the size of administrative organs and, in accordance with the law, to appoint or remove administrative officials, train them, appraise their performance and reward or punish them.

4. To exercise such other functions and powers as the National People's Congress or its Standing Committee may assign to it. Ministries, commissions, the People's Bank of China and administrations are departments that make up the State Council. Under the unified leadership of the State Council, they are in charge of directing and administering the administrative affairs in their respective areas and exercise prescribed state administrative powers.

Departments of the State Council

The following ministries, commissions, and the People's Bank of China, which were set up by the NPC for the period from 2008 to 2013, are departments that make up the State Council. Under the unified leadership of the premiership, they are in charge of directing and administering the administrative affairs in their respective areas and exercise prescribed state administrative powers:

- Ministry of Foreign Affairs
- National Development and Reform Commission
- Ministry of Finance
- People's Bank of China
- Ministry of Railways

---

3. Cited from http://www.cpcchina.org/2011-10/19/content_13934964.htm. Accessed on November 14, 2011.

- Ministry of Transport
- Ministry of Construction
- Ministry of Agriculture
- Ministry of Water Conservancy
- Ministry of Commerce
- Ministry of Industry and Information
- Commission of Science, Technology, and Industry for National Defense
- Ministry of Labor and Social Security
- Ministry of Personnel
- State Family Planning Commission
- Ministry of Land and Resources
- Ministry of Environmental Protection
- State Commission of Ethnic Affairs
- Ministry of Civil Affairs
- Ministry of Justice
- Ministry of Public Security
- Ministry of State Security
- Ministry of National Defense
- Ministry of Supervision
- National Auditing Office
- Ministry of Education
- Ministry of Science and Technology
- Ministry of Culture
- Ministry of Health.

The ministers assume overall responsibility for the work of the ministries and ministry-level bureau, commissions, and administrations. They direct the work of their respective ministries and commissions, convene and preside over ministerial meetings or general and executive meetings of the commissions, and sign important reports to the State Council and decrees and directives issued to lower levels. In addition, these are also organs that are in charge of administrative affairs in special areas, under the leadership of the State Council. Usually, the administrative rankings of these organs are lower than those of the commission and ministries listed above. Leaders of these organs are decided by the executive meeting of the State Council, appointed and removed by the premier:

- State Administration of Sports
- Xinhua News Agency
- State Administration of Industry and Commerce
- Chinese Academy of Sciences
- Chinese Academy of Engineering
- Chinese Academy of Social Sciences
- Development Research Center of the State Council
- China Meteorological Administration
- China Intellectual Property Office.

In addition, some coordinating organs and provisional organs may be set up by the State Council to deal with special affairs. These organs normally have special committees or leading groups headed by the premier, or vice premiers, or state councilors or the secretary-general. They do not, in most cases, have independent working offices while the day-to-day work is placed under permanent ministries, commissions, administrations or other departments. These organs include:

- Working organs set up for directing the work in certain special areas
- Coordinating organs
- Consulting organs composed of specialists and leaders of departments concerned.

5.2.2 Provincial Administrations

The entire country is divided into provinces, autonomous regions, and municipalities directly under the central government. The provinces and autonomous regions are further divided into autonomous prefectures, counties, autonomous counties, and cities. The counties and autonomous counties are divided into townships, ethnic townships and towns. The municipalities directly under the central government and large cities in the provinces and autonomous regions are divided into districts and counties.

China's provincial governments comprise 22 provinces, five autonomous regions, four municipalities directly under the central government, and two special administrative regions (SARs) – Hong Kong and Macau – which returned to China in 1997 and 1999, respectively (see Table 5.1 for the names of various administrative divisions in China). It was agreed on handover that the existing political and economic systems that prevailed prior to these dates would be maintained for 50 years. Governments at this level (with the exception of the SARs) are indirectly elected for five years at plenaries of their respective People's Congresses. The system of governments of SARs is prescribed by laws enacted by the NPC. In addition, government organs may also be set up for special economic zones, development zones, mining industrial zones, and nature reserves.

Provincial governments are the first-level local state administrative organs in China. Provincial governments must accept the unified leadership of the State Council which has the power to decide on the division of responsibilities between the central government and provincial administrative organs. The State Council also has the power to annul inappropriate decisions and orders of provincial governments. Provincial governments implement local laws, regulations, and decisions of the provincial people's congresses and their standing committees, are responsible to and report on their work to provincial people's congresses and their standing committees. Provincial people's congresses and their standing committees have the power to supervise the work of provincial governments, change, and annul inappropriate decisions of the provincial governments.

TABLE 5.1 The Names of Various Levels of Administrative Divisions in China

Level	Type	Names
1[a]	Provincial-level administrative division (shengji xingzheng qu) (33)	Provinces (shěng) (22)[b] Autonomous regions (zìzhì qū) (5) Municipalities (zhíxiá shì) (4) Special administrative regions (tèbié xíngzhèng qū) (2)
2[a]	Prefectural-level administrative division (diji xingzheng qu) (333)	Prefectures (dìqū) (17) Prefecture-level cities (dìjí shì) (283) Autonomous prefectures (zìzhì zhōu) (30) Leagues (méng) (3)
3	County-level administrative division (xianji xingzheng qu) (2,858)	Counties (xiàn) (1,464) Districts (shìxiá qū) (855) County-level cities (xiànjí shì) (367) Autonomous counties (zìzhì xiàn) (117) Banners (qí) (49) Autonomous banners (zìzhì qí) (3) Special districts (tèqū) (3) Forestry area (línqū) (1)
4	Township-level administrative division (xiangji xingzheng qu) (40,859)	Towns (zhèn) (19,141) Townships (xiāng) (14,646) Sub-districts (jiēdào bànshìchù) (6,686) Ethnic townships (mínzú xiāng) (1,098) Sumu (sūmù) (181) District public offices (qūgōngsuǒ) (2) Ethnic sumu (mínzú sūmù) (1)
5	Village-level administrative division (cunji xingzheng qu)	Village committees (cūnmín wěiyuán hùi) (623,669) Neighborhood committees (jūmín wěiyuán hùi) (80,717)

Notes: *The figures within parentheses indicate the number of relevant administrative divisions (as of 2009).*
[a]*Between the provincial- and prefectural-level administrative divisions, there is a sub-provincial division (cities). At present, China's sub-provincial ranking cities include Shenyang, Dalian, Changchun, Harbin, Jinan, Qingdao, Nanjing, Ningbo, Hangzhou, Xiamen, Wuhan, Guangzhou, Shenzhen, Xi'an, and Chengdu.*
[b]*Taiwan is claimed by the Chinese government as a province.*
Source: NBS (2010).

Provincial governments have the power to exercise unified leadership over the work of governments at the levels of the cities, counties, townships, and towns under their jurisdiction, and to exercise unified administration over economic, social, and cultural affairs.

Provincial governments may send out agencies, upon approval of the State Council. Their agencies are normally called 'administrative offices'. The administrative offices, as agencies of the provincial governments, are not governments themselves. The regions under their jurisdiction are not administrative divisions either. The basic responsibilities of the administrative offices are to provide guidance and coordinate the work of the counties and cities within the regions, on behalf of provincial governments. An administrative office has a commissioner, vice commissioners and advisors, appointed and removed by the provincial governments. The working meetings of administrative offices are attended by the commissioners, vice commissioners, advisors, assistant advisors, secretaries-general, and deputy secretaries-general to discuss major issues in the work of the administrative offices.

Governments of municipalities directly under the central government are first-level local state administrative organs in China. In China, there are currently four municipalities directly under the central government, namely Beijing, Chongqing, Shanghai, and Tianjin. Governments of these municipalities must accept the unified leadership of the State Council which has the power to decide on the division of power and functions between the central government and state administrative organs of municipalities directly under the central government. The State Council also has the power to alter or annul decisions and orders made by governments of municipalities directly under the central government.

Governments of municipalities directly under the central government implement local laws, regulations, and decisions of the people's congresses and their standing committees of the municipalities, are responsible for and report on their work to the people's congresses and their standing committees. People's congresses and their standing committees in the municipalities have the power to supervise the work of the governments of municipalities, change and annul inappropriate decisions and orders of municipal governments. Municipal governments have the right to exercise unified leadership over the work of the districts, cities, counties, townships, and towns and exercise unified administration over the economic, social, and cultural affairs in areas under their respective jurisdictions.

Provinces and municipalities directly under the central government have governors, vice governors, mayors, vice mayors, secretaries-general, directors of departments (or bureaus), and commissions.

Provincial governors, vice governors, mayors, and vice mayors are elected by the people's congresses of the provinces and municipalities. Within two months after their election, provincial governors and municipal mayors shall nominate secretaries-general and directors of departments, bureaus, and commissions to people's congresses of the provinces and municipalities for appointment, and report to the State Council for the record. When the people's congresses in provinces or municipalities are not in session, provincial governors or mayors cannot assume their posts, the standing committees of the people's congresses may decide on the acting governors or mayors, selected from among the vice governors or vice mayors to serve until the by-election at the next session of the people's congresses.

When the people's congresses in provinces or municipalities are not in session, the appointment or removal of individual vice governors or vice mayors are carried out by the standing committees of the people's congresses. Provincial and municipal governments serve a term of five years.

5.2.3   Sub-Provincial and Prefectural Administrations

In addition to provincial-level administrations, China has sub-provincial (fu shengji) and prefectural (diji) administrations. City governments with sub-provincial ranking refer to governments of relatively large cities whose economic plans are separately listed in the national planning, whose administrative status is lower than that of a full provincial government and which are not administratively controlled by provincial governments. At present, China's sub-provincial ranking cities are Shenyang, Dalian, Changchun, Harbin, Jinan, Qingdao, Nanjing, Ningbo, Hangzhou, Xiamen, Wuhan, Guangzhou, Shenzhen, Xi'an, and Chengdu.

Prefectural-level cities are large and medium-sized cities not including sub-provincial level cities. Normally, they are cities with a non-farming population of more than a quarter of a million. Furthermore, the seats of cities have a non-farming population of more than 200,000 each, and

their industrial production value exceeds 2 billion yuan. They have a relatively advanced tertiary industry whose production value is more than that of the first industry, and makes up more than 35 percent of the GDP in these cities. The revenue in their local budget is beyond 200 million yuan and they have grown into centers of a number of cities or counties.[4]

Governments of prefectural-level cities consist of mayors, vice mayors, secretaries-general, and directors of bureaus and commissions. Mayors and vice mayors are elected by the people's congresses of the cities. When the people's congresses are not in session, the appointment and removal of individual vice mayors are carried out by the standing committees of the people's congresses. Governments of prefectural-level cities serve a term of five years.

These governments are responsible for and report on their work to the people's congresses and their standing committees at the same level. They are responsible for and report on their work to provincial-level governments and accept the unified leadership of the State Council at the same time. They direct the economic, cultural, and administrative work of their cities. They also direct the administrative affairs of their entire regions and the work of the counties and county governments in areas under their jurisdiction.

Governments of cities where provincial or autonomous regional governments are located and large cities recognized by the State Council may formulate their administrative regulations in accordance with the law and administrative regulations of the State Council. The system of placing counties and county-level cities under the administration of prefectural-level cities means establishing an administrative organ between the province and counties (county-level cities). This mechanism requires the prefectural-level city to have the dual functions of administering both rural and urban areas. The main models of this mechanism are:

- To merge the administrative office of a prefecture with the government of the prefectural-level city where the office is located to establish a new prefectural-level city government to administer the counties and county-level cities
- To incorporate a number of counties and county-level cities in the vicinity of a prefectural-level city into the administration of the latter which previously did not administer the counties
- To elevate the status of county-level cities or towns into prefectural-level cities, or turn the organs of the administrative office directly into the organs of the prefectural-level city, so as to establish a prefectural-level city government to administer counties and county-level cities.

---

4. Source: http://www.china.org.cn/english/Political/28842.htm. Accessed on November 14, 2011.

5.2.4 County-Level Administrations

County governments are local governments established in rural areas. County governments administer the governments of townships, ethnic townships, and towns. They may also establish neighborhood offices. When necessary, county governments may, upon approval of provincial, autonomous regional, or municipal governments, set up district offices as their agencies.

In areas implementing the system of prefectural-level cities administering counties and county-level cities, and in ethnic self-governing areas, county governments receive leadership from prefectural-level city or autonomous prefectural governments. In areas where prefectural-level cities are not established, and in the four municipalities directly under the central government (i.e., Beijing, Tianjin, Shanghai, and Chongqing), county governments receive direct leadership from provincial, autonomous regional, or municipal governments.

County-level cities normally grow from towns within a county or are established in place of what was originally a county which has now been dissolved. These are places with a relatively strong rural administrative color. Governments of county-level cities administer governments of townships, ethnic townships, and towns. Neighborhood offices may also be established under their leadership. Governments of county-level cities are mainly in the following two categories:

A. In areas without an administrative office, they receive leadership directly from provincial or autonomous regional governments
B. In areas implementing a system of prefectural-level city administering the county and county-level city, or in ethnic self-governing areas with county-level city governments, they receive leadership from the prefectural-level city or the autonomous prefectural government.

District governments are urban governments established in districts in municipalities directly under the central government, sub-provincial-level cities, and prefectural-level cities. They receive leadership from the governments of municipalities directly under the central government, sub-provincial-level cities, and prefectural-level cities.

District governments consist of urban district and suburban district governments. Urban district governments are located within the urban districts and function as grassroots governments in urban areas. They may have agencies in the form of neighborhood offices. Suburban district governments, naturally located within suburban areas of cities, administer governments of townships, ethnic townships, and towns. They may also establish neighborhood offices.

Governments of counties, county-level cities, and districts are composed of county governors, vice governors, mayors, vice mayors, district heads, deputy heads, and directors of bureaus or sections. County governors, vice governors, mayors, vice mayors, district heads, and deputy heads are elected by the people's congresses of the counties, cities, and districts. When the people's congresses of the counties, cities, and districts are not in session, the standing committees of the people's congresses may decide on the appointment and removal of individual vice governors of counties and vice heads of districts and vice mayors. Governments of counties, county-level cities, and districts serve a term of five years.

5.2.5 Grassroots Administrations

Governments of townships, ethnic townships (both referring to rural areas), and towns (urban centers in rural China) are grassroots governments in rural areas. They receive leadership from governments of counties, autonomous counties, county-level cities, and districts.

A township, ethnic township, or town government has a head and several deputy heads. The head of an ethnic township government must be a citizen of an ethnic minority origin. Heads and deputy heads of townships, ethnic townships, and towns are elected by the people's congresses in the townships, ethnic townships, and towns. Governments of townships, ethnic townships, and towns serve a term of three years.

It is the provincial-level governments' duty to establish and decide the geographic division of townships, ethnic townships, and towns. People's governments of townships, ethnic townships, and towns carry out the resolutions of the people's congress at the corresponding level, as well as the decisions and orders of the state administrative organs at the next higher level. They also conduct administrative work in their respective administrative areas.

Local people's governments at various levels are responsible for and report on their work to the state administrative organs at the next higher level. Local people's governments at various levels throughout the country are state administrative organs under the unified leadership of the State Council and are subordinate to it. Local people's governments at and above the county level direct the work of their subordinate departments and of people's governments at lower levels, and have the power to alter or annul inappropriate decisions of their subordinate departments and of the people's governments at lower levels.

In addition, there are also systems of governance that operate beneath the various levels of state administration described above. These are the village committees (*cunweihui*) in rural areas and the resident committees (*juweihui*) in urban areas. The village committees deal with all administrative matters, including budgets, public services, order, welfare, and dispute resolution (see Figure 5.3).

In contrast to their attitude with regard to levels of government that are considered part of the state, the

Notes: (1) The party branch office tablet is written in red and located on the right side, denoting that the CCP is always in a superior position in China.
(2) The office tablet of the villagers' committee is written in black and located on the left side.

FIGURE 5.3   The office of a village-level administrative division. *Copyright © 2012 by Rongxing Guo.*

authorities have shown some willingness over the past two decades to countenance direct elections to these committees. There have been attempts to introduce direct elections to village committees. These innovations were part of wider efforts to restore some form of governance at village level. Urban residents' committees usually cover anywhere between 100 and over 1,000 households. Reformers have suggested that urban electoral reform should begin with direct elections.

5.3   LEGAL SYSTEM

5.3.1   Legislation with Chinese Characteristics

The current Chinese Constitution was adopted for implementation by the 5th Session of the 5th National People's Congress (NPC) on December 4, 1982. Amendments were made to the Constitution at the 1st Session of the 7th NPC on April 12, 1988, the 1st Session of the 8th NPC on March 29, 1993, and the 2nd Session of the 9th NPC on March 15, 1999, respectively. It is clear that the leadership of the CPC is stressed in the Constitution. Also, the

guidance of Marxism-Leninism and Mao Zedong thought is regarded as the proper intellectual framework and ideology for leading the country to a socialist state under the people's democratic dictatorship.

The National People's Congress (NPC) is deemed to be the 'highest organ of state power' in Article 57 of the Constitution of the People's Republic of China (1982). The NPC is partially composed of a permanent body called the Standing Committee of the NPC (Articles 57 and 65–69). The NPC is the unicameral body vested with the authority to establish the laws in China pursuant to Article 58. Deputies to the NPC are elected to their positions for five-year terms (Art. 60). Some powers of the NCP are to amend the Constitution, enact laws, elect the President and Vice President of the PRC, elect the Chiefs of the Supreme People's Court, decide issues of war and peace, and they also have various removal powers (Arts 62–63). When the NPC is not in session, the Standing Committees can enact amendments and additions to laws passed by the NPC (Art. 89).

China's legislation is also created at more local levels by the people's congresses of provinces, autonomous regions, municipalities, prefectures, and cities. The Constitution

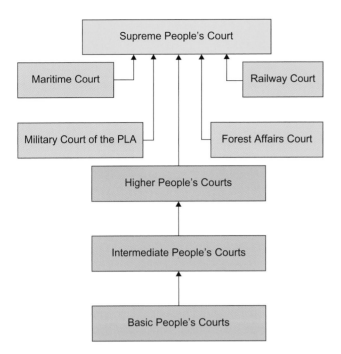

FIGURE 5.4 The legal hierarchy of China.

provides the structure, authority, and duties of the Local People's Congresses in Articles 95–111. All of the local regulations that are passed by these lower people's congresses must comply with the Constitution, laws passed by the NPC, and the people's congresses above each of the local congresses in the hierarchy.

The judicial system of the PRC is established in Articles 123–135, and consists of the people's courts, the Supreme People's Court, the people's procuratorates, the Supreme People's Procuratorate, military procuratorates and other special people's procuratorates. Article 129 refers to the people's procuratorates as 'state organs for legal supervision'. There is a hierarchy within the court structure from the top down: the Supreme People's Courts, the Higher People's Courts, the Intermediate People's Courts, and the Basic People's Courts (see Figure 5.4).

The duties of each of these Courts are as follows:

- The Supreme People's Court has the original jurisdiction over cases that have been assigned to it by law, or over cases that it decides it should try. It has jurisdiction over appeals or protests from the Higher People's Court and Special People's Courts.
- The Higher People's Courts have the jurisdiction in the first instance in cases assigned by law, or transferred from lower courts; major criminal cases which impact the entire province. The Courts also hear cases of appeals or protests against judgments and orders of lower courts.
- The Intermediate People's Courts have, in the first instance, the jurisdiction in some cases, including those

transferred from basic people's court; major cases dealing with foreign parties; counter-revolutionary cases; criminal cases subject to a sentence of life imprisonment or death; cases where foreigners have committed crimes. They also hear appeals and protests.

- Basic People's Courts are local-level courts to adjudicate criminal and civil cases of first instance. Excluded from jurisdiction are criminal cases carrying a penalty of death or life imprisonment, as well as certain foreign civil cases. The courts can request that more important cases be transferred to a higher court.

At present, the Basic People's Courts are comprised of thousands of courts at county level. There are hundreds of Intermediate People's Courts at prefectural or municipal level and 31 Higher People's Courts located in the provinces. Additionally, there are a number of specialized courts, for example, those dealing with railway transportation, forest affairs, the People's Liberation Army (PLA), and maritime issues.

Litigants are generally limited to one appeal, on the theory of finality of judgment by two trials. Cases of second instances are often reviewed *de novo* as to both law and facts. Requests for appellate review take the form of appeals and protests (in criminal cases). Appeals are lodged by parties to the case, defendants, and private prosecutors. Protests are filed by the procuratorate in criminal cases, when it is believed that an error has occurred in the law, or facts, as determined by the judgment or order of the court of first instance. In civil cases the procuratorate does not possess a right to file a direct protest, but it can initiate adjudication supervision via a protest. Adjudication supervision refers to a type of discretionary 'post-final' decision review, which may occur in certain situations in criminal cases.

5.3.2 Legalization Without Democracy

For most of the past thousands of years, the Chinese legal system was based on Confucian ideology that emphasized ethics and relationships between the people and their leaders. Disputes were settled through relationship-based methods such as mediation. The court system was undeveloped and rarely used. After 1949, a Marxist-Leninist overlay was constructed, which was also to some extent mixed with traditional adherence to Confucian-based conflict mediation. It was not until the economic reforms of the late 1970s that a true institutional legal system was introduced, mostly to deal with the demands of the growing economy. As the CCP scrambled after 1978 to train lawyers and codify laws, business law took precedence over laws pertaining to civil liberties and individual freedoms. Despite an enormous growth in the legal industry, the system is today still grossly lacking in its neutrality, capacity, and mandate, especially in poor and remote areas in China.

Box 5.1   Who Do You Speak for, the Party or the People?

In a construction area designated for the building of affordable housing in Xigang village, Xushui town, Zhengzhou city, Henan province, real estate developers have built 12 townhouses and 2 luxurious houses. In June 2009, after receiving complaints from local villagers that the land has not been developed according to its intended use (i.e., the construction of economically affordable apartments), a reporter went to Zhengzhou for an interview with Lu Jun, deputy Bureau Director of Zhengzhou Planning Bureau. Mr Lu interrogated the reporter: 'Why doesn't your radio station mind its own business? Who do you speak for, the Party or the people?'

It is well known that the land planning bureau controls the lifeline for developers to get rich, so it has become the area hardest hit by corruption. In the planning of urban construction, some corrupt officials have become the developer's spokesmen in the government because they are bribed by the developers. Officials and businessmen work in collusion with each other to form a community of common interest. For the interest of the small community, they set aside the legal interests of the country and the ordinary people, take advantage of their public power to grab state-run assets, people's benefits, and wealth, and push themselves to the opposite side of the ordinary people.

Source: www.echinacities.com. Accessed on November 5, 2011.

Most importantly, China's legal system lacks neutrality. The CCP approves all court appointments, and judges are technically responsible to the Party, not to the people (see Box 5.1). From the Basic, Intermediate, Higher Level People's Court, and Supreme People's Court, the CCP hand is evident. The CCP's Political and Legal Committee has the power to intervene in deliberations, and even to overturn verdicts issued. In addition, the infrastructure lacks capacity. For example, there is one lawyer per 10,000 people in China (the ratio is one lawyer per 550 people in the United States).[5] And finally, in many Western democracies, the ultimate arbiter of a law's constitutionality is the court system. In China, this function becomes muddled and the CCP apparatus often rules on the interpretation of its own laws.

Recently, there have been some reforms with substantive democratic content – including, for example, village elections. However, this has been unevenly implemented and often fails to live up to hopes for open and contested elections, and reaches only the most local of posts. The electoral law for village-level administrations is still weaker as an instrument of democracy, as are procedures for the indirect selection of higher-level people's congresses. The imperfectly implemented village elections law and the elections that have been held under the law allow much bounded participation, monitor potentially explosive peasant discontent, and strengthen the capacity of the regime. These 'elections serve these functions by sometimes weeding out the most ineffective and despised agents of the regime and by recruiting new cadres who can command popular support as well as their superiors' confidence' (deLisle, 2008, p. 198).[6]

Most tangible reform in China's legal system has taken place in the area of civil litigation. These primarily concern business disputes associated with China's rapid economic modernization in which people seek protection and redress from a wide array of abuses committed in the pursuit of economic competitive advantage: patent infringement, business transactions that are not honored, individuals who have been displaced by private and state-directed construction, and labor disputes, to name a few. Since 1978, prompted by the need to provide a safe environment for foreign capital, the CCP has increasingly codified business laws and sought to train its lawyers and judges to deal effectively and efficiently with the growing civil and commercial caseload. With the current system skewed toward resolving business-business and state-business disputes, the individual plaintiff is often at a significant disadvantage.

Other avenues open to individuals who feel they have complaints against the state include the petition system, mediation, and protests – however, none of these options are as effective as in the Western nations. The petition system auspiciously provides an avenue by which individuals can lodge complaints about treatment they have received from the government, other individuals, or private companies. Remember, in China the hand of the state is involved everywhere, visibly and invisibly, even when disputes seem to involve private companies. There are few private companies that do not have some form of government subsidization and/or regulation.

Another alternative to the court system includes mediation, which has been described as only somewhat effective, and for which there is not adequate capacity to process all disputes. Some instead turn to protests, mainly in rural areas where they get local attention; protesters are often disbanded, and their complaints never communicated to high-level decision-makers. And finally, an important alternative to litigation (one that is used to powerful advantage elsewhere) is severely lacking in China: free media. Many

5. Source: 'The Legal System in China.' Available at http://worldsavvy. org/monitor/index.php?option=com_content&view=article&id=113& Itemid=176. Accessed on November 15, 2011.

6. See O'Brien and Li (2000), Wang (1998), and Paler (2005) for more detailed analyses.

scandals and disputes are settled in other countries simply because they find their way to the newspaper or other public outlets. Perpetrators are shamed and agreements are negotiated. Without recourse to a free press, the Chinese are denied access to a key avenue for airing grievances.

The most important distinction between how China and many other countries deal with criminal defendants is in how they perceive presumption of guilt. In the West, criminal suspects are presumed innocent until proven guilty, and generally cannot be arrested and charged without sufficient evidence of wrongdoing. When a suspect does go to trial, it is the duty of the prosecution to prove his/her guilt beyond reasonable doubt. Abuses exist within these systems, but the underpinnings favor the individual defendant against the state until guilt is proven.

For a long period of time in China, suspects have been assumed guilty by the system and must be proven innocent. This is a critical distinction; suspects face incredible hurdles in proving their innocence; and China's appeals system similarly favors the prosecution. Freedom from unreasonable search, seizure, torture, and detention, as well as the right to a fair trial are major demands placed on China by the human rights community worldwide. The CCP aims to build the legal infrastructure of the country and has embarked on this in its technocratic manner of studying the laws of other countries and carefully codifying its 'Chinese characteristics'. However, many of the abuses occur at the hands of local and provincial officials among whom corruption is rampant and over whom the central CCP is able to exercise little control. When central CCP elites have been able to detect abuses and arrest responsible officials, the press is ordered to showcase progress for their own people and to outside critics.

Without adequate transparency within the CCP, or within the legal system in which CCP officials wield a heavy hand, reform will be difficult. While the CCP has promised that there will be movement on both laws and procedures, ordinary people in China still believe that the situation on the ground has not changed significantly. As in other areas, reform in the legal system has often served only a safety valve function – more cases processed, more complaints heard, yet the outcomes remain largely unchanged. Whether these small steps forward ultimately add up to momentum remains to be seen, but many believe that an expanding legal system could bring about true democratic progress in the PRC. For now, though, there are many who believe that such small venting in the system actually serves to strengthen the authoritarian state.

5.4 (DIS)ADVANTAGES OF CHINA'S POLITICAL SYSTEM

5.4.1 Authoritarianism, Chinese Style

Since China undertook its reforms in 1978, the Chinese economy has grown at an average rate of nearly ten percent a year. As of 2010, China's per capita GDP was already twelve times greater than it was three decades ago. Obviously, for the past three decades, the country's economic development has been reliant upon an unconventional approach – a combination of mixed ownership, basic property rights, and heavy government intervention.

The term 'Washington Consensus' was initially coined in 1989 by John Williamson to describe a set of ten specific economic policy prescriptions that he considered should constitute the 'standard' reform package promoted for crisis-wracked developing countries by Washington-based institutions such as the IMF, the World Bank, and the US Treasury Department. It is sometimes used in a narrower sense to refer to economic reforms that were prescribed just for developing nations, which included advice to reduce government deficits, to liberalize and deregulate international trade and cross border investment, and to pursue export led growth (Williamson, 1989).[7]

In 2004, Joshua Cooper Ramo, the former foreign editor of *Time* magazine, in his book entitled *The Beijing Consensus*, argues that there is a new 'Beijing Consensus' emerging with distinct attitudes to politics, development, and the global balance of power. Ramo argues that China offers hope to developing countries after the collapse of the Washington Consensus. China has provided, more or less, a more equitable paradigm of economic take-off for poor countries. According to Ramo, '[the Beijing Consensus] replaces the widely-discredited Washington Consensus, an economic theory made famous in the 1990s for its prescriptive, Washington-knows-best approach to telling other nations how to run themselves' (Ramo, 2004, p. 4).

To develop this further, Stefan Halper, in his book *The Beijing Consensus: How China's Authoritarian Model Will Dominate the Twenty-First Century*, argues that China has provided a welcome non-judgmental alternative to many nations with domestic, social, and economic conditions that are similar to China itself. This new approach to foreign aid, combined with admiration for China's economic success, is boosting its world influence, as well as access to energy and other natural resources. Meanwhile, China's autocratic leadership, which shows no sign of liberalizing, has set the foundation for future economic successes; by contrast, US economic progress seems hindered by its democratic processes (Halper, 2010).

On March 10, 2010, Singapore's www.zaobao.com published an article entitled *Comparative Politics: Why is China Superior to the West in the Political System?* (Song, 2010). In this article, the author points out that the great achievements of China result from its effective political system, which could pave a completely different way to

---

7. The Washington Consensus was most influential during the 1990s. Since then, it has become increasingly controversial.

modernization, named the China Model. The author summarizes six major advantages of China's political system, as follows.

The first advantage is that under the one-party system, China could formulate a long-term plan for national development and ensure stabilization of its policies without being affected by the alternation of parties with different positions and ideologies.

The second advantage lies in its high efficiency, and promptly effective reaction to emerging challenges and opportunities, especially in response to sudden and catastrophic accidents. The author gives the following examples: Terminal No. 3 of the Beijing Capital International Airport built for the Beijing Olympics was finished in three years, which is not enough time for the approval process in the West. In 2008, after the Wenchuan earthquake that hits once in a generation, China impressed the whole world by its quick response and efficient post-disaster reconstruction.

The third advantage is China's effective containment of corruption in the social transition period. It is generally accepted that economic prosperity and social transition were usually accompanied by large amounts of corruption throughout human history. However, the author argues that, compared with India and Russia in the same period, China has had far less corruption.

The fourth advantage is a more responsible government in China. For example, in democratic societies, many officials are elected with fixed terms, and they then will not fall out of power before the end of their term unless they break the law, make wrong decisions, or take no action. Once their term expires, they will not be blamed for any problem. In China, however, the Principal Officials Accountability System is gradually improving, and officials must be responsible for their incompetence, negligence of duty, or mistakes at any time.

The fifth advantage lies in its personnel training and Cadre-Selection System and avoiding the waste of talented people. In many Western nations, presidents and governors are elected; but in China only those who have rich and successful working experiences at the lower or local levels can be selected to be higher-ranked officials. Therefore, the author argues that China's selection of cadres from the lower to a higher level and conscious personnel training is superior to the West's election system.

The last advantage is that one party can truly represent the whole people. Under the Western multiparty system, each party represents different interest groups. But in China, since the reform and opening up, economic policies have been made by the CCP without special bias in favor of any interest groups.

5.4.2 Chinese Political Sustainability

However, the Chinese political and economic systems are far less perfect than what was just described above. In fact,

over the last 30 years, the Chinese economy has moved unmistakably toward the market doctrines of neoclassical economics, with an emphasis on prudent fiscal policy, economic openness, privatization, market liberalization, and the protection of private property (Yao, 2010). Since the beginning of its open-door policies, China has benefited increasingly from global interdependence and the modern world's free flow of goods, capital, and people. However, with those benefits have also come the responsibilities of accountability and transparency. China's party-state system has exposed the dearth of political dynamics.

Since the CCP lacks legitimacy in the classic democratic sense, it has to seek performance-based legitimacy instead. So far, this strategy has succeeded. And there was a proliferation of high-rise buildings and massive construction projects (the Three Gorges Dam, the Olympics Complex, the high-speed rail system, and so on). However, this also resulted in declining health care (hospitals, like schools, also became money-making centers for local bureaucrats), illegal expropriation of farmers' land, and more corruption, all of which have led to increasing social disorder among peasants who are finding themselves worse off (Huang, 2008). On the other hand, cadres' pay has increased rapidly, which has, as an example in 2010, induced thousands of college graduates to compete for a single government post.

The Severe Acute Respiratory Syndrome (SARS) epidemic which spread throughout China in April 2003 exposed some of China's institutional weakness.[8] Yet the greatest impact of the SARS crisis may be on China's antiquated political system. Chinese mismanagement of the outbreak has plainly exposed just how far political reform has lagged behind economic development. Beijing's long concealment of the truth is exposing political faultiness by simultaneously weakening the economy and damaging the government's credibility. The crisis has undermined traditional supporters, aggravating old demographic strains, and emboldening detractors to make more assertive protests against government policy. While the growing pressure from a more demanding public and an increasingly interdependent world has forced China to re-evaluate its political and socioeconomic policies, the extent of any resulting political reform depends upon whether or not the enhanced incentives for accountability and transparency among public officials override the traditional incentives for party and factional loyalty.

---

8. From November 2002 to 2003, SARS infected over 8,000 people in 30 countries and killed more than 500. In addition to the human toll, it was inflicting significant economic damage across Asia. Besides Hong Kong, which was among the worst hit, GDP growth rates in Taiwan, Singapore, and Thailand were also lower in 2003. Nowhere was SARS having more impact than on mainland China, where the disease started. – Guo (2007, p. 104).

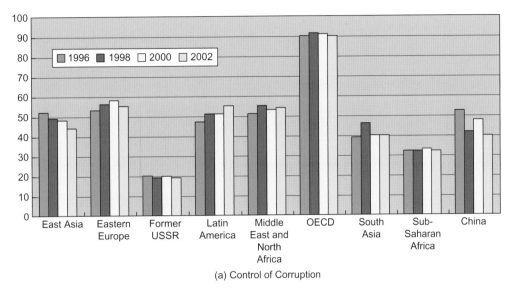

(a) Control of Corruption

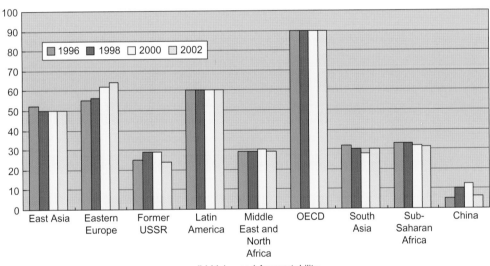

(b) Voice and Accountability

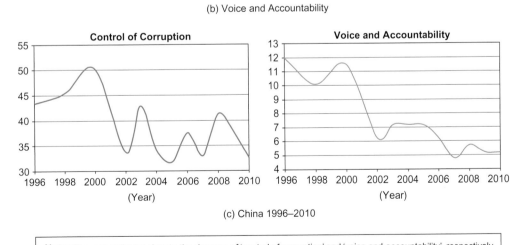

(c) China 1996–2010

Note: The y-coordinates denote the degrees of 'control of corruption' and 'voice and accountability', respectively (100 = maximum level; 0 = minimum level).

FIGURE 5.5 Social and political capacities, China and the world. *Source: Created by author based on Kaufmann et al. (2008) for (a) and (b) and the Worldwide Governance Indicators (available at http://info.worldbank.org/governance/wgi/pdf/wgidataset.xls. Accessed on October 25, 2011) for (c). Details on the data sources, the aggregation method, and the interpretation of the indicators, can be found in the methodology paper of Kaufmann et al. (2010).*

Obviously, there are signs that the Chinese model will not last because of the growing income inequality and the internal and external imbalances it has created. The CCP's free-market policies have led to increasing inequalities in China, both between different groups of people and among regions. For example, China's overall Gini coefficient – a measure of income inequality in which zero equals perfect equality and one absolute inequality – reached about 0.50 in 2010, which is higher than most of the other economies (see Figure 8.2 of Chapter 8). In addition, China also has the highest urban-rural income gap in the world. As the Chinese people demand more than economic gains as their income increases, it will become increasingly difficult for the CCP to contain or discourage social discontent.

China's astronomic growth has left it in a precarious situation, however. Other developing countries have suffered from the so-called middle-income trap – a situation that often arises when a country's per capita GDP reaches the range of $3,000 to $8,000, the economy stops growing, income inequality increases, and social conflicts erupt. China has now entered this stage, and it still remains unclear how this will affect the Chinese economy and society in the long term. At present, the Chinese government has tried to manage popular discontent by implementing

---

Box 5.2   Documentary

SCHOLARS AT RISK
N E T W O R K

People's Republic of China

Dear Sirs:

On behalf of the Scholars at Risk Network, I am writing to inquire about Dr. Guo, who until recently served as professor at the Beijing Graduate School of China University of Mining and Technology ("CUMT").

The Scholars at Risk Network is a non-governmental organization based at the University of Chicago with members at more than 70 universities and colleges in the United States and partners worldwide. Scholars at Risk is dedicated to protecting the human rights of scholars and to raising awareness, understanding of and respect for the principles of academic freedom and its constituent freedoms of thought, opinion, and expression-- freedoms essential to any healthy academic community and civil society generally. In cases such as this one, Scholars at Risk inquires on behalf of an individual scholar.

We received allegations about Dr. Guo's employment situation at CUMT, information which alleges an unwillingness to allow him to seek positions at other universities, or to accept offers received from several other prestigious academic institutions in China. We are writing to request your help in clarifying the situation. We would appreciate your responding to our letter and providing whatever information you deem appropriate.

According to the information we received, Dr. Guo had tried to accept an invitation to Peking University in 1996. Shortly thereafter, his wife's employment at CUMT was terminated. We understand she had been working there since 1981. We are also led to believe that in March 2002 Dr. Guo had been offered employment at the Chinese Academy of Sciences, and that CUMT had originally consented to his departure, but later the consent was rescinded. These allegations, if true, raise serious concerns about Dr. Guo's ability to conduct his work and to freely and openly exchange ideas and information with colleagues at other institutions. It is unclear to us at this point, however, whether the allegations are in fact true and, even if true, whether the situation is specific to Dr. Guo or is suggestive of a larger problem effecting many scholars. We therefore respectfully ask for your help in clarifying the situation.

Thank you for your urgent attention to this matter. We look forward to your reply.

Very truly yours,

Robert J. Quinn
Director

HUMAN RIGHTS PROGRAM, THE UNIVERSITY OF CHICAGO, 5828 S. UNIVERSITY AVE., CHICAGO, IL, 60637 USA
TEL: 773-834-4659 * FAX: 773-702-9286 * http://scholarsatrisk.uchicago.edu * E-MAIL: rquinn@uchicago.edu

various programs that could quickly address early signs of unrest, such as re-employment centers for unemployed workers, migration programs aimed at lowering regional disparities, and improvement of infrastructure, health care, and education in rural areas. Those measures, however, may be too weak to discourage the emergence of powerful interest groups seeking to influence the government (Yao, 2010).

5.5 FURTHER IMPLICATIONS

While China's current political system has been driving its economic growth strongly (to be discussed in Chapter 8), it has also led to the development of a series of socioeconomic problems. However, the large surge in income inequalities was not the only unwanted result of the Chinese-style reform. The worsening of social and political progress during the 1990s and the 2000s is another example. For example, China's 'control of corruption' score was more than 50 in 1996 (see Figure 5.5(a)) but it dropped to only 30 in 2007; between 1996 and 2002 its score in terms of 'voice and accountability' was among the lowest of all of the nations considered by the World Bank (see Figure 5.5(b)) and there is no sign of improvements between 2002 and 2007 (see Figure 5.5(c)). Without good reason, China's party-state political system lacked the informational and incentive roles of democracy that, working mainly through open public discussion, could be of pivotal importance for the reach of social and public policies.

Technically, China has not had an independent judiciary or a legal system that operates outside the influence of the ruling CCP. This is the so-called socialism with Chinese characteristics and the one that distinguishes China from Western democracies in which the court system is a critical component of the checks and balances placed on the other branches of government. In fact, China's lack of an independent judicial system exacerbates all the other fault lines running through the authoritarian state; there simply is no effective recourse available to individuals whose interests are harmed by the excesses of CCP officials, laws, and institutions. This situation is particularly serious in China's rural, marginal areas. The time when the average individual seeks a forum in which to officially air grievances and pursue some form of justice in China has yet to come (see Box 5.2).

Before ending our discussion about the characteristics of China's political and administrative systems, let's finish our account of the story told by Hanfeizi at the beginning of this chapter:

Feeling it strange, the Duke sent a man to ask Bianque for the reason. 'Well, an ailment lying in between the skin and the muscles remains on the surface, and so external application with warm water and ointment can cure it,' said Bianque, 'If it sinks into muscles, acupuncture will do good; if it resides in the stomach and the intestines, a decoction of herbs will take effect. But when the sickness penetrates into the bone marrow, it becomes fatal and nothing can be done about it. Now, as the Duke has come to that last stage, I have nothing to recommend.' Five days after that, the Duke felt pains and ordered his men to look for Bianque, but to find that he had fled to the state of Qin. Soon afterwards, the Duke died.

REFERENCES

deLisle, J. (2008). Legislation without democratization in China under Hu Jintao. In Cheng Li (Ed.), *China's changing political landscape: prospects for democracy.* Washington, DC: The Brookings Institution Press, 2008.

Guo, R. (2007). *How the Chinese economy works – 2E.* London and New York: Palgrave-Macmillan.

Guo, R. (2010). *An introduction to the Chinese economy works – the driving forces behind modern day China.* Singapore: John Wiley and Sons.

Halper, Stefan (2010). *The Beijing consensus: how China's authoritarian model will dominate the twenty-first century.* New York: Basic Books.

Huang, Yasheng (2008). *Capitalism with Chinese characteristics: entrepreneurship and the state.* Cambridge: Cambridge University Press.

Kaufmann, D., Kraay, A., & Mastruzzi, M. (2010). *The worldwide governance indicators: a summary of methodology, data and analytical issues.* World Bank policy research working paper no. 5430. <http://papers.ssrn.com/sol3/papers.cfm?abstract_id>.

Kaufmann, D., Kraay, A., & Mastruzzi, M. (2008). *Governance matters VII: aggregate and individual governance indicators, 1996–2007.* World Bank policy research working paper No. 4654, Washington, DC: World Bank.

NBS (2010). *China statistical yearbook.* Beijing: China Statistics Publishing House.

O'Brien, K., & Li, L. (2000). Accommodating 'Democracy' in a one-party: introducing village elections in China. *The China Quarterly, 162,* 465–489.

Paler, L. (2005). China's legislation law and the making of a more orderly and representative legislative system. *The China Quarterly, 182,* 301–318.

Pomfret, J. (2002). *Under Jiang, party changed to remain in power: communist apparatus still rules China, though Country has been transformed.* Washington Post Foreign Service, November 7. Available at <http://www.washingtonpost.com/ac2/wp-dyn?pagename=article&node=&contentId=A20178-2002Nov6&notFound=true>. Accessed on December 9, 2011.

Ramo, J. C. (2004). *The Beijing consensus.* London: The Foreign Policy Centre.

Wang, X. (1998). Administrative procedure reforms in China's rule of law context. *Columbia Journal of Asian Law, 2,* 251–277.

Williamson, J. (1989). What Washington means by policy reform. In John Williamson (Ed.), *Latin American readjustment: how much has happened.* Washington, DC: Institute for International Economics.

Yao, Y. (2010). The end of the Beijing consensus – can China's model of authoritarian growth survive? *Foreign Affairs* January/February.

Chapter 6

Economic Systems in Transition

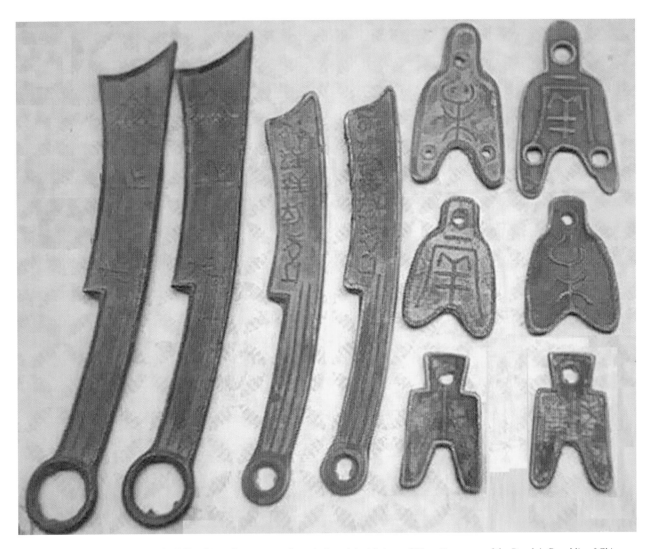

Ancient Chinese coinage. *Source: The Yellow River Conservancy Commission of the Ministry of Water Resources of the People's Republic of China.*

In ancient China, with the opening of exchange between farmers, artisans, and merchants, there came into use money of tortoise shells, cowrie shells, gold… Archeological evidence shows that the earliest use of the dao (knife) and bu (spade) monies was in the Spring and Autumn period (770–476 BC). There is no doubt that the well-known dao and bu monies were closely associated with military and agricultural activities. What is more

interesting is that these monies represented China's political and economic transformations in ancient times.

There lived a young man in the state of Yan (today's Beijing). He was at a loss as to how to behave all the time. As the days went by, he even began to doubt whether he should walk the way he did, for he felt more and more that his walking gestures were too clumsy and awkward. One day, he learnt that people in Handan

Understanding the Chinese Economies. DOI: http://dx.doi.org/10.1016/B978-0-12-397826-4.00006-8
© 2013 Elsevier Inc. All rights reserved.

85

walked most gracefully. He could not picture in what way their walking gestures were graceful and, therefore, decided to go there to learn how to walk. As soon as he arrived in Handan, he was dazzled to find that everything was novel. He learnt from the children there how to walk, because he thought the children's walking gestures were lively and pleasing to the eye. He learnt from the old people there how to walk, because he thought the old people's walking gestures were steady. He learnt from the women there how to walk, because he thought the women's walking gestures were beautiful. That being the case with him, in less than half a month he even forgot how to walk. As he had already used up his traveling expenses, he had to crawl back home.

– Zhuangzi (c. 369–286 BC)

6.1 ECONOMIC TRANSITION, CHINESE STYLE

6.1.1 An Overview

From the foundation of the People's Republic of China (PRC) in 1949, the Chinese government had uneasily followed the Soviet Union and adopted a centrally planned economy (CPE). Generally, this kind of planning system has the following problems. First of all, it makes almost all productive enterprises subordinate to administrative organs. To a large extent, this neglects the economic independence of the enterprises and thereby leads to the neglect of their material interests and responsibilities, blunting levels of initiative and enthusiasm. Secondly, the system involves excessive command planning from above and is overly rigid. So long as the enterprises meet their stipulated targets, they are considered to have performed satisfactorily – regardless of whether or not its products satisfy society's needs.

In the Third Plenum of the 11th Chinese Communist Party Central Committee (CCPCC), held on December 18, 1978, Deng Xiaoping and his senior supporters took decisive control of the CCPCC. This ended what has been described as two years of uncertainty and indecisive strategy and policy following the death of Mao Zedong. The Third Plenum of the 11th CCPCC, which was held in December 1978, marked a major turning point in China's reform and development. After a decade of turmoil brought about by the Cultural Revolution (1966–76), the new direction set at this meeting was toward economic development and away from class struggle. The course was laid for the CCP to move the world's most populous nation toward the ambitious targets of the Four Modernizations in sectors of industry, agriculture, science and technology, and national defense.

In brief, the institutional evolution in the Chinese economy since 1978 has followed a gradual path and may be outlined by the six phases listed below:

1. Centrally planned economy (before 1978)
2. Economy regulated mainly by planning and supplemented by market (1978–84)
3. Commodity economy with a plan (1985–87)
4. Combination of planned and market economy (1988–91)
5. Socialist market economy with *state* ownership as main form (1992–97)
6. Socialist market economy with *public* ownership as main form (from 1998 onwards).

6.1.2 Plan-Market Mix

Guided by the CCPCC (1984), the roles of central planning and market regulation were reversed in the modified system 'commodity economy with a plan'.[1] Generally, Phase 3 was known to be based loosely on the Hungarian model of market socialism. Nevertheless, the state continued to own the bulk of large and medium-sized enterprises and to regulate the production and pricing of a number of strategic commodities, but the market mechanism was permitted to play an increasing role in the pricing and allocation of goods and services and in the allocation and remuneration of labor in some non-strategic sectors.

In the ideological struggles between the radical reformers and the conservatives, there was a new term 'socialist commodity economy'[2] from 1988 to 1989, but this was replaced by Phase 4 ('combination of planned and market economy') immediately after the Tiananmen incidents of May–June 1989. Nevertheless, Phase 4 was extremely important insofar as it legitimized the abolition of the traditional mechanisms of the central planning system in favor of the introduction of market regulation.

During the 1980s, China's reform and open-door policy resulted in an increase in economic prosperity, but also led to some political and social instability. This can be witnessed by the CCP's 'anti-spiritual pollution' and 'anti-bourgeois liberalization' campaigns, which were launched in 1983 and 1987, respectively. This kind of political disequilibrium between the CCP conservatives and intellectuals reached its peak in 1989, and, in combination with other factors such as high inflation and official corruption, eventually became a leading cause of student protests against the CCP and central government during May–June 1989. As soon as the aftermath of the Tiananmen incident had subsided, there was a shift of power in economic decision making from the reformers to the conservatives. This led to a temporary brake being placed on China's economic reforms and also its rates of economic growth.

At the beginning of the 1990s the socialist camp in Eastern Europe and the former Soviet Union both suffered

---

1. Even though the term 'commodity' in the Chinese understanding is closely related to the concept of market economy, we may assume that it was used here to distinguish the Chinese economy from the Western-style market system.

2. The term was firstly publicized in bold headlines in the CCP's official newspapers (such as *People's Daily* and *Workers' Daily*) in early 1988.

sudden collapses. China's immediate reaction to the collapse of these communist regimes was a policy of re-centralization, but the CCP soon realized that its legitimacy could be sustained only through economic growth brought about by further reforms. Amid the political deadlock between the reformers and conservatives concerning how to combine the planned and market economic systems, Deng Xiaoping made his now famous southern tour to the province of Guangdong in early 1992. Drawing on regional support for continued reforms, Deng's visit tipped the political balance at the CCPCC and the central government. This resulted in China's official declaration in October 1992 of its intention to build a 'socialist market economy', as well as a calling for faster reforms and economic development.

In the early 1990s, some of the policies applied to the coastal SEZs were extended to a list of inland regions and cities along the Yangtze River and, thanks to the normalization of China's diplomatic relations with the former USSR, to the border cities and towns adjacent to Russia and other neighboring countries. Furthermore, many inland cities, which did not qualify for this special treatment, established numerous economic and technological development zones (ETDZs) inside their regions. It is noteworthy that the wide-ranging pro-development reforms during these years brought about not only high economic growth but also the two-digit inflationary pressures that occurred in 1993. Faced with an overheating economy, the Chinese government announced a series of banking and financial reforms in 1994, which were aimed at eliminating some of the structural inefficiencies in the financial sector.

6.1.3 Socialist Market Economy

China's ambitious agenda geared toward transforming the Chinese economy into a market-oriented one was unveiled as early as 1992, when Deng Xiaoping's Southern Speech[3] eventually had an influence on China's decision makers. On November 14, 1993, a formal document entitled 'Decision of the CCPCC on Several Issues Concerning the Establishment of a Socialist Market Economic Structure' was finally approved by the Third Plenum of the 14th CCPCC. The aim of the decision was that the government should withdraw from direct involvement in enterprise management. Instead, 'Government functions in economic management consist mainly of devising and implementing macroeconomic control policies, appropriate construction of infrastructure facilities, and creation of a favorable environment for economic development' (Article 16). The Plenum also declared that 'the government shall take significant steps in the reform of taxation, financing,

investment and planning systems, and establish a mechanism in which planning, banking and public finance are coordinated and mutually check each other while strengthening the overall coordination of economic operations' (Article 17).

The 15th National Congress of the CCP, held in 1997, witnessed a historic breakthrough in terms of the reform of the ownership structure of the national economy. The shift in the CCP's view on ownership is now enshrined in the Chinese constitution with two amendments to the constitution at the Ninth National NPC held in March 1998. The first amendment was to Article 6 of the constitution, which saw the addition of a clause stating that China is now at its preliminary stage of socialism. This amendment is used to justify having public, instead of state, ownership as the main form of ownership of the means of production. The clause further states that public ownership will develop alongside other forms of ownership. The second constitutional amendment was to Article 21, with the addition of a clause stating that individual, private, and other forms of non-public ownership are 'important components of a socialist economy' and they 'supplement the system of socialist public ownership'.

China's commitment to the creation of a market-oriented economy has been the central plank of its program of economic reform, and considerable progress toward this end has been achieved since 1978, through the gradual withdrawal of the government from the allocation, pricing, and distribution of goods. To date the reforms introduced have achieved remarkable results. Particularly praiseworthy is the fact that the Chinese-type reforms have avoided the collapse in output characteristic of transitions in other former CPEs and generated unprecedented increases in living standards across the country. Over the course of the past few decades, China has successfully implemented a stable economic reform and opening up to the outside world and, in particular, it has achieved faster economic growth than any other socialist or former socialist country in the world.

6.2 GETTING OUT OF PLAN

6.2.1 How the Planned Economy Worked

In traditional socialist countries, economic development is realized mainly through a plan worked out by the central planning authorities. The plan, however, is a mental construct which may or may not correctly reflect the objective requirements of economic development. If the plan is correct, economic development is smooth; if it is incorrect, not only is it of no help – it may even lead to stagnation and decline. Obviously this has been proven in China's economic sphere, especially during the pre-reform period.

During the early 1950s, the transformation of private ownership of the means of production into public

---

3. For details of the Speech, see Deng (1992, pp. 370–83).

Box 6.1   What is the Five-Year Plan?

China's basic national development policy is embodied in the 'Five-Year Plan for National Economic and Social Development'. This plan mainly serves to outline the physical/geographical distribution of large-scale construction projects and centers of productivity, as well as how resources are to be apportioned out to different sectors of the national economy. The plan also sets objectives and attempts to lay out a course for the national economy.

The First Five-Year Plan was started in 1953. The current plan is the 12th and runs from 2011 to 2015 (it is colloquially called 'Twelfth Five'). The five-year plans are approved by the National People's Congress (NPC), the highest legislative body in the PRC. The National Development and Reform Commission (formerly the National Planning Commission,

which was established in 1952) is responsible for drafting plan proposals.

As of the 'Eleven Five-Plan', the Chinese government replaced the Chinese term corresponding to the English 'Plan' with the equivalent 'Guidelines'. Although still informally referred to as a 'five-year plan', the new terminology implies a set of guidelines with longer lasting ramifications. This name change reflects a desire to keep abreast of the shift in focus towards the establishment of a market economy as well as reforms and paradigm shifts in the systems of government in China. Put differently, the only kind of plans that the relevant authorities can draft and execute are guidelines that take a market economy as a given, so the name was changed to reflect the evolving nature of the plan itself.

---

ownership and the establishment of a powerful socialist sector paved an effective way for planned development of the national economy. During the first Five-Year Plan (FYP) period (1953–57), much attention was paid to industrial construction, especially in heavy industry (see Box 6.1 for the definition of China's 'First-Year Plan'). At the same time, the socialist transformation of agriculture, handicrafts, and capitalist industry and commerce was effectively carried out. In line with these goals, 156 key projects and other items were arranged with the guidance of the Soviet Union. The first FYP was generally known by the PRC's central planners and economists to be very successful because all scheduled targets were fully met.[4]

Facing the economic difficulties during the late 1950s and early 1960s, the CCPCC and the State Council advanced a policy entitled 'Readjustment, consolidation, filling-out, and raising standards' (*tiaozheng*, *gonggu*, *chongshi*, *tigao*). The production targets for heavy industry were reduced and investment in capital construction was cut back. The accumulation rate, which had risen to its highest level (39.9 percent) in 1960, was adjusted sharply downwards, reaching only 10.4 percent by 1962. The enterprises with high production costs and large losses were closed or switched to other products. With these adjustments, the economy rapidly returned to normal in the following years.[5]

In contrast to the first FYP and the readjustment period (1963–65), the years 1958–60 provided a typical case of errors in planning, resulting in serious economic imbalances. During this period, the Great Leap Forward movement was effectively launched by the establishment of a series of high targets within a given period, most of which, however, were incapable of being fulfilled due to the limitation of resources and production capacities. To accomplish its ambitious target for an overnight entrance to the 'communist heaven', large quantities of raw materials and the labor force were diverted toward heavy industry while, in contrast, the development of agriculture and light industry received less attention. This situation lasted until 1960 when the serious imbalances between accumulation and consumption, and between heavy industry on one hand and agriculture and light industry on the other hand, occurred suddenly. Despite this profound lesson, similar problems arose again thereafter.[6]

Since a socialist economy is rigorously directed by state planning, as soon as errors occur in the plan, this will have an effect on every economic activity. China bore witness to this point by its experience and lessons. Theoretically, it is essential to make a 'perfect' plan for the healthy operation of the economy. However, it is almost impossible for the state planners to accurately manage a balance between social production and social needs and efficiently distribute the scarce resources even with the use of sophisticated computers. In fact, because of information constraints and asymmetries, the central planners could never obtain complete and accurate information on economic activities from which to formulate plans. Furthermore, the centrally planned system also generated a number of other problems. For example, as wages

---

4. For example, the gross value of industrial output (GVIO) grew at 18 percent annually, higher than the planned rate (14.7 percent); the annual gross value of agricultural output (GVAO) growth rate (4.5 percent) also exceeded the planned rate (4.3 percent) during this period (SSB, 1990).
5. From 1962 to 1965, the GVIO was growing at an annual rate of 17.9 percent, GVAO at 11.1 percent, and national income at 14.5 percent (Liu, 1982, p. 31).

6. See, for example, Liu (1982, pp. 28–51) for more detail.

were fixed, workers had no incentive to work after they had reached the factory's output quota. Any extra production might have led to the increase of the following year's quota while the level of salaries would remain unchanged. Factory managers and government planners frequently bargained over work targets, funds, and material supplies to be allocated to the factory. Usually, government agencies allocated less than managers requested so managers would, in turn, request more than they needed; when bargaining over production, the managers, however, proposed a smaller quota than they were able to finish, and so they were usually ordered to fulfill a larger quota than requested.[7]

China's decentralization of its mandatory planning system and the introduction of market mechanisms, which began in 1978, first focused on a gradual transition from the people's commune system (PCS) to the household responsibility system (HRS), under which farmers were free to decide what and how to produce in their contracted farmlands and, having fulfilled the state's production quotas, were permitted both to sell the excess of their produce on the free market and also to pursue some non-agricultural activities. In 1984, when urban reform was implemented, China aimed to regulate industrial production through the operation of market forces. In a similar manner to the system adopted in the agricultural sector, after fulfilling their output quotas, enterprises could make profits by selling their excess products at free or floating prices. It is worthwhile noting that the above efforts resulted inevitably in dual prices for commodities during the transition period and had both positive and negative effects (this will be discussed in detail in the next chapter).

6.2.2 Double-Track System

China's economic reform has followed a double-track system in which the reform was first implemented in agricultural products and thereafter spread slowly to consumer goods and intermediate goods. In each case, a free market, in which the price was subject to market regulations, developed in parallel with a controlled market, in which the price was kept almost unchanged at an officially fixed level. Because the price was higher in the market-regulated track than in the state-controlled track, the free market supply grew rapidly, and its share of total output rose steadily. Meanwhile, the planned price was able to rise incrementally until it approached the market price, when there was a narrowing of the gap between supply and demand.

During the 1980s and early 1990s the double-track system extended across almost every sphere of the Chinese economy, from agriculture, industry, commerce, transportation, post and telecommunications to healthcare, education, and so on. By the end of 1986, the number of key industrial products under the direct control of the State Planning Commission (SPC) had fallen from 120 to 60; accordingly, the share of industrial production fell from 40 percent to 20 percent; the number of commodities and materials distributed by the state (i.e., *tongpei wuzhi*) dropped from 250 to 20, and the number of goods controlled by the Ministry of Commerce (MOC) decreased from 188 to 25; the share of prices which were 'free' or 'floating' increased to about 65 percent in agriculture and supplementary products, 55 percent of consumer goods and 40 percent of production materials (State Council, 1988, p. 198). By the late 1990s, the dual-pricing system had decontrolled the majority of retail prices and agricultural and intermediate product prices and removed the mandatory plans of a large number of products including fuel and raw materials.

However, the dual-pricing system also created various distortions and speculative transactions. Specifically, this dual market provided opportunities for people who had access to state-controlled goods and materials to make large profits by buying them at an officially fixed low price and reselling them at a market-based price. This often led to unequal competition, as well as official corruption, especially at the early stage of reform.

6.2.3 Regional Differences

Between regions there are some slight differences in the process toward the decentralization of mandatory planning. Roughly speaking, the Eastern belt is more marketized than the Central belt, while the Western belt is the least marketized. For example, the share of the marketized agricultural products ranged between 20.3 percent (in Qinghai province) and 43.3 percent (in Jilin province) in 1988 and between 60.0 percent (in Henan province) and 98.8 percent (in Guangdong province) in 1994 (see Figure 6.1). It is more interesting to note that some developed provinces (such as Shanghai, Beijing, and Jiangsu) were not so highly marketized as the poor provinces (such as Anhui, Guangxi, and Hainan) in 1988. This probably stems from the fact that China's agricultural reform was first carried out in Anhui and other poor and agriculture-based provinces, whereas Shanghai and Beijing – the centrally administered municipalities with strong industrial bases – lagged behind those agriculture-based provinces. (More detailed analysis of China's agricultural reform will be conducted in Section 7.1.1 of Chapter 7.)

We observe that, from 1980 to 1988, the ratio of market-regulated price to state-controlled price was

---

7. This repetitive bargaining between the state planners and the managers usually reached a high tide during the national annual planning meetings arranged by the State Planning Commission (SPC).

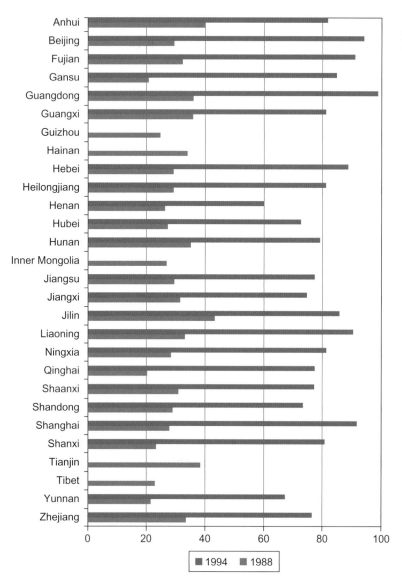

FIGURE 6.1 Shares of agricultural marketization by province, 1988 and 1994. *Sources: SSB (1989b, p. 130) and Riskin (1994, p. 350).*

negatively related to the share of the marketized agricultural products (the coefficient of correlation is 0.367, as shown in Figure 6.2a). This was reasonable and reflected to some extent the government's efforts to stabilize the market (that is, letting the provinces with market-regulated prices close to or lower than the state-controlled one share a higher proportion of the market-oriented reform in the agricultural sector during the earliest period of reform).

However, between 1988 and 1994, since the government allowed the speed of the market-oriented agricultural reform to be positively determined by the ratio of market-regulated price to state-controlled price (the coefficient of correlation is 0.0884, as shown in Figure 6.2b), high inflation and other macroeconomic risks occurred accordingly during this period. This is mainly due to the fact that, as will be discussed in detail later in subsection 6.4.1, China's agricultural reform was usually accompanied by

prices rising, since the prices of agricultural products were always kept at a very low level, especially during the early period of reform. In other words, during the late 1980s and early 1990s, had the agricultural reform followed the spatial pattern shown in Figure 6.2a, the Chinese economy would not have encountered so many problems.

6.3 LABOR AND EMPLOYMENT

6.3.1 Job Allocation During the Pre-Reform Era

Following the establishment of the new China, the labor market was officially eliminated because, according to Marxist theory, labor is not a commodity to be bought and sold. From the late 1950s, a system of state allocation of all urban employment was gradually introduced. After 1966,

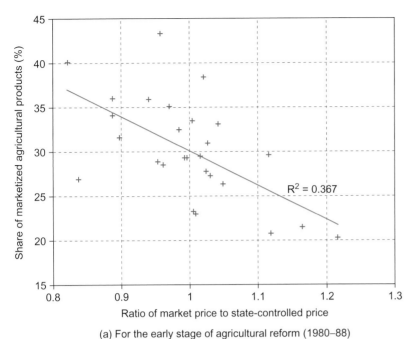

(a) For the early stage of agricultural reform (1980–88)

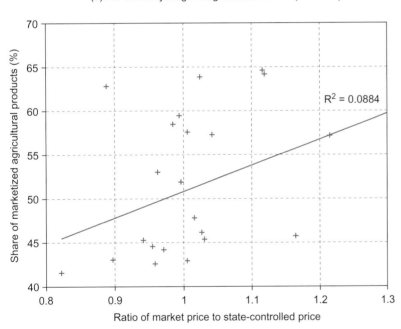

(b) For the later stage of agricultural reform (1988–94)

FIGURE 6.2 Market and state-controlled prices and agricultural reform. *Sources: Figure 6.1 and PYC (1995, p. 19).*

the state became responsible for the allocation of jobs for the entire urban labor force. All labor was allocated either to units owned by the states or to large collectives which were essentially the same as the state-owned units.

In the centrally planned system, the labor force was allocated to enterprises by the state and lifetime employment was guaranteed. Wages were also determined by the state on the principle of 'distribution according to working performance' (*anlao fenpei*). There is no doubt that this kind of system eliminated the widespread occurrence of unemployment that had usually existed in the 'old' China and that exists in all capitalist countries. It also effectively equalized wages and led to a considerable reduction in the gaps between the 'haves' and the 'have-nots'.

This rigid system of job allocation, however, has resulted in some disadvantages. Once people were employed in the state sector, their jobs were secure, regardless of the quality of their work. The system thus became known as the 'iron rice bowl' (*tie fanwan*) because of the employment security it implied. Under the equal

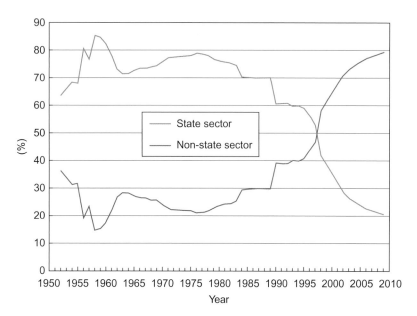

FIGURE 6.3 Employment shares of the state and non-state sectors in urban areas. *Source: NBS, various years.*

wage system (labeled 'eating from the same pot', or *daguo fan*) human resources were not allocated in an efficient manner. Egalitarianism, a lack of interest in economic outcomes, and a low sense of economic responsibility are among the expressions of this mentality. Employing units could not exercise free choice over who they selected and they also had to provide almost equal pay to workers whose performance might differ widely. This hindered the improvement of labor productivity.

Furthermore, the system did not encourage people to develop their talents and enthusiasm fully, since they could not choose the work which best suited them (see Box 5.2 of Chapter 5 for a case on this kind of situation).

6.3.2   Employment During the Transition Era

Recognizing the negative effects of this labor system, in the early 1980s the government began to introduce a series of reforms. The earliest efforts included the introduction of a contract system – setting up a production quota for each employee. Nevertheless, this system was not as successful in the industrial (mainly state-owned) sector as it was in the agricultural sector as a result of the complicated production processes in the former. In July 1986, the NPC announced four laws concerning employment. According to these laws, the governmental allocation of workers and lifetime employment were abolished and, simultaneously, a contract system (*hetong zhi*) was introduced. In the contract system, all employees were hired as contractual workers (*hetong gong*) and the employed terms varied from less than one year to more than five years. Naturally, when the contract expired, either the worker was laid off or the contract was renewed. Unfortunately, in practice, the contract system has not worked better in the state sector than in the non-state sector.

Since the introduction of its reform and its opening up to the outside world, the pattern of employment in China has been experiencing structural changes, along with the decline of the state sector and the expansion of the non-state sector in urban areas (see Figure 6.3). This kind of employment structure was the result of China's institutional transformations. Particularly noteworthy in this respect was China's large-scale privatization, or its policy of contracting out the operations of small and poorly performing SOEs, or letting them go bankrupt during the late 1990s and the early 2000s. For example, from 1995 to 2001, there were 45 million laid-off staff (excluding those who were normally retired from their current posts) in the urban state sector, of which about 30–35 million were re-employed, mostly in the non-state sector (Hu, 2002).

It should be noted that this dramatic decline in the share of employment in the state sector must have reflected China's social problems to some extent, although the Chinese government has made various efforts to secure the welfare of those workers who were laid off from the state sector. For example, there were a number of major protests organized by the SOE workers during the late 1990s when the number of laid-off workers reached a record level:

- More than 10,000 retrenched and retired SOE workers held sit-down protests and demonstrations in April 1997 (Panzhihua city, Sichuan province)
- About 100,000 retrenched workers and their relatives protested on the streets against the withdrawal of housing benefits and the misappropriation of their retirement funds in June 1997 (Mianyang city, Sichuan province)
- 30,000 textile workers protested against the non-payment of wages. They interrupted local traffic and surrounded the airport on December 3, 1997 (Jiamusi city, Heilongjiang province)

• 100,000 workers in four cities rioted during protests against retrenchments, non-payment of wages, official corruption, and other grievances during November–December 1997 (Heilongjiang province).[8]

6.4 PRODUCTION OWNERSHIP

6.4.1 Agriculture

More than two thousand years ago, there was a very special land management system in China, called 'jintian-zhi' (well-field system), whose structure looks like two Chinese characters 'jin' (or well) and 'tian' (or land) combined. This system, as described by Mencius (372–289 BC), reads:

Each block of land should be divided into nine plots, the whole containing nine hundred mu. The central plot will be the public field and the eight households, each owning a hundred-mu farm, will collaborate in cultivating the public field. Not until the public land has been properly attended to may each household attend to its private plot. This is how the countrymen should be required to learn.

After the founding of the PRC, the Chinese government reformed the ownership of land (*tugai*) and distributed the cultivated land proportionally among farmers. As a result, the farmers' incentives to work increased significantly. However, the new leadership only took this land reform as a provisional measure and did not consider it to be proper for a socialist economy. In the second half of the 1950s, China began to transform its private ownership of land into a collective one. As a result, the people's commune system (PCS) had been adopted as a universal form of agricultural production throughout mainland China.[9]

Under the PCS, land was owned collectively and the output was distributed to each household according to the work points (*gongfen*). The state purchased a major share of the grain output and distributed it to the non-agricultural population through government agencies. For much of the pre-reform period, the independent accounting unit was the production team. In the Great Leap Forward and the high tide of the Cultural Revolution, the production brigade (usually including several production teams) and even the people's commune (usually including several production brigades) were selected as independent accounting units in some 'advanced' areas where peasants were persuaded to pool their resources. Naturally, the PCS has been generally known to provide disincentives for the farmers to work harder.

The PCS lasted for more than 20 years before the Chinese government began to introduce a household-based and production-related responsibility system – the household responsibility system (HRS) – in the early 1980s. Under the HRS each rural household was able to sign a contract with the local government to obtain a certain amount of arable land and production equipment, and have a production quota, depending on the number of people in the family. As long as the household completed its quota of products to the state, it could decide freely what to produce and how to sell. Although the land was still owned by the state, the HRS and the PCS were definitely different from each other.

In the rural sector, although the system of collective ownership of land has been retained, farmers' rights and responsibilities are now clearer since the leasing period is long (15 years for the initial stage with an extension of a further 30 years). Before the reform, farmers had to sell to the government all the remaining gains (which was seen as being vital to the large Chinese population at that time) and other important agricultural products at a very low price. Following the reforms, there were two main additional benefits to farmers: (i) one that arises from 'price adjustment' within the planned price framework; and (ii) the other that arises from 'price release' (Zhao, 1999, p. 194). The policy of 'price adjustment' entailed the government gradually increasing the planned purchase price and changing the relative price of agricultural goods to manufactured goods. 'Price release', which in fact implies alteration of the price mechanism from planned pricing to market pricing, involved a gradual reduction in the quota that farmers were required to sell to the government.

Figure 6.4 provides a broad picture of the benefits to farmers through price and ownership reform. The benefit is represented by the area AEFD. The 'price adjustment' within the planned price framework is represented by the area HIBA; and the reduction in the production quota set by the government is represented by the area LMEB. 'Price adjustment' is depicted by the three little arrows in Figure 6.4. In addition, the reduction in the production quota set by the government (as shown by arrow 1 in Figure 6.4) enabled farmers to sell, given that total production is fixed, a larger proportion of their products in the market at market prices. Since market prices are usually higher than the government-adjusted prices, farmers can obtain extra benefits (which are not illustrated in the figure).

The reduction in the quota enabled farmers to sell part of their products in the market at market prices. The policies behind rural price reform were thereafter introduced as part of many urban sector reforms during the 1980s.

The HRS has been largely recognized as a success (see subsection 7.1.1 for detailed evidence). However, this system has also encountered some problems since the 1990s, especially since the late 1990s. This can be witnessed by the increasingly wider gaps between rural and urban

---

8. See Liew (2000), which also gives other references.

9. By 1958, about 150 million rural households were grouped into five million production teams which, in turn, were organized nationwide into 50,000 people's communes (Minami, 1994, p. 77).

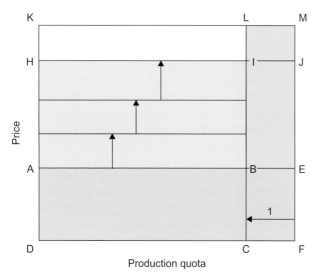

Notes: AD = price before reform; AH = government-adjusted price after reform; HK = market-based price; DF = production quota set by the government before reform; DC = production quota set by the government after reform; CF = additional products that farmers can sell at free market. AEFD = farmers' benefit before reform; HIBA = farmers' additional benefit by selling their products to the government after reform; LMEB = farmers' additional benefit by selling their products at free market; 1 = reduction in the production quota set by the government.

FIGURE 6.4 How farmers gain from the agricultural reform.

incomes during the 1990s and 2000s (see Figure 9.3 in Chapter 9). In brief, there have been two shortcomings for the HRS. First, since the management of agricultural production has been restricted within each household (note that the average size of the Chinese rural household has been reduced substantially as a result of the birth control policy implemented during the past decades), large-scale, mechanically-based modern agriculture cannot be easily realized and, consequently, labor productivity has not been able to increase. Secondly, and as a result of the emigration of rural laborers into urban areas, a certain amount of arable land has been abandoned.

In order to solve these problems, Chinese policy makers have brought forward two countermeasures:

1. Within three years, starting from 2004, agricultural tax, which had been applied since 1958, was abolished; and
2. A *de facto* land privatization scheme for rural areas, called *tudi liuzhuan* (land circulation), was proposed in the Third Plenum of the 17th CCPCC in October 2008. The scheme has been termed the 'third land reform' in China, and it is anticipated that it will be implemented throughout the nation over the course of the coming years.

6.4.2 Industry

Generally, China's industrial organization experienced a period of over-centralization and then a period of decentralization. In much of the pre-reform period, China's industrial

organization was implemented via a centrally planned system, which offered the advantages of rapid structural transformation through direct and strong government participation and large-scale mobilization of resources to priority sectors. Such a system enabled the industrial sector to grow at highly creditable rates between 1953 and 1978. The advantages of rapid structural change under a centrally planned system, however, were soon outweighed by the problems of low efficiency, slow technological progress, sectoral imbalances, and sharp annual fluctuations in growth rates.

In general, the state-owned enterprises (SOEs) were established to serve five essential roles in the Chinese economy:

1. In many cases they had led to improved efficiency and increased technological competitiveness
2. They had generally taken a more socially responsible attitude than the purely private enterprises
3. They had helped to prevent oligopolistic collusion by refusing to collude
4. They had helped the government to pursue its regional policy by shifting the investment to the poor west of the country
5. They had been used by the government as a means of managing aggregate demand to enable it to operate its counter-cyclical policy.

Closely copying the Soviet prototype, the Chinese SOEs followed a 'unified supply and unified collection' system in which the state supplied all inputs (such as labor, funds, raw material, power supply, and so on) necessary to execute production targets and claimed all output and financial revenues.[10]

The main substantive difference between the collectively owned enterprises (COEs) and the SOEs lies in the extent of government control that is exerted over the organizations. The SOEs serve, to some extent, as the concrete manifestation of the socialist principle of public ownership of the means of production by the whole population. Local governments are responsible for the provision of inputs to the COEs within their jurisdiction and, conversely, have first, if not sole, claim to their output and revenues. Usually, the COEs are classified into two types: urban COEs are directly controlled by local governments and subjected to state plans; rural COEs are fully under the jurisdiction of

---

10. As noted by Lin (1995), China's SOEs enjoyed far less autonomy than their Soviet antecedents, since the Soviet enterprises operated under the Economic Accounting System (*khozraschet*) which endowed state enterprises with a limited degree of financial autonomy with them being allowed to retain a proportion of profits, depreciation reserves, and major repair funds. However, national shortages of productive resources and severe weaknesses in enterprise management in China during the 1950s compelled a much more centralized system which left SOEs without any substantive decision-making or financial autonomy.

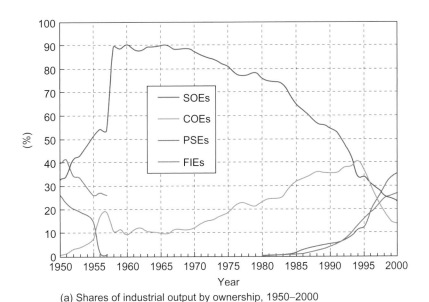

(a) Shares of industrial output by ownership, 1950–2000

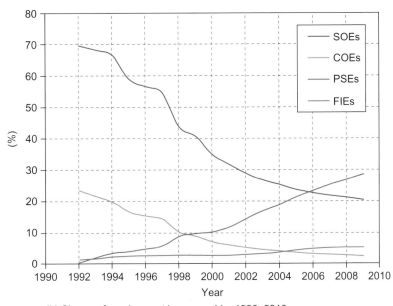

(b) Shares of employment by ownership, 1990–2010

FIGURE 6.5 China's industrial ownership in transition. *Source: NBS, various years.*

Notes: COEs = collectively-owned enterprises; FIEs = foreign (Taiwan, Hong Kong and Macau) invested enterprises; PSE = private, share-holding and other enterprises; SOEs = state-owned enterprises.

the township and village government units (this will be discussed in detail in Section 11.2 of Chapter 11).

Obviously, the private, shareholding or other enterprises (PSEs) were the most freely able to decide on investment, labor, output, and pricing and, above all, they were the most market-oriented. China's PSEs practically ceased to exist from 1958, when the socialist transformation of national capitalist industry was completed, up until 1979, when the Chinese government began to reform its CPE (see Figure 6.5). During the reform era, the PSEs have experienced a recovery during the period 1978–88, a

period of consolidation during 1989–91, and a mushrooming since 1992.

The foreign-invested enterprises (FIEs) mainly comprise joint ventures and wholly foreign-owned enterprises. Like the PSEs, the FIEs have also grown rapidly since the early 1980s, as a result of the dramatic inflows of foreign capital into China. We will discuss this issue in detail in Section 13.2 of Chapter 13.

Since 1978, industrial reforms in China have sought to improve the enterprise incentive systems, to utilize indirect economic levers (price, tax, interest rate, credit, and banking) to regulate industrial production, to endow enterprises with greater relative decision-making autonomy and, above all, to compel enterprises to operate according to market regulations. The positive effects of reform on industrial performance are evident from the dramatic industrial growth that was observed during the reform period (see Section 11.2 in Chapter 11 for more details).

The dynamism of the industrialization may be attributed to a variety of reform measures. One such measure was the shift in sectoral priorities within industry, which allowed a greater share of resources to be diverted away from the input- and capital-intensive producer goods industries, toward the more efficient and profitable consumer goods industries. Another measure was the lifting of previous restrictions on the development of the non-state sectors and the policy of promoting a diversified ownership structure. This has led to the explosive growth of the non-state sectors which are acting increasingly as the engine of industrial development, particularly since the early 1990s, when China formally tried to transform its economy to a socialist market system.

From 1978 to 2000, the shares of industrial output produced by the SOEs, COEs, PSEs, and FIEs changed greatly, with the growth in the gross value of industrial output (GVIO) being much slower in the SOEs than in the COEs, PSEs, and FIEs. It is particularly noteworthy that the SOEs' share in GVIO first began to rank after the PSEs' and FIEs' in 1997 and 1998, respectively (see Figure 6.5).

The substantial reform of the state industrial organization began in 1984 when the CCPCC and the central government decided to shift the emphasis of reforms from the agricultural sector to the non-agricultural sectors. On May 10, 1984, the State Council issued the 'Provisional Regulations on the Enlargement of Autonomy of State-owned Industrial Enterprises' which outlines ten specific decision-making powers to be enjoyed by enterprises. The 'invigoration' of large and medium-sized SOEs and the application of indirect means to regulate SOEs were adopted as policy in the State Council's governmental report to the Fourth Session of the Sixth NPC on 25 March 1986. In December, the 'Bankruptcy Law Concerning the State Enterprises' was adopted by the NPC. However, the Bankruptcy Law was not effectively applied until the early 1990s due to fears of unemployment and social instability as China does not have a relatively complete social security system.[11]

Following Deng Xiaoping's call for faster economic growth and reform, after 1992 the government began to accelerate and intensify market-oriented reforms. Industrial reform was focused on the issue of property right reform by granting more autonomy to the SOEs. In June 1992, the State Commission for Restructuring the Economic Systems (SCRES), the State Planning Commission (SPC), the Ministry of Finance (MOF), the People's Bank of China (PBC), and the Production Office of State Council jointly issued the 'Provisional Regulations on Joint-Stock Companies' to govern the formation of shareholding companies. The regulations cover the standardization of joint stock companies, their accounting system, financial management, taxation and auditing, labor, and wage systems. This was followed by the State Council's 'Regulations on the Transformation of the Operating Mechanisms of State-owned Industrial Enterprises' on 22 July 1992, which codified the independent decision-making powers of the SOEs in 14 key areas (including production, investment, labor, marketing, independent profit and loss accounting, assets, mergers, closures, bankruptcy and so on).

Since the formal adoption in 1993 of Deng Xiaoping's theory on the construction of a socialist market economy with Chinese characteristics, there have been rapid and substantial changes in the country's industrial management. One important policy is the importation of the 'modern enterprise system' which, in practice, follows the modern Western-style and market-based corporate system. In addition to its critical role in the sustainable improvement of productivity in the industrial sector, industrial reform is also the institutional *sine qua non* in terms of establishing an effectively functioning competitive market system.

The reform on non-performing SOEs was debated once more in the Fifth Plenum of the 14th CCPCC held during September 1995. The outcome was the policy of 'grasping the large and releasing the small' (*zhua da fang xiao*). To 'grasp the large' (*zhua da*) is to turn a select group of 300 out of a list of 1,000 already successful large enterprises and enterprise groups into world-class businesses. To 'release the small' (*fang xiao*) is to privatize or to contract out small SOEs or to let them go bankrupt. This policy allows most small SOEs to be sold off to private individuals and the management of those not sold is contracted out. The majority of the remaining large and medium-sized SOEs are to be turned into corporations with various forms of ownership, ranging from corporations with 100 percent private ownership to those with a mixture of private and state capital, and others with 100 percent state capital.[12] The central government, however, will continue to be the only shareholder in companies that produce 'special-category' and defense-related products.

---

11. Notice that as soon as the Tiananmen incident (May–June 1989) was calmed down, the Chinese leadership began to re-emphasize the role of the working class in the Chinese economy.

12. A case study of the ownership reform of the SOEs can be found in Chapter 8.

One example of the policy of 'grasping the large' is the restructuring of China's oil industry and the four state-owned oil companies – China National Offshore Oil Corporation (CNOOC), China National Petroleum Corporation (CNPC), China Petrochemical Corporation (Sinopec), and China National Star Petroleum Corporation (CNSPC):

- In August 1999, the CNOOC grouped the shares of all of its subsidiaries into the newly formed China Offshore Oil Corporation (COOC);
- In November 1999, the CNPC formed China Oil & Gas Stock Co. Ltd, with a new name, Petrochina;
- Late November 1999, China National Star Petroleum Corporation (CNSPC), the smallest state-owned oil company, was merged with Sinopec.

The aim behind the formation of the new companies and the merger was to reduce the four state oil companies into three state holding companies and to consolidate the shares of their subsidiaries into three companies for overseas listing. As part of the restructuring, the core and non-core businesses of the state oil companies are to be separated, some debt is to be converted to equity and their workforce is to be reduced with state financial help. Adverse stock market reactions towards the end of 1999 led to the postponement of the initial public offering (IPO) of CNOOC in Hong Kong and New York. But despite continuing uncertainties over the potential success of their IPOs, CNOOC, CNPC, and Sinopec were pushed ahead with their restructuring plans in 2000 because of China's expected entry into the WTO after its successful negotiation with the USA (Liew, 2000).

State ownership, which had been defined as the classic feature of socialism, was discussed at the 15th CCP National Congress during October 1997. The CCP's final conclusion was that public (*gongyou*), instead of state (*guoyou*), ownership is to be the dominant form of ownership.[13] In addition, it encouraged the development of every other form of ownership, including private ownership. Furthermore, private and individual businesses are not only tolerated but are now considered to be making valuable contributions to the economy.

The three aspects of the adjustment were:

1. To reduce the scope of the state sector and to withdraw state capital from industries that were considered non-essential to the national economy
2. To seek various forms for materializing public ownership that can generally promote the growth of productive forces and to develop diverse forms of public ownership

3. To encourage the development of nonpublic sectors of the economy such as the individual business sector and the private sector and to make them important components of a socialist market economy (Wu, 2005, p. 86).

In September 2003, as the 'Decision on Issues Regarding the Improvement of the Socialist Market Economic System' was adopted by the Third Plenary Session of the 16th CCPCC, it indicated that China's economic, social, and political reforms will continue to advance comprehensively in the years to come.

As part of its efforts to restructure state-owned enterprises, the Chinese government established the State-Owned Asset Supervision Administration Commission (SASAC) in 2003. The SASAC operates through several equity exchanges such as CBEX (China Beijing Equity Exchange), which is the largest and most prestigious in terms of trading volume. In general, the SASAC's responsibilities include:

1. Supervision and evaluation of state-owned enterprises
2. Oversight of state-owned assets
3. Recruiting of top executive talent
4. Drafting of laws, administrative rules and regulations that promote increased development of corporate law in China
5. Coordination of local state-owned assets as prescribed by law.[14]

6.5 PUBLIC FINANCE

To a large extent public finance determines the use of a nation's aggregate resources and, together with monetary and exchange rate policies, it influences the macro balance of payments, the accumulation of foreign debt, the rates of inflation, interest, and so on. However, the degree of impact may differ significantly and it may also depend upon whether the economy is managed under the market-oriented system or under the centrally planned system. Public finance usually plays an important role in promoting balanced development and equilibrium in both wealth accumulation and distribution for a planned economy in which central government collects and directly dispenses much of its budget for society, while the local budget is collected from and used for local administrative organs, factories, enterprises, and welfare facilities. As the market economy is a private-ownership system, the channels of policy influences are much more indirect and occur mainly through the *laissez-faire* approach.

---

13. Note that state ownership only includes the SOEs, while public ownership includes the SOEs and COEs.

14. Source: http://www.sasac.gov.cn/n2963340/n2963393/2965120.html. Accessed on November 23, 2011.

6.5.1 Central–Local Fiscal Relations (1980–93)

Since the early 1980s, public finance, as an important component of the Chinese economic system, has undergone a series of reforms in terms of the development of central–local relations.[15] The goals of these reforms were to decentralize the fiscal structure and to strengthen the incentive for local government to collect more revenue for themselves and for the central government to maintain an egalitarian fiscal redistribution among the provinces. Briefly, China's efforts towards this end have experienced different stages, all of which sought to find a rational revenue-raising formula between the central and the local governments. In 1980 the Chinese government began to implement the fiscal system entitled 'huafen shouzhi, fenji baogan' (divide revenue and expenditure, set up diversified contract system). The main contents of the fiscal reform included:

- Transformation from the traditional system of 'having meals in one pot' (yizhao chifan) to that of 'having meals in different pots' (fenzhao chifan)
- Transformation of financial redistribution from mainly through sectors directly under the central government to mainly through regions
- Transformation of the divisions of revenue and expenditure and the proportion of revenue sharing between the central and local governments from being fixed annually to being fixed every five years.

In general, China's central–local fiscal relations from 1980 to 1993 can be summarized as three stages:

- The first stage (1980–84)
- The second stage (1985–87)
- The third stage (1988–93).

The First Stage (1980–84)

During this period, the basic structure of the central–local fiscal relations was framed and amended frequently.

In 1980, there were ten provinces (Inner Mongolia, Fujian, Guangdong, Guangxi, Guizhou, Yunnan, Tibet, Qinghai, Ningxia, and Xinjiang) on which the central government taxed a zero marginal rate. Specifically, Guangdong – a coastal province with close proximity to Hong Kong and Macau – was required to pay a lump-sum (LT) tax to the central government; Fujian – another coastal province with close proximity to Taiwan – was able to retain all the revenue it collected plus a lump-sum

subsidy (LS) from the central government; the remaining eight poor provinces and ethnic minority-based autonomous regions could retain all the revenue they collected and additionally receive a lump-sum but growing subsidy (GS) from the central government.

In five provinces (Beijing, Tianjin, Liaoning, Shanghai, and Jiangsu), the total revenue collected was to be shared with the central government in fixed proportions (SOR), varying from 12 percent to 90 percent (Oksenberg and Tong, 1991, p. 24).[16]

In the remaining provinces, revenue was shared between the central and local governments in more complicated ways and, as a result of considerable and frequent politicking, negotiating, and bargaining with central government, the fiscal arrangements were amended and the shares of these provinces were generally raised in 1982 and lowered in 1983 in accordance with central government's revenue requirement (see Table 6.1).

The Second Stage (1985–87)

The fiscal system entitled 'huafen shuizhong, heding shouzhi, fenji baogan' (divide the categories of tax, verify revenue and expenditure, and set up a diversified contract system) was introduced from 1985. This system, which was to strengthen the method of 'having meals in different pots', divided revenue into three parts: the centrally fixed revenue, the locally fixed revenue, and the revenue shared by the central and local governments. Among other changes of the central–local fiscal relations, Jilin, Jiangxi, and Gansu provinces moved from DRS to LS, Shaanxi province from SOR to LS, Heilongjiang province from DRS to SOR in 1985, and LT in 1986, respectively. Simultaneously the favorable fiscal policies were still applied in Guangdong and Fujian provinces and other minority-based autonomous regions, as demonstrated in Table 6.1.

The Third Stage (1988–93)

A fiscal responsibility system was introduced through two sub-stages below:

1. *1988–90*: Seven methods were introduced during this period: (1) STR (shouru dizheng baogan); (2) SOR (zhong'e fencheng); (3) GT (shangjie'e dizheng baogan); (4) LT (ding'e shangjie); (5) LS (ding'e buzhu); (6) GS (ding'e buzhu, meinian dizheng); and (7) ROR (zhong'e baogan).
2. *1991–93*: Six methods were introduced during this period: STR, SGT, SOR, GT, LT, and LS (see Table 6.1 for a detailed account of these fiscal policies).

---

15. The literature of the evolution in central–local fiscal arrangement over the pre-reform era includes Lardy (1975, pp. 25–60), Donnithorne (1976, pp. 328–54), and Oksenberg and Tong (1991, pp. 1–32).

16. That is, the marginal and average propensity to tax each province from its collected revenue ranged between 12 per cent and 90 per cent.

TABLE 6.1 Changes of China's Central–Local Fiscal Relations, 1980–93

Province	1980–81	1982	1983–84	1985	1986–87	1988–90	1991–93
Anhui	DR	SOR	SOR	SOR	SOR	SOR	SOR
Beijing	SOR	SOR	SOR	SOR	SOR	STR	STR
Fujian	LS	LS	LS	LS	LS	LS	LS
Gansu	DR	SOR	DRS	LS	LS	LS	LS
Guangdong	LT	LT	LT	LT	LT	GT	GT
Guangxi	GS	GS	GS	GS	GS	GS	LS
Guizhou	GS	GS	GS	GS	GS	GS	LS
Hainan						GT	LS
Hebei	DR	SOR	SOR	SOR	SOR	STR	STR
Heilongjiang	DRS	DRS	DRS	SOR	LT	LT	LT/STR
Henan	DR	SOR	SOR	SOR	SOR	STR	STR
Hubei	DR	SOR	SOR	SOR	ROR	ROR	LT/SGT
Hunan	DR	SOR	SOR	SOR	SOR	GT	GT
Inner Mongolia	GS	GS	GS	GS	GS	GS	LS
Jiangsu	SOR	SOR	SOR	SOR	SOR	STR	STR
Jiangxi	DRS	DRS	DRS	LS	LS	LS	LS
Jilin	DRS	DRS	DRS	LS	LS	LS	LS
Liaoning	SOR	SOR	SOR	SOR	SOR	STR	STR/SGT
Ningxia	GS	GS	GS	GS	GS	GS	LS
Qinghai	GS	GS	GS	GS	GS	GS	LS
Shaanxi	DR	SOR	SOR	LS	LS	LS	LS
Shandong	DR	SOR	SOR	SOR	SOR	LT	LT/SGT
Shanghai	SOR	SOR	SOR	SOR	SOR	LT	LT
Shanxi	DR	DR	SOR	SOR	SOR	SOR	SOR
Sichuan	DR	SOR	SOR	SOR	ROR	ROR	LS/STR
Tianjin	SOR	SOR	SOR	SOR	SOR	SOR	SOR
Tibet	GS	GS	GS	GS	GS	GS	LS
Xinjiang	GS	GS	GS	GS	GS	GS	LS
Yunnan	GS	GS	GS	GS	GS	GS	LS
Zhejiang	DR	SOR	SOR	SOR	SOR	STR	STR

Notes: (1) DR = dividing revenue; DRS = dividing revenue and receiving growing subsidy; GS = receiving lump-sum but growing subsidy; GT = paying lump-sum but growing tax; LS = receiving lump-sum subsidy; LT = paying lump-sum tax; ROR = retaining overall revenue; SGT = sharing overall revenue and paying growing tax; SOR = sharing overall revenue; and STR = sharing target revenue but retaining residual revenue. (2) A detailed description of these fiscal policies can be found in the Annex.
Sources: World Bank (1990, p. 89), Oksenberg and Tong (1991, pp. 24–5), Agarwala (1992, p. 68), Wei (1994, p. 298), and Knight and Li (1995).

During the post-reform period the economic incentives facing the provinces appeared to improve over time. In 1980, for example, no fewer than 19 provinces were involved in some form of revenue sharing or division, whereas by 1985, revenue division had ceased and 15 provinces shared their respective revenues. In the 1988 reforms, most of these provinces were switched to lump-sum taxation or the sharing of target revenues, while only three provinces remained on a revenue-sharing formula. In sum, this account of the fiscal relationship between the central and local governments highlights four problems: first, the non-uniform treatment of provinces appeared neither efficient nor equitable; secondly, the uncertainty associated with changing rules and bargaining had disincentive effects on the revenue collection of the province governments; thirdly, the high marginal tax rates faced by some provinces could be expected to deter revenue collection, and; finally, the result of various efforts to reform the centralized fiscal system was to reduce the share that central government received of the revenue collected by the provinces (Knight and Li, 1995, p. 5).

6.5.2   Tax-Sharing System (1994–)

Since 1994, China has implemented a so-called 'tax-sharing system' (*fenshui zhi*). At this stage, Chinese fiscal policy, through transferring much of the revenue collection function from local to central government, attempted to tackle the principal–agent problem of the revenue-contracting period. The solution was essentially to transpose the principal and agent. Under this system, China's tax revenues have been collected by and shared between central and local governments, as follows:

- 'Central taxes' (i.e., those that are collected by the central government): these include customs duties; the operations tax paid by the railways, various banks, and

insurance companies; and import-related VAT and consumption tax collected by the customs
- 'Local taxes' (i.e., those that are collected by local governments): these include operation tax (excluding the part paid by railway, various banks, and insurance companies) and city and township land use tax
- 'Shared taxes' (i.e., those that are shared between central and local governments): these include domestic VAT (75 percent for central government); income tax (60 percent for central government); resource tax (except the tax paid by offshore oil enterprises, all the rest goes to local government): and stamp tax in the stock market.

It can be shown that since the early 1980s China's diversified fiscal systems have resulted in differences in central–local relations. During the period 1980–84, during the implementation of the first stage of fiscal reform, China's share of local revenue to total revenue decreased from 75.5 percent to 59.5 percent; over the course of the same period its share of local expenditure to total expenditure increased from 45.7 percent to 47.5 percent. In the following years, both of these shares had increased considerably (see Figure 6.6). It can also be seen from Figure 6.6 that since the implementation of the 'tax-sharing system' in 1994, China's fiscal transferring mechanism has been reversed from its previous pattern (i.e., the 'local-to-central transference' during the 1980s) to the present 'central-to-local transference' pattern. As a result, China's central government has become more powerful than it was in the 1980s.

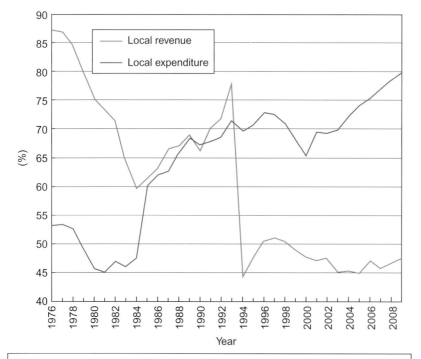

FIGURE 6.6   China's local revenue and expenditure shares. *Source: NBS, various years.*

Notes: (1) 'revenue' excludes borrowing from domestic and abroad, 'expenditure' excludes repayment of the principal and payment of interest, borrowing from domestic and abroad.

6.6 BANKING SYSTEM

6.6.1 Chinese Banks in Transition

The central bank of the PRC is called the People's Bank of China (PBC), which formulates and implements monetary policy. The PBC maintains the banking sector's payment, clearing and settlement systems, and manages official foreign exchange and gold reserves. It oversees the State Administration of Foreign Exchange (SAFE) for setting foreign-exchange policies. According to the 1995 Central Bank law, PBC has full autonomy in applying the monetary instruments, including setting interest rates for commercial banks and trading in government bonds. The State Council maintains oversight of PBC policies.

China has four state-owned banks. The Industrial & Commercial Bank of China (ICBC) is the largest bank in China by total assets, total employees, and total customers. The Bank of China (BOC) specializes in foreign-exchange transactions and trade finance. The China Construction Bank (CCB) specializes in medium- to long-term credit for long-term specialized projects, such as infrastructure projects and urban housing development. The Agriculture Bank of China (ABC) specializes in providing financing to China's agricultural sector and offers wholesale and retail banking services to farmers, township and village enterprises, and other rural institutions.

Three 'policy' banks, the Agricultural Development Bank of China (ADBC), China Development Bank (CDB), and the Export-Import Bank of China (Chexim), were established to take over the government-directed spending functions and state-invested projects.

In addition, there are smaller commercial banks in China. The largest ones in this group include the Bank of Communications, China CITIC Bank, China Everbright Bank, HuaXia Bank, China Minsheng Bank, Guangdong Development Bank, Shenzhen Development Bank, China Merchants Bank, Shanghai Pudong Development Bank, and Industrial Bank. Other city commercial banks include Shenzhen City Commercial Bank, Taizhou City Commercial Bank, Bank of Beijing, and Bank of Ningbo.

China Banking Regulatory Commission (CBRC) was officially launched on April 28, 2003, to take over the supervisory role of the PBC. The goal of the landmark reform was to improve the efficiency of bank supervision and to help the PBC to further focus on the macro-economy and currency policy. The CBRC is responsible for 'the regulation and supervision of banks, asset management companies, trust and investment companies, as well as other deposit-taking financial institutions'. Its mission is to maintain a safe and sound banking system in China.

Since 1978 banking reforms have played an important role in China's overall efforts to transform a centrally planned economy into a market-based economy. Although the banking sector has undergone remarkable changes over the course of this period, deep-seated structural problems of asset quality, capital adequacy, and profitability continue to pose considerable challenges. Arguably, the major problem in the present-day Chinese banking sector is the high level of non-performing loans (NPLs) – and the continued lending to loss-making SOEs. Until recently, banking reforms were focused mainly on introducing competition, broadening the channels of financial intermediation, and providing a legal framework for bank supervision. In 1995, two notable developments in this respect were introduced: the promulgation of the Central Bank law that firmly established the PBC as the sole government agent to supervise and regulate the banking sector; and the enactment of the Commercial Banking law that clearly defined the scope of business for the four state-owned banks – the Bank of China (BOC), the China Construction Bank (CCB), the Agricultural Bank of China (ABC), and the Industrial and Commercial Bank of China (ICBC).

China's entry into the WTO has created opportunities for foreign banks. As a milestone move to honor its WTO commitments, China released the Rules for Implementing the Regulations Governing Foreign Financial Institutions in the People's Republic of China in January 2002. The rules provide detailed regulations for implementing the administration of the establishment, registration, scope of business, qualification, supervision, dissolution, and liquidation of foreign financial institutions. They also stipulate that foreign bank branches conducting full aspects of foreign-currency business and full aspects of RMB business to all categories of clients are required to have operating capital of at least 600 million RMB, of which at least 400 million RMB must be held in RMB and at least 200 million RMB in freely convertible currency.[17]

Client restriction on foreign currency business was lifted immediately after China's entry into the WTO on December 11, 2001. Since then, foreign financial institutions have been permitted to provide foreign currency services to Chinese enterprises and individuals, and have been permitted to provide local currency business to all Chinese clients by the end of 2006. In 2007 five non-mainland banks were allowed to issue bank cards in China, with Bank of East Asia also allowed to issue UnionPay credit cards in the mainland (United Overseas Bank and Sumitomo Mitsui Financial Group have only issued cards in their home countries; they are not yet allowed to issue cards within the mainland). In May 2009 Woori Bank became the first Korean bank allowed to issue UnionPay debit cards on the mainland (it issues UnionPay credit cards in Korea only). Furthermore, when China entered the WTO, geographic restrictions placed on

---

17. Data source: http://english.cri.cn/855/2005/09/04/269@16838.htm. Accessed on December 6, 2011.

RMB-denominated business was phased out in four major cities – Shanghai, Shenzhen, Tianjin, and Dalian. Since then, foreign-funded banks were allowed to commence RMB-denominated business in more Chinese cities.

6.6.2 Progress and Problems

The 1997 Asian financial crisis accelerated the pace of reform in China's banking system. China quickened the pace of reform in 1998 and seems to be aware of two lessons that can be drawn from the Asian financial crisis. The first lesson is that a sound banking system is crucial for an economy to withstand external shocks. The second lesson from the Japanese banking saga is that delays will only allow NPLs to grow and to erode the levels of bank capital. Under the reforms that began in December 1998, the directors of the regional branches of the PBC would be appointed directly by its headquarters in Beijing without consultations with the provincial governments. Instead of the previous arrangement of a PBC branch being established in each province and SEZ, the regional PBC branches were now located in only nine cities.[18] Furthermore, powers that had previously been delegated to PBC branches to control the volume of credit were concentrated in the central PBC headquarters. Moreover, projects above a certain scale would now have to be approved by central bank headquarters. However, the above reform effort alone was not enough for the construction of a healthy banking and financing system, since there had been too many bad loans advanced to the SOEs.

The reform of the SOEs was delayed as a result of the 1997 Asian financial crisis.[19] Two years later, in 1999, China introduced a debt–equity swap scheme (*zhai zhuan gu*) which would convert a portion of SOEs' bank debt into equity. China's four largest state-owned commercial banks set up their own state asset management companies to deal respectively with their bad loans to selected SOEs that have potential as going business concerns but are burdened by heavy debts. The four state asset management companies are:

- Cinda (of the China Construction Bank)
- Huarong (of the Industrial and Commercial Bank of China)
- Great Wall (of the Agricultural Bank of China)
- Oriental (of the Bank of China).

The bad loans are converted into equity and then sold at a discount to investors. The immediate objectives of debt–equity swaps are to improve the balance sheet of the commercial banks and reduce the debt service of the SOEs. In the longer term, it is hoped that investors in these debt–equity swaps would have the managerial and technical expertise to turn the SOEs around permanently.

There are strict guidelines specifying conditions that the first enterprises have to fulfill before they are allowed to have their debts converted into equity. The conditions under which enterprises were chosen include:

1. They must have good marketing records and competitiveness
2. Their technical equipment must be in line with environmental protection
3. They must have high quality management and good accounting systems
4. Their leadership must be specialized in business and administration
5. They must take 'effective reform measures', including plans to 'cut the number of employees to increase efficiency'.

On this basis, following stringent screening, the State Economic and Trade Commission (SETC) has reviewed and recommended as many as 601 enterprises for debt-to-equity swaps and the amount planned for debt-to-equity swaps is expected to total RMB 459.6 billion. Most of those enterprises are the key enterprises and enterprise groups. Quite a few of them are the leading enterprises in their respective sectors. Financial asset management companies have assessed the recommended enterprises one by one independently. By January 24, 2000, 78 enterprises had signed debt-to-equity swap agreements, framework agreements or letters of intent with financial asset management companies or banks with a transaction value of more than RMB 112.2 billion (SETC, 2000).

On April 1, 2000, China introduced a 'real-name' banking system under which all of the household bank deposits require a depositor's ID. This is an important step in moving from anonymous banking to real-name banking, an international practice. In reality, this change was concerned not so much with increasing tax revenue, as with reducing political corruption, by making the flow of money transparent.

Since the late 1990s, especially since China joined the WTO in 2001, several measures have been taken to establish a strong prudential framework that encompasses all types of banking and non-bank financial institutions. Specifically, these institutional improvements include:

- Liberalizing interest rates for bank deposits and bank loans; improving indirect policy tools; abolishing directed, political lending

---

18. They are Shanghai, Tianjin, Shenyang, Nanjing, Ji'nan, Wuhan, Guangzhou, Chengdu and Xi'an, with additional two administrative departments housed in Beijing and Chongqing municipalities.

19. Before the crisis, there had been a crying call for the SOEs to be reconstructed according to the Korean model. But obviously this idea has been abandoned as soon as South Korea's chaebols met difficulties.

- Continuing the commercialization process by allowing more competing and accepting diversified ownership structure; improving the quality of banks' assets through debt destructing and debt transfer; increasing operational efficiency while reducing overstaffing and overbranching
- Screening and rectifying the numbers and business scope of local trust and investment corporations; modernizing the payment system; supporting new financial products while dealing carefully with associated risks
- Continuing to develop securities markets by simplifying trading procedures, improving information disclosure procedures, and upgrading the legal framework
- Strengthening prudential supervision; clarifying and harmonizing operational standards, provision requirements, and accounting rules; developing a new law for closure and bankruptcy of financial institutions
- Further simplifying the foreign exchange administration; allowing more exchange rate flexibility; starting a gradual removal of capital controls; permitting foreign banks and other financial institutions to enter China, in accordance with the WTO agreement.

China's banking system has undergone significant changes. Even though still retained in the government's hands, China's banks are now functioning more like banks than before. However, in the coming years, more banking and financial reforms are still required:

- *Monetary policy* (adopting a fully market-based strategy of demand management; exploiting new channels of monetary transmission; adopting policies of greater independence and accountability; adopting a fully flexible exchange rate regime)
- *Banking* (finishing the process of cleaning up banks' balance sheets and introducing uniform capital adequacy ratios based on internationally accepted standards; giving up majority state ownership; allowing foreign banks and other financial institutions to compete on a level playing field with domestic banks)
- *Financial services* (streamlining the structure of the financial service industry; expanding the supply and improving the quality of products; liberalizing asset prices and allowing the stock market to reflect borrowers' financial conditions and to execute corporate control)
- *Regulation/supervision* (finishing the process of replacing direct state intervention and state protection with a market-oriented regulatory framework; reconsidering the segmentation of banking, investment, and insurance; continuing the gradual and cautious removal of capital control and, ultimately, adopting full capital account convertibility).

6.7 SUMMARY

The advocates of new institutional economics recognize that a good market economy requires 'getting institutions right' (Coase, 1992; North, 1997; Williamson, 1994). This is because institutions in general set the rules to affect the behavior of economic agents in a fundamental way. The institutional economists thus regard the conventional wisdom of transition focusing on stabilization, liberalization, and privatization as inadequate, because it overlooks the important institutional dimension. To them, a set of institutions are critical for sustained growth, including secure private property rights protected by the rule of law, the impartial enforcement of contracts through an independent judiciary, appropriate government regulations to foster market competition, effective corporate governance, transparent financial systems, and so on (Qian, 2002). Standing in marked contrast with the failures of Russia, which was to some extent based on a 'blueprint' or 'recipe' from Western advisors, has been the enormous success of China, which created its own transition path (Stiglitz, 1999, p. 3).

Many efforts have attempted to probe into the characteristics of the Chinese reform that has been introduced since the late 1970s. For example, Montinola et al. (1995) suggest that the system of federalism and the inherent jurisdictional competition places striking limits on this system of patronage and political spoils. As defined by McKinnon (1991a) and Weingast (1995), the Chinese system provides a partial basis for a special kind of federalism called *market-preserving federalism*. Central to the success of market-preserving federalism is the element of political durability that is built into the arrangements, meaning that the decentralization of power is not merely at the discretion of the central political authorities. In an extensive discussion of the topics central to the success of China's economic reforms, Shirk (1994) included the importance of gradualism, the initial role of agrarian reform, and the political mechanisms underpinning reform within the central government. In comparison with other researchers, Shirk placed greater weight on the political organization of local governments and their control over the economy, arguing that local political officials should be viewed as creating systems of patronage and loyalty.

Obviously, experience of the Chinese reform defies conventional explanations. In the late 1950s, the same authoritarian regime was waging a massive campaign under the name of the 'Great Leap Forward', which resulted in the loss of a large number of lives. From 1966 to 1976, the same regime was launching a so-called 'Great Cultural Revolution', causing serious cultural and economic damages to the nation. Furthermore, influential theories of the political economy of the former socialist systems emphasize that unless the one-party (Communist Party) monopoly is abolished, reforms are doomed to fail (Kornai, 1992). Consequently, this will lead to the asking of questions such as: Why has Chinese-style reform worked during the past decades? Can China's market-oriented reform be sustained in the long run? If China's reform had adopted a 'big bang' approach instead of the gradual approach that it has utilized, how would the Chinese economy have performed in the past decades?

China's reform experience has provided ample and valuable narrative to give answers to some of these questions. But narrative alone cannot give a sufficient answer to the above questions since they relate to events that did not occur and the motivation for *not* behaving in a particular way. Addressing these questions requires an appropriate model for linking what we observe with what we do not observe. A full understanding of China's economic reform cannot be based solely on theories. The narrative matters because from the historical point of view some specific events can yield a multiplicity of equilibria. To be sure, the Chinese reform has been shown to be a complicated process in which a series of endogenous and exogenous factors are interlinked and play differing roles in the institutional changes. Thus, in order to evaluate such issues as what have determined or influenced the Chinese reform process and how well the Chinese reform has performed, we require a theoretical underpinning of any empirical analysis.

ANNEX

Definition and Formulation of China's Fiscal Policies

Fiscal Policy	Definition	Revenue Goes to Provincial Gov.	Revenue Goes to Central Gov.	Marginal Tax Rate
DR	dividing revenue	$\sum \alpha_i C_i$	$\sum(1-\alpha_i)C_i$	$\sum(1-\alpha_i)C_i/\sum C_i$
DRS	dividing revenue and receiving growing subsidy	$\sum \alpha_i C_i + S_0(1+r)^t$	$\sum(1-\alpha_i)C_i - S_0(1+r)^t$	$\sum(1-\alpha_i)C_i/\sum C_i$
GS	receiving lump-sum but growing subsidy	$C + S_0(1+r)^t$	$-S_0(1+r)^t$	0
GT	paying lump-sum but growing tax	$C - T_0(1+r)^t$	$T_0(1+r)^t$	0
LS	receiving lump-sum subsidy	$C + S$	$-S$	0
LT	paying lump-sum tax	$C - T$	T	0
ROR	retaining overall revenue	C	0	0
SGT	sharing overall revenue and paying growing tax	$(1+\alpha)C - T_0(1+r)^t$	$-\alpha C + T_0(1+r)^t$	$-\alpha$
SOR	sharing overall revenue	αC	$(1-\alpha)C$	$1-\alpha$
STR	sharing target revenue but retaining residual revenue	$C - (1-\alpha)C_0(1+r)^t$	$(1-\alpha)C_0(1+r)^t$	0

Notes: (1) C = revenue collected by province (C_0 denotes C at time zero); C_i = revenue collected by province from source i (i = 1, 2, 3 denote revenue from source i goes to central government, to provincial government, and is shared between them respectively); S = lump-sum subsidy from central government (S_0 denotes S at time zero); T = lump-sum tax to central government (T_0 denotes T at time zero); r = annual growth rate; α = fixed share of revenue accruing to province ($0 < \alpha < 1$); $\alpha_i = \alpha_1, \alpha_2, \alpha_3$ (where $\alpha_1 = 0$, $\alpha_2 = 1$, $0 < \alpha_3 < 1$). (2) As for the period from 1991 to 1993, the above fiscal policies are as the following (Wei, 1994, pp. 297–9): (1) STR: Beijing (α = 50%, r = 4%), Hebei (α = 70%, r = 4.5%), Liaoning (α = 58.25%, r = 3.5%), Jiangsu (α = 41%, r = 5%), Zhejiang (α = 61.47%, r = 6.5%), and Henan (α = 80%, r = 5%) and Shenyang of Liaoning (α = 30.29%, r = 4%), Harbin of Heilongjiang (α = 45%, r = 5%), Ningbo of Zhejiang (α = 27.93%, r = 5.3%), and Chongqing of Sichuan (α = 33.5%, r = 4%); (2) SOR: Tianjin (α = 46.5%), Shanxi (α = 87.55%), and Anhui (α = 77.5%); (3) GT: Guangdong (T_0 = ¥1.413 billion, r = 9%) and Hunan (T_0 = ¥0.8 billion, r = 7%); (4) LT: Shanghai (T_0 = ¥10.5 billion), Shandong (T = ¥289 million), and Heilongjiang (T = ¥299 million); (5) LS: Jilin (S = ¥107 million), Fujian (S = ¥50 million), Jiangxi (S = ¥45 million), Shaanxi (S = ¥120 million), Gansu (S = ¥125 million), Inner Mongolia (S = ¥1.852 billion), Guangxi (S = ¥608 million), Yunnan (S = ¥673 million), Guizhou (S = ¥742 million), Qinghai (S = ¥656 million), Hainan (S = ¥138 million), Hubei (S = 4.78% of Wuhan's revenue), and Sichuan (S = 10.7% of Chongqing's revenue); and (6) SGT (zhong'e fencheng jia zhengzhang fencheng): Dalian of Liaoning (α = 27.74%, α' = 27.26%), Qingdao of Shandong (α = 16%, α' = 34%), and Wuhan of Hubei (α = 17%, α' = 25%).

REFERENCES

Agarwala, R. (1992). China: reforming intergovernmental fiscal relations. In *World bank discussion papers* (No. 178). Washington DC: World Bank.

Coase, R. (1992). The institutional structure of production. *American Economic Review*, 82(September), 713–719.

Deng, X. (1992). The key points of the speeches in Wuchang, Shenzhen, Zhuhai, Shanghai, etc. [zai wuchang, shenzhen, zhuhai, shanghai deng di de jianghua yiaodian] Literature Editing Committee of CCPCC (Ed.), *Selected works of Deng Xiaoping* [Deng Xiaoping wenxue] (pp. 370–383). Beijing: The People's Press, 1993.

Donnithrone, A. (1976). Centralization and decentralization in China's fiscal management. *China Quarterly*, 66, 328–354.

Hu, A. (2002). *Some opinions concerning the employment situation in China* [guanyu woguo jiuye wenti de ruogan kanfa]. draft, available at <www.cpric.org.cn>.

Knight, J., & Li, S. (1995). *Fiscal decentralization, redistribution and reform in China*. Working Paper, No. 168, Institute of Economics and Statistics, Oxford University.

Kornai, J. (1992). *The socialist system*. Princeton, NJ: Princeton University Press.

Lardy, N. R. (1975). Centralization and decentralization in China's fiscal management. *China Quarterly*, *61*, 25–60.

Liew, L. (2000). China's economic reform experience: the end of a pareto-improving strategy. *China Information*, *14*(2), 129–168.

Lin, C. (1995). *The reform of state-owned enterprises in China*. unpublished draft, Oxford: University of Oxford.

Liu, S. (1982). Economic planning. In D. Xu et al. (Eds.), *China's search for economic growth: the Chinese economy since 1949* (pp. 28–51). Beijing: New World Press.

McKinnon, R. (1991a). Financial control in the transition from classical socialism to a market economy. *Journal of Economic Perspectives*, *5*, 107–122.

Minami, R. (1994). *The economic development of China: a comparison with the Japanese experience*. London: The Macmillan Press. English edition.

Montinola, G., Qian, Y., & Weingast, B. (1995). Federalism, Chinese style: the political basis for economic success in China. *World Politics*, *48*, 50–81.

NBS. (various years). *China statistical yearbook*. various issues, Beijing: China Statistics Publishing House.

North, D. (1997). The contribution of the new institutional economics to an understanding of the transition problem. *WIDER Annual Lectures*, March.

Oksenberg, M., & Tong, J. (1991). The evolution of central–provincial fiscal relations in China, 1971–1984: the formal system. *The China Quarterly*, *March*, 1–32.

Price Yearbook of China. (1995). Beijing: China Price Press.

Qian, Y. (2002). How reform worked in China, draft, also In: D. Rodrik (Ed.), *In search of prosperity: analytic narratives on economic growth* (pp. 297–333). Princeton, NJ: Princeton University Press, 2007.

Riskin, C. (1994). The distribution of income and poverty in rural China [zhonguo nongchun de shouru fenpei yu pingkun]. In R. Zhao, & K. Griffin (Eds.), *The household income distribution in China [zhongguo de jumin shouru fenpei]* (pp. 313–351). Beijing: China Social Science Press.

SETC (2000). *The three-year reform and difficulty relief efforts for the SOEs have taken a favorable turn*. Beijing: State Economic and Trade Commission (SETC). January 25. Available at <http://www.china.org.cn/e-fabuhui/download/news/English/PressConferences/200125/01.htm>. Accessed on December 7, 2011.

Shirk, S. (1994). *How China opened its door*. Washington, DC: Brookings Institution.

SSB (1989b). *China yearbook for price statistics* [zhongguo jiage tongji nianjian]. Beijing: China Statistics Publishing House.

SSB (1990). *A compilation of historical statistical materials of China's provinces, autonomous regions and municipalities (1949–89)*. [quanguo ge sheng, zizhiqu, zhixiashi lishi tongji zhiliao huibian 1949–1989]. Beijing: China Statistics Publishing House.

SSB. (various years). *China statistical yearbook*, various issues, Beijing: China Statistics Publishing House.

State Council (1988). A retrospect on the reforms of the economic system and the prospects on the basic thought of the future reforms [jingji tizhi gaige de huigu yu jinhou gaige de jiben shilu]. In CCPCC Party School (Ed.), *The basic plans for China's economic reform, 1979–87*. Beijing: the CCPCC Party School Press.

Stiglitz, J. E. (1999). *Whither reform? – ten years of transition*. Keynote address to the world bank annual bank conference on development economics, Washington, DC: World Bank.

Wei, S. (1994). Comrade Deng Xiaoping's concept of 'One country, two systems' and its Practice. *Foreign Affairs Journal*, *33*(September), 1–7.

Weingast, B. R. (1995). The economic role of political institutions: market-preserving federalism and economic growth. *Journal of Law, Economics, and Organization*, *11*, 1–31.

Williamson, J. (1994). In search of a manual for technopols. In J. Williamson (Ed.), *The political economy of policy reform*. Washington DC: Institute for International Economics.

World Bank (1990). *China: revenue mobilization and tax policy*. Washington DC: World Bank.

Zhao, R. (1999). Review of economic reform in China: features, experiences and challenges. In R. Garnaut & L. Song (Eds.), *China: twenty years of reform* (pp. 185–200). Canberra: Asia Pacific Press.

Chapter 7

Understanding Chinese Economic Reform

A roadside billboard of Deng Xiaoping in Shenzhen. *Source: http://en.wikipedia.org*

Because of the Tiananmen Square protests of 1989, there was a growing formalist faction opposed to Deng Xiaoping's reforms within the Communist Party. To reassert his economic agenda, in the spring of 1992, Deng spent the New Year festival in Shanghai and visited Wuchang, Shenzhen, and Zhuhai, in order to use his travels as a method of reasserting his economic policy after his retirement from office. On his famous southern tour (*nanxun*), Deng made various speeches and generated large local support for his reformist platform. He criticized those who were against further economic and openness reforms in China, and stressed the benefits of economic reform and opening up to the outside world.

Doctor Bianque went to see King Wu of the state of Qin. The King told the doctor about his poor health and Bianque was ready to give him a treatment. The ministers at the King's sides said to him: 'Your Majesty, the malady is in front of your ears and below your eyes. Even with treatment it might not be cured and very likely you will lose your hearing and sight.' The King passed these messages to Bianque. Bianque was enraged and threw down the stone needle which he used for giving treatment, saying: 'Sire, you discuss your illness with one who knows how to effect a cure but you allow those who know nothing about medicine to spoil the whole thing. If the Qin is governed in this way, then a single such mistake on your part is enough to bring down the state.'

– Zhanguoce (475–221 BC)

7.1 RADICAL REFORM: THE SUCCESSFUL CASES

7.1.1 Agricultural Reform

China's agricultural reform began in September 1980 and had been successfully completed before the end of 1982. The CCP and the Chinese government took only about two years to decollectivize about 700 million farmers throughout the huge nation, through a method known as the Household Responsibility System (HRS). Under the HRS, each rural household may be able to sign a contract with the local government: it will then obtain a certain amount of arable land, production equipment, and a production quota in line with the number of people in the family. Once the household fulfills its quota, it can decide freely what to produce and how to sell. Although land is still owned by the state, the incentive for agricultural production has increased significantly. The decollectivization of agriculture, which has been recognized as a radical reform by Sachs and Woo (1994) and Zhao (1999, p. 192), has been universally recognized as a success. For example, from 1978 to 1984, grain output increased by 56 percent (Lin, 1992). Even more rapid was the growth in the output of other agricultural commodities (during the pre-reform period, the growth in grain output had been at the expense of these commodities). Over the longer period of reform from 1978 to 2002, gross agricultural output had grown in real terms at an average annual rate of more than 5 percent (NBS, 2003).

The special political and economic features of China determine the driving forces and the outcomes of the reform in agricultural ownership. First, more than 80 percent of China's population still lived in rural areas in 1978 – a backward and autarkical society.[1] Secondly, China's agricultural sector had been dominated by collectivist ownership before the reform – which did not fit a standard socialist model.

As a result, the reform of the collective sector (while keeping the state-owned sector unchanged) would not have been regarded by the conservatives as fundamentally affecting China's socialist orthodoxy. Thirdly, and most importantly, the Chinese policy makers – from both reformist and conservative cliques – still remembered the three-year famine (1959–61) during which millions of farmers died of starvation. They probably recognized that the horrible famine had been attributed, at least partially, to China's highly centralized agricultural system, and that if such a disaster occurred again, the CCP would lose its power base in China.

Since the initial and external conditions of the agricultural sector were similar to those of the industrial sector (especially those of the small state-owned and collectively owned industrial enterprises), we argue that at least some of the industrial reforms – which had followed a too gradual/partial pace (as will be discussed in subsection 7.2.2) – were misguided during the early 1980s. Had the industrial reform followed a more radical approach in terms of speed and scope during the early stage of reform, there would have been more positive economic performance in the industrial sector.

7.1.2 Reform of Chinese Bureaucracy

Another successful case relates to the reform of Chinese bureaucracy. The first task undertaken by Deng Xiaoping after he resumed his job was to reform the bureaucratic institutions. Manned by millions of workers, the system was officially acknowledged to be overstaffed and sluggish. There was an intensification of the drive to weed out tens of thousands of aged, inactive, and incompetent personnel. In an even more revolutionary move, the life tenure system for state and party cadres was abolished, and age limits for various offices were established. On a less restrictive basis, an educational requirement was established for each level of government position (see Table 7.1 for a summary of the reform). While removing superfluous personnel, the reform leaders stressed the importance of creating a 'third echelon' of younger leadership to enter responsible positions and be trained for future authority.

The major and direct consequence of the bureaucratic reform was that many younger and better-educated bureaucrats replaced the older revolutionary veterans. The new, younger officials were generally more supportive of the government reforms, as well as being more adaptable and more pragmatic. Being better educated in almost all cases, they were also generally more competent than their predecessors (Li, 1998, p. 394). Clearly, the Chinese-style reform of bureaucracy served as a stable political foundation for the implementation of the economic reform during the past decades. Without that reform, in which younger cadres were able to play an important role, the later reforms would have been impossible.

---

1. Note that as a result of three decades of effective CCP control, on the one hand, and of the closed-door policy, on the other, most (if not all) peasants in rural China had been accustomed to obeying political and economic orders coming from Beijing.

TABLE 7.1 Chinese Bureaucratic Reform (February 1982 to September 1984)

Statistic	Provincial Governors	Ministers	City Mayors or Department Chiefs	County Sheriffs or Division Chiefs
Mandatory retirement age (years)	65	65	60	55
Average retirement age (years)				
– Before reform	62	64	58	–
– After reform	55	58	50	<45
Percentage with college degree (%)				
– Before reform	20	37	14	11
– After reform	43	52	44	45
Average tenure (years)				
– Pre-1982	6.43/6.23[a]	6.56	–	–
– Post-1982	3.84/4.05[a]	4.44	–	–

Notes: *By 1988, 90% of government officials above the county level were newly appointed after 1982; 60% of those government officials had college degrees. This was a result of retiring 3.4 million revolutionary veterans.*
[a]*Governor/party secretary.*
Source: Li (1998, p. 394), which also gives other references.

Although the two reforms outlined above have been regarded as successful, they also had some negative effects. For example, the cooperative medical care system, which had worked quite well before the reform in rural areas, was abandoned as a result of the HRS.[2] The implementation of the policy of 'buying-out' the ageing bureaucrats also had some negative effects. An implicit and informal arrangement for most senior officials was that their children were allowed to enter politics in senior positions, which resulted in the birth of the infamous *taizidang* (party of crown prince) in China. It is worth noting that the rise of the *taizidang* often happened in parallel with political and economic corruption. However, the above problems were not because the reforms were too radical but that they were too mild (especially in the case of bureaucratic reform) and too limited in scope (especially in the case of agricultural reform).

7.2 RADICAL REFORM: THE UNSUCCESSFUL CASES

7.2.1 Price-Release Reform

During the 1980s, the dual-pricing system (which is discussed in subsection 6.2.2 of Chapter 6) provided opportunities for people who had access to state-controlled goods and

materials to make large profits by buying them at an officially fixed low price and reselling them at a market-based price. Consequently, it created various distortions and speculative transactions, which have often led to unequal competition as well as instances of official corruption.

After nearly ten years of reforms and debates over the relative merits of plan and market, a radical price reform was suddenly introduced in June 1988. This was based on the idea that 'long pain is not better than short pain', and that market prices should be implemented at once. Theoretically, if price subsidies are a significant cause for deficits, and if supply is highly elastic, then fiscal stabilization calls for early and speedy price liberalization (Liew et al., 2003). According to this theory, the greater the fiscal deficits (if they are not due to price subsidies) and the value of forced savings, and the smaller the supply elasticities, the longer should be the lag between fiscal and monetary stabilization and price liberalization. The macroeconomic environment was not favorable to the implementation of any such radical price reforms: the level of inflation was very high (18.5 percent in 1988) and friction from dual pricing was at its worst (for example, the planned price for steel was 700 yuan per ton while the market price was 1,800 yuan per ton) (Zhao, 1999, p. 195).

From 1985 to 1988, the level of price subsidies increased (Jin et al., 2001), as did the resulting fiscal deficit. The supply was constrained as a result of the decreasing marginal return from the early reform in the agricultural sector on the one hand, and the unsuccessful reform in state-owned

---

2. For example, according to a World Bank report, before reform, China's 'barefoot doctor' approach in its rural areas had been an important model for primary healthcare worldwide (Hammer, 1995).

industrial sector (as will be discussed in subsection 7.2.2) on the other. The implementation of price reform in China under these circumstances was both politically and socially impractical.[3]

7.2.2   The SOE Reform During the 1990s

Another notable case concerned China's various attempts to achieve radical SOE reform during the late 1980s and the 1990s. This had been delayed on several occasions, owing to serious concerns about the social instability that might result from the reform. The SOE reform was sufficiently extensive to cause large increases in unemployment. In December 1986, the 'Bankruptcy Law Concerning the SOEs' was adopted by the NPC. However, the law was not effectively applied until 1994 due to fears of unemployment and social instability, as China had only a relatively primitive social security system at that time.

The reform on non-performing SOEs was debated once again in the Fifth Plenum of the 14th CCPCC which was held during September 1995. The outcome was the policy of 'grasping the large and releasing the small'. To 'grasp the large' (zhuada) is to turn a select group of 300 out of a list of 1,000 already successful large enterprises and enterprise groups into world-class businesses. To 'release the small' (fangxiao) is to privatize or to contract out small SOEs or to allow them to go bankrupt. This policy allows most small SOEs to be sold off to private individuals; the management of those not sold is contracted out (Liew, 1999, p. 93). During the first two years, when the government began to release small and non-performing SOEs and to lay off superfluous workers, there was serious resistance to these reforms.

Notice that since the mid-1990s the CCP and the central government had been particularly concerned about the increasing number of illegal organizations established to organize protests against the radical SOE reform (see the final paragraph of subsection 4.4.2 in Chapter 4 for some detailed evidence). This can be seen, for example, in Jiang Zemin's speech at the meeting commemorating the twentieth anniversary of the Third Plenum of the Eleventh CCP National Congress (Jiang, 1998, p. 2). In contrast to the Western democratic countries in which protests against government were a regular occurrence, such protests were unusual in the PRC, especially during the post-reform period. They could easily remind the CCP and central government of the Tiananmen incident in June 1989. Consequently, they could hamper any further efforts on the radical reforms of the SOEs.

We are not able to verify if – or to what extent – the SOE reform, if it had been implemented earlier, could have been more successful. But, arguably, if the substantial ownership reform of the small and rural-based SOEs was introduced in parallel with, or immediately following, the radical agricultural ownership reform during the early stages (that is, in the late 1970s or the early 1980s), there would have been similar, positive economic performance. The primary reason lies in the fact that the market culture based on private ownership – the main form of ownership before the 1950s – still remained in the memories of most middle-aged SOE workers in China in the early 1980s. The critical role that the retired SOE workers played in the dramatic growth of the township and village-based enterprises (McMillan and Naughton, 1992; and World Bank, 1996, p. 51) indicates that the SOEs and the SOE workers could become more productive if the property right and incentive system moved away from the model of state ownership.

7.3   GRADUAL/PARTIAL REFORM: THE SUCCESSFUL CASES

7.3.1   Introduction of the Dual-Track System

The key component of China's gradual/partial reform was the introduction of a dual-track system, which was implemented first in agricultural products, before spreading slowly to consumer goods and intermediate goods. In each case, a free market in which the price was subject to the market regulations developed in parallel with a controlled market in which the price was kept almost unchanged at an officially fixed level. Because the price was higher in the market-regulated sector than in the state-controlled sector, the supply in the free market grew rapidly, so that its share of total output rose steadily. Meanwhile, the planned price was able to rise incrementally until it approached the market price when there was a narrowing of the gap between supply and demand.

The dual-track system extended through almost every sphere of the Chinese economy, from agriculture, industry, commerce, transportation, post, and telecommunications to healthcare, education, and so on, during the transition. For example, between 1979 and 1992, the proportion of industrial goods and materials distributed under the central plan system declined from 95 percent to less than 10 percent. There was a parallel reduction in the planned allocation of consumer goods: the number of first-class goods distributed by the state dropped from 65 to 20 and that of the production of materials distributed by the state was reduced from 256 to 19 during the same period (Liu, 1995, p. 53).

The smooth implementation of the dual-track system depended on the material compensation of, and the spiritual consolation for, various losers. For example, although

---

3. I still remember that, upon hearing the news about price reform in August 1988, I rushed to an electrical appliances shop to buy a radio-recorder, which was worthy of my ten-month salary but seldom used in the following years.

consumers have been able to buy foodstuffs on the free market since 1980, urban food coupons (for the purchase of grain, meat, oil, and so on) were finally removed only in the early 1990s. Guangzhou completed the removal of the above coupons in 1992 and spent on average 103 yuan in 1988, 113 yuan in 1990, and 43 yuan in 1992 per urban resident for compensation. Beijing also spent 182 yuan in 1990, 185 yuan in 1991, and 123 yuan in 1994 per head before its removal of the coupons (Qian, 2002). In addition, when the reformists decided to reduce the share of the centrally planned economy during the 1980s, spiritual consolation also applied to the conservatives who had strongly believed that the Chinese economy must be regulated mainly by planning and secondly by the market mechanism (see Box 7.1).

In short, a brief review of the gradually declining trend of the plan track throughout the 1980s provides evidence that, *ex post*, there is no 'ratcheting up' of the plan. Moreover, recent data reveal that the plan track in the product market has been largely 'phased out' in the 1990s, and that this phasing out of the plan track was accompanied in general by explicit compensation. With rapid growth, the plan track becomes, in no time at all, a matter of little consequence to most potential losers, which in turn reduces the cost required for compensating them (Lau et al., 2000, p. 142). In general, the dual-track reform has been regarded as being successful, since it not only avoided the decline of output but also improved the level

of efficiency (Wu and Zhao, 1987; and Li, 1997). It must be noted that the dual-track system did not always work well, especially when a large gap existed between market-regulated and officially fixed prices (we will discuss this point later).

7.3.2 Decentralization of Authority

Another key initiative of China's gradual reform was the decentralization of authority, that is, transferring economic management and decision making from central government to the provincial and local governments (see Chapter 6 for details). How did the reform work in practice, and to what extent had the provincial governments' fiscal incentives been strengthened as a result of this reform? Jin et al. (2001), based on the panel data of 28 provinces between 1982 and 1992, found that the marginal fiscal incentives of provincial governments increased during the reform period between 1982 and 1992, compared with those during the pre-reform period from 1970 to 1979.

A comparison of these findings with parallel investigations in Russia is also revealing. Zhuravskaya (2000) examined the fiscal incentives of city governments in the region–city fiscal relationship in post-reform Russia (in which the city is one level below the region, which in turn is one level below the federal government). Using the data from 35 cities for the period 1992–97, she found that increases in a city's own revenue were almost entirely

---

Box 7.1   The Art of Reforming a Planned Economy

During the 1980s there had been extensive and heated arguments about how plan and market could be appropriately combined in the Chinese economy. While the CCP conservatives strongly believed that the Chinese economy should be regulated mainly by planning and secondly by the market, some economists advocating a laissez-faire approach suggested an increase in market regulation. In order to resolve this dispute, Chinese reformists invented a term – 'guided plan'. Compared to 'commanded plan' (under which both the price and the quantity of each commodity are strictly controlled by the central government), 'guided plan' only relates to those that are under the loose control of the central or local government.

It is interesting to note that the definition of the term 'guided plan' is quite fuzzy. In practice, commodities under the 'guided plan' scheme can be treated either as part of those regulated by 'plan' or as part of those regulated by 'market' (see figure opposite). What the reformists intended to do, while not violating the principle of 'regulation mainly by planning', was to move Line B closer to Line A so as to reduce the scope of the 'commanded plan' (Zhao, 1998). Even though the conservatives still wanted to move Line B closer to Line C, in order to retain a larger portion of purely commanded plan

for the Chinese economy, confrontations between the reformists and conservatives were reduced substantially.

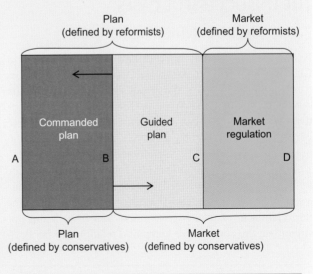

Source: *Based on a discussion with Professor Zhao Renwei, CASS.*

offset by decreases in shared revenues from the region to the city.[4]

7.3.3 Reform of Foreign Exchange System

China's foreign exchange system used to be strictly controlled by the central government. Yet since China began its economic reform in the late 1970s, the foreign trade system has been liberalized gradually. In the early 1980s, Chinese currency RMB was non-convertible and the foreign exchanges were strictly supervised by the state. Two exchange rates were in operation during that period: an official rate published by the government and another special one for foreign trade. Such a system was aimed at enhancing the country's exports and restricting its imports, as China suffered from a serious lack of foreign exchange at that time.

In 1984, as a result of improved performance in foreign trade and the economy as a whole, the government adopted a new policy of exchange retention. This policy allowed domestic enterprises and institutions to retain some of their foreign currency earnings, in contrast to the previous one in which these units turned over all of their foreign currency earnings to the state. Although a larger proportion of foreign exchanges were still under the control of the government, the new retaining policy stimulated domestic enterprises to increase their exports, and hence there was a significant improvement in China's foreign trade performance. However, this kind of gradual/partial reform, together with other gradual and partial reforms in external economic sectors, has also faced difficulties, as will be discussed in detail in Section 7.4.

7.4 GRADUAL/PARTIAL REFORM: THE UNSUCCESSFUL CASES

7.4.1 The SOE Reform in the 1980s

Not all gradual/partial reforms have performed well in China. Among the most typical unsuccessful examples were the introduction of the responsibility system and the contract system in the SOEs in 1983 and 1986, respectively. These reforms had some positive impacts on SOEs' performance, but overall they still did not achieve the objective of turning SOEs into efficient enterprises.

In brief, there were at least the following problems for this system. First, the operating mechanism of the contract system strengthened the vertical one-to-one bargaining relationship between government and firm. It did not strengthen the competitive horizontal relationship between

firms, and therefore was inconsistent with market-oriented reform (Zhao, 1999, p. 196). Secondly, it did not guarantee that the SOEs became independent economic identities. Finally, the contract did not solve the long-term behavioral problems of the managers and employees. Their behavior was still driven by short-term motivations, impinging on the interests of the owner, the state, and damaging firms' long-term development (Huang, 1999, p. 103).

7.4.2 Decentralization of Authority in the 1980s

In order to develop a full understanding of the characteristics of the Chinese-style reform, one must keep in mind two important facts: first, China's vast territorial size and wide diversity of physical environments have inevitably resulted in great differences in regional economic conditions; secondly, with China's population of 1.3 billion and its 56 distinct ethnic groups, most provinces, which would be equivalent in size to a medium-sized country, are considerable political and economic systems in their own right. The differences between these provinces have long been a defining characteristic of China's politics since, in most instances, their boundaries were created more than two thousand years ago (Gottmann, 1973; Goodman, 1997). Furthermore, Chinese culture is not homogeneous across provinces, in terms of ethnic and linguistic groups, or provincial politics. As a result, the chances of the adoption of a common standard and interprovincial coordination between different groups of people are not likely to be enhanced if there are markedly differing religious beliefs and cultural values.

The Chinese-style decentralization of economic authority (which has been defined as a successful case of reform in subsection 7.3.2) did not always work well, especially during the earliest stages of the reforms. Specifically, from the late 1970s to the early 1990s, China's early reform was characterized by a recurring pattern: 'decentralization immediately followed by disorder, disorder immediately followed by concentralization, concentralization followed by rigidity, and rigidity followed by decentralization', a cycle of 'decentralization (fang)–disorder–over-centralization (shou)–rigidity'. This is the so-called *shou-fang* circle.[5]

Since the advent of administrative decentralization, China's national economy had become effectively 'cellularized' into a plethora of semi-autarkic regional enclaves

---

4. The resulting near-zero incentives in post-reform Russia look similar to pre-reform China, but stand in sharp contrast to post-reform China (Qian, 2002).

5. For example, Baum (1994, pp. 5–9 and pp. 369–76) offers a plausible explanation of the fang–shou cycle during 1978–93: the decentralization (fang) policy was concentrated on 1978, 1980, 1982, 1984, 1986, 1988, and 1992; while the concentralization (shou) policy was concentrated on 1979, 1981, 1983, 1985, 1987, 1989, and 1993. Shirk (1993), Dittmer, and Wu (1993, pp. 10–12) reach a similar conclusion, sketching out four relatively complete, synchronous cycles of fang and shou during 1980 to 1989: fang predominated in 1979–80, 1984, and 1988, while shou predominated in 1981, 1985–86, 1987, and 1988–89.

during the 1980s. In order to protect local market and revenue sources, it became common practice in China that provinces restricted import (export) from (to) other provinces by levying high, if informal, taxes on commodities and by creating non-tariff barriers. Xinjiang autonomous region, for example, effectively banned the import of 48 commodities on the grounds that they would harm its domestic economy. Jilin refused to market beer produced in its neighboring provinces of Heilongjiang and Liaoning. Hunan province prohibited exporting grain to its neighbor, Guangdong province. In some provinces, local authorities established, and provided finance for, a variety of schemes in order to promote the sales of local products. Enterprises from other provinces, however, often had difficulties in finding office spaces, accommodation, or land for their business activities.[6]

7.4.3 Reform of China's Banking System

Another case is the reform of China's banking system, which is generally recognized to lag well behind China's dramatic moves toward a market economy that are so evident in other sectors. Prior to the commencement of reforms in 1983, the People's Bank of China (PBC), China's central bank, dominated the country's highly centralized financial scene. Not only did it control the money supply; it also managed all banking and savings activities. In effect, before the reforms the PBC was only the accounting department of the Chinese central government.

At the end of 1993, the State Council issued a new plan to spur changes in the monetary and financial system that would strengthen the PBC's grip on the macroeconomic environment, create specialized banks to serve priority sectors, and push the other banks towards becoming true commercial banks. The overall objective was to separate monetary policy from normal banking functions and to convert most banks into truly independent financial entities. However, the PBC remains subservient to the finance ministry and thus cannot refuse to finance government expenditure. Branches of the PBC in the provinces and districts are also subject to the dictates of both PBC and local government officials. As a result, it is very difficult for them to refuse loans to local government entities that demand more and more credit (Xu, 1995).

In the late 1990s, the Asian financial crisis served a very useful function: it alerted Chinese leaders to the dangers of operating a weak financial system. Aware of the lessons drawn from the Asian financial crisis, in 1998 China wanted to quicken the pace of banking reform. The major measure was that RMB270 billion (US$33 billion) in special bonds was issued in 1998 in order to recapitalize the state

banks. In the following year it created an asset management company (AMC) for each of the big four state banks. The AMCs received RMB400 billion (US$48 billion) in seed capital from the Ministry of Finance (MOF) and issued RMB1 trillion (US$121 billion) worth of MOF-guaranteed bonds. They then used these funds to buy RMB1.4 trillion (US$170 billion) of bad loans from the state banks at face value. But the program failed to cure the banks' woes, since other relevant financial and economic reforms had not been implemented. Since 1998, the percentage of bad loans on the banks' books has not fallen much, and the AMCs have had limited success in recovering or selling off the bad assets. Meanwhile, corporate governance, transparency, and risk management at the state banks have only shown slight improvement (Lo, 2004).

China's gradual/partial open-door policy has serious implications for its legal system and its lack of transparency, and problems of assimilating a non-market economy.[7] Furthermore, in accordance with the requirements of the WTO, banks, insurance companies, telecommunications, and other service industries from the rest of the world will be allowed to operate in China according to the negotiated timetable. The impact may eventually break up the status of monopoly and state control that have existed in China for around half a century. The new banking reforms, which started on December 1, 2003, opening the sector further to foreign competition, have still been too mild and limited in scope. Pressing banking and financial reforms are needed in the years to come.

7.5 WHITHER CHINESE-STYLE REFORM?

7.5.1 Political Economy of Reforms

In the previous sections, we have examined various successful and unsuccessful cases of Chinese-style reform (see Table 7.2 for a qualitative comparison of major reform programs). It should be noted that the judgment of a reform as being 'successful' or 'unsuccessful' is based on available data and literature. Frankly speaking, there is no mandatory standard for this definition since each reform – whether or not it has been 'successful' or 'unsuccessful' – has both positive and negative effects on the Chinese economy. In addition, the terms 'radical' and 'gradual/partial' reforms used in these sections are also defined elastically, since judged by international standards, over the course of the past three decades China's reforms as a whole have been implemented only via a gradual/partial approach.

---

6. More detailed analysis can be found in Shen and Dai (1990), Li (1993), and Wedeman (1993).

7. For example, there have to be changes to about 220 Chinese laws that are incompatible with WTO rules (Reti, 2001). Discussions in this regard include, for example, Garnaut and Huang (1995), Corbet (1996), Keidel (1995), Wu (1996), Mastel (1996, 1998), and Morici (1997).

TABLE 7.2 A Comparison of Selected Reform Programs

Strategy	Successful Cases	Unsuccessful Cases
Gradual/partial approach	Dual-pricing system reform (1979–92); Foreign exchange system reform (1984–)	Industrial contract system (1983; 1986); Administrative decentralization (1980s–early 1990s); Banking reform (1983–)
Radical approach	Agricultural reform (1980–82); Bureaucratic reform (1982–84)	Price-release reform (1988–89); SOE Ownership reform (1980s; 1990s)

Source: Defined in the text.

During the twentieth century the failure of the centrally planned economies (CPEs) to keep pace with their market-oriented counterparts demonstrated quite clearly that planning entire economies at the level of central government does not offer a productive path to long-term development. Since 1978, economic reforms in China have sought to improve, among other things, enterprise incentive systems with greater relative decision-making autonomy.[8] The dynamism of the Chinese economy may be attributed to a variety of reform measures. One such measure was the lifting of previous restrictions on the development of non-state sectors and the policy of promoting a diversified ownership structure. This has led to the explosive growth of the non-state sectors that are acting increasingly as the engine of economic development, particularly since the early 1990s when China formally tried to transform its economy to a market-oriented system.

It is now generally believed that the Chinese outward-oriented development policy was borrowed in part from the experiences of the newly industrialized economies (NIEs) in East Asia. On the one hand, the reformist leaders were also deeply aware that their rivals from the Chinese Civil War across the Taiwan Strait, their compatriots in colonial Hong Kong, and their Cold War enemies in South Korea were enjoying sustained economic success that raised deeply challenging questions about China's own continuing levels of backwardness (Garnaut, 1999, pp. 2–3). On the other hand, China and the USA saw the former Soviet Union as their common enemy and this led Mao and Nixon to normalize Sino-US relations in 1971, which paved the way for China's re-engagement with the non-communist world. Later the defeat of the US forces in Vietnam meant that the West appeared to be a less threatening place to China's leaders, facilitating China's re-entry into the global economy (Liew et al., 2003).

Let's consider a reform program consisting of two reform measures that can be carried out either simultaneously or sequentially. Suppose that the economic outcome of the full reform is, in most circumstances, better than that of each partial reform measure. Without considering the cost of implementation, a big bang reform may have an advantage over a gradual one.[9] However, once reforms are reversed, which sometimes happens due to political and economic uncertainties, the reversal is more costly for the full reform than the partial one, which means that reversing the full reform sometimes costs more than reversing a single partial reform measure.[10]

Figure 7.1 shows how a variety of factors interact in the market-oriented reforms in a centrally planned economy in which:

1. A reform scheme may be either accelerated or reversed, depending upon the improvement or deterioration of political stability, respectively.
2. Political stability is associated with public satisfaction (which is positively related to the increment of income level), social shock resulting from the reform, and external irritation.
3. Open-door policy has two effects: economically, it will promote economic growth through foreign trade and FDI inflows; politically, it will affect political stability through external irritation.

Essentially, China's economic reform has provided fewer incentives and opportunities for provincial and local governments to make use of the comparative advantages for inter-regional cooperation in the 1980s than in the 1990s. The following research evidence can confirm this phenomenon. Young (2000), based on the pre-1990s data, finds that China's economic reform resulted in a fragmented internal market with fiefdoms controlled by local officials whose economic and political ties to protect industry resembled those observed in Latin American economies in previous decades. It seems plausible that the endogenous response of actors to the rent-seeking opportunities created by gradualist reform could give rise to new distortions, whose lifespan far exceeds that of the rents which had motivated their initial arrival (Young, 2000). Using the data from 1988 to 2000, Cai et al. (2002), however, argue that the decentralization of authority has already generated comparative advantages for inter-regional cooperation in the manufacturing

---

8. See Annex for a list of major reform programs and their outcomes.

9. Examples that support big bang reforms include Lipton and Sachs (1990), Åslund (1991), Berg and Sachs (1992), Boycko (1992), Murphy et al. (1992), Sachs (1993), Frydman and Rapaczynski (1994), and Woo (1994).

10. Examples that support gradual reforms include Svejnar (1989), Portes (1990), McKinnon (1991b), Roland (1991), Dewatripont and Roland (1992a, 1992b, and 1995), McMillan and Naughton (1992), Murrell (1992), Aghion and Blanchard (1994), Litwack and Qian (1998), and Wei (1993).

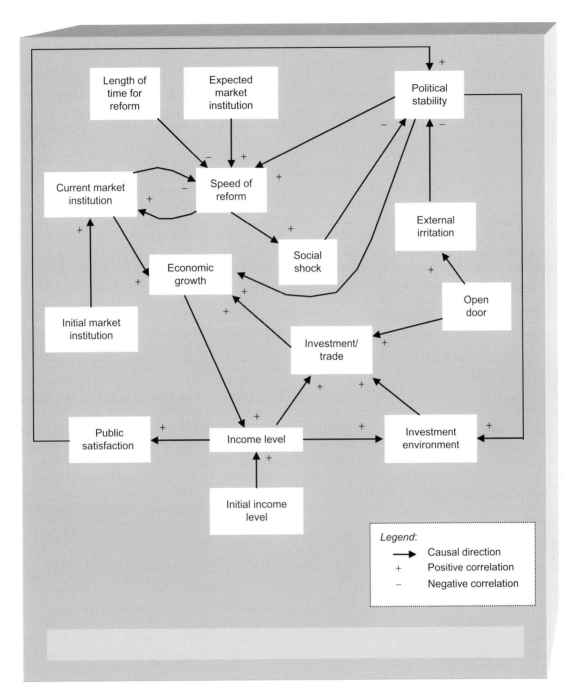

FIGURE 7.1 A feedback model of market-oriented reform in a centrally planned economy.

sector during the reform period. If both results are correct, the Chinese reform might suggest that 'big bang' tends to be optimal in the early stage of reform and that gradualism tends to be optimal in the late stage of reform.

7.5.2 WTO and the Chinese Reform

The economic reforms introduced in many former CPEs followed domestic political crises (such as the collapse of the Soviet Union in the case of Russia, and the death of Mao Zedong and the fall of the leftist 'Gang of Four' in the case of China). However, successful reforms are also promoted by a favorable international environment. Haggard and Webb (1994) have found that international factors influence reform through a number of channels, such as the prospect of trade concessions and agreements, as well as conditionality and ideas brought by external advisers and technocrats trained abroad. The significant role of the open-door policy in market-oriented reform can be witnessed by the Chinese experience. China's application to get access to the GATT/WTO lasted for 16 years – from 1986 to 2002. After each of the long-running negotiations, China's centrally planned system on foreign trade had a gradual reform toward the market-oriented economic system. During the 1990s, almost all major Chinese reforms of the foreign trade system were influenced by the WTO accession negotiations (Chi, 2000).

It is almost certain that the Chinese reforms will not be reversed in the foreseeable future. This is not only because these reforms have become a win–win situation for all who are in power, but also because it has meant that the Chinese economy is increasingly dependent on the outside world. Since China's entrance into the WTO in November 2001, external stakeholders (such as international financial organizations and foreign-invested enterprises) have been exerting an increasing influence on Chinese economic reform. However, the collective actions of these stakeholders on the Chinese reforms are much more complicated than those of Chinese domestic stakeholders. For example, with regard to the reform of the current exchange rate system under which the Chinese currency, as generally recognized, has been devalued, there are two different voices from the outside world. While countries having large trade deficits with China have requested that the level of the Chinese currency should be more freely determined by the market, their overseas enterprises in China have benefited significantly from this currency devaluation through the export of their products to the outside world.

China is now facing the dilemma of whether to follow the past tune (that is, the gradual and partial strategy) in order to minimize the risk of macroeconomic transition, or to proceed more quickly in order to satisfy the WTO requirements with the fixed timetable. However, it seems that the Chinese government is not prepared to bear the potential risk of any substantial or radical reforms. One example is the reform of the foreign exchange system. As stated in subsection 7.3.3, China's gradual/partial reform of its foreign exchange system has contributed significantly to its robust foreign trade performance on the one hand and its domestic economic stability on the other. However, since 1994 when a unitary and floating exchange-rate system was established, there has been no substantial reform. Obviously, this system is to a large extent determined by the government; the foreign exchange rate is controlled officially and the central bank is one of the biggest participants in the market.

7.6 SUMMARY

This chapter has explored the elements underpinning the design and implementation of the Chinese economic reform from 1978 onwards. It sets out to provide an explanation for the causes and timing of the major reform programs, as well as for how the successes and failures of the various reform efforts were associated with the initial conditions and the reform strategies.

The importance of initial conditions and strategies for economic reforms has been noted (Fischer and Gelb, 1991; and De Melo et al., 1997). The question of how such issues affect the final results of economic reforms still remains unresolved, however (Campos and Coricelli, 2002, p. 828). For example, when considering the remarkable differences between the reforms pursued in China and Russia, one must not overlook the initial institutional conditions in each of the countries. Prior to reform, the central planning system in China lasted only a relatively short period of time (that is, from the late 1950s to the late 1970s) compared to that in the former Soviet Union (FSU) (that is, from the early twentieth century to the late 1980s). As a result, the capitalist ideology and market culture still had a strong base in China vis-à-vis the FSU.[11]

In comparison to those reforms introduced in Eastern Europe and the former Soviet Union, the reforms in China have some distinctive characteristics. First, the degree to which the economic system derived from the former Soviet Union has exerted an influence on the Chinese economy varied from sector to sector. The sector that was most affected was the industrialized sector of the national economy, while there was less influence on the disaggregated agricultural sector and small industries. Secondly, the economic reforms in China started at a time when China was regarded as a quasi-militaristic model of communism (Zhao, 1999, p. 186), which was different to the patterns of reforms in Eastern Europe. Thirdly, the economic reform in China preceded political reform.

Except for a few cases in which reform followed an approach similar to that of the 'big bang', most Chinese economic reforms can be identified as being gradualist in nature. To date the Chinese-type reform introduced since 1978 has achieved remarkable results. Particularly praiseworthy are the facts that the Chinese-type reform has avoided the collapse in output that has been characteristic of transitions in other former centrally planned economies and that it has generated unprecedented increases in living standards across the country.

Over the course of the past three decades, China has successfully transformed its centrally planned system and has achieved a more rapid economic growth than any of the world's other socialist or former socialist countries. However, China's unusual reform experience might not be generalizable to other transition economies, since it has been shaped by a set of unique initial conditions.

---

11. With regard to the FSU's relative weakness of the market economy, Mikhail Gorbachev's speech on September 11, 1990 might be revealing: 'Our brains just could not handle this idea of a market.' Cited in Hwang (1993, p. 147).

A particularly intriguing and under-studied factor is the legacy of the Great Famine (1959–61) and of the notorious Cultural Revolution (1966–76), two major events that not only boosted Deng Xiaoping's credibility and authority as a reformer, but also laid a foundation for the smooth implementation of agricultural and bureaucratic reforms.

In short, for the majority of the past three decades, China's reforms have achieved two objectives simultaneously: to improve economic efficiency by unleashing the standard forces of incentives and competition on the one hand; and to make the reform a win–win situation, and therefore in the interests of those in power, on the other

(Qian, 2002). They also take into consideration China's specific political and cultural conditions. With its impressive economic achievements, today the Chinese reforms are rarely called into question.

Despite these successes, there still remained problems from social and political perspectives throughout the reform era. Ironically, China's economic growth was obtained at the cost of a retardation of political reforms, not to mention worsening income inequalities as well as other social problems. As China continues to integrate with the world economy and accepts other global values, there are continuing mounting pressures for political reform.

ANNEX

A List of China's Major Reforms and Their Outcomes Since 1978

Year/M/D	Organizer(s)	Program	Outcome(s)
1978/ 12/18	Third Plenum of the 11th CCPCC	'Decision of the CCPCC Concerning the Reform of Economic System'	Starting of China's economic reforms
1979	NPC	'Law of the People's Republic of China Concerning Joint Ventures with Chinese and Foreign Investment'	Promotion of the FDI and international trade
1979	CCPCC and State Council	Guangdong and Fujian provinces were granted with 'special policies and flexible measures' in foreign economic affairs	Ibid, especially in Guangdong and Fujian provinces
1979/ 12/26	People's Congress of Guangdong province	Shenzhen next to Hong Kong, Zhuhai next to Macau, and Santou were designed as the SEZs, to experiment with a market-oriented economy	For example, they have the authority to approve foreign investment projects up to US$30 million, while other regions' authority remained much lower
1980	State Council	Starting of the fiscal contract system	Transformation from 'having meals in one pot' to 'having meals in different pots'
1980/ 8/26	NPC	Xiamen in Southeast Fujian province vis-à-vis Taiwan became an SEZ	Promotion of economic ties with Taiwan
1980/9	CCP and State Council	Household Responsibility System (HRS)	Agricultural growth in rural areas
1984	State Council	'Provisional Regulations for the Management of "Small-volume" Border Trade'	Promotion of inland border trade of China
1984/4	CCPCC and the State Council	'Design of 14 coastal open cities'	Promotion of the FDI inflows into Tianjin, Shanghai, Dalian, Qinhuangdao, Yantai, Qingdao, Lianyungang, Nantong, Ningbo, Wenzhou, Fuzhou, Guangzhou, Ganjiang, and Beihai
1984/ 5/10	State Council	'Provisional Regulations on the Enlargement of Autonomy of State-owned Industrial Enterprises'	
1984/ 10/21	CCPCC	'Decision of the CCPCC Concerning the Reform of Economic Structure'	Formal start of economic reform in urban areas and in the industrial sector
1985/2	State Council	The Yangtze River, Pearl River, and South Fujian were approved as coastal economic development zones	Increase of FDI and foreign trade in the related areas
1986	State Council	Regulations of Issues Concerning the Extensive Regional Economic Cooperation	Promotion of interprovincial cooperation
1986/12	NPC	'Bankruptcy Law Concerning the SOEs'	Not applied until 1994 due to fears of unemployment and social instability

(Continued)

A List of China's Major Reforms and Their Outcomes Since 1978 (Continued)

Year/M/D	Organizer(s)	Program	Outcome(s)
1986/12	State Council	Encouraging the SOEs to adopt the contract system	By the end of 1988, most SOEs had adopted various forms of the contract system
1988/3	State Council	Liaodong and Shandong peninsulas and Bohai Basin area were allowed to open up to the outside world	Increase of FDI in the related areas
1988/4	NPC	Hainan province was approved as an SEZ with even more flexible policies than other SEZs	
1988/8	State Council	Attempt of radical price reform	Ended with bankruptcy
1990/4	CCPCC and the State Council	Shanghai's Pudong area was granted permission to enjoy some of the SEZ's mechanisms	
1991	Yunnan province	'Provisional Regulations Concerning Border Trade'	Promotion of cross-border trade in related areas
1992/7/14	Tibet autonomous region	'Resolutions Concerning Further Reform and Opening up to the Outside World'	Promotion of cross-border trade in related areas
1991/4/20	Inner Mongolia autonomous region	'Resolution of Some Issues Concerning the Extension of Open-door and Promotion of Economic Development'	Promotion of cross-border trade in related areas
1992	State Council	'Notification Concerning the Further Opening up of the Four Frontier Cities of Heihe, Shuifenhe, Hunchun, and Manzhouli'	Promotion of cross-border trade in related areas
1992/1/25	Office of Custom, PRC	'Measures Concerning the Supervision and Favorable Taxation for the People-to-People Trade in Sino–Myanmar Border'	Promotion of cross-border trade in related areas
1992/2/9	Xinjiang autonomous region	'Notification of Promoting Trade and Economic Cooperation with the Neighboring and Eastern European Countries'	Promotion of cross-border trade in related areas
1992/6	State Commission for Restructuring the Economic Systems	'Provisional Regulations on Joint-Stock Companies'	
1992/6	State Council	'Notification Concerning Further Opening up of the Five Frontier Cities and Towns of Nanning, Kunming, Pingxiang, Ruili, and Hekou'	Promotion of cross-border trade in related areas
1992/6	Heilongjiang province	'Some Favorable Policies and Economic Autonomy Authorized to the Frontier Cities of Heihe and Shuifenhe'	Promotion of cross-border trade in related areas
1992/7/22	State Council	'Regulations on the Transformation of the Operating Mechanisms of State-owned Industrial Enterprises'	
1993/11	Third Plenum of the 14th CCPCC	Establishment of the Modern Enterprise System	
1993/11/14	Third Plenum of the 14th CCPCC	'Decision of the CCPCC on Several Issues Concerning the Establishment of a Socialist Market Economic Structure'	Ideological victory of reformers over conservatives
1994	People's Bank of China	Separation of commercial banking from policy lending; reduction in the number of the central bank's regional braches from 30 or more to only six	The elimination of some of the structural inefficiencies of the financial system
1994	State Council	Introduction of 'tax-sharing system' into all provinces	The central government collects all shares as central taxes, and local government collects only those designated as local taxes
1994/1/1	People's Bank of China	Establishment of a new unitary and floating exchange-rate system	Devaluation of the RMB and promotion of export

(Continued)

A List of China's Major Reforms and Their Outcomes Since 1978 (Continued)

Year/M/D	Organizer(s)	Program	Outcome(s)
1995/9	Fifth Plenum of the Fourteenth CCPCC	Policy of 'grasping the large and releasing the small'	To turn a select group of 300 out of a list of 1000 already successful large enterprises and enterprise groups into world-class businesses; and to privatize or to contract out small SOEs or let them go bankrupt
1998/3	The Ninth NPC	Amendment to Article 6 of the Chinese Constitution: 'public, instead of state, ownership as the main form of ownership of the means of production'	Individual, private, and other forms of non-public ownership are 'important components of a socialist economy' and they 'supplement the system of socialist public ownership'
1999	State Council	Debt-equity swap scheme (*zhai zhuan gu*) in four large state-owned banks	The bad loans to SOEs are converted into equity and then sold at a discount to investors
2000/4/1	People's Bank of China	Adoption of 'real-name' banking system	All the household bank deposits require a depositor's ID
2001/11	WTO	China's entry to the WTO	Increase in the opportunity for China to integrate into the world economic system
2003/12	State Council	Transformation of Bank of China and China Construction Bank into joint stock ownership	
2004/4	State Council	The abolishment of agricultural tax within 3 years	
2008/7	State Council	Privatization of forestland for 70 years of tenure in selected areas	
2008/8	People's Bank of China	More flexible foreign exchange policies	
2008/10	Third Plenum of the 17th CCPCC	*De facto* land privatization in rural areas	

Sources: (1) Bulletins of the State Council, People's Republic of China, various issues; (2) Bulletins of the National People's Congress, various issues; and (3) the author's collection.

Case Study 5

Interest Groups, Stakeholders, and Reform in China

In this case study, we allow reform to be determined endogenously. Our task is to find out how the interest groups and stakeholders interact with each other throughout the whole of the reform process and also how they have had a decisive influence upon the outcomes of the reform. For the sake of simplicity, we assume that the CCP is the only player (policy maker), and that it can be further divided into different cliques (such as radicals and conservatives) in different reform periods. Interest groups can be defined as collections of individuals who share a specific common interest. It is noteworthy that the various interest groups can overlap. For instance, the same individual can be both an entrepreneur and a university professor. Stakeholders then are members of an interest group whose interests are affected by a particular decision.

The evidence described below will demonstrate how Chinese economic reform has evolved from the collusion of the CCP radicals and conservatives (during the early stages of reform) to the collusion of all political, economic, and cultural elites (during the later stages of reform) as well as how this evolution has influenced the outcomes of the Chinese reform *per se*.

I.   Radicals and Conservatives in the Early Reforms

To understand the implications of the incentives for the implementation of reform in China, we must make a point of the relationship between the CCP radicals and conservatives.[12] Both Deng Xiaoping and his senior supporters in

---

12. In fact, it is difficult to consistently identify the radicals and conservatives throughout the whole period of reform. Those who had been treated as radicals during one period might become conservatives at a later stage; furthermore, a CCP senior who can be a radical reformer in respect of one agenda (such as agricultural or other domestic sector reform) might be considered as a conservative in another (such as external economic sectors or political reform in general).

power had been victims of the Cultural Revolution (1966–76) during which Mao criticized them for economic liberalism. The special events of the Cultural Revolution meant that – regardless of their liberal or conservative ideology – they must unite or, at the very least, refrain from challenging each other in mutually tolerable matters during the early period of reform.

One of the initial challenges facing the Chinese leadership was to provide for the creation of a rational and efficient governing system in order to support economic development. In pursuit of that goal, the cult of personality surrounding Mao Zedong was unequivocally condemned and was replaced by a strong emphasis on collective leadership. An example of this new emphasis was the CCP's restoration in February 1980 of its Secretariat, which had been suspended since 1966. The new CCP constitution, adopted in 1982, abolished the post of CCPCC chairman – a powerful post held by Mao Zedong for more than four decades, thereby providing a degree of balance between the CCP radicals and conservatives.

The most striking feature of the Chinese reform during the 1980s was the collusive game between the radicals and the conservatives. In considering a reform strategy, the radicals must take into account not only the benefit from the reform but also the political cost stemming from the possibility of losing their coalition with the conservatives. Since deterrence implies cost, the reform strategy on which both players (radicals and conservatives) would find it optimal to cooperate, does not equate the marginal economic benefit with the marginal economic cost. Instead, a player's optimal strategy of reform equates the marginal economic cost with the marginal economic and political costs. In other words, it is political cost that creates a wedge between the efficient and optimal strategies of reform.

Although the strategy of pursuing faster reforms maximizes the radicals' gross payoff, it does not maximize its net payoff. The radicals would find it optimal to have a strategy involving slower reform in which the marginal economic gains from cooperation equal the marginal political and economic costs.[13] For example, Li Peng's long-lasting political career as premier is one of the outcomes resulting from the collusion of the radicals and conservatives. In 1987, Li became a member of the Politburo's powerful Standing Committee, and a year later, Deng Xiaoping picked Li to succeed Zhao Ziyang as premier after Zhao had become the CCPCC's general secretary. This choice might have been seen as unusual because Li Peng did not appear to share Deng's advocacy of

economic reform. However, it illustrated clearly that Deng had to seek compromises with the conservatives.[14]

As a matter of fact, during the massive mandatory retirement program which was facilitated by a one-time buyout strategy (this has been stated in subsection 7.1.2), the outgoing CCP officials were partially compensated, in both economic and political terms. For example, a special name was coined for this kind of retirement, *lixiu* – literally 'to leave the post and rest'. After *lixiu*, retired officials continued to enjoy all of their former political privileges, such as reading government circulars of the same level of confidentiality. Some served as special counselors for their successors. As economic compensations, they could keep using their official cars with chauffeurs and security guards. In addition, officials under *lixiu* received an extra month's wages each year and extra housing that their children and grandchildren were entitled to enjoy after their death (Li, 1998, p. 394). Without that reform, in which many younger cadres were able to play an important role, the reforms that followed afterwards would have been impossible.

Past reform events show that in China the institutional improvement toward a market-oriented system followed a non-linear pattern, called the *shou-fang* circle (as was discussed earlier in subsection 7.4.2). As a matter of fact, the *shou-fang* circle represents the dynamic process of the political games between radicals and conservatives. Specifically, the *fang* (decentralization) was initiated by the radicals, while the *shou* (over-centralization) was insisted upon by the conservatives. As a result of their very nature (as stated at the beginning of this section), both radicals and conservatives have compromised with each other's initiatives during most of the reform era.

When dealing with the early reforms, it is necessary to mention other stakeholders as well as their attitudes toward reforms. Farmers and urban workers – two groups that benefited from the reform-driven economic growth – did not oppose the CCP, or the reform in particular. Intellectuals, especially those who had received Westernized training and who had been seriously mistreated during the Cultural Revolution, adopted a more critical stance. They had a strong desire for Western democracy. On the other hand, however, the CCP elites, especially the CCP conservatives, could not at all accept a totally Western-oriented reform (Kang, 2002). Since the radical reformers had been much less powerful than the CCP conservatives at the time when most CCP seniors were still alive, their attempt at uniting with the intellectual elite failed during the Tiananmen incident in June 1989.

It seems likely that, as a result of the disappearance of the CCP seniors and the conservatives on the one hand and

---

13. Note that this result does not depend on the process through which the redistribution of incomes from the radicals and conservatives has been determined.

14. Cited from http://edition.cnn.com/SPECIALS/1999/china.50/inside. china/profiles/li.peng/. Accessed on November 12, 2008.

the emergence of more young and Western-learning officials on the other, the Chinese reform should have become increasingly radical since the mid-1990s. What does the evidence tell us?

II. Political, Economic, and Cultural Elites in the Later Reforms

As the initiation and sustainability of a reform requires political, economic, and cultural support, the identification of interest groups and stakeholders of the reform in general, but especially those who are politically (and otherwise) active as allies and opponents of reform, is an important step toward the successful completion of the reform. An important distinction is whether interest groups and stakeholders are organized – in other words, whether they pursue their common interest jointly in a coordinated fashion. It is natural to believe that stakeholders will exert pressure on policy makers. This, however, need not always be the case, as not all stakeholders are organized (Fidrmuc and Noury, 2003). Because organized interest groups are better informed than the citizenry at large, they can provide key personalities (the government officials, legislators) with intelligence of various kinds.

Beginning in the mid-1980s, the bureaucratic reform generated a large surplus of government officials. At the same time, many government agencies began to establish business entities, and bureaucrats became managers of these businesses. As a result, a phenomenon that later came to be known as *xiahai* ('jumping into the ocean'). Since the early 1990s, *xiahai* has been an immensely popular phenomenon among Chinese government officials.[15] By joining the business world, the former bureaucrats obtain much higher economic payoffs as well as a higher degree of personal freedom, despite being exposed to increased economic uncertainty. On the other hand, there is a high demand for those bureaucrats, since in the half-reformed economy many non-state enterprises need their knowledge and skills in order to deal with the remaining government regulations.

Since the 16th National Congress of the CCP, held in Beijing in November 2002, CCP membership has been formally opened to China's business elite. The removal of the clause in the CCP's constitution that officially prohibited private businessmen from becoming party members and serving in the government is intended to bring the CCP constitution into line with the reality of the party's character and social composition as it prepares to accelerate the pace of market reforms. In a rambling opening address to the Congress,

Jiang Zemin articulated the class interests of the new Chinese elite. He called for the Beijing regime to persevere in opening up to the capitalist market and declared that the CCP should protect the 'legitimate rights and interests' of businessmen and property owners (Jiang, 2002). The formal opening of the CCP to different levels of businesspeople in 2002 represented a turning point. The fact that Jiang's 'Three Represents' theory formalizes what has already emerged was highlighted by the year 2002 *Forbes* magazine list of China's 100 richest multi-millionaires. One-quarter of those on the list declared that they were CCP members (Chan, 2002). In addition, many Chinese CEOs of private companies or transnational corporations also have connections with the CCP.

Since the mid-1990s, cultural elites (including noted intellectuals, popular entertainers and ethnic minority-based social elites) have been establishing closer links to the political and economic elites in China.[16] The factors resulting in the collusion of the political and cultural elites might include the following. First, the disappearance of senior CCPCC members has weakened the power of the conservatives since the early 1990s, while the younger political leaders are usually more highly educated than their predecessors. Secondly, after the Tiananmen incident, radical intellectuals were subjected to serious retaliation, most of them either fleeing the country or disappearing from academic circles. Thirdly, the changing external environment (such as the collapse of the former Soviet Union followed by the unsuccessful 'big bang' reforms introduced in Russia and also the USA transferring from standing against the CCP to against China) helped most, if not all, intellectuals to cooperate with the CCP and the government.

Several books have portrayed the post-Tiananmen period as one of intense political disagreement (see, for example, Fewsmith, 1999; and Lam, 1999). Certainly, this was true until the mid-1990s. Yet disagreements since this time have been expressed increasingly through non-sanctioned means by non-sanctioned actors. The elite battles evident today are based upon illegitimate end-running, rather than legitimate contestation. Thus the politics of contestation – legitimate competition within the structures of the polity properly used by a range of agreed actors – remains absent. The earnestness of contestation in the early reform era has been replaced by the anomie of compliance or the intrigue of crypto-politics in the post-reform era (Gilley, 2004, p. 121).

Among China's rural peasantry and the industrial working class, a seething hostility is building up over official corruption, poverty, the loss of services, unemployment, and the widening income gap between rich and poor. After several years of factional debate within the CCP,

---

15. In a survey conducted in 1992, 30 percent of surveyed officials were thinking about *xiahai* (Chen, 1993). In another survey of local government officials in 1995, close to 20 percent were planning on *xiahai* (SCSR, 1996). Of those, 35 percent were looking for joint-venture enterprises, 21 percent for private enterprises, and 1.5 percent for SOEs. Tang and Parish (1998) find in their large survey that 99 percent of those officials who planned to quit the bureaucracy wanted to join businesses. – Cited from Li (1998).

16. This can be witnessed by, for example, Yu's (2004) article in which some influential Chinese economists are criticized for their favoritism to the rich over the poor.

a consensus has emerged that the lesson to be drawn from the Tiananmen events is that the regime must build a solid base among the urban upper and middle classes, while making no democratic concessions to the masses (Chan, 2002). The government believed it could weather the opposition of workers and peasants by keeping them like 'scattered sand' – that is, lacking any national organization or coherent political program (Kang, 2002). Commenting on the sentiment of the political establishment, Kang (2002) points out:

There is a stable alliance between the political, economic, and intellectual elite of China. The main consequence is that the elite won't challenge the CCP and the government. The economic elite love money, not democracy. Their vanity will also be satisfied as the CCP has promised them party membership and government positions.

How has the Chinese reform been linked to the collusion of the political, economic and cultural elites? First of all, faced by the example of the failure of the radical reforms in the former USSR, the political elite – no matter how radical they had been during the previous period of reform – has become increasingly pragmatic over time. In essence, they would now be more likely to choose a more gradual/partial (or alternatively, less radical) reform strategy than they had chosen in the 1980s. Secondly, the political, economic and cultural elites have increasingly become beneficiaries of the existing system that was based upon the past gradual and partial reforms. As a result, there will be less and less incentive for them to see any (radical and thorough) political and economic reforms that could affect their existing benefits. Last but not least, in contrast to the reforms that had been merely decided by the

political elite (including both CCP radicals and conservatives) before the mid-1990s, the reforms that have been decided by the political elite in cooperation with the economic and cultural elites since then have been far more limited in scope (as shown in Figure 7.2).

REFERENCES

Aghion, P., & Blanchard, O. (1994). On the speed of transition in central Europe: *National Bureau for Economic Research Macroeconomics Annual*. Cambridge, MA: NBER. pp. 283–319.

Åslund, A. (1991). Principles of privatization. In L. Csaba (Ed.), *Systemic change and stabilization in eastern Europe* (pp. 17–31). Aldershot: Dartmouth.

Baum, R. (1994). *Burying Mao: Chinese politics in the age of Deng Xiaoping*. Princeton: Princeton University Press.

Berg, A., & Sachs, J. (1992). Structural adjustment and international trade in eastern Europe: the case of Poland. *Economic Policy, 14*, 117–174.

Boycko, M. (1992). When higher incomes reduce welfare: Queues, labor supply, and macroeconomic equilibrium in socialist economies. *Quarterly Journal of Economics, 107*, 907–920.

Cai, F., Wang, D., & Wang, M. (2002). China's regional specialization in the course of gradual reform. *The Economic Research, 9*, 24–30. (in Chinese).

Campos, N. F., & Coricelli, F. (2002). Growth in transition: what we know, what we don't and what should. *Journal of Economic Literature, 40*(September), 793–836.

Chan, J. (2002). *Chinese communist party to declare itself open to the capitalist elite*. Available at: <http://www.wsws.org/articles/2002/nov2002/chin-n13.shtml>. Accessed on November 11, 2011.

Chen, R. (1993). *The craze of Xiahai* [xiahai kuangchao]. Beijing: Tuanjie Chubanshe.

Chi, F. (2000). The WTO accession and the second reform in China. *Business Management, 11*, 11–12.

Corbet, H. (1996). Issues in the accession of China to the WTO system. *Journal of Northeast Asian Studies, 15*(3), 32–45.

De Melo, M., Denizer, C., Gleb, A., & Tenev, S. (1997). Circumstances and choice: the role of initial condition and politics in transition economies. Policy Research Working Paper No. 1866, Washington, DC: The World Bank.

Dewatripont, M., & Roland, G. (1992a). Economic reform and dynamic political constraints. *Review of Economic Studies, 59*, 703–730.

Dewatripont, M., & Roland, G. (1992b). The virtues of gradualism and legitimacy in the transition to a market economy. *Economic Journal, 102*, 291–300.

Dewatripont, M., & Roland, G. (1995). The design of reform packages under uncertainty. *American Economic Review, 85*, 1207–1223.

Dittmer, L., & Wu, Y. (1993). *The political economy of reform leadership in China: macro and micro informal politics linkages*. Paper presented to the Annual Meeting of the Association of Asian Studies. Los Angeles.

Fidrmuc, J., & Noury, A. G. (2003). Interest groups, stakeholders, and the distribution of benefits and costs of reform. Thematic Paper. Washington DC: GDN.

Fischer, S., & Gelb, A. (1991). The process of socialist economic transformation. *Journal of Economic Perspectives, 5*, 91–105.

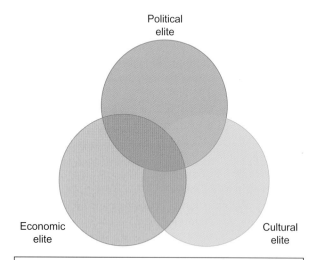

Political elite

Economic elite

Cultural elite

Notes: (1) Each circle denotes the scope of reform that is proposed by and in favor of an elite.
(2) The area that is overlapped by the three circles denotes the scope of reform that is in favor of all three elites concerned.

FIGURE 7.2   Collective actions of the Chinese elites on reforms.

Frydman, R., & Rapaczynski, A. (1994). *Privatization in eastern Europe: is the state withering away?* London: Central European University Press.

Garnaut, R. (1999). Introduction. In R. Garnaut, & L. Song (Eds.), *China: twenty years of reform* (pp. 1–20). Canberra: Asia Pacific Press.

Gilley, B. (2004). The "End of Politics" in Beijing. *The China Journal, 51,* 115–135.

Goodman, D. S. G. (1997). China in reform: the view from the provinces. In D. S. G. Goodman (Ed.), *China's provinces in reform – class, community and political culture.* London: Routledge.

Gottmann, J. (1973). *The significance of territory.* Charlottesville: University of Virginia Press.

Haggard, S., & Webb, S. (1994). What do we know about the political economy of economic policy reform? *The World Bank Research Observer, 8*(2), 143–168.

Hammer, J. S. (1995). Public expenditure and health status in China. Washington, DC: Policy Research Department, The World Bank.

Hwang, E.-G. (1993). *The Korean economies: a comparison of north and south.* Oxford: Clarendon Press.

Jin, H., Qian, Y., & Weingast, B. R. (2001). *Regional decentralization and fiscal incentives: federalism, Chinese style.* mimeo, Stanford University.

Kang, X. (2002). An analysis of Mainland China's political stability in the coming 3–5 years. *Strategy and Management, 3,* 1–15. (in Chinese)

Keidel, A. (1995). *China's regional disparities.* Washington, DC: World Bank.

Lau, L., Qian, Y., & Roland, G. (2000). Reform without losers: an interpretation of China's dual-track approach to reforms. *Journal of Political Economy, 108,* 120–163.

Li, D. (1998). Changing incentives of the Chinese bureaucracy. *American Economic Review, 88*(2), 393–397.

Li, W. (1997). The impact of the Chinese reform on the performance of Chinese state-owned enterprises, 1980–89. *Journal of Political Economy, 105,* 1080–1106.

Li, Z. (1993). In-depth exploration of the question of regional blockades. *Chinese Economic Studies, 26*(5), 23–36.

Liew, L. (1999). The impact of the Asian financial crisis on China: the macro-economy and state-owned enterprise reform. *International Management Review, 39*(4), 85–104.

Liew, L., Bruszt, L., & He, L. (2003). *Causes, national costs, and timing of reform.* Thematic Paper, Washington DC: GDN.

Lin, J. (1992). Rural reforms and agricultural growth in China. *American Economic Review, 82,* 34–51.

Lipton, D., & Sachs, J. (1990). Creating a market economy in eastern Europe: the case of Poland. *Brookings Papers on Economic Activity, 1,* 75–133.

Litwack, J., & Qian, Y. (1998). Balanced or unbalanced development: special economic zones as catalysts for transition. *Journal of Comparative Economics, 26,* 117–141.

Liu, T. (1995). Changes to China's economic system structure [zhongguo jingji tizhi jiegou de yanbian]. *Management World, 3,* 51–56.

Lo, C. (2004). Bank reform: how much time does China have? *The China Business Review* available at: <http://www.chinabusiness-review.com/public/0403/chilo.html>. Accessed on November 11, 2011.

Mastel, G. (1996). Beijing at bay. *Foreign Policy, 104*(Fall), 27–34.

McKinnon, R. (1991b). *The order of economic liberalization.* Baltimore: Johns Hopkins University Press.

McMillan, J., & Naughton, B. (1992). How to reform a planned economy: lessons from China. *Oxford Review of Economic Policy, 8,* 130–143.

Morici, P. (1997). Barring entry? China and the WTO. *Current History, 96,* 274–277. September

Murphy, K., Shleifer, A., & Vishny, R. (1992). The transition to a market economy: pitfalls of partial reform. *Quarterly Journal of Economics, 107,* 889–906.

Murrell, P. (1992). Evolution in economics and in the economic reform of the centrally planned economies. In C. Clague, & G. Raisser (Eds.), *The emergence of market economies in eastern Europe* (pp. 35–53). Cambridge: Blackwell.

NBS (various years). *China statistical yearbook.* various issues, Beijing: China Statistics Publishing House.

Portes, R. (1990). Introduction to economic transformation of Hungary and Poland. *European Economy, 43,* 11–18.

Qian, Y. (2002). How reform worked in China. draft, also In D. Rodrik (Ed.), *In search of prosperity: analytic narratives on economic growth* (pp. 297–333). Princeton, NJ: Princeton University Press, 2007.

Reti, P. (2001). China's path toward a market economy: interview with a prominent reformer. *Transition Newsletter,* Oct.–Nov.–Dec., 17–19.

Roland, G. (1991). Political economy of sequencing tactics in the transition period. In L. Csaba (Ed.), *Systemic change and stabilization in eastern Europe* (pp. 47–64). Aldershot: Dartmouth.

Sachs, J. (1993). *Poland's jump to the market economy,* Lionel Robbins Lectures. London: MIT Press.

Sachs, J., & Woo, W. T. (1994). Structural factors in the economic reforms of China, eastern Europe, and the former Soviet Union. *Economic Policy, 18*(1), 102–145.

Shen, L., & Dai, Y. (1990). Chinese federal economy: mechanisms, impacts, and sources [zhongguo de zhuhou jingji: jizhi, houguo he genyuan]. *Jingji Yanjiu [Economic Research Journal], 3,* 10–13.

Shirk, S. (1993). *The political logic of economic reform in China.* Berkeley, CA: University of California Press.

Svejnar, J. (1989). A framework for the economic transformation of Czechoslovakia. *Planning Economic Report, 5,* 1–18.

Wedeman, A. H. (1993). Editor's introduction to Chinese economic studies. *Chinese Economic Studies, 26*(5), 1–2. (special issue on regional protection)

Wei, S. (1993). *Gradualism vs. big bang: speed and sustainability of reforms.* Cambridge, MA: mimeo, Harvard University.

Woo, W. (1994). The art of reforming centrally planned economies: comparing China, Poland and Russia. *Journal of Comparative Economics, 21,* 276–308.

World Bank (1996). *From plan to market: world bank development report 1996.* New York: Oxford University Press.

Wu, J., & Zhao, R. (1987). The dual pricing system in China's industry. *Journal of Comparative Economics, 11*(3), 309–318.

Wu, R.-I. (1996). Importance of integrating China and Taiwan into the WTO system. *Journal of Northeast Asian Studies, 15*(3), 23–43.

Young, A. (2000). The Razor's edge: distortions and incremental reform in the People's Republic of China. *Quarterly Journal of Economics, 115*(4), 1091–1136.

Zhao, R. (1999). Review of economic reform in China: features, experiences and challenges. In R. Garnaut, & L. Song (Eds.), *China: twenty years of reform* (pp. 185–200). Canberra: Asia Pacific Press.

Chapter 8

Economic Growth and Income (Re)distribution

The high-speed railway. *Photo released by the Chinese Ministry of Railways, Beijing, 2011*

During the early 1990s, the commercial train service in China averaged less than 50 km/h. High-speed rail (HSR) service was introduced in China in 2007. The HSR provides a fast, reliable, and comfortable means of transporting large numbers of travelers in a densely populated country over long distances. By the end of 2011, China's HSR network had reached over 13,000 km. China is the first and only country to have a commercial train service on conventional rail lines that can reach 350 km/h. Regardless of this achievement, critics both in China and abroad have also questioned the necessity of having an expensive high-speed rail system in a largely developing country, where many ordinary workers are still trying to improve their basic living conditions.

Zigong asked what was needed for government. Confucius said, 'Sufficient food, excellent armaments, and people's trust in the government.' Zigong asked, 'Suppose you were forced to get rid of one of the three, which one would you get rid of first?' 'Armaments,' said Confucius. Zigong went on asking, 'Which one would you get rid of if you were to get rid of one of the remaining two?' Confucius answered, 'The food. Although man will die

Understanding the Chinese Economies. DOI: http://dx.doi.org/10.1016/B978-0-12-397826-4.00008-1
© 2013 Elsevier Inc. All rights reserved.

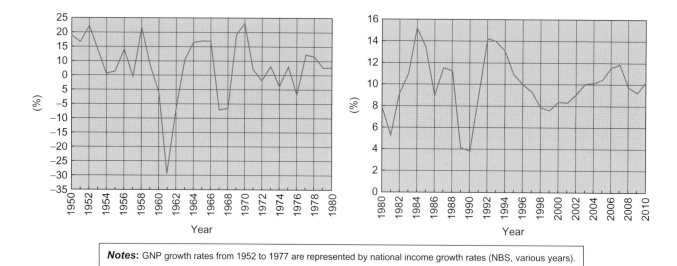

Notes: GNP growth rates from 1952 to 1977 are represented by national income growth rates (NBS, various years).

FIGURE 8.1 China's economic growth rates.

of hunger without food, man has been destined to die since time immemorial. But if people lose their trust in the government then the state has lost its basis.'

– Analects of Confucius (12:7)

8.1 MACROECONOMIC PERFORMANCE

8.1.1 How Large is China's Economy?

Over the past few decades, the Chinese economy has experienced a number of dramatic changes. Specifically, China's macroeconomic performance experienced a steady growth in the first Five-Year Plan (1953–57), a short leap forward followed by a sudden economic disaster in the period 1958–62, a rapid growth period (1963–65), a chaotic period stemming from the 'Cultural Revolution' movement (1966–76), and a fast period of growth during the post-reform era, with a few exceptions in 1981 and 1989–90 (see Figure 8.1).

While several of the world's leading economies, including the United States and the European Union, experienced negative or stagnant gross domestic product (GDP) growth in 2008 and 2009, China achieved real GDP growth rates of 9.6 percent and 9.2 percent, respectively. China's GDP already exceeded that of Japan, behind only that of the United States in 2010 (see Table 8.1). In 2010, China was the world's second largest economy, largest merchandise exporter, second largest merchandise importer, second largest recipient of foreign direct investment (FDI), and largest holder of foreign exchange reserves.

Particularly praiseworthy in the light of all of these developments is that the economic growth of China has sustained an average annual rate of about 10 percent since 1978, making it one of the most dynamic economies in

TABLE 8.1 A Comparison of Chinese, Japanese, and US GDPs, 2010

Indicator	China	Japan	United States
Nominal GDP ($ billions)	5,824	5,461	14,660
GDP in PPP ($ billions)	10,203	4,299	14,660
Nominal Per Capita GDP ($)	4,440	43,060	47,260
Per Capita GDP in PPP ($)	7,770	33,900	47,260

Source: Economist Intelligence Unit (www.eiu.com).

the world during this period. This average growth rate is approximately three times that of the developed nations, more than double that of India, whose conditions are similar to those of China, and even higher than that of the newly industrialized economies (NIEs) including South Korea, Taiwan, Hong Kong, and Singapore. What is more important, however, is the trend per se, rather than any specific figure. If the current growth trend continues, China's GDP will overtake that of the US within the next decade or so, although US per capita GDP levels are expected to remain much higher than those of China for many years to come.

Although China's total GDP is large, its per capita GDP is lower than that of South Korea, Malaysia, and Thailand, only higher than that of other neighboring nations such as India, Mongolia, North Korea, and Vietnam.[1] In addition, according to the standards of the World Bank, China has just moved from the least developed economy to a lower-middle income economy by per

---

1. All data are estimated according to World Bank Atlas method of converting national currency to current US dollars.

capita GNP.[2] It should be noted, however, that if it is calculated by the purchasing power parity (PPP) rates, China's economic size would be much larger than it is when measured by the current exchange rate.

Many economists contend that the ability of China to maintain a rapidly growing economy in the long run will depend largely on the ability of the Chinese government to implement comprehensive economic reforms that hasten China's transition to a free market economy, and to rebalance the Chinese economy by making consumer demand, rather than exports, the main engine of China's economic growth. China faces numerous other challenges as well that could affect its future economic growth (as well as internal political stability), such as widespread pollution, growing income disparities, an undeveloped social safety net, poorly enforced economic regulations, and extensive involvement of the state in several economic sectors.

Generally, even though they differ greatly, the per capita GDPs adjusted by PPP rates are between two and four times that of the figures measured by exchange rate. Of course, the optimistic estimations of Chinese GDP have not been widely accepted, because of the incomplete price statistics. Nevertheless, it is unbelievable that the gaps in real living standards between China and the advanced nations are as large as the per capita GNPs in US dollars between them.

8.1.2   Is Chinese GDP (Under-)Over-Estimated?

Arguably, the size of the Chinese economy may have been underestimated if international statistical standards are applied. For example, there is a report that China's actual GDP could have been more than 30 percent larger than the current figure, the gap being comprised of the following:

1. Real estate sector (10 percent)
2. Government, science and technology, education, culture, and healthcare sectors (4 percent)
3. Self-service within enterprises (3 percent)
4. Rural construction (2.2 percent) and other rural economic activities (2 percent)
5. National defense and underground economic activities (10 percent).[3]

The size of underground economic activities varies enormously from country to country. Obviously, it is impossible to get precise estimates because, by their very nature,

the details have been largely hidden from the authorities. Nevertheless, the following factors determine the size of the underground economy (Sloman, 1991, p. 574):

1. The level of taxes and regulations. The greater their level, the greater the incentive for people to evade the system and 'go underground'.
2. The determination of the authorities to catch up with evaders, and the severity of the punishments for those found out.
3. The size of the service sector relative to the manufacturing sector. It is harder for the authorities to detect the illicit activities of motor mechanics, gardeners, and window cleaners than the output of cars, bricks, and soap.
4. The proportion of the population that is self-employed. It is much easier for the self-employed to evade taxes than it is for people receiving a wage where taxes are deducted at source.

More detailed analysis of the accuracy of China's GDP data and its national accounting system will be conducted in the next chapter.

8.2   UNDERSTANDING ECONOMIC GROWTH

8.2.1   Literature Review

If we are to explain why economic performance has been so diverse among nations, it is necessary for us to consider political and institutional influences. Institutions in economic research are analyzed as formal (laws, regulations) and informal (customs, traditions, norms) rules in a society that structure and simplify human interactions. Historically, institutions have been devised by human beings to create order and reduce uncertainty in exchange. They evolve incrementally, connecting the past with the present and the future (North, 1991). Various efforts have been made to provide a theoretical and empirical explanation of economic growth at the 'institutional' level.[4] It is, however, very difficult to conduct any meaningful economic comparison especially when a large number of economies with different political, historical, and cultural backgrounds are taken into account.

Following Gastil's (1987, p. 210) division of countries into economic systems with respect to the role of government, Barro (1991), for example, tried to differentiate quantitatively the primarily socialist, mixed between socialist and free enterprise and primarily free enterprise economies. His estimated coefficient for socialist economies is negative on growth but that for mixed systems is

---

2. The World Bank (1996, pp. 394–5) defined low-income economies, lower-middle income economies, upper-middle income economies and high-income economies with per capita GNPs of US$725 or less, US$726–2,895, US$2,896–8,955 and US$8,956 or more, respectively.

3. See *Asia-Pacific Economic Times* (1996).

4. See, for example, Holesovsky (1977), Hwang (1993), Carson (1996), Kohler (1996), Schnitzer (1997), Gregory and Stuart (1998), McMahon and Square (2003, eds), and Rodrik (2003, ed.).

essentially zero. Because the division of economic systems into groups is subjective and because there are only nine 'socialist' countries in the sample, these results are not very reliable.

During the past decades the vast majority of countries of the world have undertaken 'market-oriented reforms'. Although this movement in favor of markets embraced both developed and developing countries, the changes in the developing world have been by far the most striking. However, the reform outcomes can only tell the story that establishing a fully-fledged market system proved to be far more complex than had been envisaged. A global research project, launched by the Global Development Network (GDN) in 2002, presents cases of similar reforms with varied outcomes. The market reforms considered in this project are privatization, pension reform, external trade, foreign direct investment (FDI) regulations, and financial reforms. In fact, a variety of countries obtained the same 'good' outcomes applying dissimilar strategies of institutional engineering. The contrasting features of the reforms in China and India exemplify this latter point well.[5]

Might political stability be a better factor to explain the engines for economic development than the political system? To measure political stability, Barro (1991) included two variables (the number of revolutions and coups per year and the number of political assassinations per million of the population per year). Using Bank's (1979) data set, Barro found that each of these variables is significantly negative for economic growth. Then, what determines political stability? Naturally, economic factors, such as economic growth and income distribution, may play a very critical role. Londregan and Poole (1989), for example, found a negative association between economic growth and political instability. But what is the primary cause driving this political and economic feedback loop? In fact, although Barro's (1991) results do reflect a positive influence of growth on political stability, rather than (or in addition to) the effects of stability on growth, further statistical proof is still needed to support the hypothesis that economic growth more decisively influences political stability rather than *vice versa*.

To conclude, existing growth theories and evidence in development experience are conflicting. Furthermore, from the standpoint of political economics, we still lack any convincing evidence to explain, for example, why Latin America's economic performance has been worse than North America's. Why were the ancient civilizations of Asia so tardy in fully exploiting possibilities for growth? Why is the African area stuck at the income level that most of the Western economies had more than one century ago?

Nor can we find any convincing evidence for the differing economic performance between countries that have the same or similar geographical, economic, or political conditions.

8.2.2 Factors Contributing to Growth

A breakdown of the economic growth in China in the second half of the twentieth century is shown in Table 8.2. Physical capital was always the factor that made the greatest contribution to economic growth. However, the percentage points of the GDP growth rate contributed by physical capital were almost doubled after the launch of the reform in 1978. The gap can be further decomposed into the increase of the savings rate, foreign capital, and the more efficient use of money. The contribution of the final one of these factors was the largest but the least mentioned. For example, the ratio of formulated capital to savings increased from about 50 percent for the pre-reform era to more than 60 percent for the reform era. It seems that it is not proper to describe the economic growth of China as being simply 'inputs-driven' since considerable efficiency improvement, which cannot be covered by total factor productivity (TFP), is hidden by the growth in input. In addition, the contribution of foreign capital will be 0.6 percentage points if its direct and indirect impacts are considered (Wang, 2000, p. 4).

Table 8.2 also shows that the average annual GDP growth rate contributed by labor input was as high as 0.84 (or about 25 percent of the GDP growth rate) between 1961 and 1978, but was only 0.48 (6 percent of the GDP growth rate) from 1991 to 1999 after the effects of the strict population control policy became apparent. As happens in other counties, the contribution of human capital was of little importance, especially from 1953 to 1960 and from 1991 to 1999, but the period from 1961 to 1978 was an exception, with a surprisingly high share of 40 percent of the GDP growth rate. It is quite impressive that TFP contributed 1.34 (16 percent of the GDP growth rate) and 1.77 percentage points (22 percent of the GDP growth rate) for the periods of 1979 to 1990 and of 1991 to 1999, respectively.

It should be clarified that the TFP covers not only technological innovation, but also management improvement, resource reallocation, and even the provision of incentives. For example, the period 1961–78 witnessed negative contribution from the TFP due to the turmoil of the 'Cultural Revolution' period (1966–76).

The high rate of capital accumulation has its basis in the liberalization of a labor-surplus economy that has a high savings rate. Investment is highly profitable because the surplus labor prevented the real wage from rising significantly and the large pool of domestic savings prevented a rise in the interest rate. The importance of the latter is

---

5. A more detailed account can be found in Fanelli and McMahon (2006, p. 28).

TABLE 8.2 Decomposition of Chinese Economic Growth (%)

	1953–60	1961–78	1979–90	1991–99
Average annual GDP growth rate	9.40	4.70	9.00	10.30
Average annual GDP growth rate (adj.)	6.63	3.31	8.50	8.10
Factor contribution to average annual GDP growth rate (adj.)				
Capital contribution	2.90	2.40	4.85	5.45
Labor contribution	0.84	0.84	0.99	0.48
Human capital contribution	0.58	1.32	1.32	0.40
TFP contribution	2.31	−1.25	1.34	1.77

Notes: *GDP=gross domestic product; TFP=total factor productivity.*
Source: Wang (2000).

seen in that household savings as a proportion of disposable income in China have been higher than those in most developed and developing nations. China's savings rate has been extremely high during the reform period.[6]

This rapid increase has been attributed to the following factors:

- Expected uncertainty
- Income increase
- Monetization in the economy
- Capital market development
- High level of income inequality.

Other factors that help to explain the rapid growth of private financial savings in China could include corporate savings in private accounts and illegal income.

Another key factor behind China's impressive economic growth is its integration into the global economy. This factor operates through four channels. First, the access to international markets for labor-intensive manufactured goods accelerated the movement of labor out of low-productivity agriculture into high-productivity industry. Secondly, China could now buy modern technology (some of which were previously denied to China). Thirdly, foreign

direct investment (FDI) increased the level of capital stock, transferred new technology, made available global distribution networks, and introduced domestic firms to more efficient management techniques. Fourthly, the competition from international trade forced Chinese enterprises to be more efficient and innovative (Woo, 1998).

8.3 INCOME DISTRIBUTION AND INEQUALITY

8.3.1 How (Un)Equal is the Chinese Society?

Economic difference (or inequality) has several dimensions. Economists are mostly concerned with the income and consumption dimensions. Several inequality indices include the most widely used index of income inequality. Non-income inequality includes inequality in skills, education, opportunities, happiness, health, wealth, and other similar factors. Results from a review of the literature suggest a relationship between inequality in income and non-income dimensions. This indicates that one should account for the interrelationship between the different dimensions in the measurement and analyses of inequalities. Although other approaches are also useful in economic analysis, the Gini coefficient has been most frequently applied by economists worldwide to measure levels of income inequality (see Annex for a detailed description of the calculation of the Gini coefficient).

While China's reform has been a strong driver of its economic growth, it has also derived a series of socioeconomic problems. Prior to the reform, China was an egalitarian society in terms of income distribution. In the initial stage of the reform, the policy of 'letting some people get rich first' (*rang yi bufen ren xian fu qilai*) was adopted in order to overcome egalitarianism in income distribution, to promote efficiency with strong incentives, and to ultimately realize common prosperity based on an enlarged pie. But this policy has quickly enlarged income gaps between different groups of people (see Table 8.3).

Compared with other countries, China's Gini coefficients have already been very high. China is only better than a few nations in Latin America and Africa (such as Mexico, Cameroon, Madagascar, Rwanda, Uganda, and Ecuador), while the latter have usually been treated as the most unequal economies in the world. A number are currently embroiled in or just emerging from deeply destabilizing conflicts, some of them linked to income inequality: Côte d'Ivoire, Sri Lanka, Nepal, and Serbia. Figure 8.2 shows the Gini coefficients of selected nations during the post-World War II period. Perhaps more damning are Brazil, Mexico, the United Kingdom, and the United States, whose Gini coefficients were much larger than China's for most of the previous decades. However,

---

6. From 1978 to 1997, the average savings rate was 37.1 percent. By contrast, governmental savings kept falling in both absolute and relative terms. Its share of domestic savings was more than 50 percent in 1978, but fell below zero in the 1990s, showing a reversal from the circumstances of the command economy. From 1978 to 1988, the annual growth rate of private financial savings (including security assets) was more than 30 percent, and a similar increase occurred in the period from 1989 to 1998 (Wu, 2000).

TABLE 8.3 China's Income Gini Coefficients, Selected Years

Year	Rural Areas	Urban Areas	China as a Whole
1952	0.230	0.165	0.255
1979/80	0.310	0.160	0.330
1988	0.338	0.233	0.382
1995	0.381	0.280	0.437
2002	0.366	0.319	0.454
2007	0.370	0.399	0.496

Sources: (1) World Bank (1983, pp. 83 and 92) for 1979/80; (2) Zhao (2001) for 1988 and 1995; (3) Li (2004) for 2002, and (4) www.ahpc.gov. cn for 2007.

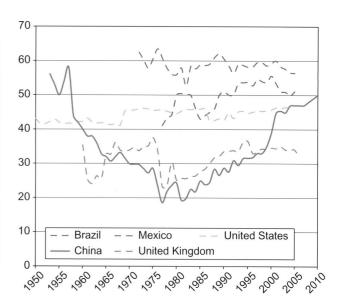

FIGURE 8.2 Gini coefficients since World War II, selected nations. *Source: Author based on the data provided by the UNU-WIDER, Helsinki, Finland (China's data for years 2009–2010 are estimated by author).*

China's income inequality has been increasing at a higher rate than all of these nations; and in recent years it is going to exceed those of the United Kingdom and the United States; both of the latter have seen either a decreasing or unchanged rates of tendencies toward income inequality.

Nevertheless, there have been two different views with respect to the current situation of income inequality in China. One view supposes that China's Gini coefficients have been underestimated since in most, if not all, cases the earnings of the low-income groups were usually overestimated, whereas those of the higher-income groups were usually underestimated. For example, in some poor agricultural households a portion of earnings had to be used for productive investment and, as a result, the earnings that can be used for consumption will be reduced. By contrast, in the urban, high-income group, some earnings and welfare payments were not included in the current reckoning of incomes (Ge, 2000).

However, there is a different view in respect of this issue: China's current income inequality has been overestimated and, if measured in terms of purchasing power parity (PPP) rates, China's income Gini coefficients should have been reduced considerably. In most cases, the price levels in poor areas are much lower than those in rich areas. We will analyze this issue in more detail in Chapter 9.

8.3.2 Income Inequality: Causes

During recent decades, and through an uneven (in both spatial and industrial terms, as will be discussed in Chapters 10 and 11, respectively) development strategy, China has achieved rapid economic growth. In the meantime, China's income inequality has also increased. What are the causes and consequences of the increasing levels of income inequality? Table 8.4 shows the positive and negative effects of such factors as economic growth and various

institutional changes and policy reforms on China's income inequality. It should be noted that some, if not all, of these factors have influenced the income inequality jointly and, therefore, it may be difficult to accurately clarify the directions of these influences.

In determining the changes in income inequality (represented by the Gini coefficient or by the ratio of quintile income shares), Xu and Zou (2000) consider the role played by output growth, increasing exposure to international trade, urbanization, taxation, government spending, inflation, human capital formation, geography, and the structure of the different sectors of the economy. The estimated results show that income distribution has been affected by the changing structure of the economy, the role of the state, and increasing levels of urbanization. Inequality increased with a reduction of SOE share of output, higher inflation, higher growth rate, and foreign trade. Government spending tends to shift resources from the rich and the poor to the middle class. Provinces furthest from the coast had higher levels of inequality, probably reflecting greater imperfections in their capital markets. Schooling and increasing urbanization did not affect the levels of income inequality. It has not been possible to identify determinants of differences in inequality across different provinces.

Using a set of survey data, Riskin et al. (2001) provide a comprehensive analysis of inequality and poverty in China for the years of 1988 and 1995; and Gustafsson et al. (2008) extend this analysis through the year 2002. They observe major changes in the composition of income between the two survey dates. Rural household income, mainly from farming, declined from 74 percent to 56

TABLE 8.4 Determinants of Income Inequality for the Reform Era

Item	Inequality Within Urban or Rural Areas	Inequality Between Urban and Rural Areas
1. Economic growth or development		
Faster growth of urban non-state owned economy	+	+
Faster growth of rural non-agricultural economy	+	−
Development of agriculture	?[a]	−
2. Economic reform or institutional changes		
Order changes		
Price reform in rural areas	−	−
Household responsibility system in rural areas	−	−
Internal migration of rural laborers	?[b]	−
Commercialization of urban housing	+	+
Disorder changes		
Rent-seeking activities	+	?
Insider control[c]	+	+
Monopoly	+	+
Corruption	+	+
3. Economic policy and its changes		
Low purchasing price for agricultural products	?	+
Taxation on agricultural products	?	?
Extra-taxational burden on peasants	?	+
Personal income tax	−	−
Reduction of urban subsidies		
a) Per head	+	−
b) By position	−	−
Transfer of urban residents' benefits to private property	+	+
Access to the WTO	?	+[d]

Notes: (1) Usually, if an item is related to urban (or rural) areas, its effect on inequality is also related to the urban (or rural) areas. (2) '+' denotes increase of inequality; '−' denotes decrease of inequality; '?' denotes difficulty in judging.
[a]According to Li et al. (1997), although inequality within rural areas had slightly increased from 1979 to 1984, it is hard to attribute this result to the development of agriculture.
[b]Generally, internal migration of rural laborers has enlarged income differentials within rural areas as a whole, but it has narrowed the gap in some specific rural areas (Zhao, 2001, p. 38).
[c]'Insider control' is described here as a mechanism through which public assets can be appropriated to serve the interests of particular departments, regions, work units, and individuals (Massahiko and Qian, 1995, p. 17).
[d]Based on Li and Zhai (2000). However, Wei and Wu (2003) conclude that there is a negative relationship between urban–rural disparity and the trade/GDP ratio.
Source: Zhao (2001, p. 36) except those that are noted otherwise.

percent, while non-farming wages increased from 9 percent to 22 percent, resulting in increasing levels of income inequality. The Gini ratio for rural income grew by 23 percent from 0.34 to 0.42 due to the unequal distribution of faster-growing wage components of rural income. The corresponding increases in inequality in the urban areas were 43 percent in seven years from 0.23 to 0.33. The increasing inequality of distribution of income caused a rise in the level of urban income inequality. The wage share of income grew from 44 percent to 61 percent. Other components of income such as income of retirees and housing rental were subject to fast growth as well. Subsidies declined from 20 percent to 1 percent of urban income.

Previous studies have suggested that non-agricultural activities have been the major cause of rural income inequality. The increase in agricultural income was considered to be a key policy measure to reduce rural inequality in China. Cheng (1996), using household data from five grain-producing Chinese regions in 1994, finds that inequality within the grain-producing areas was also very high, with differences in crop income as the major source of inequality. The decomposition of inequality indicates that 61 percent of the income inequality of peasant households is as a result of intra-provincial, while the remaining 39 percent is as a result of interprovincial inequality components.

8.3.3 Income Inequality: Consequences

A substantial body of literature has analyzed the effects of income inequalities on macroeconomic performance, as reflected in rates of economic growth.[7] Most argue that greater income inequality is actually an impediment to economic growth. A seemingly plausible argument points to the existence of credit market failures such that people are unable to exploit growth-promoting opportunities for investment.[8] With only limited access to credit, the exploitation of investment opportunities depends upon individuals' levels of assets and incomes. Specifically, poor households tend to forego human capital investments that offer relatively high rates of return. In this case, a distortion-free redistribution of assets and incomes from rich to poor tends to raise the quantity and average productivity of investment. With declining marginal products of capital, the output loss from the market failure will be greater for the poor. So the higher the proportion of poor people there are in the economy, the lower the rate of growth (Ravallion, 2001).

A second way in which inequality could affect the future levels of economic growth is through political channels. The degree of inequality could affect the median voter's desired pattern of policies or it could determine individuals' ability to access political markets and participate in costly lobbying. If the mean income in an economy exceeds the median income, then a system of majority voting tends to favor the redistribution of resources from rich to poor.[9] As the median voter's distance from the average

capital endowment in the economy increases with the aggregate inequality of wealth, he or she will be led to approve a higher tax rate. This in turn could reduce incentives for productive investment, resulting in lower levels of growth. If this is correct, democratic societies with a more unequal distribution of wealth should be characterized by the exploitation of the rich by the poor – that is, high taxes and, consequently, low investment and growth, whereas undemocratic ones with similar characteristics would not (Deininger and Squire, 1998).

Indeed, the negative effects of income inequality might exist in almost every sphere of human life. But there also exists some evidence that supports the view that income inequality could encourage economic growth – both directly and indirectly. The most intuitive thesis is that a lower degree of inequality would mean a greater amount of redistribution from rich to poor. It is this redistribution that would become an impediment to the creation of incentives for people (especially the poorest and richest groups) to work hard (Li and Zou, 1998). There is also a positive view for the effect of inequality on economic growth: if individual savings rates rise with the level of income, then a redistribution of resources from rich to poor tends to lower the aggregate rate of savings in an economy. Through this channel, a rise in income inequality tends to raise the level of investment.[10] In this case, greater inequality would enhance economic growth. However, there is an argument that inequality may lead to higher fertility rates, which could, in turn, reduce economic growth (Perotti, 1996).

Using the panel data on Chinese income inequality at the provincial urban level, Xu and Zou (2000) find that the correlation between the growth rate and the Gini coefficient is consistent with Kuznet's (1955) inverted U-curve. This contradicts the findings of Alesina and Rodrik (1994), and Persson and Tabellini (1994) who, based on a cross-section of international data, observed a negative association between income growth and inequality. In analyzing the causal mechanism relating to inequality and growth in China, Quah (2002) highlighted that there is no evidence about such a relationship. In addition to inequality, the rate of economic growth is also influenced by many other macroeconomic, technological, political, and institutional factors. Ravallion (1998) suggests that the aggregation can bias tests of whether inequality impedes growth.

Worsening levels of inequality of wealth and income motivate the poor to engage in crime, riots, and other disruptive activities (see, for example, Hibbs, 1973; Venieris and Gupta, 1986; Gupta, 1990; and Alesina and Perotti, 1996). In a civilized world the existence of millions of

---

7. Recent surveys of the theories on the economic effects of income inequality include Benabou (1996), Aghion et al. (1999), and Barro (2000).
8. See, for example, Benabou (1996), Aghion et al. (1999), and Barro (2000).
9. See Perotti (1993), Alesina and Rodrik (1994), Persson and Tabellini (1994), and Benabou (1996) for detailed analyses.

---

10. This effect arises if the economy is partly closed, so that domestic investment depends, to some extent, on desired national saving (Barro, 2000, p. 8).

> **Box 8.1   A Heterodox Approach to Economic Growth**
>
> In existing literature relating to the determinants of economic growth, the explanatory variables of income inequality and cultural diversity have been treated separately. As a result, their joint effects have not been clear.
>
> Evidence from a broad panel of nations reveals somewhat ambiguous results in that economic growth is quite independent from the variables of inequality and cultural (linguistic and religious) diversity. But for the post-Cold War era there is also an indication that religious diversity tends to retard growth in high inequality nations and to encourage growth in low inequality places. In addition, there is some evidence that supports the view that inequality tends to encourage growth in low religious diversity nations, but not in high religious diversity nations.
>
> How does one explain these findings? In many circumstances, higher religious diversity may become a source of productive factors contributing to economic growth for low inequality nations; but in nations with high degrees of religious diversity, high inequality could seriously affect economic growth. In nations with low degrees of religious diversity, income inequality could generate higher economic growth since there are very few, if any, intercultural barriers within each religiously homogeneous nation.
>
> **Source**: *Guo (2009, p. 103).*

starving people is not only unacceptable from an ethical point of view but can hardly be expected to lead to conditions of peace and tranquility. As a consequence, it is widely believed that inequality could become an impediment to economic development.

Unfortunately, the existing empirical analyses, using data on the performance of a broad panel of countries, have yielded conflicting results. Perotti (1996) and Benabou (1996), for instance, report an overall tendency for income inequality to generate lower economic growth in cross-country regressions, whereas some panel studies, such as that of Forbes (1997) and Li and Zou (1998), find relationships with the opposite sign. Nevertheless, Deininger and Squire (1998) provide evidence in support of the view that inequality retards economic growth in poor countries but not in richer countries. Using a large bulk of time-series and cross-national data, Barro (2000) also supports this hypothesis.[11] However, other carefully conducted research projects, such as Eichera and Garcia-Penalosab (2001) and Ravallion (2001), provide little evidence that supports the above views.

It seems very likely that we need to seek another approach to testing the non-linear relationships between economic growth and income inequality (see Box 8.1).

8.3.4   Poverty Alleviation

For most of our human history poverty has existed widely throughout the world. This has been mostly accepted as inevitable, as traditional modes of production were insufficient to give an entire population a comfortable standard of living. Generally, 'poverty' can be defined as the lack of a certain amount of living necessities. It can be further classified as 'absolute poverty' and 'relative poverty'. Absolute poverty refers to the inability to afford basic human needs, which includes, *inter alia*, clean water, nutrition, health care, education, clothing, and shelter. Relative poverty only refers to the lack of a usual or socially acceptable level of resources or income as compared with others within a society.

With regard to the term 'absolute poverty', there have been two separate definitions – 'broad poverty' and 'deep poverty'. Specifically, broad poverty refers to the threshold which is based on the cost of 2,100 kilocalories per person per day with an adjustment for non-food purchases, broadly consistent with the preference of low-income consumers; deep poverty relates to the threshold, which is defined as 80 percent of the broad poverty threshold (Khan and Riskin, 2001).

China experienced rapid economic growth after economic reform, accompanied by increased income levels (see Box 8.2 for a personal case). However, the reduction in poverty is still a challenging task in China. Until the mid-1980s, the total number of poor had been reduced; since then, however, it has grown continuously, especially in urban areas. From 1988 to 1995, for example, the incidence of 'broad poverty' in urban areas fell by only 2.4 percent – from 8.2 percent to 8.0 percent of the total urban population. Moreover, the urban population itself grew rapidly. As a result, the total number of urban broad poor rose rapidly during the period. This situation persists into the early twenty-first century and some scholars have put the total number of China's urban poor at more than 30 million people.[12]

---

11. There is an indication in Barro's (2000) study that growth tends to fall with greater inequality when per capita GDP is below around $2,000 (1985 US dollars) and to rise with inequality when per capita GDP is above $2,000.

12. Sources: Khan et al. (2001, p. 128) and www.fubusi.com/2006/3-14/142426956.html (accessed on December 1, 2008).

Box 8.2 Xing's Happiness Index

Before her retirement in 2003, Ms Xing had worked at a garden center in Changping district, northern Beijing. Now a materfamilias, Ms Xing is counting her 'happiness index' based on the pay she collected over the past 30 years:

- During the 1970s, her husband and herself each received a monthly pay of about 60 yuan, which remained almost unchanged until the early 1980s.
- In 1985, and as a result of increases in food prices, her monthly wages increased from 60 yuan up to 82 yuan, the net increase of which could now even cover her family's food expenditure for an entire month.
- In 1993, her monthly pay was 103 yuan, including 30 yuan of subsidy, 20 yuan of 'baogan jiang' (reward for a task until it is completed), 20 yuan of fees for gloves, 12 yuan of administrative fees, 8 yuan of unemployment fees, among others.

- In 1995, her pay increased to more than 400 yuan, which was a really big surprise to her.
- In 2000, her monthly pay exceeded 1,000 yuan for the first time; during this year, she replaced her color TV set with a new, larger one, upgraded her 10-year-old refrigerator, and installed an air conditioner in her apartment.
- In 2003, Ms Xing retired, with a pension amounting to around 1,200 yuan per month, which continued to increase in subsequent years.
- In 2008, her retirement pension, after an increase of over 200 yuan, reached 1,800 yuan per month; though facing an exceptionally higher level of inflation than that of previous years, Ms Xing was very satisfied with her life.

Source: Ma (2008).

According to a report undertaken by the Asian Development Bank (2002), China's urban poverty has varied considerably from province to province. Specifically, China's provinces can be classified into five groups by the incidences of 'broad poverty', as follows:

1. The incidences of 'broad poverty' are lower than 2 percent (including Beijing, Jiangsu, Zhejiang, and Guangdong).
2. The incidences of 'broad poverty' range from 2 percent to 4 percent (including Shanghai, Fujian, Hunan, Guangxi, Yunnan, Anhui, and Jiangxi).
3. The incidences of 'broad poverty' range from 4 percent to 6 percent (including Hebei, Hubei, Guizhou, Chongqing, Qinghai, Shandong, and Sichuan).
4. The incidences of 'broad poverty' range from 6 percent to 8 percent (including Tianjin, Inner Mongolia, Liaoning, Jillin, Hainan, Xinjiang, Shanxi, Heilongjiang, and Gansu).
5. The incidences of 'broad poverty' are higher than 8 percent (including Henan, Shaanxi, Ningxia, and Tibet).

A simulation exercise conducted by Khan et al. (2001, p. 127) shows that, by 1995, this high level of income growth in the urban area would have reduced the broad poverty rate to under 1 percent of the urban population, had the distribution of urban income remained unchanged between 1988 and 1995. In other words, had there been no rise in inequality, such a rapid increase in average incomes would have sufficed virtually to eradicate urban poverty. This rise in inequality, however, offset the rise in per capita income and, as a result, the estimated effect on the incidence of poverty ranges from an insignificant improvement to a significant deterioration, depending on the poverty indicator used and the cost of living index chosen to adjust the poverty income threshold.

8.4 INCOME REDISTRIBUTION AND SOCIAL SECURITY

8.4.1 China's Existing Tax System

As the most important source of fiscal revenue, tax is a key economic player of macro-regulation in China's economic and social development. Since the 1994 tax reform, China has preliminarily set up a tax-sharing system (see subsection 6.5.2 of Chapter 6).

Under the current tax system, China now has 26 types of taxes, which, according to their nature and function, can be divided into the following eight categories:

- Turnover taxes. These include three kinds of taxes, namely, Value Added Tax (VAT), Consumption Tax, and Business Tax. The levies of these taxes are normally based on the volume of turnover or sales of the taxpayers in the manufacturing, circulation, or service sectors.
- Income taxes. These include Enterprise Income Tax and Individual Income Tax. These taxes are levied on the basis of the profits gained by producers or dealers, or the income earned by individuals.
- Resource taxes. These consist of Resource Tax and Urban and Township Land Use Tax. These taxes are applicable to those engaged in natural resource exploitation or to the users of urban and township land.[13]
- Taxes for special purposes. These taxes include City Maintenance and Construction Tax, Farmland Occupation Tax, Fixed Asset Investment Orientation Regulation Tax, Land Appreciation Tax, and Vehicle

---

13. These taxes reflect the chargeable use of state-owned natural resources, and aim to adjust the different profits derived by taxpayers who have access to different availability of natural resources.

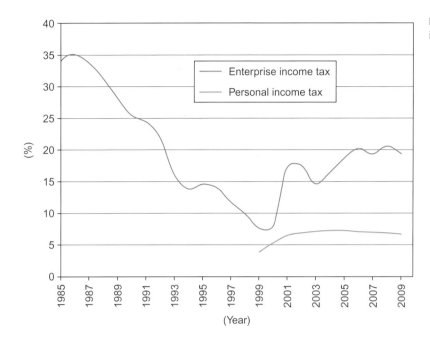

FIGURE 8.3 Ratios of enterprise and personal income taxes to GDP. *Source: NBS, 2010.*

Acquisition Tax. These taxes are levied on specific items for special regulative purposes.

- Property taxes. These taxes encompass House Property Tax, Urban Real Estate Tax, and Inheritance Tax (not yet levied).
- Behavioral taxes. These taxes include Vehicle and Vessel Usage Tax, Vehicle and Vessel Usage License Plate Tax, Stamp Tax, Deed Tax, Securities Exchange Tax (not yet levied), Slaughter Tax, and Banquet Tax. These taxes are levied on specified behavior.
- Agricultural taxes. Taxes belonging to this category are Agriculture Tax (including Agricultural Specialty Tax) and Animal Husbandry Tax which are levied on the enterprises, units and/or individuals receiving income from agriculture and animal husbandry activities.
- Customs duties. Customs duties are imposed on the goods and articles imported into and exported out of the territory of the People's Republic of China, including Excise Tax.

It seems that China's introduction of, and reform on, the income tax system was to promote the development of industrial enterprises during the early period of reform. For example, prior to January 1, 2008, there was a more favorable (and sometimes even exemption of) tax applicable to foreign invested enterprises, in parallel to a relatively higher one applied to such domestic enterprises as state-owned enterprises, collectively owned enterprises, private enterprises, joint operation enterprises, and joint equity enterprises. This can be witnessed by the declining ratios of enterprise income tax to China's total GDP from 1985 to 2000; since the early 2000s, China has increasingly levied taxes on enterprises.

8.4.2 Personal Income Tax

The personal income tax (PIT) was not introduced until the 1990s (see Figure 8.3). China is now levying 3–45 percent on personal income from a salary; income from other business is taxable at 5–35 percent; and passive income (such as interest and royalties) is taxable at a standard rate of 20 percent.

However, fundamental reforms of the PIT are still expected. These reforms are likely to introduce, as in other countries such as the United States, a tax system based not only on a person's annual income but also on economic burdens or expenses in families. China's existing PIT system, by contrast, sets a unified nationwide threshold and does not take individual economic expenses into account.

In 1990 China promulgated the Personal Income Tax Law and decided to set the taxation threshold at 800 yuan per month. During the past years, in a bid to boost domestic consumer demand and bridge income disparities, China has raised its PIT threshold three times as follows:

- From 800 yuan per month up to 1,600 yuan per month (since October 2005)
- From 1,600 yuan per month up to 2,000 yuan per month (since March 2008)
- From 2,000 yuan per month up to 3,500 yuan per month (since September 2011)

These reforms, under which the rich population has been more heavily taxed than the poor, have still been too 'superficial' as they failed to deal with the essential problems of China's taxation system. Another shortcoming of the current taxation system is that it does not tax extra-wage earnings, while the latter can constitute a substantial part of income for those working in monopoly industries.

8.4.3   Social Security

Before reform, China's social security system had been a 'pay-as-you-go' system, in which the funding to the older generation had to come from the contributions of the younger generation. In addition, this kind of system was operated by enterprises or organizations (which is commonly called *danwei* in Chinese). The *danwei* form of social security system had at least the following defects (Zhao and Tang, 2002):

- First, since China's first implementation of a strict family planning policy in the early 1980s, most families, especially those in the urban areas, have had only one child, and the burden of supporting the old generation under a 'pay-as-you-go' system was high and placed an unfair burden on the younger generation.
- Secondly, workers in newly founded *danwei* would have a lower burden of old workers than those in the previously founded *danwei*. This is unfair on the latter.
- Thirdly, some *danwei* might become bankrupt. If so, the right of its workers to social security would be threatened.
- Fourthly, it was very hard for workers to change locations and jobs.

According to the 'Decision on Issues Concerning the Establishment of a Socialist Market Economic Structure', which was adopted by the Third Plenum of the Fourteenth Party Congress in November 1993, the aim of the reform of the social security system was to establish the criterion of efficiency as the first priority while considering fairness at the same time and to change the 'pay-as-you-go' system to a funding system, which is based upon the contribution of the recipients themselves. In addition, the collection and payment of social security funding was to be unified. Administrative management and funding management were also to be separated.

Improvements in pension insurance were among the most rapid. Currently, it covers all state-owned and other ownership enterprises in urban areas and also some non-public owned enterprises and rural areas. The challenge of this reform comes from the funding of the pensions of older workers, who had received relatively low salaries during the course of their working lives. A large proportion of their salary was channeled into investment and construction while they were promised pensions after they retired. Following the implementation of the funding system, their pension will come from the selling of some state-owned enterprises or assets. The medical care system consists of four parts: compulsory basic medical insurance; supplementary medical insurance freely chosen by enterprises; commercial medical insurance freely chosen by individuals and social medical rescue systems. The principle of compulsory basic medical insurance is 'low level, wide coverage'.

In September 1997, the State Council promulgated a document relating to the safeguarding of minimum living standards for urban inhabitants in China. The criterion of minimum living standards and the entailing fund are the tasks of local governments. However, the majority of people, rural inhabitants, still face a weak, if any, social security system. They have to rely on their own deposits or the support of their relatives and offspring.

8.5   SUMMARY

Since the fall of the socialist system in 1990, old institutions which had provided a degree of economic and social stability to society have been rapidly destroyed and new market-oriented ideologies have spread rapidly throughout the economic environment of the former Soviet Union. By the late 1990s, however, while many elements of a formal market-based framework had been established, its implementation was often weak. The enforcement of new laws and regulations has been constrained by the presence of old informal institutions – the strong bureaucracy, the weak respect for law, informal networking, and other social factors, which were historically rooted in the behavior of the Soviet society. As a result the speed and sequencing of the economic reforms, which were important at the beginning of the transition, seem to be becoming less important in comparison with the necessity of institutional transformation.

During the twentieth century the failure of the centrally planned economies (CPEs) to keep pace with their market-oriented counterparts demonstrated clearly enough that planning entire economies at the central government level is not a productive path to long-term development. But the experiences of East Asia, especially of Japan, South Korea, and China make clear that it is possible for a country to have an interventionist government and still enjoy extremely rapid economic growth over a period of decades. Nevertheless, certain policies that helped Japan develop in the 1950s and 1960s, generated growth in East Asia in the 1970s and 1980s, and, more recently, sparked China's economic boom from the 1980s onwards, were specific to the time and place. However, they may not have worked well in other countries, nor are they likely to be appropriate in the time to come.

After the introduction of economic reform China experienced a period of rapid economic growth, accompanied by increased levels of income. As a result, China's rapid economic growth has sharply improved Chinese living standards and helped raise hundreds of millions of people out of extreme poverty.

Prior to the reform, China was an egalitarian society in terms of income distribution. In the initial stage of the reform, the policy of 'letting some people get rich first' was adopted to overcome egalitarianism in income distribution, to promote efficiency with strong incentives and ultimately to realize common prosperity based on an enlarged pie. But this policy has quickly increased income gaps between different groups of people. Compared with other countries, China's Gini coefficients have been very high, only being lower than those of a few nations in Latin America and Africa.

While China's reform has been a strong driver of its economic growth, it has also caused a series of socioeconomic problems. However, the level of income inequality has also increased dramatically during recent decades and the reduction of poverty is still a considerable challenge in China. China's income inequality can be further analyzed in terms of provincial components and their determinants can, in turn, be identified. An analysis of within-country regional inequality can reveal the effects of openness, marketization, and convergence due to factor mobility, and it may also indicate regional polarization, or disintegration and widening inequality driven by structural differences between regions, issues that will be discussed in Chapter 9. Furthermore, it is important to consider heterogeneity in income inequality in terms of both its level and its development over time, as well as different characteristics of sub-group dimensions (we will discuss this issue in a case study later in this chapter).

ANNEX

The Gini Coefficient and its Calculations

Developed in 1912 by Corado Gini – an Italian statistician – the Gini coefficient is most prominently used as a measure of inequality of income or wealth distribution. It is defined as a ratio with values between 0 and 1: a low Gini coefficient indicates more equal income or wealth distribution, while a high Gini coefficient implies a more unequal pattern of distribution.

In the extreme cases, 0 corresponds to perfect equality (when everyone has exactly the same income) and 1 corresponds to perfect inequality (when one person has all the income, while all remaining people have zero income).

Mathematically, the Gini coefficient is defined as a ratio of the areas on the Lorenz curve diagram (see Figure 8.4). If the area between the line of perfect equality and the Lorenz curve is A, and the area under the Lorenz curve is B, then the Gini coefficient is A/(A+B). Since A+B=0.5, the Gini coefficient becomes A/(0.5)=2A=1−2B.

If the Lorenz curve is represented by the function $y=L(x)$, the value of B can be found with integration. As a result, the Gini coefficient becomes:

$$\text{Gini} = 1 - 2\int_0^1 L(x)\,dx \qquad (8.1)$$

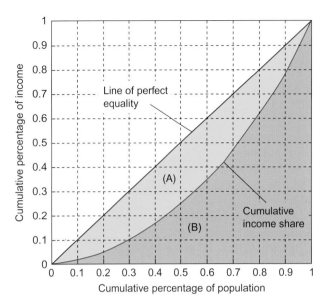

FIGURE 8.4 The Lorenz curve.

Sometimes the entire Lorenz curve is not known, and only values at certain intervals are given. In that case, the Gini coefficient can be approximated by using various techniques for interpolating the missing values of the Lorenz curve.

Assume that (x_k, y_k) are the known points on the Lorenz curve, and that:

- x_k (for $k=0, 1, ..., n$, with $x_0=0$, $x_n=1$) is the cumulated proportion of the population variable, with the increasing order (i.e., $x_{k-1} < x_k$).
- y_k (for $k=0, 1, ..., n$, with $y_0=0$, $y_n=1$) is the cumulated proportion of the income variable, with the non-decreasing order (i.e., $y_k > y_{k-1}$).

If the Lorenz curve is approximated on each interval as a line between consecutive points, then the area B can be approximated with trapezoids. Therefore, the Gini coefficient, denoted in the equation above, can be approximately computed by the following formula:

$$\text{Gini} = 1 - \sum_{k=1}^{n} (x_k - x_{k-1})(y_k + y_{k-1}) \qquad (8.2)$$

More accurate results can be obtained using other methods to approximate the area B, such as approximating the Lorenz curve with a quadratic function across pairs of intervals, or building an appropriately smooth approximation to the underlying distribution function that matches the known data. If the population mean and boundary values for each interval are also known, these can also often be used to improve the accuracy of the approximation.

Case Study 6

Transition and Growth: a Tale of Two Companies[14]

Located in Shandong province, the Zibo Mining Group (ZBM) is a large conglomerate which has been in operation for more than one hundred years. It has therefore experienced every stage of China's political and economic transformations during the twentieth century. After the 1970s, the ZBM entered into serious recession; up to 1996, it had operated with deficits for a continuous period of 24 years.

At the end of June 2001, the ZBM had a total of 36,447 registered staff, along with 25,922 retired personnel and 10,198 dependents of deceased members of staff. It had 4.249 billion yuan of fixed assets and 3.325 billion yuan of debts, with a debt/asset ratio of 78.25 percent. During the late twentieth century, the ZBM had for a long time been treated as one of the 36 worst performing state-owned enterprises (SOEs) in China.

In September 1995, the State Council put forward a series of guidelines on the reforms of SOEs. Following the opinions of the Ministry of Coal Industry (MCI) concerning the reconstructions of SOEs as shareholding and partnership companies (MCI, 1997), the ZBM decided to introduce ownership reforms in its two money losing subsidiary companies (Guangzheng and Chuangda) in 1997 and the Fall of 1999, respectively. Following the reforms in ownership, both companies were able to make profits in 2001. In September 2001 and March 2002, and requested by the Development Research Center of the State Council and by the State Development and Reform Commission, respectively, we conducted two field surveys of these two companies.[15] Our goals are: (i) to assess how well the ownership reform performed in the SOEs; and (ii) to clarify the relationships between ownership reform, output growth, and the distribution of earnings within the SOEs.

Guangzheng company, formerly called the Shigu coalmine, is located at Chawang township, Zichuan district. The coalmine was initially established by the Japanese in 1921 and was reconstructed by the ZBM in March 1958 and went into operation on September 29, 1960, achieving an annual production capacity of 250,000 tons of raw coal. Restricted by complicated geological and hydrological conditions, the coalmine produced only a total amount of 8.1 million tons of raw coal between 1960 and 1990. As a result, its operations had been based

on the subsidies from the central government, with a highest annual deficit of 13.0 million yuan, before 1996. After ownership reform was finalized in 1997, Guangzheng's staff held about 90 percent of its total shares. By 2001, Guangzheng had been successfully transformed from a single coal producer to one capable of manufacturing dozens of labor- and capital-intensive goods, with a total number of 1,785 registered staff.

Chuangda company, also formerly a coalmine with the name of Hongshan, is located at the town in Luocun, Zichuan district. The coalmine, initially established by the Germans in 1904, was occupied by the Japanese in 1914 after Germany was defeated by Japan in China during World War I. In 1953 the Hongshan coalmine was incorporated with the ZBM. From 1949 to 1990, the coalmine produced 36.27 million tons of raw coal, with the highest output of 2.24 million tons in 1960. As a result of the exhaustion of coal resources, the coalmine was closed in 1996.

Facing increasingly worsening performances in coal production, the coalmine experimented with a three-year contract system and between 1987 and 1989 it introduced a series of reforms on wages. This experiment, although not entirely successful, provided some experience for the later reforms in the late 1990s. Following the corporate reconstruction (its name was changed from Hongshan coalmine to the Chuangda company) in 1996, the state ownership was changed to one entitled shareholding partnership in 1999, with 90 percent of its total shares being held by the company's staff. As at the end of 2001, the Chuangda company was composed of 15 independent subcompanies and other economic units, with a total of 2,150 registered staff.

In brief, during the late 1990s and the early 2000s, the Guangzheng and Chuangda companies went through a process of dual transformation – structural change in production and ownership reform. How have these transformations influenced the system of earnings distribution and its outcomes within each company? In this research, we collected the samples of 391 and 446 workers from Guangzheng and Chuangda companies, respectively. The principle of the sample collection is that we try to include workers from all age groups, sex, educational backgrounds, and positions. In addition, in order to differentiate performance between the pre- and post-reform period, we include two years: 1997 (representing the pre-reform year) and 2001 (representing the post-reform year). Our data on workers' earnings are as of December. 1997's earnings only include wages, while those for 2001 also include share bonuses.

From 1997 to 2001, the distributional policies of earnings underwent significant changes in both companies. In Guangzheng company 11 kinds of wage distribution policies were established: these included 'contracted wages for

---

14. A full version of this research can be found on the companion website (http://www.elsevierdirect.com/companions/9780123978264).

15. The team members involved in the two field surveys are Zhao Renwei, Li Shi, He Dingchao, Zhao Gongzheng, Zhang Yong, Zhu Shumiao, Xing Youqiang, Wang Xiaoping, Xie Yanhong and myself.

fixed posts', 'floating wages according to profit', 'functional wages of posts', 'wages taking a percentage of profits', 'awards based on the ratios of funds tied up by purchases or sales', 'wages taking a percentage of the ratios of payments actually received to total sales', 'awards on special contributions', 'sharing out bonus according to both work performance and shares of capitals', and 'fuzzy awards'.

In the Chuangda company, following reforms in ownership, all time-based wages that had been applied during the pre-reform period were abolished. The piece rate wage system was applied to those employees whose work performance was quantifiable; in addition, the annual salary system was applied to all office workers and top managers of all economically independent units. In addition, a system of 'post-based wages' is applied to all supplementary staff and a system of 'wages taking a percentage of profits' is applied to all marketing personnel.

In order to compare the structural changes of wages between Guangzheng and Chuangda, we classify all the items of wages into three groups – basic wage, bonus, and subsidy.

First of all, the total earnings (wages) are not significantly different between Guangzheng and Chuangda

in 1997, with Chuangda's being slightly higher than Guangzheng's. But, in 2001, although the total earnings had increased greatly in both companies, differences did exist: Guangzheng's average annual growth rate of earnings is 40 percentage points higher than Chuangda's from 1997 to 2001. What is more important, there were some structural changes. After ownership reforms, workers from both companies received share bonuses in addition to wages. Specifically, in Chuangda the proportion of share bonuses to total earnings was about 15 percent, while this proportion was much higher (near 25 percent) in Guangzheng. It is also worth noting that these two companies are different from each other in terms of the structure of wages from 1997 to 2001. For example, in Guangzheng the proportions of basic wages and subsidies were reduced and a bonus was introduced as an incentive. From Table 8.5, we can see that Guangzheng's proportions of 'basic wage' and 'subsidy' are 5 and 10 percentage points lower than those of Chuangda, respectively.

Secondly, we also calculated the Gini coefficients of earnings (see Table 8.5) in order to measure the inequality index of earnings. A noticeable fact is that,

TABLE 8.5 Level, Composition, and Inequality of Earnings Per Worker, December 1997 and 2001

	Guangzheng			Chuangda		
	1997	2001		1997	2001	
		All Staff	Excl. Laid-off Staff		All Staff	Excl. Laid-off Staff
Total earnings (yuan) (%)	490.64 (100.0)	723.39 (100.0)	735.54 (100.0)	493.97 (100.0)	528.20 (100.0)	660.63 (100.0)
Wages (yuan) (%)	490.64 (100.0)	552.07 (76.3)	563.63 (76.6)	493.97 (100.0)	447.14 (84.7)	566.38 (85.7)
Share bonus (%)	NA	171.32 (23.7)	171.91 (23.4)	NA	81.06 (15.3)	94.25 (14.3)
Of wages						
Basic wage (yuan) (%)	340.36 (69.4)	376.60 (52.1)	384.48 (52.3)	354.90 (71.8)	260.86 (49.4)	330.42 (50.0)
Bonus (yuan) (%)	NA	49.89 (6.9)	50.95 (6.9)	NA	NA	NA
Subsidy (yuan) (%)	150.28 (30.6)	125.58 (17.4)	128.20 (17.4)	139.07 (28.2)	186.28 (35.3)	235.96 (35.7)
Earnings inequalities (Gini coefficients)						
Total earnings	0.265	0.345	0.326	0.186	0.414	0.276
Wages	0.265	0.362	0.320	0.186	0.405	0.247
Share bonus	NA	0.595	0.601	NA	0.592	0.590
Of wages						
Basic wage	0.355	0.423	0.411	0.247	0.394	0.233
Subsidy	0.524	0.387	0.373	0.419	0.594	0.461
Samples	229	390	382	36	437	345

Notes: (1) Monetary values are represented by current prices. From 1997 to 2001, the consumer price index (CPI) decreased by 2 percent (NBS, 2002, p. 296). (2) 'NA' denotes not available. (3) The samples of Chuangda only come from office workers in 1997, which are not comparable to those in 2001.

following ownership reforms, the inequality of total earnings increased considerably. Between 1997 and 2001, Guangzheng's Gini coefficient of total earnings increased from 0.265 up to 0.326 (for samples excluding laid-off workers) or 0.345 (for all samples). Even though Chuangda's samples are not representative of its entire staff in 1997, its data do show great inequalities of earnings in 2001, with a Gini coefficient of 0.276 (for samples excluding laid-off workers) or 0.414 (for all samples). Obviously, the ownership reforms have led to an increasingly big gap in earnings between workers in each company.

The differences in production patterns and internal organizations between the two companies may influence, to a certain extent, the earnings gaps with each company. For example, Guangzheng was still able to rely on its coal production as a stable source of revenue, while Chuangda had to develop other new businesses since its coal resources were already exhausted in 1996. After losing its comparative advantages in coal production, Chuangda faced more challenges than Guangzheng during the period of ownership reforms.

Finally, the Gini coefficients of the share bonus (about 0.60) are much higher than those of the wages in both companies. This indicates that a small proportion of staff in both companies secured most of the share bonuses. We can thus conclude that the unequal distribution of share bonuses is the major source of the increasing gaps in earnings. Taking Chuangda as an example, the unequal distribution of share bonuses enlarged the Gini coefficient of total earnings by 2.2 percent (for all samples) or 11.7 percent (for samples excluding laid-off workers). On the other hand, the laid-off workers were also affected by the increasing inequalities of earnings. According to our estimates, between 1997 and 2001 Guangzheng's Gini coefficients of total earnings and of wages rose by 6 percent and 13 percent, respectively, affected by laid-off workers. This influence was more obvious in Chuangda. From 1997 to 2001, Chuangda's Gini coefficients of total earnings and of wages increased by 50 percent and 64 percent, respectively.

Past empirical studies have demonstrated that human capital is the most important factor in the determinants of compensations of labors. Human capital, embodied in each laborer, is composed of knowledge and skills, as well as other capabilities. According to Schulz (1961), these capabilities are the major factor contributing to the growth of production. Economic growth relies on the quality of human capital, not on the abundance of natural resources. The empirical studies on the earnings of laborers show that, along with the process of marketization of the Chinese economy, human capital's influences on earnings have increased (Li and Li, 1993; Knight and Song, 1993; Lai, 1999; and Gustafsson and Li, 2001). According

to Gustafsson and Li (2000), gender gaps in earnings rose in urban China during the 1990s. It is more noticeable that the increased share of the earnings gaps have stemmed from society's prejudices and discrimination against women.

The average earnings of different groups of workers (see Table 8.6) show that workers with higher levels of education also experience a more rapid growth in earnings. In Guangzheng, for example, the average earnings of the workers who had graduated from colleges and senior high schools in 2001 are 2.65 and 1.86 times the levels observed in 1997. Chuangda's average earnings of workers who had graduated from colleges and senior high schools in 2001 are 2.13 and 1.11 times those in 1997. From the perspective of positions, the average earnings of three groups of high- and middle-ranking staff and office workers changed more quickly than those of the other workers. For example, in Guangzheng these three groups' average earnings in 2001 were 1.82, 2.72 and 3.32 times those in 1997; while they were 3.07, 2.31 and 2.02 times those in Chuangda.

It must be noted that the different levels of earnings among various groups of workers, shown in Table 8.6, do not offer a sufficient reflection of the influences of these group variables (such as age, sex, education, and position). In fact, some group variables are related to each other. For example, many high-ranking managers are also highly educated, while physical workers are often young. In order to estimate how these explanatory variables have individually contributed to the changes in earnings, let's borrow a simple model that has been widely used by labor economists:

$$\ln(\text{Wage}) = \beta_0 + \beta_1 \text{Experience} + \beta_2 \text{Experience}^2 + \beta_3 \text{Male} + \beta_4 \text{Education} + \beta_5 \text{Position}$$

In the above model, ln(Wage), the dependent variable, is the natural log of wages.[16] 'Experience' and 'Experience^2' denote the length of work experience (in working years) and its square. 'Male' denotes male workers; and 'Education' is represented by the length of education in years. 'Position' includes four dummies: 'high-ranking staff', 'middle-ranking staff', 'office workers' and 'technical workers'. 'Physical workers' are treated as a comparison variable and are thus excluded from regressions.

The detailed description of this model and the estimated results can be found on the companion website (http://www.elsevierdirect.com/companions/9780123978264).

---

16. Since 'share bonus' has nothing to do with workers' performance, we will not test the regression in which the dependent variable is represented by either 'share bonus' or 'total earning'.

TABLE 8.6 Average Earnings by Groups of Workers (Yuan/Person, December 1997 and 2001)

		1997		2001			
		Wages		Wages		Total Earnings	
		Guangzheng	Chuangda	Guangzheng	Chuangda	Guangzheng	Chuangda
All staff		490.64	493.07	552.07	447.14	723.39	528.20
Sex	Male	582.46	533.42	709.67	475.11	933.65	576.55
	Female	435.93	404.29	358.03	390.76	501.26	437.13
Education	College (3 and 4 years)	509.46	562.69	1,163.06	857.61	1,348.53	1,198.52
	Senior high or technical school	493.76	442.17	671.03	402.36	916.99	492.77
	Junior high school	513.45	530.89	469.07	415.19	637.66	460.38
	Primary	484.90	–	533.42	733.65	740.60	787.82
	Others	467.75	–	498.05	505.04	560.71	506.25
Age group	20 year or younger	–	277.90	426.27	–	426.27	24.17
	21–30 years	494.85	339.28	584.80	345.76	679.72	389.63
	31–40 years	493.48	512.43	511.22	485.55	665.72	582.45
	41–50 years	614.23	560.30	660.64	465.48	1,018.20	549.90
	50 years or older	–	–	572.72	356.36	688.50	429.91
Position	Physical workers	477.66	515.52	438.46	515.38	581.00	563.99
	Technical workers	515.10	–	534.25	433.80	699.17	482.88
	Office workers	312.38	348.21	777.17	640.24	1,036.71	703.18
	Middle-ranking staff	1,066.96	457.90	1,742.14	754.04	2,910.69	1,056.02
	High-ranking staff	1,416.65	885.02	2,281.74	1,654.73	2,575.06	2,721.39

From the estimated results, we may find that some explanatory variables are playing differing roles in the determinants of wages from 1997 to 2001. In 1997, for example, the estimated coefficient on 'Education' is not statistically significant, indicating that educational background was not taken into account in the determination of wages within Guangzheng. Might the education variable exert an influence on wages through various position variables? Our estimated results do not support this hypothesis. The estimated coefficients of 'Office workers' and 'Technical workers' are negative, indicating that, in 1997, the average level of monthly wages of office and technical workers was, *ceteris paribus*, lower than that of physical workers in Guangzheng. In addition, 'Experience', also a factor contributing to human capital and, of course, to the level of a worker's earnings under a market-oriented system, only had a negative coefficient in 1997. That is to say, a worker's level of wages is negatively related to his or her work experience (represented by working years) at the beginning of employment in Guangzheng. The coefficient of 'Male', which is positive, is only statistically insignificant, showing that gender discrimination did not exist in the determination of wages in 1997.

Different from 1997's estimated results, Guangzheng's 'Experience' and 'Experience^2' are insignificantly estimated in 2001, suggesting that, after ownership reform, the level of wages was no longer related to work experience in Guangzheng. This may also indicate that the influences of work experience on labor productivity in traditional, labor-intensive industries are much less than that in other, especially capital-intensive, industries. The estimated coefficient of 'Education' (i.e., 0.0536), which is statistically significant, is quite large, especially given that some position variables included in the regression also have positive effects on wages.

Note that education's influences on workers' earnings may be partially included in the coefficients of position variables. In other words, if the position variables are not taken into account, the estimated coefficient of 'Education' would rise accordingly. Obviously, Guangzheng's coefficient of education is even larger than those in other empirical studies, all of the latter have omitted position variables in their regressions.[17]

The estimated results also show that the coefficients of the high- and middle-ranking staff in 2001 are not only larger than those of office and technical workers, they are also larger than those in 1997. We can thus conclude that, as a result of ownership reform, high-ranking staff received a higher level of wages. Lastly, the estimated coefficient of 'Male' is 0.303 (which is statistically significant at the 1 percent level), showing that, *ceteris paribus*, male workers' wages were 35.4 percent higher than female workers in 2001. It seems very likely that ownership reform might have resulted in some kind of gender discrimination in Guangzheng!

Compared with those of Guangzheng, Chuangda's estimated results have several differences in 2001. First, its coefficient of 'Education' is not statistically significant, indicating that educational background was not emphasized in the determination of wages. Secondly, the estimated coefficients of other explanatory variables are different from those of Guangzheng. For example, the coefficient of 'Experience' is positive and statistically significant, with a ratio of return to work experience (in years) of about 3 percent. Although gender difference existed in Chuangda, it is much less than that in Guangzheng in 2001. In addition, the gaps in wages between high- and middle-ranking staff and the technical and physical workers in Chuangda are smaller than those in Guangzheng.

REFERENCES

Aghion, P., Caroli, E., & Garcia-Penalosa, C. (1999). Inequality and economic growth: the perspective of the new growth theories. *Journal of Economic Literature*, 37(4), 1615–1660.

Alesina, A., & Rodrik, D. (1994). Distribution politics and economic growth. *The Quarterly Journal of Economics*, 109, 465–490.

Alesina, A., & Perotti, R. (1996). Income distribution, political instability and investment. *European Economic Review*, 81, 1170–1189.

Asian Development Bank. (2002). *Research on poverty in Urban China*. unpublished report, Manila: Asian Development Bank.

Asia-Pacific Economic Times, October 22, 1996.

Barro, R. J. (1991). Economic growth in a cross section of nations. *The Quarterly Journal of Economics*, 106(May), 407–443.

Barro, R. J. (2000). Inequality and growth in a panel of countries. *Journal of Economic Growth*, 5, 5–32.

Benabou, R. (1996). 'Inequality and growth,' *NBER macroeconomics annual*. Cambridge, MA: National Bureau of Economic Research (NBER). pp. 11–73.

Carson, R. L. (1996). *Comparative economic systems: market and state in economic systems* (2nd ed.). New York: M.E. Sharpe.

Cheng, Y.-S. (1996). A decomposition analysis of income inequality of Chinese rural households. *China Economic Review*, 7(2), 155–167.

Deininger, K., & Squire, L. (1998). New ways of looking at old issues: inequality and growth. *Journal of Development Economics*, 57, 259–287.

Eichera, T. S., & Garcia-Penalosab, C. (2001). Inequality and growth: the dual role of human capital in development. *Journal of Development Economics*, 66, 173–197.

Fanelli, J. M., & McMahon, G. (2006). Introduction to the regional syntheses and country case studies. In J. M. Fanelli & G. McMahon (Eds., 2006), *Understanding market reforms* (pp. 1–67). Volume 2 (Motivation, Implementation and Sustainability). London and New York: Palgrave Macmillan.

Forbes, K. (1997). *A reassessment of the relationship between inequality and growth*. Unpublished paper, MIT.

Gastil, R. D. (1987). *Freedom in the world*. Westport, CT: Greenwood Press.

Ge, Y. (2000). *Probe into countermeasures: a path to reducing the unequal distribution of incomes* [duice yanjiu: huanjie shouru fenpei maodun de silu]. Beijing: Development and Research Center of the State Council.

Gregory, P. R., & Stuart, R. C. (1998). *Comparative economic systems* (6th ed.). New York: Houghton Mifflin College.

Guo, R. (2009). *Intercultural economic analysis: theory and method*. New York: Springer.

Gupta, D. (1990). *The economics of political violence*. New York: Praeger.

Gustafsson, B., & Li, S. (2000). Economic transformation in urban China and the gender earnings gap. *Journal of Population Economics*, 13(2), 305–329. July.

Gustafsson, B., & Li, S. (2001). The anatomy of rising earnings inequality in urban China. *Journal of Comparative Economics*, 29(1), 118–135.

Gustafsson, B., Li, S., & Sicular, T. (Eds.) (2008). *Inequality and public policy in China*. Cambridge: Cambridge University Press.

Hibbs, D. (1973). *Mass political violence: a cross-sectional analysis*. New York: Wiley.

Holesovsky, V. (1977). *Economic systems: analysis and comparison*. New York: McGraw-Hill.

Khan, A. R., & Riskin, C. (2001). *Inequality and poverty in China in the age of globalization*. New York: Oxford University Press.

Khan, A. R., Griffin, K., & Riskin, C. (2001). Income distribution in urban China during the period of economic reform and globalization. In C. Riskin, R. Zhao, & Li Shi (Eds.), *China's retreat from equality: income distribution and economic transition* (pp. 125–132). New York: M.E. Sharpe.

Knight, J., & Song, L. (1993). Why urban wages differ in China. In K. Griffin, & Zhao Renwei (Eds.), *The distribution of income in China*. London: Macmillan.

Kohler, H. (1996). *Economic systems and human welfare: a global survey*. Cincinnati, Ohio: South-Western College Publishing Co.

Kuznets, S. (1955). Economic growth and income inequality. *American Economic Review*, 45, 1–28.

Lai, D. (1999). In Zhao et al. (Eds., 1999), *Education, labor and income distribution* [jiaoyu, laodongli yu shouru fenpei]. pp. 451–474.

---

17. For example, the estimated ratios of return to education are 0.038 for urban China and 0.020 for rural China in 1988 (Li and Li, 1994, p. 445) and 0.042 for SOEs, 0.032 for collectively-owned enterprises, and 0.0791 for foreign-invested enterprises in 1996 (Zhao, 2001).

Li, H., & Zou, H. (1998). Income inequality is not harmful for growth: theory and evidence. *Review of Development Economics*, 2, 318–334.

Li, S. (2004). China's urban and rural income surveys. *Journal of Financial Economics* [caijing zazhi], No. 3.

Li, S., & Zhai, F. (2000). Access to the WTO and its influences on the Chinese economy [jiaru shijie maoyi zuzhi dui zhongguo jingji de yingxiang]. *Yuce (forecasting), No. 3*, 12–21.

Li, S., & Li, W. (1994). Estimating the ratios of return to investment in education in China [zhongguo jiaoyu touzi de geren shouyilv de guji]. In Zhao et al. (Eds., 1994), *Studies in income distribution in China* (pp. 442–456). Beijing: China Social Science Press.

Li, S., Zhao, R., & Zhang, P. (1997). *The changes of China's income distribution during the transition*. Dissertation for the International Workshop, Institute of Economics, Chinese Academy of Social Sciences, Beijing, August.

Londregan, J. B., & Poole, K. T. (1989). *Coups d'Etat and the military business cycle*. Working paper No. 36-88-89, Carnegie Mellon University, March.

Ma, L. (2008). A 'Happiness Curve' is drawn by ten pieces of pay-notes [shizhang gongzitiao huichu shenghuo 'xingfu quxian']. *Changping Weekly, September 2*, 5. (in Chinese).

Massahiko, A., & Qian, Y. (Eds.). (1995). *Corporation management structure in the transitional economy*. Beijing: China Economics Press.

McMahon, G., & Squire, L. (Eds.). (2003). *Explaining growth: a global research project*. London and New York: Palgrave-Macmillan.

NBS. (various years). *China statistical yearbook*, various issues, Beijing: China Statistical Publishing House.

North, D. C. (1991). Institutions. *The Journal of Economic Perspectives*, 5(1), 97–112.

Perotti, R. (1993). Political equilibrium, income distribution and growth. *Review of Economic Studies*, 60, 755–776.

Perotti, R. (1996). Growth, income distribution, and democracy: what the data say. *Journal of Economic Growth*, 1, 149–187.

Persson, T., & Tabellini, G. (1994). Is inequality harmful for growth? Theory and evidence. *American Economic Review*, 84, 600–621.

Quah, D. (2002). *One third of the world's growth and inequality LSE economics department*. CEPR Discussion Paper 2002:3316.

Ravallion, M. (1998). Does aggregation hide the harmful effects of inequality on growth? *Economics Letters*, 61, 73–77.

Ravallion, M. (2001). Growth, inequality and poverty: looking beyond averages. *World Development*, 29, 173–197.

Riskin, C., Zhao, R., & Shi, Li (Eds.) (2001). *China's retreat from equality: income distribution and economic transition*. New York: M.E. Sharpe.

Rodrik, D. (2003). Institutions, integration, and geography: in search of the deep determinants of economic growth. In D. Rodrik (Ed.), *In search of prosperity: analytic narratives on economic growth* (pp. 1–20). Princeton, NJ: Princeton University Press.

Schnitzer, M. C. (1997). *Comparative economic systems* (7th ed.). Cincinnati, Ohio: South-Western College Publishing Co.

Schulz, T. W. (1961). Investment in human capital. *American Economic Review*, 51(March), 213–226.

Sloman, J. (1991). *Economics*. Hemel Hempstead: Harvester Wheatsheaf.

Venieris, Y., & Gupta, D. (1986). Income distribution and sociopolitical instability as determinants of savings: a cross-sectional model. *Journal of Political Economy*, 94, 873–883.

Wang, X. (2000). Sustainability of China's economic growth and institutional changes. *Economic Research Journal*, 7, 1–12. (in Chinese).

Wei, S., & Wu, Y. (2003). *Globalization and inequality: evidence from within China*. NBER Working Paper No. 8611, Cambridge, MA: NBER.

Woo, W.-T. (1998). Chinese economic growth: sources and prospects [zhongguo quan yaosu shengchan lv: laizi nongye bumen laodongli aai peizhi de shouyao zuoyong]. *Jingji Yanjiu*, 3, 16–23.

World Bank (1983). *China: the development of a socialist economy*. Washington DC: World Bank.

World Bank (1996). *From plan to market: world bank development report 1996*. New York: Oxford University Press.

Wu, J. (2000). Saving, investment and economic growth. In X. Wang, & G. Fan (Eds.), *Sustainability of China's economic growth*. Beijing: Economic Science Press.

Xu, L. C., & Zou, H.-F. (2000). Explaining the changes of income distribution in China. *China Economic Review*, 11, 149–170.

Zhao, J., & Tang, J. (2002). *Explaining growth: the case of China*. draft, Global Development Network (GDN), New Delhi.

Zhao, R. (2001). Increasing income inequality and its causes in China. In C. Riskin, R. Zhao, & Li Shi (Eds.), *China's retreat from equality: income distribution and economic transition* (pp. 25–43). New York: M.E. Sharpe.

Chapter 9

A Multiregional Economic Comparison

Bianzhong – a percussion instrument in ancient China. *Source: http://en.wikipedia.org*

The Bianzhong of Marquis Yi of Zeng (or Zenghouyi bells), made in 433 BC, were unearthed in 1978 in the Zenghouyi tomb in Sui county, Hubei province, China. The bianzhong comprise a total of 64 bells (with the largest bell being 153.4 cm high and 203.6 kg in weight and the smallest one being 20.4 cm high and 2.4 kg in weight), which are hung at three levels and divided into eight groups. Each bell can play two tones (from C2 to D7) with three degree's interval between them. These bells are currently on display at the Hubei Provincial Museum in Wuhan.

A man from the state of Zheng (in today's Henan province) wanted to buy a pair of shoes. He measured his foot and put the measurement on a chair. When he set out for the market he forgot to bring it along. It was only after he had found the pair he wanted that it occurred to him, 'I forgot the measurement.' He

went home to get it, but when he returned, the market had broken up and he did not get his shoes after all. 'Why didn't you try on the shoes with your feet?' someone asked. 'I would rather trust the measurement than trust myself,' he replied.

— Hanfeizi (c. 280–233 BC)

9.1 CHINA'S STATISTICAL SYSTEMS

9.1.1 Material Product System

The lack of high quality and comparable cross-sectional data is always a major hurdle in any study of multiregional economic issues, particularly in the centrally planned economies (CPEs). After the foundation of the PRC, China adopted the so-called Material Product System (MPS) to measure its national and regional economic performance. In fact, the

Understanding the Chinese Economies. DOI: http://dx.doi.org/10.1016/B978-0-12-397826-4.00009-3
© 2013 Elsevier Inc. All rights reserved.

MPS only records productive activities. As a result, China only published a fragmentary set of data covering such indicators as national income, gross value of social product (GVSP), gross value of agricultural output (GVAO), and gross value of industrial output (GVIO), the reliability of which, however, is uncertain. The recent research environment has been increasingly improved, along with the transformation of the Chinese economy from the centrally planned system to a market-oriented system. Since the early 1980s, an increasingly complete set of data on national regional economic performance has been released. Regardless of this progress, many problems, however, still exist when one tries to apply the officially published data to conduct a multiregional comparison of the Chinese economy.

Difficulties may arise from the multiregional economic comparison between the pre-reform period, during which China was virtually a CPE, and the post-reform period, during which China has been transforming gradually into a market economy. In market economies, GNP is the total value of all final products and services generated and national income is the total of all incomes received by all factors of production during a defined period of time. In the CPEs, however, the national income accounts record only productive activities carried out in their territories, rather than incomes received by their residents. China's national income accounts during the pre-reform period were virtually based on the MPS, whose most important aggregate is net material product (NMP). The NMP comprehensively covers value added in the 'material' sectors of production. The sum of the outputs of all separately enumerated production units multiplied by the relevant prices of outputs is called the gross value of social product (GVSP). As GVSP also includes the values of intermediate products which are simply the material costs for consecutive production units, the values of products were often counted more than once.

Obviously, the use of the GVSP concept might result in a series of negative effects, particularly when it is used as an indicator to make a multiregional evaluation of the sizes of the economies, as a part of the GVSP is contributed by intermediate products that are never meaningful to social welfare – no matter how large it is. In the MPS, the national income was only created in China by material production sectors, such as industry, mining, agriculture, forestry, animal husbandry, building construction, and service trades that were productive in nature and carried out such activities as assembly, processing, and repairs during a given period. In terms of value, it is equivalent to the value of the total social product within the time period minus the value of the means of production consumed during that period; in terms of materials, it is equivalent to the total social product (including means of production and means of consumption) within the given period minus the means of production consumed during

that period.[1] However, it ignored the contributions from non-productive labors, particularly in such non-material spheres as banking, insurance, science, education, culture, health, administration, the military, and so on.

9.1.2   System of National Accounts

Since the mid-1980s, China has begun to compile national income statistics according to the United Nations' System of National Accounts (SNA).[2] However, many theoretical and practical problems on how to adopt the SNA to Chinese economic accounting still remain unresolved. For instance, the sum of the regional GDPs may not equal the national GDP published by the central government, the reason for which is that the statistical data compiled by the State Statistical Bureau (SSB) or, as it has been renamed, the National Bureau for Statistics (NBS), are derived from the records of the various ministries in charge of their related sectors, whereas the regional statistical data are compiled by the regional statistical bureaux.[3]

The compilation of the GDP data left many unpersuaded in China, especially under the dual-pricing system. With the exception of the data on the tertiary sector, the transformation of NMP data to the corresponding GDP data were simply devised by the SSB (NBS) and, therefore, raised some questions as to whether the GDP data may be arrived at by multiplying the NMP by some conversion factors. In fact, since the socialist accounting system does not take into account the output value of the service sector, historical records of this sector were very fragmentary. China has published the GDP indices at constant prices with 1978 being the base year. The GDP data at constant prices are inextricably linked to the real NMP data collected by the old system. Unlike Western countries that derive real GDP using a system of price indices, the basic production units at the lowest level of the statistical reporting system are responsible for computing the real output value based on a catalog of fixed prices (*bubian jia*) handed down from above. The raw data are then reported back to the higher level of the system to be further aggregated. Many analysts argue that problems may arise in this reporting process in the compilation of GDP data.[4]

---

1. Therefore, national income equals GVSP minus all material costs including depreciation of capital.
2. It is worth noting that the SNA has some shortcomings and is not a complete measure of economic welfare from which humankind may benefit. In fact, as illustrated in the United Nations (1990a, b), the SNA-based GNP (or GDP) indicator ignores the costs of both the depletion and degradation of natural and environmental resources.
3. More evidence may be found in Tsui (1993, pp. 30–1).
4. See, for example, Guo and Han (1991, pp. 10–21) for a more detailed explanation and a critical evaluation on the quality of Chinese GDP data.

Notes: (1) The equivalents include: Albania = Hebei, Algeria = Jilin, Angola = Hubei, Armenia = Sichuan, Azerbaijan = Zhejiang, Belarus = Jiangsu, Belarus = Jiangsu, Congo (Brazzaville) = Tibet, Costa Rica = Liaoning, Cuba = Fujian, Egypt = Xinjiang, El Salvador = Henan, El Salvador = Hunan, Guatemala = Ningxia, Guyana = Jiangxi, Hungary = Tianjin, India = Guizhou, Iraq = Gansu, Jordan = Anhui, Kazakhstan = Guangdong, Mauritius = Chongqing, Mauritius = Shaanxi, Namibia = Shanxi, Qatar = Macau, Saudi Arabia = Shanghai, Singapore = Hong Kong, Slovakia = Beijing, South Africa = Shandong, Swaziland = Guangxi, Turkmenistan = Hainan, Turkmenistan = Qinghai, Ukraine = Heilongjiang, Vanuatu = Yunnan.
(2) Figures are inpurchasing power parity (PPP) dollars and as of 2010.

FIGURE 9.1 Which countries match the GDP per capita of Chinese provinces? *Source: Author based on http://www.economist.com/content/all_parities_china*

There is another question: should real or nominal GDP/ NMP data be used for a multiregional comparison of the Chinese economy? Ideally, the adjusted GDP/NMP based on the purchasing power parity (PPP) method should be used in China because of the vast range of natural and social environments and varying price levels and inflation rates across the country (see Figure 9.1). Unfortunately, few such efforts have been made on the measurement of China's regional GDPs using the PPP methodology due to the lack of sufficient and up-to-date information and data. Hsueh (1994a, pp. 22–56) modifies the nominal NMP data of 29 provinces using the 1980s fixed prices of industrial and agricultural products, of which Beijing's relative price index is assumed to be 100 in 1981, while the data on national income (NI) of the remaining provinces are converted by their Beijing-based price levels, respectively. Hsueh's attempt to estimate China's NMP, although heroic,

is surely controversial and will leave many unpersuaded, particularly when the provinces' industrial structures differ so greatly from one another.

9.1.3 Credibility of Chinese Statistics

Some authors have questioned the credibility of Chinese statistics (see, for example, Rawski, 2001 and Holz, 2008). In 2010, the overall score for China's data in the World Bank Statistical Capacity Indicator (SCI) was 58 on a scale of 0–100, fairly well below the international average of 65.[5] In addition, Zheng (2001) notes that China's

5. See World Bank (2011). Note that the World Bank Statistical Capacity Indicator (SCI) consists of three assessment areas: methodology (where China's score is 50), data sources (score 40), and periodicity and timeliness (score 83).

quarterly national accounts, which rely heavily on estimates and excessive aggregation, are particularly weak with respect to the transportation and real estate sectors and the price system. Therefore, some care should be taken in the use of China's published time-series data.

In respect of such official publications as do exist, economic data with political implications such as income distribution, inflation, credit rationing, shadow interest rates, the use of foreign capital, and military expenditure have been under partial government control, particularly during the 1980s and the early 1990s. Furthermore, the decline in the professional ability and ethical standards of some local officials in charge of the collection and processing of economic data could largely discredit the quality of data. For instance, it is not uncommon for rural industrial enterprises to report nominal output under the rubric of output at constant prices; government cadres and business officers in rural areas whose promotion is partly based on agricultural and industrial growth may falsify the statistical data by enlarging the output valuation.[6]

9.2 MACROECONOMIC PERFORMANCE

9.2.1 Estimating China's Time-Series Data

Since the foundation of the PRC, China has adopted two different systems to measure its national and regional economic performance: the material product system (MPS) and the system of national accounts (SNA). As explained in Section 9.1, the concept of NI (national income) deviates from that of GNP *ex facto*, because the former is based on the traditional MPS used by most centrally planned economies (CPEs), while the latter is based on the SNA used by the market economies. Different approaches have been suggested to arrive at an estimate of the GNP/GDP data (see, for example, Marea, 1985, pp. 15–16 and 27–119). None of these could be applied to the CPEs with no comprehensive, consistent, and up-to-date statistical information on the NMP or physical aggregation data for direct use (Hwang, 1993, p. 108).

The Penn World Table (PWT) v6.2 (see the fifth column of Table 9.1 for selected years) provides consistently estimated time-series data for China's per capita GDP under constant prices (Heston et al., 2006), but it does not include provincial and regional data. In 1997, China's State Statistical Bureau (SSB) estimated the country's provincial GDP data for the years from 1952 to 1995 (SSB, 1997). However, many shortcomings exist in these officially estimated data (Xu, 2004). As China has adopted the SNA since the mid-1980s, while it did not abandon the MPS until 1994, it is possible for us to make a quantitative estimate of their correlations.

Using the data from 1985 to 1993 (SSB, 1989, p. 29; 1994, p. 33; 1996, p. 42; and 1996, pp. 13 and 15), we may

TABLE 9.1 Various Estimates of China's GDP Per Capita, Selected Years

Year	NBS (2005)		Equation (9.2)	PWT[c]	Other Sources[d]
	RMB (yuan)[a]	US$[a]	RMB (yuan)[b]	PPP ($)	PPP ($)
1979	417	268	455	724	1,000
1986	956	277	974	1,293	2,440
1988	1,355	364	1,406	1,489	2,472
1990	1,634	342	1,668	1,678	1,031; 2,140
1991	1,879	353	1,895	1,798	1,680
1992	2,287	415	2,288	1,983	1,600
1993	2,939	510	2,753	2,131	2,120
1994	3,923	455		2,453	2,510

[a]All are measured at current prices (the exchanges rates of RMB yuan to US dollars are shown in Figure 12.1 in Chapter 12).
[b]Estimated by author at current prices.
[c]Penn World Table (PWT) v6.2 (Heston et al., 2006) at constant prices.
[d]World Bank (1996, p. 21) and Zheng (1996, p. 1).

---

6. For example, according to a survey conducted by JPSB (1990, pp. 27–8), the rural GVIO data reported to the National Bureau of Statistics (NBS) in Beijing might have been 21.8 percent higher than the real data in Jilin province in 1989.

estimate three linear equations between GNP and GVSP (gross value of social product), NI (national income) and GVIO (gross value of industrial output), as the following:

$$GNP = 0.4837GVSP \quad (1985 - 93, R^2 = 0.991)$$
$$(78.456)$$
(9.1)

$$GNP = 1.3259NI \quad (1985 - 93, R^2 = 0.993)$$
$$(84.587)$$
(9.2)

$$GNP = 0.5799GVIAO \quad (1985 - 93, R^2 = 0.967)$$
$$(39.210)$$
(9.3)

By replacing the NI series into Equation 9.2 (as it is the most significantly estimated among the three equations), the GNP derivation is shown in the second column of Table 9.1. It is worth noting that China's NI/GNP ratio ($1/1.3259 \approx 0.7542$) estimated in Equation 9.2 is less than North Korea's (0.8) estimated by Hwang (1993, p. 118). The causes of the difference between China and North Korea need to be explored in detail. The differences between the estimated GNP per capita (the fourth column of Table 9.1) and the SSB's GNP per capita (the second column of Table 9.1) may be possibly explained by: (1) the estimation errors produced in Equation 9.2; and (2) the official miscalculation arising from the incomplete application of the SNA.

If China's national income data are more accurately stated by SSB than GNP from 1986 to 1993, we may conclude that China's actual GNP must have been understated before 1992 and overstated since then (especially during the first half of the 1990s) by the SSB.[7]

9.2.2 China's Interprovincial Differences

Let's first of all consider the poorest and richest provinces in China. In 1952, the per capita national income of Shanghai was estimated at 584.15 yuan, which is 10.67 times that of Guizhou (54.77 yuan). In 1979, Shanghai's per capita national income, at constant prices, had risen to 2,860.92 yuan, 27.85 times the figure for Guizhou (102.72 yuan) (SSB, 1990). Obviously, during the pre-reform period, there was a rapid widening of the economic gap between the richest and poorest provinces. How large is this gap during the post-reform period? Briefly, if we consider per capita GDP, the economic gap has experienced two different patterns. Shanghai's per capita GDP was 27.88 times of Guizhou's in 1979 and 7.34 times of Guizhou's in 1990, which implies that the per capita GDP ratio of Shanghai to Guizhou decreased greatly during the above period. From 1990 to 2000, however, the per capita GDP ratio of Shanghai to Guizhou increased once again to 12.6.

Obviously, even though not taking into account its two Special Administrative Regions (Hong Kong and Macau) (an economic comparison of Taiwan, Hong Kong, Macau, and mainland China will be conducted in Chapter 15), China has still been among the countries with the largest spatial inequality (see Box 9.1).

The provinces' national income (NI) statistical data were only reported for the period between 1952 and 1993, while their GDP statistical data have been available since 1978. In order to conduct a consistent multiregional comparison of the Chinese economy across the pre- and post-reform periods, we have to apply the national income data and Equation 9.2 in order to arrive at an estimate of the

---

Box 9.1 An International View of China's Spatial Economic Gaps

China's vast size and social and cultural diversities have also resulted in great regional economic differences. Even though not taking into account its two Special Administrative Regions (Hong Kong and Macau), China still had a per capita GDP ratio of more than 12 for the richest (Shanghai) to the poorest (Guizhou) at the end of 1990s. This figure is only lower than Indonesia (20.8 in 1983), but much higher than many other countries, such as:

- The former Yugoslavia (7.8 in 1988)
- India (3.26 in 1980)
- Netherlands (2.69 in 1988)
- Italy (2.34 in 1988)
- Canada (2.30 in 1988)

- Spain (2.23 in 1988)
- France (2.15 in 1988)
- West Germany (1.93 in 1988)
- Greece (1.63 in 1988)
- UK (1.63 in 1988)
- South Korea (1.53 in 1985)
- Japan (1.47 in 1981)
- USA (1.43 in 1983; 2.31 in 2009)
- Australia (1.13 in 1978).

Data sources: *Ottolenghi and Steinherr (1993, p. 29), Savoie (1992, p. 191), Smith (1987, p. 41), Higgins (1981, pp. 69–70), Nair (1985, p. 9), Hill and Weidemann (1989, pp. 6–7), Kim and Mills (1990, p. 415), Hu et al. (1995, p. 92), and author.*

---

7. For more evidence of the overstatement on China's GNP for the post-1992 period, one may also refer to Ling et al. (1995, pp. 18–19), *China Youths* (1995, p. 2), *The Economist* (1995, p. 19), *People's Daily* (1995, p. 2), and Huang (1996, pp. 157–62).

GDP indicators for the pre-reform period. In addition, during the early period, when the MPS was transferred to the SNA, the GDP data were not reported by a few provinces (including Liaoning in 1978 and 1979, Qinghai in 1979 and 1981–84, Guangxi in 1979, 1981–85 and 1987, and Tibet in 1978–84). As a result, we have to make some approximations of per capita GDP for these provinces according to their national income data and Equation 9.2.

Finally, there still exists an obstacle to the multiregional comparison of the Chinese economy: Tibet had not officially reported any statistical data before 1980. The only possible method we can use is to estimate Tibet's per capita GDP by making reference to other provinces with which it shares a number of similarities in terms of economic conditions. In 1980, the per capita national income of Tibet was 266 yuan, approximately 1.127 times that of Yunnan. Using Yunnan's GDP data and a conversion factor of 1.127, we obtain Tibet's per capita GDP data for the period from 1952 to 1979.

Using the per capita GDP data of the selected years (1952, 1979, 1990, 2000, and 2010), we may compare the changes of provincial ranking over time (see Table 9.2):

(1) 1952–1980 (29 provinces):
- 15 provinces (Beijing, Hebei, Shanxi, Liaoning, Jilin, Jiangsu, Zhejiang, Shandong, Henan, Hubei, Sichuan, Yunnan, Tibet, Shaanxi, and Qinghai) ranked higher than before
- ten provinces (Tianjin, Inner Mongolia, Heilongjiang, Anhui, Fujian, Jiangxi, Hunan, Guangxi, Ningxia, and Xinjiang) ranked lower than before
- four provinces (Shanghai, Guangdong, Guizhou, and Gansu) remained unchanged.

(2) 1980–1990 (29 provinces, with the exclusion of Hainan):
- ten provinces (Jiangsu, Zhejiang, Anhui, Fujian, Shandong, Hubei, Guangdong, Yunnan, Tibet, and Xinjiang) ranked higher than before
- 11 provinces (Hebei, Shanxi, Inner Mongolia, Jilin, Heilongjiang, Guangxi, Sichuan, Guizhou, Shaanxi, Gansu, and Qinghai) ranked lower than before
- eight provinces (Beijing, Tianjin, Liaoning, Shanghai, Jiangxi, Henan, Yunnan, and Ningxia) remained unchanged.

(3) 1990–2000 (30 provinces, with the exclusion of Chongqing):
- nine provinces (Fujian, Hebei, Henan, Hunan, Inner Mongolia, Jiangsu, Shandong, Sichuan, and Zhejiang) ranked higher than before
- 13 provinces (Gansu, Guizhou, Heilongjiang, Jiangxi, Jilin, Liaoning, Ningxia, Qinghai, Shanxi, Shaanxi, Tibet, Yunnan, and Xinjiang) ranked lower than before
- eight provinces (Anhui, Beijing, Guangdong, Guangxi, Hianan, Hubei, Shanghai, and Tianjin) remained unchanged.

TABLE 9.2 Provincial Ranks by Per Capita GDP, Selected Years

Province	1952[a]	1980	1990	2000	2010
Anhui	22	27	24	24	25
Beijing	3	2	2	2	2
Chongqing	NP	NP	NP	19	18
Fujian	14	20	12	7	9
Gansu	16	16	27	30	30
Guangdong	18	18	5	5	6
Guangxi	27	28	29	29	26
Guizhou	29	29	30	31	31
Hainan	NP	NP	15	15	22
Hebei	9	7	17	11	12
Heilongjiang	4	5	8	10	14
Henan	23	21	28	18	15
Hubei	20	17	13	13	13
Hunan	21	22	20	17	20
Inner Mongolia	7	14	18	16	7
Jiangsu	13	10	7	6	5
Jiangxi	11	24	23	25	27
Jilin	8	6	10	14	11
Liaoning	5	4[a]	4	8	9
Ningxia	10	19	19	22	19
Qinghai	15	9	14	20	23
Shaanxi	24	12	21	27	17
Shandong	19	13	11	9	8
Shanghai	1	1	1	1	1
Shanxi	17	15	16	21	16
Sichuan	28	26	26	23	24
Tianjin	2	3	3	3	3
Tibet	25[b]	23[b]	22	26	28
Xinjiang	6	11	9	12	21
Yunnan	26	25	25	28	29
Zhejiang	12	8	6	4	4

Notes: (1) Per capita GDP data are measured at current prices; (2) 'NP' denotes 'not a province for the year'.
[a]Per capita GDP is estimated based on the data of national income (SSB, 1990) and Equation 9.2 of Section 9.2.
[b]Per capita GDP is estimated by the author based on the Tibet/Yunnan ratio of national incomes (1.127) and Yunnan's GDP data.
Sources: SSB (1986, 1991) and NBS (2001; 2011) except for [a] and [b].

(4) 2000–2010 (31 provinces):

- ten provinces (Chongqing, Jiangsu, Shandong, Guangxi, Henan, Jilin, Ningxia, Shanxi, Inner Mongolia, and Shaanxi) ranked higher than before
- 14 provinces (Xinjiang, Hainan, Heilongjiang, Hunan, Qinghai, Fujian, Jiangxi, Tibet, Anhui, Guangdong, Hebei, Liaoning, Sichuan, and Yunnan) ranked lower than before
- seven provinces (Beijing, Gansu, Guizhou, Hubei, Shanghai, Tianjin, and Zhejiang) remained unchanged.

9.3 REAL LIVING STANDARDS

9.3.1 General Situation

The standard of living improved significantly in China during the period of the first Five-Year Plan (FYP), from 1953 to 1957, but suffered a sudden decline thereafter due to the failures of the Great Leap Forward (1958–60). It did not start to improve significantly until the end of the Cultural Revolution (1966–76) during which period people were largely encouraged to be rich in 'spirit' but *not* 'material'. Since the early 1980s, Chinese living standards have improved steadily. Among China's ten FYPs, the eighth FYP (1991–95) is the one in which the per capita personal consumption growth rate is the highest for China as a whole, while the sixth FYP (1981–85) is the one in which per capita personal consumption growth rate is at its highest level for the agricultural households. This was not only because of economic growth but also because of continuous reduction in population growth.

If China's per capita personal consumption is measured in terms of US dollars, the figure is still quite small. However, China's commodity prices are very low. If measured in terms of purchasing power parity (PPP) instead of exchange rates, the recorded standard of living in China would definitely be higher. For instance, after having calculated personal consumption in China and Japan using exchange rates, Mizoguchi et al. (1989, p. 28) find that China's per capita personal consumption expenditure is only 3.1 percent of Japan's. However, when per capita personal consumption expenditure is recomputed using purchasing power, China's figure is 21.5 percent of Japan's when Japan's consumption structure is used for weighting and 15.7 percent when China's consumption structure is used for weighting (see Figure 9.2).[8]

China's data on people's livelihoods (including information such as employment, the disposable income and expenditure of residents, the level of consumption, housing conditions, the quantity of consumer goods owned, and so on) have been compiled annually by the SSB (NBS) based on surveys of different samples. Some questions and ambiguities remain when different samples and measurements are chosen. For instance, the SSB (NBS) makes no allowance for the rental value of housing. Furthermore, the SSB coverage of income in kind and subsidies also appears to be much less comprehensive than it is.

Moreover, Khan et al. (1993, pp. 34–7) explain in detail why their estimates are different from those of

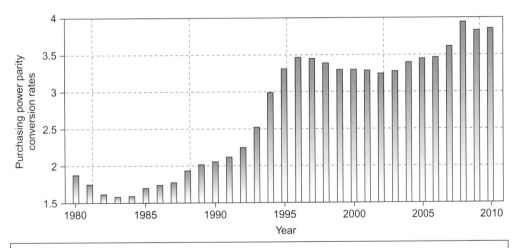

> **Notes:** These data form the basis for the country weights used to generate the World Economic Outlook (WEO) country group composites for the domestic economy. For primary source information, please refer to one of the following sources: the Organization for Economic Cooperation and Development; the World Bank; or the Penn World Tables.

FIGURE 9.2 China's purchasing power parity (PPP) conversion rates, 1980–2010. *Source: IMF.*

8. The PPP conversion rate in China was reported to be around 3.9 yuan per US dollar in 2010.

the SSB: the difference in the case of the rural sample is almost certainly due to differences in the definition of income and the method of estimation rather than differences in sampling method or in measurement errors; for the urban areas, as the sample is much more weakly related to the SSB sample, the difference between the two estimates could therefore be due in part to differences in sampling and to measurement errors. If we assume that their calculations are more accurate than those of the SSB, we may thus conclude that the national income under China's macroeconomic accounting was underestimated during the 1980s, which is consistent with the hypothesis advanced in Section 9.2.

When comparing China's living standards with those of other countries, one should remember that China has had a very comprehensive social welfare system (even if it is not available to all Chinese citizens), especially during the pre-reform period.[9] In addition, urban residents also have access to low-cost housing.[10]

One important indicator reflecting real living standards is the measure of 'life expectancy at birth'. In demography, the term 'life expectancy at birth' is expressed in terms of the number of years newborn children would live if subject to the mortality risks prevailing for the cross section of population at the time of their birth. During the 1980s and 1990s, China's economic growth was faster than that of the rest of the world. However, its life expectancy did not improve in line with this.

Table 9.3 shows that in 1980 five economies in the Asia-Pacific region had a higher level of life expectancy than China. Between 1980 and 2007 China's level of life expectancy rose by 4.88 years, while Australia, Hong Kong, Japan, New Zealand, and Singapore, each of which had a higher base level of life expectancy than China, achieved increases of more than six years. During the same period Sri Lanka, which had the same level of life expectancy as China in 1980, had increased its life expectancy by 6.8 years. The infant mortality rate in China was higher than that of the Asia-Pacific economies during the same period.

In addition, after comparing China and an Indian state, Kerala, Sen (2004) points out:

At the time of economic reforms, when China had a life expectancy of about 67 years or so, the Indian state of Kerala had a

TABLE 9.3 Life Expectancy and Infant Mortality Rates, Selected Economies

Country	Life Expectancy (years)		Infant Mortality Rate (‰)	
	1980	2007	1980	2007
China	68	72.88	42	21.16
Australia	74	80.62	11	4.51
Hong Kong	74	81.68	11	2.93
Japan	76	82.20	8	2.80
South Korea	67	79.10	26	5.94
Malaysia	67	72.76	30	16.39
New Zealand	73	78.96	13	4.99
Singapore	71	81.80	12	2.30
Sri Lanka	68	74.80	34	19.01
World average	61	65.82	67	42.65

Sources: Wang (2003, p. 55) and CIA (2008).

similar figure. By now, however, Kerala's life expectancy of 74 years is very considerably above China's 70. Going further, if we look at specific points of vulnerability, the infant mortality rate in China has declined very slowly since the economic reforms, whereas it has continued to fall very sharply in Kerala. While Kerala had roughly the same infant mortality rate as China – 37 per thousand – at the time of the Chinese reforms in 1979, Kerala's present rate, below 14 per thousand, is less than half of China's 30 per thousand (where it has stagnated over the last decade).

9.3.2 Rural–Urban Disparity

Since the reform, the income differentials between urban and rural China have experienced different patterns. In the early period of the economic reform, which was focused on the introduction of the household responsibility system (HRS) to the agricultural sector, the level of rural income increased very rapidly and the gap between the rural and urban areas narrowed until 1985. Since then, the rural–urban gap has begun to increase again as a result of the diminishing marginal returns of the agricultural sector on one hand and the urban industrial reforms on the other. As demonstrated in Figure 9.3, the ratio of urban to rural per capita income fell from 2.36 in 1978 to 1.70 in 1983; it has been in excess of 3.0 since 2000.

Before beginning our in-depth analysis for the causes, there should be clarification of some issues relating to the definition of rural and urban income. The estimates of China's rural and urban incomes conducted by both the

---

9. Ma and Sun (1981, p. 568), for example, estimate that the total work-related insurance and other types of social welfare expenditure might have been as high as 526.7 yuan per year for each worker, or 81.7 percent of the average wage before 1980.

10. According to the urban surveys conducted by the SSB, the per capita expenditure for residence in most urban areas is only 32.23 yuan in 1985 and 250.18 yuan in 1995, which accounts for approximately only 4.3 percent and 5.8 percent of the total per capita incomes, respectively, far lower than that of the market economies (SSB, 1986, p. 563 and 1996, p. 282).

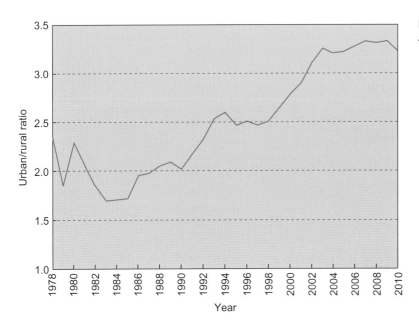

FIGURE 9.3 China's rural–urban income gaps. *Source: NBS, various years.*

SSB and the World Bank are based on the conventional definition of income, which excludes several items such as subsidies and payments in kind, and undervalues others (production for self-consumption). The understatement of income sources will, of course, artificially decrease both rural and urban true incomes and may miscalculate the income gap between the two.[11]

Before the reform, there was a rather uneven distribution of income between rural and urban areas. In 1957 when the Chinese economy was at its most prosperous, the per capita personal income in urban area was 3.48 times that found in rural areas (SSB, 1986, pp. 667 and 673). As shown in Figure 9.3, the income gap between the rural and urban areas continued to decrease until 1983, but after 1985 the gap began to widen again and by 1994 the rural–urban inequalities were even greater than during the mid-1960s and 1970s. How can one explain these changes in the relative incomes of the rural and urban populations in China?

Zhao (1993, pp. 82–3) argues that China's income differentials between rural and urban areas have been largely the result of government policy. For example, in the pre-reform era, it was the policy to keep agricultural prices low in order to accumulate funds for industrialization. The migration of labor from the low-income countryside to the high-income cities was strictly controlled by the government through a system of registration of urban residents. The consequence of these policies, however, was to aggravate rural–urban inequalities.

Engel's law, which was named after the statistician Ernst Engel (1821–1896), states that as income rises, the proportion of income spent on food falls, even if actual expenditure on food may rise. In economics, the proportion of income spent on food is called the Engle coefficient. It is used to illustrate the difficulty of people acquiring basic needs of life. Thus, this indicator can be used to represent people's living standard. However, Engel's law doesn't imply that food spending remains unchanged as income increases. It suggests that consumers increase their expenditures for food products (in relative terms) less than their increases in income. One application of this statistic is treating it as a reflection of the living standard of a country. As this proportion or 'Engel coefficient' increases, the country is by nature poorer, conversely a low Engel coefficient indicates a higher standard of living.

A brief look at the composition of personal consumption in China shows that the proportion of total expenditure on food and beverages has dropped in both rural and urban areas since the reform, reflecting Engel's law (see Figure 9.4); by contrast, demand for housing, furniture and utensils, clothing, health care, and education is seen to be more income-elastic, as is suggested by the law. Since 1978, the Engle coefficients of China's urban and rural households show a downward trend. In 1978, the Engle coefficient of urban households was 58 percent and it fell to its lowest level of 36 percent in 2006. With regards to rural households, the Engle coefficient decreased from 68 percent in 1978 to its lowest level of 41 percent in 2009.

---

11. For example, according to Khan et al. (1993, p. 34), the difference between the incomes of an average urban household and an average rural household are much higher than the official estimate. The true ratio of urban to rural incomes, for instance, would be 2.42 in 1988 as compared to a ratio of 2.05 estimated by the SSB (1989, p. 719). Li (2004) further argues that, if taking into account the subsidies and other earnings in kind, the actual urban-to-rural ratio of incomes would have been as high as 5–6 times during the early 2000s, which was the largest in the world.

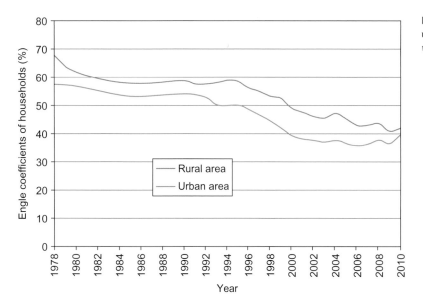

FIGURE 9.4 The Engle coefficients of China's urban and rural households, 1978–2010. *Source: NBS, various years.*

Along with its increasing income levels in both urban and rural areas, China's Engle coefficients should have been reduced. China's worsening income inequalities could be a key factor to explain the above dilemma. In addition, the economic transformation in China has raised some problems in relation to the application of the law. For instance, when estimating the Engel coefficients with respect to the per capita net incomes, we obtain a significant regression for the rural area and an insignificant regression for the urban area:

$$REC = 69.47 - 5.87 \times 10^{-5} RNI$$
$$(-5.06) \qquad\qquad (9.4)$$
$$(N = 30, R^2 = 0.48, F = 25.64)$$

$$UEC = 50.20 + 9.75 \times 10^{-5} UNI$$
$$(0.15) \qquad\qquad (9.5)$$
$$(N = 29, R^2 = 0.001, F = 0.02)$$

where RNI and UNI are the per capita rural and urban net incomes; REC and UEC are the rural and urban Engel coefficients, the data of which are calculated based on SSB (1996, pp. 288–9, 303 and 305).

Equation 9.4 demonstrates a negative correlation between the rural Engel coefficient (REC) and per capita net income (RNI), which is consistent with Engel's law. It should be noted that the insignificant and positive correlation between UEC and UNI, with far smaller t-statistical values in parentheses, R^2 and F-values in Equation 9.5, does not mean that Engel's law has been disproved by the Chinese urban data; rather, it implies that the Chinese data need to be further clarified in detail. Perhaps the miscalculation of the Engel coefficients for Chinese urban areas might be due to the subsidies from the government which

have usually been ascribed to the personal consumption in housing and health care.

9.3.3 Spatial Differences in Purchasing Power

China's vast landmass, together with an underdeveloped transport system and rigid spatial economic barriers (as will be discussed in Chapter 10), differentiates regional purchasing powers. That is, the same level of monetary income may result in different real living standards from region to region. Theoretically, if the price indices and consumption structures are known, the personal consumption expenditure can be recomputed for different regions of China based upon purchasing power. Due to the difficulties in collecting comparable regional data, however, we have to leave this ambitious task.

Nevertheless, one is still able to witness the regional differences in purchasing power based on the retail prices of agricultural products at free markets. The following demonstrate the price-tags for some foodstuffs in different provinces in China:

- 1 kg of chicken costs ¥12.06 in Jiangxi but ¥32.00 in Shanghai
- 1 kg of fish costs ¥10.04 in Jiangxi but ¥20.10 in Tibet
- 1 kg of pork costs ¥21.76 in Xinjiang but ¥32.00 in Beijing
- 1 kg of eggs costs ¥6.8 in Shanghai but ¥10.96 in Hainan
- 1 kg of milk costs only ¥3.78 in Xinjiang but ¥17.4 in Shanghai
- 1 kg of apples costs only ¥4.12 in Henan but ¥13.16 in Chongqing

- 1 kg of oranges costs only ¥3.04 in Henan but ¥7.00 in Qinghai and Tibet
- 1 kg of bananas costs only ¥2.98 in Jiangxi but ¥7.00 in Chongqing.[12]

9.4 REGIONAL ECONOMIC DISPARITY

9.4.1 Literature Review

One of the most influential theories on regional economics has been the 'inverted-U' hypothesis in which economic development is at first accompanied by an increase in regional disparties and then followed by a decrease. The analysis of the convergence hypothesis has a long history that dates back to the work of Kuznets (1955) and the subsequent empirical work of Williamson (1965). At a basic level, this hypothesis is based on a theory in which growth initially occurs in some regions, but not in others, with the result that inter-regional disparities widen as growth proceeds. At a later stage, the high-growth regions become saturated and more and more of their industrial activities are shifted to the less developed regions, thereby enabling the latter to catch up.

China's regional inequalities have had a long history, resulting from the diversified natural and social conditions among the country's different regions. It is generally acknowledged that the Eastern belt has a relatively higher per capita GNP and, of course, higher living standards than the Western belt. It is noticeable that different results have emerged in the estimates of regional economic inequalities in China. Some researchers believe that China's regional inequalities have definitely increased, reflecting the first stage of the inverted-U hypothesis as well as China's uneven regional development strategy.[13] In contrast, others argue that only the gaps between the Eastern, Central, and Western belts have widened in recent years, while the interprovincial gaps have been narrowed substantially since the introduction of economic reform in 1978.[14] Given the use of different data and measurements, it seems that there is not likely to be any emerging consensus on this issue.

Since the late 1970s, China's experience with trade liberalization and with rapid economic growth in the coastal provinces has given an indication of widening income inequalities among China's regions. Jian et al. (1996) examine the tendency towards convergence in real per capita income among the provinces of China during the period 1952–1993. No strong convergence or divergence during the initial phase of central planning (1952–65) was observed. There is strong evidence of divergence during the period of the 'Cultural Revolution' (1965–78) with social planning in favor of richer industrial regions widening the levels of inter-regional inequality. Regional inequality is equalized with the extent of marketization and openness that began in 1978. Convergence as the result of factor mobility, the flows of labor, capital, and technology, increased productivity among the rural regions and convergence within the coastal provinces. A policy to promote the further liberalization of the country's interior will also promote convergence. Variance decomposition of the log of real GDP in each province is obtained.

Zhang et al. (2001) investigate the time-series properties of per capita income in China's regions during the period 1952 to 1997 and compare the consistency of results with cross-sectional methods. The results based on the Gini coefficient, the ratio of per capita income between regions, and the coefficient of variation suggest that eastern and western regions have converged to their own specific steady states over the course of the past 40 years. The regional gap between the east and other regions had widened before the reforms, but the economic reforms have served only to worsen the gap still further.

Demurger et al. (2002) examine the growth in GDP per capita for the period 1952–98 and decompose the location and policy growth rates in the provincial growth regressions in order to quantify the contribution of each factor in the period 1996–99. Their respective contribution varies with the interval of 0–2.8 percent and 1.6–3.5 percent. The highest and lowest rates are associated with the coastal and northwestern provinces, respectively. The authors list a number of policy measures to solve the unbalanced growth and to reduce the regional disparity. The policy measures include:

- The extension of the deregulation from coastal areas to include other provinces
- The introduction of a registration system to prevent movement of the rural poor to prosperous areas
- Changes in the policy of the monopoly state bank system to allocate more resources to the western provinces
- Improvements in the infrastructure to overcome geographical barriers and also to increase the level of human capital formation.

Obviously, the regional inequalities will demonstrate differing patterns if different approaches to measurement are employed. In addition, care should be taken when one uses the official data to estimate China's regional inequality index for the pre- and post-reform periods during which different statistical systems were employed.

12. Source: China Price Information Network (www.chinaprice.gov.cn. Accessed on September 29, 2009).
13. See, for example, Guo and Wang (1988), Yang (1990), Denny (1991, pp. 186–208), Dong (1992), Lyons (1992), Tsui (1991), Wei (1992), Yang (1992a; 1992b), Zhang (1994, pp. 296–312), Wei and Liu (1994), and Song (1996).
14. See, for example, Yang (1991, pp. 504–9, and 1993, pp. 129–45), Liu et al. (1994, pp. 141–66), and Tsui (1993).

For example, Zhang (1994, p. 300) uses 27 provinces (excluding Qinghai and Tibet) for 1980, 28 provinces (excluding Tibet) for 1981–88 and 28 provinces (excluding Tibet and Hainan, a new province established in 1988) for 1989–90 and obtains an increasing regional inequality in terms of per capita income in rural China. Using the multiregional data in which three municipalities directly under the central government are incorporated into their neighboring provinces (Beijing and Tianjin into Hebei, Shanghai into Jiangsu) and Tibet and Hainan are excluded from the analysis, Tsui (1993) shows that the level of interprovincial inequality declined from the late 1970s to the mid-1980s and a reversal in the trend preceded the reform era. Jian et al. (1996, pp. 1–22) use the data of 28 provinces (Tibet and Hainan are excluded) and obtain a V-shaped pattern for China's multiregional inequalities from 1978 to 1993.

9.4.2 Regional Inequality Index

Natural and human resources are distributed irregularly in China. Specifically, the Eastern belt is blessed with a mild climate and rich soil, while the Western belt has a vast area and a sparse population. The Northern part is much richer in mineral resources than the Southern part, except for a few non-ferrous metals. In contrast, most of the Southern part, given its favorable climate and terrain, has an agricultural advantage over most of the Northern part (especially the desert North and Northwest regions) and, in particular, dominates most of the nation's rice production. All of the above regional characteristics in the distribution of resources, together with the spatially diversified regional economic development policies that China has pursued during recent decades and other historical and cultural factors, have unevenly decided the spatial structure of the Chinese economy.

The vast size and diversified natural conditions in China have generated many regional differences in terms of climate, geography, soil fertility, and other resource endowments, which in turn mean that the living standards vary from region to region. In particular, South and East regions have natural advantages for agriculture over the Northwest region. Minerals and energy resources are much richer in the North than in the South. In other aspects, the eastern coastal area, because of its geographical proximity to market economies, may find it easier to introduce the laissez-faire approach than would be the case for the central and the western inland areas. All of these factors have inevitably resulted in great economic disparities among regions.

China is now the world's second-biggest economy, but some of its provinces by themselves would rank fairly highly in the global league. For example, Guangdong's GDP (at market exchange rates) is almost as big as Indonesia's; the output of both Jiangsu and Shandong exceeds Switzerland's. Some provinces may, however, exaggerate their output: for example, the sum of their reported GDPs is 10 percent higher than the national total. But, over time, the latter has consistently been revised up, suggesting that any overstatement is modest. Figure 9.1 shows the nearest equivalent country. As the richest province, Shanghai has a GDP per capita similar to Saudi Arabia's (at purchasing power parity), though still well below that of China's special administrative regions, Hong Kong, and Macau. At the other extreme, the poorest provinces, Guizhou, Gansu, Yunnan, and Tibet, have an income per capita of less than $5,000, close to that of India, Iraq, Vanuatu, and the Congo, respectively.[15]

A more systematic comparison is presented in Table 9.4. The ratio of per capita GDP for the top five to the bottom five provinces has been in the range of 3.98 in 2010, if all provinces are taken into account. Even if Beijing, Shanghai, and Tianjin are excluded, the ratio of the top five to the bottom five provinces is still higher than 3.00, which is seen to have a continuous increase from 1990 to 2010. By way of comparison, the ratio of the top five to bottom five states for the USA is 2.46, if Washington DC is included, or 1.84 if Washington DC is excluded (Groeneworld et al., 2008, p. 27).

Until now, we may conclude that there have been very large gaps between the richest and the poorest provinces in China. It is tempting to draw conclusions from Table 9.4 concerning the trend of the disparities over time. Let's turn to measure China's year-to-year regional inequalities after all provinces are taken into account. Using the provinces' per capita GDP data which have been officially reported and are estimated by the author (based on the method in Section 9.2) for the provinces whose GDP data are not reported officially, we may calculate the coefficients of variation (CV) for the years from 1952 to 2010 (see Figure 9.5).

Generally, regional inequalities (measured by CV) have fluctuated frequently over recent decades. With the exception of a few years (such as 1954–55, 1957, 1961–62, and 1967), China's regional inequalities increased steadily from the early 1950s to the late 1970s. For instance, the CV is 0.339 in 1952; in 1980, however, it increases significantly to 0.621. Obviously, during this period China's egalitarian policy did not bring about any economic egalitarianism among any of its provinces. From the early 1980s to the mid-1990s, with the exception of a few years in the early 1990s, regional inequalities decreased among the provinces; however, they have increased steadily since then.

---

15. Note that these figures use the same PPP conversion rate for the whole of China, but prices are likely to be lower in poorer provinces than in richer ones, slightly reducing regional inequality.

TABLE 9.4 Gaps Between the Top Five and Bottom Five Provinces (in Per Capita GDP, Yuan)

GDP Per Capita	1952	1980	1990	2000	2010
Panel A: All provinces					
Top five (yuan)	397	1,766	3,833	20,129	61,956
Bottom five (yuan)	81	176	979	3,991	15,548
Absolute gap (yuan)	315	1,590	2,854	16,138	46,407
Ratio of top five to bottom five	4.87	10.04	3.92	5.04	3.98
Panel B: Excluding Beijing, Shanghai, and Tianjin					
Top five (yuan)	226	502	2,136	11,981	49,126
Bottom five (yuan)	81	176	979	3,991	15,548
Absolute gap (yuan)	144	326	1,157	7,990	33,577
Ratio of top five to bottom five	2.77	2.85	2.18	3.00	3.16

Source: SSB (1986, 1991) and NBS (2001; 2011); calculated by author.

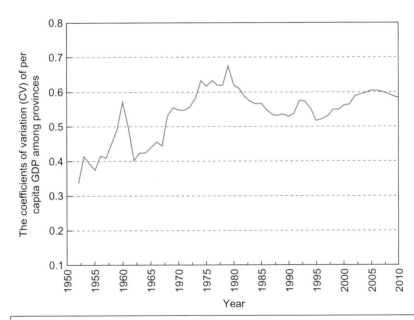

Notes: (1) Calculated based on Annex. (2) 29 provinces are considered from 1952 to 1988 (during which Hainan is included in Guangdong province) while 30 provinces are considered from 1989 to 1997 and 31 provinces from 1998 onwards (since then Chongqing has been separated from Sichuan province).

FIGURE 9.5 The coefficients of variation (CV) of per capita GDP among provinces.

9.5 SUMMARY

Since economic reform and open-door policies were implemented in the late 1970s, the Chinese economy has demonstrated an increasing asymmetry between different regions. This has resulted in a series of regional economic problems which need to be addressed properly by policy makers. In this chapter, the Chinese economy is analyzed generally and compared via multiregional dimensions. Due to the application of different statistical systems in the pre- and post-reform periods, as well as the unavailability of statistical data in some provinces, a complete multiregional comparison of the Chinese economy is extremely difficult and, to some extent, meaningless. Using the best data and the regression approach, Section 9.2 tries to estimate a set of time-series data on GDP for all provinces, on which the multiregional comparison of the Chinese economy is based. In Section 9.3, efforts of consistent economic comparison are attempted based on the indices of real living standards. Finally, in Section 9.4, regional economic disparity indexes are computed for the past decades.

Beginning with a common background of ideological system and history, but proceeding with differing paces of economic reform and with different development policies, China has developed its provinces and promoted the welfare of urban and rural people differently. Not surprisingly, China's economic reform and open-door policies have over the past decades disproportionally aided the coastal provinces where per capita GDPs are several times higher than those in the poorer inland provinces. When addressing the Chinese economy from a multiregional perspective, at least two issues should be noted.

First, China's rural–urban inequalities are very high compared with other developing countries. For example, in Indonesia the ratio of urban to rural income was 1.66 in 1987. In Bangladesh the highest observed ratio during the 1980s was 1.85, whereas the typical ratio was close to 1.5 (Khan et al., 1993, p. 69). Admittedly, the household surveys on which these estimates are based do not give full weight to subsidies and incomes in kind. However, in Indonesia and Bangladesh, these components are tiny compared to those in China.

Secondly, even though not taking into account its two Special Administrative Regions (Hong Kong and Macau) (an economic comparison of Taiwan, Hong Kong, Macau, and mainland China will be conducted in Chapter 12), China still had a per capita GDP ratio of more than 12 for the richest (Shanghai) to the poorest (Guizhou), which is much higher than many other countries.

How much will China's regional inequalities eventually affect the Chinese economy and society? We are watching with open eyes.

ANNEX

Methods of Measuring Multiregional Economic Disparities

The simplest measurement for economic differences is standard error (SR). SR is a statistical approach by which economic differences are measured in absolute terms.

Other approaches, such as the Gini coefficient (already discussed in the Annex of Chapter 8), the coefficient of variation (CV), and the weighted coefficient of variation (MCV), may also be used to derive the economic differences in relative terms. The following two formulas demonstrate how the CV and MCV are measured mathematically:

$$CV = \frac{\sqrt{\frac{1}{n}(x_i - \bar{x})^2}}{\bar{x}} \qquad (9.6)$$

$$MCV = \frac{\sqrt{\rho_i(x_i - \bar{x})^2}}{\mu} \qquad (9.7)$$

Where x_i is the value of the variable of interest for the ith province, there are n provinces; $\bar{x}$ is the sample mean for all x, ρ_i is a weight for the ith province and μ is the weighted mean of all x using the ρ_i weights.

The CV is reported as a percentage and calculated from the average and standard deviation. For example, a CV of 3 percent means the standard deviation is equal to 3 percent of the average. For some measures, the standard deviation increases as the average increases. In this case, the CV is the best way to summarize the variation. In other cases the standard deviation does not change with the average. In this case, the standard deviation is the best way to summarize the variation. The advantage of the CV is that it is unit-less. This allows CVs to be compared to each other in ways that other measures, like standard deviations, or root mean squared residuals, cannot be.

There are some requirements that must be met in order for the CV to be interpreted in the ways we have described. The most obvious problem arises when the mean of a variable is zero. In this case, the CV cannot be calculated. Even if the mean of a variable is not zero, but the variable contains both positive and negative values and the mean is close to zero, then the CV can be misleading. The CV of a variable or the CV of a prediction model for a variable can be considered as a reasonable measure if the variable contains only positive values. This is a definite disadvantage of the CV approach.

The CV is useful because the standard deviation of data must always be understood in the context of the mean of the data. Instead, the actual value of the CV is independent of the unit in which the measurement has been taken, so it is a dimensionless number. For comparison between data sets with different units or widely different means, one should use the CV instead of the standard deviation. When the mean value is close to zero, the CV will approach infinity and is hence sensitive to small changes in the mean. This is often the case if the values do not originate from a ratio scale.

Usually, the results of economic differences derived from CV and Gini approaches are consistent with each other, while, in some instances, an inconsistency of measurements may be generated by the two approaches. For instance, after having mathematically illustrated the Gini and CV indices through the use of the Lorenz curve, Zhou (1994, pp. 193–200) concludes that when the Gini coefficient changes slightly, it may not be consistent with the CV, whereas when the Gini coefficient changes at a relatively large rate, it may be consistent with the CV.

In contrast to the Gini and CV approaches, generalized entropy (GE) is a family of measures depending on a parameter (c). Users may adjust the value of the parameter to suit their ethical preferences. As described in Shorrocks and Foster (1987, pp. 485–97), the parameter (c) determines the relative sensitivity of distribution: when $c = 0$ and 1, the GE family becomes two versions of Theil's entropy (TE) measure. In the extreme case when $c \to -\infty$, the ranking of the corresponding GE is same as that of Rawls' maximum criterion, i.e., to focus exclusively on the well-being of the worst-off province (Shorrocks, 1980, pp. 613–25).

It must be noted that the SR, Gini, CV, and MCV approaches can only deal with the measurement of economic differences in terms of a single index. However, it is necessary sometimes for one to conduct a joint analysis of the various disparities according to different indices, particularly when these indices contradict one another. For instance, Nolan and Sender (1992, pp. 1279–303) and Sen (1992, pp. 1305–12) argue that China has paid more attention to economic growth rather than education, health care, and other service sectors since the early 1980s. Thus, when evaluating the various inequalities in China, one should take different indices into account.

Literature of the multidimensional measurement of regional inequalities includes Atkinson (1970), Atkinson and Bourguigon (1982), Maasourmi (1986), and Kolm (1976a, 1976b, and 1977).

Case Study 7

Similar Initial Conditions, Varied Results

The process of choosing different regional development strategies is always followed by the comparison of results. During the 1980s and 1990s, this kind of scenario occurred in many similar prefectures just across the provincial borders in China: these pairings included Xiangfan (Hubei province) and Nanyang (Henan province); Shangrao (Jiangxi province) and Quzhou (Zhejiang province); and Shaoguan (Guangdong province) and Chenzhou (Hunan province). Below is the example of two twin prefectures, but stories of this type can be replicated in many other cross-province areas.

Shaoguan is a prefecture-level city in the north of Southern China's Guangdong province. It is about 221 km north of the provincial capital of Guangzhou. Shaoguan is also readily accessible by road as it is adjacent to the Jingzhu Expressway running from Beijing to Zhuhai. At Shaoguan, the Wu River from the northwest and the Zhen River from the northeast join up to create the North River (bei jiang) which flows south to Guangzhou. The downtown part of Shaoguan is located on a peninsula between the Wu and Zhen Rivers.

Chenzhou is situated at the juncture of Hunan and Guangdong provinces at the foot of Qitianling Hill of the Nanling Mountain Range. It is located on the Beijing–Guangzhou Railway. As a prefecture-level city located in the southern area of Hunan province, Chenzhou covers an administrative area of 19,317 sq. km. Places of interest, natural scenic spots, ancient relics, and buildings make for various tourism spots in the city. The major ones are the Suxian Hill, the Wanhuayan, the Dongjiang Lake, and the Wugai Mountain Hunting Field.

Shaoguan and Chenzhou are similar with each other in terms of natural and geographic features and resource endowments; but they have experienced very different economic transitions during the early period of economic reform. For example, after the first adoption of reforms in Guangdong in 1980, many commodity prices in Shaoguan rose above the levels of those in Chenzhou, since the reforms had not been carried out in Hunan province. As a result, resources were attracted to Shaoguan from Chenzhou. The Chenzhou government set up tax offices on the border in an attempt to stop this outflow. These attempts did not bring prosperity to Chenzhou; rather, they led to an increase in the levels of underground and 'illegal' cross-border trading.

Shaoguan had possessed a relatively higher degree of 'autonomy' in terms of public finance, credit and banking, trade, price, labor, and wage systems, while Chenzhou's transition had lagged behind. For example, when Guangdong's provincial government began to implement a new fiscal policy entitled '*dizheng baogan*' (fix the increased rate of the revenue turned over to the state), Hunan province continued to follow a policy of '*zhong'e fencheng*' (proportionally share the total revenue) policy to Chenzhou. Apparently, the latter lacked the incentive for local government to accumulate its wealth. In addition, Shaoguan had a more elastic tax system than Chenzhou. For example, in Shaoguan the ore mining business was only taxed by 3 percent, but in Chenzhou the total rate of taxes and fees for the same business was as high as 20 percent (Li, 1988, pp. 338–9). The unequal policies have produced many differences between the two sides of the provincial border. In the 1950s, the two neighbors developed with almost the same pace of growth. Both of them had 580 million yuan of gross value of industrial and agricultural output (GVIAO) coincidentally in 1958 and with little significant difference in the 1960s and 1970s. During the 1980s, the economic performance of these two areas had become increasingly different: Shaoguan had 918 million yuan of GVIAO higher than Chenzhou in 1980. But in 1987, the GVIAO gap reached 2,213 million yuan.[16]

When people in Chenzhou compared themselves with their neighbors in Shaoguan, they found that, although both had started from similar initial economic conditions, Shaoguan had benefited significantly from economic

---

16. Data sources: *Yearbook of Provincial Statistics* (Guangdong and Hunan), related issues.

reform policies. People in Chenzhou urged that they should follow the reforms that had been implemented in Shaoguan. In 1988, Chenzhou was allowed to adopt some reform measures. This enabled Chenzhou to enjoy the benefits of opening markets to Shaoguan. The prefecture government withdrew all its tax offices along the border with Guangdong. Soon the adjacent areas between Chenzhou and Shaoguan were experiencing an economic boom and inter-regional trade reached record levels. Importantly, the Chenzhou government obtained far higher tax revenues from these businesses than they had ever received from border tax offices.

REFERENCES

Atkinson, A. B. (1970). On the measurement of inequality. *Journal of Economic Theory, 2*, 244–263.

Atkinson, A. B., & Bourguignon, F. (1982). The comparison of multidimensional distributions of economic status. *Review of Economic Studies, 49*, 183–201.

China Youth, January 3 1995.

CIA (2008). *World factbook 2007*. Washington, DC: Central Intelligence Agency.

Demurger, S., Sachs, J. D., Woo, W. T., Bao, S., Cheng, G., & Mellinger, A. (2002). *Geography, economic policy, and regional development in China*. NBER Working Paper 8897.

Denny, D. L. (1991). Provincial economic differences diminished in the decade of reform US Congress Joint Economic Committee (Ed.), *China's economic dilemmas in the 1990s: the problems of reforms, modernization, and interdependence* (Vol. 1, pp. 186–208). Washington DC: the U.S. Government Printing Office.

Dong, F. (1992). Some comments on analyses of interregional income gaps [guanyu diqu jian shouru chaju biandong fenxi de jidian shangque yijian]. *The Economic Research* [jingji yanjiu], *7*, 63–64.

Economist, The (1995). p. 19.

Groeneworld, N., Chen, A., & Lee, G. (2008). *Linkages between China's regions: measurement and policy*. Cheltenham: Edward Elgar.

Guo, F., & Wang, W. (1988). *Poverty and development* [pinkun yu fazhan]. Hangzhou: Zhejiang People's Press.

Guo, S., & Han, W. (1991). *The distribution and utilization of China's GNP* [zhongguo GNP de fenpei he shiyong]. Beijing: The People's University of China Press.

Heston, A., Summers, R., & Aten, B. (2006). *Penn world table version 6.2*. Center for International Comparisons of Production, Income and Prices at the University of Pennsylvania, September.

Higgins, B. (1981). Economic development and regional disparities: a comparative study of four federations. In R. L. Mathews (Ed.), *Regional disparities and economic development* (pp. 69–70). Canberra: The Australian National University Press.

Hill, H., & Weidemann, A. (1989). Regional development in Indonesia: patterns and issues. In H. Hill (Ed.), *Unity and diversity: regional economic development in Indonesia since 1970* (pp. 1–7). Singapore: Oxford University Press.

Holz, C. A. (2008). China's 2004 economic census and 2006 benchmark revision of GDP statistics: more questions than answers? *The China Quarterly, 193*, 150–163.

Hsueh, T. (1994). A synthesized development index system for China's regions [zhongguo diqu zhonghe fazhai zhibiao tixi]. In S. Liu, Q. Li, & T. Hsueh (Eds.), *Studies on China's regional economic development [zhongguo diqu jingji yanjiu]* (pp. 22–56). Beijing: China Statistics Publishing House.

Hu, A., Wang, S., & Kang, X. (1995). *Regional disparities in China* [zhonguo diqu chayi baogao]. Shenyang: Liaoning People's Press.

Huang, W. (1996). *The hidden economy in China* [zhongguo de yinxing jingji] (2nd ed.). Beijing: China Commercial Press.

Hwang, E.-G. (1993). *The Korean economies: a comparison of north and south*. Oxford: Clarendon Press.

Jian, T., Sachs, J. D., & Warner, A. M. (1996). Trends in regional inequality in China. *China Economic Review, 7*(1), 1–22.

JPSB. (1990). *Please read the results of an investigation to evaluate the quality of data for the three indices* [sanxiang zhibiao shuju zhiliang ruhe, qingkan diaocha pinggu jieguo]. By Jilin Provincial Statistical Bureau, *China Statistics [zhongguo tongji]*, No. 2, pp. 27–28.

Khan, A. R., Griffin, K., Riskin, C., & Zhao, R. (1993). Household income and its distribution in China. In K. Griffin & R. Zhao (Eds.), *The distribution of income in China* (1993, pp. 25–73). New York: St Martin's Press.

Kim, K.-H., & Mills, E. S. (1990). Urbanization and regional development in Korea. In J. K. Kwon (Ed.), *Korean development*. New York: Green Press.

Kolm, S.-C. (1976). Unequal inequalities I. *Journal of Economic Theory, 12*, 416–442.

Kolm, S.-C. (1976). Unequal inequalities II. *Journal of Economic Theory, 13*, 82–111.

Kuznets, S. (1955). Economic growth and income inequality. *American Economic Review, 45*, 1–28.

Li, S. (2004). China's urban and rural income surveys. *Journal of Financial Economics* [caijing zazhi], 3.

Ling, Y., Xu, F., & Chen, J. (1995). Be attention to the overstatement wind! [jingti! fukua feng]. *Economic Tribune* [jingji luntan], *7*, 18–19.

Liu, S., Gong, Y., Li, Q., & Wu, Y. (1994). The regional income disparity in China: measurement, analysis, and policy suggestions [zhongguo ge diqu shouru chayi de jishuan, fenxi yu zhengze jianyi]. In S. Liu, Q. Li, & T. Hsueh (Eds.), *Studies on China's regional economic development* [zhongguo diqu jingji yanjiu] (1994, pp. 142–143). Beijing: China Statistics Publishing House.

Lyons, T. (1992). Interprovincial disparities in China: output and consumption, 1952–1957. *Economic Development and Cultural Change, 39*, 471–506.

Ma, H., & Sun, S. (Eds.). (1981). *A study of the economic structure of China – part 2* [zhongguo jingji jiegou yanjiu, xia]. Beijing: The People's Press.

Maasoumi, E. (1986). The measurement and decomposition of multidimensional inequality. *Econometrica, 54*, 771–779.

Marea, P. (1985). *Dollar GNPs of the USSR and eastern Europe*. Baltimore: Johns Hopkins University Press.

Mizoguchi, T., Wang, H., & Matsuda, Y. (1989). A comparison of real consumption level between Japan and the People's Republic of China: the first approach to the application of the ICP method to Chinese data. *Hitotsubashi Journal of Economics*, June.

Nair, K. R. G. (1985). Inter-state income differentials in India, 1970–71 to 1979–80. In G. P. Mishra (Ed.), *Regional structure of development and growth in India*. New Delhi: Ashish Publishing House.

NBS. (various years). *China statistical yearbook*, various issues, Beijing: China Statistics Publishing House.

Nolan, P., & Sender, J. (1992). Death rates, life expectancy and China's economic reforms: a critique of A. A. Sen. *World Development*, *20*, 1279–1303.

Ottolenghi, D., & Steinherr, A. (1993). Yugoslavia: was it a winner's curse? *Economies of Transition*, *1*(2), 209–243.

People's Daily, January 18, 1995.

Rawski, T. G. (2001). What is happening to China's GDP statistics? *China Economic Review*, *12*, 347–354.

Savoie, D. J. (1992). *Regional economic development: Canada's search for solution* (2nd ed.). Toronto: University of Toronto Press.

Sen, A. (1992). Life and death in China. *World Development*, *20*(9), 1305–1312.

Sen, A. (2004). *Remarks at the inaugural meeting of the GDN conference on understanding reform*. Global Development Conference, New Delhi, January 27.

Shorrocks, A. (1980). The class of additionally decomposable inequality measures. *Econometrica*, *48*, 613–625.

Shorrocks, A., & Foster, J. E. (1987). Transfer sensitive inequality measure. *Review of Economic Studies*, *54*, 485–497.

Smith, D. M. (1987). *Geography, inequality and society*. Cambridge: Cambridge University Press.

Song, X. (1996). China's regional economic development and its convergence. *The Economic Research*, *9*, 38–44.

SSB (1990). *A compilation of historical statistical materials of China's provinces, autonomous regions and municipalities (1949-89).* [quanguo ge sheng, zizhiqu, zhixiashi lishi tongji zhiliao huibian 1949–1989]. Beijing: China Statistics Publishing House.

SSB (1996). *China industrial economic statistical yearbook 1995*. Beijing: China Statistics Publishing House.

SSB. (various years). *China statistical yearbook*. various issues, Beijing: China Statistics Publishing House.

Tsui, K. (1991). China's regional inequality, 1952–1985. *Journal of Comparative Economics*, *15*, 1–21.

Tsui, K. (1993). *Economic reform and interprovincial inequalities in China*. Working paper no. 31, Economics Department. Hong Kong: the Chinese University of Hong Kong.

United Nations. (1990a). *SNA handbook on integrated environmental and economic accounting*, Part I ('General Concept'), New York: United Nations.

United Nations (1990b). *Revised system of national accounts*. New York: United Nations.

Wang, S. (2003). China's public health care: crisis and transitions [zhongguo gonggong weisheng de weiji yu zhuanji]. *Comparative Analysis* [Bijiao], *4*, 52–88.

Wei, H. (1992). On the changing pattern of the interregional income gaps in China [lun woguo quji shouru chaju de biandong geju]. *The Economic Research* [jingji yanjiu], *4*, 61–65.

Williamson, J. (1965). Regional inequality and the process of national development: a description of the patterns. *Economic Development and Cultural Change*, *13*(4), 165–204.

World Bank (1996). *From plan to market: world bank development report 1996*. New York: Oxford University Press.

World Bank (2011). *Bulletin board of statistical capacity*. Washington, DC: The World Bank. available at <http://go.worldbank.org/6EIB0ZUV00>, accessed on December 11, 2011.

Xu, X. (2004). China's gross domestic product estimation. *Chinese Economic Review*, *15*(3), 302–322.

Yang, D. (1990). Patterns of China's regional development strategy. *The China Quarterly*, *122*, 230–257.

Yang, K. (1991). The theory and application of regional structure – an application of the regional structure in China [quyu jiegou lilun yu yingyong – zhongguo quyu jiegou yanjiu]. In S. Sun (Ed.), *The economic structure: theory, application and policy* [jingji jiegou de lilun, xingyong yu zhengce]. Beijing: China Social Science Press.

Yang, W. (1992). An empirical analysis of the changes in interregional income inequalities [Diqu jian shouru chaju biandong de shizheng fenxi]. *The Economic Research* [jingji yanjiu], *1*, 70–74.

Yang, W. (1992). Answers to comrade dong fan's comments [dui dong Fan tongzhi shangque de dafu]. *The Economic Research* [jingji yanjiu], *7*, 65–66.

Zhang, P. (1994). The peasant income distribution among rural areas [nongchun jian de shouru fenpei]. In R. Zhaoand, & K. Griffin (Eds.), *The household income distribution in China* [zhongguo de jumin shouru fenpei] (pp. 296–312). Beijing: China Social Science Press.

Zhang, Z., Liu, A., & Yao, S. (2001). Convergence of China's regional incomes, 1952–1997. *China Economic Review*, *12*(2/3), 243–258.

Zhao, R. (1993). Three features of the distribution of income during the transition to reform. In K. Griffin & R. Zhao (Eds.), *The distribution of income in China* (1993, pp. 74–94). New York: St Martin's Press.

Zheng, J. (1996). How large is China's per capita GDP in US dollars? [zhongguo de renjun GDP wei duoshao meiyuan]. *Economic Highlights* [jingjixue xiaoxi bao], September 13, *193*, 1.

Zheng, J. (2001). China's official statistics: growing with full vitality. *China Economic Review*, *12*, 333–337.

Chapter 10

Regional Diseconomies and Development Strategy

Mt. Huangshan. *Copyright © by Arne Hückelheim, September 23, 2009.*

Understanding the Chinese Economies. DOI: http://dx.doi.org/10.1016/B978-0-12-397826-4.00010-X
© 2013 Elsevier Inc. All rights reserved.

To take the road to socialism is to realize common prosperity step by step. Our plan is as follows: where conditions permit, some areas may develop faster than others; those that develop faster can help promote the progress of those that lag behind, until all become prosperous. If the rich keep getting richer and the poor poorer, polarization will emerge. The socialist system must and can avoid polarization. One way is for the areas that become prosperous first to support the poor areas by paying more taxes or turning in more profits to the state. Of course, this should not be done too soon. At present, we don't want to dampen the vitality of the developed areas or encourage the practice of having everyone 'eat from the same big pot'. We should study when to raise this question and how to settle it.

– Deng Xiaoping (1992, 374)

10.1 SPATIAL COMPARATIVE ADVANTAGES

10.1.1 General Overview

A glance at modern Chinese history reveals that China's economic development has been focused on three geographical areas: the Bohai Sea rim (BSR) area, the Pearl River delta (PRD) area, and the Yangtze River delta (YRD) (see Table 2.3 of Chapter 2 for more details about these three areas). It is evident that complementary economic conditions exist in these three areas. In general, the BSR area has advantages in terms of agricultural products, energy, industrial materials, some high-tech products, and education. However, this area possesses obsolete equipment, lacks management experience for small and medium-sized enterprises, and lacks capital.

The PRD area neighbors Hong Kong and Macau and so has the advantages of accessing international markets and attracting foreign direct investment (FDI). Most overseas Chinese, many of whom were sources of FDI in China during the 1980s and 1990s, originated from this area. It is also the area which was the first to open its doors to the outside world. For example, among the original four special economic zones (SEZs), three (Shenzhen, Zhuhai, and Shantou) were established in this area. With favorable conditions for international trade, the PRD area has the freest market; and considerable management experience for small and medium-sized enterprises. The disadvantages of the area are, among others, the less-developed education, and shortage of industrial materials, especially of energy and some mineral resources.

The YRD area has advantages in terms of education, management experience for large modern industrial bases, and rural industrial enterprises. A lack of industrial resources, especially minerals and energy, is one of the many disadvantages in this area.

Table 10.1 shows the advantageous and disadvantageous industrial sectors for the three areas.

TABLE 10.1 Comparative Advantages of China's Three Economic Engines

Area	Advantageous Industrial Sectors	Disadvantageous Industrial Sectors
Bohai Sea rim	Petroleum and natural gas extraction; coal mining; ferrous and nonferrous metals mining; petroleum processing and coking	Timber and bamboo logging; apparel; chemical fibers; electric, telecommunication, instruments, meters, and other measuring equipment
Pearl River delta	Apparel; electric, telecommunication equipments, leather, furs, and manufactured goods; palm fiber and straw products; timber and bamboo logging; fresh water	Petroleum and natural gas extraction; smelting and pressing of ferrous metals; coal mining and preparation; universal machines
Yangtze River delta	Chemical fibers; textile; instruments, meters and other measuring equipment; smelting and processing of nonferrous metals; universal machines	Petroleum and natural gas extraction; ferrous and nonferrous metals mining; coal mining; timber logging

Note: *Bohai Sea rim = Beijing, Tianjin, coastal Hebei and Shandong and Liaodong peninsulas; Pearl River delta = Guangdong and northern Hainan (Hong Kong and Macau are excluded); Yangtze River delta = Shanghai, Zhejiang, and southern Jiangsu.*
Source: Author.

10.1.2 Location Quotient

The Location Quotient Technique is the most commonly utilized spatial economic analysis method. It was developed in part to offer a slightly more complex model to the variety of analytical tools available to economic base analysts (Isserman, 1977). This technique compares the local economy to a reference economy, in the process attempting to identify specializations in the local economy. Location quotient compares the regional share of economic activity in a particular industry to the national share of economic activity in the same industry. The result reveals the degree of regional specialization in each industry.

If the location quotient for a particular industry is less than one, the region is less specialized than the nation, while location quotients greater than one reveal greater specialization of the industry in the local economy than in the national economy. Also, observing location quotients over time shows if an industry is becoming more or less specialized in the region.

To calculate any location quotient the following formula is applied. Note that in this formula we are comparing the regional economy (often a province) to the national economy. The location quotient (*LQ*) of region *j* in industry *i* can be calculated as:

$$LQ(i,j) = \frac{\text{Region } j\text{'s output in industry } i \Big/ \text{Total regional output}}{\text{National output in industry } i \Big/ \text{Total national output}}$$

Mathematically, if x_{ij} is the output value of the *i*th industry ($i = 1, 2, \ldots$) in the *j*th province ($j = 1, 2, \ldots$), the values of *LQ* can be calculated as follows:

$$LQ(i,j) = \frac{x_{ij} \Big/ \sum_i x_{ij}}{\sum_j x_{ij} \Big/ \sum_i \sum_j x_{ij}} \quad (10.1)$$

Interpreting the Location Quotient (*LQ*) is very simple. Only three general outcomes are possible when calculating location quotients: i.e., *LQ* < 1.0, *LQ* = 1.0, and *LQ* > 1.0). Their implications are as follows:

An *LQ* that is less than one suggests that the local economy is less than was expected for a given industry. Therefore, that industry is not even meeting local demand for a given good or service.

An *LQ* that is equal to one suggests that the local economy is exactly sufficient to meet the local demand for a given good or service. Therefore, that industry is meeting local demand for the given good or service.

An *LQ* that is greater than one suggests that the local economy is greater than expected and it is therefore assumed that there is an 'extra' part of goods and services. This extra economy must then export their goods and services to other areas.

10.1.3 Empirical Evidence

There exist many multiregional differences in terms of natural and social resources, industrial structure, and economic development in China. For example, Shanxi (the western part of Mount Taihang) province has abundant coal resources but poor mineral, petroleum, and agricultural resources; except for petroleum, non-metal and agricultural resources, metals and coal resources are relatively poor in the province of Shandong (the eastern part of Mount Taihang); Hebei (the northern part of the Yellow River) province has a surplus supply of metals and coal resources but lacks petroleum and non-metals; Henan (southern part of the Yellow River) province has rich coal, metal, and agricultural resources but has only a low supply of non-metals.

In order to have a better understanding of the multiregional comparative advantages in China, let's calculate the location quotient (LQ_{ij}) of China's provinces. According

to the results shown in Table 10.2, we can classify China's provinces into three groups for each sector:

(i) Coal sector:
- Shanxi, Ningxia, Guizhou, Henan, Hebei, Inner Mongolia, Anhui, Shaanxi, and Hunan provinces have extra coal products.
- Production almost meets demand in Sichuan, Jiangxi, Liaoning, and Shandong provinces.
- Production cannot meet local demand in Jiangsu, Jilin, Gansu, Yunnan, Beijing, Heilongjiang, Fujian, Xinjiang, Guangxi, Qinghai, Hubei, Guangdong, Zhejiang, Hainan, Tibet, Tianjin, and Shanghai provinces.

(ii) Petroleum sector:
- Xinjiang, Heilongjiang, Qinghai, Gansu, Tianjin, Liaoning, and Hebei provinces have extra petroleum products.
- Production almost meets demand in Shandong, Jilin, and Henan provinces.
- Production cannot meet local demand in Hubei, Sichuan, Shaanxi, Ningxia, Yunnan, Inner Mongolia, Guangdong, Jiangsu, Anhui, Beijing, Fujian, Guangxi, Guizhou, Hainan, Hunan, Jiangxi, Shanghai, Shanxi, Tibet, and Zhejiang provinces.

(iii) Metal sector:
- Tibet, Hainan, Shaanxi, Jiangxi, Yunnan, Guangxi, Hunan, Hebei, Inner Mongolia, Guizhou, and Henan provinces have extra metal products.
- Production almost meets demand in Liaoning, Qinghai, Gansu, Shandong, Anhui, and Shanxi provinces.
- Production cannot meet local demand in Guangdong, Hubei, Zhejiang, Jilin, Beijing, Xinjiang, Sichuan, Fujian, Jiangsu, Heilongjiang, Ningxia, Tianjin, and Shanghai provinces.

(iv) Non-metal sector:
- Hubei, Zhejiang, Tibet, Jiangsu, Anhui, Guangdong, Fujian, Hunan, Qinghai, Jiangxi, Sichuan, and Shandong provinces have extra non-metal products.
- Production almost meets demand in Guangxi, Liaoning, Guizhou, Inner Mongolia, and Gansu provinces.
- Production cannot meet local demand in Hainan, Hebei, Yunnan, Shaanxi, Beijing, Tianjin, Jilin, Henan, Xinjiang, Ningxia, Shanxi, Heilongjiang, and Shanghai provinces.

(v) Timber sector:
- Tibet, Jilin, Fujian, Inner Mongolia, Heilongjiang, Guizhou, Yunnan, Sichuan, and Jiangxi provinces have extra timber products.
- There is no province in which the production exactly meets demand.

TABLE 10.2 Interprovincial Comparative Advantage Indices (Q_{ij}), by Industrial Sector

Province	Coal	Petroleum	Metal	Non-Metal	Timber	Food
Anhui	1.42	0.00	0.93	1.61	0.18	1.34
Beijing	0.63	0.00	0.44	0.62	0.00	1.90
Fujian	0.43	0.00	0.33	1.55	6.23	1.45
Gansu	0.75	2.22	1.01	0.92	0.83	0.46
Guangdong	0.21	0.16	0.82	1.58	0.14	1.78
Guangxi	0.32	0.00	2.58	1.16	0.34	1.59
Guizhou	2.63	0.00	1.30	0.97	1.94	0.76
Hainan	0.04	0.00	3.58	0.83	0.54	1.59
Hebei	1.51	1.30	2.05	0.75	0.00	0.57
Heilongjiang	0.58	2.79	0.12	0.16	3.12	0.32
Henan	1.57	0.94	1.24	0.37	0.00	0.91
Hubei	0.23	0.71	0.66	2.45	0.17	1.37
Hunan	1.21	0.00	2.53	1.44	0.43	1.19
Inner Mongolia	1.48	0.38	1.33	0.95	5.60	0.78
Jiangsu	0.79	0.14	0.16	1.62	0.00	1.66
Jiangxi	1.08	0.00	3.43	1.36	1.38	1.05
Jilin	0.79	0.95	0.56	0.54	6.50	0.88
Liaoning	1.03	1.51	1.18	0.99	0.00	0.75
Ningxia	3.70	0.42	0.05	0.25	0.00	0.52
Qinghai	0.26	2.70	1.13	1.37	0.09	0.37
Shaanxi	1.22	0.58	3.47	0.64	0.67	0.82
Shandong	0.90	1.13	0.97	1.22	0.00	1.01
Shanghai	0.00	0.00	0.01	0.07	0.04	2.31
Shanxi	4.70	0.00	0.89	0.25	0.03	0.20
Sichuan	1.10	0.61	0.43	1.35	1.74	1.16
Tianjin	0.01	2.05	0.02	0.56	0.00	1.12
Tibet	0.03	0.00	5.05	1.88	10.7	0.53
Xinjiang	0.35	3.11	0.44	0.26	0.21	0.37
Yunnan	0.71	0.40	3.24	0.66	1.83	1.09
Zhejiang	0.21	0.00	0.62	2.21	0.01	1.82

Source: Author based on Equation (10.1) and SSB (1996, pp. 118–36).

- Production cannot meet local demand in Gansu, Shaanxi, Hainan, Hunan, Guangxi, Xinjiang, Anhui, Hubei, Guangdong, Qinghai, Shanghai, Shanxi, Zhejiang, Beijing, Hebei, Henan, Jiangsu, Liaoning, Ningxia, Shandong, and Tianjin provinces.

(vi) Food sector:
- Shanghai, Beijing, Zhejiang, Guangdong, Jiangsu, Guangxi, Hainan, Fujian, Hubei, and Anhui provinces have extra food products.

- Production almost meets demand in Hunan, Sichuan, Tianjin, Yunnan, Jiangxi, Shandong, and Henan provinces.
- Production cannot meet local demand in Jilin, Shaanxi, Inner Mongolia, Guizhou, Liaoning, Hebei, Tibet, Ningxia, Gansu, Qinghai, Xinjiang, Heilongjiang, and Shanxi provinces.

Generally, China's resource demand and supply may be classified into four different geographical zones which are labeled as follows: (1) $S_L D_L$ (low supply, low demand), (2) $S_H D_L$ (high supply, low demand), (3) $S_H D_H$ (high supply, high demand), and (4) $S_L D_H$ (low supply, high demand). Obviously, Zones $S_L D_L$ and $S_H D_H$ can reach their respective optimum equilibrium point of social welfare even under the condition that inter-zone trade is not available, as their resource supplies can meet their resource demands. However, under the disequilibrated supply–demand conditions, neither Zone $S_L D_H$ nor Zone $S_H D_L$ can optimize its social welfare. As a matter of fact, as these two Zones' resource supply–demand structures are complementary with each other, the optimization of their social welfare can benefit greatly from their inter-zone trade, more specifically, from the import from Zone $S_H D_L$ to Zone $S_L D_H$, or the export to Zone $S_L D_H$ from Zone $S_H D_L$.

There have been two potentially contradictory metaphors pervading contemporary commentary on the nature and trajectory of the Chinese political economy. First, there is the more benign metaphor of the 'nationalization' of economic activities, which presents a picture of an environment in which economic agents, in particular multiregional firms, are increasingly indifferent to political boundaries, competing in the 'national market' and satisfying the demands of consumers whose tastes are increasingly homogeneous across borders. Secondly, there is the view of the national economy as being increasingly defined by different 'regional blocs' which are marked by high levels of intra-regional interdependence but which compete at the national level.

10.2 SPATIAL ECONOMIC SEPARATION

In principle, spatial economic separation may effectively be reduced to a minimum level within a sovereign country by the central government. As a result of the diversified natural, geographical environments and the heterogeneous social and cultural conditions in China, however, the Chinese economy has been spatially separated by a series of natural and artificial barriers. This kind of spatial separation became particularly serious during the period when the centrally planned system was transformed into a decentralized administrative system. Let's look briefly at this spatial separation and its negative effects on the Chinese economy through a consideration of three aspects — geographical, administrative, and cultural.

10.2.1 Geographical Barriers

In terms of its topography and physical environment, China is one of the most complex countries in the world. Glancing at the map of China, one may find that many administrative regions, especially provinces, have natural geographical barriers such as mountains, rivers, lakes, and so on. This kind of geographical separation between

adjacent provinces could have a serious effect on regional economic development if the interprovincial transport and communication linkages are established inefficiently. After checking the highway networks of ten provinces (Beijing, Shanghai, Tianjin, Hebei, Shanxi, Liaoning, Gansu, Qinghai, Inner Mongolia, and Ningxia) in *China Atlas* published in 1983, for example, we may observe that, of the 453 highways in the peripheral areas, around 60 percent were transprovincially connected, whereas about 40 percent did not reach their respective province's border (Guo 1993, p. 119). Obviously, the fragmentary nature of the highway networks has exacerbated the inconveniences for every sphere of the local inhabitant's lives and has had a particularly adverse effect on the Chinese economy.

Many provinces, autonomous regions, and municipalities directly under the central government have been informally demarcated in China. As a result, cross-border relations between the relevant provinces have never been easily coordinated and, sometimes, could become a destabilizing source for social stability and economic development, even though the regulations concerning the resolution of the border disputes have been issued and revised by the State Council (1981, 1988). After 1986, the Ministry of Civil Affairs (MCA) conducted a series of field surveys on the provinces of Xinjiang, Inner Mongolia, Ningxia, Gansu, Shaanxi, Qinghai, Jilin, Hebei, and Shandong in order to provide legal, formal, geographical boundaries for those provinces. Many interprovincial border problems, however, still remained unresolved.[1]

Moreover, there is another geographical characteristic in the Chinese economy: many provinces' borders are naturally marked by mountains, rivers, and lakes which bless the border regions with abundant natural and environmental resources. Given the cross-border *imbroglios* between the provinces, the sustainable exploitation and utilization of natural resources (such as energy, metals, forests, fisheries, and so on) as well as environmental protection in the border regions, will undoubtedly pose problems and disputes for both central and local governments in China. Non-cooperative cross-border relations between provinces could eventually become a source of disturbance to economic development. Even worse, some interprovincial disputes led to armed conflicts and seriously affected the social security and economic sustainability in border regions (see Box 10.1). This has seriously affected the social security and sustainability of economic development in China.

---

1. For example, after having compared the locally mapped borders, Zhang (1990, p. 8) points out that among China's 66 cross-province border lines (totaling about 52,000 km), 59 cross-province borders have been the subject of controversy and 54 cross-province borders, amounting to around 9,500 km, have been disputed by the relevant local governments.

Box 10.1   The Interprovincial Border Disputes in China

Of China's interprovincial borderlines, many are disputed and have even been published, according to their own preferences, by the provincial-level authorities in their official maps and documents. According to the statistics released by the Ministry of Civil Affairs, of the 52,000 km of interprovincial borders in the PRC, only 5 percent are legally fixed; 77 percent are regarded as informal (or customary borderlines); and about 18 percent (about 9,500 km) remain the subject of active disputes (*Beijing Youth*, 2 December 2002).

There were more than 800 cases of cross-border disputes in 333 of the 849 interprovincial border counties of almost all provinces. The total disputed areas (about 140,000 km²) include grassland (about 96,000 km²), mining areas (about 5,000 km²), water (about 1,000 km²) and mixed grass-mining-forestland (about 30,000 km²) and are distributed unevenly in the Western belt (about 130,000 km²), the Central belt (about 17,000 km²) and the Eastern belt (about 700 km²) (*Baokan Wenzhai*, 1989, p. 4). In defiance of the State Council (1981, 1988) regulations concerning the resolution of interprovincial border disputes, many disputes were the subject of armed fights between different groups of people.

10.2.2   Administrative Barriers

One of the key initiatives of China's economic reform that began in the late 1970s was the promotion of decentralization in economic operations, i.e., transferring economic management and decision making from central government to provincial and local governments. For example, retail trade, which used to be under the control of local government, is now determined by collectively and individually owned enterprises. Decentralization and the introduction of market forces together imply that the centers of economic power are moving away from central government to the localities. Since the advent of administrative decentralization, China's national economy had become effectively 'cellularized' into a plethora of semi-autarkic regional enclaves.

The uneven distribution of natural resources and industrial structure among different provinces enhances the mutual complementarities of the Chinese economy. However, to a certain extent, administrative separation had formed a rigid self-reliant agricultural and industrial system for each province and had a serious effect on cross-border economic relations, particularly during the high tide of administrative decentralization stemming from economic reform. In order to protect local market and revenue sources, it became very common that in some provinces, local authorities established, and provided finance for, a variety of schemes that promoted the sale of local products. Enterprises from other provinces, however, often have difficulties in finding office spaces, accommodation or land for their business activities. These protectionist measures, which were often in violation of central directives, were enforced through a patchwork system of roadblocks, cargo seizures, *ad hoc* taxes, commercial surcharges, and licensing fees, and in a number of well-publicized cases, highway robbery across the interprovincial borders.[2] Moreover, this unfair competition between

provinces could be fierce in the 'battlegrounds' of their border regions and there were numerous tales of 'trade embargoes' or 'commodity wars' between provinces over, among other items, rice, wool, tobacco, soy beans, and mineral products.[3]

Experience and lessons from advanced countries have shown that the success of a nation in promoting its economic development depends to a large extent on a complete legislative structure and effective instrumental incentives of its own. China's efforts to this end have achieved much progress, but some detailed work still remains to be done. In fact, China's 'commodity wars' between provinces stemmed from the fact that China does not have any constitutional clauses to specifically prohibit barriers against interprovincial commerce, even though the relevant regulations and laws have been issued time and again.[4] More often than not, the state's orders were not accorded the priority status of a self-contained law, but took the form of less formal circulars, or were included as minor elements of larger pieces of portmanteau legislation (Young and Ho, 1993, pp. 9–13).

The negative economic impacts of interprovincial separation are obvious. Here is an example. With a land area of 167 thousand square kilometers and a population of about 100 million, Henan is one of the largest provinces in China. It has a great deal of diversities in terms of natural topography and social and economic developments. Henan province has 3,130 km of long land boundaries with six provinces (i.e., Hebei in the north, Shanxi in the northwest, Shaanxi in the west, Hubei in the south, Anhui in the southeast, and Shandong in the northeast). Among the 42 border counties (or county-level municipalities), 35 are adjacent to one province (here, we define them as '2-d border counties'), and seven are adjacent to two provinces (here, we define them as '3-d border counties').

---

2. This phenomenon has been described as Zhuhou Jingji (feudal prince economy) or Duli Wangguo (independent kingdom). See, for example, Shen and Dai (1990, p. 12), Li (1993, pp. 23–36), and Wedeman (1993, pp. 1–2) for more detailed analyses.

3. More detailed evidence may be found in Sun (1993, pp. 95–104), Feng (1993, pp. 87–94), Guo (1993, pp. 201–5), and Goodman (1994, pp. 1–20).
4. See, for example, State Council (1980, 1982, 1986, and 1990) and NPC (1993).

TABLE 10.3 Average Income Level (Yuan/Person) by Type of Region

Topographical Type	Core Counties	Peripheral Counties	
		2-d Border	3-d Border
Plain area	623.46	733.50	411.03
Mountain area	774.24	532.95	623.01
All	746.10	607.44	501.88

Note: *An i-d border county is one which is bordered by i provinces.*
Source: Guo (1996, 73–4).

Table 10.3 supports the view that income level was higher in core counties (746.10 yuan) than in peripheral counties. Furthermore, the income level was higher in the 2-d border counties (607.44 yuan) than in the 3-d border counties (501.88 yuan), suggesting that border complexity is not helpful to the economic development of border regions.

Note that Table 10.3 shows some inconsistencies. For example, for the samples of plain area, core counties have a lower income level than the 2-d border counties; and for the samples of mountain area, 2-d border counties have a lower level of income than the 3-d border counties. These inconsistencies may be explained by Henan's transprovincial border economic cooperation (this will be discussed in the next section, especially as shown in Table 10.6).

10.2.3 Ethno-Cultural Barriers

Cultural differences have had a decisive influence on economic and marketing decisions. Although it is not the only tool in building trusting relationships, doors usually open more quickly when knocked on by someone who shares a familiar culture. The differences between intra- and intercultural behaviors can be summarized as consisting of four aspects: (1) feelings of superiority (and occasionally inferiority) toward people who are perceived as being very different; (2) fear of and lack of trust in such people; (3) communication difficulties resulting from differences in language and accepted civil behavior; (4) lack of familiarity with the assumptions and motivations, such as relationships and social practices of other people (Huntington, 1996, p. 129).

In addition to the Han-Chinese, which account for more than 90 percent of the nation's total population, 55 other minority groups also exist in mainland China. Geographically, the Han majority are dominant in the Eastern and Central belts, with the only exception being Guangxi, which is a Zhuang autonomous region. The other minority-dominated autonomous regions include Ningxia (Hui minority-based) and Xinjiang (Ugyur minority-based) in the Northwest region, Inner Mongolia

TABLE 10.4 China's Ethnic and Linguistic Differences, by Province

Province	Main Ethnic Groups	Main Languages (Dialects)
Anhui	Han, Hui, She	Mandarin
Beijing	Han, Hui, Manchu	Mandarin
Chongqing	Han, Yi	Mandarin
Fujian	Han, She, Hui	Min, Kejia
Gansu	Han, Hui, Tibetan	Mandarin, Mongolian
Guangdong	Han, Yao, Zhuang	Cantonese (Yue), Kejia, Miao-Yao
Guangxi	Zhuang, Han, Yao	Chinese dialects, Dai
Guizhou	Han, Miao, Buyi	Chinese dialects, Dai
Hainan	Han, Li, Miao	Chinese dialects, Kejia, Dai
Hebei	Han, Hui, Manchu	Mandarin
Heilongjiang	Han, Manchu, Korean	Mandarin
Henan	Han, Hui, Mongol	Mandarin
Hubei	Han, Tujia, Hui	Chinese dialects
Hunan	Han, Tujia, Miao	Xiang (Chinese dialects), Miao-Yao
Inner Mongolia	Mongol, Han	Mongolian, Mandarin
Jiangsu	Han, Hui, Manchu	Chinese dialects, Mandarin, Wu
Jiangxi	Han, Hui, Miao	Gan (Chinese dialects)
Jilin	Han, Korean, Manchu	Mandarin
Liaoning	Han, Manchu, Mongol	Mandarin
Ningxia	Hui, Han, Manchu	Mandarin
Qinghai	Han, Tibetan, Hui	Tibetan, Mongolian
Shaanxi	Han, Hui, Manchu	Mandarin
Shandong	Han, Hui, Manchu	Mandarin
Shanghai	Han	Wu
Shanxi	Han, Hui, Mongol	Mandarin
Sichuan	Han, Yi, Tibetan	Mandarin, Tibetan
Tianjin	Han, Hui, Korean	Mandarin
Tibet	Tibetan, Han, Menba	Tibetan
Xinjiang	Uighur, Han, Kazak	Turkish dialects, Mongolian
Yunnan	Han, Yi, Bai	Mandarin, Tibetan
Zhejiang	Han, She, Hui	Chinese dialects, Wu

Source: Author.

(Mongolian minority-based) in the North region, Tibet (Tibetan minority-based) in the Southwest region, and so on. In addition, there are also dozens of minority-based sub-provincial administrations (such as autonomous prefectures and prefecture-level municipalities) and even more minority-based autonomous counties and county-level municipalities under the administrations of the above autonomous regions and other provinces in China.

Most of China's provinces, autonomous regions, and municipalities directly under the central government, which are each the average size and scale of a European country in terms of both population and land area, are considerable political and economic systems in their own right. The differences between these provinces have long been a defining characteristic of China's politics since, in most cases, their boundaries were created more than some two thousand years ago. Besides, Chinese culture is not homogeneous across provinces, in terms of ethnic and linguistic groups (see Table 10.4).

More importantly, there are various religiously based areas in China. For example, people in Tibet and its adjacent autonomous areas in Southwest China usually adhere to Tibetan Buddhism, while most minorities in Northwest China have close connections to Islam. The Han-Chinese, representing the majority of Chinese population in the Central and Eastern belts, are traditionally in favor of a mix of Buddhism, Confucianism, and Taoism, with the exception of a few others. Naturally, it is unlikely that people with markedly differing attitudes, as well as different cultural values, could emphasize the adoption of a common standard and socioeconomic coordination. Apart from abstract questions of justice, this circumstance would not lead itself to an agreement between the cultural regimes concerned.

10.3 SPATIAL DISECONOMIES AND CHINA

10.3.1 China's Quest for Spatial Integration

Rooted in a single culture, the Chinese economic area is politically separated. Hong Kong (until 1997) and Macau (until 1999) were two colonial territories ruled by the United Kingdom and Portugal. Long before their return to China under the principle of 'one country, two systems', these two capitalist economies had set up close and efficient economic links with their communist rival on the mainland. Traditionally, mainland China supplied most of Hong Kong's food and fresh water, and Hong Kong traditionally served as China's main port. After 1978 the links between the two economies were extended to production, investment, provision of services, and financial relations (Dodsworth and Mihaljek, 1997). Regardless of the political and military tensions between Taiwan and mainland

China, bilateral trade and economic exchanges across the Taiwan Strait have grown dramatically, as have tourism, technological, and labor cooperation. It is seems extraordinary that economic ties of this kind could have been sustained between two such politically distrustful and hostile economies.

However, the large size of the Chinese nation does impose some negative influences on its economy, especially in its huge and less developed inland areas. Since the advent of administrative decentralization in the early 1980s, China's national economy had become effectively 'cellularized' into a plethora of semi-autarkic regional enclaves. Public finance, as an important component of the Chinese economic system, has undergone a series of reforms on central–local relations. The main goals of these reforms were to decentralize the fiscal structure and to strengthen the incentive for local governments to collect more revenue for themselves. While the economic decentralization has been a major factor in China's current economic success, it also had negative impacts on interprovincial relations. For example, in order to protect local market and revenue sources, it became common in China for some provinces to restrict imports (exports) from (to) other provinces by levying high, if informal, taxes and by creating non-tariff barriers on commodities whose production was seen as important to their provincially 'domestic' economies.[5]

Most of China's provinces, autonomous regions, and municipalities that are under the direct control of the central government are on a size and scale equivalent to a European country in terms of both population and land area, meaning that they are considerable political and economic systems in their own right. The differences between these provinces have long been a defining characteristic of China's politics. In most cases their boundaries were created thousands of years ago. In addition, Chinese culture is not homogeneous across provinces. There is a broad range of ethnic and linguistic groups as well as religious adherents in the nation. The holding of markedly differing religious beliefs and values implies that the chances of the adoption of a common standard between different groups of people are not likely to be enhanced. Consequently, China's great diversity in terms of physical geography, resource endowment, political economy, and ethnic identity has given rise to many difficulties in interprovincial administration.

10.3.2 Multiregional Economic Cooperation

Since the late 1970s, the Chinese government has recognized the importance of transprovincial trade and economic cooperation and attempted to tear down its internal

---

5. See, for example, Shen and Dai (1990, pp. 1–13) and Li (1993, pp. 23–36).

trade and economic barriers. In 1979 the CCPCC and the State Council implemented a new spatial development strategy entitled 'evading weakness, exerting advantages, protecting competitiveness, and promoting unification'. This strategy first attempted to replace the traditional economic method by which the Chinese economy was constructed into several self-supported regional systems. On October 20, 1984, the Third Plenum of the 12th CCPCC claimed that 'All administrative divisions should open up to each other, the barriers between economically developed and lagging regions, between coastal, inland, and frontier regions, between urban and rural areas, and between different sectors and enterprises should be removed for economic unification according to the principle of evading weakness, mutual complementarity, and joint development' (CCPCC, 1984). Generally, it is believed that multiregional economic cooperation was promoted substantially during the above period. Between 1981 and 1985, more than 30 regional economic and technological cooperative organizations were established in China.

China's spatial economic integration drive was further promoted by the 'Regulations on Some Issues Concerning the Further Promotion of Horizontal Economic Unification' promulgated by the State Council in 1986. According to the Chinese Academy of Social Sciences (CASS) (1992, pp. 561–7), central and local governments have established more than 100 multiregional economic cooperative zones. Generally, China's multiregional economic cooperative zones are voluntarily established and jointly administered by adjacent local governments. Many of them also have liaison officers and convene regular (annual) meetings co-chaired by the participating sides. The main tasks of the meetings include:

- Discussion of the key issues related to all sides concerned, such as the regional economic development strategy, regional economic structure, and so on
- Coordination of the policies and measures concerning the promotion of regional economic development
- Development of bilateral and multilateral economic cooperation
- Study of reconstruction and unification in the fields of production, circulation, science, and technology
- Implementation of the specific coordination between all sides concerned.

According to their objectives and functions, the multiregional economic cooperative zones can be classified into seven categories:

- Synthesized economic cooperative zones
- Resource-exploiting cooperative zones
- Open economic zones
- Municipal economic cooperative zones
- Municipal economic cooperative networks

- Cooperative zones for economically lagging areas
- Sectoral economic cooperative zones.

In addition, these economic cooperative zones can be classified into three general categories in terms of administrative level:

- First-class economic cooperative zones, each of which is usually composed of two or more provincial administrations
- Second-class economic cooperative zones (trans-province border economic cooperative zones, or BECZs), each of which is composed of two or more adjacent prefectures, municipalities, or counties under different provincial administrations
- Third-class economic cooperative zones, each of which is composed of two or more adjacent prefectures, municipalities, or counties within a single provincial administration.

10.3.3 Trans-Province Border Economic Cooperation

Of the economic cooperative zones listed above, the BECZs are worthy of further note, because of their special geographic locations and multidimensional administrative structures. In 1983 the BECZs were new entries to the regional economic sphere. By the end of 1989, the total number of these BECZs had increased dramatically to 41.[6] Table 10.5 gives some basic natural and social conditions for selected Chinese trans-provincial BECZs.

In China, the proliferation of trans-provincial BECZs has provided an efficient channel for provincially peripheral areas to develop cross-border economic ties and cooperation. From Table 10.6, we can see that the average level of per capita income is always higher in the border counties that have joined the BECZs than in the other border counties. Specifically, the per capita income was only 473.79 yuan and 391.61 yuan in 2-d and 3-d border counties (an i-d border county is one which is bordered by i provinces), respectively, given the unavailability of trans-province border economic cooperation. As a result of trans-province border economic cooperation, however, the per capita income in the 2-d and 3-d border counties increased by 44.88 percent and 49.17 percent, to 686.42 yuan and 584.18 yuan, respectively.

To further investigate the mechanisms and functions of the trans-provincial BECZ, let's take the Zhongyuan Association for Economic and Technological Coordination (ZAETC) as an example.

---

6. Examples of the literature include CASS (1992) and Guo (1993, pp. 189–95; 1996, pp. 146–50).

TABLE 10.5 Selected Trans-Provincial Border Economic Cooperative Zones (BECZs) in China

Border Economic Cooperative Zone (BECZ)	Participating Provinces	Land Area (1,000 Sq. Km)	Population (Millions)[a]	Natural Resources
Zhongyuan Association for Economic and Technological Coordination	Shanxi, Hebei, Shandong, Henan	97.3	4.42	Coal, petroleum, agricultural resources
The Yellow River Delta Economic Zone	Shanxi, Shaanxi, Henan	36.6	10.00	Coal, bauxite; copper; hydraulic power
The Huaihai Economic Zone	Jiangsu, Shandong, Henan, Anhui	176.0	100.00	Coal, agricultural resources
The H-H-S-S Border Zone for Economic Cooperation	Hubei, Henan, Sichuan, Shaanxi	153.8	32.91	Petroleum; coal; phosphor; iron ore; natural alkali; crystal; mercury
The S-G-G Border Economic Zone	Shaanxi, Gansu, Sichuan	162.0	22.60	Lead; zinc; petroleum; natural gas; pottery
The F-G-J Border Zone for Economic and Technological Cooperation	Fujian, Guangdong, Jiangxi	74.6	11.39	Coal; manganese; hydraulic power; copper; gold; silver
The Joint Congress for Promotion of Economic Development in the Dabieshan Area	Anhui, Henen, Hubei	123.0	25.69	Biological and agricultural resources

[a]*Data as of the 1990s.*
Source: Guo (1996).

TABLE 10.6 Average Income Level (Yuan/Person) by Type of Border Region

Topographical Type	2-d Border Counties			3-d Border Counties		
	(1) non-BECZ	(2) BECZ	(2)–(1)	(1) non-BECZ	(2) BECZ	(2)–(1)
Plain area	489.79	942.40	452.61	391.61	467.69	76.08
Mountain area	460.07	566.96	106.89	NA	623.01	NA
All	473.79	686.42	212.63	391.61	584.18	192.57

Notes: *(1) An i-d border county is one which is bordered by i provinces. (2) BECZ = trans-provincial border economic cooperative zone.*
Source: Guo (1993).

The border areas of Shanxi, Hebei, Shandong, and Henan provinces in central China play a leading role in the economic interdependence between China's East and West regions. On September 27, 1985, wishing to promote the trans-provincial economic cooperation, the nine municipal mayors of Changzhi, Xinxiang, Anyang, Handan, Jincheng, Jiaozuo, Xingtai, Hebi, and Puyang and five prefectural governors of Xinxiang, Xingtai, Handan, Liucheng, and Hezhe of the border-region met in Handan, Hebei province, to establish a multi-governmental association, namely ZAETC.

As a permanent body housed in Handan city, Hebei province, ZAETC's Liaison Office is operated jointly by representatives from the participating municipalities and prefectures under the leadership of ZAETC. ZAETC has been convening its regular annual meetings co-chaired by the municipal mayors and prefectural governors, with the participation of heads of the Economic Commission, Planning Commission, Office of Economic Cooperation, and Center for Economic Research from each municipality or prefecture, while the chairpersons of which are to be appointed as the mayors (governors) of the participating municipalities (prefectures) in turn, from 1986, in the following order: Changzhi municipality, Xingtai (municipality and prefecture respectively), Anyang municipality, Handan (municipality and prefecture respectively), Jincheng municipality, Liucheng prefecture, Jiaozuo municipality, Xinxiang (municipality and prefecture respectively), Hebi municipality, Puyang municipality, and Hezhe prefecture. The main topics of the annual meetings have included:

- Discussion of key issues relating to the economic developments of all parts of the border area
- Formulation of regulations and measures concerning the promotion of socio-economic development in the border area
- Development of bilateral and multilateral cooperation
- Formulation of reciprocal measures for trans-border trade.[7]

According to the working manual released from ZAETC's Liaison Office, 11 fields of cross-border cooperation have been agreed to start between the 14 municipalities and prefectures in the border region:

a) Joint exploitation and utilization of underground resources to develop coal, petroleum, power, and metallurgic industries
b) Joint exploitation and synthetic utilization of agricultural resources to promote the development of aquatic, forestry, and livestock products
c) Promotion of cooperation and trans-border combination in the sectors of textile, chemistry, machinery, electrics, building materials, etc.
d) Reinforcement of urban–rural combination in terms of the joint development of feed-processing plants, food-processing industry, and the production of meat, egg, chicken, milk, etc.
e) Joint establishment of trading centers and setting up of liaison offices in each other's provinces
f) Cooperation in science and technology by establishing joint research projects
g) Cooperation in capital, technology, and equipment to develop cross-border railway, highway, and air transports
h) Cooperation in education and exchange of personnel
i) Mutual assistance to each other's urbanization
j) Establishment of cross-border information networks
k) Promotion of cross-border financial and labor markets.

10.4 REGIONAL DEVELOPMENT STRATEGIES

10.4.1 Historical Review

After three years of recovery (1950–52), the PRC government began to construct its economy through a centrally planned approach. In order to effectively overcome the disequilibrated industrial distribution between the coastal and inland areas, the government shifted investment to the inland area from the coastal area. During the period 1953–78, basic construction funded by the state was split with 35.7 percent in the coastal area and 55.2 percent in the inland area

TABLE 10.7 Spatial Distribution of Investment, 1953–90

Period	Coastal (%)	Inland (%)	Coastal/ Inland
1953–57 (1st FYP)	36.9	46.8	0.788
1958–62 (2nd FYP)	38.4	56.0	0.686
1963–65	34.9	58.3	0.599
1966–70 (3rd FYP)	26.9	64.7	0.416
1971–75 (4th FYP)	35.5	54.4	0.653
1976–80 (5th FYP)	42.2	50.0	0.844
1981–85 (6th FYP)	47.7	46.5	1.026
1986–90 (7th FYP)	51.7	39.9	1.296
1953–78 (pre-reform)	35.7	55.2	0.647
1979–90 (post-reform)	49.9	43.2	1.155
1953–90	45.0	46.8	0.962

Notes: *The total investment of coastal and inland areas is less than 100.00% due to the exclusion of the spatially 'unidentified' investment which includes (1) the trans-provincial investment in railway, post and telecommunication, electric power, etc.; (2) the unified purchase of airplanes, ships, vehicles, etc.; and (3) the investment in national defense.* **Sources:** (1) SSB (1991, 1992), and (2) Li and Fan (1994, p. 65).

(see Table 10.7). As a result, industrial production grew unevenly between the coastal and inland areas. From 1952 to 1978, the inland area's share of gross value of industrial output (GVIO) increased from 31.8 percent to 40.2 percent, while the coastal area's share of GVIO decreased from 68.2 percent to 59.8 percent accordingly (Liu, 1994, p. 3).

After 1978 when the Chinese government began to realize the importance of reforming its centrally planned system and paying more attention to efficiency, rather than regional equality, capital investment had been concentrated in the coastal area. Between 1979 and 1990, the coastal area accounted for 49.9 percent of the nation's capital investment, while the inland area's share decreased accordingly to 43.2 percent, as demonstrated in Table 10.7.

Since the late 1970s, China has adopted an uneven spatial development strategy, encouraging a proportion of regions to go one step further to get rich.[8] This included differing development preferences among different regions and during different periods.

10.4.2 Coastal Area Development Strategy

To date, the most successful regional development strategy is the so-called 'Coastal Area Development Strategy'.

---

7. Based on the author's interviews with the officers of ZAETC in Handan, Hebei province, China, in May 1990.

8. For further details about China's regional development strategies and policies during the pre-reform period (viz., from the 1950s to the 1970s), see Section 11.1 of Chapter 11.

This strategy, which will be discussed in detail in subsection 12.2.1 of Chapter 12, has benefited significantly from China's open-door policy. The final, major outcome of this strategy, a fact well known by us, has been the dramatic growth of foreign direct investment and foreign trade, which have been substantial drivers of the Chinese economy – and of the coastal area in particular. The additional outcome of this strategy is the increasing economic disparity between China's coastal and western areas in recent decades.

The idea of Western Taiwan Straits Economic Zone (WTSEZ) was first proposed by the Fujian government in 2001. The WTSEZ includes the coastal cities of Xiamen, Zhangzhou, Quanzhou, and Fuzhou of Fujian province. It aims to integrate the economies, transport, infrastructure, and policies from the coastal cities west of the Taiwan Straits for competitiveness, social development, and increased and strengthened economic cooperation with Taiwan. The proposal was also supported by the Chinese central government, wishing to facilitate political and economic relationships across the Taiwan Straits.

The proposed economic zone will accelerate economic development along the coastal cities in Fujian province. Fujian's economy is China's 11th largest provincial economy. The zone will help Fujian province catch up to Taiwan's economic development. Fujian province has already received a large amount of Taiwanese investment. With the opening of direct transport links between Taiwan and Mainland China, it is expected that this would increase economic activity in the economic zone as well as for Taiwan. This will mean reduced costs for aviation, shipping, and postal services. This is expected to increase as cross-straits bilateral ties improve. The economic zone would promote better use of resources of the economic belt in Eastern China and enhance its overall economic strength.

10.4.3   Western Region Development Strategy

In the middle of 1999 the members of the CCPCC, headed by Jiang Zemin, started to talk publicly about the introduction of changes to China's regional development policy. For just over twenty years, ever since the establishment of Mao's principles of equal development and regional self-sufficiency – encapsulated in the description of 'The whole country is a chessboard' (*quanguo yipan qi*) – had been set aside, a more differentiated approach to regional development policy had privileged the eastern and coastal economies of the PRC. Without abandoning the regional development policy of the previous twenty years, the new policy initiative has placed greater emphasis on the development of the interior.

While the policy to develop 'West China' has clearly been introduced from the top down, and under the leadership of a dedicated office of the State Council, the wider political environment is very different from that of the 'Third Front Strategy' (see subsection 11.1.3 of Chapter 11). Not only has the project been discussed more openly, but there has been greater lower-level involvement in its development. Even at the planning stage, provinces such as Shaanxi, Sichuan, and Chongqing were centrally involved. A West China Development Research Institute was established in Xi'an as a cooperative project of the central government's Ministry of Science and Technology, the Shaanxi Province Committee of the CCP, the Science Commission of the Shaanxi Provincial People's Government and Northwest University in order to provide advice on strategy and policy.

One challenge facing China in the era of globalization is to prevent its uneven growth pattern. In order to narrow the gap with the prosperous coastal area, the CCPCC propagated a campaign called the 'Western Region Development Strategy' (*xibu da kaifa*), which constitutes a cornerstone of the 10th Five-Year Plan (2001–2005) and is intended to foster the future development of the inland regions. The stated goals were to bring about social and economic development of the interior and western regions of China. In November 1999, the State Council appointed the newly formed 'State Council Leading Group for Western Region Development' to define a new policy. The 'Office' was established in January 2003 to deal with day-to-day business. The main goals of the Western Region Development Strategy set out by the central government are as follows:

- To promote the development of the Western and Central regions
- To gradually eliminate regional disparities
- To consolidate the unity of ethnic groups
- To ensure border security and social stability
- To promote social progress.

It is anticipated that the strategy will initiate a number of programs and projects to stimulate domestic demand, expand the market, and maintain sustained, rapid, and healthy development of the national economy. The main tasks are as follows:

- to construct the infrastructure
  - water conservancy, communications, energy, telecommunication, and urban infrastructure
- to improve the environment
- to convert cultivated land back into forestry and pasture
- to protect natural forests, recover and increase the vegetation of forestry and pasture
- to reduce water loss and soil erosion, and
- to develop agriculture with local characteristics.

Rural poverty alleviation is also on the agenda. Enterprises are called to be active players in restructuring and upgrading traditional industries, to take advantage of military industries concentrated in the Western region, and to develop high-tech industries in fields such as biology, engineering, aerospace, renewable energy, new materials, electronic information processing, and advanced manufacturing.[9]

10.4.4 Resurgence of the Old Industrial Base

In 2002 a new spatial initiative entitled the 'Resurgence of the Old Industrial Base in the Northeast Region' was announced. As is suggested by the name of the policy, its purpose was to address the increasing obsolescence of the industrial base of the three provinces of Jilin, Heilongjiang, and Liaoning in the Northeast region. This region, formerly called Manchuria, had been relatively more industrialized than other Chinese regions at the beginning of the People's Republic. The main reasons for this are twofold: the first is that much of its industrial capacity was preserved after the Japanese were defeated at the end of World War II; and the second relates to China's close ties with the former USSR during the 1950s, which had put most of their cooperative, industrial projects within the Northeast region. Since the early 1960s, however, as a result of the worsening relations between China and the former USSR, the Northeast region had become the first-front area facing a high probability of wars that China must prepare for (see subsection 11.1.3 of Chapter 11 for details).

Since the 1980s, the Chinese economy has benefited substantially from both reform and its open-door policy. However, the Northeast region has lagged behind other regions (especially the southeast and coastal provinces) during this period. In order to implement a coordinated regional development during the entire Tenth Five-Year Plan (2000–2005), the State Council spent 100 billion yuan in the Northeast region as part of its proposal to upgrade industry and to provide greater incentives for modernization. This interpretation of both the 'Western Region Development Strategy' and the 'Resurgence of the Old Industrial Base in the Northeast Region' provides another point of contrast with the Third Front strategy that was implemented during the pre-reform period. Inevitably because the Third Front strategy was less openly announced and more tightly focused with a highly specific policy goal (defense in the event of invasion) the projects implemented in the twenty-first century have been considerably more contested in their formulation and may also be in their implementation.

10.5 SUMMARY

The experiences and lessons from both developed and developing countries in the post-war period have demonstrated that the success of a nation in promoting its economic development depends, to a large extent, on a complete legal system and effective management and supervision mechanisms of its own. China's efforts to this end have achieved some progress, but some large-scale changes are still needed. In fact, the 'commodity wars' between provinces and autonomous regions are derived from the fact that China has no constitutional clauses which specifically prohibit restraints on interprovincial commerce.

Despite the mutually complementary conditions between many of its different regions, the Chinese economy has been internally affected by various geographical, administrative, and cultural barriers that exist between provincial administrations. Following an empirical analysis of the spatial efficiency of the Chinese economy, this chapter studies the possibilities and conditions under which the Chinese economy can (or cannot) be optimized spatially. In this chapter, we have also analyzed the economic impacts of China's sub-political borders. The result shows that the multiregional complementarities have not been utilized fully and that because of this existing cross-border separation, the Chinese economy cannot be spatially optimized. As a practical measure to overcome the inter-regional barriers and to provide a 'bridge' for spatial economic integration, since the early 1980s China has established different forms and levels of multiregional economic cooperative zones. The particular focus of the final part of this chapter has also examined China's various efforts on the search for spatial economic integration.

In theory, multiregional economic cooperation and trade must be mutually beneficial to all of the provinces concerned, given the complementarity in natural resource endowments as well as other economic attributes. However, in China the costs arising from the transactions between provinces cannot be underestimated. Among the factors that hinder attempts at coordination are the differing sub-administrative systems of Chinese provinces and their specific internal social and cultural conditions. Thus, the extent of progress in economic cooperation between the provinces must depend upon the extent to which the related sides pragmatically reorganize and respond to the economic and non-economic benefits and costs involved.

If China's regional and local economies may be easily regulated by means of unified economic policies, the inefficiencies in allocation of production factors can, therefore, be eliminated. But as the Chinese economies are administered by different regional authorities, this problem cannot be solved so easily.

---

9. http://www.westchina.gov.cn/english/asp/showinfo.asp?name=2.11.11. 2003. Accessed on November 29, 2011.

Case Study 8

Fighting for Rainfalls?

On an overcast day in the western vicinity of Beijing, you will hear the booming sound of anti-aircraft guns from the mountainside of Xiangshan Hills Park. Please don't be startled. That was neither an air raid drill, nor preparation for a coming war. Rather, it was the sound of Beijing meteorologists shooting canisters of silver iodide into the gathering clouds. The Beijing municipal government has instructed the meteorological workers to shoot at any clouds that could enhance the levels of rainfall over the drought-stricken city. In addition to Beijing, other major cities such as Tianjin have also called in soldiers to scan the sky for signs of clouds.

China's first man-made precipitation enhancement was conducted in 1958. It has now become the world's largest cloud seeder, using an array of methods to disperse chemicals into cloud layers in order to make rain. Between 1995 and 2003, China spent a total of US$266 million on rainmaking technology in 23 provinces, autonomous regions, and municipalities, with some 35,000 people working in the field. In 2003 alone, China spent about US$50 million to disperse chemicals into clouds through the use of 30 airplanes, 3,800 rockets, and 6,900 high artillery shells (CMB, 2004). In addition, numerous aircraft, old anti-aircraft guns, balloons, and even mountaintop dispersal devices have been employed by provincial and local meteorological bureaus and rainmaking authorities (note that by law private companies are not entitled to conduct rainmaking activities in China) to fire chemicals into the clouds.

This man-made precipitation has also been part of the efforts of local meteorological authorities to establish a long-term mechanism aimed at minimizing the losses caused by bad weather such as prolonged heatwaves or heavy fogs. China experiences almost all of the problems related to water resources faced by countries across the world. China's rapid economic growth, industrialization, and urbanization have outpaced infrastructure investment and management capacity, and have created widespread problems of water scarcity. The degradation of groundwater resources and the deterioration of groundwater quality have become striking environmental problems in many Chinese cities. In the areas of the North China Plain, where about half of China's wheat and corn is grown as well as plenteous peach orchards, drought is an ever-looming threat.

Scientific rainmaking or precipitation enhancement began in 1946 when the American scientists Vincent Schaefer and Bernard Vonnegu at General Electric (GE), following up on some laboratory observations, 'seeded' a cloud with dry ice and then watched snow fall from its base. Until recent times it was thought that rain might be induced by explosions, updrafts from fires, or by giving the atmosphere a negative charge. Research showed that rain forms in warm clouds when larger drops of condensed water grow at the expense of smaller ones until they become large enough to fall; furthermore, in cold clouds super-cooled water below $-15°C$ freezes into ice crystals that act as nuclei for snow (Battan, 1962).[10] It was also important to determine what kinds of clouds were suitable for seeding. It was found that, for reasons that were not very well understood, there were important differences between clouds formed over land and over sea, with many more but much smaller droplets in continental clouds. Since larger droplets are needed if rain is to form, this meant that continental clouds were much less likely than maritime ones to be a good source of rain, a discovery of considerable significance to would-be Australian rainmakers. The temperature of the upper levels of the cloud was found to be another critical factor. In the case of both cumulus and stratiform clouds, provided this temperature was lower than $-7°C$, seeding would inevitably be followed by precipitation within 20–25 minutes (Ryan and King, 1997, p. 21).

The factors controlling the distribution of rainfall over the earth's surface include the belts of converging-ascending airflow, air temperature, moisture-bearing winds, ocean currents, the distance inland from the coast, and the presence of mountain ranges. Ascending air is cooled by expansion, which results in the formation of clouds and the production of rain. Conversely, in the broad belts of descending air are found the great desert regions of the earth, descending air being warmed by compression and, consequently, absorbing instead of releasing moisture. If the temperature is low, the air has a small moisture capacity and is able to produce little precipitation. When winds blow over the ocean, especially over areas of warm water (where the evaporation of moisture into the air is active) toward a given coastal area, that area receives more rainfall than a similar area where the winds blow from the interior toward the oceans. Areas near the sea receive more rain than inland regions, since the winds constantly lose moisture and may be quite dry by the time they reach the interior.

The production of rain by artificial means is now generally disregarded by many Western countries, although it is probable that rainmaking hastens or increases rainfall from clouds suitable for natural rainfall. The existing rainmaking techniques have been only moderately successful. Without clouds, there can be no rainfall. So rainmaking activities cannot be relied upon in cases of drought. On the other hand, it should be noted that some clouds would

---

10. On this basis, three methods were developed: (i) spraying water into warm clouds; (ii) dropping dry ice into cold clouds (where the dry ice freezes some water into ice crystals that act as natural nuclei for snow); and (iii) wafting silver iodide crystals or other similar crystals into a cold cloud from the ground or from an airplane over the cloud (UWRL, 1971).

almost certainly result in rainfall, regardless of the artificial seeding. To judge the viability of a rainmaking program, it is important to establish that seeding made a difference – that is, it results in rain from clouds that would not otherwise have yielded it naturally. It was difficult to determine whether fluctuations in rainfall that occur at the time of cloud-seeding were produced by seeding or would have occurred naturally. Besides, the over-seeding can sometimes dissipate a cloud. Research conducted in China showed that even the best efforts of China's rainmakers produce an increase in rainfall of only 10–15 percent (CMB, 2002). In addition, the vagaries of nature, such as wind direction and velocity, mean the effect of cloud-seeding on any given locality is difficult to predict.

In China, when rare clouds appear over this often-parched region, it has been common practice for workers at the local weather bureau to roll out anti-aircraft guns and blast away at the sky. The exploding shells contain fine particles of silver iodide, which scatter through the moisture-laden clouds. Provincial, county, and municipal governments in almost all of the country's 32 provinces, autonomous regions, and municipalities have set up weather modification bureaus assigned to regularly bombard the heavens with chemicals in the hopes of squeezing out more rainfall for demanding farmers and thirsty city dwellers.

With persistent drought still plaguing China, some neighboring regions have begun to squabble about clouds. The most hotly debated topic is around the issue of upwind neighbors unfairly intercepting clouds for seeding, and as a result depriving downwind areas of rainfall. Given the severity of water shortages in northern China, such sensitivity is unsurprising. In a large part of central and northern China, the annual rainfall has decreased significantly in the past three decades, while the level of population has soared. Rivers run dry at certain times of year. A typical case of the accusation of 'rain theft' arose in central China's Henan province, after a heavy rainstorm in mid-2004.

Between July 9 and 11, 2004, a moisture-laden cloud drifted northeast across the sky of Nanyang in southern Henan province. This was very good news for all of the northeastern administrative areas (including Pingdingshan, Zhumadian, Luohe, and Xuchang cities and Zhoukou prefecture), since most of these areas were experiencing serious droughts during that period. In order to obtain a larger share of rainfall for themselves, the five cities and prefectures competed, using thousands of rocket shells and old anti-aircraft guns to shoot canisters of chemicals into the cloud. The final result of the rainmaking was significant but uneven in geographical distribution: the largest rainfall occurred in Pingdingshan and Xuchang cities (each recording a rainfall of 100 mm or more); while Zhoukou prefecture, with the same input as the other four cities, had only

a 27 mm rainfall in its urban area and a paltry 7 mm in the rural area where the need for rainfall was the most urgent (Liu, 2004).

Zhoukou officials complained to a provincial newspaper *Dahe Bao* (Big River News) and to the national Xinhua news agency that the neighboring cities had milked the cloud system nearly dry even before it arrived in their area. Municipal officials later demanded legislation to regulate how to divvy up the clouds (*China Daily*, 2004). Meteorologists in Zhoukou were accusing their counterparts in Pingdingshan of overusing natural resources by intercepting clouds that would have been likely to drift on to other places – such as Zhoukou. 'Some places have abused rainwater resources', said a Zhoukou expert who asked not to be named. Zhoukou's meteorological officials stated that the Pingdingshan Weather Modification Office had repeatedly seeded clouds that, if nature had been allowed to follow its course, would have scudded along to other places – such as Zhoukou – before delivering their rainfall.

The Pingdingshan office responded. 'We didn't grab the clouds away from other cities', declared the office director, who gave his name only as Wang. 'What we are doing is quite a scientific thing. And we reported our cloud-seeding schedule to the provincial government. I believe other cities also did so', Wang said in a telephone interview with the *Washington Post* correspondent, Edward Cody. 'The water vapor resource is not like water resources in a river, which could be intercepted from points upstream. Nor is it like a cake – if I have a bite, others get only a smaller piece. Besides, clouds change while floating in the sky, so it is quite complicated.'[11]

Over the next two decades, China's economy is expected to grow at a higher rate than the global average. This rapid economic growth, along with continued increases in population, will place an increasing stress on China's natural resource base, especially in relation to the availability of fresh water. Over the next few decades sustainable growth depends in part upon how China deals properly with issues and policies relating to water resources. The demands of intensive farming and burgeoning industrial development, as well as waste and pollution, add to the area's problem of low rainfall. In 2001, China consumed four times as much water for each unit of GDP than the world average (NBS, 2002). China has the opportunity to increase its available water supplies through careful management. Initiatives to encourage the more efficient use of existing water supplies are already under way in some areas. The difficulties will be for national and local governments to craft policies and rules within China's complex cultural and legal-administrative system that

---

11. Cited from *Washington Post* (2004, p. A12).

provide incentives for users to increase the efficiency of water use, and for polluters to clean up the water they use and return clean water to stream flows (Crook and Diao, 2000, p. 28).

Facing this projected increasing shortage of water supplies, China is experimenting with various precipitation enhancement technologies: as we have shown earlier, airplanes, rocket shells, and old anti-aircraft guns are used to shoot canisters of chemicals such as silver iodide, liquid nitrogen, and calcium chloride into the sky in order to build up moisture in the clouds and increase the levels of rainfall. Better water management can increase the available water supply. China abhors open feuding between government bodies. But China's increasingly acute water shortage is causing tempers to fray. On the basis of historical climate data, some Chinese and Western scientists predicted, at an international conference held in Beijing in May 2002, that eastern and central China (the location, for instance, of those regional rivalries in rainmaking in Henan province discussed earlier) would experience a hotter and drier climate from 2001 till 2030, by which time the available water will decrease by 20 percent (Sun et al., 2002).

The period since the 1980s has seen the introduction of a number of pieces of legislation relating to the exploitation and protection of natural and environmental resources. But the legislative foundation is still weak. For example, China has not introduced any comprehensive weather modification laws. It has only enacted the 'Regulations of the People's Republic of China on Meteorological Services' promulgated by the State Council on August 18, 1994, and the 'Regulations on Administration of Weather Modification' adopted at the 56th Executive Meeting of the State Council on March 13, 2002. The Meteorological Law was adopted at the 12th Meeting of the Standing Committee of the Ninth National People's Congress of the People's Republic of China on October 31, 1999 and came into effect as of January 1, 2000 (NPC, 2000). However, there are many contradictory articles in the law. For example, in Article 5, the law states:

The competent meteorological department under the State Council is responsible for meteorological work nationwide. Local competent meteorological departments at different levels are responsible for meteorological work in their own administrative regions under the leadership of the competent meteorological departments at a higher level and the people's governments at the corresponding level.

This article defines a dual-track system of leadership for the provincial and local meteorological departments. The problem with this system is its administrative inefficiency, given that provincial and local meteorological departments are simultaneously subordinate to two different administrative organs. Regarding the prevention of meteorological disasters, Article 28 of the law states:

Competent meteorological departments at all levels shall make arrangements for joint monitoring and forecasting of significant weather events among regions or departments, propose timely measures for preventing meteorological disasters and make assessment of severe weather disasters, which shall serve as the decision making basis for the people's governments at the corresponding levels to arrange prevention of meteorological disasters.

Obviously, this article does not define the geographic scopes of and manners for inter-regional coordination in case a meteorological disaster occurs. Our most serious concern now arises from the fact that there is no article relating to cross-border activities of weather modification in the Chinese laws. In 2002, it appears in the 'Regulations on Administration of Weather Modification' (*rengong yingxiang tianqi guanli tiaoli*) adopted at the 56th Executive Meeting of the State Council on March 13 (State Council, 2002). As defined in Article 14 of these Regulations:

Where weather modification operations are to be implemented crossing the boundaries of different provinces, autonomous regions or municipalities directly under the Central Government, the relevant people's governments of the provinces, autonomous regions, or municipalities directly under the Central Government shall make a decision thereon through consultation; if no agreement is reached through consultation, the decision shall be made by the competent meteorological department of the State Council in consultation with the relevant people's governments of the provinces, autonomous regions, or municipalities directly under the Central Government.

Clearly, this is an invalid article. And, therefore, its enforcement is weak. In most circumstances, the weather modification activities of a province may not be carried out across land borders, but they could have a serious impact on the neighboring provinces. Because of the geographical proximity in cross-border areas, weather modification activities carried out within each side of a border may affect the territory of the other side.

In contrast to the Chinese regulations on weather modification, the 'Agreement between the United States of America and Canada Relating to the Exchange of Information on Weather Modification Activities', signed by the Government of the United States of America and the Government of Canada, is much more clearly defined.[12] For example, in Article I(b) of the Agreement, the term 'weather modification activities of mutual interest' is defined as:

...carried out in or over the territory of a Party within 200 miles of the international boundary; or such activities wherever

---

12. This Agreement is available at www.americansovereign.com/articles/weather.htm. Accessed on November 23, 2011.

conducted, which, in the judgment of a Party, may significantly affect the composition, behavior, or dynamics of the atmosphere over the territory of the other Party.

In Article IV, 'each Party agrees to notify and to fully inform the other concerning any weather modification activities of mutual interest conducted by it prior to the commencement of such activities. Every effort shall be made to provide such notice as far in advance of such activities as may be possible....' Furthermore, the agreement states:

The Parties agree to consult, at the request of either Party, regarding particular weather modification activities of mutual interest. Such consultations shall be initiated promptly on the request of a Party, and in cases of urgency, may be undertaken through telephonic or other rapid means of communication.

Indeed, the rational and optimal utilization of cloud resources among the neighboring administrative areas is becoming an increasingly pressing legal and institutional problem that must be solved appropriately by the Chinese authorities at both central and local levels. To date, China, like most other countries, has not had any laws and administrative regulations dealing with cloud resources or the rational application of man-made precipitation enhancement. However, if this disordered competition in rainmaking continues to exist among the neighboring administrative areas, perhaps someday in the future, the anti-aircraft guns and missiles that are currently used to shoot clouds to make rainfall might be turned to more militaristic purposes.

REFERENCES

Baokan Wenzhai (1989). The armed disputes in China's internal borders [zhongguo bianjie da xiedou]. *The Digest of Newspapers and Magazines*, June 13, p. 4.

Battan, L. J. (1962). *Cloud physics and cloud seeding.* San Francisco: Doubleday.

CCPCC. (1984). *Decision of the CCPCC concerning the reform of economic structure.* Beijing: the Third Plenum of the 12th CCPCC, Beijing, October 21.

China Daily (2004). Hey, you! get off of my cloud. July 14, Beijing: China Daily.

CMB (China Meteorological Bureau) (2002; 2004). *China meteorological report (in Chinese).* Beijing: China Meteorological Bureau.

CASS (Chinese Academy of Social Sciences) (1992). *China's yearbook for horizontal economy* [zhongguo hengxiang jingji nianjian]. Beijing: China Social Sciences Press.

Crook, F. W., & Diao, X. (2000). Water pressure in China: growth strains resources. *Agricultural Outlook*, January–February, 25–29.

Dodsworth, J., & Mihaljek, D. (1997). *Hong Kong, China: growth, structural change, and economic stability during the transition.* International Monetary Fund Occasional Paper No. 152, Washington, DC: IMF.

Feng, L. (1993). On the 'Wars' over the purchase of farm and subsidiary products. *Chinese Economic Studies*, 26(5), 87–94.

Goodman, D. S. G. (1994). The politics of regionalism: economic development conflicts and negotiation. In D. S. G. Goodman & G. Segal (Eds.), *China deconstructs: politics, trade, and regionalism* (1994, pp. 1–20). London and New York: Routledge.

Guo, R. (1993). *Economic analysis of border-regions: theory and practice of China* [zhongguo shengji bianjie diqu jingji fazhan yanjiu]. Beijing: China Ocean Press.

Guo, R. (1996). *Border-regional economics.* Berlin and New York: Springer.

Huntington, S. P. (1996). *The clash of civilizations and the remaking of the world order.* New York: Simon & Schuster.

Isserman, A. M. (1977). The location quotient approach for estimating regional economic impacts. *Journal of the American Institute of Planners*, 43, 33–41.

Li, J., & Fan, M. (1994). A comparison of the regional structures for the economic development in China during pre- and post-reform periods [gaige kaifang qianhou zhongguo jingji fazhan quyu jiegou de bijiao]. In S. Liu, Q. Li, & T. Hsueh (Eds.), *Studies on China's regional economic development* [zhongguo diqu jingji yanjiu] (pp. 57–73). Beijing: China Statistics Publishing House.

Li, Z. (1993). In-depth exploration of the question of regional blockades. *Chinese Economic Studies*, 26(5), 23–36.

NBS. (various years). *China statistical yearbook*, various issues. Beijing: China Statistics Publishing House.

NPC (1993). *Anti-unfair competition law* [fan bu zhengdang jingzhen fa]. Beijing: National People's Congress of China.

NPC. (2000). *Meteorological law of the People's Republic of China.* Beijing: the 12th Meeting of the Standing Committee of the Ninth National People's Congress of the People's Republic of China, October 31.

Ryan, B. F., & King, W. D. (1997). A critical review of the Australian experience in cloud seeding. *Bulletin of the American Meteorological Society*, 78, 239–254.

Shen, L., & Dai, Y. (1990). Chinese federal economy: mechanisms, impacts, and sources [zhongguo de zhuhou jingji: jizhi, houguo he genyuan]. *Jingji Yanjiu* [Economic Research Journal], 3, 10–13.

SSB (1996). *China industrial economic statistical yearbook 1995.* Beijing: China Statistics Publishing House.

SSB. (various years). *China statistical yearbook*, various issues. Beijing: China Statistics Publishing House.

State Council (1980). *Provisional regulations relating to the development and protection of socialist competition* [guanyu fazhan yu baohu shehui zhuyi jingzheng de zhanxing tiaoli]. Beijing: State Council.

State Council (1981). *Regulations of the P. R. China concerning the resolutions of the disputes on borders of the administrative divisions* [zhonghua renmin gongheguo xingzhengqu bianjie zhengyi culi tiaoli]. Beijing: State Council.

State Council (1982). *Notice relating to the prohibition of blockades in the sale of industrial products* [guanyu jinzhi gongye chanpin xiaoshou bilei de tongzhi]. Beijing: State Council.

State Council (1986). *Regulations on some issues concerning the further promotion of horizontal economic unification.* Beijing: State Council. March 26.

State Council (1988). *Regulations of the P. R. China concerning the resolutions of the disputes on borders of the administrative divisions.* Beijing: State Council. revised version.

State Council (1990). *An administrative order to remove all regional blockades to trade.* Beijing: State Council.

State Council (2002). Regulations concerning the artificial weather modification: *Rule of the state council of the People's Republic of China.* Beijing: State Council. No. 248, March 19.

Sun, G., MacNulty, S. G., Moore, J., Bunch, C., & Ni, J. (2002). *Potential impacts of climate change on rainfall erosivity and water availability in China in the next 100 years.* The 12th International Soil Conservation Conference, Beijing, China, May.

Sun, Z. (1993). Causes of trade wars over farm products, their effects, and suggested solutions. *Chinese Economic Studies, 26*(5), 95–104.

UWRL (Utah Water Research Laboratory) (1971). *Development of cold cloud seeding technology for use in precipitation management.* Logon: Utah State University. available at <www.encyclopedia.com/html/r1/rainmaki.asp>. Accessed on December 12, 2004.

Washington Post. (2004). *Chinese rainmakers competing for clouds: widespread drought leads to regional rivalries* (by Edward Cody). Foreign Service, August 2, p. A12.

Wedeman, A. H. (1993). Editor's introduction to Chinese economic studies. *Chinese Economic Studies, 26*(5), 1–2. (special issue on regional protection).

Young, J. C., & Ho, H. H. (1993). China moves against unfair competition. *East Asian Executive Report* September.

Zhang, W. (1990). Reform well China's administrative division for the continuous peace and stability of the nation [chong guojia changzhi jiu'an chufa, gaohao xingzheng qu hua de gaige]. *Journal of East China Normal University, 2,* 1–9.

Chapter 11

Industrialization and Technological Progress

A model of a Chinese ladle-and-bowl type compass used for geomancy in the Han dynasty (202 BC–220 AD). *Source: http://zh.wikipedia.org/zh/File:Antic_Chinese_Compass.jpg*

The Four Great Inventions (papermaking, gunpowder, movable-type printing, and the compass) are celebrated in Chinese culture for their historical significance and serve as symbols of China's advanced science and technology. These four discoveries had an enormous impact on the development of Chinese civilization and also had a far-ranging global impact. For example, paper was introduced in China in the second century AD, came to Japan in the seventh century, and was then diffused westward to Central Asia in the eighth century, North Africa in the tenth, Spain in the twelfth and northern Europe in the thirteenth. Printing was invented in China in the eighth century AD and movable type in the eleventh century, but this technology only reached Europe in the fifteenth century. Another Chinese invention, gunpowder, made in the ninth century, disseminated to the Arabs after a few hundred years and reached Europe in the fourteenth century.

A man of the state of Song was worried about his seedlings growing too slowly. He pulled up the seedlings one by one and came home exhausted, saying to his family 'I am tired out today because I have helped the seedlings to grow'. Hearing this, his

Understanding the Chinese Economies. DOI: http://dx.doi.org/10.1016/B978-0-12-397826-4.00011-1
© 2013 Elsevier Inc. All rights reserved.

son hurried to the fields and found that all the seedlings had shrivelled up. There are very few in the world who will refrain from helping the seedlings grow. But there are some who think it useless to give any help and give up. They are those who do not weed the fields. Whereas there are others who want the shoots to grow quickly by pulling them upward. In their case, not only is it of no help, it actually does harm.

– Mencius (372–289 BC)

11.1 INDUSTRIALIZATION DURING THE PRE-REFORM ERA

11.1.1 Economic Recovery

Before the foundation of the People's Republic of China (PRC) in 1949 China had been a typical agrarian society, with more than 90 percent of its population living in rural areas. Thereafter, the Chinese government abandoned the old political and economic systems through the socialist transformation of capitalist industry and commerce.[1] During the early period of the PRC, the development of modern and comprehensive industry was given a high priority. With the direct involvement of central and local government, the targets of the first Five-Year Plan (FYP), from 1953 to 1957, were fully completed.

Among the pre-reform FYPs, the first FYP (1953–57) has been generally acknowledged to be the most successful, because many key macroeconomic issues, such as the relationship between industry and agriculture and the setting of an appropriate rate of accumulation, were properly handled in this FYP. However, some economic problems in relation to over-centralized administration and non-economic methods of management that have been reformed since the late 1970s had their origins in that period.

The time of the first FYP saw national income increase annually by an average of 8.9 percent and the annual growth rate of gross value of industrial output (GVIO) was 18.0 percent (see Table 11.1).[2] As the first FYP was nearing its completion, Mao Zedong pointed out at an expanded meeting of the Political Bureau of the CCPCC held on April 25, 1956: 'The emphasis in our country's construction is on heavy industry. The production of the means of production must be given priority, that's settled. But it definitely does not follow that the production of the

means of subsistence, especially grain, can be neglected' (Mao, 1956, p. 285).

In subsequent years, however, the construction of heavy industry was overheated.

11.1.2 Great Leap Forward (1958–60)

Guided by Mao's general line of building socialism with 'greater, faster, better, and more economical results' (*duo kuai hao sheng*), the Great Leap Forward (GLF) movement was launched by the Chinese government, who called for a doubling of output within one year (Mao, 1957, p. 491).[3] Obviously, the achievement of this target was impossible because of the limitations of production capacity and resource bases. Nevertheless, the fulfillment of the quota was stubbornly insisted upon and consequently tens of millions of people had to be mobilized for steel production. The scale of capital construction grew dramatically so that the rate of accumulation suddenly rose from 24.9 percent in 1957 to 33.9 percent in 1958 (SSB, 1990).

Stimulated by the arbitrary directions given by the central authorities, many heavy industrial enterprises were set up during the GLF period (1958–60), with no consideration being given to their sources of raw materials and their technological requirements. The quality was low and many unwanted and unusable goods were produced, resulting in great losses. Even worse, as large quantities of materials and labor were diverted toward the development of heavy industries, the development of agriculture and light industry received accordingly less attention. Millions of peasants abandoned farming to dig for ore and fell trees in order to make steel using indigenous methods.

This situation lasted until 1960, resulting in serious imbalances between accumulation and consumption and also between heavy industry and agriculture, on the one hand, and light industry on the other. In the rural areas, however, the harvest was poor despite the high yields. Consequently, from 1959 onwards, there was a spectacular fall in the levels of agricultural production.[4] Although natural disasters and the deterioration of Sino-Soviet ties played some role in these setbacks, the major cause was attributed to China's overheated industrial policy.

In the following years, attempts were made to achieve economic readjustment in order to correct some of the previous errors. Factories were closed, suspended, merged, or

---

1. Between 1949 and 1956, some 123,000 capitalist enterprises were transformed into 87,900 industrial units under joint state–private ownership and, at the same time, many small workshops run by individual laborers were reorganized as collectives (Liao, 1982, p. 130).

2. Note that during the pre-reform period, China applied the material product system (MPS) under which only such indicators as national income, gross value of social product (GVSP), gross value of agricultural output (GVAO), and gross value of industrial output (GVIO) were reported. See Section 9.1 of Chapter 9 for more details.

3. For example, in 1958, the target for steel production was raised from the planned output of 6.3 million tons to 10.7 million tons (Liu, 1982, p. 32).

4. The gross value of agricultural output (GVAO) in 1961 was 26.3 percent below that in 1958; compared with the preceding year, industrial production dropped by an incredible 38.2 percent in 1961 and then again by 16.6 percent in 1962. The productivity of industrial labor was 5.4 percent lower in 1962 than in 1957, while the level of national income declined by 14.4 percent over the same period (Liang, 1982, p. 60).

TABLE 11.1 Major Economic Indicators During the Pre-Reform Period

Item	1950–52	1953–57	1958–62	1963–65	1966–70	1971–75	1976	1977	1978
1. Annual growth rate (%)									
1.1 National income	19.3	8.9	–3.1	14.5	8.4	5.6	–2.7	7.8	12.3
1.2 Gross value of agricultural output (GVAO)	14.1	4.5	–4.3	11.1	3.9	4.0	2.5	1.7	9.0
1.3 Gross value of industrial output (GVIO)	34.8	18.0	3.8	17.9	11.7	9.1	1.3	14.3	13.5
(1) Heavy industry	48.8	25.4	6.6	14.9	14.7	10.2	0.5	14.3	15.6
(2) Light industry	29.0	12.9	1.1	21.2	8.4	7.7	2.4	14.3	10.8
2. Accumulation/national income (%)		24.2	30.8	22.7	26.3	33.0	30.9	32.3	36.5
3. National income growth/ investment ratio (%)		35.0	1.0	57.0	26.0	16.0	–10.0	26.0	34.0
4. Distribution of capital construction									
4.1 Agriculture (%)		7.8	12.3	18.8	11.8	11.3			
4.2 Light industry (%)		5.9	5.2	3.9	4.0	5.4			
4.3 Heavy industry (%)		46.5	56.1	49.8	57.4	54.8			

Sources: Liang (1982, p. 63, tab. 4); Dong (1982, pp. 88–9, tab. 9).

Box 11.1 World Dynamics: a Pessimistic Viewpoint

In the early 1970s, and based on system dynamics – a technique based on conceptions in control theory, organization theory, and on the available techniques of computer simulation – developed by Jay W Forrester, an MIT research team constructed a computer model to simulate likely future outcomes of the world economy. The most prominent feature of system dynamics is the use of feedback loops to explain behavior. It is a unique tool for dealing with questions about the way in which complex systems behave over time. The standard model run assumes no major change in the physical, economic, or social relationships that have historically governed the development of the world system. All variables included in the model follow historical values from 1900 to 1970. One end result of this ambitious study was originally published in 1972 under the title *The Limits to Growth* (Meadows et al., 1972) and was subsequently updated and revised in 1992 under the title *Beyond the Limits* (Meadows et al., 1992).

Three main conclusions were reached by this study. The first suggests that within a time span of less than 100 years, society will run out of the non-renewable resources on which the world's industrial base depends. When the resources have been depleted, a precipitous collapse of the economic system will result, manifested in massive unemployment, decreased food production, and a decline in population. The characteristic behavior of the system is collapse. The second conclusion of this study is that piecemeal approaches to resolving the individual problems will not be successful. As its final conclusion, the study suggests that overshoots and collapse can be avoided only by an immediate limit on population and pollution, as well as a cessation of economic growth. Thus, according to this study, growth will eventually cease, one way or another. Still, the authors conclude that it is possible to avoid the collapse if we make the right choices now.

switched to other lines of production. The construction of some large plants was either cancelled or delayed. Many industrial workers were redeployed to the countryside (*xiafang*). During the readjustment period (1963–65), some sound progress towards industrial construction was made. The launching of the Cultural Revolution in 1966 and the

ten years of social chaos that followed, however, disrupted this process. Similar errors of blind and subjective leadership of industrialization were committed. Many large-scale industrial enterprises were constructed which lacked adequate sources of raw materials and gave no consideration to either the availability of transport or social needs.

11.1.3 Preparing for War

From the early 1960s to the late 1970s, China undertook a spatial division of its economy into three fronts according to the principle of 'preparing for wars':

- The eastern (coastal) provinces were defined as the first front because of their proximity to the capitalist world
- A number of inland provinces (such as Sichuan, Guizhou, Shaanxi, Gansu, Qinghai, Ningxia, Yunnan, the western parts of Hubei, Hunan, Henan, Shanxi and Hebei, the northern part of Guangdong, and the northwest part of Guangxi) – most of which are covered by mountains – were treated as the third front
- The remaining provinces were treated as the second front.

During the Cultural Revolution period (1966–76), the development of the third front area was given priority in Chinese industrialization as it was believed that World War III would occur very soon and that the first front area could inevitably become the battlefield. As a result of the government's involvement, the third front area's share of China's capital investment increased sharply from 30.60 percent in the first FYP (1953–57) to 52.70 percent in the third FYP (1966–70) and the per capita GVIO increased from 22.04 yuan in 1952 to 373.97 yuan in 1983, while the coastal area increased from 93.77 yuan to 871.3 yuan during the same period (Jao and Leung, 1986, pp. 3 and 6). Promoted by the third front development strategy, many large and key enterprises (principally in the military, aeronautical, electronic, and other high-tech industries), universities, and research institutions were transferred from the coastal (urban) area (called the 'first front') to the remote, mountainous, and usually rural inland area (called the 'third front').[5]

The third front area development policy rapidly industrialized some areas of China's inland provinces (see Table 11.2) and provided a template for developing countries to avoid the 'polarization' between rich and poor areas.[6] However, this has not been identified as a successful approach to the modernization of the Chinese economy as a whole. This can be demonstrated by the fact that the average annual capital output coefficient (that is, output/investment ratio) of the third front area was only 0.256, far less than that of the coastal area (0.973) during the period

TABLE 11.2 Industrial Outputs of the Third Front Area as a Percentage of China's Total

Item	1952	1965	1978
Gross value of industrial output (GVIO)	17.9	22.3	25.7
Steel	13.9	19.4	27.9
Coal	33.0	40.9	47.6
Electricity	10.5	25.2	33.5
Machine tools	2.2	15.7	27.3
Car	–	–	12.1
Tractor	–	77.4	30.6
Cement	14.1	13.6	37.0
Clothing	15.9	27.9	30.7
Paper	7.1	14.5	23.0
Cigarette	28.6	34.5	42.0

Source: Liu (1983).

1953–79 (Liu, 1984, p. 270). In addition, there would have been an increase of approximately 45 percent of China's total GVIO had the investment been distributed in the coastal area rather than the third front area during that period (Yang, 1989, p. 76).

11.1.4 Great Leap Outward

Following the death of Mao Zedong in September 1976, the Chinese government once again tried to accelerate the rate of economic development by setting targets that were much higher than any possible maximum capabilities. These impetuous and unrealistic plans began in 1978 and resembled, in many ways, those of the Great Leap Forward that had begun two decades before. Proposals were enthusiastically made by the post-Mao leadership to produce 400 million tons of grain, 60 million tons of steel, 250 million tons of oil, and to develop 120 large and medium-sized projects, including ten major oilfields, ten major steel plants, and ten major coal mines, and to import large amounts of modern equipment and technology by the end of the Sixth FYP (1981–85).[7] It was not until the Third Plenum of the 11th CCPCC in December 1978 that the Chinese government began to shift the main focus of its national task from the 'class struggle' to the realization of socialist economic construction, calling on the entire

---

5. Examples of literature on the third front area include Lardy (1978), Leung (1980), Maruyama (1982, pp. 437–71), Liu (1983), Riskin (1987), Naughton (1988, pp. 227–304), Bo (1991, pp. 1202–3 and 1209), and Chen (1994, pp. 329–42).

6. For example, between 1953 and 1978, the annual GVIO growth rates of Shaanxi, Qinghai, Shanxi, Guizhou, and Sichuan provinces reached 20.1 percent, 16.3 percent, 12.0 percent, 11.2 percent, and 11.8 percent, respectively, which were much higher than that of the coastal provinces (Hu et al., 1995, p. 5).

---

7. Cited from Liang (1982, pp. 61–2). Clearly this went too far beyond the real capacities of this country.

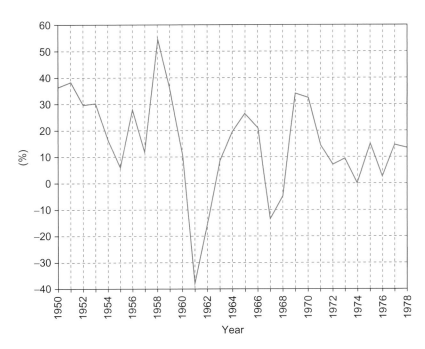

FIGURE 11.1 Industrial growth during the pre-reform period. *Source: NBS, various years.*

people to strive to achieve the four modernizations of: industry; agriculture; national defense; and science and technology by the end of the twentieth century. However, many economic problems had been cyclically generated by the previous political struggles and could not be immediately resolved. In late 1979, China decided to call a temporary halt to industrial expansion and carried out a policy entitled 'readjustment, reform, consolidation, and improvement' (*tiaozheng, gaige, gonggu, tigao*) in order to properly tackle the existing structural imbalances of the Chinese economy. This policy lasted for three years and many industrialization programs did not start to work until 1984.

During the pre-reform period, China's industrialization was implemented mainly through a system of central planning. Direct and strong government participation and large-scale mobilization of resources to priority sectors enabled the industrial sector to grow at an average rate of over 10 percent annually (with a few exceptions in 1961–62, 1967–68, and 1974), resulting in a dramatic increase of its share in national income from 19.5 percent in 1953 to 49.4 percent in 1978 (see Table 11.1 and Figure 11.1). The advantages of rapid industrial expansion from a centrally planned mechanism, however, were soon outweighed by the problems of low levels of efficiency, an unbalanced industrial structure dominated by heavy industry, sluggish technological progress, sectoral imbalances, and sharp annual fluctuations in growth rates. In addition, the self-reliant and inward-looking policies that had been implemented by the Chinese government for most of the pre-reform period bore responsibility for this poor industrial performance.

11.2 INDUSTRIALIZATION DURING THE REFORM ERA

11.2.1 General Background

'Industry' can be defined as the material production sector which engages in the extraction of natural resources and the processing and reprocessing of natural resources and agricultural products. With regard to the division between light and heavy industry, definitions vary from country to country. According to China's official definition (SSB, 1996, p. 405), 'light' refers to an industry that produces consumer goods and tools. This comprises two categories: (i) using farm products as raw materials; and (ii) using non-farm products as raw materials. Heavy industry refers to general products used by other manufacturers. According to the purpose of production or use of products, heavy industry is divided into three separate branches:

1. The extraction of petroleum, coal, metal and non-metal ores, and timber felling
2. Smelting and processing of metals, coke making and coke chemistry, chemical materials and building materials such as cement, plywood, and power, petroleum, and coal processing
3. Machine-building industry which equips sectors of the national economy, metal structure industry and cement works, industry producing the means of agricultural production, and the chemical fertilizers and pesticides industry.

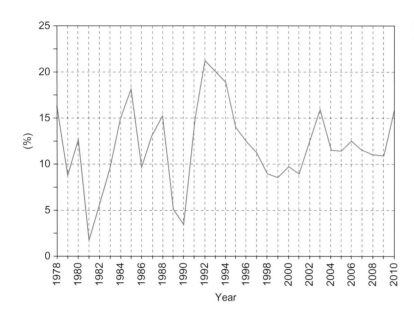

FIGURE 11.2 Industrial growth during the post-reform period. *Source: NBS, various years.*

Between the early 1950s and the end of the Cultural Revolution, China devoted much of its energy to heavy industrialization at the expense of agriculture and light and service sectors (see the last rows of Table 11.1). Since the early 1980s, the Chinese government has effectively shifted the emphasis away from heavy industry to industries that have a more direct connection with people's lives. This is the correct approach for China to undertake, not only because those industries can meet people's demands, but also because they are *labor-intensive* and therefore more appropriate for the conditions prevailing in China – a country which benefits from a cheap and abundant labor supply.

Since the end of the Cultural Revolution, industrial fluctuations have been reduced significantly. At the beginning of the economic reform, the industrial output increased by over 10 percent annually, but this declined to a meager 5 percent in 1981. The industrial growth rate rose by over 20 percent in 1985, followed again by less than 10 percent during 1989–90 as a result of the conservative and tight monetary policy employed by the government. Since the early 1990s, China's industrial output has achieved the longest and fastest growth rate of the post-reform period (see Figure 11.2).

Since the early 1980s, there has been a fundamental change in the investment system, characterized mainly by decentralization and regional autonomy. In respect of decentralization, the responsibilities are shared proportionally between central and local governments: (1) projects which are closely related to the overall structure of the national economy, such as key energy, raw material industry bases, transprovincial communication and transportation networks, key mechanical, electronic, and other high-tech development projects, key agricultural bases as well as the national defense industry, are still financially controlled by the state; (2) the primary industrial and local projects, such as agriculture, forestry and wood, local energy, raw material industries, regional communication and transportation networks, mechanical and light industries, science and technology, education, culture, public health, urban public infrastructure and services and so on, are mainly managed by local government.

In the case of regional autonomy, the quotas of industrial construction and technological remolding items that needed to be approved by the State Planning Commission (SPC) were increased: from 30 million yuan or more to 50 million yuan or more for energy, communication, and raw materials industries; and from 10 million yuan or more to 30 million yuan or more for light and other industries (Yang, 1993, p. 179). Production of construction items and non-productive construction items beyond the above limits are to be determined by the provinces themselves.

Industrialization makes a direct contribution to economic development through an increase in income levels, job opportunities, exports, the availability of foreign capital and technology, and other related factors. In the newly industrialized economies (NIEs), industrialization has served as the key engine in the early period of economic take-off. Therefore, most developing nations (especially poor and agrarian nations) have placed great emphasis upon it. Economic development, the end result of industrialization, also determines the industrial structure of a country.[8] Increases in per capita income usually lead to increased consumption, which in turn shifts the industrial structure away from agriculture toward manufacturing and service sectors. This also determines the distribution of the labor force among the industries.

---

8. See Annex A for a quantitative comparison of the Chinese and international cases.

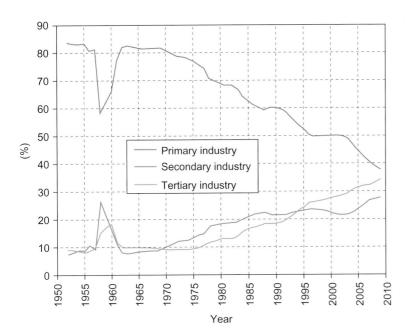

FIGURE 11.3 Employment by type of industry.

Over the course of the past decades, China's employment shares have changed significantly. In the early 1950s, more than 80 percent of China's labor force relied on the primary sector (i.e., agriculture), while less than 20 percent relied on either secondary or tertiary industry (shown in Figure 11.3). In 2010, the primary sector accounted for less than 40 percent of the total labor force. Regardless of the increasing shift toward secondary and tertiary industries, Chinese employment has still been dominated by primary industries, especially in the western provinces (such as Tibet, Yunnan, Guizhou, and Guangxi), with the exception of a few provinces whose employment is dominated by secondary industries (for example, Shanghai, Tianjin, and Liaoning) and tertiary industries (such as Beijing) in the coastal area.

11.2.2 Multiregional Differences

Industrialization in China differs considerably from region to region. As shown in Table 11.3, the average number of employees and the average size in fixed assets in the Eastern belt were 62.6 percent and 105.9 percent higher than those in the Central belt, and 249.2 percent and 292.6 percent higher than those in the Western belt, respectively. Also the capital/labor ratio, output/capital ratio and labor productivity in the Eastern belt were higher than those in the Central and Western belts. However, Table 11.3 shows that the profit/output and profit/capital ratios of the Western belt were the best among the three belts and that the Eastern belt had the lowest profit/output ratio and Central belt had the lowest profit/capital ratio.

In Annex B the effects of labor and capital on industrial performance are quantitatively tested for three geographical

TABLE 11.3 Differences in Industrialization of the Eastern, Central, and Western Belts

Item	Eastern Belt	Central Belt	Western Belt
Average size in fixed assets (million yuan)	7.87	5.98	7.53
Average number of employees (persons)	183.3	176.4	197.3
Capital/labor ratio (yuan/person)	4,29,196	3,39,031	3,81,680
Output/capital ratio	0.47	0.41	0.37
Labor productivity (yuan/person)	2,02,178	1,39,111	1,41,881
Profit/output ratio (%)	32.80	33.13	38.32
Profit/capital ratio (%)	15.45	13.60	14.25

Note: *For industrial enterprises under independent accounting system only.*
Source: Calculated by the author based on SSB (1996b, pp. 79–81).

belts. The estimated results show that: (1) capital's contribution to the industrial growth of the Western belt is larger than that of the Central belt, which is in turn larger than that of the Eastern belt, which suggests that the Western belt has the highest efficiency for capital input in large enterprises; (2) labor's contribution to the industrial growth of the Eastern belt is larger than that of the Central belt, and the latter is larger than that of the Western belt, which suggests that the Eastern belt has the highest efficiency for labor input.

From the perspective of the industrial sector, we observe that: (1) capital's contribution to industrial growth of the resource-exploiting enterprises is larger than that of the resource-processing enterprises, and the latter is larger than that of the high-tech enterprises, which suggests that the resource-exploiting enterprises have the highest efficiency for capital input in the large enterprises; (2) labor's contribution to industrial growth of the high-tech enterprises is larger than that of the resource-processing enterprises, and the latter is larger than that of the resource-exploiting enterprises, which suggests that the high-tech enterprises have the highest efficiency for labor input.

11.2.3 Rural Industrialization

In the early 1950s, almost 90 percent of the Chinese population lived in the countryside and earned their living from the land. During the period to the end of the 1990s, this proportion decreased gradually to two-thirds, although the total rural population increased during the same period. It is inevitable that the situation of a rapidly increasing rural population combined with limited cultivable land will generate a large rural labor surplus, particularly given the increased productivity that has resulted from the introduction of advanced technologies.

In 1978, more than 80 percent of the population in China still lived in rural areas. This resulted to a large extent from the long-standing government policy that exercised strict control over rural–urban migration. With little prospect for expanding cultivated land and a large and still growing population, the Chinese government began to recognize the urgency of shifting the rural labor force from farming to more productive non-agricultural sectors. In the following years, the rural population as a percentage of the total population in China experienced a substantial reduction as a result of industrial expansion. However, the government also remained convinced that this occupational shift must be achieved without significantly enlarging the urban population through rural–urban migration. Accordingly, the period since the 1970s has witnessed the implementation of the policy entitled 'litu bu lixiang, jinchang bu jincheng' (leave the soil but not the countryside, enter the factory but not the city).

The growth of the rural industrial sector has been extremely rapid and is largely responsible for the dramatic increases in income levels in rural China. Almost overnight, a large number of new industrial activities emerged and millions of private, shareholding, or other enterprises (PSEs) and collectively-owned enterprises (COEs) were established in the countryside. Of particular importance in this respect is the rapid growth of enterprises that are collectively owned and operated by the townships and villages. The proliferation of township- and village-based enterprises (TVEs) has had far-reaching consequences, because millions of rural workers have shifted from farming to industrial activities and in the process have helped to transform the economic structure of rural China.

The growth in the number of the TVEs in China is extraordinary.[9] The TVEs also created a large number of jobs for the surplus rural workers and contributed significantly to the growth of the Chinese economy during the 1980s and 1990s. Total factor productivity in the TVEs is much higher than in the state sector and is growing by 5 percent a year, more than twice the rate in the SOEs (World Bank, 1996, p. 51). The factors that have contributed to the remarkable growth and superior efficiency record of the TVEs include the following:

1. *Decentralization plus financial discipline.* The 1984 decentralization of fiscal power in China allowed subnational governments to retain locally generated revenues, creating powerful incentives for the development of local industry. Under this system a non-performing TVE becomes an unaffordable drain on a limited local budget. In the end persistent money-losers are closed and the workforce is transferred to more profitable lines.
2. *Competition.* Studies also show intense competition for investment (including foreign investment) among communities with TVEs. Success in attracting investment is affected by reputation and local economic performance.
3. *Market opportunities and rural saving.* A past bias against light industry and services has created vast market opportunities, buttressed by high rural savings and demand following the agricultural reforms of 1978 and by the limited scope for emigration from rural areas.
4. *Links with the state enterprise sector.* The large state-owned industrial sector provides a natural source of demand, technology, and raw materials for many TVEs.

Kinship and implicit property rights were characteristics of the TVEs. Strong kinship links among rural Chinese villagers, although encouraging responsibility in entrepreneurs, especially during the 1980s, have had potential risks thereafter since they do not exhibit the basic principles of market economic systems. The system of implicit, if fuzzy, property rights was improved compared to the people's commune system (PCS) of the pre-reform period and this led to a productive combination of risk and reward sharing between entrepreneurs and local government. However, the incentives facing TVEs are less than those of private firms. In addition, the proliferation of industrial activities in rural China stemming from rural reform created

---

9. In 1978, there were only 1.524 million TVEs in rural areas, whereas by 1995 the number of TVEs had increased dramatically to 22.027 million. Output has grown by over 30 percent per annum from 1978 to 1995; and the share of value-added output in GDP rose from about 10 percent in the early 1980s to more than 30 percent in 1995 (SSB, 1996, pp. 387–90).

numerous opportunities for China's rural population. The rural residents have seized these opportunities aggressively and shifted large amounts of resources from agricultural to more profitable non-agricultural activities. It appears that large amounts of 'surplus labor' existing in China have facilitated the rapid rural industrial development.

The problems that have emerged in the process of rural industrialization are, *inter alia*, the occupation of farmland by TVEs, the possible adverse effects of rural industrial production on agriculture, the waste of energy by TVEs, and environmental pollution.[10]

In the late 1990s, increasing institutional checks and balances increased the security of foreign investors, and FDI replaced the TVEs as a major driver of manufacturing growth (Winters and Yusuf, 2007, p. 29). A detailed analysis of the FDI and its contributions to the development of the Chinese economy is given in Chapter 13.

11.3 TECHNOLOGICAL PROGRESS

11.3.1 An Overview

Technological innovation has been the most fundamental element in the promotion, either directly or indirectly, of economic development and social change. Although it is very difficult to measure its short-term impact precisely, nobody would reject the notion that technological progress is changing the world at an incredible rate. The most obvious contribution is transport and communication that have changed from the primitive means (such as horses, carriages, and hand-written letters) to advanced methods such as super jets, telephones, and faxes, as well as the increasingly efficient computer networks, of which the Internet has become the most important means for transmitting information.

The mechanism of competition in securing technological leadership has been characterized by a leapfrogging process. Leapfrog is a game in which one player kneels or bends over while the next in line leaps over him or her. Economists have applied it to explain the international patterns of incremental technological change.[11] Theoretical and empirical analyses have concluded that, given their extensive experience with older technologies, leading nations may have no incentive to adopt new ideas; lagging nations, however, have less experience with the old technologies, and may grasp the opportunity to break into the market. If the new techniques eventually prove to be more productive than the old, there is a reversal of leadership.

When a new technology becomes available, however, it may not initially seem much better than the old one – and

to a nation that has established a commanding lead in the old technology, it may well seem worse. Thus eighteenth-century Holland, with its established lead in shipping, banking, and trading, was not attracted by the prospects of cotton spinning; it was the somewhat poorer English who moved into the new area and exploited its eventually far greater potential (Brezis et al., 1993, p. 1212). Such a failure to take advantage of new technologies may seem in retrospect like short-sightedness. In fact, however, it may have been an entirely rational decision from the point of view of individual entrepreneurs. A country with an established lead will be a high-wage nation; new technologies or industries that are initially less productive than the old one are therefore not profitable. It is only in a lagging nation, where the old technology is less well developed and hence wages are lower, that the new, relatively untried techniques seem attractive.

Such technological 'leapfrogging' could be essentially random: lagging countries may simply get lucky, leading countries may be unlucky. And, indeed, the divergent patterns could be explained, at least partially, by what has been noted in Landes (1966, p. 563): 'Prosperity and success are their own worst enemies.' However, the above situation does not exist in all circumstances. Brezis et al. (1993, p. 1219) give a number of conditions necessary for a leapfrogging process to occur:

(i) The difference in wage costs between the leading nation and potential challengers must be large.

(ii) The new technology must, when viewed by experienced producers, appear initially unproductive compared with the old one.

(iii) Experience in the old technology must not be too useful in the new technology.

(iv) The new technology must ultimately offer the possibility of substantial productivity improvement over the old.

Before the early twentieth century, technological innovations had been mainly developed by individual inventors or small-scale entrepreneurs. But now the great bulk of it – such as the invention of the space shuttle and the Internet, to list but two – has been conducted by prominent firms with substantial budgets, as well as by governments. As a result, the process of technological innovation becomes more complicated than ever before. Specifically, the technological and related products are positively related to capital stock of, and personnel engagement in, technological innovation. In addition, technological innovation is also related to educational level, as the content of education changes over time to accommodate the growing stock of knowledge. There has been a proliferation of specialized intellectual disciplines to facilitate the absorption of knowledge and to promote its development through research.

---

10. More details may be found in He et al. (1991, pp. 124–41).
11. Examples include Brezis et al. (1993), Jovanovic and Nyarko (1994), and Barro and Sala-i-Martin (1995, ch. 8).

11.3.2 China's Efforts on Innovation

China's ancient inventions, such as papermaking, gunpowder, movable-type printing, and the compass, have made enormous contributions to world civilization. For example, paper was introduced in China in the second century AD, came to Japan in the seventh century, and was then diffused westward to Central Asia in the eighth century, North Africa in the tenth, Spain in the twelfth and northern Europe in the thirteenth. Printing was invented in China in the eighth century AD and movable type in the eleventh century, but this technology only reached Europe in the fifteenth century. Another Chinese invention, gunpowder, made in the ninth century, disseminated to the Arabs after a few hundred years and reached Europe in the fourteenth century (Braudel, 1981, p. 14).

In recent centuries, however, China has lagged far behind Western nations in terms of industrialization and technological innovation. Regarding the causes of China's backward state in technological innovation, Lu Xun, a well-known writer, ironically noted that while Western nations used powder to make firearms and the compass for navigation, China used powder to make firecrackers for entertainment and the compass to align the spiritual location within the landscape (*fengshui*).

After the foundation of the PRC in 1949, China began to import advanced technology from the Soviet Union. Unfortunately, this process came to an abrupt halt following the deterioration of Sino-Soviet relations in the late 1950s. Following its *rapprochement* with the United States and Japan, China began the gradual importation of advanced technology from the capitalist nations. But economic relations between China and the technologically advanced nations did not improve significantly until the late 1970s when the new CCP and the state leaders tried to abandon the 'leftist' ideology (of self-reliance and independence). By the early 1980s, China's production technology in the iron and steel industry was only comparable to that of the advanced nations in the 1950s; similarly, the scientific and technological level of the electronic industry was approximately 15 to 20 years behind advanced international standards (Liao, 1982, p. 138).[12]

It must be noted that some important advances in science and technology had been achieved during the pre-reform period. Notable technological milestones include the development of the atomic bomb in 1964 and of artificial satellites in 1970, which granted China a political seat in the superpowers. However, as this kind of technology has been controlled by the Science and Technology Commission for National Defense (STCND) and guided by the State Council and the Military Commission of the CCPCC, the transfer of military technology to social and economic uses is to some extent limited. Other sectors of the economy, such as China's metallurgical, coal, machine-building, oil, chemical, power, electric and precision instrument industries, had acquired a stock of relatively advanced equipment. This provided the foundation for industrial modernization. Taken as a whole, however, the level of productivity still remained very low, as did the level of labor productivity.

For a considerable period of time, China followed an extensive development pattern and paid more attention to the construction of new industrial projects than to the renovation of old ones. It is often reported that outdated machinery and equipment is still used by many Chinese factories. Technologically outdated machinery and equipment implies low levels of labor productivity and high levels of energy consumption. In Table 11.4 the labor productivity in the Chinese steel, electricity, and petrochemical industries is shown to be only between 3 and 25 percent that of the advanced nations; while the energy consumption level of China is 16 to 100 percent higher than that found in advanced nations. The technologically outdated machinery and equipment also lead to the manufacture of poor quality products. According to the sample survey conducted by the State Technological Supervision Bureau in 1995, only 86.8 percent, 75.1 percent, and 24.2 percent of the commodities

TABLE 11.4 Some Industrial Production Indicators, China and the Advanced Nations

Item	Advanced Nations (1)	China (2)	(2)/(1) (3)
A. Labor productivity			
Steel (ton/person)	600–900	30	0.03–0.05
Electricity (kW/person)	2,132[a]	244	0.114
Synthetic rubber (ton/person)	200–300	20–50	0.067–0.25
Ethylene (ton/person)	150	30	0.2
B. Energy consumption[b]			
Steel (kg/ton)	629	1,034	1.64
Oil refinery (kg/ton)	19	22	1.16
Ethylene (1000 kal)	420–550	840	1.53–2.0
Electricity (g/kWh)	150	30	1.28

[a]USA
[b]Standard coal equivalent
Source: IIE (1996, p. 40).

---

12. According to the national industrial census conducted in 1985, 23 percent of the machines and equipment used by 8,285 large and medium-sized companies were produced during the period from 1949 to 1970 (SSB, 1987, p. 100).

of the SOEs, the TVEs, and the PSEs, respectively, had met national standards (Huang, 1996, p. 11).

The large number of small-scale plants, particularly those in the energy and heavy industries, contribute widely to this high level of energy consumption. In addition, the use of inefficient facilities and equipment has been encouraged by the country's low energy prices. In market economies, the energy price provides an incentive for the efficient production and use of energy resources. However, for a long period, especially during the pre-reform era, China's energy price was fixed at an artificially low level. These lower energy prices encouraged people to operate those facilities in ways that used more energy than they would have done if managers had taken account of the true cost of energy. This has resulted in the wasteful production of excess energy, idle factories and other facilities when sufficient energy is not available, and emission of more CO_2, SO_2, and other pollutants than necessary.

The Chinese economy has been regarded as very efficient in terms of energy consumption. As of 2004, China's energy intensity – a term that refers to the total primary energy consumption per dollar of GDP at market exchange rates – was 1.53 times that of India, 2.71 times that of South Korea, 4.26 times that of the USA, and 8.69 times that of Japan (EIA, 2006). If all of the above assumptions and projections hold up, China's oil consumption will increase continually and will account for an increasing proportion of global oil demand in the coming decades. This will place energy security at the top of China's economic agenda, and thus China will be more eager than ever before to compete and secure cheap and stable overseas energy supplies.

Research and development (R&D) refers to all activities related to fundamental research, applied research, and experimental development. In fact, Chinese policy makers clearly recognized the increasing role of technology in the Chinese economy and have also paid considerable attention to the acceleration of R&D. Since the mid-1980s, China has implemented a package of plans for the development of new technology, high technology and traditional technology. These plans include, *inter alia*:

- *The '863' Plan*, which aims to track the frontiers of the high and new technologies and research and development
- *The Torchlight Plan*, which aims to promote the commercialization, industrialization, and internationalization of the high-tech products
- *The Climbing Plan*, which aims to organize the research and application of new and high technologies
- *The Spark Plan*, which aims to spread applicable technologies to small and medium-sized enterprises, TVEs, and other rural areas
- *The Harvest Plan*, which aims to popularize various kinds of technology contributing to agriculture, animal husbandry and fishery.

However, many problems still exist in the Chinese science and technology sector, particularly during the 1990s. For example, China's R&D/GNP ratio declined rapidly alongside its GNP growth from the late 1980s to the mid-1990s. In 1995, China's expenditure on R&D was only 0.50 percent of GNP, compared with the R&D/GNP ratios of 0.93 percent in 1979 and 1.12 percent in 1986.[13] Minami (1994, p. 116) found that the R&D/GNP ratio rises sharply with respect to per capita GNP in developing countries when the per capita GNP is less than US$11,000 and in the newly industrialized economies (NIEs). However, this did not apply in the case of China in the years from the late 1980s to the mid-1990s.

Nevertheless, since the late 1990s, there have been continuous increases of government expenditure on R&D activities, with the R&D/GDP ratio having grown at the rate of about 0.1 percentage points per year. In 2009, for example, China's R&D/GDP ratio was already 1.7 percent (see Figure 11.4). Consequently, technological innovation has been accelerated significantly. Between 2001 and 2010, the patent office of China has seen the most dramatic increases in application levels (see Figure 11.5).

11.3.3 Institutional Constraints

Innovation has been the most fundamental element in promoting, either directly or indirectly, economic development and social change. In China, there were great thinkers such as Confucius, Mencius, Laozi, and Zhuangzi. But these achievements go back to the periods of the Spring and Autumn (770–476 BC) and of the Warring States (475–221 BC), and there has not been a similar breakthrough within the past 1,000 years. Throughout its history, Chinese culture has two obvious historical traits. One is that it had a very long period of feudalism. The second trait is that the Imperial Examination (*keju*) system – which had largely promoted creativity and academic development during the Tang (AD 618–907) and Song (AD 906–1279) dynasties – was widely recognized as too rigid and deeply entrenched during the following centuries.

In addition, the feudal period in Europe was shorter and was followed by over 200 years of the Renaissance (from the fourteenth to the sixteenth century AD), a revolutionary movement in intellectual thought and inventiveness spurred on by the call to revive the arts of classical Greece. The

---

13. Data sources: (1) SSB (1996, p. 661) for the 1995 data; (2) SSTC (1988, p. 267) for the 1986 data; (3) As Ma and Sun (1981, p. 614) estimate that China's R&D expenses were 0.54 percent of GVIAO in 1979, using the estimated GVIAO/GNP ratio (0.5799) in Equation 9.3 of Chapter 9, we can obtain an approximation of the R&D/GNP ratio (0.54/0.5799≈0.93). According to UNESCO (1995, tab. 5), the R&D/GNP ratio of China was much lower than that of many advanced countries, including the USA (2.9 percent, 1988), Japan (3.0 percent, 1991), France (2.4 percent, 1991), and the UK (2.1 percent, 1991).

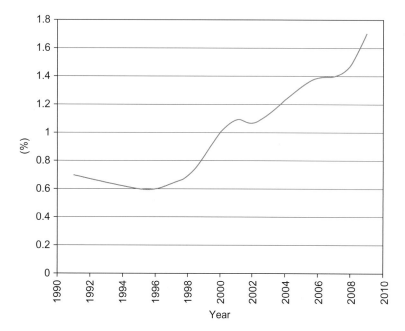

FIGURE 11.4 China's R&D/GDP ratios. *Source: NBS, 2010.*

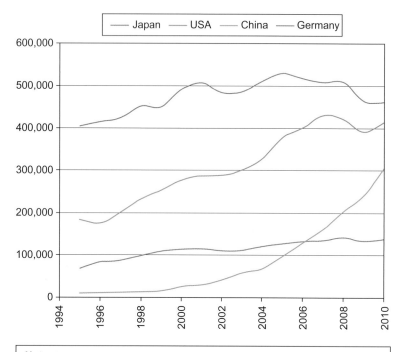

FIGURE 11.5 Patent applications by selected countries (1995–2010). *Source: WIPO (2011).*

Note: Counts are based on the patent filing date. Country of origin is the residence of the first-named applicant (or assignee). Data by origin might be incomplete.

Enlightenment and the Industrial Revolution that followed caused a tumultuous transformation in Europe. Shaking off its feudal shackles in ideology and social systems, Europe created a brave new world for itself. Under such circumstances, Europe produced many new creations and inventions in the realms of art, science, music, architecture, and so on. Over the course of the past 200 years, the United States has attracted many high caliber immigrants and provided very favorable conditions for creativity and inventiveness, making it the world's only present-day superpower.

11.4 INTELLECTUAL PROPERTY RIGHTS

11.4.1 General Situation

Historically, intellectual property rights (IPR) was not a serious topic in Chinese society. As a result, copyright violations were common, and intellectual property violations were even committed by prominent members. This can be witnessed in Lu Xun's story '*Kong Yiji*' in which there is an aphorism, 'to steal a book is an elegant offense' (*qieshu bushuan tou*). The enforcement of protection of IPR is difficult in China. Without adequate education, there is little awareness that infringement is a crime.

Since the early 1980s, China has acceded to various major international conventions on protection of IPR. In 1980, the PRC became a member of the World Intellectual Property Organization (WIPO). It has patterned its IPR laws on the Berne Convention for the Protection of Literary and Artistic Works and the Agreement on Trade-Related Aspects of Intellectual Property Rights (TRIPS). China acceded to the Paris Convention for the Protection of Industrial Property on November 14, 1984, and to the Madrid Agreement for the International Registration of Trademarks in June 1989. In January 1992, China entered into a Memorandum of Understanding with the United States government to provide copyright protection for all American 'works' and for other foreign works. At the conclusion of a series of negotiations in 1995, the Sino-US Agreement on Intellectual Property Rights was signed. In June 1996, the two governments reached another agreement protecting American intellectual property in the PRC.

The legal framework for protecting intellectual property in China is built on three national laws passed by the National People's Congress (NPC):

- Patent law, which was enacted in 1984 and has been amended in 1992 and 2000 to extend the scope of protection (the latest amendment extended the duration of patent protection to 20 years from the date of filing a patent application).
- Trademark law, which was first adopted in 1982 and subsequently revised in 1993 and 2001, with implementing regulations taking effect on September 15, 2002 (the new trademark law extended registration to collective marks, certification marks, and three-dimensional symbols, as required by TRIPS).
- Copyright law, which was established in 1990 and amended in October 2001, with the new implementing rules coming into force on September 15, 2002.

At the same time, a great number of regulations, rules, measures, and policies have been made by the NPC Standing Committee, the State Council and various commissions, ministries, and bureaux. The circulars, opinions, and notices of the Supreme People's Court also form part of the legal framework. All this has led to the creation of a comprehensive legal framework to protect both local and foreign intellectual property.

To enforce IPR protection, an administrative system has been established within the government. After the reshuffle of the State Council in March 1998, the Patent Office became part of the State Intellectual Property Office (SIPO). The Trademarks Office is still under the authority of the State Administration for Industry and Commerce (SAIC). The Copyright Office falls within the State Administration for Press and Publication (SAPP). A similar system exists at various levels of local government.

Commonly, enforcement of IPR will be carried out by local IPR personnel, assisted by police from the local Public Security Bureau (PSB).

To handle cases of infringement of IPR more efficiently, special intellectual property courts have been established in some cities and provinces. At the level of the Higher People's Court in Beijing, Shanghai, Guangdong, Fujian, and Hainan, intellectual property courts have been separated from the economic division. Beijing, Shanghai, and Tianjin have also established intellectual property courts within the Intermediate People's Court. In 1992, the Supreme People's Court also established an intellectual property division.

11.4.2 Unresolved Problems

Even though the first intellectual property law was drafted in 1982, the first IPR training center wasn't established until 1996. In 1998, China established the SIPO, with the vision that it would coordinate China's IP enforcement efforts by merging the patent, trademark, and copyright offices under one authority. However, this has yet to occur. Today, SIPO is responsible for granting patents (national office), registering semiconductor layout designs (national office), and enforcing patents (local SIPO offices), as well as coordinating domestic foreign-related IPR issues involving copyrights, trademarks, and patents. Sometimes local protectionism may dilute the strength of central legislation or the power of law enforcement. For example, local governments might not want to genuinely support the work of anti-piracy supervisors. They may create obstacles during IPR investigation and assist local counterfeiters by letting them hide their production lines in safer places. When counterfeiters have good connections with local governmental or law enforcement officials, they may find an umbrella for their counterfeiting activity (Priest, 2006).

Since joining the World Trade Organization (WTO), China has strengthened its legal framework and amended its IPR and related laws and regulations to comply with the WTO Agreement on TRIPS. Despite stronger statutory protection, China continues to be a haven for counterfeiters and pirates.[14] Though we have observed commitment on the part of many central government officials to tackling the problem, enforcement measures taken to date have not been sufficient to deter massive IPR infringements effectively.

There are several factors that undermine enforcement measures, including China's reliance on administrative instead of criminal measures to combat IPR infringements,

---

14. According to one copyright industry association, the piracy rate in China remains one of the highest in the world (over 90 percent) and US companies lose over one billion dollars in legitimate business each year to piracy. On average, 20 percent of all consumer products in the Chinese market are counterfeit (ITA, 2003).

TABLE 11.5 Industrialization at Different Economic Stages, Chinese and International Cases

Variable	International Case[a]			Chinese Case[b]		
	US$100 (1)	US$400 (2)	(2)–(1) (3)	¥250 (4)	¥1000 (5)	(5)–(4) (6)
Va	0.452	0.228	−0.224	0.513	0.196	−0.317
Vm	0.149	0.276	0.127	0.276	0.584	0.308
Vl				0.118	0.282	0.164
Vh				0.164	0.303	0.139
Lp	0.658	0.438	−0.220	0.892	0.462	−0.431
Lm	0.091	0.135	0.144	0.041	0.323	0.282
Ls	0.251	0.327	0.076	0.067	0.215	0.149

[a]Chenery and Syrquin (1975, pp. 20–1).
[b]Hsueh (1994b, p. 80).
Variables: Va = ratio of value-added agricultural output in NI (national income); Vm = ratio of value-added industrial output in NI; Vl = ratio of value-added light industrial output in NI; Vh = ratio of value-added heavy industrial output in NI; Lp = ratio of labor of primary sector to total social labor; Lm = ratio of labor of manufacturing sector to total social labor; and Ls = ratio of labor of service sector to total social labor.

local protectionism at provincial levels, and lack of public education regarding the economic and social impact of counterfeiting and piracy.

ANNEX

A. An International Comparison of Industrialization

In order to conduct an international comparison of China's industrial performance during the post-reform period, one may simply employ the results estimated by Hsueh (1994, pp. 74–99) for China and the results estimated by Chenery and Syrquin (1975, pp. 20–1) for the international case. Both results are based on the same specification shown below:

$$X = \alpha + \beta_1 \ln Y + \beta_2 (\ln Y)^2 + \gamma_1 \ln N + \gamma_2 (\ln N)^2 + \sum (\delta_i T_i) \quad (11.1)$$

where X denotes each of the variables shown in the first column of Table 11.5; Y is the per capita national income (RMB yuan) at 1980 constant prices in the case of China and per capita GNP (US dollar) in the case of other countries; N is population size (million persons); and T_i denotes the time period. In Hsueh's analysis, two periods (i.e., 1980–84 and 1985–89) were selected. Arguably this is reasonable, because the year 1985 was generally regarded as a watershed for China's HRS-based agricultural reform and its urban industrial reform, while it was the latter that significantly influenced industrialization. For most provinces, per capita national income ranged between ¥250 and ¥1,000 during the 1980s, which can be converted

approximately to the per capita GNP of US$100 to US$400 for the international case during the period 1950 to 1970 in the analysis by Chenery and Syrquin (1975).

From Table 11.5, we find that the industrial structure of China was similar to that found in many other countries. For both versions, the ratios of value-added agricultural output were in decline, while those of industrial output were increasing. However, the only difference is that China had larger marginal changes in industrial structure with respect to economic growth than the international version. For example, when the per capita GNP ranged from US$100 to US$400, the changes of the ratio of value-added agricultural output and the ratio of value-added industrial output in GNP were −0.224 and 0.127, respectively, for the international case; while the changes of the ratio of value-added agricultural output and the ratio of value-added industrial output in national income for the Chinese case were −0.317 and 0.308, respectively, during approximately the same development stage.

Furthermore, when the per capita national income increased from 250 yuan to 1,000 yuan, the ratio of value-added light industrial output and the ratio of value-added heavy industrial output in national income increased by 0.164 and 0.139, respectively, implying that light industry served as a stronger engine in the Chinese economy than heavy industry. In Table 11.5, when the per capita national income increased from 250 yuan to 1,000 yuan, the ratio of value-added agricultural output in national income decreased from 0.513 to 0.196, and the ratio of primary sector labor to total social labor decreased from 0.892 to 0.462 accordingly; in contrast, when the per capita national income increased from 250 yuan to 1,000 yuan, the ratio of value-added industrial output to national income increased from 0.276 to 0.584, while the ratio of labor of the industrial sector to total social labor increased from 0.041 to 0.323 accordingly.

B. A Multiregional Production Function

In order to conduct an in-depth comparison of industrial performances between different regions, we may build a multiregional production function. The general form of a Cobb–Douglas function can be written as $Y = e^{\lambda}K^{\alpha}L^{\beta}e^{u}$, where, Y=output, K=capital, L=labor, α=elastic coefficient of capita, β=elastic coefficient of labor, λ=factor of technological progress, and μ=system error.

If we use a regional variable, D_1 (where, $D_1 = -1$ denotes the Western belt, $D_1 = 0$ denotes the Central belt, and $D_1 = 1$ denotes the Eastern belt) and a sectoral variable, D_2 (where $D_2 = -1$ denotes the resource-exploiting enterprises, $D_2 = 0$ denotes the resource-processing enterprises, and $D_2 = 1$ denotes the high-tech enterprises), the modified Cobb–Douglas production function may be written in the log form:

$$\ln Y = \lambda_0 + (\alpha_0 + \alpha_1 D_1 + \alpha_2 D_2)\ln K \\ + (\beta_0 + \beta_1 D_1 + \beta_2 D_2)\ln L \quad (11.2)$$

where, λ_0, α_0, α_1, α_2, β_0, β_1, β_2 are constants to be estimated. Using the data of 500 top industrial enterprises compiled by CEEC (1990), we obtain a log-form regression:[15]

$$\ln Y = 6.87 + (0.50 - 0.02 D_1 - 0.17 D_2)\ln K \\ (10.11)(-4.53)(-2.40) \\ + (-0.10 + 0.03 D_1 + 0.09 D_2)\ln L \quad (11.3) \\ (-17.0)(4.94)(2.51)$$

$$(N = 500, R^2 = 0.76, F = 1\,94.98)$$

where ln represents a natural logarithm, R^2 is a multiple correlation coefficient, F is the F-statistic and the figures in parentheses under the parameters are the t statistics. Using Equation 11.3, we may obtain the elasticities of capital (K) and labor (L) on production for each geographical belt and industrial sector:

(1) Eastern belt (D1 = 1):
Resource-exploiting sector (D2=−1): K=0.64; L= −0.23
Resource-processing sector (D2=0): K=0.48; L= −0.07
High-tech sector (D2=1): K=0.31; L=0.02

(2) Central belt (D1=0):
Resource-exploiting sector (D2=−1): K=0.66; L= −0.30
Resource-processing sector (D2=0): K=0.50; L= −0.10
High-tech sector (D2=1): K=0.33; L=−0.01

(3) Western belt (D1=−1):
Resource-exploiting sector (D2=−1): K=0.68; L= −0.32
Resource-processing sector (D2=0): K=0.51; L= −0.13
High-tech sector (D2=1): K=0.35; L=−0.04

Note that since the labor elasticity is negative for all enterprises, with the exception of high-tech enterprises in the Eastern belt of China, this implies that China's industrial enterprises have experienced some problems in relation to labor productivity during the 1980s (from which the data are collected).

REFERENCES

Barro, R. J., & Sala-i-Martin, X. (1995). *Economic growth*. New York: McGraw-Hill.

Bo, Y. (1991). *A retrospect of some key decisions and incidents of China* [ruogan zongda juece yu shijian de huigu] (Vol. 1). Beijing: The CCPCC Literature Press.

Braudel, F. (1981). *The structure of everyday life, civilization and capitalism 15–18th century* (Vol. 1). New York: Harper and Row.

Brezis, E., Krugman, P., & Tsiddon, D. (1993). Leapfrogging in international competition: a theory of cycles in national technological leadership. *American Economic Review, 83*(3), 1211–1219.

CEEC (China Enterprise Evaluation Center) (1990). *China's Top 500 enterprises*. Beijing: Development Research Center of the State Council.

Chen, G. (1994). *China's regional economic development: a comparative study of the east, central, and west belts* [zhongguo quyu jingji fazhan: dongbu zhongbu he xibu de bijiao yanjiu]. Beijing: Beijing University of Technology Press.

Chenery, H., & Syrquin, M. (1975). *Patterns of development, 1950–1970*. New York: Oxford University Press.

Dong, F. (1982). Relationship between accumulation and consumption. In D. Xu (Ed.), *China's search for economic growth: the Chinese economy since 1949* (pp. 79–101). Beijing: New World Press.

EIA (Economist Intelligence Agency) (2006). *International energy outlook 2006*. London: Economist Intelligence Agency.

He, B., Gu, R., Yan, Y., & Bao, Z. (1991). *Studies on the non-agricultural development in Jiangsu's rural area* [jiangsu nongcun feinonghua yanjiu]. Shanghai: Shanghai People's Press.

Hsueh, T. (1994). The regional economic development pattern in China and its international comparison [zhongguo diqu jingji fazhan de xingtai, jianyu guoji jian de biaojiao]. In S. Liu, Q. Li, & T. Hsueh (Eds.), *Studies on China's regional economic development [zhongguo diqu jingji yanjiu]* (pp. 74–99). Beijing: China Statistics Publishing House.

Hu, A., Wang, S., & Kang, X. (1995). *Regional disparities in China* [zhonguo diqu chayi baogao]. Shenyang: Liaoning People's Press.

Huang, W. (1996). *The hidden economy in China* [zhongguo de yinxing jingji] (2nd ed.). Beijing: China Commercial Press.

Institute of Industrial Economics (1996). *China's industrial development report* [zhongguo gongye fazhan baogao]. Beijing: The Economics and Management Press.

ITA (2003). *Protecting your Intellectual Property Rights (IPR) in China: a practical guide for U.S.* U.S. Department of Commerce, International Trade Administration (ITA). Available at <www.mac.

15. The units used are yuan for Y and K and person for L.

doc.gov/china/docs/businessguides/intellectualpropertyrights.htm>. Accessed on November 11, 2011.

Jao, J. C., & Leung, C. K. (Eds.). (1986). *China's special economic zones: policies, problems and prospects*. Oxford: Oxford University Press.

Jovanovic, B., & Nyakro, Y. (1994). *The Bayesian foundations of learning by doing*. New York University. unpublished paper.

Landes, D. (1966). Technological change and development in western Europe, 1750–1914. In H. Habakkuk & M. Posten (Eds.), *The Cambridge economic history of Europe* (Vol. 6). Cambridge: Cambridge University Press.

Lardy, N. R. (1978). *Economic growth and income distribution in the People's Republic of China*. New York: Cambridge University Press.

Leung, C. K. (1980). *China: railway patterns and national goals*. Department of Geography, The University of Chicago. Research Paper no. 195.

Liang, W. (1982). Balanced development of industry and agriculture. In D. Xu (Ed.), *China's search for economic growth: the Chinese economy since 1949* (pp. 152–178). Beijing: New World Press.

Liao, J. (1982). Size of industrial enterprises operation and choice of technology. In D. Xu (Ed.), *China's search for economic growth: the Chinese economy since 1949* (pp. 130–144). Beijing: New World Press.

Liu, S. (1982). Economic planning. In D. Xu (Ed.), *China's search for economic growth: the Chinese economy since 1949* (pp. 28–51). Beijing: New World Press.

Liu, Z. (1983). *On the construction of the third-front area* [lun shanxian jianshe]. Beijing: Department of Planning and Statistics, The People's University of China.

Mao, Z. (1956; 1975). On the ten major relations. In *Selected works of Mao Tse-tung* (Vol. 5). Beijing: Foreign Languages Press.

Maruyama, N. (1982). The mechanism of China's industrial development: background to the shift in development strategy. *The Developing Economies*, 20, 437–471.

Meadows, D. H., Meadows, D. I., & Randers, J. (1972). *Limits to growth: a report of the club of Rome's project on the predicament of mankind*. Rome: the Club of Rome.

Meadows, D. H., Meadows, D. I., & Randers, J. (1992). *Beyond the limits: confronting global collapse, envisioning a sustainable future*. Post Hills, VT: Chelsea Green Publishing Company.

Naughton, B. (1988). The third front: defense industrialization in the Chinese interior. *China Quarterly*, 115, 227–304.

NBS. (various years). *China statistical yearbook*, various issues. Beijing: China Statistics Publishing House.

Priest, E. (2006). The future of music and film piracy in China. *Berkeley Technology Law Journal*, 795(21), 796–870.

Riskin, C. (1987). *China's political economy: the quest for development since 1949*. Oxford: Oxford University Press.

SSB (1987). *Materials of the 1985 industry census in the People's Republic of China* [zhonghua renmin gonghe guo 1985 nian gongye pucha zhiliao]. Beijing: China Statistics Publishing House.

SSB (1990). *A compilation of historical statistical materials of China's provinces, autonomous regions and municipalities (1949–89)*. [quanguo ge sheng, zizhiqu, zhixiashi lishi tongji zhiliao huibian 1949–1989]. Beijing: China Statistics Publishing House.

SSB (1996). *China industrial economic statistical yearbook 1995*. Beijing: China Statistics Publishing House.

State Science and Technology Commission (1988). *Guide to China's science and technology policy* [zhongguo kexue jishu zhengce zhinan]. Beijing: Science and Technology Compilation Press.

Winters, L. A., & Yusuf, S. (2007). Introduction: dancing with giants Winters Yusuf (Eds.), *Dancing with giants: China, India, and the global economy* (pp. 1–34). Washington, DC: World Bank Publications.

World Bank (1996). *From plan to market: World Bank Development report 1996*. New York: Oxford University Press.

Yang, K. (1989). *A study of regional development in China* [zhongguo quyu fazhan yanjiu]. Beijing: China Ocean Press.

Yang, K. (1993). *For a spatial integration: China's market economy and regional development strategy* [maixiang kongjian yiti hua: zhongguo shichang jingji yu quyu fazhan zhanlue], 'Across the Century Series'. Chengdu: Sichuan People's Press.

Chapter 12

International Economic Engagement

The ruins of an ancient watchtower, located in Dunhuang, Gansu province. *Copyright © The Real Bear, January 27, 2008*

The Silk Road (Silu) is the most well-known trading route in ancient China. Trade in silk grew under the Han dynasty (202 BC–AD 220) during which the Chinese traded silk for medicines, perfumes, and slaves, in addition to precious stones. The Silk Road was an important path for cultural, commercial, and technological exchange between traders, merchants, pilgrims, missionaries, soldiers, nomads, and urban dwellers from different parts of the world. Trade on the Silk Road was a significant factor in the development of the great civilizations of India, China, Egypt, Persia, Arabia, and Rome, and in several respects helped lay the foundations for the modern world. During the Tang dynasty, trade along the Silk Road had declined. It revived tremendously during the eleventh and twelfth centuries when China became largely dependent on its silk trade. In addition, trade to Central and Western Asia as well as Europe recovered for a period of time from 1276–1368 under the Yuan dynasty when the Mongols controlled China. As overland trade became increasingly dangerous, and overseas trade became more popular, trade along the Silk Road declined...

Understanding the Chinese Economies. DOI: http://dx.doi.org/10.1016/B978-0-12-397826-4.00012-3
© 2013 Elsevier Inc. All rights reserved.

A frog that lived in a shallow well said to a turtle coming from the East Sea: 'I am so happy! When I go out, I jump about on the railing beside the mouth of the well, and I rest in the holes on the broken wall of the well when I come home. If I jump into the water, it comes up to my armpits and holds up my cheeks. If I walk in the mud, it covers up my feet. I look around at the wriggly worms, crabs, and tadpoles and none of them can compare with me. Moreover, I am lord of this trough of water and I stand up tall in this shallow well. My happiness is full. Why wouldn't you come here often and look around my place?'[1]

– Zhuangzi (c. 369–286 BC)

12.1 HISTORICAL REVIEW

12.1.1 How Autarkic Was China?

For thousands of years, Chinese culture, which aims at achieving a harmonious balance between Confucianism, Buddhism, and Taoism, had worked quite well for a very long time. Probably as a result, the Chinese were too intoxicated with its past prosperity and still had proudly treated themselves at the 'center of the world' even when it was clear that in both economic and technological terms the 'central kingdom' (zhongguo) had lagged well behind those barbarians in the Western world. This kind of ethnocentrism and self-satisfaction meant that China remained a typical autarkic society. With regards to the cultural differences between the Chinese and Japanese economies, Maddison (1996, p. 53) states:

In China, the foreigners appeared on the fringes of a huge country. The ruling elite regarded it as the locus of civilization, and considered the 'barbarian' intruders as an irritating nuisance. In Japan, they struck in the biggest city, humiliated the Shogun and destroyed his legitimacy as a ruler. The Japanese had already borrowed important elements of Chinese civilization and saw no shame in copying a Western model which had demonstrated its superior technology so dramatically.

Indeed, China had been a typical autarkic society for a long time before it was forced to open up to the outside world at the end of the First Opium War (1840–42). In the later period of the Qing dynasty (AD 1644–1911), there was a *haijin* (ban on maritime voyages) which included the following:

1. The export of cereals and five metals (gold, silver, copper, iron, and tin) were strictly prohibited.
2. Private trade and contacts between Chinese and foreign business people were illegal.
3. Foreigners' activities in China were only allowed on the conditions that 'at most ten foreigners may take a walk together near their hotel on the 8th, 18th, and 28th days a month', 'overseas businessmen should not stay in Guangdong in winter', and 'women from foreign countries are prohibited to enter this country'.
4. Chinese businessmen going abroad were subject to the conditions that 'at most one liter of rice may be carried by a seaman a day' and 'at most two guns may be installed in a ship'.
5. Manufacture of seagoing vessels of more than 500 *dan* (hectoliters) in weight and eight meters in height was prohibited.[2]

12.1.2 External Influences

Western influence in China came about at the beginning of the fifteenth and sixteenth centuries due to the increased trade in Chinese products, such as silk and tea, through the Silk Road that stretched from northwestern China to Eastern Europe. The Europeans were interested in Hong Kong's safe harbor located on the trade routes of the Far East, thus establishing a trade enterprise between Western businessmen and China. The Portuguese were the first to reach China in 1555, but the British dominated foreign trade in the southern region of Guangdong during the early stages of Western connection in China. Ships from the British East India Company were stationed on the Indian Coast after Emperor Kangxi (reign 1654–1722) of the Qing dynasty (1644–1911) opened trade on a limited basis in Guangzhou. Fifteen years later, the company was allowed to build a storage warehouse outside Guangzhou. The Westerners were given limited preferences and had to adhere to many Chinese rules and policies. In addition, Chinese rulers also banned foreigners from learning the Chinese language for fear of their potential bad influences.

Chinese commodities, principally porcelains, were popular among European aristocrats. However, the levels of European imports from China were far greater than its exports. As a result, the British East India Company tried to equalize its huge purchases from China by doubling its sales of opium to China. The sale of opium saw a great increase by the turn of the nineteenth century. Fearful of the outflow of silver, the Chinese emperor banned the drug trade in 1799 but to no avail. Following the end of the first Opium War, the Treaty of Nanjing in 1842 ceded Hong Kong to Britain in perpetuity. With the involvement of the British, many companies transferred from Guangzhou to Hong Kong, enabling the British colony to begin a prime Asian entrepôt. Hostilities between the British and the Chinese of China continued to heighten, leading to the Second Opium War. In 1860, under the 'Convention of Peking', Britain gained Kowloon, Stonecutters Island, and some other small islands.

---

1. To be continued at the end of this chapter.

2. Cited from *Guangxu Da Qing Huidian Shili* (vol. 775, p. 4 and vol. 776, p. 13).

Since the middle of the nineteenth century, the Chinese economy has been transformed as a result of the gradual destruction of the feudal system. There was a gradual flow of foreign capital into the mainland, which was followed by the penetration of Western culture, which represented the first stirrings of Chinese industrialization. Unfortunately, because of long civil wars as well as the invasion by the Japanese, China's economic development had not been given a high priority during the first half of the twentieth century. During the period of the first Five-Year Plan (1953–57), some economic progress was achieved. Thereafter, however, difficulties arose due to China's frequent domestic political struggles and the 'closed-door' policies towards both the US-dominated capitalist bloc and the USSR-dominated socialist bloc.

As soon as the PRC was founded on October 1, 1949, the Chinese government severed almost all economic ties with the capitalist world. Affected by the Korean War (1950–53) and the Taiwan Strait crisis, the Eastern belt stagnated, in comparison with most parts of the Western belt – which benefited geographically to a large extent from China's close relations with the former USSR. However, it should be noted that China's foreign trade with the centrally planned economies (CPEs) usually remained at a minimum level, aiming at just supplementing any gap between domestic supply and demand. Such trade reflected natural resource endowments more than anything else. Therefore, China's close ties with the socialist economies did not result in significant economic effects on the Western belt. During the period from the early 1960s to the late 1970s, China practiced autarkic socialism as a result of the Sino-USSR disputes as well as the implementation of the 'self-reliance and independence' strategy thereafter.

12.2 TOWARD AN OPEN ECONOMY

12.2.1 China Opens its Door

For a long period after the foundation of the PRC in 1949, the Chinese economy was characterized as a closed economy. China's external economic strategy began to experience dramatic changes in the late 1970s when the top Chinese policy makers suddenly found that the Chinese economy, having been constructed along socialist lines for almost 30 years, had lagged far behind not only the Western nations but also those once-ever undeveloped economies along the western coast of the Pacific Ocean.

In order to attract foreign investment, China enacted, in 1979, the 'Law of the People's Republic of China Concerning the Joint Ventures with Chinese and Foreign Investment'. Also in this year, the CCPCC and State Council decided to grant Guangdong and Fujian provinces 'special policies and flexible measures' in foreign economic affairs. On December 26, 1979, the People's Congress of Guangdong province approved the proposal of the provincial government that a part of Shenzhen next to Hong Kong, Zhuhai next to Macau, and Santou should all be permitted to experiment with a market-oriented economy with Chinese characteristics, namely, special economic zones (SEZs). This proposal was finally accepted by the NPC on August 26, 1980. At the same time, Xiamen in Southeast Fujian province, with its close proximity to Taiwan, also became an SEZ with the approval of the NPC.

Subsequently, Guangdong and Fujian gained substantial autonomy in developing their regions as the central government granted them authority to pursue reform 'one step ahead' (*xian zhou yibu*). As a result, not only did these areas enjoy lower tax rates, but they also gained more authority over economic development. The four cities are below the provincial level, but have independent budget agreements with the central government; they have the authority to approve foreign investment projects up to US$30 million, while other regions' authority remained much lower.

Thereafter, a series of open-door measures were implemented in the coastal area: in October 1983, Hainan island, Guangdong province, was allowed to conduct some of the special foreign economic policies granted to the SEZs; in April 1984, 14 coastal cities (Tianjin, Shanghai, Dalian, Qinhuangdao, Yantai, Qingdao, Lianyungang, Nantong, Ningbo, Wenzhou, Fuzhou, Guangzhou, Ganjiang, and Beihai) were designated by the CCPCC and the State Council as 'open cities'; in February 1985, the three deltas of the Yangtze River, the Pearl River, and South Fujian were approved as coastal economic development zones (EDZs); in March 1988, the expansion of the EDZs of all three deltas was again approved, while at the same time some cities and counties in Liaodong and Shandong peninsulas and the Bohai Basin area were allowed to open up economically to the outside world; in April 1988, the NPC approved the establishment of Hainan province which was organized as an SEZ with even more flexible policies than other SEZs; in April 1990, Shanghai's suggestion to speed up the development of Pudong area using some of the SEZ's mechanisms was approved by the CCPCC and the State Council.

In addition to its 14,500 km coastline, China has more than 22,000 km of international land boundaries. Specifically, nine provinces are directly exposed to the outside world. These frontier provinces, the neighboring nations, and the lengths of their respective borderlines are detailed below:

- Gansu (with Mongolia, 65 km)
- Guangxi (with Vietnam, 1,020 km)
- Heilongjiang (with Russia, 3,045 km)
- Inner Mongolia (with Mongolia, 3,640 km; and Russia, 560 km)
- Jilin (with North Korea, 870 km; and Russia, 560 km)
- Liaoning (with North Korea, 546 km)

- Tibet (with India, 1,906 km; Nepal, 1,236 km; Bhutan, 470 km; and Myanmar, 188 km)
- Xinjiang (with Russia, 40 km; Mongolia, 968 km; Pakistan, 523 km; Kazakhstan, 1,533 km; Kyrgyzstan, 858 km; Tajikistan, 540 km; Afghanistan, 76 km; and India, 1,474 km)
- Yunnan (with Myanmar, 1,997 km; Laos, 710 km; and Vietnam, 1,353 km)

12.2.2 WTO Membership

China was one of the 23 original signatories of the General Agreement on Tariffs and Trade (GATT) in 1948. After China's revolution in 1949, the government in Taiwan announced that China would leave the GATT system. Although the government in Beijing never recognized this withdrawal decision, only nearly 40 years later, in 1986, did China notify GATT of its wish to resume its status as a GATT contracting party.

China's process of resumption of its GATT status and, later, of its accession to the World Trade Organization (WTO) has been guided by a Working Party whose membership consists of all interested WTO member governments. Because the Working Party makes decisions by consensus, China must be in agreement with all WTO members in that their individual concerns have been met and that all outstanding issues have been resolved in the course of their deliberations. While several areas of China's trade policies (i.e., schedules of market-access commitments in goods and specific commitments on services) have been the focus of bilateral and multilateral negotiations, it was the responsibility of the Working Party to maintain an overview of how the negotiations were progressing and to ensure that all aspects of China's trade policies were addressed.

As a result of the long negotiations, on December 11, 2001, China became the 143rd member of the WTO at the Fourth Ministerial Conference of the World Trade Organization (WTO) held in Doha, Qatar. As a precondition to entering the WTO, China accepted some restrictive clauses, one of which was that China's market economy status (MES) could not be automatically granted worldwide. In order to accede to the WTO, China agreed to take concrete steps to remove trade barriers and open up its markets to foreign companies and their exports in virtually every product sector and for a wide range of services as represented in the Protocol of Accession of the People's Republic of China (Document No. WT/L/432, 2001). Among some of the commitments undertaken by China are the following:[3]

- China will provide non-discriminatory treatment to all WTO Members. All foreign individuals and enter-

prises, including those not invested or registered in China, will be accorded treatment no less favorable than that accorded to enterprises in China with respect to the right to trade.
- China will eliminate dual pricing practices as well as differences in treatment accorded to goods produced for sale in China in comparison to those produced for export.
- Price controls will not be used for purposes of affording protection to domestic industries or services providers.
- The WTO Agreement will be implemented by China in an effective and uniform manner by revising its existing domestic laws and enacting new legislation fully in compliance with the WTO Agreement.
- Within three years of accession all enterprises will have the right to import and export all goods and trade them throughout the customs territory with limited exceptions.
- China will not maintain or introduce any export subsidies on agricultural products.

With China's consent, the WTO created a special multilateral mechanism for the purpose of reviewing China's compliance on an annual basis. Known as the Transitional Review Mechanism, this mechanism operates annually for eight years after China's accession, with a final review by the tenth year (see Box 12.1). The WTO membership will give China an improved external environment under which the import of new technologies and capital inflows have given a boost to China's industry. Exports have also been growing faster as China has been less strictly bound by trade quotas. For the first time in the last few decades China no longer needs to be concerned about the annual renewal of its most-favored nation (MFN) status by the US Congress. Furthermore, in accordance with WTO requirements, banks, insurance companies, telecommunications, and other service industries of the rest of the world will be allowed to operate in China according to the negotiated timetable. The impact may eventually break up the status of monopoly and state control that have existed in China for around half a century. In the long run the impact on social and political reforms can be highly significant.

While China will reserve the right of exclusive state trading for products such as cereals, tobacco, fuels, and minerals and maintain some restrictions on transportation and distribution of goods inside the country, many of the restrictions that foreign companies have at present in China will be eliminated or considerably eased after a 3-year phase-out period. In other areas, like the protection of intellectual property rights, China will implement the TRIPS (Trade-related Aspects of Intellectual Property Rights) Agreement in full from the date of accession. During a 12-year period starting from the date of accession there will be a special

---

3. Cited from http://www.wto.org/english/news_e/pres01_e/pr243_e.htm. Accessed on November 11, 2011.

Box 12.1   China's Quest for Market Economy Status

Like many of the countries that have been applying for WTO membership, China is in the process of implementing economic reforms and transforming its economy into one which is more market-based. Under WTO agreement, other members can invoke 'non-market economy' provisions to determine dumping cases for 15 years following accession. Non-market economy provisions imply that domestic prices cannot be used as a reference point and make it much easier to reach a positive finding in an antidumping investigation.

As a precondition to entering the WTO in 2001, China accepted some restrictive clauses, one of which was that China's market economy status (MES) could not be automatically granted worldwide until 2016.

Non-market economy status has been a source of frequent trade remedy cases against China. During the past few years, China has become the major target of trade protectionism worldwide, with the US initiating the largest number of cases. Thus, China's quest for the MES has never ceased.

New Zealand was the first nation to accept China's MES in 2004, and has been followed by 80 other nations and regions (including Australia, Brazil, and Russia), but major economies such as the US, Japan, and the European Union have yet to do so. In August 2009, the US said it appreciated China's progress in market reform, and would accept China's MES as soon as possible through cooperation. However, the US side has claimed that an undervalued Renminbi (RMB) is a major source of its huge trade deficit with China.

Ironically, during the 1980s there were heated arguments about whether China should adopt the market-regulated system (see Box 7.1, p. 111).

Transitional Safeguard Mechanism in cases where imports of products of Chinese origin cause or threaten to cause market disruption to the domestic producers of other WTO members.

On the other hand, prohibitions, quantitative restrictions, or other measures maintained against imports from China in a manner inconsistent with the WTO Agreement would be phased out or otherwise dealt with in accordance with mutually agreed terms and timetables specified in an annex to the Protocol of Accession.

The conclusion of the negotiations for market access represents a commitment undertaken by China to gradually eliminate trade barriers and expand market access to goods and services from foreign countries. China has bound all tariffs for imported goods. After implementing all the commitments made, China's average bound tariff level will decrease to 15 percent for agricultural products. The range is from 0 to 65 percent, with the higher rates applied to cereals. For industrial goods the average bound tariff level will go down to 8.9 percent with a range from 0 to 47 percent, with the highest rates applied to photographic film and automobiles and related products. Some tariffs will be eliminated and others reduced mostly by 2004 but in no case later than 2010.

12.2.3   Tariff and Non-Tariff Barriers

In pre-reform China, tariffs were high and represented the only form of protection. On the other hand, non-tariff barriers were introduced in the early 1980s. Subsequently, an increasing number of goods were placed under licensed trading and quota. In 1992, some 25 percent of imports and 15 percent of exports were managed under licenses. However, the scope of license and quota management has been narrowed down since 1992. By 1997, only 384 categories of imports, 5 percent of the total, were managed under quota and licenses. China's import-regulating tax system was finally abolished in 1992 (Yin, 1998; and Wan et al., 2004). When China initiated significant trade reforms in 1992, the rates of tariffs were still high, averaging more than 40 percent. Since 1992, China has cut its tariff rates substantially every year. For example, the average tariff rate fell to 17.5 percent in 1998 (see Table 12.1). Since that time, the Chinese government has reduced the tariffs on three occasions.

On January 1, 2002, China cut the import tariffs on more than 5,000 goods. The average tariff rate was reduced to 12 percent from a level of 15.3 percent in 2001 (see Table 12.1). The rate for manufacturing goods was reduced from 14.7 percent to 11.3 percent, while that for agricultural goods, excluding fisheries, fell from 18.8 percent to 15.8 percent (Wan et al., 2004). At the same time, China abolished the quota and license arrangement for grains, wool, cotton, chemical fertilizers and so on. In addition, China modified or abolished those laws and regulations that are inconsistent with WTO rules. Since January 1, 2002 new laws on anti-dumping and anti-subsidy have been implemented. The average tariff rate was further cut from 12 percent in 2002 to 9.3 percent in 2005. Non-tariff barriers were also removed for most manufacturing goods by the end of 2004. Small and medium-sized enterprises and foreign invested companies have also been entitled to participate directly in international trade.

12.2.4   Currency Convertibility

China's foreign exchange system used to be subject to rigid control by the government. Since the late 1970s, the foreign exchange system has been subject to a gradual process of liberalization.

In the early 1980s, the Chinese currency Renminbi (RMB) was non-convertible and foreign exchanges were strictly supervised by the state. During this period two exchange rates were in operation: an official rate published by the government and another special one for foreign trade. The intention of the system was to enhance the country's exports and to restrict its imports, for at the

time China was suffering from a serious lack of foreign exchange. In 1984, a new policy of retaining exchange was adopted by the government as a result of improvements in China's foreign trade and economy. It allowed domestic enterprises and institutions to retain a part of their foreign currency earnings, compared with the previous one in which these units handed over all of their foreign currency earnings to the state. Although a larger part of foreign exchange was still under the control of the government, the new retaining policy stimulated domestic enterprises to increase their exports, and hence there was a significant improvement in China's foreign trade performance.

On January 1, 1994, China established a new unitary and floating exchange rate system. Although it is based on market supply and demand, this system is still, to a large extent, determined by the government, as the People's Bank of China (PBC), China's central bank, takes the position of the largest demander of foreign exchange and the Bank of China (BOC), which is also owned by the state, is the largest supplier of foreign exchange. Furthermore, the newly established foreign exchange rate system is still officially controlled and the central bank is one of the biggest participants in the market in order to maintain the RMB rate at a reasonable level.

From July 2005 to July 2008, the RMB appreciated by about 18 percent against the US dollar. From July 2008 to mid-June 2010, the Chinese government halted any further appreciation because the effects of the global economic slowdown. However, on June 19, 2010, the government has allowed the RMB to appreciate. Since then (through the end of 2011), the RMB has risen by about 6 percent against the dollar (see Figure 12.1).

TABLE 12.1 China's Declining Tariffs (%), 1982–2002

Year	Unweighted Average	Weighted Average	Dispersion (SD)	Max
1982	55.6	...	...	...
1985	43.3	...	...	...
1988	43.7	...	...	...
1991	44.1	...	...	...
1992	42.9	40.6	...	220.0
1993	39.9	38.4	29.9	220.0
1994	36.3	35.5	27.9	...
1995	35.2	26.8	...	220.0
1996	23.6	22.6	17.4	121.6
1997	17.6	16.0	13.0	121.6
1998	17.5	15.7	13.0	121.6
2000	16.4	...	...	...
2001	15.3	9.1	12.1	121.6
2002	12.3	6.4	9.1	71.0

Source: Rumbaugh and Blancher (2004).

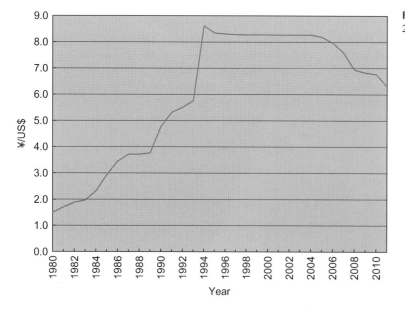

FIGURE 12.1 China's RMB exchange rates (1980–2011). *Source: NBS, various years.*

12.3 FOREIGN TRADE

12.3.1 Foreign Trade Regime in Transition

During the early stages of the PRC, China's foreign trade reflected, to a large extent, the basic characteristics of a socialist economy. To bring about socialist modernization in its own way, China did not adopt the strategy of 'founding a nation on trade' used by many industrially developed nations; rather, it was based on the principle of 'independence and self-reliance' during the first decades of the PRC. As a result, China lagged far behind the advanced nations. In order to achieve rapid economic modernization, the Chinese government has clearly recognized the importance of seeking new technologies through foreign trade and international cooperation.

China's foreign economic affairs had not been guided by a *laissez-faire* approach before, and even during the early stage of, the reform era. Intervention in the form of trade restrictions such as tariffs and licensing, subsidies, tax incentives, and active contact with the world economy exists on the sides of both imports and exports. China used to manage its foreign trade through a policy of high tariff rates. This policy had effectively promoted the developments of China's immature, domestic industries. However, it also had a negative effect upon the Chinese economy. For example, under the system of high tariff rates, products made abroad do not have an equal opportunity to enter the Chinese market as those made in China, which will inevitably prevent the importation of high-quality and cheap commodities from advanced nations, harming the interests of

Chinese consumers, and finally providing fewer incentives for Chinese producers to improve their competitiveness.

In the 1950s, because of a trade embargo imposed by the USA and other Western nations, most foreign trade was restricted to the countries of the Soviet bloc. Following the Sino-Soviet split in the early 1960s, there was a dramatic decrease in the level of foreign trade. Guided by the principle of 'self-reliance and independence', China's foreign trade and economic relations were not improved significantly before the early 1970s. Since then, its trade with the capitalist market increased gradually, as a result of the *rapprochement* with Japan, the USA, and some EU countries. However, because the autarkic economic policy was still in operation before the late 1970s, both the volume of Chinese foreign trade and the ratio of it to GDP were still very small at that time (see Figure 12.2).

Generally, China's foreign trade is facilitated by both geographical factors and also the fact that people on both sides of the border often belong to the same minority group and share many cultural characteristics. China's border development has mainly benefited from its 'open-door' policy and *rapprochement* with the neighboring countries since the mid-1980s. In 1984 the Chinese government promulgated the 'Provisional Regulations for the Management of "Small-volume" Border Trade' and opened up hundreds of frontier cities and towns. In contrast to the eastern coastal development, which was fueled principally by foreign direct investment (FDI), China's inland frontier development has been characterized by border trade with its foreign neighbors. Since the early 1990s,

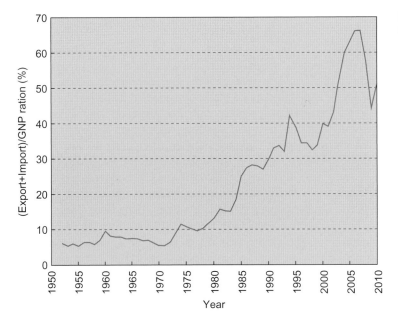

FIGURE 12.2 China's foreign trade as a percentage of GDP, 1950–2010. *Source: NBS, various years.*

a series of favorable and flexible measures to manage cross-border trade and economic cooperation have been granted to those frontier provinces.

Prior to the early 1980s, the management of foreign economic affairs rested in the hands of one government ministry that maintained an overly rigid control of matters. In the first years of the implementation of China's outward development strategy, the reform of the foreign economic system was conducted via three aspects. First, under the unified control of the state, there was a closer relationship between production and marketing and between industry and trade, which enabled production units to participate directly in foreign trade. Secondly, the special policies and measures relating to foreign trade were handed to the local governments. A third type of reform was to expand the autonomy of the state-owned enterprises (SOEs) to act on their own initiatives and have direct links with foreign traders at meetings arranged by specialized export SOEs.

In 1982, the Ministry of Foreign Trade (MFT) was renamed the Ministry of Foreign Economic Relations and Trade (MFERT). At the same time, trade bureaus were established at provincial and local levels to manage both foreign trade and FDI. The MFERT and local trade bureaus were, in principle, not allowed to interfere in the management of foreign trade enterprises. Many large SOEs received permission to engage in foreign trade. Local enterprises were also able to establish their own foreign trade companies. In 1988, foreign trade was reformed by a system of contracts under which the separation between ownership (state) and management (enterprise) was maintained and thus foreign trade enterprises were able to operate independently. Despite these reforms, the fundamental structure of central planning and state ownership has not been changed fundamentally, particularly in large and medium-sized SOEs.

Before the 1980s, international trade was in the hands of central government planning, which controlled China's foreign trade by monopolizing the imports and exports of more than thousands categories of commodities. These commodities can be classified into two categories: plan-commanded goods (in which both the value and the volume of trade are strictly controlled) and plan-guided goods (in which only the value of trade is controlled). In 1984, there was a reform of the trade management system, with foreign trade enterprises being given autonomy to deal with international trade. In 1985, the number of goods under these categories was cut to about 100 each. By 1991, almost all exports were deregulated, with only 15 percent controlled by specially appointed trading companies. Imports have also been deregulated. The proportion of plan-commanded imports in the total import volume was reduced from 40 percent in 1985 to 18.5 percent in 1991 (Wan et al., 2004).

In parallel with the gradual acceleration of its economic reforms, China has increasingly amplified its foreign-related legal system, steadily improved its trade and investment environment, and enforced the intellectual property rights protection system. With regard to the issue of trade system transparency, China has sorted out and publicized all management documents that used to be deemed confidential. In 1993, the Ministry of Foreign Trade and Economic Cooperation (MFTEC) was established to reform laws and regulations on the management of foreign trade and economic cooperation. Import restrictions were eased still further. By 1994, almost all planning on imports and exports were abolished, with only a few exceptions where extremely important goods were traded by specially appointed trading companies. One year later, by the end of 1995, China had rescinded import licensing and quota controls on 826 tariff lines.

12.3.2   China's Trade Performance

Since the late 1970s, China has made many efforts to import advanced production equipment from abroad in order to use it to kick-start its economic take-off. Except for a few years such as 1982–83 and 1989–90, China's foreign trade during the reform period has grown with exceptional speed. In 1978, China ranked 32nd in the world in terms of international trade. Its ranking improved to 15th in 1989, 10th in 1997, and 6th in 2001.

In 2000, China was the 7th leading exporter and 8th largest importer of merchandise trade. Since 2001, China has steadily increased its share of global manufactured exports. Notwithstanding the global reductions in trade, which resulted from the US financial crisis in 2008, China replaced Germany as the world's largest exporting nation in 2009. In 2010, China continued to be the leading merchandise exporter (US$1.58 trillion, or 10.4 percent of world exports), followed by the United States (8.4 percent of world exports), Germany (8.3 percent of world exports), and Japan (5.1 percent of world exports) (see Table 12.2).

China also moved ahead of Germany to become the world's second-largest importer, behind the United States last year. In spite of some correction in its external imbalances, the United States remained far and away the world's largest merchandise importer. Germany and China held onto the next two positions, with China becoming the second-largest importer and Germany falling to third. As with exports, it was because the decline for China was less dramatic than that for Germany that China moved up one spot.

China's top five trading partners, measured by the total trade volume, are the USA, Japan, Hong Kong (including re-exports), Republic of Korea, and Taiwan (see Figure 12.3).

During the early period of the PRC, the Chinese economy sustained a large trade deficit. This seems to be reasonable because, after many years of wars, China's demand for both more consumer goods and also production materials was greater than it could possibly supply. From 1955 to 1977, China obtained a high level of trade surplus, with

TABLE 12.2 Shares in World Exports of Major Economies (%), 1960–2010

	1960	1970	1980	1990	2000	2010
China	…	…	1.0	1.9	3.9	10.4
USA	19.4	15.3	12.0	11.6	12.1	8.4
Germany	10.7	12.1	10.5	12.1	8.6	8.3
Japan	3.7	6.7	7.1	8.5	7.5	5.1

Sources: Rumbaugh and Blancher (2004) and WTO (2011).

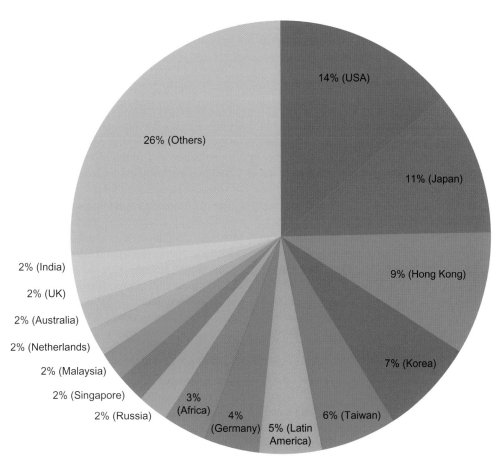

Notes: (1) Data are as of 2008. (2) Hong Kong's share includes re-exports.

FIGURE 12.3   China's major trading partners. *Source: NBS, 2009.*

the exceptions of 1960, 1970, and 1974–75. Obviously, this beneficial foreign trade pattern had to a large extent been shaped by China's 'self-reliance' policy for much of that period. China's attempt at speeding up economic development based on the 'imported' method was mainly responsible to the trade deficit in the late 1970s. A long-lasting trade deficit occurred between 1984 and 1989. Trade surplus has accompanied the strong and growing exports since 1990, with the exception of 1993 (see Figure 12.4). This has also increased China's foreign deposits. However, this trade surplus has also led to large trade deficits for its trade partners, sometimes resulting in retaliations.

China's increasing economic competitiveness and its growing exports have raised concerns in the Western

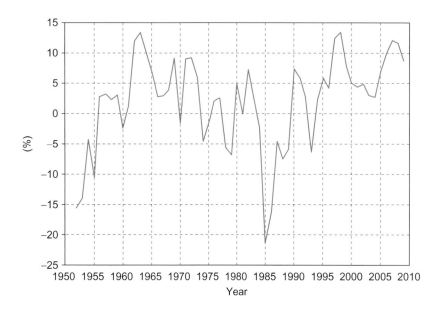

FIGURE 12.4 Foreign trade surplus (deficit) as a percentage of total trade. *Source: NBS, various years.*

nations. During the past decade, a number of specific trade issues – textiles (the infamous 'bra wars'), leather shoes, and car parts – have seen responses from the EU and the US which have been characterized as 'protectionist'. While divisions over policy responses have been seen between EU Member States and different industries, trade policy is agreed at EU level and reflects compromise positions. The EU Trade Commissioner, Peter Mandelson, has identified China as 'the biggest single challenge of globalization in the trade field […] Europe must get China right – as a threat, an opportunity, and prospective partner' (Mandelson, 2006). Fears of China as a competitor have been most obvious in the US, as the US trade deficit on goods with China has grown in recent years.[4]

12.3.3 Structural Changes

A glance at the history of the PRC reveals that China's economic stagnation and prosperity have been closely related to its policy of economic internationalization. More specifically, when the autarkic policy was implemented, economic stagnation occurred; when the outward development strategy was introduced, economic prosperity would be achieved accordingly. China's regional economic performances have also been decided in this way. Since the introduction of reform and open-door policies in 1978, China has basically formed a pattern featuring gradual advances from coastal

to the inland areas. As a result, China's spatial trade performance has also followed this pattern (see Figure 12.5a). Given the large spatial and demographic sizes of China's provinces, Guangdong exports as much as South Korea, and Jiangsu, Shangai, and Zhejiang as much as Taiwan, Austria and Thailand, respectively. On the other hand, some poorer provinces in Southwest China only match the southern African nations (see Figure 12.5b).

Generally, foreign trade can be classified into four types according to the composition of imported and exported commodities in kind: (1) both imports and exports are dominated by primary goods; (2) imports are dominated by primary goods while exports are dominated by manufactured goods; (3) exports are dominated by primary goods while imports are dominated by manufactured goods; and (4) both imports and exports are dominated by manufactured goods. Over recent decades China's foreign trade has effectively transformed from pattern (1) to pattern (4). In the early 1950s, the shares of primary and manufactured goods were about 80 percent and 20 percent of total exports, respectively. Since then, the share of manufactured products to total exports has grown steadily and it eventually overtook that of primary products in the early 1980s. Since 1995, the share of manufactured goods to total exports has increased to more than 80 percent (see Figure 12.6).

In summary, China's export of manufactured goods has accounted for an increasing share since the mid-1980s, while the corresponding level of imports has declined, although at a slow rate. Clearly, China has been industrializing and is becoming a major exporter of manufactured goods. This structural change of exports has been largely ascribed to China's strong push toward industrialization since 1949 (as discussed in Chapter 9). The composition of

---

4. According to *Foreign Trade Statistics*, released by the US Census Bureau, in 2005 the total deficit was US$201.6 billion, compared with US$161.9 billion in 2004, US$83.8 billion in 2000, and US$18.3 billion in 1992. The US-China deficit on goods of US$201.6 billion was equivalent to 26.3 percent of the value of the total US trade in goods deficit in 2005.

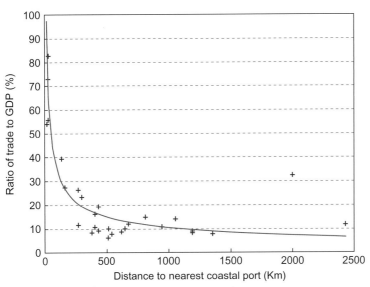

Notes: (1) Data on 'ratio of trade to GDP' are based on NBS (2002). (2) Data on 'distance to nearest coastal port' are estimated by the author based on the locations of China's 31 provincial capitals.

(a) Foreign trade versus distance in China

Notes: (1) The equivalents include: Austria = Shanghai, Bahrain = Sichuan, Belize = Tibet, Benin = Ningxia, Bosnia and Herzegovina = Shaanxi, Botswana = Jilin, Colombia = Tianjin, Congo = Hunan, Costa Rica = Henan, El Salvador = Inner Mongolia, Gabon = Guangxi, Greece = Hebei, Hungary = Shandong, Jordan = Heilongjiang, Latvia = Jiangxi, Lebanon = Chongqing, Libya = Liaoning, Mongolia = Hainan, Namibia = Yunnan, Nepal = Gansu, Nigeria = Fujian, North Korea = Guizhou, Oman = Beijing, Panama = Macau, Rwanda = Qinghai, Serbia = Anhui, Iceland=Shanxi, South Korea = Guangdong, Sri Lanka = Hong Kong, Taiwan = Jiangsu, Thailand = Zhejiang, Trinidad and Tobago = Hubei, and Uzbekistan = Xinjiang. (2) Figures are in US dollars and as of 2010. (3) The data of Hong Kong and Macau exclude re-exports.

(b) Which countries match the exports of Chinese provinces?

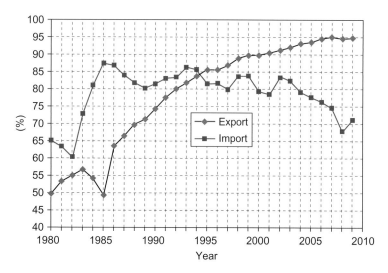

FIGURE 12.6 Shares of manufactured commodity imports and exports (%). *Source: NBS, various years.*

TABLE 12.3 China's Crude Oil Imports by Origin (%)

Origin	1990	1997	2005	2006	2008	2010
Middle East	39.0	48.0	46.0	44.0	46.0	46.0
Russia/Central Asia	–	–	11.0	11.0	10.0	10.0
Atlantic Basin	–	–	23.0	5.0	3.0	3.0
Asia Pacific	60.0	26.2	8.0	4.0	–	–
Africa	0.0	16.7	–	32.0	23.0	22.0
Others	0.0	9.6	12.0	4.0	18.0	19.0
Total	100.0	100.0	100.0	100.0	100.0	100.0

Notes: *(1) Atlantic Basin in 2010 is from Brazil. (2) The data are compiled from different sources: China General Administration of Customs (2005), US Energy Information Agency (IEA) and FACTS Global Energy (2008).*
Source: Zhang (2011).

imported commodities includes a very small share of primary products compared with that of manufactured products, as a result of China's abundance of available natural resources, as well as its large agricultural sector.

China's quest for imported oil has changed with corresponding global and regional geopolitical and economic developments over time in response to geopolitical and transportation risks. Though Middle Eastern countries continue to be the most important suppliers of almost half of China's imported oil (see Table 12.3), China has attempted to decrease its dependence on imports from the volatile Middle East through investments in African countries (such as Angola, Sudan, Libya, and the Congo) and Russia and Central Asian countries such as Kazakhstan. Investments in these Central Asian countries can also significantly decrease sea-lane transportation risks.

12.4 UNDERSTANDING CHINA'S TRADE PERFORMANCE

12.4.1 Methodology

It has been broadly assumed that a country's economic dependence on the outside world is negatively related to its land area. For example, in an estimation of international trade, Frankel and Romer (1996, Table 1) find that, for every 1 percent increase in land area, trade falls by about 0.2 percent. This may be illustrated unambiguously by the relationship between the supply and demand of some basic resources for countries differing in size (land area). Generally speaking, in comparison to large economies, small economies have a relatively limited variety of natural resources. Therefore, they have to import those resources that they lack and that are essential to meeting diversified production and consumption needs. Eventually, the increased imports will stimulate exports in order to attain a balance.

In addition to geographic area, a country's economic size (output) and population also have an influence on its external economic activities. Generally, the larger the GDPs (or GNPs)[5] of trading partners, *ceteris paribus*, the larger the volume of trade between them; by contrast, population is a negative factor in the determination of international trade. This captures the well-known phenomenon that larger countries tend to be relatively less open to trade as a percentage of GDP (or GNP). Therefore, it is easy to understand that Hong Kong, Singapore, and Luxembourg are more highly dependent on international trade than the United States, China, or India. The former lack not only natural endowments but also the room to exploit economies of scale in the domestic market, while the latter, engaging in far more trade in absolute terms (*versus* less trade as a percentage of GDP or GNP), can find an increasing number of business opportunities within their own borders.

Without considering geographic factors, it could be very difficult to understand the current patterns of both global and regional trade. For instance, bilateral trade flows across the US-Canadian border, between France, Italy, the UK, Germany and the Netherlands, and along the western coast of the Pacific Ocean (including, *inter alia*, South Korea, Taiwan, Hong Kong and the mainland of China) have risen a great deal more quickly than between more remote and isolated economies. In addition to distance, another proxy of geographic factor that influences international trade is adjacency. For example, bilateral trade between France and the United Kingdom will be the result of their proximity, but trade between France and Germany will be further boosted by their common border.[6]

Past theories of the determinants of international trade seem controversial, or at best incomplete. The Heckscher-Ohlin (H-O), or factor-endowment, theory can be expressed in terms of two theorems. According to the H-O theorem, a nation will export the commodity produced by its relatively abundant and cheap factor and will import the commodity produced by its relatively scarce and expensive factor (see Heckscher, 1919; and Ohlin, 1933). The factor-price equalization theorem was proved rigorously by PA Samuelson and is therefore also called the Heckscher-Ohlin-Samuelson

(H-O-S) theorem (Samuelson, 1948, 1949). According to the H-O-S theorem, international trade will bring about equalization in the relative and absolute returns to homogeneous factors across nations. The first empirical test of the H-O model was conducted by Leontief (1954) using 1947 US data, which demonstrates that US import substitutes were about 30 percent more capital-intensive than US exports. Since the United States is the most capital-intensive nation, this result was the opposite of what the H-O model had predicted and thus it became known as the Leontief paradox. This paradox could be explained in a number of ways: (1) 1947 being a non-representative year; (2) the use of a two-factor (labor and capital) model; (3) the fact that US tariffs gave more protection to labor-intensive industries; and (4) the exclusion of human capital from the calculations. Some empirical studies, however, give conflicting results.[7]

Past studies have raised more questions than they have answered. For example, the effects of geographic proximity on trade have not been shown to fall over time. Rather, for the period 1950–88 (Boisso and Ferrantino, 1997) and 1965–92 (Frankel et al., 1997b) these effects have been shown to strengthen over time. In their analyses of the negative correlation between distance-related costs and the interdependence for sovereign countries, Frankel et al. (1997a) use the data from the 1980s and obtain slightly larger coefficients (around 0.5 to 0.6) on distance compared with Eichengreen and Irwin's (1995) interwar estimates (around 0.3 to 0.6) based on data from the 1930s. Similarly, using panel data from 1970, 1980 and 1990, Rauch (1999) finds little evidence that the effects of distance-related barriers declined between 1970 and 1990. Clearly, this provides no evidence that, as a result of technological innovation, declining distance-related transaction costs should have led to increased trade flows. One possibility is that these analyses exclude important explanatory variables, thereby biasing the estimates. To clarify related issues, it is necessary to isolate the influences of all distance-related variables on trade. In particular, the inclusion of some relevant cultural variables might allow us to gain a better understanding of the black box containing the distance-related transaction costs that affect foreign trade.

Since the 1990s, numerous quantitative studies have examined the role that cultural factors play in international trade (for example, Havrylyshyn and Pritchett, 1991; Foroutan and Pritchett, 1993; Frankel and Wei, 1995; Frankel et al., 1997b; Rauch, 1999). These studies used linguistic links as one or more explanatory variables. The estimated results suggest that countries which have linguistic

---

5. Linnemann (1966) and Frankel et al. (1997) have estimated the effects of both GDP and GNP on trade, but no significant difference is found.

6. Frankel et al.'s (1997b, p. 66) estimated coefficients on 'adjacency' range between 0.5 and 0.7. Because trade is specified in natural logarithmic form in their estimates, the way to interpret the coefficients on adjacency is to take the exponent: that is to say, two countries that share a common border will, *ceteris paribus*, increase their trade by about 65–101 percent compared with countries that do not share a border.

---

7. See, for example, Leontief (1956), Kravis (1956a and 1956b), Keesing (1966), Kenen (1965), Baldwin (1971), Branson and Monoyios (1977), Leamer (1980; 1984; and 1993), Stern and Maskus (1981), Bowen et al. (1987), and Salvatore and Barazesh (1990).

TABLE 12.4 Determinants of Foreign Trade, China and East Asia

Coefficient	East Asia		China	
	1985	**1995**	**1985**	**1995**
Constant	−17.282 (1.666[a])	−29.303 (1.225[a])	−2.122 (7.664)	−15.220 (2.823[a])
$\ln(GDP_i GDP_j)$	1.162 (0.032[a])	1.236 (0.027[a])	1.418 (0.166[a])	1.081 (0.065[a])
$\ln(GDPPC_i GDPPC_j)$	0.722 (0.059[a])	0.868 (0.047[a])	−0.689 (0.330[b])	0.145 (0.117)
$\ln(DISTANCE_{ij})$	−1.440 (0.147[a])	−0.648 (0.103[a])	−1.364 (0.631[b])	−0.423 (0.218[b])
$LANGAUGE_{ij}$	−9.048 (2.096[a])	2.860 (0.862[a])	14.375 (4.432[a])	2.600 (1.017[a])
$RELIGION_{ij}$	0.192 (0.410)	1.242 (0.330[a])	−26.770 (11.358[b])	5.919 (4.069)
R square	0.570	0.633	0.489	0.770
F-statistic	425.917	841.41	22.737	98.54
Number of observations	1612	2446	124	152

Notes: *All regressions are based on ordinary least squares (OLS). Dependent variable is the natural log of bilateral trade (sum of exports and imports) in 1984 (since many East Asian economies suffered from bad recessions in 1985). Figures within parentheses are standard errors.* [a] *and* [b] *denote statistically significant at the 1% and 5% levels, respectively.*
Source: Guo (2007) for 'East Asia' and estimated by the author for 'China'.

similarities have been more likely to trade with each other in the postwar period. In other words, there is some evidence of linguistic barriers to trade. However, linguistic variables have been highly simplified in these studies. For example, the links between countries were only measured with dummy variables in the above studies. As most countries do not share the same language, the international (or inter-regional) links should not be simply expressed by a dummy variable.[8] Last but not least, the existing literature omits another cultural variable – religion – that could play, at least in some cases, a more important role in economic activities than linguistic variables (Guo, 2006, pp. 96–102).

12.4.2 Estimated Results

The following result is based on the data from a panel of East Asian economies and on the model built in the Annex. A comparison of the estimated coefficients on the log of DISTANCE in 1985 and 1995 (see Table 12.4) provides evidence that supports the view that geographic influence on trade also tends to be reduced in China and East Asia during the last decades of the twentieth century. One of the major driving forces contributing to this tendency might be technological advances in transportation and communications. Intuitively, the widespread application of e-commerce and the decline in distance-related transaction costs have increasingly contributed to the growth of international trade in East Asia.

The estimated results reveal that, between 1985 and 1995, five individual languages (Bahasa, Chinese, English, Khmer, and Thai) have played different roles in foreign trade in East Asia (see Table 12.5). In the case of inter-regional trade, Chinese and English, the only two languages with no missing correlation in the regressions, are statistically insignificant in 1985; but they become statistically significant in 1995. In the case of intra-regional trade, Bahasa has a decreasing role between 1985 and 1995; English and Khmer are statistically insignificant in 1995 and statistically significant in 1985. For both years, Thai is not statistically significant. By way of contrast, the Chinese language plays a dramatically increasing role from 1985 (with a statistically insignificant coefficient of only 0.056) to 1995 (with a statistically significant coefficient of 1.755).

Why does the Chinese language play a more important role in international trade than the other languages? I suspect that the reasonable force behind this is the strong effect of Chinese diaspora. Rauch and Trindade (2002), for example, find that ethnic Chinese networks have a quantitatively important impact on bilateral trade through the mechanisms of market information and matching and referral services, in addition to their effect through community enforcement of sanctions that deter opportunistic behavior. Their estimated results show that for trade between countries with ethnic Chinese population shares at the levels prevailing in Southeast Asia, the smallest estimated average increase in bilateral trade in differentiated products attributable to ethnic Chinese networks is nearly 60 percent.

---

8. There is an exception in which Boisso and Ferrantino (1997) construct a measure of linguistic distance that is a continuous scalar.

TABLE 12.5 The Growing Chinese Role in Foreign Trade

Explanatory Variable	Intra-Regional Trade		Inter-Regional Trade	
	1985	1995	1985	1995
Constant	−46.816 (4.716[a])	−39.547 (3.079[a])	−12.519 (2.232[a])	−33.077 (1.833[a])
$\ln(GDP_iGDP_j)$	1.147 (0.126[a])	1.107 (0.079[a])	1.148 (0.034[a])	1.260 (0.029[a])
$\ln(GDPPC_iGDPPC_j)$	1.313 (0.219[a])	1.093 (0.169[a])	0.642 (0.063[a])	0.742 (0.053[a])
$\ln(DISTANCE_{ij})$	1.069 (0.288[a])	0.601 (0.210[a])	−1.795 (0.217[a])	−0.112 (0.178)
$RELIGION_{ij}$	2.697 (1.659)	2.332 (0.901[b])	−0.206 (0.419)	0.454 (0.360)
BAHASA	1.893 (1.036[c])	1.478 (0.753[b])	Excl.	Excl.
CHINESE	0.056 (0.694)	1.755 (0.483[a])	0.529 (0.641)	1.012 (0.383[a])
ENGLISH	1.734 (0.710[b])	−0.419 (0.527)	0.258 (0.218)	0.679 (0.159[a])
KHMER	6.806 (2.277[a])	5.922 (1.191[a])	Excl.	Excl.
THAI	−3.406 (4.114)	−1.211 (1.137)	Excl.	Excl.
R square	0.565	0.641	0.569	0.625
F-statistic	19.341	48.71	322.188	605.96
Number of observations	143	255	1,468	2,190

Notes: *All regressions are based on ordinary least squares (OLS). Dependent variable is the natural log of bilateral trade (sum of exports and imports) in 1984 (for 1985's regressions) and 1995 (for 1995's regressions). Hong Kong is excluded from regressions in 1985. Figures within parentheses are standard errors. 'Excl.' denotes the left-hand variable is deleted from the analysis since it has missing correlation. '[a],' '[b]' and '[c]' denote statistically significant at the 1%, 5%, and 10% levels, respectively.*
Source: Guo (2007).

12.5 SUMMARY

In *The Wealth of Nations* (1776), Adam Smith explained not only the critical role that the market played in the relocation of a nation's resources but also the nature of the social order that it achieved and helped to maintain. Applying his ideas about economic activity within a country to specialization and exchange between countries, Smith concluded that countries should specialize in and export those commodities in which they had an absolute advantage and should import those commodities in which the trading partner had an absolute advantage. Each country should export those commodities it produced more efficiently because the absolute labor required per unit was less than that of the prospective trading partner. According to Smith, there is a basis for trade because nations are clearly better off specializing in their lower-cost commodities and importing those commodities that can be produced more cheaply abroad.

China's foreign economic affairs had not been guided by a *laissez-faire* approach during the early period of the open-door policy. Intervention in the form of trade restrictions such as tariffs and licensing, subsidies, tax incentives, and active contact with the world economy exists on the sides of both imports and exports. China used to manage its foreign trade through a policy of high tariff rates. This policy had

effectively promoted the developments of China's immature, domestic industries. However, it also had a negative effect upon the Chinese economy. For example, under the system of high tariff rates, products made abroad do not have an equal opportunity to enter the Chinese market as those made in China, which will inevitably prevent the importation of high-quality and cheap commodities from advanced nations, harming the interests of Chinese consumers, and finally providing fewer incentives for Chinese producers to improve their competitiveness.

Since the 1980s, China's economic liberalization has been hindered by both 'super-national remuneration' and 'sub-national remuneration'. On the one hand, the foreign-funded enterprises were greeted by a series of favorable policies such as tax exemption and low tax rates; on the other hand, they also faced some unequal treatments and economic discriminations in fields such as communication, transportation, housing, and advertising. Around the time of China's entry into the WTO, China issued new laws and regulations concerning service trade, covering legal services, telecommunications, financial institutions, insurance, audio and video products, tourism, and other related areas. Laws regarding the entry of foreign sales companies and joint ventures of stock exchange are being drawn up. However, further measures are still needed to ensure compliance with rules of the WTO on intellectual property, foreign investment, and information transmission.

Before ending, let's complete our recounting of the story told by Zhuangzi at the beginning of this chapter:

Before the turtle from the East Sea could get its left foot in the well, its right knee got stuck. It hesitated and retreated. The turtle told the frog about the East Sea: 'Even a distance of a thousand li [500 km] cannot give you an idea of the sea's width; even a height of a thousand ren [approximately 666.67 m] cannot give you an idea of its depth. In the time of King Yu of the Xia dynasty, there were floods nine years out of ten, but the waters in the sea did not increase. In the time of King Tang of the Shang dynasty there were droughts seven years out of eight, but the waters in the sea did not decrease. The sea does not change along with the passage of time and its level does not rise or fall according to the amount of rain that falls. The greatest happiness is to live in the East Sea.'

ANNEX

A Model of Foreign Trade[9]

There is a widely held view that easily observable impediments, such as transportation costs, do not adequately capture the transaction costs of international trade. One response has been to offer direct investigations of the possible role of trans-border business networks or ethnic diasporas in reducing transaction costs (Rauch, 2001; Rauch and Trindade, 2002; and Combes et al., 2005). In addition, Guiso et al. (2004) and Guo (2006) suggest that more diffuse cultural affinity or similarity may be another channel. They argue that cultural distance – as proxied by, among other things, the genetic differences across national populations – is a robust determinant of the volume of international trade in the context of a conventional gravity model.

The gravity model is most commonly used by economists to make a quantitative estimate of the determinants of foreign trade. The classic early application of the model was by Linnemann (1966), who continued work first reported in Tinbergen (1962) and then in Pöyhönen (1963).[10] Some of the most recent work on the application of the model was undertaken by Frankel et al. (1997a, 1997b), Rauch (1999), and Rose (2004), among others. Generally, a gravity model assumes that the volume of trade between any two economies will be directly proportional to the product of their economic masses (measured by GDP or GNP) and inversely proportional to the distance between them. Per capita incomes (measured by product of per capita GDPs

or GNPs) have become a standard covariate in the gravity models of, for example, Eaton and Tamura (1994), Frankel et al. (1997a, 1997b), and Rauch (1999).

In order to apply the gravity model to test the effects of the cultural influences on trade, we analyze the influences of linguistic and religious variables. The assumption here is that language is an effective tool of communication and that religion can provide the insights into the characteristics of culture. The basic form of the gravity model to be used in my empirical analysis is as follows:

$$
\begin{aligned}
\ln(\text{TRADE}_{ij} + 1) = {} & \alpha_0 + \alpha_1 \ln(\text{GDP}_i \text{GDP}_j) \\
& + \alpha_2 \ln(\text{GDPPC}_i \text{GDPPC}_j) \\
& + \alpha_3 \ln\text{DISTANCE}_{ij} + \alpha_4 \text{LANGUAGE}_{ij} \\
& + \alpha_5 \text{RELIGION}_{ij}
\end{aligned}
\tag{12.1}
$$

In Equation (12.1), 'ln' represents natural logarithm; TRADE_{ij}, measured in thousands of US dollars, is the sum of exports and imports between economies i and j. In order to make the natural logarithm of TRADE become mathematically meaningful when TRADE=0, $\ln(\text{TRADE}+1)$ is used to approximate $\ln(\text{TRADE})$.[11] This seems to be reasonable since the size of TRADE is, if not zero, always far larger than US\$1,000. $\text{GDP}_i \text{GDP}_j$ is the product of purchasing power parity (PPP)-adjusted GDP of the ith and jth economies. $\text{GDPPC}_i \text{GDPPC}_j$ is the product of PPP-adjusted GDP per capita of the ith and jth economies. DISTANCEij represents the distance between the geographic centers of gravity of the ith and jth economies (in kilometers). LANGUAGEij and RELIGIONij, the measurement of which will be discussed later, denote the extents to which the ith and jth economies are linguistically and religiously linked to each other, respectively.

Linguistic differences have clearly, to some extent, influenced international trade and marketing. Although it is not the only tool for building trusting relationships, doors usually open more quickly when knocked on by someone who speaks a familiar language. Sharing a common language, however, does not necessarily mean effective communication in technical terms. Compared to language, religion can provide more insights into the characteristics of interpersonal behavior. More importantly, religion can have a deep impact not only on attitudes toward economic matters but also on values that influence them. Specifically, religious attitudes and values help to determine what one thinks is right or appropriate, what is important, what is desirable, and so on.

As discussed later, the data on some, if not all, linguistic groups are probably subject to a wider range of errors than the other variables in Equation (12.1). Therefore, the

---

9. This section is based on the first part of my paper ('Linguistic and Religious Influences on Foreign Trade: Evidence from East Asia') published by *Asian Economic Journal*, vol. 21, pp. 100–21.

10. The earliest application of the gravity model can be traced back to the 1940s (see, e.g., Zipf, 1946; Stewart, 1948).

---

11. Note that if there are a significant number of zero values in the pairwise trade, then Tobit regressions techniques should be used. In this research, the number of observations identified by TRADE=0 is quite small.

ability to use five international languages of, in the case of East Asia, Bahasa (Indonesian or Malay), Chinese, English, Khmer, and Thai, is measured with dummy variables. Consequently, the gravity model on trade is written as:

$$
\begin{aligned}
\ln(\text{TRADE}_{ij} + 1) = {}& \beta_0 + \beta_1 \ln(\text{GDP}_i \text{GDP}_j) \\
& + \beta_2 \ln(\text{GDPPC}_i \text{GDPPC}_j) + \beta_3 \ln \text{DISTANCE}_{ij} \quad (12.2) \\
& + \beta_4 \text{RELIGION}_{ij} + \beta_5 \text{BAHASA} + \beta_6 \text{CHINESE} \\
& + \beta_7 \text{ENGLISH} + \beta_8 \text{KHMER} + \beta_9 \text{THAI}
\end{aligned}
$$

In Equation (12.2), BAHASA = 1, CHINESE = 1, KHMER = 1 and THAI = 1 means that economies i and j both speak the language in question; otherwise these dummies take the value 0. It has been recognized that most international trade contracts and documents are processed in English, especially in East Asia where different phylums exist.[12] As a result, English reading and writing ability has been an important linguistic trait that reduces trade-related transaction costs. To reflect this fact, the English dummy is defined to include not only English as a mother tongue but also lingua franca and bilingual forms of English.

Equations (12.1) and (12.2) can be estimated by using standard statistical techniques. In order to further account for the potential impacts of multicollinearity between geographical and linguistic and religious variables, additional regressions are estimated by excluding the linguistic and religious variables. Specifically, if correlation coefficients of each pair of explanatory variables are fairly large, they could suggest potential multicollinearity that can cause imprecise regression results (Greene, 2002, pp. 255–8). Because this section employs cross-sectional data, it is also necessary to conduct tests for heteroskedasticity. More specifically, while ordinary least squares (OLS)-estimated coefficients are unbiased, weighted least squares (WLS) estimation can provide more efficient results in terms of smaller coefficient standard errors (Greene, 2002, p. 499). After each OLS run, heteroskedasticity tests are performed for each individual regression model. If heteroskedasticity is significant, WLS estimation should be performed to correct this problem.

Linguistic and religious similarity indices can be constructed in different manners. The simplest method is to use a dummy index; i.e., using '1' for economies to be linguistically or religiously linked with each other, and using '0' otherwise. Although it has been applied in a number of studies (see, for example, Havrylyshyn and Pritchett, 1991; Foroutan and Pritchett, 1993; Frankel and Wei, 1995; Frankel et al., 1997b), this method cannot precisely

measure the extent to which economies are linguistically or religiously linked to each other, particularly when the economies are linguistically or religiously diversified.

A comprehensive method can be used to construct linguistic and religious similarity indices. Suppose that the population shares of N linguistic (religious) groups are expressed by $(x_1, x_2, ..., x_N)$ and $(y_1, y_2, ..., y_N)$ for economies X and Y, respectively. x_i and y_i (where, $x_i \geq 0$ and $y_i \geq 0$) belong to the same linguistic (religious) group. Mathematically, the linguistic and religious similarity indices (denoted by LANGUAGE and RELIGION, respectively) between the economies X and Y can be measured according to the following formula:[13]

$$
\sum_{i=1}^{N} \min(x_i, y_i) \quad (12.3)
$$

In Equation (12.3), min ($\bullet$) denotes the minimization of the variables within parentheses.[14] The values of LANGUAGE and RELIGION range between 0 and 1. In the extreme cases, when LANGUAGE (RELIGION)=1, the two economies have a common linguistic (religious) structure (i.e., for all i, $x_i = y_i$); when LANGUAGE (RELIGION) = 0, the two economies do not have any linguistic (religious) links with each other (i.e., for all i, x_i (or y_i) = 0 and $x_i \neq y_i$). In other words, greater values of LANGUAGE or RELIGION indicate greater linguistic or religious similarity between two economies.

REFERENCES

Baldwin, R. E. (1971). Determinants of the commodity structure of US trade. *American Economic Review*, *61*(Mar.), 126–146.

Boisso, D., & Ferrantino, M. (1997). Economic distance, cultural distance and openness in international trade: empirical pules. *Journal of Economic Integration*, *12*, 456–484.

Bowen, H. P., Leamer, E. E., & Sveikauskas, L. (1987). Multicountry, multifactor tests of the factor abundance theory. *American Economic Review*, *77*(December), 791–809.

Branson, W. H., & Monoyios, N. (1977). Factor inputs in US trade. *Journal of International Economics*, *20*, 111–131.

Combes, P.-P., Lafourcade, M., & Mayer, T. (2005). The trade-creating effects of business and social networks: evidence from France. *Journal of International Economics*, *66*(1), 1–29.

Eaton, J., & Tamura, A. (1994). Bilateralism and regionalism in Japanese and US trade and direct foreign investment patterns. *Journal of the Japanese and International Economics*, *8*, 478–510.

Eichengreen, B., & Irwin, D. (1995). Trade blocs, currency blocs and the reorientation of trade in the 1930s. *Journal of International Economics*, *38*(2), 89–106.

---

12. For example, there are five main phylums in East Asia: Sino-Tibetan phylum, Ural-Altaic phylum (such as Mongolian and Manchu-Tungas), Dravidian phylum (such as Telugu and Malay), Austronesian phylum, Austro-Asiatic phylum (such as Khmer, Mon, and Vietnamese), and other phylums (such as Japanese, Korean, and Papuan).

13. This formula has been used in Guo (2004, 2006) and Noland (2005). Several other methods can also be used to comprehensively measure linguistic and religious similarity indices.

14. Boisso and Ferrantino (1997), for example, use $\sum x_i y_i$ as the construct of similarity index. However, using Equation (12.3) can prevent the index from further reduction when the values of x_i and y_i are small.

Foroutan, F., & Pritchett, L. (1993). Intra-Sub-Saharan African trade: is it too little? *Journal of African Economics*, *2*(May), 74–105.

Frankel, J., & Wei, S. (1995). European integration and the regionalization of world trade and currencies: the economics and the politics. In B. Eichengreen, F. Frieden & J. von Hagen (Eds.), *Monetary and fiscal policy in an integrated Europe*. New York: Springer.

Frankel, J. A., & Romer, D. (1996). *Trade and growth*. NBER Working Paper No. 5476, Cambridge, MA: National Bureau of Economic Research.

Frankel, J. A., Stein, E., & Wei, S.-J. (1997a). *Regional trading blocs in the world economic system*. Washington, DC: Institute for International Economics.

Frankel, J. A., Stein, E., & Wei, S.-J. (1997b). Trading blocs and the Americas: the natural, the unnatural, and the super-natural. *Journal of Development Economics*, *47*(1), 61–95.

Greene, W. H. (2002). *Econometric analysis* (5th ed.). Upper Saddle River, NJ: Prentice-Hall.

Guangxu Da Qing Huidian Shili (vol. 775, p. 4 and vol. 776, p. 13).

Guiso, L., Sapienza, P., & Zingales, L. (2004). *Cultural biases in economic exchange*. NBER Working Paper Series 11005, Cambridge, MA: National Bureau of Economic Research, December.

Guo, R. (2004). How culture influences foreign trade: evidence from the US and China. *The Journal of Socio-Economics*, *33*, 785–812.

Guo, R. (2006). *Cultural influences on economic analysis – theory and empirical evidence*. London and New York: Palgrave Macmillan.

Guo, R. (2007). Linguistic and religious influences on foreign trade: evidence from east Asia. *Asian Economic Journal*, *21*(1), 101–121.

Havrylyshyn, O., & Pritchett, L. (1991). *European trade patterns after the transition*. Policy, Research and External Affairs Working Paper Series No. 74, Washington, DC: World Bank.

Heckscher, E. F. (1919). The effect of foreign trade on the distribution of income. *Ekonomisk Tidskirift*, *21*, 497–512.

Keesing, D. B. (1966). Labor skills and comparative advantage. *American Economic Review*, *56*(May), 249–258.

Kenen, P. (1965). Nature, capital and trade. *Journal of Political Economy*, *73*(Oct.), 437–460.

Kravis, I. B. (1956). Wages and foreign trade. *Review of Economics and Statistics*, *38*(February), 14–30.

Kravis, I. B. (1956). Availability and other influences on the commodity composition of trade. *Journal of Political Economy*, *73*(April), 143–155.

Leamer, E. E. (1980). The Leontef paradox reconsidered. *Journal of Political Economy*, *88*(June), 495–503.

Leontief, W. (1954). Domestic production and foreign trade: the American capital position re-examined. *Economia Internationale*, *February*, 2–32.

Leontief, W. (1956). Factor proportions and the structure of American trade; further theoretical and empirical analysis. *Review of Economics and Statistics*, *38*(November), 386–407.

Linnemann, H. (1966). *An econometric study of international trade theory*. Amsterdam: North-Holland.

Maddison, A. (1996). *A Retrospect for the 200 Years of the World Economy, 1820—1992*. Paris: OECD Development Center.

NBS. (various years). *China statistical yearbook*, various issues. Beijing: China Statistics Publishing House.

Noland, M. (2005). *Affinity and international trade*. Working Paper Series No. WP 05-3, Washington DC: Institute for International Economics, June.

Ohlin, B. (1933). *Interregional and international trade*. Cambridge, MA: Harvard University Press.

Pöyhönen, P. (1963). A tentative model for the volume of trade between countries. *Weltwirtschaftliches Archiv*, *90*(1), 93–99.

Rauch, J. E. (1999). Networks versus markets in international trade. *Journal of International Economics*, *48*, 7–35.

Rauch, J. E. (2001). Business and social networks in international trade. *Journal of Economic Literature*, *39*(4), 1177–1203.

Rauch, J. E., & Trindade, V. (2002). Ethnic Chinese networks in international trade. *Review of Economics and Statistics*, *84*(1), 116–130.

Rose, A. K. (2004). *Macroeconomic determinants of international trade*. NBER Working Paper, Cambridge, MA: National Bureau of Economic Research.

Rumbaugh, T., & Blancher, N. (2004). *China: International Trade and WTO accession*. IMF Working Paper WP/04/36, Washington, DC: International Monetary Fund (IMF).

Salvatore, D., & Barazesh, R. (1990). The factor content of US foreign trade and the Heckscher-Ohlin theory. *International Trade Journal*, *16*(Winter), 149–181.

Samuelson, P. A. (1948). International trade and the equalization of factor prices. *The Economic Journal*, *58*(June), 165–184.

Samuelson, P. A. (1949). International factor-price equalization once again. *The Economic Journal*, *59*(June), 181–197.

Stern, R. M., & Maskus, K. E. (1981). Determinants of the structure of US foreign trade. *Journal of International Economics*, *24*, 207–224.

Stewart, J. Q. (1948). Demographic gravitation: evidence and applications. *Sociometry*, *2*, 31–58.

Tinbergen, J. (1962). An analysis of world trade flows, the Linder hypothesis, and exchange risk. In J. Tinbergen (Ed.), *Shaping the world economy*. New York: The Twentieth Century Fund.

Wan, G., Lu, M., & Zhao, C. (2004). *Globalization and regional income inequality evidence from within China*. Discussion Paper No. 2004/10, UNU World Institute for Development Economics Research (UNU-WIDER), Helsinki, Finland, November.

WTO. (2011). *World Trade 2010, prospects for 2011.* (Trade growth to ease in 2011 but despite 2010 record surge, crisis hangover persists), World Trade Organization (WTO) Press/628, 7 April. Available at: <http://www.wto.org/english/news_e/pres11_e/pr628_e.htm>. Accessed on December 5, 2011.

Zhang, J. (2011). *China's energy security: prospects, challenges and opportunities*. CNAPS Working Papers. Washington, DC: The Brooking Institution.

Zipf, G. K. (1946). The P^1P^2/D hypothesis: on the intercity movement of persons. *American Sociological Review*, *11*(6), 677–686.

Inward and Outward Direct Investments

The above photograph (taken by Lars Plougmann in the Ibn Battuta Mall in Dubai, available at http://wikipedia.org) shows the modern model of Zheng He's ship compared to one of Columbus's ships.

In the early fifteenth century, China was an advanced country in the world. A vast Chinese fleet, under the command of Zheng He, set sail in July 1405 from Liujia Harbor near Suzhou on a distant voyage. The purpose was to establish relations with foreign countries, to expand trade contacts and to look for treasures to satisfy the desire of the sovereign for luxuries. On board the ships were large quantities of silk goods, porcelain, gold and silver ware, copper utensils, iron implements, and other daily essentials. The fleet sailed in the South China Sea and the Indian Ocean. Then the Chinese visited Yemen, Iran, and the Holy City of Islam Mecca and further west to today's Somalia in East Africa. All this had taken place about half a century before the famous European sailor Columbus's voyage to America.

A man of the state of Lu (in today's southern Shandong province) was skilled in weaving hemp sandals and his wife was good at weaving fine white silk. The couple was thinking of moving out

Understanding the Chinese Economies. DOI: http://dx.doi.org/10.1016/B978-0-12-397826-4.00013-5
© 2013 Elsevier Inc. All rights reserved.

to the state of Yue (in today's Zhejiang province). 'You will be in dire straits,' he was told.' 'Why?' asked the man of the Lu. 'Hemp sandals are for walking but people of the Yue walk barefoot. White silk is for making hats but people of the Yue go about bareheaded. If you go to a place where your skills are utterly useless, how can you hope to do well?'

– Hanfeizi (280–233 BC)

13.1   SOME BASIC CONCEPTS

When the Chinese economy was opened to foreign investors during the early stage of China's economic reform, there were various regulations permitting ventures between Chinese and foreign companies. These regulations, however, did not go so far as to permit foreign players to fully engage in cross-border activities. From the late 1970s to the early 1990s, foreign companies were effectively locked out from making investments in several areas in China. The next decade of economic liberalization saw a big increase in the number of foreign invested enterprises (FIEs) established in China.

In China all FIEs should be formed as limited liability corporations under the PRC Corporation Law. The fundamental issue in forming such an entity revolves around which party has ultimate control over company operations. In general, the FIEs may take the form of either an equity joint venture (EJV), a cooperative joint venture (CJV), or a wholly foreign-owned enterprise (WFOE).

13.1.1   Equity Joint Venture

In China equity joint ventures (EJVs) have been one of the most common manners via which foreign investors enter the Chinese market. In each EJV, all the partners involved share profits, losses and risk in equal proportion to their respective contributions to the EJV's registered capital. These escalate upwardly in the same proportion as the increase in registered capital.

Normally, the operation of an EJV is limited to a fixed period of time. In some cases an unlimited period of operation can be approved by the Chinese government, especially when the transfer of advanced technology is involved. Profit and risk sharing in an EJV are proportionate to the equity of each partner in the joint venture, except in cases of a breach of the joint venture contract. Share holdings in a joint venture are usually non-negotiable and cannot be transferred without approval from the Chinese government. Investors are restricted from withdrawing registered capital during the life of the joint venture contract. Regulations surrounding the transfer of shares with only the approval of the board of directors and without approval from government authorities will probably evolve over time as the size and number of international joint ventures grow.

TABLE 13.1 Categories of Total Foreign Investment and Investment-Capital Ratios

Category	Total Investment (TI)	Minimum Registered Capital
1	Up to $3 million	At least 70% of the TI
2	From $3 million to $4.2 million	At least $2.1 million
3	$4.2 million to $10 million	At least 50% of the TI
4	$10 million to $12.5 million	At least $5 million
5	$12.5 million to $30 million	At least 40% of the TI
6	$30 million to $36 million	At least $12 million
7	More than $36 million	At least 33.33% of the TI

Note: *The foreign investment in the total project must be at least 25%. No minimum investment is set for the Chinese partner.*
Source: www.iflr.com/Article/1984450/The-pros-and-cons-of-joint-ventures.html?ArticleId=1984450. Accessed on November 16, 2011.

There are specific requirements for the management structure of an EJV but either party can hold the position as chairman of the board of directors. At least 25 percent of the total investment must be contributed by the foreign partner(s); however, there is no minimum investment for the Chinese partner(s). It is preferable that foreign exchange accounts are balanced in order to remit profits abroad so that the repatriated foreign exchange is offset by exports from the joint venture. With the elimination of foreign exchange certificates and the further opening of the China market, this requirement is becoming more and more relaxed. The permissible debt to equity ratio of a joint venture is regulated depending on the size of the joint venture (see Table 13.1).

The EJVs have been a popular entry mode for two reasons. First, the Chinese government believes that equity joint ventures best serve the Chinese objective of foreign capital, technology and management experiences. Second, foreign investors hope through engaging in joint ventures to get local partner's assistance in the domestic markets (Zhang, 2002). For the EJVs, 'equity' can include cash, buildings, equipment, materials, intellectual property rights, and land-use rights but cannot include labor. The value of any equipment, materials, intellectual property rights, or land-use rights must be approved by government authorities before the joint venture can be approved. After an EJV is registered, the entity is considered a Chinese legal entity and must abide by all Chinese laws.

13.1.2 Cooperative Joint Venture

In China, some foreign investors may also establish cooperative joint ventures (CJVs). CJVs and EJVs are similar in many respects including approval process, approval authorities, format of agreements, tax breaks, legal standing, and the means, laws, and authorities for dispute resolution. The general management structure and governance procedures are also virtually the same.

However, the CJVs are different from the EJVs in that there are no minimum limits on the foreign partner. Other differences are as follows. A CJV does not need to be a separate legal person under PRC law.[1] The partners in a CJV are allowed to share profit on an agreed basis, not necessarily in proportion to capital contribution. (In contrast, an EJV's profit, control, and risk are divided in proportion to the equity shares invested by the parties.) This proportion also determines the control and the risks of the enterprise in the same proportion. A CJV could allow negotiated levels of management and financial control, as well as methods of recourse associated with equipment leases and service contracts. In an EJV management control is through allocation of board seats. During the term of the venture, the foreign participant can recover his investment, provided the contract prescribes that and all fixed assets will become the property of the Chinese participant on termination of the joint venture.

The CJVs may have a limited or unlimited structure – therefore, there are two versions. The limited liability version is similar to the EJVs in status of permissions – the foreign investor provides the majority of funds and technology and the Chinese party provides land, buildings, equipment, and others as accepted by all the partners involved. The other format of the CJV is similar to a partnership where the parties jointly incur unlimited liability for the debts of the enterprise with no separate legal person being created. In both the cases, the status of the formed enterprise is that of a legal Chinese person which can hire labor directly as, for example, a Chinese national contractor. The minimum of the capital is registered at various levels of investment.

CJVs have their drawbacks. For example, since all CJV contract details need to be negotiated, establishing a CJV can be time consuming and expensive (Folta, 2005). Indeed, CJV negotiations can derail potential ventures as parties discover that they cannot reach agreement on every detail. As a result, CJVs sometimes are not the most appropriate business structure for the project.

13.1.3 Wholly Foreign Owned Enterprise

During the early period of reform, China only allowed foreign investors to resort to using joint ventures companies involving a Chinese partner. And the investing sectors were also restricted. China's accession to the World Trade Organization (WTO) in 2001 has helped enormously to level the playing field in China for foreign investors, by further opening previously closed sectors of industry to foreign investment.

To implement its WTO commitments, from time to time China has promulgated an updated version of the 'Catalogue for the Guidance of Foreign Investment', by gradually lifting restrictions on foreign players, particularly in the service sector, and increasing the number of industries where wholly foreign owned enterprises (WFOEs) are now allowed. The Catalogue classifies foreign direct investment projects into three categories: encouraged, restricted and prohibited. All foreign investments that are not included in the Catalogue are permitted. The level of approval for the project and the availability of tax holidays are both derived from this all-important classification.

In China, the establishment of the WFOEs is regulated by the 'Law of the PRC Concerning Enterprises with Sole Foreign Investment'. China's entry into the WTO around 2001 has had profound effect on foreign investment. The WFOE is a Chinese legal person and has to obey all Chinese laws. As such, it is allowed to enter into contracts with appropriate government authorities to acquire land-use rights, rent buildings, and receive utility services. In this it is more similar to a CJV than an EJV. Like EJVs, the WFOEs are typically limited liability enterprises, but the liability of the directors, managers, advisers, and suppliers depends on the rules which are established by the Chinese ministries and other relevant administrations to control product liability, worker safety or environmental protection. An advantage a WFOE enjoys over the other types of FDI is the protection to its know-how but its disadvantage is absence of an interested and influential Chinese party.

Joint ventures and WFOEs have a limited capacity to become indebted. As a result, their registered capital must never be less than a certain proportion of their total investment. In this context, total investment refers to the sum of the registered capital and the amount of the company's medium- and long-term debts (see Table 13.1). Capital contributions can be made in cash, patented and unpatented technology, materials and equipment or other property rights. Investors to a CJV (usually Chinese investors with insufficient financial facilities) may also contribute cooperative conditions in exchange for an agreed share of the profits. These could consist of access to or use of certain assets or rights that are not formally transferred to the CJV, including market access rights or undertakings to supply certain services that will drum up business for the CJV.

---

1. Note that a CJV that is not a separate legal person may benefit from lower costs, but may also expose the parties to greater liability than if they were legal persons, because CJVs with legal person status confer limited liability on parties to the joint venture.

13.2 INFLOW OF FOREIGN DIRECT INVESTMENT

The trends of foreign direct investment (FDI) in China can be distinguished according to changes in policy directions. During the late 1970s and the early 1980s, the Chinese government established four special economic zones (SEZs) in Guangdong and Fujian provinces, and offered special incentive policies for these SEZs to attract FDI. China has made continuous efforts to attract foreign capital in the forms of both foreign loans and FDI. Foreign loans include foreign government loans, loans from international financial institutions, and buyers' credits and other private loans. In order to attract foreign investment, the NPC enacted the 'Law of the People's Republic of China Concerning the Joint Ventures with Chinese and Foreign Investment' in 1979. In the SEZs and other economic and technological development zones, foreign investors were afforded preferential treatment. Moreover, the government assumes responsibility for improving the landscape and constructing infrastructure such as water-supply and drainage systems, electricity, roads, post and telecommunications, warehouses, and so on.

Note that FDI inflows into China were highly concentrated in these SEZs and the amount was rather limited during this period. Although a lot of interest among foreign investors in China emerged after 1979, large FDI inflows did not occur in the initial period because of the poor infrastructure (OECD, 2000). The period of 1983–91 saw a steady growth and relatively large inflows, as the special and favorable policies and measures being expanded from the four SEZs to 14 other coastal cities.

Since the early 1980s, when 14 coastal cities across ten provinces and Hainan island were opened, the previously recorded modest FDI levels started to take off. Total FDI inflows amounted to US$10.3 billion in the 1984–88 period, with an annual average growth of US$2.1 billion. This remarkable upward trend, however, dropped steeply in 1989, mainly due to the impact of the Tiananmen incident. The growth of FDI inflows into China slowed down at a meager 6.2 percent level in 1989 and only 2.8 percent in 1990. Even though FDI resumed its growth path in 1991, by recording an increase of 25.2 percent over the previous year, the annual growth rate for this overall period fell to 11.0 percent, which paled in comparison with the 38.1 percent recorded during the period 1984 to 1988 (OECD, 2000).

The third phase began in the spring of 1992, when Deng Xiaoping went on a tour of China's southern coastal areas and SEZs. His visit, whose principal intention was to push forward China's overall economic reform process and to emphasize China's commitment to the open-door policy and market-oriented economic reform, also proved

to be a success in terms of increasing the confidence of foreign investors in China. China adopted a new approach, turning away from special regimes toward a more nationwide implementation of open policies for FDI. The government issued a series of new policies and regulations to encourage FDI inflows. The results were remarkable: Since 1992 the inflows of FDI into China have accelerated and reached the peak level in the early 2000s. Since 2001, China has become the only country that has seen its FDI increase continually. This fact suggested location factors play a critical role in China's FDI growth process, and China has unique advantages over other potential countries in attracting FDI.

Since it made its first calls for foreign capital participation in its economy in 1979, China has received a growing amount of foreign investment (see Figure 13.1). China has become the second largest FDI recipient in the world, after the United States, and the largest host country among the developing countries. China's position as a host to FDI is in fact too far removed from any other developing country – and most developed countries – to be placed under any serious challenge. China has been the largest recipient of FDI among developing countries since 1993. China's joining of the WTO in 2001 provided a strong push for a new wave of foreign investment into China. In 2003, China overtook the United States as the world's biggest recipient of FDI, attracting a figure of US$53 billion. By the end of 2010, the actual use of foreign investment has reached more than US$100 billion (see Table 13.2), which is equivalent to 10 percent of direct investment worldwide and about 30 percent of the combined investment amount for all developing countries.

Regarding the origins of FDI, Hong Kong has been the largest investor and contributed 60 percent of the total foreign investment in 2009, followed by Taiwan (7 percent), Japan (5 percent), Singapore (4 percent), USA (4 percent), South Korea (3 percent) and UK (2 percent).[2] The CJVs were initially the most important type in China. Since the late 1980s, the EJVs have become predominant and recent years have seen a proliferation of WFOEs (see Figure 13.2). In recent years many foreign investors have chosen wholly foreign owned enterprises as the preferred entry mode so as to avoid problems associated with equity joint ventures.

13.2.1 Sectoral Distribution

During the 1980s and early 1990s, most of the foreign investments came from small and medium-sized

2. Calculated by the author based on NBS (2010). Note that the data include investments sourced in these countries but made through Barbados, the British Virgin Islands, the Cayman Islands, Mauritius, and Western Samoa.

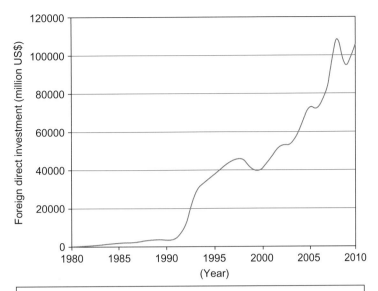

FIGURE 13.1 Annual inward foreign direct investment flows to China, 1980–2010.
Source: UNCTAD (2011).

TABLE 13.2 Non-Financial Foreign Direct Investment (FDI) Inflows to China, 2001–10

Year	Projects		Utilized FDI	
	Number	Growth (%)	US$ (billion)	Growth (%)
2001	26,140	17.0	46.9	15.1
2002	34,171	30.7	52.7	12.5
2003	41,081	20.2	53.5	1.4
2004	43,664	6.3	60.6	13.3
2005	44,001	0.8	60.3	−0.5
2006	41,485	−5.7	69.5	4.5
2007	37,871	−8.7	74.8	18.6
2008	27,514	−27.3	92.4	23.6
2009	23,435	−14.8	90.0	−2.6
2010	27,406	16.9	105.7	17.4

Source: NBS (2011).

enterprises based in Hong Kong. The dominant position of Hong Kong is apparent from several factors. First, Hong Kong is geographically adjacent to Guangdong province, where Shenzhen – the most important SEZ of China – is located. Secondly, it was in the 1980s that Hong Kong made the transfer of its export-oriented labor-intensive manufacturing industry to mainland China. This is the

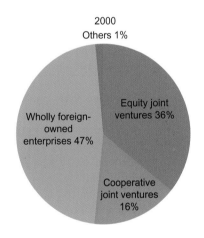

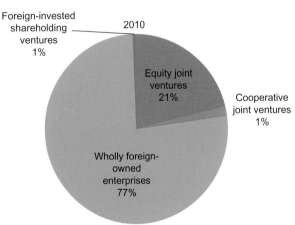

FIGURE 13.2 The structural changes of the FDI in China (from 2000 to 2010).

typical 'Flying Geese Paradigm' of the international division of labor. Thirdly, especially since 1992, investments from Hong Kong took advantage of the preferential treatment given to foreign investors.

In terms of sectoral distribution, foreign investment in China has concentrated on secondary industries, but tertiary industries have become the latest destination for China-bound FDI. The scope of foreign investment has now extended from investments in tourism, textile and building industries to cooperative ventures in oil exploration, transportation, telecommunications, machine building, electronics, and other industries.

As China fulfills its WTO commitments, it will further open up the financial, insurance, telecommunications, energy, water, commercial, accounting, auditing, and legal sectors, which are expected to absorb more foreign investment. Early investors saw China as a place to digest outdated technologies. In the 1980s, multinationals saw the world's new markets, such as China, India, and Brazil, as a venue for selling their out-dated products. But as market competition intensifies in China, many foreign firms have increasingly adopted new technologies to maintain their market shares. The number of patents registered by multinationals in China has been rising rapidly since the early 1990s. It is clear that those companies see China as a new focus of their global strategy and have put more emphasis on localization of their research and development (R&D) capacities.

Multinationals have built more R&D centers in China. According to UNCTAD (2001), by the end of 2000, they had established more than 100 such centers in China. Most of them are located in Beijing, Shanghai, and Guangzhou. Intensifying market competition has driven the localization of the R&D capacities of multinationals. It can speed up the launch of new products on the domestic market, which is crucial for grabbing market share. It can also help improve relations between multinationals and the host country, which often hopes that these multinationals can transfer more state-of-the-art technologies (Yunshi and Jing, 2005).

During the 1980s, FDI was concentrated in traditional labor-intensive manufacturing industries (light industry), especially textiles, garments and real estate companies. Since 1992, it has gradually shifted to capital- and technology-intensive sectors, such as chemicals, machinery, transport equipment, electronics and telecommunications. In the second half of the 1990s, while there was stagnation in foreign investments in traditional labor-intensive manufacturing industries, the IT industry became a new focus of investment. Investments in technology-intensive industries have become a new focus of investment. The goal to attract FDI inflows has been to introduce advanced technology, improve management and expand markets. The modes of foreign investment have undergone some systematic changes. The basic option in the early period of reform was to set up a contractual joint venture. Since 1986, equity joint ventures and wholly foreign-owned enterprise investments have become the main forms of foreign investment. Since the 1990s, the share of wholly foreign-invested enterprises has increased gradually, as has the level of foreign control of joint ventures. By 2000, the actual investment share of wholly foreign-owned enterprises exceeded that of joint ventures; the former became the main force in impelling growth in foreign trade. A related fact is that, with the exception of a few sectors, the Chinese government repealed restrictions on foreign control in joint ventures.

13.2.2 Regional Distribution

Foreign investment has been unevenly distributed in China. FDI inflows have been heavily concentrated in China's coastal provinces, while the Central and Western Regions have attracted only marginal shares. By 2000, foreign investments were felt in all parts of China, except in Tibet. Throughout the period the southeast coastal area has dominated as a recipient of inward foreign investment. Not surprisingly, the most important determinant for the irregular absorption of foreign capital is geographical location. For example, the Eastern belt received most of the foreign capital, while less than 10 percent of the total foreign capital flowed into the Central and Western belts, which cover more than 85 percent of China's territory. Nevertheless, this uneven pattern has improved gradually as a result of the government efforts to internationalize the inland economy.

This inequality stems from the FDI policies taken by the Chinese authorities at both the central and the local levels. The open door began with the creation of SEZs and preferential regimes for 14 coastal cities. This has resulted in an overwhelming concentration of FDI in the east. With the adoption of more broad-based economic reforms and open-door policies for FDI in the 1990s, FDI inflows into China have started to spread to other provinces. Among the eastern region provinces, Guangdong's performance in attracting FDI has been particularly impressive. Its share of accumulated FDI stock from 1983 to 1998 was 29.4 percent of the national total, far exceeding all other provinces including Jiangsu and Fujian, each of which possessed around 10 percent of the national total, and ranked second and third among China's thirty provinces. However, if we analyze this province group one step further, we find that the shares of each province have changed gradually. The share of Guangdong has declined from 46.13 percent in the 1980s to 27.98 percent in the 1990s. In contrast, the shares of other coastal provinces (such as Jiangsu, Fujian, Zhejiang, Shandong, Tianjin, and Hubei) have increased steadily.

In recent years the share of the central provinces in the national total of accumulated FDI stocks has increased gradually – from 5.3 percent during the 1980s to 9.2 percent during the 1990s. The main contributors are Henan, Hubei, and Hunan provinces, with their shares of accumulated FDI in the national total doubling between the 1980s and the 1990s. These figures suggest that the provincial distribution of FDI inflows has spread somewhat from the opened coastal provinces into the inland provinces. The western, less developed provinces received only a very small amount of FDI inflows, with their share in the national accumulated FDI stocks declining from 4.7 percent in the 1980s to 3.2 percent in the 1990s. However, Sichuan and Shaanxi attracted relatively higher levels of FDI inflows than the other provinces in this group. In the final analysis, FDI inflows in the 1990s have diffused from the initially concentrated southern coastal areas toward the southeastern and eastern coastal areas as well as toward inland areas.

The three provincial groups of the Eastern, Central and Western belts have experienced different patterns of FDI inflows. For the eastern region provinces FDI inflows have been increasing steadily. For the other two provincial groups, the inflows of FDI have been much lower, especially for the western region provinces. As a result, in terms of the absolute magnitude of annual FDI inflows the gap between the Eastern belt and the Central and Western belts has actually broadened.

13.2.3 Contributions to the Chinese Economy

Foreign investment has played an increasing role in the Chinese economy. What is more important, the foreign enterprises have promoted the importation of advanced technology, equipment, and management and, above all, competition mechanisms from the advanced economies. Moreover, the foreign-funded enterprises (FIEs) have generated a considerable portion of China's total tax revenues and millions of job opportunities in the urban areas. In summary, the major effects of FDI on the Chinese economy are to:

- Increase trade growth and participation in the international segmentation of production
- Build dynamic specialization
- Increase export competitiveness
- Become an important source of capital
- Create jobs, upgrade skills, and raise wages of employees
- Raise factor productivity and increased technology transfer
- Upgrade China's industrial structure
- Increase domestic competition
- Increase industrial performance.

13.3 OUTWARD DIRECT INVESTMENT

13.3.1 Historical Evolution

Although China's outward direct investment (ODI) is still smaller than its massive inward FDI, China's overseas companies have been gaining momentum in moving international capital, investing across a broad spectrum of sectors ranging from natural resources to manufacturing to telecommunications and many others. During the past decades, China's outward foreign direct investment (ODI) has gone through four stages:

Stage I (1979–85)

In August 1979, the State Council proposed 'to go abroad to do business', setting, for the first time, the development of foreign investment as a state policy. During this stage, China was just opening up to the world, and foreign trade was still in the mighty grip of government control. Only state-owned companies, as well as large provincial- and municipal-owned enterprises, could invest overseas.

Stage II (1986–91)

During the second stage, the Chinese government began gradual liberalization to allow more enterprises, including non-state owned firms, to establish investment in other countries, provided they had sufficient capital and a suitable foreign partner. As China's economic development grew, the trend of China's foreign investment started to increase. However, until the early 1990s, China's basic guiding principle of foreign direct investment was still to limit the overseas investment of Chinese enterprises. In this stage, China's outward investment was only promoted by the introduction of foreign capital, technology, equipment, and management experience, and the 'going out' businesses were still very small.

Stage III (1992–98)

During the third stage, as liberalization reforms progressed and companies began aggressively engaging in real estate and stock speculation, mostly across Asia, the Asian financial crisis struck. Many unprepared countries suffered heavy losses due to institutional weakness, corruption, and lack of management expertise. Alarmed by the hemorrhage of precious foreign exchange assets, China's Ministry of Foreign Trade and Economic Cooperation (MOFTEC) tightened approval procedures, setting up rigorous screening and monitoring processes for any overseas venture of over $1 million.

In his report at the 15th National Congress of the Communist Party of China, held in September 1997, Jiang Zemin put forward the idea to strive to improve the level of opening up and to actively explore the international market, in which China for the first time clearly stated:

…We shall encourage investing abroad in areas that can bring China's comparative advantages into play. We shall make better use of both Chinese and foreign markets and resources. We shall improve and enforce laws and regulations governing China's trade and economic relations with foreign countries.[3]

After the 1997 Asian financial crisis, in order to expand exports, China began to encourage enterprises to develop overseas processing and assembly operations. In February 1999, the State Council approved the former Ministry of Foreign Trade, the former State Economic and Trade Commission, and the Ministry of Finance 'to encourage enterprises to develop overseas processing and assembly operations'. This set the basic principles and specific policy measures to guide China's overseas enterprises.

Stage IV (1999–present)

Starting in 1999, China entered its current stage of ODI development. China's 'going out' strategy was consolidated. During this period, many important laws and regulations were enacted to aid outward investment. As a result, China's outward foreign direct investment flows have grown sharply during this period (see Figure 13.3).

13.3.2 China's 'Going Out' Strategy

The 'going out' strategy (or '*zouchuqu zhanlue*' in Chinese pinyin) is China's current strategy to encourage

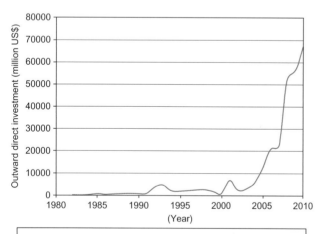

Notes: (1) Figures are measured in US dollars at current prices and current exchange rates in millions. (2) The UNCTAD figures include only non-financial FDI.

FIGURE 13.3 China's outward foreign direct investment flows, 1980–2010. *Source: UNCTAD (2011).*

its enterprises to invest overseas. The essence of the 'going out' strategy is to promote 'the international operations of capable Chinese firms with a view to improving resource allocation and enhancing their international competitiveness'.

The 'going out' strategy was initiated in 1999 by the Chinese government to promote Chinese investments abroad. The strategy was formally proposed in March 2000 during the Third Session of the Ninth National People's Congress (NPC). The 'going out' strategy was finally approved in the Fifth Plenary Session of the 15th CCP Congress held in October 2000. The session examined and adopted the 'National Economy and Social Development Five-Year Plan'. Recommendations for the first time clearly stated, 'going out' strategy, and used it as one of China's four new development strategies (i.e., the Western development strategy, the urban strategy, the talent strategy, and the 'going out' strategy). In order to promote its 'going out' strategy, the Chinese government has also implemented a series of measures including the further simplification of various procedures (see Box 13.1).

The Chinese government, together with the China Council for the Promotion of International Trade (CCPIT), has introduced several schemes to encourage and assist domestic companies to exploit opportunities in the expanding local and international markets. In October 2004, the National Development and Reform Commission (NDRC) and the Export-Import Bank of China (EIBC) jointly issued a circular to encourage overseas investment in specific areas:[4]

1. Resource exploration projects to mitigate the domestic shortage of natural resources
2. Projects that promote the export of domestic technologies, products, equipment, and labor
3. Overseas research and development (R&D) centers to utilize internationally advanced technologies, managerial skills, and professionals
4. Mergers and acquisitions that could enhance the international competitiveness of Chinese enterprises and accelerate their entry into foreign markets.

In October 2005, at the Fifth Plenary Session of the 16th CCPCC, China once again made commitments to support qualified Chinese enterprises to 'going out' in its 'Recommendations on the "Eleventh Five-Year" Plan for National Economy and Social Development'. One year later, the Central Economic Work Conference, held in Beijing in December 2006, once again stressed that China should continue to implement the 'going out' strategy. Thereafter, the 'going out' strategy was fully implemented in the 'Eleventh Five-Year' period (2006–2010). In March

---

3. Cited from http://www.fas.org/news/china/1997/970912-prc.htm. Accessed on December 7, 2011.

4. Cited from UNCTAD (2006, p. 210).

Box 13.1   A Guide to Applying for Visas

Since the late 1970s when the open-door policy was introduced, Chinese citizens have been freer to go abroad.
However, problems still remain due to both the border control policy of China and the unavailability of visa-free access
to most of the foreign nations. Chinese citizens going abroad
for public affairs are able to apply for 'public affairs passports'
(*gongwu huzhao*), while those who intend to go abroad for
private affairs have to apply for passports and visas through
a more complicated procedure. The diagram below shows a
visa application process in the mid-1990s.

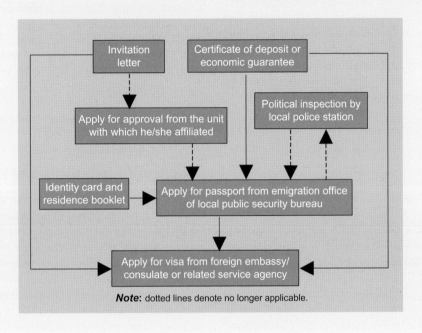

Note: dotted lines denote no longer applicable.

2010, in his government work report at the Third Session
of the Eleventh National People's Congress (NPC),
Premier Wen Jiabao stressed the need to accelerate the
implementation of the 'going out' strategy to encourage
industry to meet the needs of foreign markets and called
for an orderly transfer of production capacity to support
qualified enterprises to carry out overseas mergers and
acquisitions, and deepen mutually beneficial cooperation
and foreign resources to enhance the quality of foreign
contracted projects and labor cooperation.[5]

Since 2010, the State Council has further simplified
various types of examination and approval procedures, the
implementation of the autonomy of enterprises investing
abroad, including those to grant export tax rebates, financial and foreign exchange assistance, and other incentives
to Chinese enterprises wishing to tap overseas markets.

Since the launching of the 'going out' strategy, interest
in overseas investment by Chinese companies has increased
significantly. This boost in outward foreign investment can

also be attributed to the Chinese government's commitment
to creating the right environment for outward investment;
and China's huge production capacity. With a dynamic
economy, and a strong business-friendly culture, the outlook for Chinese companies will continue to be positive.

As part of its efforts to restructure state-owned enterprises, the Chinese government has established the
SASAC (State-Owned Asset Supervision Administration
Commission), which develops China's equity exchange
market, while supporting Chinese foreign investments. The
SASAC operates through several equity exchanges such
as CBEX (China Beijing Equity Exchange), which is the
largest and most prestigious in terms of trading volume. It
is headquartered in the heart of Beijing's financial district.
Presently, CBEX has established three international platforms in Italy, Japan, and the United States.

Realized and planned foreign direct investment deals
indicate that the government encourages Chinese enterprises to invest overseas in order to gain access to raw
materials and advanced technology from abroad, increase
foreign exchange earnings, and promote China's exports.
In general, China's 'going out' strategy has brought about
the following positive results:

---

5. Cited from http://info.e-to-china.com/investment_guide/75421.html.
Accessed on December 8, 2011.

Avoiding Intensified Competition in the Domestic Market

As domestic Chinese markets have become more competitive, the motivation for Chinese firms to invest abroad has grown in importance. These firms' efforts at overseas expansion are responses to saturated domestic markets or attempts to gain first-mover advantage in untapped overseas markets rather than attempts to further Chinese strategic interests. Investment in tax havens (such as Hong Kong, the Cayman Islands, and the British Virgin Islands) is a major component of Chinese outward direct investment and one that makes the ultimate destination of Chinese overseas investment especially difficult to track.

Easy Access to Overseas Sources of Raw Materials and Energy

The need to secure access to overseas raw materials (such as oil, aluminum, copper, nickel, iron ore, and agricultural products) to support China's high economic growth rate continues to be a key strategic driving force. Most mergers and acquisitions completed in 2007–10 were in the energy and minerals sectors, although the largest transactions tended to be purchases of minority stakes in global financial institutions (Salidjanova, 2011). A similar picture of explosive growth in demand on the part of China has also been forming in the case of petroleum. China has moved from being East Asia's largest oil exporter to becoming the world's third largest importer of oil, behind the United States and Japan. The natural resource-seeking ODI of the Chinese energy majors is intimately connected with the government's pursuit of a national energy security agenda to secure overseas assets and supply agreements. Meanwhile, the Chinese authorities have been courting the governments of host states aggressively by strengthening bilateral trade relations, awarding aid, and providing a much-needed transport and communications infrastructure.

Acquisition of Technology, Brands, and Know-How

Technologically, China is still a relatively undeveloped nation compared to the United States and the European Union. Through mergers and acquisitions (M&As), however, China does not have to spend decades building up brand names because it can simply acquire existing well-known brands. Moreover, it is also able to gain managerial and commercial experience in international marketing and advertising. Overseas investment can help Chinese firms acquire advanced technology, manufacturing processes, and managerial know-how. FIEs are encouraged to enter joint ventures or to purchase foreign companies through which they can absorb state-of-the-art technologies and thus 'leapfrog' several stages of development and upgrades.[6]

Avoiding or Overcoming International Barriers to Trade

Chinese investment abroad is also motivated to avoid foreign quotas, tariffs, and other barriers set to Chinese-made goods. This was a more compelling motivation for overseas investment before China's World Trade Organization (WTO) accession.[7] Although WTO accession has lowered the tariffs and quotas on Chinese exports, Chinese firms have continued to build factories in countries that have relatively unfettered access to the American and European markets.

13.3.3   Characteristics and Directions

The internationalization of Chinese ODI has intensified, driven by resource-, asset-, and efficiency-seeking, as well as by the 'going out' strategy. Also complicating matters is the practice of round-tripping, which many Chinese enterprises use to park a large proportion of their foreign exchange holdings in Hong Kong, with some later funneled into foreign countries as FDI and some subsequently recycled back into China as 'new FDI' in order to take advantage of China's relevant favorable policies toward 'foreign investment' in China. The Annex provides a list of major Chinese overseas investment deals from 2008 to 2010.

As shown in Figure 13.4 and Table 13.3, although geographically dispersed, a significant proportion of China's ODI (stock) is concentrated in a few countries. For example, Hong Kong, the British Virgin Islands and the Cayman Islands alone received 78.59 percent of total Chinese outbound investment, which is perhaps explained in part by their role as round-tripping hubs. The regional bias in favor of Asia may also be partially explained by Chinese companies setting up their production facilities in the region, in Southeast Asia in particular, with the aim of expanding their market share in the host countries and reducing production costs (Lunding, 2006).

Chinese outward direct investment (ODI) targets a wide variety of areas (see Figure 13.5), reflecting both the

---

6. Examples of successful M&As include Lenovo's purchase of IBM's personal computer division in 2005, and Nanjing and Geely Automotives' acquisitions of British car manufacturer MG Rover's brand in 2005 and Ford Motors' Volvo unit in 2010.

7. For example, before China became a member of the WTO, its textiles, clothing, and footwear (TCF) products had limited access to the US market. TCF firms consequently invested in Australia and then exported 'Made-in-Australia' products to the US in order to avoid American textiles quotas for non-WTO producers (Wong and Chan, 2003, p. 285).

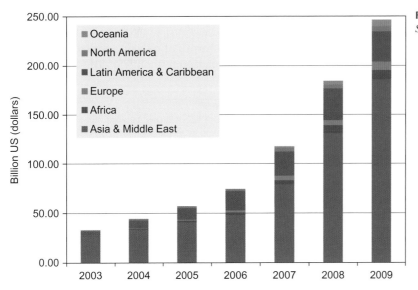

FIGURE 13.4 Chinese ODI by region, stock.
Source: MOFCOM (2010).

TABLE 13.3 Top Destinations for China's Outward Direct Investment in 2009 (Stock)

Destination	Amount (million US$)	Share (%)
Hong Kong	164,498.94	66.94
British Virgin Islands	15,060.69	6.13
Cayman Islands	13,577.07	5.52
Australia	5,863.10	2.39
Singapore	4,857.32	1.98
United States	3,338.42	1.36
South Africa	2,306.86	0.94
Luxembourg	2,484.38	1.01
Russia	2,220.37	0.90
Macau	1,837.23	0.75
Canada	1,670.34	0.68
Kazakhstan	1,516.21	0.62
Pakistan	1,458.09	0.59
Mongolia	1,241.66	0.51
South Korea	1,217.80	0.50
Germany	1,082.24	0.44
UK	1,028.28	0.42
Nigeria	1,025.96	0.42
Myanmar	929.88	0.38
Zambia	843.97	0.34
Others	17,696.57	7.20
World Total	245,755.38	100.00

Source: MOFCOM (2010).

diversified nature of the country's domestic industries and the Chinese government's policy considerations. The consistently high percentage of investment flow in the service sector (30 percent in business services and 19 percent in finance in 2009) reflects the fact that the ODI is largely used to serve and promote the export of Chinese commodities. The natural resource sector is the third biggest and has far-reaching impacts. Oil, gas, and mineral extraction in particular are important areas for the Chinese.

Since the early 2000s, China's national oil companies (NOCs) have taken a number of steps to gain access to investment opportunities in the Middle East, in such fields as exploration and exploitation, as well as in the construction of refineries (see Table 13.4). The investment comprises large oil and gas fields in the countries with rich oil and gas reserves, such as Iran, Iraq, Kuwait, Oman, Saudi Arabia, Syria, the United Arab Emirates (UAE), and Yemen. The year 2009 saw Chinese oil companies secure significant deals: China National Petroleum Corporation (CNPC) concluded an agreement with the Iranian government to replace Total to develop Phase 11 of the South Pars gas field; Sinopec launched a successful purchase of Swiss oil explorer Addax Petroleum Corporation (APC), which was producing oil fields in the semi-autonomous Kurdish region in northern Iraq; and British Petroleum (BP) and CNPC won a contract to develop the giant Rumaila oil field in southern Iraq at the end of June 2009.

While China will continue with attempts to gain access to large oil/gas reserves in the rest of the world, its NOCs may lack the technical and managerial skills for the largest and most complex projects. As a result, China's NOCs will benefit from cooperating with the major international oil companies. In this context, BP and CNPC have planned to invest approximately US$15 billion in cash over the 20-year lifetime of the contract with the intention of increasing plateau production to 2.85 million barrels a day in the Rumaila oil field for the second half of the 2010s. The consortium led by BP (38 percent) with partners CNPC (37 percent) and the Iraqi government's representative State Oil Marketing Organization (25 percent) has agreed to nearly triple the Rumaila field's output to almost 3 million barrels of oil a day, which would make it the world's second largest oilfield (BP Press Office, November 3, 2009).

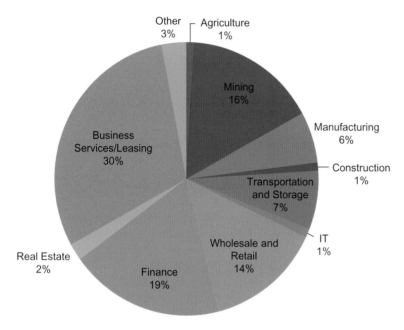

FIGURE 13.5 China's outward direct investment in 2009 (stock) by sector. *Source: MOFCOM (2010).*

TABLE 13.4 Summary of Selected Exploration, Production, and Refining Investment by Chinese NOCs in the Middle East, 2001–2010

Country	Reserves Oil (bn bb)/gas (tcm)	Project Name	Project Type	Date Signed	Company	Investment
Saudi Arabia	264/7.2	Section B (gas)	Exploration & production	2004	Sinopec	<US$5.2 bn
Iran	138/27.8	Block 3 (oil)	Exploration & production	2005	CNPC	
		Masjed-I-Suleiman (oil)	Acquisition	2004	CNPC	US$150 m
		South Pars (gas)	Development	2009	CNPC	US$2 bn
		Yadavaran (oil)	Exploration & production	2007	Sinopec	US$160 m
		Zarareh-Kashan	Exploration & production	2001	Sinopec	US$16 bn
		North Pars (gas)	Exploration & production	2006	CNPC	
		Arak (oil)	Refinery upgrade	2006	Sinopec	
Iraq	115/3.2	Al-Ahdab (oil)	Development	1997/2008	CNPC	US$190 m
		South Rumaila (oil)	Development	2009	CNPC	
		Addax assets (oil)	Exploration & production, refinery	2009	Sinopec	US$350 m

(Continued)

TABLE 13.4 (Continued)

Country	Reserves Oil (bn bb)/gas (tcm)	Project Name	Project Type	Date Signed	Company	Investment
Kuwait	101/1.8		Development	2009	Sinopec	
UAE	98/6.1	Uraq&Zora (gas)	Acquisition	2003	Sinochem	
Oman	5.6/0.7	Blocks 36&38	Exploration & production	2004	Sinopec	
		Blocks 17&40	Acquisition	2003	Sinochem	
		Blocks 5 (oil)	Exploration & production		CNPC	
Yemen	2.8/0.5	Block S2		2001	CNPC	
		Block 69&71		2005	Sinopec	
Syria	2.5/0.3	Qubibe (oil)	Development	2004	CNPC	
		Al Furat Prod Co (oil)	Acquisition	2005	CNPC	US$570 m
		Al Zour (oil)	Refinery	2008	CNPC	US$2 bn
		Block 10 (oil)	Acquisition	2008	Sinochem	
			Acquisition	2010	CNPC	US$1,500 m

Notes: *CNPC = China National Petroleum Corporation; NOC = national oil companies; Sinopec = China Petrochemical Corporation Group.*
Sources: Andrew-Speed (2009, p. 19) and Scissors (2011).

ANNEX

A List of Major Chinese Overseas Investment Deals, 2008–2010

Year	Acquiring Company	Transaction Value; Shares Acquired	Target Company, if Any	Industry	Target Country
2008	SAFE	US$180 m; 1%	Australia and New Zealand Banking, Commonwealth Bank of Australia, National Bank of Australia	Banking	Australia
2008	Wuxi PharmaTech	US$150 m	AppTec Lab Services	Pharma	USA
2008	Minmetals (20%), Xingxing Iron's (35%) with Kelachandra and Manasara	US$1,200 m	Kelachandra and Manasara	Steel	India
2008	China Metallurgical	US$370 m		Iron	Australia
2008	Sinochem	US$470 m	Soco	Oil	Yemen
2008	Chalco, with Alcoa	US$12,800 m; 12%	Rio Tinto	Aluminum	Australia
2008	CIC	US$100 m	Visa	Finance	USA
2008	China Life	US$260 m; 1%	Visa	Finance	USA
2008	Sinopec	US$560 m; 60%	AED	Oil	Australia
2008	Huaneng Power	US$3,000 m	Tuas Power	Power	Singapore

(Continued)

A List of Major Chinese Overseas Investment Deals, 2008–2010 (Continued)

Year	Acquiring Company	Transaction Value; Shares Acquired	Target Company, if Any	Industry	Target Country
2008	CIC	US$3,200m; 80%	JC Flowers	Investment	USA
2008	SAFE	US$2,800m; 1.6%	Total	Energy	France
2008	SAFE	US$2,000m; 1%	BP	Energy	Britain
2008	China Nonferrous	US$150m		Copper	Zambia
2008	Chinalco	US$2,160m		Copper	Peru
2008	CNPC	US$5,000m		Oil	Niger
2008	Zoomlion	US$250m; 60%	Compagnia Italiana Forme Acciaio	Construction	Italy
2008	SAFE	US$2,500m; 20%	TPG	Investment	USA
2008	China National Cereals, Oils, and Foodstuffs	US$140m; 5%	Smithfield Foods	Food	USA
2008	China Railway Engineering and Sinohydro	US$1,200m; 28%		Metals	DRC
2008	CNOOC	US$2,500m	Awilco Offshore	Oil	Norway
2008	China Nonferrous	US$800m; 50%		Metals	Myanmar
2008	Sinosteel	US$1,300m	Midwest	Iron	Australia
2008	China Metalurgical	US$850m; 20%		Metals	DRC
2008	Sinohydro	US$850m; 20%		Metals	DRC
2008	Shenhua	US$260m		Coal	Australia
2008	CNPC	US$3,000m		Oil	Iraq
2008	Sinopec	US$1,900m	Canada-based Tanganyika Oil	Oil	Syria
2008	China International Marine Containers	US$330m; 30%	Yantai Raffles Shipyard	Shipping	Singapore
2008	Sany Heavy Industry	US$140m		Construction	Germany
2008	Jiangsu Shagang	US$270m; 45%	Bulk Minerals and Grange	Iron	Australia
2008	CIC	US$200m; 2.6%	Blackstone	Investment	USA
2008	CNPC	US$1,280m; 51%	Myanmar Oil and Gas Enterprise	Construction	Myanmar
2008	China Metallurgical	US$1,000m		Copper	Philippines
2008	10 property companies	US$520m	Pacific Holdings	Property	Japan
2008	China Union	US$2,600m		Iron	Liberia
2009	CNPC	US$1,760m	National Iranian Oil Company	Oil	Iran
2009	Hunan Valin Iron & Steel	US$770m; 16.5%	Fortescue Metals	Iron	Australia
2009	Shougang Group	US$1,000m		Iron	Peru
2009	Wuhan Iron and Steel	US$240m; 19.9%		Iron	Canada
2009	CIC	US$800m	Investment in Morgan Stanley property fund	Property	USA

(Continued)

A List of Major Chinese Overseas Investment Deals, 2008–2010 (Continued)

Year	Acquiring Company	Transaction Value; Shares Acquired	Target Company, if Any	Industry	Target Country
2009	CNPC	US$2,600m	KasMunaigas	Gas	Kazakhstan
2009	China Nonferrous	US$450m; 85%		Copper	Zambia
2009	China Metallurgical	US$520m; 10%	Palmer's Mineralogy	Coal	Australia
2009	Guangdong Rising Asset Management	US$140m; 19.9%	PanAust	Metals	Australia
2009	PetroChina	US$1,020m; 46%	Keppel, Singapore Petroleum	Oil	Singapore
2009	AnSteel	US$130m; 24%	Gindalbie Metals	Iron	Australia
2009	Minmetals	US$1,350m	Oz Minerals	Metals	Australia
2009	CIC	US$1,210m	Morgan Stanley	Banking	USA
2009	Sinopec	US$7,200m	Addax Petroleum	Oil	Switzerland
2009	CIC	US$160m; 8%	Goodman Group	Real Estate	Australia
2009	CNPC	US$4,700m		Gas	Iran
2009	CIC	US$500m	Blackstone	Investment	USA
2009	CIC	US$530m	Blackrock	Investment	USA
2009	CIC	US$1,500m; 17%	Teck Resources	Copper	Canada
2009	Zhonghui Mining	US$3,600m		Copper	Zambia
2009	Xiyang Group	US$480m		Iron	Russia
2009	Chinalco	US$1,500m	Rio Tinto	Aluminum	Australia
2009	Shenhua Guohau Power	US$330m; 70%		Power	Indonesia
2009	CIC	US$370m; 1.10%	Diageo	Food	Britain
2009	Group of Shanxi companies	US$750m		Property	Mauritius
2009	CIC	US$450m; 19%	Songbird Estates	Property	Britain
2009	CNPC	US$1,740m; 60%	Athabasca Oil Sands	Oil	Canada
2009	CNOOC	US$100m	Qatar Petroleum	Gas	Qatar
2009	Sinochem	US$880m	Emerald Energy	Energy	Britain
2009	Yanzhou Coal	US$2,950m	Felix Resources	Coal	Australia
2009	CIC	US$1,090m	Goodman Group	Property	Australia
2009	Sinohydro	US$800m		Hydro	Cameroon
2009	PetroChina	US$1,160m	Singapore Petroleum	Oil	Singapore
2009	CIC	US$940m; 11%	JSC KazMunaiGas E&P	Gas	Kazakhstan
2009	CIC	US$600m	Oaktree Capital Management distressed asset fund	Investment	USA
2009	CIC	US$600m	Goldman Sachs distressed asset fund	Investment	USA
2009	State Construction Engineering	US$100m; 2.75%	Baha Mar Resort		Bahamas
2009	CNPC	US$2,250m		Oil	Iran

(Continued)

A List of Major Chinese Overseas Investment Deals, 2008–2010 (Continued)

Year	Acquiring Company	Transaction Value; Shares Acquired	Target Company, if Any	Industry	Target Country
2009	Hanlong Mining	US$200m	Moly Mines	Iron	Australia
2009	CIC	US$300m	Nobel Holdings	Oil	Russia
2009	Baosteel	US$240m; 15%	Aquila Resources	Iron	Australia
2009	CIC	US$1,580m; 15%	AES	Power	USA
2009	Beijing West Industries	US$100m	Delphi	Autos	USA
2009	Wuhan Iron and Steel	US$400m; 22%	MMX Mineracao	Iron	Brazil
2009	Great Wall Motor	US$120m	Litex Motors	Autos	Bulgaria
2009	Wuhan Iron and Steel	US$250m	Centrex Minerals	Iron	Australia
2009	Shunde Rixin	US$1,900m; 70%		Iron	Chile
2009	China Railway Construction and Tongling Nonferrous	US$650m	Corriente Resources	Copper	Canada
2009	Zijin Mining	US$500m	Indophil Resources		Australia
2009	CNPC	US$190m		Oil	Iraq
2009	BAIC	US$200m	Saab	Autos	USA
2009	Hebei Zhongxin	US$400m		Autos	Mexico
2009	Shanghai Auto	US$330m; 50%	GM	Autos	India
2009	Jinjiang International Hotels	US$150m; 50%	Thayer Lodging	Tourism	USA
2010	China Metallurgical	US$200m; 5%	Resource House	Metals	Australia
2010	China Nickel Resources	US$220m		Steel	Indonesia
2010	Baiyin Non-Ferrous, CITIC & Chang Xin	US$190m; 60%	Oxus	Metals	Uzbekistan
2010	Chalco	US$350m; 35%	GIIG	Aluminum	Malaysia
2010	CIC	US$960m; 2.30%	Apax Finance	Investment	Britain
2010	ICBC	US$530m	ACL Bank	Banking	Thailand
2010	CIC	US$1,500m	Lexington Partners, Pantheon Ventures, Goldman Sachs	Investment	USA
2010	Sany Heavy Industry	US$200m		Construction	Brazil
2010	Wanhua Industrial	US$190m	BorsodChem	Chemicals	Hungary
2010	CNPC	US$180m; 51%	INOVA Geophysical Equipment	Energy	USA
2010	Hudian	US$650m; 51%	Sintez	Gas	Russia
2010	Geely Auto	US$1,800m	Ford	Autos	Sweden
2010	East China Mineral Exploration and Development Bureau (Jiangsu)	US$1,200m	Itaminas	Iron	Brazil
2010	Poly Technologies	US$100m		Agriculture	Mauritania
2010	CNOOC	US$3,100m; 50%	Bridas	Oil	Argentina

(Continued)

A List of Major Chinese Overseas Investment Deals, 2008–2010 (Continued)

Year	Acquiring Company	Transaction Value; Shares Acquired	Target Company, if Any	Industry	Target Country
2010	PetroChina	1,580 m; 50%	Arrow Energy	Gas	Australia
2010	CIC	US$250 m; 13%	South Gobi Energy	Coal	Mongolia
2010	First Auto Works	US$100 m		Autos	South Africa
2010	China National Chemical Engineering	US$500 m		Agriculture	Sudan
2010	China Railway Materials	US$260 m; 13.00%	African Minerals	Iron	Sierra Leone
2010	Sinopec	US$4,650 m; 9%	ConocoPhillip	Oil	Canada
2010	CNOOC	US$270 m; 5%	BG	Gas	Australia
2010	CNPC	US$900 m		Oil	Venezuela
2010	Tencent	US$300 m; 10.00%	Digital Sky Technologies	Technology	Russia
2010	China Mobile	US$300 m		Telecom	Pakistan
2010	Chongqing Food Group	US$320 m		Agriculture	Brazil
2010	Hanlong	US$140 m; 55%	Moly Mines	Rare metals	Australia
2010	CNPC	US$1,500 m; 35%	Shell	Energy	Syria
2010	Hopu	US$100 m; 1%	Chesapeake Energy	Gas	USA
2010	CIC	US$1,220 m; 5%	Penn West Energy	Oil	Canada
2010	State Grid	US$990 m	Cobra, Elecnor and Isolux	Power	Brazil
2010	Sinochem	US$3,070 m; 40%	Peregrino field	Oil	Brazil
2010	Jinchuan Group and China-Africa Development Fund	US$230 m; 51%	Wesizwe Platinu	Metals	South Africa
2010	Tianyu Group	US$1,000 m		Property	South Korea
2010	CNPC	US$150 m		Energy	Indonesia
2010	Yunnan Chihong	US$100 m; 50%	Howards Pass	Metals	Canada
2010	Tempo Group and Beijing city	US$440 m	Nexteer Auto	Autos	USA
2010	China Merchants Group	US$550 m	Loscam	Shipping	Australia
2010	Chinalco	US$1,350 m; 45%	Rio Tinto	Iron	Guinea
2010	China Merchants Group	US$450 m; 70%	Aitken Spence	Shipping	Sri Lanka
2010	Chery	US$700 m		Autos	Brazil
2010	Bosai Minerals	US$1,200 m; 80%	Ghana Bauxite	Aluminum	Ghana
2010	Jinchuan	US$420 m	Continental Metals	Metals	Canada
2010	Shanda Games	US$100 m	Eyedentity Games	Technology	South Korea
2010	Sinopec	US$7,100 m; 40%	Repsol	Oil	Brazil
2010	CNOOC	US$2,200 m; 33%	Chesapeake Energy	Oil	USA
2010	Sinochem	US$1,440 m; 60%	Makhteshim-Agan	Agriculture	Israel
2010	Minmetals	US$2,500 m		Copper	Peru
2010	Huaneng Power	US$1,230 m; 50%	InterGen	Power	USA

(Continued)

A List of Major Chinese Overseas Investment Deals, 2008–2010 (Continued)

Year	Acquiring Company	Transaction Value; Shares Acquired	Target Company, if Any	Industry	Target Country
2010	CNOOC	US$2,470m; 30%	Pan American	Oil	Argentina
2010	CNPC and Sinopec	US$610m		Oil	Ecuador
2010	SAIC	US$500m; 1%	GM	Autos	USA
2010	Guangdong Rising Asset Management	US$400m	Caledon	Coal	Australia
2010	Sinopec	US$2,450m	Occidental	Oil	Argentina
2010	CIC	US$200m	BTG Pactual	Investment	Brazil
2010	Three Gorges	US$170m	EuroSibEnergo	Power	Russia
2010	Sinopec	US$680m	Chevron	Gas	Indonesia

Notes: *BAIC = Beijing Automotive Industry Holding Co; CIC = China Investment Corporation; CNOOC = China National Offshore Oil Corporation; CNPC = China National Petroleum Corporation; DRC = Democratic Republic of Congo; NOC = national oil companies; SAFE = State Administration for Foreign Exchange; SAIC = Beijing Automotive Industry Holding Co; Sinopec = China Petrochemical Corporation Group.*
Source: Salidjanova (2011), which is an excerpt from Scissors (2011).

REFERENCES

Andrew-Speed, P. (2009). China's energy role in the middle east and prospects for the future. In *The new energy silk road: the growing Asia-Middle East energy nexus* (pp. 13–28). The NBR Conference Report, October 2009, Washington, DC: The National Bureau of Asian Research.

BP Press Office. (November 3, 2009). *BP and CNPC to develop Iraq's super-giant rumaila field.* Available at: <www.bp.com/genericarticle.do?categoryId=2012968&contentId=7057650> Accessed on May 10, 2010.

Folta, P. H. (2005). Cooperative joint ventures: savvy foreign investors may wish to consider the benefits of this flexible investment structure. *China Business Review.* Available at <https://www.china-businessreview.com/public/0501/folta.html>. Accessed on November 23, 2011.

Lunding, A. (2006). Global champion in waiting: perspectives on China's overseas direct investment. *Deutsche Bank Research* August 4, p. 8. Available at <http://www.dbresearch.com>. Accessed on November 13, 2011.

MOFCOM (2010). *2009 statistical bulletin of China's outward foreign direct investment.* Beijing: Ministry of Commerce (MOFCOM).

NBS. (various years). *China statistical yearbook*, various issues. Beijing: China Statistics Publishing House.

OECD. (2000). *Main developments and impacts of foreign direct investment on China's economy.* Directorate for Financial, Fiscal and Enterprise Affairs Working Papers on International Investment, No. 2000/4, Paris: OECD, December.

Salidjanova, N. (2011). *Going out: an overview of China's outward foreign direct investment.* Washington, DC: U.S.-China Economic & Security Review Commission. March 30.

Scissors, D. (2011). *China global investment tracker: 2011.* Washington, DC: The Heritage Foundation. January 10. Available at <http://www.heritage.org/Research/Reports/2011/01/China-Global-Investment-Tracker-2011>. Accessed on November 29, 2011.

UNCTAD (2011). *Inward and outward foreign direct investment flows, annual.* UNCTAD Stat Database, United Nations Conference on Trade and Development (UNCTAD). Available at <http://unctadstat.unctad.org>. Accessed on October 26, 2011.

UNCTAD. (various years). *World investment report 2006: FDI from developing and transition economies: implications for development.* New York: United Nations Press.

Wong, J., & Chan, S. (2003). China's outward direct investment: expanding worldwide. *China: An International Journal, 1*(2), 279–295. (September).

Chapter 14

Doing Business in China

Qīngmíng Shànghé Tú (section).

Qīngmíng Shànghé Tú ('Along the River during the Qingming Festival') is a panoramic painting by Zhang Zeduan (AD 1085–1145). It captures the daily life of people from the North Song period at the capital of Bianliang (today's Kaifeng). The entire piece (24.8×528.7 cm) was painted in hand scroll format and the content reveals the lifestyle of all levels of society, from rich to poor, as well as different economic activities in the city and the surrounding rural areas. The painting is known for its geometrically accurate images of a variety of natural elements and architectures, boats and bridges, market places and stores, people and scenery. Currently kept at the Palace Museum in the Forbidden City, the Qingming scroll is often considered to be the most renowned work of all Chinese paintings.

In order to expand its market, one factory owner sent two marketing managers to an isolated island to investigate market potential. When the first marketing manager arrived and found that the local people were not in the habit of wearing shoes, he immediately sent a telegram to the boss, saying, 'People here do not wear shoes. There is no market here.' Two days later, the second marketing manager, after seeing that the local people were walking barefoot and that there were no shoe shops, advised the boss, 'The residents of the island do not wear shoes. There is a huge potential market here. Send one million pairs of shoes ASAP.'

– A popular MBA course case

Understanding the Chinese Economies. DOI: http://dx.doi.org/10.1016/B978-0-12-397826-4.00014-7
© 2013 Elsevier Inc. All rights reserved.

14.1 STARTING A BUSINESS

14.1.1 First Things First

Opening a business in China has become much easier than it was decades ago. But doing business does not guarantee that you will make money. Risks can exist in any time and any place. If you plan to open a business in China, consider looking into the field of providing services to other Western businesses seeking to operate in China. It will likely be easy to talk to people who have already opened offices in China. Ask them where they succeeded and especially where they failed. Because the Chinese government is tightly affiliated with various business activities, it is always helpful for you to know what the government wants. Check out the Five-Year Plan (FYP) that the Chinese government publishes, which details what types of businesses they're looking for. The economic development of the People's Republic of China is now in its twelfth FYP period (2011–15).[1]

The next step is to pick a location. You cannot set your business down anywhere and expect to be a success. If your company relies on international trade, coastal cities (such as Shanghai, Dalian, Qingdao, Tianjin, Ningbo, Xiamen, and Guangzhou) may be on the shortlist of locations. If you're running a tech company, Beijing may be the ideal place for you. The major business centers aren't your only options. Some companies find moving inland to be the better bet, as this is where they can take advantage of the low-cost labor and land inputs. (A comparison of the ease of operating a business among China's provinces will be conducted in the following section.)

In general, the following questions can help you determine an ideal location for your business (Lapowsky, 2010):

- What are your transportation needs?
- What are your logistical needs?
- Are you relying on goods that may be imported to China?
- How can you get the goods from the port to your location?
- What government inspections and restrictions will you be subject to?

14.1.2 Selecting a Business Type

After the location is fixed, you need to acquire an application for the name of the business you're planning to open. This can be done from the 'Administration of Industry and Commerce' (AIC) in your area. It's often possible to get this for free on its official website. Before deciding to invest in a business in China, you need to decide what type of business entity to register. The most common options for foreign businesses are joint ventures (JVs) and wholly owned enterprises. The investor can go it alone and form a 100% foreign-owned entity (a wholly foreign-owned entity, or 'WFOE'), or work together with an existing Chinese business and operate through some form of JV entity. Each of these two types, of course, has its pros and cons.

A JV requires a partnership between a foreign business owner and a Chinese partner. In some cases, it is more efficient to allow the Chinese side to control day-to-day management of the company. In this case, the local partners will bring their political or social connections (or *guanxi*) into play if their own people act as the representative director and general manger. Under this type of business, the experience with day-to-day management is a primary reason for operating as a JV. Though JVs may sound like the safest route, critics say the most common problem for them is simply a classic case of 'same bed, different dreams' syndrome. Despite these problems, many foreign investors still choose to enter the Chinese market through a JV, and the particular risks involved with this type of arrangement require careful planning.

In China, if a foreign investor wishes to maintain control over its businesses in a JV, he or she, as majority owner, should strive to obtain a 51% or higher share of ownership interest in the business. In addition, in order to exercise effective control over a JV in China, foreign investors must have control over the day-to-day management of it. Such control comes from the following three aspects:[2]

- The power to appoint and remove the JV's representative. The side that appoints the representative director will have significant control over operations. The usual practice of conceding the power to appoint a key officer or director to another investor is a mistake.
- The power to appoint and remove the general manager of the JV company. It must be made clear that the general manager is an employee of the JV company who is employed entirely at the discretion of the representative director. The common practice of appointing the same person as both representative director and general manager is a mistake.
- Control over the company seal, or 'chop'. The person who controls the registered company seal has the power to make binding contracts on behalf of the JV company and to deal with the company's banks and other key service providers. The power over that seal should be carefully guarded. Ceding control over it as a matter of convenience is a mistake. There is a long, documented history of this seemingly minor consideration dooming JVs.

---

1. The full content of the twelfth FYP (2011–15) can be obtained from the website (http://cbi.typepad.com/files/full-translation-5-yr-plan-2011-2015. doc. Accessed on December 23, 2011).

2. Cited from Dickinson (2008).

With the exception of some strategic sectors, China is remarkably open to foreign investment, and WFOEs have become the most common vehicle for foreign investment in the past several years.[3] Since China joined the WTO, its restrictions on foreign investment have been further reduced. The WFOE, which is much more complicated to set up than a joint venture, takes more time to get approval from the government, and requires a minimal capital investment (the actual amount can vary greatly depending on the nature of your business and where you're setting it up).

14.1.3 Drafting a Business Plan

A detailed business plan is also crucial. Once the plan is approved by the Chinese government, you will be able to operate only within its guidelines. If you start offering a product or service that is not in your business plan, the Chinese government can shut your business down. The same goes for where and how you operate.

The 'Foreign Investment Industrial Guidance Catalog' was introduced in China in 1995. It classifies foreign investment into 'encouraged', 'restricted', and 'prohibited' investment projects. Since its creation, the catalog has been updated every two or three years. The amendments reflected the policy changes in relation to foreign investment over the years. On April 6, 2010, the State Council issued the 'Several Opinions of the State Council on Further Improving Utilization of Foreign Investment'.[4] The Opinions formulate political and strategic aims in relation to foreign investment in China and target improving the legal framework for foreign investment.

According to the Opinions, the Foreign Investment Industrial Guidance Catalog shall be amended again to further open up and encourage foreign investment in the field of high-end manufacturing, high-tech modern services, new energy, energy-saving, and environmental protection. The Opinions also encourage multinational companies to set up regional headquarters, R&D centers, procurement centers, financing management centers, financial clearance centers, as well as costs and profits verification centers in China. On the other hand, foreign investment in high-energy consumption, heavy pollution, natural resources exhausting, low-end and over-capacity industries will be subject to stricter control. The Opinions further emphasize the 'Western Development' strategy. Foreign investment in labor intensive sectors fulfilling environmental protection requirements will be encouraged in the Central and Western belts of China. Foreign banks are also encouraged to set up establishments and open businesses in these regions.

The Opinions signal that the Chinese government is encouraging merger and acquisition (M&A) deals by foreign investors targeting Chinese enterprises. The Opinions further support foreign investors to acquire a stake in companies listed on the Chinese domestic stock market as 'strategic investors'. But they do not indicate any policy preference for acquisition of state-owned enterprises. Legislation regarding M&A activities of foreign investors (including the anti-trust review system) will be further improved. In this respect the establishment of a 'national security' review mechanism applicable to cross-border M&A deals will be sped up. Merger control has recently been discovered as a powerful regulatory tool. Therefore foreign investors will have to be prepared for certain political obstacles to M&A deals in sensitive areas.

The Opinions show a commitment of the State Council to further attracting foreign investment in China, in particular in certain industry sectors. They reflect China's pursuit of foreign investment in the field of innovative technology and environmental protection. This is in line with the Chinese government's general policy to have cleaner and more sustainable economic development. But they do not provide for new tax incentives which used to be the most attractive part of China's 'open door' policy in the past.

14.1.4 Multiregional Differences

The average time to start a business in China was 35 days in 2008, which is longer than in OECD nations (15 days), Eastern Europe & Central Asia (26 days), Middle East & North Africa (28 days), and South Asia (33 days), but shorter than Sub-Saharan Africa (56 days) and Latin America & Caribbean (68 days) (see Figure 14.1).

Foreign investors must be aware of the fact that the ease of starting a business also differs from province to province in China. Table 14.1 shows that: (i) internationally, in 2010 the time needed for starting a business in China (38 days, similar to that in Sri Lanka or Tajikistan) is shorter than that in Djibouti and Guatemala (39 days), but longer than that in Malawi, Nicaragua, Seychelles, and Vanuatu (37 days); and (ii) domestically, in 2006 there is significant variation among China's provinces. For example, we can see that Guangdong province is comparable to Austria; and in several other coastal provinces a business can also be started within a very short period of time. However, in some provinces, such as Ningxia, Shanxi, Qinghai, and Guizhou, the average time needed for starting a business, similar to that of Papua New Guinea and the Philippines, is almost double that of Guangdong province.

More detailed indicators on the ease of starting a business have been computed by the World Bank in its surveys for 30 provinces in China. Although commercial activities are subject to a uniform regulatory system set by the central government, provincial and local officials have a large degree of discretion in terms of the enforcement of national legislation. Generally, most provinces have at least one

---

3. See Chapter 13 for more details.
4. See Annex A for the full text of the latest government document.

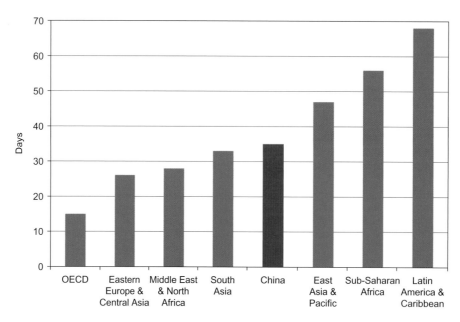

FIGURE 14.1   How long does it take to start a business in different parts of the world? *Source: World Bank (2008, p. 9).*

TABLE 14.1 Time Needed for Starting a Business, Selected Nations and Chinese Provinces

Nations	Days in 2010	Chinese Provinces	Days in 2006
Austria, Palau	28	Guangdong	28
Tanzania	29		
India, Russia	30	Zhejiang	30
Bahamas, Benin, Nepal, Nigeria	31	Jiangsu	31
Burundi, Poland, Thailand	32		
Guyana (CR), Israel, Kenya	34	Jilin	33
Cameroon, Kuwait, Paraguay	35	Shanghai, Sichuan	35
Sudan	36	Hubei	36
Djibouti, Guatemala	37	Beijing, Jilin	37
China, Sri Lanka, Tajikistan	38	Hainan	38
Malawi, Nicaragua, Seychelles, Vanuatu	39	Chongqing	39
Côte d'Ivoire, Lesotho	40	Fujian	40
Guinea, Peru	41	Liaoning, Tianjin, Henan	41
Trinidad and Tobago	43	Anhui, Heilongjiang, Hebei, Hunan, Shaanxi, Yunnan	42–43
Bangladesh, Belize	44	Xinjiang	44
Bhutan, Fiji	46	Jiangxi, Guangxi	46
Spain	47	Gansu	47
West Bank and Gaza	49	Inner Mongolia	48
Bolivia, Vietnam	50	Guizhou	50
Papua New Guinea	51	Qinghai	51
Philippines	53	Shanxi, Ningxia	55

Sources: World Bank (2011, pp. 145–205) and Annex B.1.

indicator which compares favorably with other provinces. However, the provinces of Zhejiang, Jiangsu, Guangdong, Shandong, and Shanghai have the most favorable environments for starting a business; while the provinces of Guizhou, Gansu, Guangxi, Anhui, Ningxia, and Shaanxi seem to have the most challenging business environments.[5]

14.2 EASE OF DOING BUSINESS ACROSS CHINA

14.2.1 Registering Property

Registering property and getting credit are also important steps required for a business to operate in China. Usually, the Chinese government has very low minimum requirements for the amount of capital you need to start your business.

You should apply for registration certification from your local Administration of Industry and Commerce (AIC). This requires waiting a certain period of time (which differs among different provinces, to be discussed later) and paying a number of fees. This requires that you contact the Quality and Technology Supervision Bureau for an organization code certificate, place your registration for the local statistics bureau, and submit your forms for the local and state tax bureau. You should also gain approval for, and create the company seal from, the local police department. This requires that you find a seal carving company that will create your company seal for you.

After all the above procedures are completed, you are able to open up an official company bank account with a Chinese bank and transfer capital assets to it. You must open a local bank account to hold your company's assets.

You should acquire permission to print or purchase financial invoices and receipts after the completion of tax registration. Contact the same taxation authorities to get the forms for these permits. Uniform invoices to be purchased from the tax office and register with the local career services station are also legal requirements that can't be bypassed.

In 2008 China's enterprise income tax system was reformed. China eliminated the previous preferential tax treatments for foreign invested enterprises and gradually replaced them with a new generally applicable system of tax incentives for high and new technology enterprises, irrespective of the nationality of the investor. In 2010, the Chinese government reiterated these principles by exempting products imported by foreign investment R&D centers for scientific research purposes from import customs duties, VAT, and consumption tax.[6]

Table 14.2 shows that: (i) internationally, in 2010 the time needed for registering property in China (29 days, similar to that in Luxembourg or Mali) is shorter than that in Bahrain, Chile, El Salvador, and Zimbabwe (31 days), but longer than that in Italy (27 days); and (ii) domestically, in 2006 there is significant variation among China's provinces. For example, we can see that Chongqing municipality is comparable to Italy in 2010; and in several other coastal provinces the average time needed for registering property is also very short. However, in some provinces, such as Gansu, Guizhou, Hainan, and Qinghai, the average time needed for registering property (69–78 days), which is similar to that of Czech Republic, Eritrea, Uzbekistan, Grenada, Uganda, and the Central African Republic, is more than double that of Chongqing municipality (28 days).

More detailed indicators on the ease of registering property have been computed by the World Bank in its surveys for 30 provinces in China. Generally, most provinces have at least one indicator which compares favorably with other provinces. However, the provinces of Shanghai, Guangdong, Fujian, Shandong, and Jiangsu have the most favorable environments for registering property; while the provinces of Guangxi, Gansu, Guizhou, Henan, Shanxi, and Hubei seem to have the most challenging business environments.[7]

14.2.2 Getting Credit

In China, foreign-invested enterprises (FIEs) always have very limited financing sources. Except for bank loans, direct financing via the capital market has been difficult and there were only a few successful precedents of FIEs going public. In the 'Opinions of the State Council on Further Improving Utilization of Foreign Investment' (see Annex A) introduced in 2010, the Chinese government proposed a series of measures supporting qualified FIEs to broaden their financing means by issuing shares, enterprise bonds, and middle-term instruments on the domestic capital market. The Opinions further address the feasibility of issuing RMB bonds in China by foreign entities. Such a tool, if implemented, could create a significant breakthrough in opening the Chinese capital markets to foreign investors.

More detailed indicators on the ease of getting credit have been computed by the World Bank in its surveys for 30 provinces in China. Generally, most provinces have at least one indicator which compares favorably with other provinces. However, the provinces of Fujian, Jiangsu, Guangdong, Shandong and Shanghai have the most favorable environments for getting credit; while the provinces of Guangxi,

---

5. See Annex B.1 for the specific indicators (number of procedures, time, and cost as a percent of provincial GDP per capita) on the ease of starting a business in China's provinces.
6. See Annex A for more details.

7. See Annex B.2 for the specific indicators (number of procedures, time, and cost as a percent of property value) on the ease of registering property in China's provinces.

TABLE 14.2 Time Needed for Registering Property, Selected Nations and Chinese Provinces

Nations	Days in 2010	Chinese Provinces	Days in 2006
Italy	27	Chongqing	28
China, Luxembourg, Mali	29	Shanghai	29
Bahrain, Chile, El Salvador, Zimbabwe	31	Jiangsu	31
Austria, Panama, Kosovo, Philippines	32–34		
Niger, Hong Kong, Iran	35–6	Guangdong	35
Tajikistan	37	Fujian	37
Ireland, St. Vincent and the Grenadines	38		
Gabon, Tunisia, Zambia	39	Jilin, Sichuan	39
Djibouti, Germany, Kazakhstan, Ethiopia	40–1		
Albania, Brazil, Denmark, Mozambique	42	Tianjin	42
Russia, Chad, India, Swaziland	43–4		
Latvia	45	Xinjiang	45
Paraguay	46	Anhui	46
Algeria, Morocco, Venezuela	47	Inner Mongolia	47
Liberia, Pakistan	50	Jiangxi, Shaanxi, Zhejiang	50
Iraq	51	Liaoning	51
Argentina	52	Hunan	53
Congo, Dem. Rep.	54	Jillin	55
Congo (Rep.), Jamaica, Kuwait	55	Heilongjiang	55
Cambodia, Vietnam, Macedonia	56–8	Hebei	58
Burkina Faso	59	Beijing, Ningxia	59
Belize, Dominican Rep., Rwanda	60	Hubei, Henan	60
Côte d'Ivoire, São Tomé and Principe	62	Shanxi	62
Gambia, Uruguay	66	Yunnan, Guangxi	66
Fiji	68	Qinghai	69
Central African Republic	75	Hainan	76
Grenada, Uganda	77	Guizhou	77
Czech Republic, Eritrea, Uzbekistan	78	Gansu	78

Sources: World Bank (2011, pp. 145–205) and Annex B.2.

Gansu, Shaanxi, Ningxia, Xinjiang and Guizhou seem to have the most challenging business environments.[8]

14.2.3 Enforcing Contracts

Table 14.3 shows that: (i) internationally, in 2010 the time needed for enforcing contracts in China (about 400 days,

---

8. See Annex B.3 for the specific indicators (time and cost as a percent of loan value) on the ease of getting credit in China's provinces.

similar to that in Cambodia, Eritrea, or the UK) is longer than that in Australia, Hungary, Austria, and Fiji (395 to 397 days), but shorter than that in Mexico, Iceland, Switzerland, Turkey, and Peru (415 to 428 days); and (ii) domestically, in 2006 there is significant variation among China's provinces. For example, we can see that Jiangsu province has the shortest time (112 days) needed for enforcing a contract in the world and that the time in Guangdong province (120 days) is even shorter than that in Singapore (150 days). However, in some provinces, such as Jilin, Qinghai, and Gansu, the

TABLE 14.3 Time Needed for Enforcing Contracts, Selected Nations and Chinese Provinces

Nations	Days in 2010	Chinese Provinces	Days in 2006
		Jiangsu	112
Singapore	150	Guangdong	120
Uzbekistan, New Zealand	195–216	Jilin	210
Belarus, S. Korea, Azerbaijan	225–37	Shaanxi	235
Kyrgyz Republic, Rwanda	260	Liaoning	260
Namibia	270	Ningxia	270
Lithuania, Guinea	275–6	Hubei	277
Hong Kong, Norway, Russia	280–1		
Armenia, Georgia	285	Henan, Zhejiang, Chongqing	285–6
		Heilongjiang, Shanghai	290–2
Vietnam	295	Sichuan	295
United States	300	Anhui, Shanxi, Tianjin	300
Latvia, Mongolia, Luxembourg	309–21	Hainan	310
France	331	Inner Mongolia	330
Ukraine	345	Beijing, Fujian	340–2
Japan, Moldova	360–5	Yunnan, Jiangxi	365
Macedonia, Mauritania, Finland	370–5		
Denmark	380	Hunan	382
Albania, Kazakhstan, Germany	390–4	Xinjiang	392
Australia, Hungary, Austria, Fiji	395–7	Guizhou, Guangxi, Hebei	397
China, Cambodia, Eritrea, UK	399–406		
Mexico, Iceland, Switzerland, Turkey, Peru	415–28		
Tajikistan, Lao PDR	430–43	Gansu	440
Nigeria	457	Qinghai	458
United Arab Emirates	537		
Brunei, Nicaragua	540	Jillin	540
Montenegro, Niger, Portugal	545–7		

Sources: World Bank (2011, pp. 145–205) and Annex B.4.

average time needed for enforcing contracts is four times that of Jiangsu province.

More detailed indicators on the ease of enforcing contracts have been computed by the World Bank in its surveys for 30 provinces in China. Generally, most provinces have at least one indicator which compares favorably with other provinces. However, the provinces of Guangdong, Jiangsu, Zhejiang, Shanghai, and Shaanxi have the most favorable environments for enforcing contracts; while the provinces of Gansu, Yunnan, Qinghai, Hunan, Anhui,

and Jilin seem to have the most challenging business environments.[9]

14.2.4 Summary

In China, although commercial activities are subject to a uniform regulatory system set by the central government,

---

9. See Annex B.4 for the specific indicators (time and cost as a percent of claim) on the ease of enforcing contracts in China's provinces.

TABLE 14.4 Ease of Doing Business in China – Top and Bottom Five Provinces

Rank No.	Starting a Business	Registering Property	Getting Credit	Enforcing Contracts
1	Zhejiang	Shanghai	Fujian	Guangdong
2	Jiangsu	Guangdong	Jiangsu	Jiangsu
3	Guangdong	Fujian	Guangdong	Zhejiang
4	Shandong	Shandong	Shandong	Shanghai
5	Shanghai	Jiangsu	Shanghai	Shaanxi
...	...	...	...	...
26	Ningxia	Shanxi	Xinjiang	Anhui
27	Anhui	Henan	Ningxia	Hunan
28	Guangxi	Guizhou	Shaanxi	Qinghai
29	Gansu	Gansu	Gansu	Yunnan
30	Guizhou	Guangxi	Guangxi	Gansu

Note: *Hong Kong, Macau, Taiwan, and Tibet are excluded from the rankings.*
Source: Annex B.

provincial and local officials have a large degree of discretion in terms of the enforcement of national legislation.

As measured by the four indicators (starting a business, registering property, getting credit – getting and registering collateral, and enforcing contracts) in Table 14.4, the coastal provinces (such as Guangdong, Jiangsu, Shanghai, Zhejiang, Shandong, and Fujian) have the most favorable environments for the conducting of business. The western and central provinces, however, seem to have the most challenging business environments. Nevertheless, most provinces measured have at least one indicator which compares favorably with other surveyed provinces.

14.3 UNDERSTANDING CHINA'S BUSINESS CULTURE

Each individual human being has been socialized in a unique environment. Important aspects of the environment are shared, and these constitute a particular culture. Culture poses communication problems because there are so many variables unknown to the communicators. As the cultural differences increase, communication costs and intercultural misunderstanding will appear. As noted by Gudykunst (1994):

When we travel to another culture or interact with people from another culture in our culture, we cannot base our predictions of their behavior on our cultural rules and norms. This inevitably leads to misunderstanding. If we want to communicate effectively,

we must use our knowledge of the other culture to make predictions. If we have little or no knowledge of the other person's culture, we have no basis for making predictions.[10]

14.3.1 Collectivism Versus Individualism

Individualism and collectivism are conflicting ideas in terms of the nature of humans, society, and the relationship between them. Unlike the West, in which there exists an individualist culture, China has a collectivistic culture. Collectivism is the political theory that states that the will of the people is omnipotent, an individual must obey; that society as a whole, not the individual, is the unit of moral value. Individualism, as the antipode of collectivism, holds that the individual is the primary unit of reality and the ultimate standard of value. This view does not deny that societies exist or that people benefit from living in them, but it sees society as a collection of individuals, not something over and above them.

Collectivism holds that a group – such as a nation, a community, or a race – is the primary unit of reality and the ultimate standard of value. This view stresses that the needs and goals of the individual must be subordinate to those of the group. Unlike collectivism, which requires self-sacrifice, individualism holds that every person is an end in himself and that no person should be sacrificed for the sake of another. While not denying that one person can build on the achievements of others, individualism points out that the individual is the unit of achievement. Individualism holds that achievement goes beyond what has already been done; it is something new that is created by the individual. Collectivism, on the other hand, holds that achievement is a product of society.

For most of the past many thousands of years, Confucianism has had a substantial influence on China's political culture. The ethical beliefs of Confucianism have remained consistently within the bounds of a set of orthodox principles governing interpersonal relationships in China. They have been applied officially to all strata of society: loyalty, filial piety, benevolence, righteousness, love, faith, harmony, and peace. As a result, China has developed a different culture in respect of economic development than that which is found in the rest of the world, in response to its own particular environment and social conditions (see Box 14.1). For instance, in contrast to other peoples, the Chinese pay heed to their own spiritual interests (including the richness of spiritual life and harmonization of feeling) more than the material ones. This characteristic results largely from the Confucian philosophy which emphasizes 'faithfulness', 'kindheartedness', 'trustworthiness', 'ritualism', 'peace' and so on. All of these have influenced Chinese economic life and structure, which eventually result in characterizing China's economic culture.

---

10. Cited from Harris et al. (2004, p. 42).

Box 14.1 Chinese Characteristics

More than one hundred years ago, Arthur H. Smith, who had served as the Missionary of the American Board for 22 years in China, wrote a book entitled *Chinese Characteristics*. The book was first published in Shanghai by an English newspaper in 1890. The second edition of the book was published in London in 1892. The third, fourth, and fifth revised editions were published in New York, London, Edinburgh, and London in 1894, 1895, and 1900, respectively. Based on rural Chinese life during the late nineteenth century, Smith presented an interesting description of how the Chinese were different from Westerners. To make comparison easier, we classify all the chapters in Smith's (1972) book into two types, as the following:

- *Positive type*: economy; industry; politeness; physical vitality; patience and perseverance; benevolence; mutual responsibility and respect for law; polytheism, pantheism and atheism.
- *Negative type*: disregard of time; disregard of accuracy; talent for misunderstanding; talent for indirection; intellectual turbidity; contempt for foreigners; absence of public spirits; conservation; absence of sympathy; social typhoons; mutual suspicion; absence of sincerity.

Box 14.2 News From the Brookings Institution: Who Follows Whom?

A senior fellow from the Brookings Institution, Washington, DC, told me of his unhappy experience in China when he served as a senior US government official engaged in a series of important negotiations with his Chinese partners in Beijing.

On the way toward a meeting hall, he walked behind his secretary, and when he arrived at the meeting room, a security guard stopped him impolitely at the door, but gave a welcome to his secretary (a young lady). Indeed, this was a diplomatic fault from the Chinese side. However, that situation is somewhat understandable in China (at least to those people who adhere to tradition) since it was the security guard's duty to prevent all *irrelevant* personnel from going through.

According to the security guard's reasonable judgment, senior officials should be followed by junior staff, and therefore the young American girl who was allowed to enter must have been assumed to be of the lowest rank and, definitely, the last US official to be joining that meeting. Who cares about the old man behind her? Alas, the young Chinese security guard would have had a difficult time after his boss saw the US guests off.

In Chinese business culture, the collectivist way of thinking still prevails, even in sectors experimenting with free enterprise. 'Saving face' is an important concept in order to be able to understand the Chinese. In Chinese business culture, a person's reputation and social standing rests on this concept. Causing embarrassment or loss of composure, even unintentionally, can be disastrous for business negotiations. So be careful to avoid causing someone to 'lose face' by insulting, criticizing, or embarrassing him or her in front of others, or by treating the person with less than the proper respect due his status in the organization.

14.3.2 What Can(not) Be Done in China

The concepts of good and bad luck, or auspicious and inauspicious symbols, are important emotionally to many people in China. Therefore, in order to maximize the success of your business in China, you should make use of positive symbols and avoid those with negative connotations. The following are some examples:[11]

- 4 is regarded as unlucky, as 'four' sounds similar to the word for death
- 7 also has negative connotations

- 8 is regarded as very lucky, as 'eight' sounds similar to the words for prosperity and wealth. 3 is also lucky, as it sounds similar to the word for 'life' in Cantonese
- 9 is also positive as it sounds like the word for 'eternity' or 'long term', while 6 sounds similar to 'good progress'
- Red and yellow/gold are regarded as lucky, but avoid white, which is associated with mourning
- Use images of auspicious animals: dragon, phoenix, unicorn, tortoise (the Buddhist symbol of learning), crane, and fish
- Images of the Great Wall indicate stability and reliability
- Avoid name plaques for opening ceremonies, as these are equivalent to your standing next to your tomb!
- Also avoid black borders around names or photos of people, since this is also associated with death.

In accordance with Chinese business protocol, people are expected to enter the meeting room in hierarchical order. The Chinese will assume that the first person to enter the room is head of the delegation (see Box 14.2). Since there is such a strong emphasis on hierarchy in Chinese business culture, ensure that you bring a senior member of your organization to lead the negotiations on your behalf. The Chinese will do the same. Only the senior members of your group are expected to lead the discussion.

---

11. Source: UK Trade & Investment (2011, p. 51).

Present your card with two hands, and ensure that the Chinese side is facing the recipient. When receiving a business card, make a show of reading it carefully for a few moments; then, carefully place it into your card case or on the table, if you are seated at one. Not reading a business card that has been presented to you, then stuffing it directly into your back pocket, would be a breach of protocol.

14.4 MANAGING CULTURAL DIFFERENCES

14.4.1 Obstacles to Cross-Cultural Exchanges

As well as being used to describe the content of libraries, museums, moral, and religious codes of conduct, the world 'culture' is commonly used to describe many other aspects of social life. As such, 'culture' is the living sum of symbols, meanings, habits, values, institutions, behaviors, and social artifacts which characterize a distinctive and identified human population group. It confers upon individuals an identity as members of some visible community; standards for relating to the environment, for identifying fellow members and strangers; and for distinguishing between what is important and what is unimportant to them (Goulet, 1980, p. 2).

Intercultural communication is a process whereby individuals who are culturally different from each other on such important attributes as their value orientations, preferred communication codes, role expectations, and perceived rules of social relationship. Although most cultural groups have their own communication styles, the differences of communication styles between the Asian and the Western worlds are most distinct (see Table 14.5). For example, when a Japanese manager says in a business negotiation, 'It is very difficult' (which is a polite manner of refusal in Japanese society), the American partner would probably ask the Japanese side to find a solution, finding the expression to be more ambiguous (in the American's point of view). In contemporary Chinese society, by contrast, 'We have some difficulties' implies 'It would be OK under certain conditions.'

In the West, people normally build transactions and, if they are successful, a relationship will ensue. However, the Chinese believe that prospective business partners should build a relationship and, if successful, commercial transactions will follow. This difference underlies many misunderstandings arising from business negotiations. Virtually all successful transactions in China result from careful cultivation of the Chinese partner by the foreign one, until a relationship of trust evolves.

The logical development of close relationships is the Chinese concept of *guanxi*. The kernel of *guanxi* is doing business through value-laden relationships. In a country with a strong collectivistic culture, the use of personal contacts was the only way to get things done. *Guanxi* is the counterpart

TABLE 14.5 Eastern Versus Western Cultures: Communication Styles

Western Styles	Eastern Styles
Direct	Indirect
Blunt	Diplomatic
Polite	Very courteous
Talkative	Reserved
Extrovert	Introvert
Persuasive	Recommendations
Medium-strong eye contact	Weak eye contact
Unambiguous	Ambiguous
Decisive	Cautious
Problem solving	Accepting of the situation
Interrupt	Does not interrupt
Half listens	Listens carefully
Quick to deal	Courtship dance
Concentrates on power	Concentrates on agreed agenda

Source: Lewis (2003).

of a commercial legal system. Where the latter is relatively weak, as in China, the need to rely on *guanxi* will be strong. As long as the relationship is more valuable than the transaction, it is logical to honor it. The idea of a friendship leading to business is attractive. But Easterners who are familiar with *guanxi* are more cautious than Western converts. The obligations of *guanxi* are very real. In the wrong place, at an inappropriate time, with unsuitable people, the obligations can become a trap from which it is hard to escape.

14.4.2 Tips in Cross-Cultural Negotiations

Business negotiation is a process in which two or more economic entities come together to discuss common and conflicting interests in order to reach an agreement of mutual benefit. In cross-cultural business negotiations, the negotiation process differs in language, cultural conditioning, negotiating styles, approaches to problem solving, implicit assumptions, and so on.

The following tips will help to highlight negotiation differences in distinct cultures:

- If you are Arabian, then junior managers enter first, followed by senior executives; take time to establish rapport and relationships; expect to mix business and personal information to establish individual support, trust, and commitments; utilize a go-between in the negotiation; to gain concessions, they may try to make you feel guilty and then obligated; they like to bargain and are skilled at making deals; be patient, enjoy the process, and be willing to compromise…[12]

- If you are North American, then it is a good idea to prepare an agreed agenda before the meeting; be prompt in starting on time; prepare and pass on minutes of the meeting afterwards; the chairperson presents first; focus on issues one at a time; solicit input from all attendees; expect open discussion and debate; share problem-solving ideas; assign individual action items; be direct, assertive, involved, and action oriented…[13]

- If you are Latin American, then you tend to be extrovert, impatient, talkative, and inquisitive. Interpersonal skills are often considered more important than professional competence and experience. Latin Americans are not very interested in schedules or punctuality. The pace of negotiations is slower in Latin America than in Europe. The best policy is to wait for your Latin American counterparts to initiate any 'small talk' and follow their lead in establishing rapport. Latin Americans follow a top-down decision making process, where employees follow a trusting subservience to their superior as task orientation is dictated from above. Opinions of experienced middle managers and technical staff do not always carry the weight that they would in the UK. Meeting formalities must be followed; the two senior executives should sit facing each other. Be sensitive to the fact that Latin Americans tend to stand and sit extremely close to others…[14]

- If you are Western European, then you are likely to be highly receptive to new developments that improve efficiency and reduce costs and suggest there are two key opportunities to look for: products or services borne out of a technological breakthrough and clever ways to serve needs not currently recognized or acknowledged by European customers. Marketing products to Western European customers can be approached on two levels: pan-European or country-specific. However, cultural and language barriers are making it difficult to find success with pan-European programs. To ensure messages are understood, experts recommend packaging, labeling, and promotion be created for each individual country…

- If you are Eastern European, remember that the habits and behavior inherited from the communist period may still be in evidence. When a foreign firm invests in an Eastern European country in order to maintain their competitive advantage internationally, it must be able to quickly replicate their embedded resources within the affiliate. In addition, foreign firms have to cope with specific barriers to change inherited from the

communist legacy. To make its affiliates work according to Western criteria, foreign investors have to overcome these barriers. The local firm's capacity to learn and the willingness of local workers to change skills and habits are two important factors…

- If you are Indian, then you might hesitate to say 'No' when you may actually be trying to convey that you are worried whether the job can be done; aggressiveness can often be interpreted as a sign of disrespect; only the senior person might speak, and the junior members may maintain silence; Westernized Indians, however, can be quite assertive and direct; politeness and honesty go a long way in establishing the fact that your intentions are genuine…

- If you are Japanese, then you are expected to deal with a homogeneous group of up to four junior and middle managers; try to establish harmonious, cooperative relationships, giving time to lunch and/or dinner and entertainment; follow their rules of etiquette, such as token gifts called 'presenta' which are exquisitely wrapped – use holidays to exchange greetings; focus on middle managers, who make recommendations to senior managers, who in turn make the final decisions. When a Japanese negotiator says 'It is very difficult', it usually denotes a polite manner of refusal…[15]

But when you plan to come to China to negotiate with your Chinese partners there, you will benefit from knowing about, and observing, some issues of Chinese business etiquette:

Senior managers enter into the meeting room first, followed by junior staff. On formal occasions, only senior members on both sides are expected to talk, unless junior members are invited to do so; do not interrupt, even if a mistake is made (take notes and share corrections in private); interruptions of any kind from subordinates are considered inappropriate by the Chinese; expect a large negotiating team and long lunch breaks; 'face' is important; realize that the power of the negotiator may be limited, and that assistants and secretaries to top managers are sometimes even more useful than deputy managers; remember that there is a difference in negotiating with Chinese who have received Western educations…

ANNEX

A. Several Opinions of the State Council on Further Improving Utilization of Foreign Investment

To: all provinces, autonomous regions, people's governments under direct jurisdiction of the central government, all government agencies of the state council and their affiliates.

Foreign investment utilization is a key component of the nation's basic policy of opening up to the outside

12. Based on Elashmawi (2001).
13. Based on Elashmawi (2001).
14. Based on Castle and Carrasco (2007).
15. Based on Elashmawi (2001).

world. The reform and open policy has seen an industrial boost and technological progress through attracting foreign investments, while foreign enterprises are one of the major components of our national economy. And such momentum remains up till now. To further improve the quality and level of foreign investment utilization, and fully tap its potential in advancing technological innovation, industry upgrading and regional coordination, the State Council puts forward several opinions below:

1. Improve the Structure of Foreign Investment Utilization

a. Amend the Catalog for the Guidance of Foreign Investment Industries to conform to the need of economic growth and the national plan of adjusting and rejuvenating industries. More efforts are to expand the open areas, and to encourage more investment to sectors including high-end manufacturing, high-tech industry, modern service, new energy and energy conservation, and green industries. Restrictions are imposed on resource-dependent, low-level, and overcapacity projects.

b. Policies and measures adopted in industrial adjustment and rejuvenation also apply to eligible foreign enterprises.

c. Priority in land supply is given to the land intensive foreign enterprises which are encouraged by policy, where the land may be priced at 70% of the Lowest Standard of Land Price Used for Industrial Purpose.

d. Encourage the growth of high-tech enterprises invested in by foreign capital and improve the accreditation of high-tech enterprises.

e. Encourage partnership between domestic and foreign enterprises. Encourage the joint application of national sci-tech development projects, innovative capability building projects by eligible domestic and foreign enterprises and R&D institutions.

f. Encourage setting up headquarters and other functional centers such as R&D centers, procurement centers, financial management centers, and clearing centers by multinational corporations in China. Import duty, import VAT, and consumption tax are exempted for necessary sci-tech products imported by eligible foreign-funded R&D centers.

g. Put in place and improve the supporting policy, encouraging foreign investment in the service outsourcing sector to improve the competitiveness of this sector.

2. Steer More Foreign Investment to the Central and West Regions

h. Amend and supplement the Catalog for the Foreign Investment Industries with Competitiveness in the Central and West Regions according to the progress

in amending the Catalog for the Guidance of Foreign Investment Industries, adding more labor intensive projects and encouraging foreign investment to environmentally friendly and eligible labor intensive industries in the central and west regions.

i. Continue the income tax credit to eligible domestic and foreign enterprises invested in the central and west regions. Maintain the momentum of attracting foreign investment in the west regions.

j. More open policy and technological and financial support shall be offered to foreign enterprises moving to the central and west regions from the eastern regions. More simplified administrative procedures shall be provided. Encourage and steer foreign banks to establish offices and operations in the central and west regions.

k. Encourage a joint effort by the eastern regions and the central and west regions, to build market-oriented development zones by means of entrusting investment cooperation, in a principle of complementary advantages and mutual benefit.

3. Diversify the Means of Foreign Investment Utilization

l. Encourage the participation of foreign investment in domestic enterprise restructuring and mergers by means of stakeholding and merging. Encourage introducing domestic and foreign strategic investors by share-A listing companies. Regulate foreign investment on domestic securities and enterprises acquisitions. Speed up building acquisition safety censorship by foreign investment in accordance with anti-monopoly censorship.

m. Fully benefit the potential of both domestic and overseas market resources and boost competitiveness by continuously supporting overseas listing of eligible enterprises in accordance with the strategy of national development and growth needs of their own.

n. Facilitate the trial of building guaranty companies by foreign investment for small and medium enterprises. Encourage foreign venture investment. Make the most of the private equity fund and improve the exit mechanism.

o. Support eligible foreign-invested enterprises financing by issuing stocks, company bonds, or mid-term notes domestically. Financial institutions are to be guided to extend more credit to foreign-invested enterprises. The range of subjects allowed to issue RMB bonds shall be gradually expanded.

4. Advance Reform of Administration System on Foreign Investment

p. Apart from those stipulated otherwise by the Catalog for Investment Projects Approved by the Government, the approval for projects, which are allowed and encouraged among the Catalog for Guidance of Foreign Investment Industries, with a total investment worth less than 300 million USD, shall be decided by the relative departments of local government. Except for those approvals stipulated in law, or regulations which must be made by certain agencies of the State Council, all investment approval power may be granted to the local governments by the relative agencies of the State Council. The establishment of foreign invested enterprises in the service sector (except for financial institutions and telecom service) shall be approved by the local governments.

q. Simplify the approval procedure and boost transparency.

5. Foster a Good Investment Climate

r. In order to make the most of the role of development zones as a platform and conveyor, more efforts shall be made in their regulation and promotion. Support the expansion, adjustment, and upgrading of the eligible development zones at national or provincial level. More supporting policies are in place to facilitate border area economic cooperation zones.

s. Improve the foreign exchange administration of foreign-invested enterprises and simplify the relative procedures.

t. Reinforce investment promotion and publicize our policy on foreign investment at some key sectors, regions, and countries. Actively participate in multilateral investment cooperation.

Governments at all levels and relative agencies of the State Council shall, under the principle of 'selecting the best based on our need', uphold the policy of efficient utilization of foreign investment to improve its quality by introducing both capital and intelligence.

The State Council

(Guofa (2010) No. 9, April 6, 2010)

B. Indicators of the Ease of Doing Business in China

B.1 Starting a Business

Province	Procedures (Number)	Time (Days)	Cost (% of Provincial GDP per Capita)	Rank
Anhui	14	42	19.4	27
Beijing	14	37	3.2	10
Chongqing	14	39	9.5	17
Fujian	12	40	6.7	7
Gansu	14	47	14.1	29
Guangdong	13	28	6.3	3
Guangxi	14	46	16.5	28
Guizhou	14	50	26.6	30
Hainan	13	38	12.1	13
Heibei	14	42	9.8	16
Heilongjiang	14	42	11.9	18
Henan	13	41	11.6	12
Hubei	13	36	13.6	15
Hunan	14	42	14.6	10
Inner Mongolia	14	45	7.9	11
Jiangsu	12	31	5.8	2
Jiangxi	14	46	14.6	21
Jilin	14	37	9.5	8
Liaoning	14	41	6	9

(Continued)

B.1 Starting a Business (Continued)

Province	Procedures (Number)	Time (Days)	Cost (% of Provincial GDP per Capita)	Rank
Ningxia	14	55	12	26
Qinghai	14	51	12	23
Shaanxi	14	43	15.2	25
Shandong	13	33	6	4
Shanghai	14	35	3.1	5
Shanxi	14	55	9.3	20
Sichuan	13	35	19.1	11
Tianjin	14	41	3.7	8
Xinjiang	13	44	9	14
Yunnan	14	42	13.9	23
Zhejiang	12	30	5.7	1

Note: *Each province is represented by its capital city. Hong Kong, Macau, Taiwan, and Tibet are excluded.*
Source: World Bank (2008, p. 38).

B.2 Registering Property

Province	Procedures (Number)	Time (Days)	Cost (% of Property Value)	Rank
Anhui	10	46	5.6	17
Beijing	10	59	3.1	12
Chongqing	7	28	7	9
Fujian	7	37	4.1	3
Gansu	10	78	7.8	29
Guangdong	8	35	3.7	2
Guangxi	12	68	6.8	30
Guizhou	9	77	12.6	28
Hainan	16	76	4.8	23
Heibei	10	58	3.2	21
Heilongjiang	8	55	6.1	14
Henan	11	60	5.1	27
Hubei	9	60	6.2	25
Hunan	10	53	6.9	24
Inner Mongolia	11	47	4.6	18
Jiangsu	7	31	4.6	5
Jiangxi	10	50	6.1	20
Jilin	8	55	4.2	8
Liaoning	12	51	3.1	14
Ningxia	10	59	4.4	16

(Continued)

B.2 Registering Property (Continued)

Province	Procedures (Number)	Time (Days)	Cost (% of Property Value)	Rank
Qinghai	8	60	5.3	19
Shaanxi	8	50	5.1	10
Shandong	8	39	4.1	4
Shanghai	4	29	3.6	1
Shanxi	10	62	5.4	26
Sichuan	11	39	3.9	11
Tianjin	5	42	4.4	6
Xinjiang	11	45	4.2	13
Yunnan	9	66	5.4	22
Zhejiang	8	50	3.7	7

Note: Each province is represented by its capital city. Hong Kong, Macau, Taiwan, and Tibet are excluded.
Source: World Bank (2008, p. 38).

B.3 Getting Credit – Creating and Registering Collateral

Province	Time (Days)	Cost (% of Loan Value)	Rank
Anhui	20	2.8	14
Beijing	15	2.7	7
Chongqing	15	5	19
Fujian	7	2.3	1
Gansu	20	8	29
Guangdong	11	2.4	3
Guangxi	47	3.9	30
Guizhou	17	6.9	25
Hainan	14	5.1	18
Heibei	15	2.8	9
Heilongjiang	13	3.1	10
Henan	16	3.3	17
Hubei	13	3.3	12
Hunan	20	3.7	20
Inner Mongolia	15	3.3	16
Jiangsu	10	2.1	2
Jiangxi	17	5.9	24
Jilin	22	3.3	21
Liaoning	20	2.8	15
Ningxia	25	3.6	27
Qinghai	20	3.8	22

(Continued)

B.3 Getting Credit – Creating and Registering Collateral (Continued)

Province	Time (Days)	Cost (% of Loan Value)	Rank
Shaanxi	21	4	28
Shandong	10	2.9	4
Shanghai	8	2.9	4
Shanxi	16	2.9	12
Sichuan	12	3.2	11
Tianjin	14	2.7	6
Xinjiang	24	3.4	26
Yunnan	18	4	23
Zhejiang	11	3	8

Note: *Each province is represented by its capital city. Hong Kong, Macau, Taiwan, and Tibet are excluded.*
Source: World Bank (2008, p. 39).

B.4 Enforcing Contracts

Province	Time (Days)	Cost (% of Claim)	Rank
Anhui	300	41.8	26
Beijing	340	9.6	9
Chongqing	286	14.8	8
Fujian	342	13.7	12
Gansu	440	29.9	30
Guangdong	120	9.7	1
Guangxi	397	17.1	20
Guizhou	397	23	24
Hainan	310	14.5	11
Heibei	397	12.2	14
Heilongjiang	290	31.5	20
Henan	285	31.5	16
Hubei	277	33.1	17
Hunan	382	26.6	27
Inner Mongolia	330	23.7	30
Jiangsu	112	13.6	2
Jiangxi	365	16.5	15
Jilin	540	18.4	25
Liaoning	260	24.8	10
Ningxia	270	28.7	13
Qinghai	458	24.8	28

(Continued)

B.4 Enforcing Contracts (Continued)

Province	Time (Days)	Cost (% of Claim)	Rank
Shaanxi	235	21.7	5
Shandong	210	22	5
Shanghai	292	9	4
Shanxi	300	26.4	18
Sichuan	295	35.5	23
Tianjin	300	11.3	5
Xinjiang	392	20.5	22
Yunnan	365	36.4	29
Zhejiang	285	11.2	3

Note: *Each province is represented by its capital city. Hong Kong, Macau, Taiwan, and Tibet are excluded.*
Source: World Bank (2008, p. 39).

REFERENCES

Castle, F., & Carrasco, C. G. (2007). *Doing business in central and south Latin America*. Available at <http://intercultural-training.blogspot.com>, Wednesday, 3 October. Accessed November 25, 2008.

Dickinson, S. (2008). *Avoiding mistakes in Chinese joint ventures*. Beijing: American Chamber of Commerce. Available at <www.amcham-china.org.cn/amcham/upload/wysiwyg/CB2008No3-JV.pdf>. Accessed on November 16, 2011.

Elashmawi, F. (2001). *Competing globally – mastering multicultural management and negotiations*. Burlington, MA: Butterworth-Heinemann/Elsevier.

Goulet, D. (1980, 1995). *Development ethics: A guide to theory and practice*. New York: Apex Press.

Gudykunst, W. B. (1994). *Bridging differences: effective intergroup communications*. Thousand Oaks, CA: Sage Publications.

Harris, P. R., Moran, R. T., & Moran, S. (2004). *Managing cultural differences: global leadership strategies for the 21st century*. Amsterdam: Butterworth-Heinemann.

Lapowsky, I. (2010). *How to start a business in China*. Jul 12, <www.inc.com/guides/2010/07/how-to-start-a-business-in-china.html>. Accessed on November 7, 2011.

Lewis, R. D. (2003). *The cultural imperative*. Yarmouth, ME: Intercultural Press.

Smith, A. H. (1890; 1972). *Chinese characteristics* (5th ed.). Shannon, Ireland: Irish University Press.

UK Trade & Investment (2011). *China business guide – third edition*. London: the Department for Business, Innovation and Skills, and the Foreign and Commonwealth Office, UK. February.

World Bank (2008). *Doing business in China 2008*. Washington, DC: The World Bank Group and Beijing: Social Science Academic Press (China).

World Bank (2011). *Doing business 2011*. Washington, DC: The World Bank Group.

Chapter 15

Understanding the Chinese-Speaking Economies

Mt. Hua, Shaanxi. *Source:* http://en.wikipedia.org/wiki/Mount_Hua.

Understanding the Chinese Economies. DOI: http://dx.doi.org/10.1016/B978-0-12-397826-4.00015-9
© 2013 Elsevier Inc. All rights reserved.

Mt. Hua (Huashan) is located near the southeast corner of the Ordos Loop section of the Yellow River basin, south of the Wei River valley, at the eastern end of the Qinling Mountains, in southern Shaanxi province. Mt. Hua is usually referred to as one of the birthplaces of the ancestors of the Hua-Xia (Han) Chinese now living in Hong Kong, Macau, Taiwan, and mainland China.

The king of the state of Wei intended to attack Handan. Ji Liang heard of this and went to see the king, and said: 'Your majesty, on my way here I saw a man driving his carriage which was facing north. He told me that he wanted to go to the state of Chu. 'Why are you going north?' I asked. 'I have fine horses,' he said. 'Even though you have good horses, this is not the road to Chu,' I pointed out. 'I have plenty of money for my journey,' he said. 'But this is not a right direction,' I said. 'I have an excellent driver for my carriage,' he said. The better the resources, the further he was going from Chu. Now you seek to raise above all the kings and win the support of the common people everywhere. However, you plan to extend your territories and raise your prestige by attacking Handan, relying on the powerful strength of your state and the well-trained soldiers. This is as effective as going north hoping to reach the state of Chu.'

– Zhanguoce (475–221 BC)

15.1 THE GREATER CHINA AREA

The term 'Greater China' is defined in this chapter as one which includes Taiwan, Hong Kong, Macau, and mainland China.[1] There have been different names for the greater China area, such as 'the Chinese circle', 'the Chinese community', 'the greater China community', 'China economic circle', 'Chinese economic area', 'China economic zone', and so on. Probably first used by George Cressey at least as far back as the 1930s, the term 'Greater China' was to refer to the entire Chinese empire, as opposed to China proper (Harding, 1993, p. 660). The term 'Greater China' is now generally used for referring to the cultural and economic ties between the relevant territories, and is not intended to imply sovereignty. Sometimes, to avoid any political connotation, the term 'Chinese-speaking world' is often used instead of 'Greater China'.

In order to help understand the economic mechanisms of the greater China area, let's briefly review the historical evolution of Hong Kong, Macau, and Taiwan and the current situations of their economic relations with mainland China.

15.1.1 Hong Kong

In ancient China, Hong Kong was initially included in Bao'an county, while the latter today also included Donguan county and Shenzhen municipality, Guangdong province (see Figure 15.1). In 1573, Xin'an county was established and was entitled to administer Hong Kong for more than two hundred years since that time. Following the end of the first Opium War, the Treaty of Nanjing in 1842 ceded the island of Hong Kong to Britain in perpetuity. Kowloon, Stonecutters' Island and some small islands were annexed in 1860. In 1898, Britain acquired, under the 'Treaty of Peking', what is known as the New Territories and 236 associated islands, which were mainly agricultural lands, which were leased from the Qing dynasty (1644– 1910), on a 99-year lease. At present, Hong Kong consists of the island of Hong Kong (83 sq. km), Stonecutters' Island, Kowloon Peninsula, and the New Territories on the adjoining mainland, with 1,068 sq. km of land and a population of just over six million.

Over the past few decades, there has been a special geopolitical scenario between the two sides of the Shenzhen river. Even though the Chinese character, Shenzhen, means a deep gutter, no one would have expected that the 'gutter' would serve as a forbidden frontier between the socialist mainland China and the capitalist Hong Kong in the mid-twentieth century, and that it would also create economic prosperity for Hong Kong and continue to fuel the industrialization of the South China area.

China has always maintained that the three treaties on Hong Kong were signed under coercion, and were therefore unjust. On 19 December 1984, the Chinese and British governments issued a joint declaration in relation to the question of Hong Kong. As a result, the sovereignty of Hong Kong was transferred from the UK to the PRC on 1 July 1997.[2] Upholding national unity and territorial integrity, maintaining the prosperity and stability of Hong Kong, and taking account of its history and realities, China has made Hong Kong a Special Administrative Region (SAR) of the People's Republic of China (PRC) in accordance with the provisions of Article 31 of the Constitution of the PRC. The Joint Declaration also provides that for 50 years after 1997, Hong Kong's lifestyle will remain unchanged. The territory will enjoy a high degree of autonomy, except in relation to foreign and defense affairs, and China's socialist system and policies will not be put into practice in the SAR. Under the principle of 'one country, two systems', 'the socialist system and policies shall not be practiced in the Hong Kong special administrative

---

1. See Zhou (1989), Hwang (1988, p. 924), Zheng (1988), Feng (1992, pp. 6–9), Fei (1993, p. 54), Segal (1994, p. 44), Zhou (1992, pp. 18–21), Yang (1992). In addition, Dong and Xu (1992, pp. 10–13) and Wei and Frankel (1994, pp. 179–90) add Singapore, Malaysia, Indonesia, Thailand, and the Philippines to this area.

---

2. See 'Joint Declaration of the Government of the United Kingdom of Great Britain and Northern Ireland and the Government of the People's Republic of China on the Question of Hong Kong', Beijing, 19 December 1984.

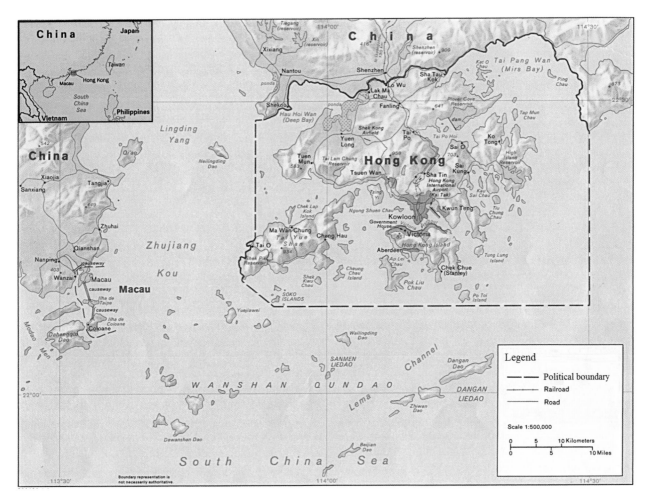

FIGURE 15.1 Hong Kong and Macau.

region, and the previous capitalist system and way of life shall remain unchanged for 50 years'.[3]

Since the Asian financial crisis, Hong Kong has tried to exploit its connections with mainland China in order to boost its economy. The measures introduced included the relaxation of controls against tourists and skilled workers from the mainland, and the promotion of economic integration with the Pearl River delta. Hong Kong also proposed the formation of an FTA (free trade area) with the mainland. On 29 June 2003, the 'Mainland and Hong Kong Closer Economic Partnership Arrangement', or 'Closer Economic Partnership Arrangement' (CEPA) was signed between the Government of the Hong Kong Special Administrative Region and the Central People's Government of the People's Republic of China.[4] In

addition, annual supplements have been signed between the Mainland and Hong Kong governments. This was the first free-trade agreement for either the mainland or Hong Kong.

15.1.2 Macau

Located in the west side the Pearl River (Zhujiang), Macau was included in Xiangshan county, Guangdong province in ancient times. In 1533 the Portuguese rented Macau from the Chinese government. After the Opium War (1840–42), they extended their possessions in Macau. Macau became a formal Portuguese colony in 1887. Bordering on Zhuhai municipality, Guangdong province, Macau now has an area of 16.92 square kilometers, including Macau peninsula and Taipa and Toloane islands. Macau has a population of more than 400,000. In accordance with the Sino-Portugal Joint Declaration signed on 15 January 1988, Macau was handed over from the Portuguese administration to mainland China on 20 December 1999. Since this time, Macau has become the second SAR of the PRC, operating like Hong Kong under the principle of 'one country, two systems'.

---

3. See 'Basic Law of the Hong Kong Special Administrative Region of the People's Republic of China', Article 5, the Third Session of the Seventh NPC, 4 April 1990.
4. For the full text of the CEPA, see http://www.tid.gov.hk/english/cepa/files/main_e_pdf. Accessed on November 29, 2011.

In order promote Macau's economic strength, a similar agreement, known as the Mainland and Macau Closer Economic Partnership Arrangement, was signed between the Government of the Macau Special Administrative Region and the Central People's Government on 18 October 2003.

15.1.3 Taiwan

With 36,000 square kilometers of land and a population of more than 20 million, Taiwan is composed of Taiwan, Penghu, Mazu, and other small islands adjacent to mainland China (see Figure 15.2). The Sino-Japanese War was ended with the signing of the Shimonoseki Treaty on 17 April 1895. Under the Treaty, Japan seized Taiwan and the Penghu islands from the Qing dynasty (1644–1911), subjecting Taiwan to colonial rule for half a century. At the end of World War II, in cooperation with the Allied forces, China defeated Japan. On 25 October 1945, Taiwan and Penghu islands returned unconditionally to the Chinese government, marking the end of Japan's colonization. However, with the civil war coming to an end, Taiwan and mainland China were again politically separated in 1949 when the Nationalist-led government fled to Taiwan and the Communists took power in the mainland.

Since the late 1940s, in practice China has been ruled by two ideologically antagonistic regimes, each of which has laid claim to the sole sovereignty of the whole nation and treated the other side as its 'rebel' local government.[5] The division of the Chinese nation extends through many phases of Chinese life – political, economic, and social. The decades-long cross-Strait separation led to a series of tragic conflicts and produced mutual distrust and many other human and national agonies. Since then, it has become the inviolable mission and long-term goal for the two regimes to maintain peaceful relations and to promote all-round revitalization of the nation.

At present, Taiwan has only maintained 23 diplomatic allies, most of which are small developing countries on Pacific islands, in Africa, or in Latin America. According to the website of the ROC Ministry of Foreign Affairs (MOFA), Taiwan currently has its own informal representations in 57 countries, while 49 countries maintain offices in Taiwan.[6] The names and levels of competence of these representations vary considerably both on the Taiwanese as well as on the foreign side, and they all stop short of being formal embassies, although many of them fulfill similar functions. In addition, MOFA's website also lists 32 international organizations of which Taiwan is a member.

Taiwan joined three quarters of them after 1987, when it started its policy of overture to international organizations.

In 2008 new President Ma Ying-jeou saw that Taiwan was fighting a losing battle with more and more states drawn into China's orbit as a fast power. He proposed a 'diplomatic truce' with the mainland, meaning in part that both sides would stop stealing each other's diplomatic allies. Since then, no country has switched sides (Winkler, 2011).

15.1.4 Summary

For a period of time, in spite of their common history, and cultural and linguistic homogeneity, the four economic areas have followed divergent political systems, which have resulted in different social and economic performances. For example, as soon as the PRC was founded in 1949, mainland China had effectively adopted and practiced a Marxist-Leninist command economy as imposed by the Soviet Union, before it decided to introduce structural reform in the late 1970s. Hong Kong and Macau – two former colonial economies under the British and Portuguese administrations, respectively – have been fundamentally incorporated into Western-style society, albeit that Chinese culture and language are still accepted by most of the citizens that live there. From an economic viewpoint, Hong Kong and Macau each have an autonomous entity, are separate customs territories and founding members of the WTO. Each has an independent fiscal and monetary system, issuing their own currencies that are linked to the US dollar. Each issues its own passport and retains its legal system, maintaining its own court of appeal. Each runs its internal affairs without interference from the central government, except in matters of defense and foreign affairs.

Taiwan had been under the colonial rule of the Japanese for 50 years before it was liberated and returned to China in 1945. With the Civil War (1946–49) coming to an end, however, the newly reunified nation was separated by two ideologically rival regimes – the Nationalists (Kuomintang, or KMT) in Taiwan and the Chinese Communist Party (CCP) on the mainland. Backed by the United States, Taiwan followed the capitalist road of economic development. While both sides of the Taiwan Strait have declared that there is only one *China* in the world and that their motherland should be reunified sooner or later, many of the political issues arising from the bloody war which was eventually detrimental to national cooperation still remain unresolved.

The end of the Cold War and the implementation of economic reform and the open-door policy in mainland China in December 1978 heralded a new era. In January 1979 the USA established diplomatic relations with mainland China and broke off its long-standing diplomatic relations with Taiwan. Ties between Hong Kong and the mainland developed very rapidly. The development of

---

5. For example, the Mainland Commission has still been established by the Taiwanese government to officially manage its 'mainland affairs', while in mainland China, the Office for Taiwan Affairs is also authorized by the State Council to deal with the 'Taiwan affairs'.

6. Data source: http://www.mofa.gov.tw. Accessed on November 22, 2011.

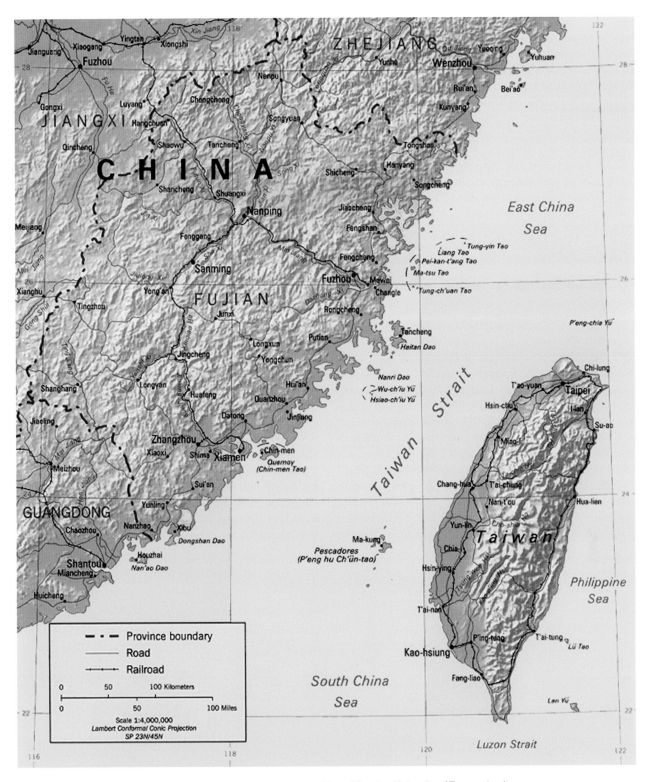

FIGURE 15.2 The Taiwan Strait. *Source: Courtesy of the University of Texas Libraries, University of Texas at Austin.*

mainland Taiwan ties mainly took place after November 1987 when Taiwan lifted its ban on visits to the mainland. Hong Kong and Macau reverted to Chinese sovereignty in 1997 and 1999, respectively, while preserving their capitalist system for 50 years under the formula of 'one country, two systems'.

It can be seen that since the 1980s the greater China area has been undergoing various political and economic transformations. Since 1997 and 1999, respectively, Sino-Hong Kong and Sino-Macau relations have no longer been treated as international in nature. Regardless of the political separation, non-governmental relations between the two sides of the Taiwan Strait have been developed gradually since 1980 when the Standing Committee of the NPC firstly publicized 'Message to the Taiwan Compatriots', especially since 1988 when private visits from Taiwan to the mainland were permitted by the Taiwanese government. In the remainder of this chapter, we will try to analyze economic performances and relations between Hong Kong, Macau, Taiwan, and mainland China.

15.2 A MULTIREGIONAL ECONOMIC COMPARISON

15.2.1 Social and Economic Differences

Despite the common historical, cultural, and linguistic homogeneity, the greater China economic area has followed different routes of economic development. Hong Kong and Macau have been under the colonial administrations of the UK and of Portugal, respectively. Taiwan was a Japanese colony between 1895 and 1945 and, following a short period of reunification with mainland China, has been operating independently from the rest of the world. As a result, significant social and economic differences have been present in the four parts of the area, especially since 1949. In what follows we will analyze them in detail.

Table 15.1 shows the basic social and economic indicators of greater China in the early years of the twenty-first century. In 2003, Taiwan's GDP was 1.8 times that of Hong Kong. The GDP of the mainland was 4.9 times

that of Taiwan and 8.9 times that of Hong Kong. The mainland's 2003 exports of US$438 billion surpassed Taiwan's exports of US$144 billion and also substantially surpassed the level of Hong Kong's domestic exports (that is, exports made domestically in Hong Kong) of US$16 billion. The figure for Hong Kong's total exports (that is, including re-exports) of US$225 billion is large because Hong Kong is re-exporting Chinese products to third countries and third-country products to China. In other words, Hong Kong is China's gateway to the world in commodity trade.

From Table 15.1, one may also note that all parts of the greater China area have enjoyed higher annual GNP growth rates than most of the remaining economies in the world. Particularly noteworthy is the fact that mainland China's GNP growth rate is among the highest of all of the world's dynamic economies. If all goes according to plan, mainland China's economic size and per capita GNP will continue to increase at a higher rate than those of the other parts.

Hong Kong's economy was seriously affected by the Japanese invasion during World War II. The population decreased sharply from 1.6 million in 1940 to 0.60 million in August 1945 and 60 percent of the buildings were destroyed (Wu and Liang, 1990, p. 235). By the 1950s and 1960s the constant influx from China of capital and manpower led to the establishment of light manufacturing in Hong Kong. At the same time, Hong Kong's tax policies began to attract growing levels of foreign investment, adding further impetus to the rapid growth of the territory. In the 1950s Hong Kong began in earnest a new career as a manufacturing and industrial center. Textiles, electronics, watches, and many other low-priced goods stamped 'Made

TABLE 15.1 Basic Indicators of the Greater China Area

Indicator	Taiwan	Hong Kong	Macau	Mainland
Area (sq. km)	36,188	1,098	19	9,600,000
Population (million persons)	22.5	6.8	0.4	1,284.5
GDP (2003, billion US$)	286.8	158.6	7.9	1,416
GDP per capita (2003, US$)	12,751	23,311	17,782	1,090
Average growth rate of GDP per capita (1978–2002, %)	5.50	3.98	2.03[a]	8.04
Exports (2003, billion US$)	144.2	224.6 (15.7[b])	2.6	438.4
Life expectancy (1990s, Female/male, years)	77/71.8	81.2/75.8		71/68
Adult literacy rate (1990s, Female/male, %)[c]	86/96	88/96	95.7[d]	73/90

[a]Growth rate for 1982–2002.
[b]Exports of Hong Kong goods (re-exports are excluded).
[c]ADB (1996, pp. 11 and 28), SSB (1996, pp. 769, 781, and 803).
[d]Xie (1992, p. 115) for labor population.
Source: Websites of the respective governments except those that are noted otherwise.

in Hong Kong' flowed from the territory in ever-increasing amounts. Restricted by the shortage of land and other natural resources of its own and the closed-door policy in mainland China, Hong Kong's economy grew very slowly in the period before the 1970s.

Since the late 1970s, Hong Kong's economy has grown rapidly, as a result of its favorable geographical location in terms of international trade and its proximity to mainland China. During the 1980s Hong Kong started to work with China on a series of joint projects that brought the two closer together. Today the financial service industries have taken over from manufacturing as Hong Kong's main enterprise. This small territory was the first developing economy to enter the world's top ten economies and the highest of the 'four Asian dragons' in terms of per capita GNP. And while much of the manufacturing is now likely to be done either in the region across the border or further afield, Hong Kong is still one of the world's largest exporters. Social programs continue to raise the standard of living, which is comparable to that found in many Western countries.

In mid-1997 the Asian financial crisis struck Hong Kong shortly after Hong Kong's reversion to China. Hong Kong's GDP contracted by more than 5 percent in 1998, the first recorded instance of negative annual growth since official GDP figures became available in 1961. Though the Hong Kong economy recovered in 1999–2000, the slowdown of the US economy and the September 11 terrorist attack led to another recession, and GDP growth fell to 0.5 percent in 2001. Recovery in the second half of 2002 was interrupted by the outbreak of SARS in March 2003. Since the Asian financial crisis, Hong Kong has tried to exploit its connections with mainland China in order to boost its economy. The measures introduced included the relaxation of controls against tourists and skilled workers from the mainland, and the promotion of economic integration with the Pearl River Delta. Hong Kong also proposed the formation of an FTA (free trade area) with the mainland, resulting in the implementation of the 'Closer Economic Partnership Arrangement' (CEPA) on 29 June 2003. The CEPA has brought positive economic benefits to both Hong Kong and the mainland.

For the past 400 years, the mixture of the Western and Chinese societies has resulted in Macau developing a unique cultural landscape. However, Macau's industrialization only began during the 1960s and it has been restricted by the trade protectionism that was imposed upon Hong Kong by the USA and the EU before the 1980s. Since the early 1980s, the economic development of Macau has benefited greatly from its proximity to both Hong Kong (one of the freest markets in the world) and mainland China (one of the world's cheapest sources of labor and raw materials). Today, Macau's three major industries are trade, tourism, casinos, property, and construction.

In recent decades, Taiwan has been successfully transformed from a colonized and agriculturally based economy to a newly industrialized economy and has become known as one of the 'four Asian economic dragons'. In 1953, its per capita GNP was less than US$200, a figure that grew dramatically to more than US$15,000 in the 2000s. Economic development in Taiwan faced many obstacles, including a lack of energy and industrial resources, high population density, and the need to fund a high level of spending on defense in order to sustain a balance with mainland China (as shown in Table 15.3), a series of failures in foreign affairs, as well as the increasing political pressure coming from the mainland, the effects of regional protectionism, and so on. The Taiwan miracle, however, has been ascribed mainly to the indomitable spirit of the Taiwanese people themselves, embodied in the phrase by Kao and Shong (1992, p. 10): 'the more difficulties they faced, the harder they would work'.

With the heterogeneous natural and social conditions, there exist substantial differences of real living standards in the greater China area. However, owing to the differing personal consumption structures, as well as their purchasing powers, it is very difficult for us to conduct a complete and reasonable comparison of the four parts. In brief, Hong Kong and Macau, as two municipal economies, have the highest living standards in the greater China area. Nevertheless, the socioeconomic gap between Taiwan and mainland China would be narrowed substantially if the purchasing power differences are taken into account.

Other indicators, such as life expectancy, literacy, and other physical quality-of-life indices, not to mention the political freedom of the individual (which is the most valuable criterion in Western nations), seem to indicate that there exist significant differences within the greater China area.

15.2.2 Complementary Conditions

Obviously, the mutually complementary conditions exist in the greater China area in terms of natural resources, labor force, technology, and industrial structure, as demonstrated in Table 15.2. For example, mainland China has adequate and various agricultural products and oil, coal, building materials, some high-tech products, excess and cheap labor, and a huge domestic market. However, mainland China lacks capital, advanced equipment, technology, and management experience, especially in its western, inland areas. Taiwan, with its high levels of capital saving, its portable advanced equipment, and vanguard agricultural and industrial products and management experience, suffers from a shortage of energy and industrial resources, and faces increasing inefficiency and high costs of labor supply. Furthermore, its economic development seems to have been restricted by the limited domestic market. As

TABLE 15.2 Mutually Complementary Conditions in the Greater China Area

Economy	Advantages	Disadvantages
Mainland China	Adequate and various agricultural products, energy, industrial materials, excess labor, some high-tech products, and huge domestic market.	Relative shortage of advanced equipment; shortage of international management experience and economic infrastructures, especially in the western, inland provinces.
Taiwan	High capital saving, advanced equipment ready to move out, vanguard agricultural and industrial products, and management experience.	Shortage of energy and industrial resources, limited domestic market, and insufficient and high costs of labor supply.
Hong Kong and Macau	Capital surplus, favorable convenient conditions for international trade, the freest economic environment, and management experience in commercial and financial markets.	Severe shortage of agricultural and industrial resources, especially fresh water, foodstuff, energy, and land and deficiency of labor; limited domestic market.

the freest economies in the world, Hong Kong and Macau have capital surplus, favorable conditions for international trade, and advanced management experience in commercial and financial markets; while they are severely lacking agricultural and industrial resources, especially fresh water, foodstuffs, energy and land. In addition, like Taiwan, Hong Kong and Macau are also facing a serious deficiency and high cost of labor.[7]

Traditionally, both Hong Kong and Taiwan are strong in labor-intensive, export-oriented industries: Hong Kong's niches are in clothing, toys, watches, and electronics, while Taiwan's are in footwear, umbrellas, textiles, and electronics. Such traditional industries have all but relocated to the mainland. The opening up of the mainland came at the right time for Hong Kong and Taiwan as they had accumulated valuable human capital in the management and manufacturing of labor-intensive products for exports from the 1950s to the 1970s. However, successful export-oriented industrialization had raised the levels of their wages, and their labor-intensive industries were threatened in the 1980s. The majority of manufacturing firms in Hong Kong and Taiwan were small, and lacked the ability to operate internationally; for example, to relocate to Southeast Asia. Without the opening of the mainland, the vast majority of these small firms would have gone bankrupt. However, the opening of the mainland allowed small firms to relocate to a culturally familiar environment and thereby utilize their valuable know-how to build a 'global factory' – that is, a production base dominating the world market (Sung, 2004, p. 3).

Under the mutually complementary conditions, the multilateral economic cooperation may generate a series of positive effects on the economic development of the greater China area. Through trade and the spatial relocation of such production factors as labor, raw materials,

technology and capital, economic optimization will be undoubtedly increased in the greater China area.

15.2.3 Summary

Despite their common history and cultural and linguistic homogeneity, over the course of recent decades the greater China area (including Taiwan, Hong Kong, Macau, and mainland China) has followed divergent political and economic systems, which has resulted in different social and economic performances. Along with mainland China's economic renaissance and the returns of Hong Kong and Macau from the British and Portuguese governments to China in 1997 and 1999, respectively, the economic ties between the three parts as a single sovereign nation have been accelerated under the principle of 'one country, two systems'.

After the return of Hong Kong and Macau from the British and Portuguese governments to mainland China in 1997 and 1999, respectively, the economic development of the PRC has been further advanced by approximately two to three years.[8] The two sides of the Taiwan Strait, however, have been politically separated for more than fifty years due to the mutual distrust and hostile strategies arising from the bloody conflict between the Nationalists and the Communists at the end of World War II.

It is close to a rule among practitioners and theorists that multilateral conflicts frequently arise from narrow individual interests and the expectations of different communities on the one hand, and a chaotic interdependent system on the other. Notwithstanding the political, economic, and social differences within the greater China economic area, it appears to be increasingly possible for all Chinese, under increasing comparative advantages, mutual complementary conditions, as well as the tendency toward the development of unanimity in relation to political,

7. During the early 1990s, average labor cost in Hong Kong, Macau, and Taiwan was 10–20 times that in mainland China (Yang, 1992, p. 3).

8. See Annex A for a detailed description of the calculations.

social, and especially economic points of view across different parts of the area, to find an appropriate approach that can maximize the benefits for all of the parties concerned, while also taking into account their respective articulated objectives.

15.3 CROSS-STRAIT ECONOMIC RELATIONS

The state of Zhao was going to assault the state of Yan. Su Dai came to see King Hui of the Zhao, and said, 'On my way here I saw a clam just coming out to bask in the sun on the shore of the Yishui river. A snipe came over to peck at the flesh of the clam, which closed its shell and gripped the snipe's beak. The snipe said, 'If it does not rain today and tomorrow, you will become a dead clam.' 'If you cannot free yourself today and tomorrow, you will become a dead snipe,' replied the clam. Neither one would give way and eventually a fisherman caught them both. Su continued, 'Now if Zhao is ready to attack Yan, but if both states were locked in a long stalemate with neither side ready to yield, I am afraid then the powerful Qin will turn up as the fisherman. Therefore, I do hope that you will give this matter careful consideration before you act.' 'Well said,' nodded the King. And he gave up his military plan.

– Zhanguoce (475–221 BC)

15.3.1 Historical Evolution

The Taiwan Strait became a forbidden boundary in 1949 when the Nationalist-led government fled to Taiwan and, at the same time, the Communist-led government was founded on the mainland. Since then, Taiwan and mainland China have been two divergent regimes. Against the common cultural and linguistic homogeneity, mainland China chose essentially to pursue a socialist line, while Taiwan followed the route of market-oriented capitalism. Furthermore, the two sides have also treated each other antagonistically, particularly during the high tide of military confrontation, when the mainland claimed that it would liberate the Taiwan compatriots from the *black* society sooner or later, while in turn Taiwan maintained that they would use the 'three democratisms' to reoccupy the mainland eventually.

Throughout the 1950s and the 1960s the Taiwan-based Nationalists had been the internationally recognized government representing China as a whole. On October 15, 1971, the United Nations seat was changed from Taiwan to mainland China in accordance with UN Resolution No. 2758. Since this time, the international positions of Taiwan and mainland China have been reversed. Following the United States' transference of its diplomatic relations with China from the KMT-led Taiwan to the CCP-led mainland in December 1978, an increasing number of Western nations began to establish their own formal ties with the mainland. As a result, Taiwan lost most of its friends.

Even though '[the cross-Taiwan Strait] reunification does not mean that the mainland will swallow up Taiwan, nor does it mean that Taiwan will swallow up the mainland' (Jiang, 1995, p. 2), many critical issues concerning the cross-Taiwan Strait relations still remain unresolved. For instance, even though both mainland China and Taiwan have declared to the outside world that they are pursuing the 'one China' policy, the contents of which are absolutely different from each other. Mainland China proudly stresses that the 'People's Republic of China' (PRC) has been one of the five permanent members of the UN's Security Council and of course should be – and has already been – the only legal government representing China of which, to be sure, Taiwan is only a province.[9]

The Taiwanese government, however, strongly argues that the 'Republic of China' (ROC) founded by Dr Sun Yatsen has existed since 1911 and is still in *rapport* with a certain number of independent nations. More importantly, in addition to Taiwan's remarkable economic growth and social progress, the Taiwanese government, after a long period of silence, has increasingly felt that it is time to expand its international presence and to let the outside world know the fact that there exists the 'Republic of China on Taiwan' at least in parallel with the 'People's Republic of China' in the mainland (see Box 15.1).

A comparison of military expenditures between Taiwan and mainland China is shown in Table 15.3.

Nevertheless, progress toward peaceful relations has been registered in negotiations over a number of specific issues. In order to find a practical way to maintain contacts, each of the two sides established a 'non-governmental' institution, viz., the Foundation of the Taiwan Straits Exchanges (FTSE) in Taiwan and the Association for the Taiwan Straits Relations (ATSR) on the mainland. During the early 1990s, the ATSR–FTSE talks represented forward steps in the relations between the two sides of the Taiwan Strait. In November 1992, the mainland China-based Association for Relations across the Taiwan Strait (ARATS) and the Taiwan-based Straits Exchange Foundation (SEF) held a meeting in Hong Kong. Three months before the meeting, the Taiwan side (on August 1, 1992) published the following statement in respect of its interpretation of the meaning of 'one China':

---

9. The PRC's attitude towards Taiwan's position in the international community may be briefly summarized by Jiang (1995, p. 2) as that '... Under the principle of one China and in accordance with the charters of the relevant international organizations, Taiwan has become a member of the Asian Development Bank, the Asian-Pacific Economic Cooperation Forum, and other international economic organizations in the name of "Chinese Taipei".'

Box 15.1 How to Solve the Cross-Straits Equation?

The two sides of the Taiwan Strait have been politically separated for more than fifty years due to the mutual distrust and hostile strategies arising from the bloody conflict between the Nationalists and the Communists at the end of World War II. With the Cold War coming to an end and the surging tide of global participation in economic development, cross-Straits trade and economic cooperation have developed rapidly. However, it is still unclear when national reunification may eventually become a possibility.

At present, there are five choices for Taiwan and mainland China: (i) PU (peaceful reunification); (ii) FU (forced reunification); (iii) peaceful independence (PI); (iv) SQ (to maintain the status quo); and (v) FI (forced independence). They are assumed to follow:

(1) PU>SQ>FU>FI>PI (preferred by mainland China)
(2) PI>FI>SQ>FU>PU (preferred by pro-independence clique in Taiwan)
(3) SQ>PI>PU>FI>FU (preferred by pro-reunification clique in Taiwan)

Given the above preference ranking, what are the most likely solutions to the cross-Straits equation?

TABLE 15.3 Military Expenses, Taiwan, and Mainland China

Item	Taiwan	Mainland China
Defense expense (US$100 million)	104	562
Forces (1,000 persons)	442	3,031
Defense expense as % of GNP	4.7	2.7
Defense expense as % of budget	20.0	16.2
Per capita defense (US$)	494	48
Forces per 1,000 population	21.0	2.6

Sources: The US Academy of Defense Agency (1993) and SSB (1996, pp. 230 and 580).

Both sides of the Taiwan Strait agree that there is only one China. However, the two sides of the Strait have different opinions as to the meaning of 'one China.' To Peking, 'one China' means the 'People's Republic of China (PRC),' with Taiwan to become a 'Special Administration Region' after unification. Taipei, on the other hand, considers 'one China' to mean the Republic of China (ROC), founded in 1911 and with de jure sovereignty over all of China. The ROC, however, currently has jurisdiction only over Taiwan, Penghu, Kinmen, and Matsu. Taiwan is part of China, and the Chinese mainland is part of China as well.[10]

The Kuomintang (KMT) led ROC government had expressed the 1992 meeting's outcome as 'one China with different interpretations': that both sides agreed that there was one China, but indirectly recognized and respected that both sides had different interpretations of that concept. By contrast, the PRC government consistently emphasizes that the 1992 meeting reached an understanding that there is 'one China'. ROC's main opposition party, the Democratic Progressive Party (DPP), however, did not see the 1992 meeting as reaching any consensus on there being only 'one China'. Instead, it saw the outcome of the meeting as establishing that the two sides had different interpretations of the status quo.

In Taiwan, supporters of the pan-Green coalition led by the DPP remained insistent that the meetings in 1992 did not come to any consensus over the one China principle. In support of this view, they point out that both Hsu Huei-yu and Koo Chen-fu, who participated in the 1992 meeting as SEF delegates, have publicly affirmed that the meeting did not result in any consensus on the 'one China' issue. Instead, they claim, both sides agreed to proceed with future meetings on the basis of equality and mutual respect. Koo stated in his biography that, 'Both sides across the strait have different interpretations of the 1992 Hong Kong meeting. Rather than using 'consensus,' the term of art should be 'understanding' or 'accord' to better reflect the fact, thus avoiding untruthful application.'

After 1996, the cross-Taiwan Strait relations became strained by two significant developments: (i) the Taiwanese president, Lee Tenghui, insistence on seeking to expand Taiwan's 'international living space' which is aimed at, as claimed by mainland China, creating 'two Chinas' or 'one China, one Taiwan'; and (ii) mainland China's missile tests within the Taiwan Strait area.

Taiwan's economy suffered from the Asian financial crisis during the late 1990s, from the September 11 terrorist attack in 2001 and from the Severe Acute Respiratory Syndrome (SARS) in 2003. While economic difficulties have spurred Taiwan toward the establishment of closer links with the mainland, Taiwan was less active than Hong Kong in capturing the mainland market, owing to high levels of political antagonism. Taiwan's GDP

---

10. This statement was published in the Mainland Affairs Council, Executive Yuan, ROC, 'Consensus Formed at the National Development Conference on Cross-Strait Relations,' February 1997. – Cited from Kan (2011).

contracted by 1.9 percent in 2001, the first record of negative annual growth since data were first made available in 1951. Taiwan's unemployment rate rose about 5 percent in 2002, the highest since 1964, when statistics on unemployment were regularly available (Sung, 2004, p. 7). While Taiwan's business community has been eager to improve relations with the mainland, the election and re-election of Chen Shui-bian (representing the pro-independence Democratic Progressive Party, or DPP) to Taiwan's presidency in 2000 and 2004, respectively, exacerbated political tensions across the Taiwan Strait.

In fact, the long-awaited breakthrough on direct links has been achieved during the second term of Chen's presidency. A brief chronology of cross-Strait relations is as follows:

On May 17, 2004, Hu Jintao made friendly overtures to Taiwan on resuming negotiations for the 'three links', reducing misunderstandings, and increasing consultation.

In March 2005, China passed the 'Anti-Secession Law' where it laid down in writing that 'the state [the PRC] shall employ non-peaceful means and other necessary measures' if Taiwan's formal secession from China becomes imminent.[11] In April, there were increased contacts culminated in the Pan-Blue visits to mainland China, including a meeting between the CCP Secretariat General Hu Jintao and then-KMT Chairman Lien Chan.

On March 20, 2008, the KMT party won the presidency in the Republic of China. It also has a majority in the Legislature. On April 12, 2008, Hu Jintao met with ROC's then vice-president elect Vincent Siew as chairman of the Cross-strait Common Market Foundation during the Boao Forum for Asia. On May 28, 2008, Hu met with KMT chairman Wu Po-hsiung, the first meeting between the heads of the CPC and the KMT as ruling parties. Dialogue through semi-official organizations (the SEF and the ARATS) reopened on June 12, 2008 on the basis of the 1992 Consensus, with the first meeting held in Beijing. Neither the PRC nor the ROC recognizes the other side as a legitimate entity, so the dialogue was in the name of contacts between the SEF and the ARATS instead of the two governments, though most participants were actually officials in PRC or ROC governments.

On May 1, 2009, the ROC's financial regulator, the Financial Supervisory Commission, announced that mainland Chinese investors would be permitted to invest in Taiwan's money markets for the first time since 1949.

On June 29, 2010, the Economic Cooperation Framework Agreement (ECFA) is signed between the governments of the People's Republic of China (mainland China) and the Republic of China (Taiwan) that aims to reduce tariffs and commercial barriers between the two sides.

On October 10, 2011, in the 100th anniversary of the Xinhai Revolution, Chinese President Hu Jintao calls for reunification with Taiwan; in Taipei, Taiwanese president Ma Ying-jeou calls on mainland authorities to remember Sun Yat-sen's founding ideals of China as a nation of freedom, democracy and the fair distribution of wealth.

15.3.2 Bilateral Economic Cooperation

Bilateral trade and economic exchanges between Taiwan and mainland China had been frozen before 1979, except for small amounts of indirect trade of, among others, Chinese medicine and other native products from mainland China to Taiwan (mainly conducted via Hong Kong). In 1979, mainland China's 'Taiwan policy' was transformed from 'liberating Taiwan' to 'peaceful reunification'. Since this time, indirect trade between the two sides of the Taiwan Strait and the Taiwanese investment in mainland China via Hong Kong and other regions have grown rapidly as a result of the cross-Taiwan Strait *détente*. In addition, tourism, technological and labor cooperation between the two sides have also achieved considerable progress.

In 1985, the Taiwanese government instituted the 'non-interference' policy to Taiwan's exportation to mainland China. Thereafter, the restrictions of the cross-Taiwan Strait trade were gradually worn away under the principle of 'indirect trading' – that is, the direct trade partners should be located outside mainland China and trade movements should be via third countries (regions). Until the 1990s, the cross-Taiwan Strait trade had still been managed through a 'concentrated' approach in mainland China, not allowing the mainland's foreign trade companies to deal directly with Taiwanese companies outside Hong Kong and Macau. This policy, nevertheless, has promoted the two sides' foreign trade companies to open up either sub-companies or branches of their own in Hong Kong and Macau.

During the early period, Taiwanese investment in mainland China was usually conducted under the names of investors from Hong Kong, Macau, overseas Chinese and others who would nominally be accepted by the two sides.[12] In order to overcome the lack of foreign capital,

---

11. The full text of the Law is posted on the website of the Taiwan Affairs Office of the State Council of the PRC (http://www.gwytb.gov.cn/en/Special/OneChinaPrinciple/201103/t20110317_1790121.htm. Accessed November 10, 2011.)

---

12. In 1985, Chen Guoshun, a Taiwanese businessman, was sentenced in Taipei to 12 years in prison for 'rebellious' activities. The prosecutor charged Chen with illegally entering mainland China in 1984, signing a contract, and engaging in direct investment in the mainland. Chen's sentence sent a shock wave to those who had engaged or intended to conduct direct business activities (*Pai Shing Semimonthly*, 1 March 1986, p. 52).

mainland China introduced a flexible policy entitled 'attraction of the Taiwanese capital via Hong Kong and overseas Chinese' (*yi gang yin tai, yi qiao yin tai*) which was intended to encourage Taiwanese businessmen to invest in mainland China. Since October 1990, when the Taiwanese government formally allowed Taiwanese businessmen to invest in mainland China, it has always required that the Taiwanese investors should be under the names of their sub-companies housed in the third areas. In order to encourage Taiwanese businessmen to invest in the mainland, mainland China promulgated the 'Regulations Concerning the Promotion of the Taiwanese Compatriots' Investment' in July 1988 and the 'Law of Protecting the Taiwanese Compatriots Investment' in March 1994, respectively.

Financial movements between Taiwan and mainland China had been prohibited strictly by the Taiwanese government before May 1990 when the South China Bank (in Taiwan) was allowed to indirectly (via a British bank in Hong Kong) offer individual financial businesses from Taiwan to mainland China. Since then the level of Taiwanese investment in mainland China has increased dramatically. In July 1993, financial movements were able to extend from individual to business activities, and furthermore banks in the Taiwan area were able to receive funds sent indirectly from mainland China. As Taiwanese businessmen were only allowed to invest in mainland China via third regions or countries, this kind of 'indirect investment' is, in theory, one between a third region (country) and mainland China, which might result in many unresolved issues.

In Taiwan, the population is identified mainly by two groups – native Taiwanese and Han- and other ethnic Chinese who fled to Taiwan when the Nationalists (KMT) lost the mainland in 1949. In addition to the cross-Taiwan Strait trade and Taiwanese investment on the mainland, other exchanges between the two sides of the Taiwan Strait have also grown rapidly since many Taiwanese have relatives in mainland China. Since November 1987, when Taiwanese citizens were first allowed to pay private visits to mainland China, there has been a considerable increase in the numbers of visitors from Taiwan to the mainland, resulting in a large amount of expenditure including traveling expenses, donations and others. In addition, there have been rapid developments in terms of the exchanges in labor, science and technology between the two sides.

In spite of the very cool political relations during the Chen Shui-bian years, economic relations continued to intensify. Mainland China replaced the United States as Taiwan's most important trading partner around 2002. In 2008 Taiwan's exports to mainland China and Hong Kong together (US$99.6 billion) were more than three times greater than Taiwan's exports to the United States

(US$30.8 billion) (Bottelier, 2009, p. 100). On June 30, 2010, the Economic Cooperation Framework Agreement (ECFA) was signed between and the ARATS and the SEF, both of which represent the governments of the People's Republic of China (mainland China) and the Republic of China (Taiwan), respectively. The ECFA is a preferential trade agreement that aims to reduce tariffs and commercial barriers between the two sides. For a long period of time, the Chinese government uses its influence on neighboring economic powers to prevent them from signing free-trade agreements (FTAs) with Taiwan. Instead, under the leadership of the Kuomintang, Taipei was motivated to sign the ECFA with mainland China partly in hope that once it has this agreement the PRC will stop pressuring other countries to avoid such agreements with Taiwan. The ECFA has been compared with the Closer Economic Partnership Arrangements (CEPA) signed by mainland China with its two Special Administrative Regions (Hong Kong and Macau).

The ECFA was seen as the most significant agreement since the two sides split after the Chinese Civil War in 1949. The deal is thought to be structured to benefit Taiwan far more than mainland China. The 'early harvest' list of tariff concessions covers 539 Taiwanese products and 267 mainland Chinese goods. The advantage to Taiwan would amount to US$13.8 billion, while mainland China would receive benefits estimated at US$2.86 billion. Mainland China will also open markets in 11 service sectors such as banking, securities, insurance, hospitals and accounting, while Taiwan agreed to offer wider access in seven areas, including banking and movies.[13]

15.3.3   Direct Air and Shipping Services

Dividing the Chinese nation into two economically complementary but politically antagonistic counterparts, the Taiwan Strait has been perhaps one of the most special borders in the world. The nearest distance between Taiwan and mainland China is less than 1.8 km. Since the 1980s, efforts have been made to promote negotiations on the basis of reciprocity and mutual benefit. These have included the signing of non-governmental agreements relating to the protection of industrialists and businessmen. For years, Taiwan businesses had been asking for direct links across the 160-km wide Strait. But the pro-independence Democratic Progressive Party (DPP) had refused to re-establish direct links with the mainland. In the past, planes from the two sides had to fly through Hong Kong or

---

13. Source: http://www.mashpedia.com/Economic_Cooperation_Framework_Agreement. Accessed on November 18, 2011.

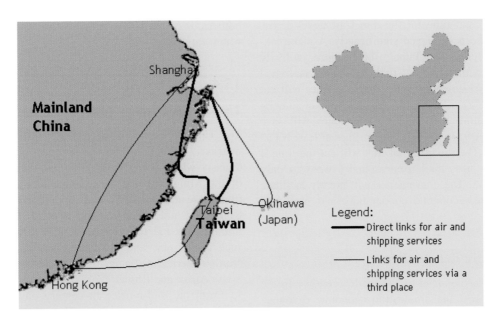

FIGURE 15.3 Links for air and shipping services between Taiwan and mainland China.

Macau airspace, and cargo ships usually sailed via Japan's waters. Direct links for postal, air and shipping services and trade between the two sides are the objective requirements for their economic development and contacts in various fields, and since they are in the interests of the people on both sides, it is absolutely necessary to adopt practical measures to speed up the establishment of such direct links.[14]

The 'three direct links' across the Taiwan Strait were finally established in 2008. According to agreements signed between Taiwan and mainland China on November 4, 2008, daily passenger flights have been launched. The two sides have agreed to increase the number of direct charter flights to 108 a week and the frequency from four to seven days a week between 21 mainland cities (Beijing, Shanghai, Guangzhou, Xiamen, Nanjing, Chengdu, Chongqing, Hangzhou, Dalian, Guilin, Shenzhen, Wuhan, Fuzhou, Qingdao, Changsha, Haikou, Kunming, Xi'an, Shenyang, Tianjin, and Zhengzhou) and eight Taiwan cities (Taipei, Taoyuan, Kaohsiung, Taichung, Penghu, Hualien, Kuemen, and Taidong).

In addition, 48 ports in mainland China have been approved for the establishment of direct air and shipping links with Taiwan: Dandong, Dalian, Yingkou, Tangshan, Jinzhou, Qinhuangdao, Tianjin, Huanghua, Weihai, Yantai, Longkou, Fengshan, Rizhao, Qingdao, Lianyungang, Dafeng, Shanghai, Qingbo, Zhoushan, Taizhou, Jiaxing, Wenzhou, Fuzhou, Shongxia, Ningde, Quanzhou, Xiaocuo, Xiuyu, Zhangzhou, Xiamen, Shantou, Chaozhou, Huizhou, Shekou, Yantian, Chiwan, Mawan, Humen, Guangzhou, Zhuhai, Maoming, Ganjiang, Beihai, Fangcheng, Qinzhou, Haikou, Shanya and Yangpu and 15 river ports of Taichang, Nantong, Zhangjiagang, Jiangyin, Changshu, Changzhou, Taizhou, Zhenjiang, Nanjing, Wuhu, Ma'anshan, Jiujiang, Wuhan, and Chenglingji. Taiwan's ports granted to set up direct links with mainland China include six ports (Keelung (including Taipei), Kaohsiung (including Anping), Taichung, Hualien, Mailiao and Budai) on Taiwan island as well as five other ports on Kuemen, Shuitou, Mazu, Baisa and Penghu islands.

On December 15, 2008, a Trans-Asia Airways jetliner took off from Taipei's Sungshan airport, carrying 148 Taiwanese tourists and businesspeople on the 80-minute flight to Shanghai. Taiwan's ERA Cable Station also aired footage of a China Eastern Airline jetliner at Shanghai airport that was preparing to depart for Taipei. The flight time is now cut by an hour because the planes are no longer required to fly south through Hong Kong's airspace, a detour that Taiwanese authorities had insisted on for security reasons. Cargo ships had been required to stop at the Japanese island of Okinawa north east of Taiwan (see Figure 15.3).

14. According to CEC (1996), the direct cross-Taiwan Strait links would have resulted in a net saving of US$731.5 million per annum for postal, remittance, air, and shipping services between the two sides of Taiwan Strait, including: (1) US$248.0 million for shipping service; (2) US$437.5 million (6.95 million hours) for air service; (3) US$24.0 million for postal service; and (4) US$22.0 million or more for remittance service. Cited from *Cankao Xiaoxi* (1996, p. 8).

The distance and time for the direct air travel across the Strait have been shortened significantly. A plane taking off from Beijing to Taipei, for instance, will fly 1,100 km less with its flying time becoming shortened by 80 minutes. Meanwhile, direct shipping lanes will cut costs and reduce time for businesspeople. Taiwan authorities are anticipating that shipping companies will save NT$1.2 billion (US$36 million) and airlines at least NT$3 billion a year.[15] The direct postal link will cut the time it takes to send express mail from around a week to only two or three days. The convenience will greatly facilitate cross-Strait trade, economic cooperation, and personnel exchanges.

15.3.4   Future Perspective

In view of the development of the world economy in the twenty-first century, the cross-Strait economic exchange and cooperation should be accelerated further. Only this can achieve prosperity for both sides and benefit the entire nation. The two sides have promised that political differences should not affect or interfere with economic cooperation between the sides. Under the principles of peace, equality and bilateralism, the Taiwanese government is willing to promote cross-Taiwan Strait economic exchanges and to treat the mainland as its hinterland. In order to seek the most efficient way of raising the level of the national economy, the PRC's government seems intent to continue to implement, over a considerable period of time, the policy of encouraging industrialists and businessmen from Taiwan to invest in the mainland. Definitely, the increasing contacts and exchanges between the two sides will further enhance the level of mutual understanding and trust.

Still, nobody can predict when the reunification of greater China will become a realistic possibility. With the Cold War coming to an end and private and semi-official cross-Taiwan Strait contacts being guaranteed by the both sides, all Chinese see no reason why their country should be left out of the surging tide of *détente* and further divided by man-made barriers.

Where there is patience and willingness to compromise, there is still hope. The hope emerges when the two sides find that their differences are not really so fundamental. Without doubt, the creation of political harmony and reunification between Taiwan and mainland China may still require time and patience on the part of both parties. It is a hopeful sign that the political regimes have promised to reunify peacefully as a single nation. Chinese people on both sides of the straits, and also the outside world, will watch carefully.

15.4   OVERSEAS CHINESE ECONOMICS

15.4.1   A History of Chinese Emigration

The Chinese people have a long history of migrating overseas. One of the migrations dates back to the Ming dynasty when Zheng He (1371–1435) became the envoy of the Ming emperor. He sent people – many of them Cantonese and Hokkien – to explore and trade in the South China Sea and in the Indian Ocean. Different waves of immigration led to subgroups among overseas Chinese such as the new and old immigrants in Southeast Asia, North America, Oceania, the Caribbean, Latin America, South Africa and Russia.

From the mid-nineteenth century onward, emigration has been directed primarily to Western countries (such as Australia, Brazil, Canada, New Zealand, the United States, and Western Europe). Many of these emigrants were themselves overseas Chinese or were from Taiwan or Hong Kong, particularly from the 1950s to the 1970s, a period during which the PRC placed severe restrictions on the movement of its citizens. In 1984, Britain agreed to transfer the sovereignty of Hong Kong to the PRC; this triggered another wave of migration to the United Kingdom, Australia, Canada, USA, Latin America, and the other parts of the world. The Tiananmen Square protests of 1989 further accelerated the migration. The wave calmed after Hong Kong's transfer of sovereignty in 1997. In addition, many citizens of Hong Kong hold citizenships or have current visas in other countries so if the need arises, they can leave Hong Kong at short notice.

15.4.2   Distribution of Overseas Chinese

There have been more than 40 million overseas Chinese living in over one hundred countries (see Annex B). Urban areas with large Chinese populations include Bangkok (2,900,000 persons; 2009 census, registered resident only), Singapore (2,800,000 persons; 2010 census), Kuala Lumpur (612,277 persons; 2000 census, city only), Penang (650,000 persons; 2005), Jakarta (528,300 persons; 2010 census), New York City Metropolitan Area (665,714 persons), the San Jose-San Francisco-Oakland Combined Statistical Area (562,355 persons; 2009), as well as the Greater Toronto Area (486,300 persons; 2006 census, metropolitan area).

Since the early twenty-first century, China has built increasingly stronger ties with African nations. As of 2010, there were more than 700,000 Chinese working or living in

---

15. Source: www.cnnb.com.cn, accessed on December 15, 2008.

different African countries. The countries with the largest Chinese communities include South Africa (with 350,000 Chinese), Angola (with 100,000 Chinese), Egypt (with 100,000 Chinese), and Madagascar (with 60,000 Chinese). Russia's main Pacific port and naval base of Vladivostok, once closed to foreigners, has been a dwelling place for 10 million and Chinese may become the dominant ethnic group in the Russian Far East region in the years to come. In addition, as of 2010, a growing Chinese community in Germany consists of around 76,000 people; and 15,000 to 30,000 Chinese live in Austria, including a significant Chinese community in Vienna.[16]

15.4.3 Global Economic Contributions

Since World War II, and especially since the 1970s, the wealth of the overseas Chinese has been growing rapidly and it has played an increasing role in the world economy. According to an incomplete estimate, the overseas Chinese already had US$223.1 billion of foreign currency deposits by the end of 1993, which is distributed mainly in Taiwan (US$90.6 billion), Hong Kong (US$32.7 billion), Singapore (US$43.7 billion), Thailand (US$23.4 billion), Malaysia (US$15.4 billion), Indonesia (US$11.0 billion), the Philippines (US$4.3 billion) and other nations (US$2.0 billion).[17]

In countries with small Chinese minorities, the economic disparity can be remarkable. For example, in 1998, ethnic Chinese made up just 1 percent of the population of the Philippines and 3 percent of the population in Indonesia, but controlled 40 percent of the Philippines private economy and 70 percent of the Indonesian private economy (Chua, 2003, pp. 3 and 43). The book *World on Fire*, describing the Chinese as a 'market-dominant minority', notes that:

Chinese market dominance and intense resentment amongst the indigenous majority is characteristic of virtually every country in Southeast Asia except Thailand and Singapore.

(Chua, 2003, p. 61)

Briefly, several factors can explain this remarkable growth of the overseas Chinese economy. These include:

(1) the thriftiness and hard-working nature of the overseas Chinese
(2) an elite group of intellectuals
(3) a positive role of overseas Chinese organizations
(4) closer socioeconomic ties with mainland China.

Since the early 1980s, when the open-door policy was implemented in mainland China, overseas Chinese have made great contributions to the economic development of mainland China, and in particular the coastal area with which they had the closest relations. Including the 'compatriots' (tongbao) of Hong Kong, Macau and Taiwan, the great majority of foreign direct investment (FDI) in China has come from the Chinese diaspora. Local development patterns have been strongly affected by the extent, or lack, of emigrant connections (Smart and Hsu, 2004). FDI in China is positively related to the population share of ethnic Chinese in the source country, and interpret this as showing the significant role of ethnic Chinese networks in FDI in China. For example, the result of an econometric analysis suggests that a one percentage point increase in the ethnic Chinese population share leads to a 3.7 percent or higher increase in cumulative FDI in China (Gao, 2003).

In addition, China's growing exports have also been widely promoted by the overseas Chinese networks (this has been discussed in Section 12.4 of Chapter 12).

ANNEX

A. Method of Estimating the Static Economic Effects of Reunification

After the return of Hong Kong and Macau from the British and Portuguese governments to mainland China in 1997 and 1999, respectively, the economic development of the PRC has been further advanced. A quantitative method by which estimate these influences is as the following:

$$\frac{GNP_{MC} + GNP_x}{POP_{MC} + POP_x} = \frac{GNP_{MC}}{POP_{MC}}(1 + R_{MC})^{T_x},$$

$$\text{with } \frac{GNP_x}{POP_x} \gg \frac{GNP_{MC}}{POP_{MC}} \text{ and } R_{MC} > 0.$$

Where $GNP =$ gross national product, $POP =$ population, $MC =$ mainland China, $x =$ Hong Kong, Macau, or Taiwan, $R_{MC} =$ the average annual growth rate of per capita GNP for mainland China within a certain period in the future, and $T_x =$ time period (in years) by which the per capita GNP of mainland China will reach that of mainland China and x combined.

Solving the above equation with the data in Table 15.1, we can obtain T_x (for a constant rate of $R_{MC} = 7\%$): $T_{\text{HongKong}} = 2.51$ years, $T_{\text{Macau}} = 0.03$ year and $T_{\text{Taiwan}} = 4.58$ years.

---

16. See Annex B.
17. Data source: *The Economic Research Materials* (1996, p. 62). Furthermore, *The Economist* (1992, p. 17) offered an even more optimistic estimation that, excluding Taiwan and Hong Kong, the total capital owned by overseas Chinese could exceed US$150 to $200 billion.

B. Statistics of Overseas Chinese Population, by Country

Country	Number (Persons)	Year	Country	Number (Persons)	Year
Asia	**31,279,797**	**2006**	Brazil	151,649	2005
Thailand	7,053,240	2005	Panama	135,000	2003
Malaysia	6,390,900	2010	Cuba	114,240	2008
Indonesia	7,000,000	2008	Argentina	100,000	2008
Singapore	2,794,000	2010	Mexico	23,000	2003
Vietnam	1,200,000	2005	Nicaragua	12,000	–
Cambodia	1,180,000	2008	Suriname	40,000	2011
Philippines	1,100,000	2005	Jamaica	70,000	–
Myanmar	1,100,000	2005	Dominican Republic	15,000	–
Japan	655,377	2008	Costa Rica	7,873	2009
South Korea	624,994	2009	Chile	5,000	–
Kazakhstan	300,000	2009	Trinidad & Tobago	3,800	2000
India	189,470	2005	Guyana	2,722	1921
Laos	185,765	2005	Belize	1,716	2000
United Arab Emirates	180,000	2009	Puerto Rico	–	–
Brunei	43,000	2006	Haiti	230	–
Israel	23,000	2001	**Europe**	**1,716,233**	**2006**
North Korea	10,000	2009	Russia	998,000	2005
Pakistan	10,000	2009	France	700,000	2010
Sri Lanka	3,500	?	United Kingdom	500,000	2008
Iran	3,000	–	Italy	201,000	2011
Kyrgyzstan	1,813	2009	Spain	128,022	2008
Mongolia	1,323	2000	Netherlands	76,960	2011
Bangladesh	1,200	2011	Germany	71,639	2004
Americas	**6,059,240**	**2008**	Serbia	20,000	2008
United States	3,500,000	2007	Ireland	16,533	2006
Canada	1,300,000	2006	Denmark	10,247	2009
Peru	1,300,000	2005	Bulgaria	10,000	2005

(Continued)

(Continued)

Country	Number (Persons)	Year	Country	Number (Persons)	Year
Portugal	9,689	2007	Angola	100,000	2007
Sweden	14,134	2010	Egypt	100,000	2010
Finland	7,546	2010	Madagascar	60,000	2007
Czech Republic	4,986	2007	Nigeria	50,000	2008
Romania	2,249	2002	Mauritius	30,000	2007
Turkey	1,000	2009	Réunion	25,000	1999
Oceania	**1,021,019**	**2003**	Zambia	20,000	2003
Australia	669,896	2006	Mozambique	12,000	2007
New Zealand	147,570	2006	Kenya	10,000	2007
Samoa	30,000	–	Tanzania	10,000	2008
Papua New Guinea	20,000	2008	Ghana	7,000	2008
Fiji	6,000	2000	Botswana	6,000	2009
Tonga	3,000	2001	Cameroon	2,000	2008
Palau	1,019	2001	Senegal	2,000	2008
Africa	**734,000**	**2009**	Seychelles	1,000	1999
South Africa	350,000	2009	Total	40,382,279	

Source: http://en.wikipedia.org/wiki/Overseas_Chinese#cite_note-ROC_date-52. Accessed on November 16, 2011.

Case Study 9

Location, Size, and Political Economy of Chinese Dynastic Cycles

Throughout history, political leaders have struggled to increase their territories through conquest. However, probably they forgot one fact: the territories per se are also an endogenous factor determining the lifespan of the regimes, particularly when the latter are authoritarian ones.

Thousands of archeological finds in China provide evidence that explains how China's dynastic cycles have been determined by its location, size and political economy.

Many historians have believed that it was the crude rule of the last king of the Shang – named Zhou – that made the dynasty collapse.[18] But there have been some historical records arguing that the war launched by the king Wu against the Shang dynasty was more a result of Wu's injustice than that of the king Zhou's cruelties.[19] Nevertheless, it is reasonable to believe that the disadvantageous geographical location of the Shang's capital in the north frontier of its territory did not enable the Shang court to keep an effective control over its remote, southwest frontiers where small tribes could grow strong enough to, under the leadership of the king Wu, eventually defeat the Shang dynasty in 1046 BC. This hypothesis can be supported by king Wu's intention to move the Zhou's capital from Hao (near Xi'an) in western China to Luoyi (now known as Luoyang) in central China in order to keep a more effective control over the whole nation.

In fact, perhaps king Wu's father, the king Wen, also recognized the crucial role of geographical locations and moved their capital from the middle reaches of the Wei River to Hao around today's Xi'an city, Shaanxi province.

---

18. Evidence from the royal tombs indicates that royal personages were buried with articles of value, presumably for use in the afterlife. Perhaps for the same reason, hundreds of commoners, who may have been slaves, were buried alive with the royal corpse.

19. See, for example, Dai and Gong (2000, vol. 1, p. 68).

TABLE 15.4 A Comparison of Selected Chinese Dynasties in Terms of Location, Size, and Other Parameters

Indicator	Zhou (1046–221 BC)	Han (206 BC–AD 220)	Jin (265–420)	Tang (619–907)	Song (960–1279)	Ming (1368–1644)	Qing (1644–1911)
Capital city	Hao (Xi'an)[a]; Luoyi (Luoyang)[b]	Chang'an (Xi'an)[c]; Luoyang[d]	Luoyang[e]; Jiankang (Nanjing)[f]	Chang'an (Xi'an)	Kaifeng[g]; Lin'an (Hangzhou)[h]	Nanjing[i]; Beijing[j]	Beijing
Distance between capital and farthest frontier (km)[k]	1,200[a]; 950[b]	3,200[c]; 3,300[d]	3,500[e]; 2,000[f]	3,500	2,000[g]; 1,700[h]	2,000[i]; 2,600[i]	3,900
Area of territory (million km²)[l]	3.4	8.9	9.2[e]; 2.3[f]	12.5–8.0	4.6[g]; 4.0[h]	7.1	13.1
Length of existence (years)	825 (571)[m]	426	155	289	319	276	267
Major force(s) for collapse	Endogenous	Endogenous	Exogenous & Endogenous	Endogenous	Exogenous	Endogenous & Exogenous	Endogenous

Notes:
[a]from 1046 to 771 BC.
[b]from 771 to 221 BC.
[c]from 206 BC to AD 25.
[d]from AD 25 to 220.
[e]from 265 to 316.
[f]from 317 to 420.
[g]from AD 960 to 1127.
[h]from AD 1127 to 1279.
[i]from AD 1368 to 1420.
[j]from AD 1421 to 1644.
[k]estimated by the author based on the maps of ancient China.
[l]available at http://bbs.zanba.com/message/122377/122377304.html.
[m]figure within parenthesis does not include the 'Warring States' period (from 475 to 221 BC).
Source: Calculated by the author except those that are specifically cited.

Although the construction of Luoyi as an alternative capital of the Zhou was eventually completed by Wu's son and successor, king Cheng (reign 1043–1007 BC), Hao continued to be the Zhou's capital till 771 BC when the king You was killed by invading barbarians from the northwest frontier.

Compared with its predecessor, the Zhou dynasty, the Qin dynasty had an enlarged territory, but it was short lived (see Tables 15.4 and 15.5 for a comparison of the two dynasties). Historians have identified many factors leading to the shortness of the Qin empire, which include, among others, Qin Shihuang's tyranny, harsh law imposed on the lives of people, large expenditure on big projects (such as the Great Wall) and persecution of Confucianism. The direct cause of the Qin's collapse, however, was initially connected with a long-distance trip of the border patrol led by Chen Sheng and Wu Guang. For example, the following was reported in Sima Qian's (104 BC) famous book *Shiji* (historical records):

In 209 BC, Huhai, the second emperor of the Qin dynasty, ordered 900 people in the region of Huaihe river to Yuyang (today's Miyun county in northeast Beijing) to serve as border patrol. Chen Sheng and Wu Guang, who were among them, were appointed leaders of the troop. When people arrived in Dazexiang (in southwest of today's Suxian county, Anhui province), due to heavy rain, the roads were damaged and their trip to the destination was delayed. According to the Qin's penal code, those in military service would be executed if they failed to keep their appointments, so these people faced the threat of death. Since Chen Sheng and Wu Guang had long been dissatisfied with their poverty-stricken life, and now faced the treats of death, they decided to initiate an uprising to 'save' themselves. Soon, many people joined (including Xiang Yu and Liu Bang) and the uprising spread across the country. They led the peasants to attack and occupy finally Chen County (today's Huaiyang in Henan province), and they established their own regime entitled Zhangchu. Then their army sent by Chen Sheng to fight against Qin army was defeated by Zhang Han. Later, Chen Sheng and Wu Guang were murdered by their subordination. And the rest of the army was surrendered to Liu Bang and Xiang Yu. In 206 BC, the Qin dynasty came to an infamous end.

The Han dynasty, after which the members of the ethnic majority in China, the 'people of Han', are named, was notable also for its military prowess. The empire expanded westward as far as the rim of the Tarim Basin (in modern Xinjiang), making possible relatively secure caravan traffic across Central Asia to Antioch, Baghdad, and Alexandria. The paths of caravan traffic are often called the 'silk route' because the route was used to export Chinese silk to the Roman Empire. Chinese armies also invaded and annexed parts of northern Vietnam and northern Korea toward the end of the second century BC. Han control of peripheral regions was generally insecure, however. To ensure peace

TABLE 15.5 A Comparison of China's Three Short-Lived Dynasties and Their Predecessors

Indicator	Qin (221–206 BC)	Sui (AD 581–618)	Yuan (1279–1368)
Capital city	Xian'yang (near Xi'an)	Chang'an[a]; Luoyang[b]	Dadu (Beijing)
Length of lifespan (years), which is	15	37	89
Less than that of its predecessor by	810 (556)[c]	118	230
Distance between capital and farthest frontier (km)[d], which is	2,000	3,200[a]; 3,100[b]	4,000
Longer than that of its predecessor (km) by	800[e]; 1,050[f]	−300[a]; 1,100[b]	2,000[g]; 2,300[h]
Area of territory (million sq. km)[i], which is	3.6	8.4	16.8
Larger than that of its predecessor (million sq. km) by	0.2	−0.8[a]; 6.1[b]	12.2[g]; 12.8[h]
Major force for collapse	Endogenous	Endogenous	Endogenous
Compared to that of its predecessor	Endogenous	Exogenous & Endogenous	Exogenous

Notes:
[a]from AD 581 to 605.
[b]from AD 606 to 618.
[c]figure within the parenthesis is based on that the Zhou dynasty does not include the 'Warring States' period (from 475 to 221 BC).
[d]estimated by the author based on relevant maps of ancient China.
[e]based on the Western Zhou dynasty (1046 to 771 BC).
[f]based on the Eastern Zhou dynasty (771 to 221 BC).
[g]based on the North Song dynasty (AD 960 to 1127).
[h]based on the South Song dynasty (AD 1127 to 1279).
[i]available at: //bbs.zanba.com/message/122377/122377304.html.
Source: Calculated by the author based on Table 15.4 except those that are specifically cited.

with non-Chinese local powers, the Han court developed a mutually beneficial 'tributary system'. Non-Chinese states were allowed to remain autonomous in exchange for symbolic acceptance of Han lordship. Tributary ties were confirmed and strengthened through intermarriages at the ruling level and periodic exchanges of gifts and goods. In 25 AD, after years of chaos, the new Han ruler moved its capital from Chang'an (today's Xi'an) to Luoyang in the east.

The collapse of the Han dynasty was followed by nearly four centuries of rule by warlords. Unity was restored briefly in the early years of the Jin dynasty (AD 265–420), but the Jin could not long contain the invasions of the nomadic peoples. In AD 317 the Jin court was forced to flee from Luoyang to Jiankang (today's Nanjing) in the south. Though militarily stronger than its predecessor, the Sui dynasty only ruled for 36 years, a much shorter period than that of the Jin dynasty. Similar to another short-lived dynasty, the Qin, the Sui dynasty also had a tyrannical ruler during its last stage. Weakened by costly and disastrous military campaigns against Korea in the early seventh century, the Sui dynasty disintegrated through a combination of popular revolts, disloyalty, and assassination.

The Tang dynasty spanned the reigns of 21 sovereigns, in total for a period of 289 years. At the height of its power (from 712–755 AD), the Tang dynasty enlarged its territory to 12.4 million square kilometers, extending to Mongolia in the north, Xinjiang in the west, to the northern part of the Korean peninsula in the east, and to the northern part of Annam (today's Vietnam) in the south, which was larger than in any previous period. In the Tang dynasty, the Chinese culture influenced as far away as India in the western side of the Himalayas and Japan in the east. For example, the traditional written language, architecture, and political institutions of Japan and Korea were to some extent imitations of the Tang model. However, at the late stage of the dynasty, the huge size of the territory and the capital's proximity to the north and the west frontiers were full with domestic chaos and invasions by barbarians. As soon as the Tang declined in the early tenth century, five dynastic changes occurred along the valley of the Yellow River and ten regional powers controlled different sections of the Yangtze River.[20]

After the founders of the Song dynasty unified China in AD 960, there had been two locations that could serve as the capital: Luoyang and Kaifeng, in the western and the eastern Henan province, respectively. Economically, Kaifeng was a better choice, given its convenient transport and communication facilities. This can be witnessed by the

rapid economic, commercial, and technological developments enjoyed by Kaifeng and by China as a whole during the North Song dynasty (AD 960–1127). However, Kaifeng was not an ideal city for military purposes, since it was so near to its northern enemies that no geographical barriers (with the exception of the Yellow River) could protect it from invasions. Clearly, this has been witnessed by the forced abandonment of Kaifeng and northern and central China by the Song court in 1127; as a result, the Song's capital was moved from Kaifeng southwardly to Lin'an (today's Hangzhou). By contrast, Luoyang is an ideal city for military, but not for economical, purposes. Transportation between Luoyang and the economic center in southeast provinces was very costly since there was no convenient waterway.

Under the Mongol rule, China's territory increased to 16.8 million square kilometers, covering areas of Korea and the Muslim kingdoms of Central Asia. Effective control over this huge territory was always a difficult task. But this short-lived empire collapsed suddenly due to rivalry among the imperial heirs, natural disasters, and peasant uprisings. Then, why was Yuan's capital transferred from Karakorum (in modern Mongolia) to Beijing? The first possible driving force for the southward move of the capital might be the change in territorial size. As a result of the fall of the Jin and the Song courts, most of Chinese territory, formerly under the control of the Jin and the Song dynasties, had been under the Mongol's control. If Karakorum is a geographically optimal location as the capital for the Mongol state (AD 1206–1271), *ceteris paribus*, the optimal location for the capital of the newly established, spatially enlarged dynasty, the Yuan should move to the south.

There are many factors that could result in a short lifespan for the Yuan dynasty, which include natural disaster, misgovernment, as well as rivalry among the Mongol imperial heirs, among others. But it was the large territory and the long distance between Beijing and the southern fields of peasant uprisings that eventually led to the collapse of the Yuan dynasty. A comparison of selective parameters in Table 15.5 shows that the huge area of territory of the Yuan dynasty, which is much larger than that of its predecessor, the Song dynasty, should have been one of the major factors responsible for its shorter lifespan.

The Ming dynasty (1368–1644) moved its capital from Nanjing (southern capital) to Beijing (northern capital) in 1420, in order to help the Ming court to effectively control its northern territory with close proximity to the Mongols and to the Manchus. Long wars with the Mongols and the Manchus in the north and the harassment of Chinese southeast coastal areas by the Japanese in the sixteenth century weakened Ming rule. However, in 1644, Li Zicheng and his peasant rebels from western China took Beijing, though they were defeated by the Manchus shortly

---

20. The period from AD 907 to 960 is known as the Five Dynasties and Ten Kingdoms (*wudai shiguo*).

afterwards. To some extent, the Ming is not a successful dynasty in terms of military and culture (if compared with the Tang) or in terms of industry, trade, science and technology (if compared with the Song). Like the Song, the Ming fell suddenly, partly as a result of its capital being adjacent to the northern enemies.

The Qing dynasty's moving of its capital from Shengjing (now named Shenyang) to Beijing also provides evidence to support, and can be further explained by, geo-economics. This is similar to that of the Yuan dynasty. But, different from the Yuan, the Qing court applied the Han-Chinese way to govern China, which enabled it to sustain a longer period than the Yuan. Entering the nineteenth century, the Chinese society became a totally autarkic one. The Chinese nation fell behind the Western nations in science and technology. After the Opium War in the mid-nineteenth century, China declined into a semi-colonial and semi-feudal country. Britain and other Western powers such as Belgium, the Netherlands, Prussia, Spain, Portugal, the USA, and France, seized 'concessions' and divided China into 'spheres of influence'. During the second half of the nineteenth century, many peasant leaders and national heroes rose time and again, eventually resulting in the disintegration of this nation.

Indeed, each dynasty has a different lifespan; but no dynasty can last forever. A comparison of the Chinese and Korean dynasties (see Figure 15.4) indicates that the Korean dynasties did sustain a much longer average lifespan than the Chinese ones during approximately the same period of time. If political and economic factors were not quite responsible for these differences, geographical factors (size and location) must have contributed. Furthermore, we can find that the three Korean dynasties had significantly different lifespans. For example, the Koryo dynasty (915–1392 AD), with its capital in Kaesong, and the Chosen dynasty (1392–1910), with its capital in Seoul, lasted for 477 and 518 years, respectively, and could have been even longer had the two dynasties not been invaded by external forces. By contrast, the unified Shilla dynasty (668–915 AD), with its capital in Kyongju, only lasted for 247 years, which is less than that of the Koryo, and even less than half that of the Chosen.

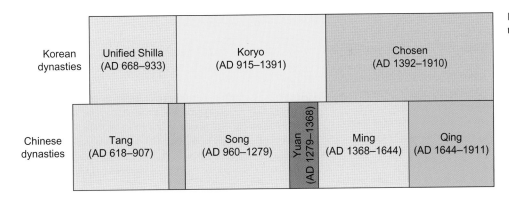

FIGURE 15.4 A comparison of the Chinese and Korean dynasties.

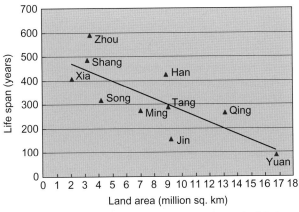

(a) Chinese dynasties: lifespan versus territorial size
Source: Tables 15.4 and 15.5 and the author's calculation.

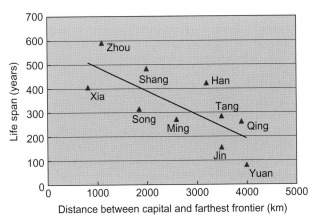

(b) Chinese dynasties: lifespan versus distance
Source: Tables 15.4 and 15.5 and the author's calculation.

FIGURE 15.5 Location, territorial size, and Chinese dynasties.

It is reasonable to believe that it was the disadvantageous (southeast coastal) location of the capital that made the Shilla court gradually lose efficient control over the northern peripheries and eventually the whole country as well.

In short, a historical review of the national development of China has left many issues unexplained. They include such important problem as: Why were China's political centers usually located at the geographical peripheries during its prosperous periods, and located at the geographical centers during its stagnant periods? Besides, why have various forms of economic integrations existed between Hong Kong, Macau, Taiwan, and mainland China, while cultural and economic separations existed between China's western, less developed provincial administrations? The geographical location of capital cities and the territorial size of the Chinese nation have mattered very much to the dynastic changes in the Chinese history, as shown in Figure 15.5.

REFERENCES

Asian Development Bank (1996). *Key indicators of developing and Asian Countries 1996* (vol. 27). Manila: Economics and Development Resource Center, Asian Development Bank (ABD). published by Oxford University Press.

Bottelier, P. (2009). China and International financial crisis. In A. J. Tellis, A. Marble, & T. Tanner (Eds.), *Economic meltdown and geopolitical stability* (pp. 70–102). Seattle, WA: National Bureau of Asian Research.

Cankao Xiaoxi (1996). *Reference News–Taiwan*. October 16, p. 8, Beijing.

Chua, A. (2003). *World on fire: how exporting free market democracy breeds ethnic hatred and global instability*. New York: Doubleday.

Dai, Y., & Gong, S. (Eds.). (2000). *A history of China* [zhongguo tongshi]. Zhengzhou: Haiyan Press. a four-volume edition (in Chinese).

Dong, S., & Xu, C. (1992). Some issues relating to the greater China economic cooperation [da zhongguo jingji xiezuo de jige wenti]. Youths Committee of China Society of Natural Resources (Ed.), *The Cross-Taiwan strait: sustainable development of the issues of resources and environment* (pp. 10–13). Beijing: China Science and Technology Press.

Fei, W. (1993). Economic analysis of China economic area [dui zhongguo jingji quan de fenxi]. *Asia-Pacific Economic Review, 2*, 54–59.

Feng, Y. (1992). The trends of Asian–Pacific regional cooperation and the formation and development of the Chinese economic circle. Youths Committee of China Society of Natural Resources (Ed.), *The Cross-Taiwan strait: sustainable development of the issues of resources and environment* (pp. 6–9). Beijing: China Science and Technology Press.

Gao, T. (2003). Ethnic Chinese networks and international investment: evidence from inward FDI in China. *Journal of Asian Economics, 14*, 611–629.

Harding, H. (1993). The concept of 'Greater China': themes, variations and reservations. *The China Quarterly, 136*(Special Issue: Greater China), 660–684.

Hwang, Z. (1988). *The United States' 203 years: an analysis of the history and future for the 'American System'* [meiguo 203 nian: dui 'meiguo tixi' de lishi yu weilai xue de fenxi]. Hong Kong: Zhongliu Press.

Kan, S. A. (2011). *China/Taiwan: evolution of the 'One China' policy – key statements from Washington, Beijing, and Taipei*. Washington, DC: Congressional Research Service. June 3. Available at <http://fpc.state.gov/documents/organization/166825.pdf>. Accessed on November 12, 2011.

Kao, C., & Shong, E. (1992). *A positive analysis of the indirect trade between the two sides of the Taiwan strait via third areas*. Taipei: Chunghua Institution for Economic Research, September.

Pai Shing Semimonthly, March 1, 1986.

Segal, G. (1994). China's changing shape. *Foreign Affairs, 73*, 40–65.

Smart, A., & Hsu, J. (2004). The Chinese diaspora, foreign investment and economic development in China. *The Review of International Affairs, 3*(4), 544–566.

SSB. (various years). *China statistical yearbook*, various issues. Beijing: China Statistics Publishing House.

Sung, Y.-W. (2004). *Greater China: an emerging economic reality*. New York: Palgrave Macmillan.

The Economic Research Materials, no. 6, 1996, p. 62, in Chinese.

The Economist (1992), p. 17.

US Academy of Defense Agency (1993). *US arm control and disarmament*. Washington, DC: US Academy of Defense Agency.

Winkler, S. (2011). *Biding time: the challenge of Taiwan's international status*. The Brookings Institution. Available at <http://www.brookings.edu/papers/2011/1117_taiwan_international_status_winkler.aspx>. Accessed on November 22, 2011.

Wu, R., & Liang, Y. (1990). Hong Kong – the first financial and trade center in the far east [yuandong diyi jinrong maoyi zhongxin–xianggang]. In N. Hu & R. Yang (Eds.), *Studies of the disequilibrated development issues in the Chinese economy* [zhongguo jingji feijunheng fazhan wenti yanjiu] (1994, pp. 234–244). Taiyuan: The United Press of Shanxi Universities.

Xie, H. (1992). The industrial development in Macau Youths Committee of China Society of Natural Resources (Ed.), *The Cross-Taiwan strait: sustainable development of the issues of resources and environment* (pp. 110–116). Beijing: China Science and Technology Press.

Yang, X. (1992). The resource exploitation and economic development in the greater China economic circle [da zhongguo jingji quan de ziyuan yu jingji fazhan]. Youth Committee of China Society of Natural Resources (Ed.), *The Cross-Taiwan strait: sustainable development of the issues of resources and environment* (pp. 1–5). Beijing: China Science and Technology Press 1992.

Zheng, Z. (1988). 'A Framework of the Greater China Community' (da zhonghua gongtong ti shichang de gouxiang). *Economic Review. June*, 13.

Zhou, B (1989). The Chinese community and southeast China free trade zone [zhongguo ren gongtongti hua dongnan zhiyou maoyi qu]. *Economic Review*, November 6.

Zhou, J. (1992). To establish the greater China economic area between Hong Kong, Macau, Taiwan and Mainland China: a basic framework [zhongguo dalu yu gang ao tai goujian da zhonghua jingji quan de jiben gouxiang]. Youths Committee of China Society of Natural Resources (Ed.), *The Cross-Taiwan strait: sustainable development of the issues of resources and environment* (pp. 18–21). Beijing: China Science and Technology Press.

- 1949: The People's Republic of China (PRC) is proclaimed. It is not recognized by the US and many other Western nations. The Kuomintang (KMT) still holds Taiwan and continues to claim legitimacy as the government of China as a whole.
- 1950: Chinese People's Liberation Army (PLA) occupies Tibet. The Korean War begins.
- 1951: Chinese and North Korean armies occupy Seoul. The Tibetan government signs an agreement with the Chinese government in Beijing.
- 1952: The administrative divisions are readjusted in China.
- 1953: The First Five-Year Plan begins. The Chinese Buddhists' Association is established.
- 1954: The first direct Beijing-Moscow passenger train opens. China and India sign a joint declaration on principle of peaceful coexistence. The Central Military Committee of the CCPCC is established.
- 1955: China and Yugoslavia establish formal diplomatic relations. The new currency of RMB is issued.
- 1956: The tropical storm (named 'Wanda') kills c. 5,000 people in Zhejiang province.
- 1957: The CCPCC puts forward the 'Hundred Flowers' movement to allow limited freedom and criticism of the government.
- 1958: The 'Great Leap Forward' movement. The PCS becomes a universal form of agricultural production. As peasants neglect their fields and try to produce steel in small-scale furnaces, agricultural production slumps dramatically in following years.
- 1959: An uprising by Tibetans against Chinese rule is suppressed and the Dalai Lama flees to northern India with 10,000 supporters.
- 1960: The Russians withdraw their technical advisers and aid.
- 1961: Three-year famine ends, with millions of people dead from starvation.
- 1962: Border war with India.
- 1963: China's first computer (named '109') is successfully made. China's birth rate reaches a highest record.
- 1964: Development of atomic bomb.
- 1965: Tibet is formally made an autonomous region of China.

- 1966: The 'Great Proletarian Cultural Revolution' begins. Universities are closed.
- 1967: China's Cultural Revolution movement reaches Hong Kong. China declares the shutting down of American spy planes.
- 1968: Liu Shaoqi, the Head of State, is imprisoned, dying a year later in jail.
- 1969: Border clashes with the USSR.
- 1970: Launch of artificial satellite.
- 1971: The PRC is admitted to the United Nations in place of the ROC regime in Taiwan. An attempted coup takes place, led by the Defense Minister, Lin Biao.
- 1972: US president Nixon visits China. Japan establishes diplomatic relations with China.
- 1973: China and Japan jointly construct undersea cable line in East China Sea. China first convenes national environmental protection conference. The 35th Guangzhou Exhibition, now the largest scale, opens.
- 1974: China attacks the South Vietnamese army in, and occupies, the Paracel islands. Daqing and Shengli Oilfields go into operation in North China, which is followed by Dagang Oilfield. The Chinese government calls for the implementation of population control policy.
- 1975: A new constitution is adopted. The position of Head of State is abolished.
- 1976: An earthquake of 7.8 on the Richter scale occurs at Tangshan city, Hebei province, on 12 May 2008, with over 200,000 victims. Death of Chinese Premier Zhou Enlai. Mao Zedong dies and his widow, along with 3 radical members of the Politburo (the 'Gang of Four'), are arrested. Hua Guofeng succeeds Mao as Party Chairman and Premier.
- 1977: Deng Xiaoping wrestles power from Hua Guofeng and is restored to his former posts. University entrance examination resumes.
- 1978: Third Plenum of the 11th CCPCC passes the 'Decision of the CCPCC Concerning the Reform of the Economic System'.
- 1979: China sets up diplomatic relations with the USA. People's Congress of Guangdong province approves the creation of Shenzhen next to Hong Kong, Zhuhai next to Macau, and Santou as the SEZs, to experiment with a market-oriented economy. The NPC passes

'Law of the People's Republic of China Concerning the Joint Ventures with Chinese and Foreign Investment'. Shenzhen next to Hong Kong, Zhuhai next to Macau, and Santou are made into special economic zones (SEZs). One year later, Xiamen, with close proximity to Taiwan, also became an SEZ with the approval of the NPC. The CCPCC and State Council grant Guangdong and Fujian provinces 'special policies and flexible measures' in foreign economic affairs.

- 1980: Hua Guofeng resigns as Premier and is replaced by Zhao Ziyang, confirming the ascendancy of Deng's moderate supporters. Deng takes over as Chairman of the Central Military Commission. The NPC grants Xiamen in Southeast Fujian province vis-à-vis Taiwan status of SEZ. China introduces Household Responsibility System (HRS).

- 1981: The CCPCC chairman Fa Guofeng is replaced by Hu Yaobang. Deng Xiaoping puts forward 'One Country, Two Systems' policy.

- 1982: The post CCPCC Chairman is abolished.

- 1983: The CCP is purged of Maoists and those who oppose Deng's pragmatic policies.

- 1984: The CCPCC passes 'Decision of the CCPCC Concerning the Reform of Economic Structure'. The CCPCC and the State Council choose 14 coastal open cities. The State Council passes 'Provisional Regulations on the Enlargement of Autonomy of State-owned Industrial Enterprises'. The State Council passes 'Provisional Regulations for the Management of "Small-volume" Border Trade'.

- 1985: The State Council approves the Yangtze River, Pearl River, and South Fujian as coastal economic development zones.

- 1986: Chinese government applies to resume GATT status. The NPC passes 'Bankruptcy Law Concerning the SOEs'. The SOEs are encouraged to adopt the contract system. The State Council passes 'Regulations of Issues Concerning the Extensive Regional Economic Cooperation'.

- 1987: Deng resigns from the CCPCC but retains other influential posts.

- 1988: The Hainan island becomes a province and is approved as an SEZ with even more flexible policies. Liaodong and Shandong peninsulas and Bohai Basin area are allowed to open up to the outside world.

- 1989: Former Party General Secretary Hu Yaobang dies in April. Tiananmen Square becomes the focus and at one stage a million people assemble there. The People's Liberation Army attacks the protesters. Zhao Ziyang is dismissed from his post as Party General Secretary and placed under house arrest. Jiang Zemin takes over as the CCPCC General Secretary.

- 1990: Jiang Zemin succeeds Deng Xiaoping as Chairman of the CCP Central Military Commission.

Shanghai's Pudong area is granted some of the SEZ's mechanisms. Asian Olympic Games in Beijing.

- 1991: Jiang Zemin calls for opposing 'peaceful evolution'. NPC promotes Zhu Rongji to Vice Premier.

- 1992: Deng Xiaoping embarks on a famous Southern Tour. China passes 'Measures Concerning the Supervision and Favorable Taxation for the People-to-People Trade in Sino–Myanmar Border'. Tibet autonomous region passes 'Resolutions Concerning the Further Reform and Opening up to the Outside World'. 'Provisional Regulations on Joint-Stock Companies'. 'Notification Concerning the Further Opening up of the Five Frontier Cities and Towns of Nanning, Kunming, Pingxiang, Ruili, and Hekou'. 'Some Favorable Policies and Economic Autonomy Authorized to the Frontier Cities of Heihe and Shuifenhe'. 'Regulations on the Transformation of the Operating Mechanisms of State-owned Industrial Enterprises'.

- 1993: Third Plenum of the 14th CCPCC passes 'Decision of the CCPCC on Several Issues Concerning the Establishment of a Socialist Market Economic Structure'. The constitution is changed to confirm the State's aim of running a 'socialist market economy'. Modern enterprise system is introduced.

- 1994: People's Bank of China separates its banking from policy lending and reduces the number of the central bank's regional branches from 30 or more to only six. Introduction of 'tax-sharing system' into all provinces. Establishment of a new unitary and floating exchange rate system.

- 1995: Policy of grasping the large and releasing the small is applied to Chinese SOEs.

- 1996: China tests surface-to-surface missiles into sea off the coast of Taiwan.

- 1997: Deng Xiaoping dies in February and Jiang Zemin and Li Peng both announce that his economic policies will be maintained. Hong Kong is transferred to Chinese sovereignty.

- 1998: Amendment to Article 6 of the Chinese Constitution: 'public, instead of state, ownership as the main form of ownership of the means of production'. China signs (but does not ratify) the International Covenant on Civil and Political Rights. Dissidents attempt unsuccessfully to set up an opposition party, the China Democracy Party.

- 1999: Western Region Development Strategy (*xibu da kaifa*). Debt-equity swap scheme (zhai zhuan gu) in four large state-owned banks (China Construction Bank, Industrial and Commercial Bank of China, Agricultural Bank of China, and Bank of China). The Falun Gong cult is banned as a threat to society. The Chinese embassy in Belgrade is bombed by NATO. Macau is transferred from Portuguese to Chinese sovereignty.

- 2000: Adoption of 'real name' banking system. The government publishes new rules allowing it to control material on the Internet. A census records the population at 1,242,612,226.
- 2001: The International Olympic Committee awards the 29th Olympic Games to Beijing. The Shanghai Cooperation Organization (SCO) is established. A US spy plane is forced to land on Hainan island after colliding with a Chinese fighter aircraft. China joins the World Trade Organization (WTO).
- 2002: 'Resurgence of the Old Industrial Base in the Northeast Region' is announced. The South-North Water Diversion project begins. China is by now the world's third largest Internet user, with a growth of 72 percent over the previous year.
- 2003: Transformation of the Bank of China and of the China Construction Bank into joint stock ownership. China's first manned spaceship, Shenzhou V, is launched on October 15, which makes China take its place alongside Russia and the United States in the elite circle of countries able to send people into space. The Three Gorges Dam project leads to the relocation of 1.5 million residents of the area. China records a trade surplus of US$44.6 billon despite the outbreak of Severe Acute Respiratory Syndrome (SARS). China overtakes USA as the world's biggest recipient of FDI.
- 2004: China decides to abolish agricultural tax within 3 years. Foreign investment in Chinese media companies is allowed under preconditions. China becomes the biggest trade partner of Japan, surpassing the US.
- 2005: The NPC passes the anti-secession law on Taiwan. KMT Chairman (Lien Chan) and CCP General Secretary (Hu Jintao) meet in Beijing. A new system is announced under which the RMB is pegged against a basket of currencies and will be allowed to fluctuate by 0.3 percent a day.
- 2006: 'Freezing Point' (a weekly supplement to the *China Youth Daily*) is closed down and three editors removed from their positions. First oil from a new pipeline connecting China and Kazakhstan arrives in China.
- 2007: China's GDP growth rate reaches 12 percent (the highest level since 1995), while its inflation rate also rises sharply. Amended property rights law passes at the 5th Session of the 10th NPC.
- 2008: An earthquake of 8.0 magnitude on the Richter scale occurs at Whenchuan county and its surrounding areas of Sichuan province, southwest China on 12 May 2008, with over 80,000 victims. The 29th Olympic Games take place in Beijing. Three direct links are set up between Taiwan and mainland China. China becomes the world's second largest exporter. Privatization of forestland for 70 years of tenure in selected areas. More flexible foreign exchange policies.
- 2009: China has now more than 360 million Internet users. Deadly violence occurs in Muslim-dominated Xinjiang, with about 1,000 people (mostly Han-Chinese) being killed or wounded. China celebrates the 60th anniversary of the PRC at Tiananmen Square. After overtaking Germany, China becomes the world's largest exporter. China also becomes the largest producer and consumer of passenger cars and trucks.
- 2010: The world's fastest supercomputer – Tianhe-1A – is made, with 2,507 trillion calculations per second. China surpasses Japan as the second largest economy in terms of GDP, behind only the USA. ECFA was signed between Taiwan and mainland China. Liu Xiaobo was awarded the Nobel Peace Prize. The Beijing-Shanghai high-speed railway reaches a record high speed of 486.1 km/hr.
- 2011: On 23 July, two high-speed trains collide on a viaduct in the suburbs of Wenzhou, Zhejiang province, with 40 people killed and at least 192 injured; China decides to slow its average train speed running along the high-speed railways. The Shenzhou 8 spacecraft was remotely docked with the Tiangong 1 space module (launched on 29 September). This unmanned docking – China's first – will be followed in 2012 with the manned Shenzhou 9 mission, which will perform a manned docking (also China's first) with the Tiangong 1 module. Only the Soviet Union (Russia) and the European Space Agency had achieved automatic rendezvous and docking prior to China's accomplishment. October 10, the 100th anniversary of the Xinhai Revolution. On December 11, China celebrates the 10th anniversary of its accession to the WTO in the Great Hall of the People.

Centrally Planned Economy (CPE): This is based upon the supposition that 'society' (in practice the planning agencies, under the authority of the political leadership) knows or can discover what is needed, and can issue orders incorporating these needs, while allocating the required means of production so that the needs are economically met.

Chinese Communist Party Central Committee (CCPCC): This has been virtually the most important power body in China. Seated at Zhongnan Sea in central Beijing, Political Bureau (PB) is the standing organ of the CCPCC. The PB's members and its more powerful standing members can be frequently found in the evening news of China's official media, including the CCTV.

Chinese People's Political Consultative Congress (CPPCC): Under the leadership of the CCPCC, the CPPCC consists of representatives of the CCP, several democratic parties, democrats with no party affiliations, various people's organizations and ethnic groups, and other specially invited individuals. The primary functions of the CPPCC are to conduct political consultations and democratic supervisions, and to discuss and manage state affairs.

Comparative Advantage: A comparative advantage prevails for products which have the lowest opportunity cost of production. According to the law of comparative advantage, a country or region should specialize in the production of those commodities for which it has a comparative advantage.

Debt–Equity Swap Scheme: Under the scheme, a portion of SOEs' bad loans are converted into equity and then sold at a discount to investors. The immediate objectives of debt–equity swaps are to improve the balance sheet of the commercial banks and reduce the debt service of the SOEs.

Democratic Centralism System: This system was first described by Lenin as 'freedom of discussion, unity of action'. The democratic aspect of this organizational method describes the freedom of members of the political party to discuss and debate matters of policy and direction, but once the decision of the party is made by majority vote, all members are expected to uphold that decision. This latter aspect represents the centralism.

Dual Pricing System: Under this system, price was subject to market regulations developed in parallel with a controlled market in which price was kept almost unchanged at an officially fixed level. Because the price was higher in the market-regulated track than in the state-controlled track, supply in the free market grew rapidly, so its share of total output rose steadily. Meanwhile, the planned price was able to increase incrementally until it approached the market price when the gap between supply and demand narrowed.

Economies of Scale: The percentage increase in output exceeds the percentage increase in all inputs. Equivalently, average cost falls as output expands.

Engel's Law: Named after the statistician Ernst Engel (1821–1896), this law states that as income rises, the proportion of income spent on food falls, even if actual expenditure on food may rise. In economics, the proportion of income spent on food is called the Engel coefficient. It is used to illustrate the difficulty of people acquiring basic needs of life. Thus, this indicator can be used to represent people's living standards.

Gini Coefficient: This is prominently used as a measure of the degree of inequality in income or owned assets such as land or financial wealth. It is defined as a ratio with values ranging from 0 (perfect equality – every household or person is the same) to 1 (perfect inequality – one household or person owns everything).

Gradualism: This is the belief that change ought to be modified in small, discrete increments rather than abrupt changes. Without considering the cost of implementation, a big bang (or shock therapy) reform may have an advantage over a gradual one. However, reversing the full reform sometimes costs more than reversing a single partial or gradual reform measure.

Great Leap Forward (GLF): During the period from 1958 to 1960, large quantities of materials and labor were diverted towards heavy industry in China. This resulted in serious imbalances between accumulation and consumption and between heavy industry and agriculture and light industry. During the early stage of the GLF, harvest was poor despite high yields in the rural areas. Consequently, from 1959 onwards, agricultural production dropped spectacularly, followed by a three-year famine.

Greenhouse Gases (GHGs): They include such pollutants as carbon dioxide, methane, and chlorofluorocarbons, among others. The GHGs are believed to have contributed to climate modification by absorbing the long-wave (infrared) radiation, thereby trapping heat which would otherwise radiate into space.

Household Responsibility System (HRS): Under this system, each rural household may be able to sign a contract with the local government to obtain a certain amount of arable land and production equipment and have a production quota, depending on the number of people in the household. As long as the household completes its quota of products to the state, it can decide freely what to produce and how to sell.

Kuznets Curve: Also called the 'inverted-U' hypothesis in which economic development is at first accompanied by an increase in income disparities (or inequalities) and later a decrease.

Market Economy: An economic system in which resource allocation decisions are guided by prices resulting from the voluntary production and purchasing decisions made by private producers and consumers.

National People's Congress (NPC): This is the supreme legislative organ of China. The NPC's representatives, coming from different regions and sectors, meet regularly in the Great Hall of the People in Beijing to discuss state affairs, to approve those who are recommended by the CCPCC as central government officials, and to issue laws and regulations.

'One Country, Two Systems': This concept was originally proposed by Deng Xiaoping for the reunification of China during the early 1980s. He suggested that there would be only one China, but that Hong Kong, Macau, and Taiwan could have their own capitalist economic and political systems, while the rest of China uses the socialist system. Under the suggestion, each of the three regions could continue to have its own political system, legal, economic, and financial affairs, including commercial and cultural agreements with foreign countries, and would enjoy 'certain rights' in foreign affairs.

People's Commune System (PCS): Under this system, land was owned collectively and the output was distributed to each household according to work points (*gongfen*). The state purchased a major share of the grain output and distributed it to the non-agricultural population through government agencies. The PCS has generally been known to provide disincentives for the farmers to work harder.

Rent-Seeking Behavior: The use of resources in lobbying and other activities directed at securing increased profits through protective regulation or legislation.

Special Economic Zone (SEZ): In 1980, Shenzhen next to Hong Kong, Zhuhai next to Macau, and Santou were designated as SEZs to exercise 'special policies and flexible measures' in foreign economic affairs. At the same time, Xiamen in Southeast Fujian province, with its close proximity to Taiwan, also became an SEZ.

Total-factor Productivity (TFP): This is an economic variable which accounts for effects in total output not caused by traditionally measured inputs such as capital input and labor input. If all inputs are accounted for, then TFP can be taken as a measure of an economy's long-term dynamism. TFP cannot be measured directly; instead it accounts for effects in total output that are not caused by inputs. Technological growth and efficiency are regarded as two of the biggest contributors to TFP.